GLADIO

NATO's Dagger at the Heart of Europe

The Pentagon-Nazi-Mafia Terror Axis

BY

RICHARD COTTRELL

FIRST EDITION

2012

GLADIO

NATO'S DAGGER AT THE HEART OF EUROPE
THE PENTAGON-NAZI-MAFIA TERROR AXIS

Masquerading as a rear guard against Soviet invaders, NATO's covert forces warped into psychological and physical terrorism. These were the 'years of lead,' in which hundreds perished in a synthetic war in the streets of Europe. NATO commander General Lyman Lemnitzer ordered serial attacks on French president Charles de Gaulle. Sacked from the Pentagon by John F. Kennedy for rank insubordination, then exiled to Europe, Lemnitzer reaped revenge in Dallas. The secret armies forged bonds with organized crime and neo-fascists. NATO-backed coups struck down governments in Greece and Turkey; the island state of Cyprus was sundered amid bitter genocide. Urban guerrillas like the Red Brigades and Baader-Meinhof Gang were cunningly manipulated. Italy gained a deep-state government, the ultra-secret P2 pseudo-Masonic lodge founded by former Blackshirts. Swedish PM Olof Palme and Italian ex-PM Aldo Moro were assassinated. Pope John Paul II was shot by Turkish gangsters who had regular work as Gladio guns for hire. In 2009 a Gladio copy-cat outfit codenamed Ergenekon came to light in Turkey. The shootings in Norway in July 2011, and in Belgium, France and Italy in 2012, all bore the classic stripe of Gladio false-flag operations.

TABLE OF CONTENTS

Author's Preface

In July 2011, a calm and studious risk-assessment analyst working for the South Yorkshire Police was summarily fired. He had filed a report with his superiors which openly contradicted the official narrative compiled by the British authorities to explain the 7/7 London Transport bombings. Tony Farrell's allotted task was to assess the degree of risk posed by terrorism. Starting with a clean sheet, he worked to the electrifying conclusion that the London attacks were — in all probability — staged by the secret state. Furthermore, he dismissed the danger posed by Islamic extremists as virtually non-existent. Despite rigorous carpeting by his bosses, pleas, arm-twisting and threats, Farrell refused to budge. He was convinced the story of suicide bombers responsible for London's day of infamy was a concoction of 'monstrous lies.' The sole purpose of the carnage on 7th July 2005 was to terrify the population to such an extent that the United Kingdom could be moved closer to a state of regimented tyranny.

As this book will explain, we have been here before. In the 1970s and '80s, the spectre of officially orchestrated terror stalked the European landscape. Gladio was the name of the Italian branch of the secret Guerrilla armies that NATO established to 'stay behind' in the event of a Russian invasion. Every NATO state, and some that were not, had such a secretive force. As the prospect of an attack from the East receded, so did fear of the Soviets. To preserve the myth of the Red Peril, these secret, or 'sleeping,' soldiers were released in a wave of synthetic violence against innocent European citizens. It lasted two decades, the years remembered by Italians as the *anni di piombo* — the years of lead.

The modern-day manufactured 'war on terror' comes from the same stable of synthetic violence. With the communist bogey exhausted, we are told of an insidious new peril in our midst: the fearful prospect of minarets and Sharia law marching across the European landscape, destroying Christian civilization. But for fear to work in a tangible form, as was discovered in the years of lead, we must have the visible impact of terror all around us. That is where we are now.

Now, the author's special thanks to those who have brought five years' work to the printed page: foremost to my wife, Diana, for her brilliant efforts in assembling the work and her constructive aid and criticism, always when it was needed. Special words for Giulio Piovesan, for his many splendid insights, and to Jeffrey Simmons of London for his unflagging encourage-ment. And not least my publisher, John-Paul Leonard, unrelenting symbol of independent investigative publishing. Finally, I shall certainly miss Gordon Logan's startling e-mails.

Introduction:
Lambs to the Slaughter

'The deep state refers to a parallel secret government, organized by the intelligence and security apparatus, financed by drugs, and engaging in illicit violence, to protect the status and interests of the military against threats from intellectuals, religious groups, and occasionally the constitutional government.'

— Professor Peter Dale Scott

An entire post-war generation grew up in Europe and North America in the shadow of a war that seemed never to end. The spy novels that date from this period of perpetual uncertainty, notably John le Carré's fantastically rich plots, gave rise to its own counter-culture. Why were we fighting this enormous game of shadow boxing on our respective sides of the Iron Curtain? Le Carré wrote about strange men of the shadows — often rather sad individuals hatched in the English public school system — essentially unhinged freaks, which is very largely the nature of spies. The James Bond movies, freely adapted from Ian Fleming's novels, turned the Great Game to hot pursuit conducted in the name of *cherchez la femme*. In retrospect they now seem enormously silly. One could not even describe it as an intelligence war to gain an accurate picture of the other side's capabilities. At a time in the '60s when the Soviets were supposed to possess a massive missile superiority over the United States, we now know that they had exactly four rockets, of doubtful range.

When Nikita Khrushchev made his epic foray to the United States in 1959 for the famous summit with President Richard Nixon, he flew in a largely unproven new model of Tupolev long distance jet. It took off on an educated guess by the flight crew that it carried sufficient fuel to complete the flight. The manufacturers and the Politburo held so much faith in this magnificent example of Soviet enterprise that a line of trawlers stretched across the Atlantic, to fish the General Secretary and his companions from the icy waters should anything go amiss. The Russians were bluffing. This was the essence of the Cold War. The two potential combatants, the Soviets and the western camp led by the United States, used up a great deal of bellicose language, but kept their swords sheathed. If there had never been such a thing as the Cold War, we might have been spared Richard Nixon, Ronald Reagan and Margaret Thatcher. And, for that matter Leonid Brezhnev and the bumbling clown Nikita Khrushchev.

We were told that we were 'fighting' for the ultimate truths and freedoms represented by western democracy. If we at any moment dropped our guard, then the Soviet menace, coiled and ready to spring, would strike. Only the ceaseless vigilance of the North Atlantic Treaty Organisation spared us from the monstrous and tyrannical Soviet Empire. It was taken for granted by millions that the atomic mushroom cloud was tinged a bright hue of red.

But there is a quite different version.

At the peak of Cold War paranoia in the late 1960s, NATO unsheathed its weapons on the very people it was chartered to protect. The sole motive was the preservation of a massive war machine, which in a world governed by common sense, would have gone to the scrapheap: the very essence of swords beaten into ploughshares. Instead, NATO lurched into a guerrilla war against ordinary Europeans going about their daily lives, a psychological campaign of brutal, synthetic violence. Europeans were terrorised by NATO's secret soldiers and their underworld allies. This is the story of Gladio, NATO's secret army that really did go to war in Europe. The battle cry was the enemy within, the phantom Red Menace gnawing at the entrails of the western democratic system. The Alliance for Peace and Progress became a distorted and cruel reflection of its high and lofty constitution. The NATO axis of domestic terror hinged on the military-industrial complex controlled by the Pentagon, the cultivated revival of neofascism, and hired hands drawn from the Mafia criminal underworld.

During World War Two, the Allies prepared for the possibility of a German victory by creating so-called 'stay behind' guerrilla warfare units. They were intended to menace enemy supply routes in each of the occupied countries, working with local partisans to blow up bridges and generally harass troop movements. The challenge called for highly trained volunteers, skilled in handling explosives and accustomed to living rough among the local populations. Their tasks would extend to espionage and reconnaissance conducted in tricky and dangerous environments. The model was the British Special Operations Executive, or SOE, a top-secret guerrilla-commando force established in 1940. It was the brainchild of Winston Churchill, who characteristically issued the command 'set Europe ablaze!'

Churchill seems to have copied the idea from the Dutch-speaking Afrikaner rebels known as the Boers, who were fighting the British in South Africa at the close of the 19th century. The young Churchill reported on the war for London newspapers, and came away very impressed by the Boers' highly successful hit-and-run sabotage tactics. These succeeded brilliantly in tying down the much larger but cumbersome and slow-moving British occupation forces. Only a few select insiders knew that the SOE units existed, but those who did were inclined to call them 'Churchill's secret army.' The name and the idea stuck, to be adopted in due course by NATO.

After the Allied victory of 1945, these units were not disbanded. On the contrary, they were strengthened and expanded in almost every European country, with the direct aid and encouragement of the United States. The task was now to deploy the same wartime guerrilla and espionage tactics against Soviet invaders. Each country had a code name for its clandestine sleeping soldiers. In Italy it was Gladio, from the two-edged sword that gladiators once carried to the Coliseum. After NATO was established in April 1949, the secret armies gradually came under the direct control of the new military alliance. NATO carefully established departments of clandestine warfare, which managed the secret armies and allocated their tasks. In each NATO country only a few close, trustworthy intimates were permitted to know of their existence. As each secret unit was eventually exposed or dragged reluctantly to the daylight, the striking generic name 'Gladio' came to be applied to all of them.

The possibility of a Soviet attack on Western Europe seemed real enough to warrant preparations of an extremely secretive nature. Arms dumps were scattered around each NATO country, to which the Gladiators could have recourse once war broke out. Secret lairs in caves, deep forests, cemeteries, basements of government offices, freight yards of country railway stations, or abandoned fortifications dating from WW2, were filled with abundant supplies of munitions and explosives, including in some instances chemical weapons. The anticipated invasion failed to materialise, but the enormous infrastructure created to nourish and support the secret armies was now seen as another kind of investment for the future. This was expressly political. Gladio was to turn against the people. Banking on herd behaviour, the orchestrators hoped the resulting panic and revulsion would send voters flocking to the welcoming arms of safe Right-wing governments. The Alliance for Peace and Progress was now enmeshed with forces of darkness.

Mimicking vintage anarchist techniques lifted, virtually intact, from the 19th century, and copied by the secret warfare arm of NATO, bands of secret soldiers and their cohorts were ordered to shoot, bomb, maim and kill their own citizens. It was the new age of the scapegoat. The United States forbade any sovereign European state to seat communist ministers in government. All movements of the Left fell under suspicion as cloaks for Moscow — even the milk-and-water British socialist variety. In Turkey, bizarrely, the logic was wrenched inside out. Secular movements in thrall to Kemal Atatürk's long shadow joined with the army, both driven by imaginary fears in a struggle to prevent resurgent Islamic forces from seizing a keystone of the Alliance. Turkey's dirty war on its own people cost some 5,600 lives, one prime minister his head and the destruction of the few struggling shoots of democracy in that unpromising climate.

Unfortunate Italians were selected as the main brunt of a campaign of deadly violence that stretched over the better part of two decades. They shudder when they recall the 'years of lead' — the *anni di piombo*. They remember the smoking ruins of Bologna railway station one summer day in

1980. On the morning of 2nd August, 85 Italians eagerly setting off for their annual vacations were blown up by a huge bomb placed in the main station waiting room. It was air-conditioned, unusually for Italy, and crowded in the heat; which the perpetrators callously calculated would maximize casualties. Two hundred passengers and railway staff were injured. A train waiting to depart was completely wrecked, and a large part of the station collapsed. A pair of English sweethearts fresh with graduate laurels was among the victims. The government rushed to claim the device was planted by the *Brigate Rosse* — the Red Brigades, Italy's legendary band of self-proclaimed urban revolutionaries. Almost within hours, the truth emerged, subsequently confirmed by the courts. The atrocity at Bologna was conceived in the bowels of the Italian Deep State, in short by the Italian government itself. The attack was carried out by secret intelligence services with the aid of their associates in the murky world of resurgent Italian neofascism — and the secret army code-named Gladio. Giuseppe Valerio Fioravanti, a former child actor in the Italian cinema, was sentenced to life imprisonment for his role in the outrage. Fioravanti was among the founders of the neofascist *Nuclei Armati Rivoluzionari* (NAR), which could be traced to a series of terrorist attacks.

Bologna was intended to convince Italians their country was under siege by sinister revolutionary forces working in their midst, acting on instructions from Moscow. Francesco Cossiga, the Right-wing Christian Democrat premier who so hurriedly denounced the Red Brigades, was in a rather compromising position. Cossiga was among the godfathers at the founding of the Gladio secret army in Italy. Later he was himself among the commanders of Gladio, as Minister of the Interior, embracing public order, the police and security. In that position, he had known for many years of the secret state's links with violent terrorist organisations, including NAR. Just over two years earlier, in May 1978, Cossiga was among the council of Christian Democrat elders who coldly sentenced their kidnapped former colleague, ex-premier Aldo Moro, to death. Moro was another victim of the black-on-red war of deceptions. This gentle and conciliatory figure died because he was the father of the 'historic compromise,' his long gestating plan to bring the communists in from the Italian political wilderness. The project ran full counter to the NATO imperial mission. So he was seized and murdered by a criminal gang acting on secret orders from the highest levels in the Italian state. This conflict of interest studded the connections between Italian neofascism and the so-called respectable Christian Democrats throughout the *anni di piombo*.[1]

---

[1] In June 2011, an unnamed source (citing self-protection) within the Swiss financial community informed the NewWorldOrder website that the payoff for the murder of Aldo Moro was arranged by US funds shifted through secret Gladio accounts held in Swiss banks. The interview took place against the background of the Bilderberg gathering in St. Moritz.

On 18th October 1980, two months after the Bologna station bombing, Cossiga resigned. He was replaced by the weak caretaker premier Arnaldo Forlani, another member of the Christian Democrat hierarchy who knew precisely where real responsibility lay for the massacre.

There was another name invented by strategists for this fabricated looking-glass war, which went on for nearly two decades against imaginary Soviet infiltrators. It was the 'Strategy of Tension.' Italy was the home of the largest and most powerful communist party to be found anywhere in Europe.[2] The United States entertained nightmares that communists might win power in a country deemed an essential rampart of European defences against the Soviet Union. The communist party was thus to be destroyed and along with it, much of the fabric of frail Italian democracy. The stunted sapling which is modern Italy today is a notional, weakened apology for a democratic nation. In such a climate the Bilderberg/Trilateral Commission/EU coup of November 2011 was accomplished with ease. For Italians, this is their legacy from the years of lead.

The sound of bullets, screams, the whumpf of great explosions, shattering glass, the scream of emergency vehicles, fell cross Europe. Bombs planted in a prominent city bank, in railway stations and trains, and in beer tents overflowing with jolly drinkers. Snipers fired at will into squares heaving with crowds of peaceful demonstrators, or supermarkets as weekend shoppers queued to pay for their groceries. A slaughter of the innocents. To meet its own political ends, the United States fostered the mirage of communist subversion of the European continent. In so doing it worked through the CIA and secret war departments of every NATO country, and ruthlessly milked and nourished latent forces of fascism left over from WW2. The extreme Right once more flooded the European mainstream political spectrum, corroding and polluting existing structures and cultures. In time, the slipstream sucked in Canada, Australia and New Zealand, which became dependencies of NATO, the emerging global military colossus.

A military pact ostensibly grounded on the principle of common deterrence, but turning instead to aggressive belligerence, was foreseen with astonishing clarity by the American political and social visionary James Burnham. His seminal work *The Struggle for the World* appeared in 1947. In this he glimpsed an American empire exercising 'decisive world control,' and a US-sponsored European Federation, with the Marshall Plan as the warm-up act. The English-speaking powers and the Euro federation would

---

[2] In the mid '60s the Italian communist party outshone its nearest rival, the Parti communiste français (PCF), in terms of membership, with over 1,500,000 members against the PCF's quarter of a million. The Italian party was the largest anywhere in the capitalist world. It drew the allegiance of a third of the electorate. Hence NATO's nightmares of the enemy within.

eventually fuse as a Universal State, with the United States occupying the central role of 'semi-barbarian, unifying power.' For easy consumption the arrangement would be sugar-coated as 'the policy of democratic world order,' an early insight of the emerging mercantile-military globalism we recognise all around us today. Burnham viewed this splendid project favourably. His pulse quickened at the sound of war drums. He imagined a planetary NATO, the prospect of 'winged soldiers, air cavalry, able to raid two thousand miles behind the lines tonight and be gone before the defence arrives tomorrow.' In short, the promised land of perpetual war.[N1]

Burnham grass-hoppered across the American political landscape, from his friendship with Leon Trotsky, thence to his own brand of American Marxism, a brief sabbatical as a mild anti-war socialist, before he flowered as a full-blown neocon. He was an important source of inspiration for George Orwell and *Nineteen Eighty-Four*. Orwell, fearing the stain of plagiarism, characteristically wrote a sarcastic essay denouncing him. Burnham is the true godfather of war *ad infinitum* and the American *imperium rex*. He deserves to be a revered icon in the annals of the North Atlantic Council.

The Strategy of Tension functioned at three basic levels. The guerrilla war fought in the streets formed a classic demonstration of synthetic terrorism. It was intended to stiffen loyalties in those countries considered at the greatest risk of falling under the sway of the Soviet Union.

The second level, the political front, involved NATO-inspired conspiracies to evict democratically elected governments and replace them with more pliable puppet regimes. Two governments were toppled in this fashion in Turkey. Greeks awoke one bright spring morning in 1967 to find the cradle of democracy under the heel of a trio of sadistic junior army officers. They seized power using a NATO blueprint code-named Prometheus, designed to forestall a communist take-over. All the officers were members of the local Gladio offshoot called Sheepskin. Thus Fascism was replanted on European soil, even as it wilted in Spain and Portugal. Cyprus was forcibly ruptured as a unitary state, at the price of bitter ethnic pogroms between Turkish and Greek Cypriots. NATO planners convinced themselves that Archbishop Makarios, the island state's deeply conservative priest-president, was the emerging Castro of the Mediterranean. In Italy, an aristocratic wartime naval hero, famous for his exploits with midget submarines and daring frogmen, staged an abortive Gladio-sponsored coup just before Christmas 1970. A second putsch was scheduled for 1981, betrayed when all the secret plans were suddenly exposed at the last moment. The plotters belonged to Italy's parallel clandestine government, a quasi-Masonic lodge called *Propaganda Due* (infamously recorded in history as P2). The grand master of P2 was Licio Gelli, a serial conspirator and prominent acolyte of Benito Mussolini, the pre-war Italian dictator. His sole aim was the restoration of Italian fascism. To this end he assembled a host of Italy's senior politicians, businessmen, journalists, military and police officers, born-again fascists and creatures from the criminal underworld. This virtual alternative state formed an integral part of the Gladio structure.

The third level required assassination of figures deemed obstructive to NATO's aims. Thus high political leaders were culled: in Italy, ex-premier Aldo Moro, and in Sweden the prime minister Olof Palme. We later examine their fates in detail. In Turkey, the briefly reigning Adnan Menderes was lynched by the military high command on 17th September 1961, together with two cabinet colleagues. The executions followed a NATO and US-supported putsch. Menderes was thought to be flirting with a more Islamist form of republic, but we encounter radically different explanations in a moment.

The venerable Greek politician Georgios Papandreou (Sr.), who had the temerity to stand up to the bullying of President Lyndon Johnson over US plans to dismember Cyprus, was all but assassinated. Imprisoned under house arrest by the military junta in 1967, he was denied some of the essential life-supporting medicines necessary for his heart condition. President Charles de Gaulle of France was the target of repeated assassination attempts by renegade secret army guerrillas and their criminal cohorts acting on NATO orders. In revenge, the furious general ordered the alliance to close down its central command headquarters located near Paris, and then to quit French soil entirely. De Gaulle restored full sovereignty over French forces to the government in Paris. Effectively, France abandoned NATO. The Cypriot president Mikhail Makarios III had a narrow escape from Gladio units who invaded the island in 1974 with orders to kill him. The attack on Pope John Paul II in May 1981 was an audacious example of false-flag tactics designed to divert attention from an intended fascist putsch in Rome. The failed shooting offered the added bonus of doubling as a perfect opportunity to discredit the Soviet Union.

Other political weapons were extraordinarily sophisticated. In the UK of the mid 1970s, MI5, working in close affiliation with NATO and the CIA, achieved the 'soft assassination' of the moderate socialist prime minister, Harold Wilson. He was the target of destabilisation techniques on the specious grounds that he was in secret league with the Kremlin (See chapter XI: Frolics in the Forest: A Very British Coup). In this very odd interlude of British history, extreme Right-wing forces came close to staging a *coup d'état*. A senior member of the Royal Family, Earl Mountbatten, was sounded out by the plotters, but failed to take the bait. (This strange business, and the circumstances of Mountbatten's death at the hands of Irish Republican terrorists, is explored in Chapter XX, The Strange Tale of Two Earls.)

Following Wilson's abrupt fall on 16th March 1976, British big business allied with *agents provocateurs* — planted in the trades unions by the secret services — to invoke the infamous 1978-79 'Winter of Discontent.' Garbage choked the streets, practically every public service spluttered out. Britons were invited to see that their main enemy was the very socialism that had given them the National Health Service, medicines that everyone could afford, and free education for all — the full panoply of the cradle-to-the-grave welfare state. This final sabotage of the Labour government culminated in the election victory which catapulted the dependable US ally Margaret Thatcher to power. Her first actions sacrificed the long-standing cross-party commitments to welfarism in favour of the rising gods of the free market, privatization and crude competition in all forms of public services. Her famous stock market 'Big Bang' deregulation exercise in 1986 introduced the corrosive forces of rampant corporatism at the expense of old fashioned, outmoded manufacturing. People who actually make things, as distinct from providing so-called services, became a redundant species. The ruined landscape lies exposed for all to see in Britain today.

In Belgium, paedophiles linked to espionage services and the country's secret deep state were enlisted to undermine the state and blackmail prominent citizens. The techniques and the gross depravity of the abuse suggest an overhang from the CIA's horrific mind-bending experiments known as the MK-Ultra program, conducted in the 1960s and '70s.

Copycat violence and murders marked the rash of Marxist urban guerrillas who appeared in Germany, Italy, Turkey and Greece. These were branded as Soviet-manipulated Fifth Columns, burrowing away at the foundations of democracy. A crop of radical subversive movements — led by disgruntled intellectuals, students and other disaffected members of the young post-war generation — began to express angry frustration with soulless and exploitative capitalist militarism. In the United States the outcome was Bob Dylan and Flower Power; in Europe, the 'armed struggle.' Today we remember these times through names such as Germany's legendary Baader-Meinhof Red Army Faction, Britain's anarcho-Marxist Angry Brigades and Italy's Red Brigades. In Greece the terrorist band November 17 was to remain in business, so to speak, for almost 30 years, a peculiar story of eluding detection in such a small country. This was only possible with full sanction at the highest levels of the Greek state (see Chapter VIII). N17 took its name from an especially infamous date in Greek history. On that day in 1973, twenty-four demonstrators were gunned down when military police panicked during an anti-Junta demonstration at the Athens Polytechnic. The band were gleefully dubbed the 'false teeth guerrillas' by the Greek media when the ringleaders were finally rounded up, or more plausibly offered up for sacrifice, as the new century began.

A common stripe ran through all the urban revolutionary forces that arose in Europe. They were riddled with double agents planted by the secret intelligence services to provoke takeaway terror to order.

The architect of these tactics was an elusive and extremely dangerous Frenchman called Yves Guérin-Sérac. In a black sense, the man was a genius. A small and wiry figure, he was a decorated veteran of the French colonial wars in Indo-China and Algeria. He was in thrall to his personal vision of a Christian-Fascist New World Order. He was also the intellectual mentor of Gladio terrorism. He wrote the basic training and propaganda manuals which can be fairly described as the Gladio order of battle. He devised the 'steering' of urban revolutionaries by planting interlopers. These could in turn incite acts of terror. They could also uncover plots that were then 'just allowed to happen.' When we analyse all the European terrorism committed during the Cold War, it appears that many atrocities were in fact intercepted by the authorities well in advance. They sat on their hands and looked the other way. In the subsequent disorder, they appeared as statues of calm. The bullet and the bomb were foremost intended to destroy the existing political order and fix the blame on the communists. Here is an extract describing the strategy, picked out in Guérin-Sérac's typically cold, emotionless prose.

Two forms of terrorism can provoke such a situation [breakdown of the state]: blind terrorism (committing massacres indiscriminately which cause a large number of victims), and selective terrorism (eliminate chosen persons)...

This destruction of the state must be carried out under the cover of 'communist activities.' Popular opinion must be polarized... that we are the only instrument capable of saving the nation.

But from whom precisely? There was no popular will for a communist uprising anywhere in Europe, least of all in devoutly Catholic Italy. Guérin-Sérac understood that perfectly well. Despite its well-organised communist mass, Italy was out of bounds to a Leftish revolution. His real target was the western liberal and tolerant model of democracy. Thus new meaning is bestowed on the old proverb warning that supping with the devil calls for a long spoon. Stefano Delle Chiaie, a prominent Italian neofascist and close confederate of Guérin-Sérac, admitted that all his acts were foremost intended to destabilise the liberal state. He mentioned very little about the communists. All the prominent European dictators of the 20th century — Vladimir Ilyich Lenin, Benito Mussolini, Adolf Hitler, Spain's General Francisco Franco and António de Oliveira Salazar of Portugal — made the extinction of the vacuous, bourgeois state their leading priority.

The communists had become an increasingly vexing problem in Italy. They were deploying their increasing strength to demand a position in the mainstream consensus. In a wider sense, beyond Italy, this was known as the period of 'Euro-communism,' summarised as defanged communism with a smiling face. The charismatic young Italian communist leader, Enrico Berlinguer, offended Moscow by striking out independently with a new European brand of modern, updated communism. Berlinguer was a child of two momentous events that shook the communist world, the Hungarian Revolution in the autumn of 1956 and the Prague Spring twelve years later. The brutal crushing of popular uprisings in both countries by troops drawn from NATO's alter ego, the Warsaw Pact, seared the spirit of the essentially humanist communist cause all over Europe. Berlinguer's response was to invoke the phrase that later became such a favourite with British politicians of the Right: namely, 'back to basics.'

To the NATO command's entire satisfaction, the Italian Communist Party was ultimately destroyed by Guérin-Sérac's classic infiltration ruse. As we noted, the kidnap and murder of the former Italian premier Aldo Moro in 1978 was attributed to the urban Marxist guerrillas calling themselves the Brigate Rosse. His death clearly belonged with Guérin-Sérac's dictum of 'selective terrorism (eliminate chosen persons).' Portrayed as allied to the Brigate Rosse, the communist party never recovered. But the prize was even greater in transforming the culture of Italian politics. The burgeoning spirit of Eurocommunism, the banner flown by Enrico Berlinguer, perished with Aldo Moro. Here was one resounding victory for the Strategy of Tension.

The lesson that we learn is this. NATO's commitment to post-war Europe did not include the preservation and nourishment of genuinely deep-rooted democracy, despite all the cross-my-heart pretensions of that nature. After WW2, the United States industrially harvested unreconstructed fascists in Germany, Belgium, Italy, France, Austria, Greece and Turkey. This was part of the imperial mission to join Europe and the United States in a combination of global power. In such a picture, 'bourgeois liberal democracy' — in Europe, the United States, or anywhere else — is a hindrance that has no place whatsoever.

The Turkish Prime Minister Adnan Menderes was hanged on the orders of a military kangaroo court in 1961, because he threatened to choke the highly profitable contraband trails passing through Turkey. These were in part controlled and organised by the CIA and their confederates in the Turkish Mafia, the powerful army high command, the rogue Turkish state secret service MIT, and violent Far Right mercenaries. Menderes' counterfeit leanings to an Islamic republic were a confection manufactured by US intelligence. The murder of Olof Palme, the Swedish premier, in Stockholm on 28th February 1986, was only peripherally connected to the theme of anti-communism. Often described as the 'Swedish JFK,' Palme was cut down because he obstructed US geopolitical interests. These notably featured the Iran-Iraq war. The US at first promoted the war, then took positions on both sides. Palme was the UN umpire trying to stop this pointless bloodshed. He compounded his sins by his firm attachment to the cause of Palestinian sovereignty. His star pupil, Social Democrat premier-in-waiting Anna Lindh, was savagely murdered in a Stockholm supermarket on 11th September 2003. She had also adopted the Palestinian cause, and openly turned against the US-inspired war on terror.

Throughout these pages we shall read of the intricate involvement of the Vatican with the machinations of Gladio, organised crime and resurgent neofascism. The extraordinary events that led up to the attempted assassination of Pope John Paul II on 13th May 1981 belong to this category (St. Petersgate, Chapter XII). One of the memorable episodes dating from this time is the image of Roberto Calvi, the suave Italian financier known as God's Banker, dangling from a noose beneath Blackfriars Bridge across the River Thames in London. The Vatican's internal bank, the Institute of Religious Works (*Istituto per le Opere di Religione*, IOR) had been effectively hi-jacked by criminal interests holding strong affinities with the Italian and American Mafia, the Italian secret state and the Gladio sleeping soldiers. This was to cost Calvi his life in a spectacular fashion.

Michele Sindona was the brains behind the Sicilian-born Carlo Gambino's US money laundering networks, and a leading figure in P2 as well. He wormed his way into virtual control of the Vatican's secretive heavenly bank, thanks to the unworldly Pope Paul VI, who sincerely believed this son of a Sicilian farm hand was some kind of gifted accountant. In terms of purely down-to-earth practicalities, the IOR was the perfect priest-hole to conceal the profits of the contraband industry. After the usual cut for himself and the Holy Father's good works, Sindona, the wizard working the levers behind the curtain, used these sacred chutes to shuttle millions of dollars to fund death squads propping up venal US-backed Latino dictators. Their brave exploits in the Argentine 'Dirty War' of the mid 1970s included the so-called 'shrimp cocktail,' the grim description of naked, semi-drugged victims hurled to their deaths from helicopters flapping over gray Atlantic waves. The last comforting words victims often heard were murmured by chaplains of a messianic sect of Christian Fascists, known to inspire some of Gladio's high princes of terrorism (notably the Frenchman Yves Guérin-Sérac), incanting the virtues of 'sorting the wheat from the chaff.'

The Vatican State was in the thick of laundering money pouring from all directions: the Sicilian-American Mafia, mysterious shelf companies hiding the illegal activities of secret services, powerful mainstream banks with deeds to conceal — with the proceeds calmly skimmed by Pope John Paul II. The Vatican's profit, so to speak, lubricated his sacred duty of buying the freedom of East European Catholics, most prominently those in his own Polish homeland. This is the extraordinary story of the Vatican, the Kremlin and the Red Gold, which appears for the first time in these pages. It is no exaggeration to state that the Holy See has always been a holy ghost within the structure of NATO, even to the extent of hosting its own Gladio unit, drawn from the Swiss Guard, the Pontiff's personal protection squad, and the private Vatican police. From a miniature kingdom only three times or so larger than New York's Grand Central Station, the Pope of the day exercises temporal authority on the scale of a great power. One crowned head of the CIA, Bill Colby, famously remarked that the global intelligence services maintained by the Vatican left his own modest efforts entirely in the shade.

The attempt on the Pope's life was promoted by western intelligence as a headline-grabbing KGB-Bulgarian conspiracy, for which there was not one shred of hard supporting evidence. Mehmet Ali Ağca, the gunman convicted of shooting the Pope, was a well-known Turkish criminal connected to Gladio and the CIA's narcotics chains. Behind the scenes nearly all the key players in the St. Petersgate drama were drawn from the Turkish Mafia, with the exception of two prominent figures associated with known CIA assassination programmes. Both were in Rome that day. Ağca's companion in St. Peter's Square was Abdullah Çatlı, a senior Turkish gangster holding an official 007 licence to kill. He travelled on a diplomatic passport, containing a note that he was allowed to carry guns. Both Ağca and Çatlı belonged to the Gray Wolves, a Right-wing paramilitary organisation, known for fits of wild howling when they gathered en masse. The Gray Wolves formed an essential element of the Turkish Gladio structure known as Counter-Guerrilla. The German investigative writer Jürgen Roth has stated that killers such as Çatlı and Ağca were allowed to roam Europe without hindrance by the authorities, whatever the pretensions of Interpol to the contrary.

Çatlı's fabulous career as gangster, mercenary, government *agent provocateur* and Gladio contract killer came to a sudden end on 3rd November 1996, in what became known as the Susurluk Incident. He died in a car crash in the undistinguished small town of that name in western Anatolia. The Mercedes he was driving in some haste smashed into the back of a heavy truck. He died instantly, along with his girl friend, an attractive fashion mannequin called Gonca Us. A third body pulled from the wreckage was that of Hüseyin Kocadağ, the former deputy chief of the Istanbul gendarmerie. He was also closely connected to Counter-Guerrilla, the Turkish Gladio, and frequently given ultra-secret assignments for the special operations department of the national police force. Sedat Bucak, a powerful Kurdish clan leader, whose men were armed by the state to fight against separatist violence, survived with little more than a broken leg and a fractured skull. As investigators got to work, it emerged that Çatlı possessed a clutch of eight national identity cards, each with a different alias. These included documents made out in the name of Mehmet Ozkay, the same alias that Mehmet Ali Ağca often used on his travels. He also held two Turkish diplomatic passports which had been approved by none other than the interior minister Mehmet Agar, who was also a high True Path party official. One of these stated that he was permitted to travel while carrying firearms.

The Susurluk Incident struck Turkey with all the force of Watergate in Richard Nixon's America. It brought to light for the first time the existence of a deep state organisation with links to organised crime, the police and secret intelligence services and the NATO Gladio organisation. The lady prime minister, Tansu Çiller, resigned but she expressed no regrets that her government had been caught out consorting with subversive forces. The secret state closed ranks. No prosecutions followed from the ensuing investigation, for one very good reason. Between them the dead and injured at Susurluk represented the 'Mafia-Gladio' coalition responsible for waging a dirty war on the minority Kurdish nationalist community. This is one of the oldest running sores in the history of modern Turkey, and from present events we see that the Kurdish struggle for self-determination is far from resolved, to this day. What Susurluk told the world was that many so-called Kurdish attacks on prominent symbols of the Turkish state were in fact performed by the Mafia-Gladio alliance, on the orders of the *derin devlet* (deep state). In short, false-flag synthetic violence. But the real explosive force behind Susurluk was the revelation that Çatlı was a long-time contract killer, reporting to the highest offices of the state. Small surprise then that one of the most infamous gunmen in the Gladio story received a send-off with such pomp and circumstance it might have been a full-blown state funeral.[3]

The Susurluk affair also served to expose the wiring of the narcotics chains winding across Turkey and the many hands vigorously competing for a piece of the action. The scramble included, in no particular order, the CIA, the Turkish state intelligence agency MIT, the Gray Wolves, the Counter-Guerrilla Gladio outfit, Kurdish secessionists, the national and border police, and the Mafia of course — not to mention the government itself, which was short of revenues after the loss of export markets in the Iran-Iraq war. Yet there was plenty for all — the racket was said to be worth £3 millions an hour. One of these trails wound its way through the secretive Soviet bloc state of Bulgaria, with the full knowledge and complicity of western

---

[3] Susurluk retains all the features of a constantly erupting volcano. The exposure in 2009 of a new Turkish deep state organization called Ergenekon brought together many characters who had been connected to Counter-Guerrilla. A top Mafioso called Yaşar Öz, imprisoned for offences related to the Susurluk investigation, delivered a six-page dossier to the judge investigating the Ergenekon affair. In it he claimed that Abdullah Çatlı was assassinated to ensure his silence on dangerous affairs of state. It seemed to confirm the reports after the crash that experts found very skilled hands had meddled with the car's braking system.

intelligence at the highest levels. The role of the hugely criminalised Bulgarian state as effectively a fiefdom of Gladio and side actor in the Strategy of Tension is revealed, for the first time, in Chapter IX.

The appointment of the much-decorated General Lyman Lemnitzer as supreme commander of all NATO forces in Europe in 1963 brought one of the US Army's most committed enthusiasts for black warfare into the highest seat of power within the Alliance. The Pentagonian chief of staff had recently been rudely sacked and effectively exiled by President John F. Kennedy, on justifiable grounds of rank insubordination. With Lemnitzer's arrival, *gli anni di piombo* erupted with a vengeance. Lemnitzer's colossal ego had permitted him to coldly propose a scheme to JFK calling for Mafia hoodlums to shoot Americans walking about the streets and then blame Cuban subversives (the Northwoods Plot, chapter III). A looking-glass war fought on European soil with identical methods and similar alliances came quite naturally to such a twisted mind. Lemnitzer could quietly nod when Trotsky spoke of combining all available means to meet the desired ends. In good time he reaped revenge on the man he despised as a closet communist, a president he demeaned as 'with no military experience — some kind of patrol boat captain.' Kennedy revealed his fatal weakness, in Lemnitzer's arid gaze, by bowing to the Soviets in the Cuban Missile Crisis of October 1962.

Lemnitzer was among the chief architects of the Strategy of Tension, and brought with him a wealth of experience gained from earlier commands in Southeast Asia. There and later in the Pentagon he was under the spell of the immensely unorthodox air force colonel (later general) Edward Lansdale. His speciality lay in bizarre voodoo-like schemes of psy-war and false-flag operations. Lansdale was likely the inspiration for the manic Northwoods conspiracy. The probability that both men were arms linked in Dallas on 22nd November 1963 is also explored in detail (again, chapter III). It was no accidental coincidence between Lemnitzer's fascination for Lansdale's eclectic methods and the morbid orders that went out to Gladio units under NATO command to kill innocent citizens quietly going about their lives. This was the selfsame blueprint Lemnitzer had proposed to the appalled John F. Kennedy to justify invading Cuba.

Lemnitzer was a seminal figure in other ways. NATO was of course a rib cut from the American Adam, an offshoot of Pentagonia, but at least until Lemnitzer's time there was some mood of a coalition with a common righteous cause. An alliance constructed on the basis of mutual defence, drawing on the ideas of Niccolò Machiavelli concerning well-organised but non-aggressive deterrence, is not without just cause. Lemnitzer changed all that to a zealous crusade pursued in the ruthless interests of the United States. He saw no moral hazards or ambiguity because America had, after all, saved (conquered) Europe, and was thus entitled to claim rightful homage by *droit du seigneur*. Henceforth European states must select governments conforming to the American imperial mission, or the consequences could be painful. Lemnitzer's poisoned chalice handed down to the current generation is an alliance without a cause, a penfold of obedient sheep who bray hosannas at every motion from the gods of war in Washington. However, as this book was preparing for press, NATO's Libyan war raised issues with blind obedience to the imperial writ by Turkey, Italy's Berlusconi government and peripherally, Germany.

So far we have pursued the theme which suggests that the Gladio secret armies were the main agent in manufacturing synthetic terrorism, in order to ward off the latent appeal of communism to the European masses. Thanks to Yves Guérin-Sérac, we see that NATO happily dramatised a non-existent threat of Soviet subversion. This is an opportune moment to introduce some famous words uttered by the American president, former general of the army and D-Day invasion commander, Dwight Eisenhower. Here is the legendary tablet of stone that the great national monument handed down (somewhat belatedly) to the American people on 17th January 1961, his last day in office.

> *In the councils of government, we must guard against the acquisition of unwarranted influence, whether sought or unsought, by the military-industrial complex. The potential for the disastrous rise of misplaced power exists and will persist. We must never let the weight of this combination endanger our liberties or democratic processes. We should take nothing for granted. Only an alert and knowledgeable citizenry can compel the proper meshing of the huge industrial and military machinery of defense with our peaceful methods and goals so that security and liberty may prosper together.*

A war machine without wars to fight or even prospective enemies is a contradiction in terms. Yet these were the discomfiting circumstances in which NATO now found itself when the Berlin Wall collapsed, followed by the entire Soviet order. Shortly before his death in 1946, the great economist and new-world-order progenitor John Maynard Keynes expressed the gloomy view that post-war America might find it difficult to sustain lasting economic prosperity without maintaining a war machine in full working order. The late Professor Seymour Melman of Colombia University described the US war machine and all its components including NATO as 'permanent war socialism.'[4] Matters had been moving in the direction of

---

[4] To be exact, Keynes argued that by 1944 the US was spending more on war production than the entire value of GNP ten years earlier. In the same year GNP reached $183 billions, from $110 billions in 1929. Nearly all of this increase was accounted for by war spending that began on a serious scale in 1942. Keynes posed the question how on earth a country that could not find work for 47 million people

Eisenhower's valedictory warning since 1947. In July that year, the National Security Act established a permanent military hierarchy in the form of the imperial high command — the Joint Chiefs of Staff — as an emerging parallel government. For good measure, America was blessed with its first peacetime espionage organisation, the Central Intelligence Agency. It would become the personal praetorian guard of every future president. At the stroke of his pen President Harry Truman invented the Cold War.

Over time, the military-industrial-complex metastasized to the sprawling military-security-industrial-media complex that we see today, driven by the manufactured fear of Islamic terrorism. The Cold War agenda, which supposedly crumbled along with the Berlin Wall, we find resurrected in all its dreary, sterile imbecility. At the University of California, Dr. William Robinson, Professor of Sociology and Global Studies, has been thinking about the 'hysterical global scape-goating and criminalization of Muslims,' which at heart is precisely what the illusory war on terror is all about. He sees it as deliberately orchestrated by the emerging fascist-minded World Corporate Order composed of big business, the financial élites and the ravenous military-industrial complex. They play on escalating world tensions arising from global poverty, swelling populations and the finite limits of food, oil and minerals. In other words, the manufacture of synthetic fear, exactly like the original Gladio Strategy of Tension, refreshed and revived to drive people everywhere into submitting before a global security system, and to relentless draconian restraints on their individual lives and privacies. Professor Robinson believes forces already loosed in the US will not be easily extinguished: 'A neofascist insurgency is quite apparent in the United States.....[America] cannot be characterized at this time as fascist. Nonetheless, all of the conditions and the processes are present and percolating, and the social and political forces behind such a project are mobilizing rapidly.' The Canadian-born Professor Peter Dale Scott drives the stake a little harder. For him, the political system of the United States exhibits a deceivingly democratic and legal appearance on the surface, but in reality is now little different from any other dictatorial regime in the world.

---

before the war would manage in peacetime with 55 millions looking for work. As Keynes feared, the United States went right back to militarism after the war.

Yet WW2 is a poor example to follow for economic stimulus. It was highly labor-intensive on all sides, while modern weapons production creates few jobs. Major wars can only be paid for by unsustainably high budget deficits. Military spending does much less for the real economy than investment in education or infrastructure. In a 1961 essay, 'The Economic Effects of Disarmament,' Nobel-prize-winning economist Professor Wassily Leontief showed that alternative domestic spending creates twice as many jobs as dollars on 'defence.' Melman's findings were similar.

Take all the elements of waging perpetual war. A rash of so-called humanitarian interventions underpin and drive forward the massive capacity of the NATO/US war machine. Endless cycles of destruction and re-building, and indulgence in gratuitous waste. $20 billion a year simply to chill US army tents in Afghanistan; almost $7 billion earmarked for the 'reconstruction' of Iraq vanished altogether. Meanwhile public infrastructure crumbles, schools and hospitals across the US and in the UK are in decay. What is left is the Orwellian *Nineteen Eighty-Four* total war economy — all in the service of the criminalization of Islam described by Dr. Robinson.

The communist menace having inconveniently evaporated, the frustrated conquistadores wheeled around to attack the Balkans, unpicking the work of ages by destroying Yugoslavia, one of the few practical fruits surviving the post-WW1 Versailles peace conference. NATO's first real war (leaving aside the shadow assault on Cyprus) was conducted without a shred of legality, since no attack had been suffered by any member state to justify invoking the kernel Article 5 solidarity clause.

As a humanitarian intervention, it fell distinctly short of advance billing. Clumsy meddling with ancient accommodations and loyalties along the fault lines of two combative world religions sparked grisly racial pogroms and genocide, which are not yet exhausted. The spectacle of NATO warplanes raining bombs on non-combatants and Chinese diplomats (eerily paralleled by the bombing of North Korea's embassy in the Libyan campaign) trashed illusions of a sober and benign Alliance for Peace — yet this was unerringly close to James Burnham's futuristic eye. All the characteristics of Gladio and the Strategy of Tension were laid bare once again. Chapter XIX — Appointment at Račak — displays these tactics in full play in one tragic episode in the hotly disputed enclave of Kosovo in January 1999. All through the Big Push to tame the Balkans, NATO hitched up with the mainstream corporate media to hosepipe public opinion with distorted accounts of the glorious crusade, soaked with stories of horrific atrocities performed by Serbian monsters and their cronies. For sure nobody was playing paintball in this squalid scrap. The calamities that befell former Yugoslavia and its ethnic divides guaranteed horrors on both sides. Until however a Dutch academic named Cees Wiebes came up with the incontrovertible facts in 2002, nothing was admitted on the Alliance side of calumnies performed by their imported Mujahedeen fighters. Bloodied in struggles against the Russian forces in their Afghan homeland, they were let loose by the Pentagon on the selfsame communities the NATO avenging angel was supposed to defend.

This is the inconvenient truth concerning Al Qaeda, remnant of the CIA's made-to-measure Afghan resistance movement (its name means literally 'The Platform' in Arabic). Honed and hardened in the epic and ultimately victorious struggle with the Russians, these same fighters were transferred to the Balkans to tip the balance towards Muslim forces. As a strategy this was certain to guarantee friction with other NATO powers such as the Greeks, who smiled favorably on the Serbs. The presence of Afghan guerrillas and Iranian specialists and arms, with the direct connivance of the United States, defied a string of UN resolutions. The West's hear-no-evil, see-no-evil media barons conspired to suppress the Dutch study because these revelations, coming on the heels of 9/11 twenty months before, raised serious questions concerning the *casus belli* of the war on terror.

For five years, Professor Cees Wiebes, of Amsterdam University and senior analyst at the Office of the National Coordinator for Counter-Terrorism (NCTB) in the Netherlands, was allowed complete freedom to mine Dutch military and secret service files. His devastating report, which he turned into a book, undermined all the arguments for sending Dutch troops to the Balkans.[5] The government instantly collapsed. In one of the few published comments to appear in the UK corporate media, Professor Richard Aldrich, the noted British expert in peace and international security studies at Warwick University, explained to *Guardian* readers on 22nd May 2002:

> *It includes remarkable material on covert operations, signals interception, human agents and double-crossing by dozens of agencies in one of dirtiest wars of the new world disorder. Now we have the full story of the secret alliance between the Pentagon and radical Islamist groups from the Middle East designed to assist the Bosnian Muslims — some of the same groups that the Pentagon is now fighting in the war against terrorism.*

The late Richard Holbrooke — Washington's chief point man in the Balkans — described these accommodations as a 'necessary pact with the devil.' Subsequently despatched as US special envoy to the Afghan snake pit, it seems the devil may have followed hot on his footsteps. Reports speak of curious material shipments reaching Taliban insurgents, designed to prolong the conflict and justify a long-term NATO stake in the country. The finger of suspicion points to so-called security contractors, including one owned by the Afghan president's warlord brother, who were paid tens of millions of dollars by NATO and the CIA to escort convoys of essential supplies to the troops. When they are not busily bribing Taliban commanders, or selling them fuel and other supplies, favoured pastimes include staging fake attacks to dramatise instability, and false-flag attacks against competitors who get in their way. 'One way or another,' an exasperated NATO official informed a

---

[5] *Intelligence and the War in Bosnia 1992-1995*. The professor makes the excellent point that no war ever proceeds according to plan. Expect then chaos and confusion caused by unexpected developments, inferior intelligence, confused strategizing. NATO's first hot war witnessed all of these confusions and more.

correspondent from the AllGov open source site, 'we are funding both sides in this conflict.' The only security element is the safe conduct of dope convoys heading for the NATO-EU principality of Kosovo, centrifugal pump for nearly all heroin reaching European streets. The chief entrepreneur is the great freedom fighter and prize Pentagonian princeling, pocket state Prime Minister Hashim Thaçi. The Balkan campaign was to find a sequel in Libya, NATO's desert war of 2011. The alliance was compelled to admit the presence of Al Qaeda fighters in the ranks of their Libyan rebels — another convenient 'pact with the devil.' The Alliance abandoned all pretence of respect for formal protocols to attack Libya. There had been of course no attack by Libya on any NATO member state that would justify an action, so the ruse was adopted of yet another humanitarian intervention authorized by the UN Security Council. The original no-fly-zone patrols supposed to clear the skies of Gaddafi's jet fighters soon gave way to a full-scale bombing campaign. The most modern state in the Arab world was bombed back to the stone age. The precedent thus established, the real business began of looting resources deemed crucial to the West: Libyan oil, the country's massive hoard of cash and bullion and (not least in these parched desert wastes) water. It was NATO's third war of aggression: first the Balkans, then Afghanistan, and now North Africa.

Dr. William Robinson dates the emergence of fascism in the United States to the militarist posture of the George H. W. Bush years, although others — including myself — prefer a steady evolutionary process that began much earlier with the creation of the CIA in 1947. From the outset, the so-called intelligence-gathering agency bore the distinctive features of a lawless, state-within-a-state mercenary organisation. The truly Gothic presidency of Richard Nixon, then Reagan's semi-detached watch, the respective turns of Bush the Elder, Bill Clinton and then Bush Junior, witnessed the accelerating extinction of American democracy.

The same drift is evident everywhere that one looks within the Atlantic Alliance. Under Nicholas Sarkozy, France clearly owed more to Vichy's Marshal Philippe Pétain of WW2 than Charles de Gaulle. Silvio Berlusconi and his Northern League separatist consort Umberto Bossi eventually pushed Italy to the brink — and over, into the underworld beneath the veneer of democracy. In November 2011 the globalist EU-Bilderberg-sponsored *coup d'état* collapsed Berlusconi's government like a pack of cards. Psychologically, the moment was finely judged. Italians had sickened of the gaffe-prone premier's sexual peccadilloes and bruising encounters with the courts. The incoming techno-government headed by the free-market economist Mario Monti, rector of an expensive private university in Milan, effectively suspended parliamentary rule 'for the duration of the emergency.' The excuse was presented that Italy's problem of public debt had blossomed to such an extent that it threatened the euro currency. Early in January,

Professor Monti himself made the rather astonishing admission that there had not been a euro crisis, and that Italy's problems were purely 'systemic.' A similar coup occurred in Greece at exactly the same time. Another economist, Professor Loukas Papademos, formed a coalition government that provoked uproar by including four members of the extreme Right Popular Orthodox Rally party. Its leadership views the former Greek military junta with benign approval.

Both Monti and Papademos are loaded with New World Order credentials. Monti is associated with the Bilderberg club and chairs the European branch of the Trilateral Commission. Among his other garlands he advises the board of Goldman Sachs. The speed with which he assembled a government of technocrats suggests well-laid plans. Was it any co-incidence that Sig. Monti was an Italian representative at the Bilderberg conclave in St. Moritz in June that year? Papademos is the central banker *par excellence*: Boston Federal Reserve economist, Bank of Greece governor, European Central Bank vice president. He has been a Trilateral member for twelve years. Greece clung to a fragment of democracy, the pretence of politicians still pulling the levers. But the government was chosen by Papademos and decided in Brussels and Frankfurt, and along the underground corridors of the secretive Bilderberg Club, just like Italy's.

The affairs of backwater Hungary rarely disturb the international commentariat. So it passed unnoticed that Prime Minister Viktor Orban — 'The Great Viktator' to his detractors — was allowed to impose full-blown press censorship and the creeping evolution of a one-party state. Orban is a glowing Bilderberg alumnus whose ruthless rape of democracy — 'the Second Hungarian Rising' — was timed with brute cheek to mark the start of Hungary's six-month presidency of the European Union on 1st January 2011. He attracted the warm approval of fellow Bilderberger Herman van Rompuy, then the Belgian president of the EU governing council (who strangely resembles one of the goblin clerks in the Potterland wizard bank). Van Rompuy instantly shot off to Budapest to shake the splendid Viktator's hand. On 1st January 2012, a new constitution came into force which effectively ended the country's twenty year flirtation with democracy.

Sweden is on the slope to such an extent that sober commentators wonder if democracy will survive there another ten years. Neofascists have emerged as a strong force in the Riksdag. The government of Fredrik Reinfeldt, for all its pretence to moderate centralism, is actually closer to the Blair-Cameron everlasting war axis. Thanks to the stealthy abandonment of neutrality (joyously cheered at the CIA's website), Sweden's 'peacekeepers' mustered in the Balkans and Afghanistan. Her jets screamed through Libyan skies. Stephen Harper's Canada is falling like a captured planet into the magnetic suction of the United States. It is no longer eccentric to talk of a union between the two countries.[6] Slippage to the Right in both major parties has levered the United Kingdom inexorably towards a parafascist, total-surveillance society. Absolutely no people on earth are more closely scrutinised by their masters as the British. With one per cent of the world's population, this small country has amassed more than 20% of all closed-circuit cameras on the planet. A visitor to London can expect to be spotted and recorded up to 6,000 times every day by one of these sneaking eyes. It is no coincidence that much of this paraphernalia was installed following the London Transport bombings on 7th July 2005, which occurred at a time of rising opposition to the British military presence in Iraq and Afghanistan.

During the 1997 general election, that brought the purely notional socialist Anthony Charles 'Tony' Blair to power, his Conservative opponents got into hot water for playing low tactics. Conservative strategists pasted billboards all over the country portraying their opponent with maniacal demon eyes. Some might argue with the benefit of hindsight it was not far short of an accurate character assessment. The rise of New Labour, a designer fiction invented and dominated by Blair — a figure of no precise centre of political gravity — was the decisive factor. Under his successive governments, parliament was — and a strong word is needed — raped. A series of bills went through that effectively emasculated the powers of members of parliament to enact legislation. Henceforth the *fiat* rule of whoever dwelt in Downing Street prevailed. Ancient provisions such as *habeas corpus*, the Magna Carta and the ancient Statutes of Westminster were elbowed aside as so much historical junk, for which the Great Moderniser Blair had no time or patience. As everyone now recognises, the illegal invasion of Iraq was constructed from cooked evidence concerning Saddam Hussein's alleged possession of weapons of mass destruction. Iraq was about oil and the strategic safety screen around Israel. Dr. David Kelly, contrarian arms assessment expert found dead in a glade near his Oxfordshire home in July 2003, expired from the equivalent of a shaving nick and a few aspirins. We learnt in October 2010 that one crucial document, the incident report by the paramedics who arrived first on the scene, had vanished into oblivion. Such affairs hover over the Blair era like thunderclouds.

Those traditional bastions of tolerance, free love and hash, Denmark and Holland, veered off to extremities of the Right, impelled by issues of race and religion stirred by the 'war on terror.' Denmark inspired the famous Mohammed cartoons affair. This is the same country where the royal family

---

[6] In February 2011 it was announced that Canada — of all countries — was to develop a new forward operational base in Germany. I regard this as a symbolic example of the developing North American imperialism and in the longer term, a step towards James Burnham's vision of a global military and political Euro-American colossus.

and most of the population defiantly adorned themselves with yellow stars in solidarity with persecuted Danish Jews during the Nazi occupation. Holland is undoubtedly exposed to the pressures of large-scale migration from her former colonies in Asia and South America. Yet all went peaceably enough until a series of events which bear an unmistakeable common thread.

First the despatch of nearly 2,000 Dutch soldiers to a second unpopular foreign war, in Afghanistan; then the appearance of the damning Wiebes Report in April 2002 on the catastrophe in the Balkans. A month later (on 6th May 2002), the murder of Pim Fortuyn, charismatic contender for the premiership, allegedly by a Dutch eco-activist and so-called sympathiser with persecuted Muslims. Finally came the gruesome slaughter in November 2004 of the film director Theodore Van Gogh, a member of the iconic Van Gogh family tree. He courted notoriety with cinematic rages against the Dutch Islamic immigrant community. His killer had been under secret service scrutiny for months. Again we divine the Guérin-Sérac Gladio ordinance to 'eliminate chosen persons.' Fortuyn died because he threatened to upset the existing political order and block Dutch participation in the Lockheed Martin Joint Strike Fighter project. Van Gogh was killed to dramatise the threat of Islamic terrorism. (See Chapter XVII, The Return of Gladio: In the Shadow of the Minaret). As the American Gothic fantasy writer Emma Bull so rightly observes, 'Coincidence is the word we are inclined to employ when we cannot see who is tugging the levers and pulleys.'

The penumbra of Lemnitzer's madness clings to Europe like a nightmare. Despite grudging avowals from NATO command, there is no concrete evidence that the Gladio units were shut down. Why should they be, given that the propaganda and secret policy committees of the alliance remain in full working order? There are too many fresh sightings and green shoots of Gladio redux to ignore. There is trouble brewing in Turkey, a country which exhibits similar characteristics to the US: apparently democratic on the surface, while old forces hold sway underground. For the last ten years Turks have lived with a soft Islamic political power, the populist but broadly pro-western Justice and Development (AK) Party. The new rulers revitalised the economy and struck out with radical foreign policies and associations with pariah states, including Iran. People began to speak of the rise of the New Ottomans. The Israeli commando attack on the Turkish-sponsored Gaza aid mission flotilla on 31st May 2010, in which nine Turkish citizens were killed by the boarding party, provoked the previously unthinkable breach with the Jewish state. For the first time since the man-god founder, Kemal Atatürk, Turkey is under non-secular rule.

The year 2011 was a momentous one in the on-going struggle between the rigidly secular whisky generals of the armed forces and the Islamist civilian state. On 29th July, the entire Turkish High Command resigned *en masse* in protest at the arrrest of officers in the ongoing investigation of the Ergenekon deep state organisation, which has dominated Turkish politics and media headlines since its exposure in 2007. Ergenekon is widely seen as the successor to Counter-Guerrilla, the former Gladio operation in Turkey, with the same taste for interfering in the affairs of state. There was no better example of a magnificently calculated exercise in misjudgement. Prime Minister Recep Tayyip Erdoğan promptly replaced the entire command with appointments more to his liking. Turks then sat back in rapt astonishment as Erdoğan aimed two more powerful blows at the military establishment, with all the skill of a prize fighter. The government arrested an ex-chief of the general staff, General Ilker Başbuğ, on charges of plotting with the Ergenekon organisation to overthrow the government. In the past any prime minister who dared lay hands on such an exalted figure would expect to meet the same fate as poor Adnan Menderes, at the end of a rope. But these were merely warm-up acts to the main performance. Early in the New Year 2012, the former Turkish president-dictator General Kenan Evren (aged 94) and his chief surviving collaborator, General Tahsin Şahinkaya (86), were placed on trial for overthrowing the civilian government of Süleyman Demirel on 12th September 1980. Both NATO and the US (specifically, the CIA) were directly involved through Counter-Guerrilla in the coup — one of the bloodiest episodes in contemporary Turkish history — and they find Erdoğan's actions highly sensitive and contentious.

Turkey, as we shall see in following pages, was always a popular Gladio playground. The outing in 2007 of the organisation code-named Ergenekon was followed by scores of arrests of serving and retired military officers. The Islamists had been in power for scarcely two years when the *Balyoz* or 'Sledgehammer' Plot was exposed in 2003. Sledgehammer was devised by the Turkish High Command and the state secret service MIT, with the connivance of the CIA. It came straight from the Gladio pedigree stables. A Turkish fighter plane would be shot down and blame fixed on the Greeks. The AK Party would then be branded as 'weak' for allowing the Aegean to be brought to the brink of war. The same plan called for mosques in Istanbul to be bombed during Friday prayers to ensure the maximum number of casualties. Military guard posts were to be attacked by 'shariah-dressed persons.' Caught in the spotlights, the red-faced generals explained that they were 'just planning' for possible eventualities. Elements of Sledgehammer bore a startling resemblance to General Lyman Lemnitzer's Northwoods insanity. All the more interesting, then, that Turkey's military leadership held a conclave with visiting US top brass just before a series of bomb explosions shook Istanbul in 2003. Attributed to Al Qaeda and an obscure Islamist fringe group, the bombs targeted two synagogues, the local headquarters of the HSBC Bank and the venerable British Consulate, a noted architectural monument dating to Ottoman times. The explosions killed 57 people, including the Consul General, Roger Short, and injured 700. The attribution to a gang of suspects purportedly in thrall to Osama bin Laden would have been more convincing, but for the plain fact that Al Qaeda affiliates were at precisely that moment fighting on behalf of the US and NATO in the Balkans. As it is, another pack of stooges were led quietly away to reflect on the penalties of trusting the promises of western intelligence agencies. It is difficult to prevent fools from their own folly when they step so willingly into lethal minefields. This tale has not run its course. Bombs continue to explode with depressing frequency in Turkey's major cities, but their provenance is another matter altogether. The affair at Susurluk is probably our best guide to a repeat of the Mafia-Gladio Counter-Guerrilla axis.

There are ominous signs developing in Germany. In the summer of 2011, a rash of bombings at electrical transformer stations serving the German State Railway were blamed on 'socialist guerrillas.' According to informed whispers from government spokesmen, the saboteurs 'knew what they were doing.' Respectable organs like *Der Spiegel* rattled skeletons in the Baader-Meinhof cupboard, reminding Germans how the RAF started in a modest fashion and ended up holding the entire country to ransom. The guilt-by-association reference to socialists implies we should expect a new wave of Gladio-type terrorism to send German voters flocking to the safe bosom of the Right.

Certainly, Gladio's story is one of steady evolution to meet contemporary strategies. An 'information unit' called DSSA, consisting of Right-wing police officers, came to the surface in Italy. The same organisation was reputedly traced as supplying *agents provocateurs* to the prefabricated 'Black Bloc' of anarchists who appeared, bang on cue, to tear down a statue of the sacred Madonna at the peak of anti-austerity protests in Rome in autumn 2011. In December that year a bomb exploded in a package delivered to the central tax-collecting office in Rome, injuring an official sitting at his desk. In this case the blame fell upon a conveniently shadowy organisation calling itself the *Federazione Anarchica Informale* (Informal Anarchist Federation). The same group was blamed for sending a letter bomb to the headquarters of the Swiss Nuclear Industry Association and another to the office in Frankfurt of Josef Ackerman, CEO of Deutsche Bank and standard hate figure of purported anti-globalists. The subtle implication of these bomb incidents was to remind Italians and Europeans of the *anni di piombo* — with a refreshed story line: Only underworld anarchists opposed the march to a new world order. Thus was the retired scape-goat of communism replaced.

Controversy refuses to subside concerning the mysterious murder on 22nd July 2005 of a Brazilian jobbing electrician by clandestine army and police units, plainly bearing a Gladio-type James Bond licence to kill. Jean Charles de Menezes was tailed in a leisurely fashion around South London and then shot dead like a hunted sewer rat on a crowded rush hour tube train, for no apparent reason. According to Scotland Yard (and the rare stage appearance of weeping secret policemen) it was all a tragic blunder. Menezes was supposedly mistaken for an Ethiopian sought in connection with the failed bombings on the transport network the day before (two weeks after the deadly 7/7 attacks blamed on four young 'suicide bombers'). The victim was comprehensively libelled by the police as a potential suicide bomber, wearing bulky clothes and fiddling with wires. In fact he was setting off for work in his usual casual gear. In Chapter XVI (The Return of Gladio: Death in the Underworld) I explore the alternative case that the killing of Menezes was no accident or blunder but a premeditated take-out. He quite possibly encountered knowledge of engineered voltage changes to track circuits that may have played an important role in the deadly London Underground bombings of 7th July, quite sufficient to place his life in danger.

Indeed who were the real authors of the London transport bombings that day, given that a parallel security exercise involving the same trains and stations that were bombed was under way at precisely the same time? (Chapter XV Ghost Trains: London and Madrid). Police and forensic accounts of the alleged backpack bombers raise many disturbing questions. So does the evidence that the bright blue flashes and noxious fumes reported by many survivors point to an engineered overload of the electrical current feeding power to the trains. As one highly reputable source that I have consulted has explained, this would cause any 'combustible material' attached to the trains to ignite. We move to the question of who commissioned and performed the highly sophisticated Spanish train bombings on 11th March 2004, at the peak of a bitterly contested nationwide election campaign, if it was not the strange and wholly unconvincing cast of characters assembled by the *Guardia Civil*? The courts failed to secure a single conviction that pointed clearly to an Islamist plot. The so-called mastermind walked from the court a free man.

Why there always seems to be a 'P' in Italy is a good question about a country eternally hovering in the everglades between the secret deep state and the one presented to the world. In July 2010, the Roman political establishment was rocked by the exposure of a new parallel state basement society, instantly christened P3 in a logical numerical sequence. P3 specialized in graft to influence a number of judges sitting on contentious cases, or swing lucrative government contracts the right way. Troubles, Romans always say, generally blow in with the scorching summer blasts from the Sahara known as the *sirocco*. So, unsurprisingly, these revelations appeared as the mercurial Silvio Berlusconi's latest coalition approached the rocks, burdened with a fractious crew and hugely unpopular austerity baggage. A year later, P4 broke surface. Like P's 2 and 3 before it, P4 operated as an underworld clique connected to the highest quarters of the state including the police, the military and powerful state corporations. The new Licio Gelli was named Luigi Bisignani, whose pedigree could be traced to the great political corruption *mani pulite* ('clean hands') scandals of the 1990's. He was said to have been a P2 member. The media (largely controlled by Berlusconi's companies or his political rope tricks) waxed loquaciously of the unknown man of the shadows — *L'uomo nell'ombra* — treading Italy's halls of power. It transpired however that signor Bisignani was a member of the chosen ones known as the *intoccabili* — the untouchables — a privileged caste permitted to wield power and influence on a scale close to the prime minister himself. The exposure of P4 served to confirm, yet again, that Italy is an entirely conditional state with no firm roots in democratic institutions. Whether she will recover from the Monti regency is an important question.

Another intriguing peep behind the curtain exposed theoretically neutral Switzerland's P26 secret soldiers — long associated in cloaked alliance with NATO — awaiting the call to arms should any socialist force dare to approach power in the land of Mammon. The summer of 2011, a vast hoard of explosives was suddenly discovered beneath a quiet street in Lucerne, placed it was said by the Swiss army even as the Soviet empire tottered to collapse. An odd story made odder by the explanation that it was supposed to impede the advance of Soviet tanks — down a minor street. The treasure trove made far better sense as a Swiss secret army munitions dump of far greater antiquity. In Athens, revolutionary urban guerrillas again stirred the Strategy of Tension, bombing symbols of western capitalism, as protests and strife spread against enforced IMF/EU austerity (looting) programs. These incidents bore a strong impression of November 17 fished from history for a new walk-on role.

Scarcely a day passes without some new fear-stoking headline delivering authorities the opportunity to stage another expedition of looting our collective liberties. At the height of the great poisoned cucumber scare in the summer of 2011, MI6 solemnly invoked the hand of Al Qaeda — yet the evidence pointed to a live test of yet another laboratory-created designer plague. If anyone is really looking for hard clues to the risible car bomb incident in New York's Times Square on 1st May 2010, there is the fact that yet another 'training exercise' was by strange coincidence in progress at exactly the same time — certainly the hardest nugget of evidence pointing to the actual culprits. The devastating Norwegian holiday island massacre of 22nd July 2011 and the huge bomb that exploded in the capital city Oslo's government quarter that same day were blamed in the familiar pattern on a lone, deranged terrorist. These incidents claimed the lives of 77 innocents. Like 9/11 and 7/7, these terrible events occurred against a background of preparatory and parallel security exercises. These drills were simply ignored by the media, and dismissed by the authorities as remarkable co-incidences, if mentioned at all.

Each time we are told that in order to be free, we must revere our chains and shackles. Sodomised by political rhetoric and corporate media plainsong, we fall for it. From Aldous Huxley's *Brave New World*:

> '*And that,*' *put in the Director sententiously,* '*that is the secret of happiness and virtue — liking what you've got to do. All conditioning aims at that: making people like their inescapable social destiny.*'

Evolution is the key to the unfolding Gladio story. In Era One of the Strategy of Tension, manufactured synthetic violence spread the fear of communist subversion. Era Two led to the demonization of the Muslim minority in Europe, the inflamed acts of religious war conducted in the shadow of the minaret. In 2011, we reached Era Three. The target has shifted again. The new, refreshed-for-duty Public Enemy Number One, complete with recharged batteries of rage and anger, is resurgent anarchism aimed at the overthrow of nothing less than the entire fabric and system of western capitalism. From closet communists and suicide bombers we have moved on to dystopian black-masked anarchists attacking the ramparts of globalism, represented by the Wall Street-enforced austerity programmes. As we shall see in Chapter IV, The Propaganda of the Deed, there is very little that is fresh and original under the Gladio sun. Depressingly, public opinion once again follows the line propagated by the establishment media, of mindless thugs and villains who hate progress attacking civilisation's prominent symbols. The communists were consumed by jealousy of the West's prosperity. Maddened Islamic Jihadists attacked 'our way of life.' Now it is resurgent anarchism that would do away with all the blessings of civilisation and the New World Order. Has anyone noticed the sum of those who benefit from these disorders: namely strong, centralised power that consistently acts in our name — but without our authority?

We now know how all this began. In the summer of 1959, the top secret Clandestine Committee of NATO circulated the famous 'smoking gun' communication to all the Allied powers. Quite simply, the 'stay behind' task was explicitly declared redundant. Henceforth it would be the duty of the Gladio secret armies to switch to the task of combating 'internal subversion' within each NATO state. Moreover, the secret armies were to play 'a determining role... not only on the general policy level of warfare, but also on the politics of emergency.' The 'emergency' was the enemy within, the phantom of the communist menace purportedly eating away like a vicious termite at the foundations of western democracy. Thus began the wholesale invention of synthetic fear and the *anni di piombo* — the years of lead.

I.
The Outcomes Business

'Although tyranny, because it needs no consent, may successfully rule over foreign peoples, it can stay in power only if it destroys first of all the national institutions of its own people.' — Hannah Arendt

---

One consequence of the emerging new world order is the triumph of total secrecy in almost every quarter of government. For all the pretentious claims, what 'Freedom of Information' Act is worth more than the paper it is printed on? As the Canadian open government campaigner John Reid once remarked, secrecy is now the principal activity of government: a tool of social control so powerful, with barricades so high, that few ordinary citizens may hope to scale them. For all the valiant efforts of well-meaning bodies such as the American Civil Liberties Union (ACLU), what lasting testaments have they secured in the defence of personal freedoms and the public right to know what elected officials are doing?

The use of secrecy to conceal a criminal conspiracy famously came to a head as Ronald Reagan entered the last lap of his second term. It was 1986 and the Iran-Contra scandal had just broken. Here was the bizarre story of a clandestine arms-for-cash carousel in which munitions were sold to the Iranians (then at war with America's current ally of convenience, Iraq). The proceeds were used to arm the Contra guerrilla forces fighting the Left-wing Sandinista government in the diminutive state of Nicaragua. How Richard Nixon, who was still alive to rejoice in this deliciously complex muddle, a close cousin of Gladio in so many respects, must have chuckled archly.

No one to this day really knows why Tricky Dicky authorised the Watergate break-in. Was it out of paranoia, or as the late Christopher Hitchens speculated, some kind of launch pad for a quasi-coup to save America from revolutionary anti-war flower power. Some observers noted the legendary burglary served to drown out the public loudspeaker blaring the state murder of leading black rights activists, Black Panthers Fred Hampton and Mark Clark, by the FBI and Chicago's Finest. In both cases, it came down to the question of the respective chief executives, first Nixon and then Reagan, lying to cover up deeds that were wholly criminal in American law. If Watergate was in essence concerned with personal greed for untrammelled power, then Iran-Contra turned on a key mission of the Reagan agenda, namely to pursue the struggle against godless communism wherever the beast showed its head. This required a mind-boggling and deliberate deception of the American people and their elected representatives, the Congress of the United States.

The Iran-Contra affair and Reagan's role in it reduced Watergate to almost a minor demeanour in comparison, yet Reagan the teflon president left office beaming and unsullied. As Haynes Johnson wrote in *Sleepwalking through History,* the CIA and a previously-obscure Marine Corps lieutenant colonel, Oliver North, knitted a network known loosely as 'The Enterprise,' composed entirely of hand-picked 'private brokers' off-radar to the Congress. To achieve his government's secret policy goals, Reagan had already given his personal commitment to maintain the Contras in the field at any cost, with the assistance of friendly — if unlikely — partners such as Saudi Arabia and Israel.

In a matter of months, The Enterprise blossomed as a full-scale world-straddling octopus. It could count on its own airline, ships, and front companies, nourished by hundreds of secret offshore bank accounts, the whole business up to its neck in the murky netherworld of organised crime. Significant quantities of munitions were sent to Latin America in direct defiance of the Boland Amendment. Approved by Congress in October 1984, this unambiguously ordered an immediate halt to all aid by any branch of the US government to the Right-wing guerrillas renowned for brutal human-rights abuses. The crew assembled by Oliver North and friends included the usual tinkers and tailors of the black global economy: arms dealers, narcotics smugglers, money launderers, soldiers of fortune and Mafioso wholesalers. The original Iran-Contra concept was eclipsed by an extraordinary extension of The Enterprise. Shipments of NATO munitions and narcotics by rackets associated with the CIA were funnelled through the hard-line communist state of Bulgaria (see Chapter IX), as well as neighbouring Romania.

In the usual way of these things, Iran-Contra was accidentally exposed when a lone supply plane ditched in the rain forest. Every individual involved, right up to the president himself, lied copiously. Daniel Ellsberg, the State Department whistleblower who exposed the US military's best-kept Vietnam secrets (immortalized as the Pentagon Papers) denounced Iran-Contra as 'quite the worst covert operation in US history.' Reagan, transparently guilty as charged, dodged an impeachment rap by invoking the 'took an afternoon nap' immunity clause. It surely befitted the image of a venerated public institution metaphorically rocking his chair on the front porch of the White House, sucking on a hickory pipe and nodding warmly at passers-by. Iran-Contra was a natural offshoot of the years of lead which rocked the European continent for more than twenty years. Many players had dual roles and loyalties in different camps, including NATO, the Pentagon, the CIA, the Holy See, Eastern bloc states Bulgaria and Romania, Turkish criminal gangs and the Mafia. Supporting roles were reserved for Mossad, British, German and Italian intelligence.

I am not an especial admirer of the US diplomat-turned-historian George Frost Kennan, who seems to me grandly over-promoted in the post-war record. Although unintentional, his intellectual legacy is the resurgence of fascism, driven by the contrived war on terror that we see all around us today. The elegant Princeton-taught Kennan, *chargé d'affaires* at the embassy in immediate post-war Moscow, was just as much an enigma as the problems he tried to solve. A rather confused upbringing left him awkward and introverted in company. But he was one of the few genuine Eastern European hands in the pre-war US State Department, a backwater not exactly brimming with promotional opportunities. He gained a Pentecostal grasp of a string of European languages (including excellent Russian and German), yet there was a sense with Kennan of the thinker who looked and reasoned without absorbing vital insights. Most of all, he wanted someone to listen to him — irrespective of what he said — which arose from his experiences coping with life at Princeton. Never a man to go for the rabbit punch when he could use up eight thousand or so spare words, Kennan composed in 1946 the famous nocturnal 'long telegram' (actually, one of a series) to the State Department, analysing the causes of Soviet mistrust of the West. These, he concluded somewhat unoriginally, arose from 'the traditional and instinctive Russian sense of insecurity.'

This might have been the end of it, had Kennan not awakened his masters to the beguiling theory of internal subversion — the enemy within. He was the Cassandra who thoroughly disturbed Washington with his warnings of a communist menace that would spread from the East and disappear underground like an incubus, with the power to subvert the social fabric of the western alliance. This alarming prospect fanned the Red Scare sweeping the United States, the rise of Red-Hunter General Senator Joe McCarthy, J. Edgar Hoover's Messianic persecutions, the House Un-American Activities Committee and the Hollywood purge. Each of these was an ironic reflection, though few confessed it at the time, of look-alike Soviet pogroms and show trials.

Kennan was ambitious, a man in a hurry, and his windy epistle was a barely-disguised job application. He saw himself as the one-eyed man in the kingdom of the blind — otherwise known as the Truman administration — eager to exploit American bewilderment over Russia's exact aims. At many points he betrayed his innate lack of feel for the Russian soul. He allowed himself to imply that Stalin might be a maddened involuntary hermit roaming the draughty corridors of the Kremlin, victim of a conspiracy within a conspiracy to imprison him in ignorance of the outside world. He skirted, too, massive boulders lying in the path of all his arguments: Russia's historical isolation from liberating European trends such as the Enlightenment and the Renaissance, and her well-grounded wariness of foreign troops trampling the sacred soil of the Motherland. These included forces from Sweden, Poland, Napoleon, Hitler, and not least the United States. Moscow still nursed smouldering grievances over the 'Polar Bear Expedition,' authorised by President Woodrow Wilson, which appeared in Arctic Russia between 1918 and 1919 to fight on the side of the White Russians.

Kennan's initial error was failing to detect the fine line of distinction between Russian nationalism and the Soviet banner that flew over it. In this way, he created a cul-de-sac in American strategic thinking for decades to come. He was conditioned chiefly by the horrors of Stalin's pre-war purges. It seemed impossible for Kennan to grasp that despite savageries performed by an obvious megalomaniac, Stalin was considered a rock of salvation to the vast majority of Russians following the Great Patriotic War (as Stalin's cunning spinners smartly re-branded WW2).

His final solution was to seal the Russians and communism in general inside a quarantined political sanatorium, ring-fenced by massive military power. It was not especially elegant or even original (Napoleon's anti-British Continental System was one precedent, for example). The United States and its NATO allies did not break off diplomatic or trading relations with the USSR nor any of its satellites. But to the Truman administration, desperate for any stick to beat off Republicans berating it as soft on communism, 'containment' dropped like manna from heaven. The Cold War left the quayside. Kennan smarted for the rest of his much-extended life from accusations that he was personally responsible (he was not to die until 2005, a venerable 101). He largely recanted once he realised that placing East-West relations in a perpetual deep freeze was fraught with perils. He began to oppose NATO and eventually recognised that wars of liberation raging in Asia were driven by latent anti-colonial nationalism rather than Marxist-Leninism. But it was much too late. Lasting damage had been done. No practical lessons were learned. Kennan originally argued that Russia's aggressiveness arose from envy of better-organised and economically more successful societies of the West. Since very little in politics is ever really fresh and original, this was exactly the same charge subsequently levelled post-9/11 at the Islamic world.

The usual travelling companion of containment is invariably mission creep. If the Alliance for Peace had announced ten years ago that it was rethinking its defensive posture to allow pre-emptive nuclear strikes, to halt the 'imminent' spread of nuclear weapons, the result would have been uproar. When General John M. Shalikashvili, former chairman of the US Joint Chiefs of Staff and lately NATO's supreme commander, and General Klaus Neumann, Germany's former top soldier and ex-chairman of NATO's military committee, said exactly that in Brussels in January 2008, there was scarcely a ruffle.[N1] The brief summer war that same year between Russia and the Georgian pocket state supplied a further instalment. From Moscow's perspective, it was an unmistakeable message of 'thus far, no further' — a demonstration of retaliatory Kennanist containment in reverse, following the proposed NATO anti-ballistic missile system in Poland supported by ABM detector screens in the Czech Republic and Romania. It will be surprising if the Shalikashvili-Neumann pronouncement is not read by future historians, assuming of course there are any, as the first chapter and verse of the Second Cold War.

Shalikashvili, whose parents were Georgian immigrants, was a leading protagonist arguing that this Caspian hot spot should be allowed fast-track alliance membership. This was an incendiary proposition in Russian eyes, following on the extended process of enlarging NATO and the European Union. Viewed from the Kremlin, it was Kennanist encirclement, initiated by the hawkish Secretary of State, Madeleine Albright. In this light, was the Brussels statement devised as a cunning flyer to indicate a subtle shift to a first strike nuclear posture — which would thereafter be taken for granted?

Some five hundred years before Christ, the Chinese master warrior-philosopher Sun Tzu wrote a manual of war extolling the virtues of the skilful leader who 'subdues the enemy's troops without a fight... who overthrows their kingdom without a lengthy fight in the field.' Even before WW2 was over, the future American counter-intelligence chief Allen Welsh Dulles, Winston Churchill and European leaders including Paul Spaak of Belgium and future president Francesco Cossiga of Italy, laid the basis of a network of 'stay-behind armies,' pop-up guerrillas intended to wreak havoc among Soviet invaders behind the lines. They drew on the practical experience of the 'Jedburgh Teams,' or 'Jeds,' — established early in 1944 — to join the talents of Britain's Special Operations Executive, the US Office of Strategic Services (forerunner of the CIA) and commandos drawn from Dutch, Belgian and Free French forces. Small specialised units were dropped on moonless nights deep into enemy-occupied territory to liaise with local resistance groups, arrange airdrops of arms and ammunition and generally stir up acts of sabotage against the Germans. The American 'Jeds' included Bill Colby, future chief of the CIA spookocracy during the imperial reigns of Nixon and Gerald Ford.[7] Colby was credited with much of the

---

[7] As chief of the CIA's Far East bureau, Colby ran the murderous Phoenix squad in Vietnam, blamed for thousands of targeted assassinations. He got into trouble by disclosing the agency's dirty laundry (or 'family jewels') in his book, letting slip the sleeping armies, including those in neutral non-NATO states. Late one stormy night in May 1996, he stepped away from a half-eaten supper of clams and white wine at his Maryland riverside home, apparently gripped by a sudden fancy to go fishing,

footwork in setting up the Gladio secret army programme across Europe, including theoretically neutral Sweden, actually a shadow NATO member. He confided in his memoirs *Honourable Men* (1978) that only an exclusive coterie of insiders in each country were entrusted with the knowledge that these forces existed within their own national boundaries. He regarded Gladio as a straightforward strategic decision with little in the way of moral complexity. Victory over the Axis powers did not eliminate the potential for conflict with the victors' former ally, the Soviet Union.

Ambiguity did arise. As Professor John Duffield of Atlanta State University has observed, where any collection of countries opts for an internationalised co-operative to oversee their security, invariably such a body 'will reflect the calculations of self-interest of the most powerful member state.' Duffield's theory implied NATO was effectively designed by a committee of one, which Richard Nixon seemed to confirm when he remarked: 'The only collective body that ever worked was NATO and that was because it was a military alliance and we were in charge of it.' In short, NATO was pursuing policy ends that chiefly met American interests to supervise the international order. These pastures were thoroughly tilled by half-American Winston Churchill, peerless prose-master of propaganda. Churchill shamelessly fanned the Red Menace in his best cultivated bulldog growl before an audience in Fulton, Missouri (Harry Truman's home state, by useful coincidence) in 1947. He painted a lurid description of the 'Iron Curtain' the Soviets had slammed down across Europe 'from Stettin in the Baltic to Trieste in the Adriatic.' Churchill's sole purpose was to lock the United States into Europe, in alliance with the British Empire. As Roy Jenkins put it in his biography of Churchill: 'He believed in single shot salvoes, and for Fulton he decided to put a great weight of explosive behind it.' As usual, Churchill was sparing with the truth. He did not explain to his riveted audience that all those countries finding themselves locked behind the 'Iron Curtain' (a phrase which the arch-plagiariser pinched from Goebbels) had been surrendered as war booty by none other than himself and Franklin Roosevelt, even before the conflict ended. The speech, a classic example of Churchillian theatrical rhetoric, nevertheless served its intended aims. Thereafter the image of the Iron Curtain as a physical property was etched in the minds of Americans and Europeans alike, along with the chilling image

---

minus his usual life jacket. Despite multiple sweeps, it took a week to find his body, a few meters from the empty skiff.

[7] *Churchill*, Macmillan, 2001. 'If the population of the English-speaking Commonwealth be added to that of the United States with all that such co-operation implies in the air, on the sea, all over the globe and in science and industry, there will be no quivering, precarious balance of power to offer its temptations to ambition or adventure.'

of the mushroom cloud. It was the deliberate inculcation of fear resting on deception — the vital component of the Strategy of Tension.

1947 was a vintage year for the policy of containment. Six months after Churchill's bombardment at Fulton, the Central Intelligence Agency and the National Security Agency received their articles of incorporation from Congress. These were developments destined to alter fundamentally the nature of America herself and her relations with the world. Less than a year later, on 21st June 1948, National Security Council Directive (NSC 10/2) granted the newborn CIA sweeping powers under the so-called cloak-and-dagger clause (and patently the Gladio birth certificate) to perform

covert operations against hostile foreign states or groups, or in support of friendly foreign states or groups, but which are so planned and conducted that any US Government responsibility for them is not evident to unauthorized persons.

The shrinking violet Kennan was among the varied godparents of this new offspring of containment. He was by now swept up in the smart Washington set of glittering élites and aspiring wannabees known as the Georgetown Crowd. Mostly loyalist Roosevelt Democrats, they formed a kind of supporters' club, dreaming up initiatives to fend off increasingly effective salvoes aimed at Truman's wobbly foreign policies. As political cross-dressers, the Georgetowners would set the scene for the forthcoming American neoconservative revolution. Their ranks included a number of refugees suffering severe withdrawal symptoms from the redundant wartime Office of Strategic Services (OSS), where they acquired an appetite for unrestrained buccaneering in foreign parts.

The CIA was pure Georgetown. Americans were calmly assured that the collective talents of the new agency, some of the best brains to be found in America, would prevent another Pearl Harbor rearing up from nowhere. As former CIA consultant and unofficial agency historian Chalmers Johnson observed, matters turned out differently. Very quickly the tail began to wag the dog, thanks to secret codicils granting the CIA virtually unlimited powers to act as the 'personal, secret, unaccountable army of the president.' From the outset, the CIA was steeped in subversions and manipulations, including clandestine sources of funding, screened from oversight by Congress and all but a select few insiders among America's chosen allies. The 'outcomes business,' or as the late Chalmers Johnson memorably described it, 'presumptive intervention,' was henceforth to work chiefly in favour of advancing American strategic interests.

The great exponent of cloak-and-dagger was a figure whom J. Edgar Hoover wrote off as a 'weirdo.' For once, Hoover was broadly objective. His target was Frank Wisner, who by any standards was very peculiar. Wisner cut his wartime espionage teeth unsuccessfully trying to save Romania from communism, enjoying relaxing interludes in a pleasing *divertissement* with the Transylvanian crown princess. He hailed from a fraternity of Wall Street lawyers cooling their heels after wartime revels in the OSS, who eagerly leapt at this recall to exhilarating new adventures. Wisner was overlord of the CIA's Office of Policy Co-ordination — 'the dirty tricks brigade' — from 1948 until the late 1950s, heading the roll-out of the European stay-behind armies, which he regarded as extension battalions and therefore foot-soldiers of the CIA itself. There was never any doubt in Wisner's mind that these secret fighters were America's fifth column to undermine the potential for communist subversion of Europe, which called for every serviceable method of unorthodox warfare and black operations.[8]

By mid-1953, Wisner directed a covert action wing of several thousand clones of himself, who between them consumed three-quarters of the CIA's official budget (besides a good deal more squirreled illegally from the Marshall Aid European reconstruction programme). There was no limit to what Wisner could spend and no restrictions on whom he could hire, or what they or he could do. In 1954, Wisner calmly siphoned money from CIA coffers to promote the Hollywood cartoon production of George Orwell's *Nineteen Eighty-Four*. The Agency's spy-catcher-in-chief James Jesus Angleton suspected Wisner was a double agent, but on that score he suspected just about everybody around him. Wisner was much too conspiratorial by nature to chain himself to the mundane task of forking through the muck heaps of espionage. Here was a pyrotechnic personality raging in full technicolor, hovering in undemarcated territory, somewhere between a screwball and darkly-gifted impresario of a madcap rodeo. The stamp he left on the culture and general mischief-making capacity of the CIA remains indelible. Within the portals of mission control in Langley, Virginia, he retains the status of a saint.

Wisner's fertile imagination ran amok even on American soil, strictly speaking outside the Agency's purview, according to its founding articles. He dreamt up Operation Mockingbird, after the Texan song thrush that artfully mimics the calls of other birds. It was a disinformation highway, featuring Wisner the ideological traffic cop directing the re-writing of history. He proudly called his creation the 'Mighty Wurlitzer.' Wisner's

---

[8] Initiate of Virginia State University's ultra-secretive, pseudo-Masonic lodge known as the Seven Society, whose memberships are revealed only after death, and then by placing a bunch of magnolias on the grave of the departed one. For the enlightenment of non-American readers, secret societies are not only endemic in the culture of American universities, but invariably act as incestuous recruiting quarters for future élites. Looking at the subsequent manic behavior of the CIA, which displays all the obviously ritualistic signs of a Knights Templar-like structure, clearly Wisner was going to find himself very much at home.

mockingbirds included some of America's best-known reporters and commentators, who eagerly signed on to the CIA's subsidy to exaggerate the Russian threat. The Wurlitzer hummed with great irony from the offices of the future Watergate-busting Washington Post, whose publisher, Philip Graham, and his powerful spouse, Katherine 'The Great,' jointly reigned as king and queen of the Georgetown set.

In 1953, Wisner finally got the chance to test-run his covert warfare skills in a working laboratory. The Iranian caper of that year was much less about ideology than the first postwar casting of dice in the Great Game of Oil. An international crisis ignited when the elected government in Teheran, headed by the austere Dr. Mohammad Mossadegh, nationalised the Anglo-American Oil Company (the future BP) in a complex dispute. It involved the fair apportioning of oil revenues, amid large hints of wholesale cheating by the British side. Harnessed somewhat reluctantly to MI6, Kermit Roosevelt, gung-ho grandson of the boisterous 26th president Teddy Roosevelt, toppled a freely elected and extremely popular leader, whom the masses regarded as taking a principled stand against foreign robber barons.[N2] Mossadegh, a conservative-minded moderate and aristocrat of ancient Persian lineage, got the full Soviet gulag treatment. He was tossed into solitary confinement and left to rot for three long years to reflect on his foolish error in thinking that Iran was a sovereign state. All that the world learnt of the affair was the official line: a popular royal coup by Shah Reza Pahlavi to foil the plots of a prime minister in cahoots with the Soviet Union.

Iran was a stark example of the new policy of planning, co-ordinating and implementing America's foreign policy goals in complete secrecy, and then pretending afterwards the outcome was entirely due to the natural selection of events. But there was an additional and significant factor which far outweighed the secrecy. This was the new primacy of deception, to falsify and distort factual circumstances on the ground. American secret services and MI6 employed the full gamut of black propaganda alongside acts of outright terrorism, sabotage and psychological warfare. These included carefully prepared actions designed to stir unrest, such as the false-flag bombing of a prominent ayatollah's home, made to appear as the work of government agents.

The year 1956 might well be described as the fulcrum of Wisner's technicolor life, when he let go of the ropes. It was also the year of the Hungarian Rising. On 23rd October simmering discontent with the puppet communist regime overflowed into riots, then full-scale popular insurrection. Russian armour crushed the rising with great brutality. Imre Nagy, the previously rather grey party conformist who found himself cast in the unfamiliar role of revolutionary leader, foolishly gushed that Hungary had unilaterally abandoned the Warsaw Pact. As the tanks rolled into Budapest, he was arrested and quickly executed. Wisner's subsequent depressions were blamed on the depth of his distress over Hungary. Perhaps, but he was hardly the sentimental sort. What is yet to be dragged into daylight is the CIA's manipulation of the uprising, and to what extent the agency acted independently, for example, of the State Department, where Secretary John Foster Dulles displayed distinct signs of being caught off balance by the turn of events (even though he had proved a master at running agents inside Nazi Germany).

Was this Wisner's biggest gamble, far eclipsing Iran, a freelance effort ripping out an important coping piece of the Warsaw Pact, after which all else would tumble? Nationalist outrage is of itself rarely the full explanation for the oxygen which drives revolutions. There are invariably actors with another script altogether. There is some evidence which points to Hungary as a sort of proving ground for the forthcoming 'color' or 'flower power' rebellions popular in the 21st century, nearly all with the backing of CIA technicians and advisers, not to mention special forces. Wisner gave every impression of being crushed, and never regained a semblance of his old irrepressible confidence. He was side-lined on permanent sick leave. A genius of a certain black school, it was perhaps scarcely surprising that behind all this hyperactivity, he nursed a condition of undiagnosed mental illness. He gradually surrendered to the lure of chronic clinical depression. In 1965 he placed his own son's shotgun in his mouth and pulled the trigger.[9] An important Gladio godfather was laid to rest.

Despite the novelty of the word 'central,' the CIA was never granted an exclusive monopoly. Over the course of time, the field expanded to the crowded pitch that it is today, with some twenty visible players at last count, who were never issued a clear set of rules, let alone notified of precise

---

[9] Wisner must be beaming down from his celestial balcony with considerable satisfaction, watching the same tricks being rolled out all over again to topple the current Iranian regime. Pulitzer Prize winner Seymour Hersh revealed US special forces have been in Iran since 2005 on reconnaissance missions, while a restive ethnic minority, the Baluch, are blamed for numerous attacks on military and civilian targets. Many sources, including Hersh, Tarpley, ABC News and the *Daily Telegraph* claim the Baluch armed wing, the *Jundallah* or Soldiers of God, is a front for American, British and Pakistani secret services. A bomb attack on Islamic Revolutionary Guard commanders in 2009, attributed to the Soldiers of God, killed five senior officers and left many others seriously wounded. Abdulmalik Rigi, the Jundallah leader, was hanged by the Iranians in June 2010.

The Curse of the Wisners is not easily exorcised. In February 2011, Wisner's son (also named Frank) was despatched as Obama's personal envoy to Egypt, as Webster Tarpley and others suspected, with the task of levering long-time strongman Hosni Mubarak from power, in the service of wider US interests to encircle Iran.

territorial boundaries. This inevitably provokes constant internecine tribal rivalries, confusion and petty jealousies. According to CIA observer Thomas Powers,[N3] the Pentagon had only itself to blame for lagging behind in the intelligence wars. Its senior officers disdained dreary nuts-and-bolts analysis, which offered scant opportunities to shine before the glorifying American public, bewitched by battle garlands. The US Army's Counter Intelligence Corps (established in 1917) was traditionally a languid backwater for those lacking the stamina for more challenging roles in the front-line fame factory. In any event it drifted into a forgotten bureau of little more than twenty men, marooned in the doldrums between the two world wars.[10]

The outcome was a long-lasting civil war between close neighbours camped on the banks of the Potomac. Both sides prickled each other with differing intelligence assessments. The CIA invariably presented a strong counterpoint to the Pentagon's inflated estimates of the Soviet arsenal and extreme pessimism about Soviet intentions, which fed the military's appetite for continuous upgrades in arms-spending. Serious displays of bicep flexing between these sparring protagonists arose from the fountains of tax dollars pouring unregulated from clandestine budgets into the booming unorthodox warfare industry. The CIA claimed grandfather rights, glaring dismissively at the junior and inexperienced rookies of the Army's counter-intelligence and covert specialist teams. The Pentagon sneered at the CIA and its minions as soft-shoe civilian meddlers in military affairs. Finally, in 1961, the old army counter-intelligence corps was retrieved from a dusty Pentagon loft, brushed up and re-christened the Defence Intelligence Agency, the near similarity in titles an intentionally snide dig at the CIA. The DIA's first practical test arose during the 'Red October' Cuban missiles crisis in 1962, with middling results (though much trumpeted by General Lyman Lemnitzer). Next came alluring prospects of big-budget covert warfare operations in Southeast Asia. Both the CIA and the Pentagon, through the DIA, vied to subvert North Vietnam by flooding the communist stronghold with hundreds of agents

---

[10] A feud without end. In 2004, the arch-neoconservative and long-time CIA foe Paul Wolfowitz (then No 2 to Donald Rumsfeld at the Pentagon), signed off an edict creating yet another secret purse called the Counter Intelligence Field Agency. By 2008, it amassed some 2,000 agents with powers to spy on American citizens on their own soil, a direct affront by the military to the FBI. Obviously, this quite possibly unconstitutional act could only have taken place with the knowledge and consent of the president. The *Washington Post* (July 2010) estimated the 'intelligence community' number more than 800,000 with no clear oversight, remit or boundaries. In the same camp, the widely-despised TSA body snatchers, scourge of America's airports, are inexorably morphing into a paramilitary arm of the Department of Homeland Security, with heavy implications for the rapidly shrinking freedoms of all Americans.

versed in psychological warfare, as well as sabotage and selective assassinations.

Practically all these efforts proved to be calamitous failures. Virtually every infiltrator demonstrated an amazing ability to instantly dematerialise once north of the 17th parallel. One can but imagine the glee in Hanoi as all these operatives trained at huge expense to the US taxpayer arrived in droves, only to be turned around and sent back in streams to cause havoc in the south. This flourishing export-import industry lasted for almost seven years. By then, at least several hundred million dollars had disappeared down the drain. Bear in mind that at least 40% of all expenditures of the Pentagon and CIA generally rate as 'black' and thus free from scrutiny by nosey outsiders.

The Pentagon and the National Security Council sought justification for America's Asian wars in the Kennanist policy of containment dating from the Truman era, with China promoted to Public Enemy No. 2, after the USSR. The scarcely 200-something-years-old Washington mind was intellectually incapable of reading Vietnam as a highly complex culture whose multi-layered patina was acquired over thousands of years, like viewing slices cut through the cake of the ancient geological record. Regarding all resistance as promoted and led by ideological terrorists and fanatics simply underlined the invaders' inability to understand themselves as unwanted guests. Yet more absurd was the illusion that it was possible to ignore the constraints of race, culture, history and language, the curse of the unlearnt lessons of 'nation-building' that returned to haunt Afghanistan and Iraq. Despite his suspicion of the Pentagon's underlying motives, John F. Kennedy initially fell for the superficially appealing delusion that a cheap short cut to pacify Vietnam could be thrown open by means of well-planned destabilisation exercises. These would chiefly require selected sabotage and fraternisation with friendly natives — a soft war of minds rather than pitched and costly conventional warfare requiring vast numbers of troops.

The secret war in Europe was of course different from the Asian quagmire, while flowing from the same desire to secure America's position as the hub of a global system resting chiefly on American values, culture and power. This conflict was an ideological reflection of the petrified trench system of the Great War, with two sides glaring at each other over the parapets of Churchill's Iron Curtain. If lacking specific pitched battles of the intensity witnessed in the Far East, moments of extreme tension continually arose around divided Berlin. There were three powerful anti-Soviet uprisings, in East Germany, Hungary and Czechoslovakia. Poland constantly rumbled like an awakening volcano, and eventually gave way to a military coup when the *Solidarnosc* ('Solidarity') free labour union seemed to threaten counter-revolution. In Asia, black warfare was an adjunct in a supporting role of the conventional fighting. In Europe, the roles were precisely reversed, something akin to the plot of a John le Carré novel gone haywire.

We owe it to the brilliant Polish sociologist Professor Zygmunt Bauman for a perceptive analysis of these mysterious realms. Surveying the landscape of modern nation states, he pointed to the existence on their fringes of shadowy borderlands characterised by 'indistinction and lawlessness, whose inhabitants cannot be clearly distinguished as friends or foes.' There is no more fitting description of the Deep State. In the summer of 2010, the Pentagon pronounced an adjustment to terminology which subliminally indicated the stay-behind armies are alive and busy. A small-print announcement declared 'psy-ops' behind enemy lines would henceforth be redesignated Military Information Support Operations, or MISO. The sinews led as before to the Fort Bragg secret warfare base, with the emphasis on the unchanged role of shaping attitudes in the public sphere. But, a spokesman declared, hand on heart, there was to be nothing sinister, an unmistakeable inference to the spectre of Gladio. The exact meaning of 'behind the lines' retained the same elusive and fluid lack of definition.[N4] The victims of the secret war waged in Europe were ordinary folk stepping out for everyday business, shopping and waiting for trains, visiting the bank or sipping a beer. They were not trapped in the cross-fire; they were the selected targets of manic psychological terror pursued to extremes.

In 1998, a young Swiss political history graduate, Daniele Ganser, began looking for a high-profile subject as a doctoral thesis. An American contact, the CIA critic William Blum (another who resigned from the State Department over Vietnam) pointed him to NATO's Gladio secret army network, of which little of substance had yet appeared in Europe or America. Ganser grasped the astonishing unity of the Gladio network spanning the entire European continent, from the Atlantic to the Black Sea. He produced the first clear evidence showing how it was designed to penetrate terrorist organisations of both Left and Right. The manipulators then exploit the resultant disorder to discredit and disable established Left-wing forces in Europe from posing a threat to the established political order. Excavating intelligence history is a painfully slow process, resisted by officialdom every step of the way. Ganser was not the first sleuth to delve into this twilight zone and, like all previous investigators, he encountered a wall of silence from every official source, including NATO itself, the CIA and Britain's MI6, between them the godfathers of Gladio.[N5]

There is no clear modern copyright to the term 'Strategy of Tension,' but the surest claim lies with the Italian deep state researcher Claudio Celani, author of numerous studies on the structures of the Italian Gladio operation and its links to western intelligence, organised crime, the Vatican and the powerful Italian neofascist community. But it was Ganser who succinctly captured the essence of exactly how the strategy was applied in practice.

If you infiltrate a group and then carry out terror operations with that group, without that group knowing that it has been infiltrated and is being 'steered,' that is one of the strategically most sophisticated operations imaginable. To any strategist that is beautiful, just as it is ugly from a moral perspective.

In the Balkans, an alliance ostensibly dedicated to the high humanitarian ground instead waded in moral ambiguities and manipulations of groups and interests (see Ch. XIX, Appointment at Račak). Former NATO Secretary General Baron Robertson once spoke glowingly of his charge as a 'unique partnership... forged during half a century's fight against tyranny.' Might this be that same George Robertson, former Blairite MP and Defence Secretary, in his own chosen words a human rights activist, who declared under inquisition in a BBC radio interview that NATO's bombing of Serbia's TV HQ on 23rd April 1999, was justified to silence a propaganda mouthpiece? Sixteen people going about their normal duties on the night shift died when several air-fired missiles slammed into the four-storey building in the centre of Belgrade. NATO jets and gunships thundered across Serb skies for almost eighty days, hammering non-military 'targets of opportunity' such as bridges on the Danube, the ruling party's offices, railways, homes of Serbian officials, Belgrade's power grid and water supply, and even by accident — or so it was claimed — the Chinese legation. These were the tactics of Gladio and the Strategy of Tension transferred to the air, the targets again citizen bystanders. As his Lordship Robertson wriggled to avoid admitting, such collective punishment of civilians is against all established laws of war, and expressly forbidden by the Geneva and Hague Conventions.[N6] Nor was this the sole instance where NATO's mask of spreading democracy backed with armed might — Chalmers Johnson's 'presumptive intervention' — slipped badly.

As the report of Professor Cees Wiebes clearly demonstrated, the Balkan imbroglio was nothing less than a direct continuation of the great armaments merry-go-round that came to be known as Iran-Contra, otherwise as 'The Enterprise.' Professor Wiebes figured that once again the Pentagon was gaily playing fast and loose with its allies, with the UN and all the warring Balkan factions. Quoting from the Wiebes Report, Professor Richard Aldrich filled in the detail:

The UN protection force, UNPROFOR, was dependent on its troop-contributing nations for intelligence, and above all on the sophisticated monitoring capabilities of the US to police the arms embargo. This gave the Pentagon the ability to manipulate the embargo at will: ensuring that American AWACS aircraft covered crucial areas and were able to turn a blind eye to the frequent night-time comings and goings at Tuzla [The chief airlift base located in Bosnia-Herzegovina].

Weapons flown in during the spring of 1995 were to turn up only a fortnight later in the besieged and demilitarised enclave at Srebrenica. When these shipments were noticed, Americans pressured UNPROFOR to rewrite reports, and when Norwegian officials protested about the flights, they were reportedly threatened into silence.[N7]

To complicate matters further, there is evidence that the British — in the shape of MI6 — were out of line themselves, running guns through Hungary and Croatia to arm the anti-Muslim front as a kind of correction mechanism. This was to prove a significant factor in the forthcoming turf war between the CIA and MI6 in Greece (exhumed in Chapter VIII) which led to the murder of a senior British intelligence officer recently transferred from the Balkans to Athens.

The 'just war' launched on Serbia was explained as a demonstration of force to protect threatened and terrified minorities. To the historian Robert Skidelsky, NATO's adoption of 'ethical imperialism' was nothing less than blatant 'overturning of the doctrine of national sovereignty.' This excuse was rolled out once again to justify the brutal mauling of Libya in 2011, the perfect example of regime change via 'humanitarian intervention.' To discover the flesh on Skidelsky's words, hark back to the protocols of Generals Shalikashvili and Neumann, enunciated in the spring of 2008. There we find a shift to majority voting, to over-ride national vetoes on military expeditions, and the exclusion of any members that refuse to co-operate in campaigns ordered by NATO war chiefs. It is easy to see that a Doomsday-style first strike becomes an accomplishable act when an unelected body acquires the authority of a military autocracy, in which political judgement and caution are bullied to the sidelines. Countries that might be opposed or nervous about going to war find themselves unwitting victims of the ruling consensus. The grand vizier of NATO, Anders Fogh Rasmussen, stated in March 2010 that NATO is a 'permanent alliance' whose self-appointed duties will include intervening in the affairs of so-called failed states. The unmistakable inference is that NATO is now a world policeman. What he did not say, although it is true, is that no member will be easily permitted to exit the alliance, unlike the Warsaw Pact which lost Albania and, effectively Romania. (Tito's Yugoslavia — champion of the non-aligned club — never took the bait.)

Skidelsky's remarks struck to the inherent contradiction at the heart of NATO's personality and structure, namely the extent to which a confederal power can act to override the spirit of democracy it was designed to protect.

The perfect illustration was a vintage stroke of Kennanist containment, the shift of Europe's and NATO's boundaries to scoop up all Balkan territories of the former Austro-Hungarian Empire (as extant in 1917). Ex-Yugoslavia was destined to be consumed by the omnivorously state-eating European Union and the North Atlantic Alliance. We can see North Africa heading for the same fate.

It is now incontestable that NATO is shape-shifting to acquire global ambitions. The earliest evidence can be detected in the small print of the huge re-jig of the Atlantic Charter, which was compressed into just two days in Washington in April 1999. Both the conference and the concluding winding-up communiqué received far less scrutiny than they deserved. Aside from the neutering of the catch-all Articles 5 and 6, the language pointed unmistakeably to the emphasis that the Alliance would henceforth place on 'asymmetrical threats to European security, arising chiefly from terrorism and related acts of sabotage, friction thrown up by mass population shifts and global competition for shrinking resources, particularly oil.' Such operations would be conducted 'out of theatre' (beyond Europe) or even within the bounds of Alliance territory (a clear warning to back-sliders). In 2003, the US ambassador to NATO, Nicholas Burns, told the Senate Foreign Relations Committee:

> *NATO needs to pivot from its inward focus on Europe. We have to deploy our... military forces east and south. NATO's future, we believe, is east, and is south. It's in the Greater Middle East.*

To understand why Tripoli and many more Libyan communities lie in ruins, with Syria to come, here is the explanation. As Madison Ruppert has argued at his web site *End The Lie*, NATO is on the march worldwide. He sees the resurrection of the old South East Asia Treaty Organization (SEATO) linking Japan, India and Australia, in order to 'contain' China. James Burnham himself might have written the script. All these factors are now major geopolitical preoccupations, justified by the war on terror foreseen with such remarkable prescience eighteen months *before* 9/11.

The world changed when the Twin Towers fell. Yet here are the strategic planners of NATO forecasting just such an eventuality that could be used as a cover story to invade Afghanistan, on the pretext of capturing former CIA asset Osama bin Laden (significantly never charged by the FBI with any crime committed in the United States, but supposedly assassinated just the same). Bin Laden and Al Qaeda masked the urgency to strategically secure pipeline access to the vast oil reserves of the Caspian Basin. 'Shrinking resources' are the words that matter. This is what Obama meant when he talked about Afghanistan as 'the war of necessity.' He was certainly not fretting about women's rights or little Muslim girls trotting off to school in crisply-pressed uniforms.

In January 2008, unmistakeable signs of a massive destabilisation exercise appeared in Turkey, NATO's crucial watchtower sandwiched between the Balkans and the unstable triangle composed of Iraq, Iran and Afghanistan. As though the Titanic had been raised from the seabed and found in perfect working order, the visible superstructure appeared of an entire Gladio-type deep state organisation (*derin devlet* in Turkish). This creature from the depths was clearly operating under protection at the highest levels in the military, the secret services and secular political groups brooding miserably over their loss of power. The government ordered a thorough-going inquiry by a team of state prosecutors, amid astonishing allegations concerning its activities.[N8] The media quickly filled with stories that Ergenekon conspired to create a chaotic atmosphere which the armed forces and the secular establishment could then exploit to oust the Islamist government. The outing of Ergenekon (its name inspired by a Turkish foundation myth akin to Moses and the Promised Land) is instructive on many levels. Turkish commentators immediately recognised the re-incarnation of the former Gladio operation in Turkey, code-named Counter-Guerrilla. As before, this creature from the depths clearly owed its loyalties to forces such as the CIA, the Pentagon, NATO, the Turkish High Command and the country's gin-and-tonic swilling secular élites — an alliance jointly responsible for the endless contamination of Turkish political culture. This time, the Islamist newcomers struck first.

In the last decade, Turkey has witnessed a miraculous transformation brought about by the Justice and Development (AK) Party. Admirers speak of an Islamic take on Protestant values and work ethics. Detractors suspect a secret agenda to Islamise Turkey by stealthily chipping away at Atatürk's precious secular legacy. Either way, these new arrivals with their crisp tailored suits and confident smiles immediately launched a charm offensive. The country's business class reacted warmly to the pledge of concrete deeds to free up markets and promote private enterprise, in extraordinary contrast to the ousted sclerotic secular politicians who ushered Turkey from one fiscal calamity to the next. Under new management, she rocketed from a middling third-world backwater to seventeenth in the world GNP league table. She belongs to a select group of countries whose sovereign credit ratings actually rose amid the global slump. Turkey's photogenic premier and later President, Abdullah Gül — the very image of Islam with a human face — was soon darling of the international chattering circuit. On the other hand, AK's new foreign policies disturbed the powerful troika composed of Washington, Tel Aviv and Brussels. NATO members are not supposed to practice impudently independent foreign policies. Ankara, however, began talking to Hezbollah and Hamas. Both organisations received red-carpet treatment in Ankara. At the UN in September 2011, on the eve of the contentious debate on the highly charged issue of Palestinian sovereignty, Prime Minister Recep

Tayyip Erdoğan delivered a powerful admonishing lecture to the world for its collective shame over tortured Somalia, a vast racial pogrom which has rumbled unabated for twenty years. Few doubted his finger-pointing was especially directed at the United States, whose special forces and grisly regional warrior-lord allies have continually meddled in this miserable land.

After years as the compliant poodle of US policies, Turkey (or the New Ottoman Empire, should you prefer) was out of step with the American agenda right across the Middle East. Her prized $10-billion-worth of trade with Iran — much of it tied up in oil and gas deals — spoke volumes louder than sanctions or bombs, or the Israelis. President Ahmadinejad, Washington's replacement bogeyman for Saddam Hussein, is regularly feted in the Turkish capital, another red rag waved at the US and the Zionist Likudniks. In May 2010, Turkey and Brazil, brash new kids on the global block, jointly brokered a deal to ship Iran's controversial uranium to Turkey for onward processing by Russia and China, thereby dealing an unexpected blow to the Israeli-American war party. Then came the Gaza convoy raid of 2nd June 2011, in which eight Turkish citizens and one Turkish-American died at the hands of Israeli assault forces. In January 2012, the Turkish government offered further provocations, by its willingness to fund Hamas, and signing a new compact with Russia. In all these events, US policy-makers demonstrate they are blinded by the cold logic of the Bush Doctrine: that anyone who is not entirely with us is automatically against us. In passing, remember this was Lenin's refrain too.

Seventy-two million Turks have witnessed the only real prosperity this enormous country has known since Atatürk died in 1938. Istanbul — billed Istan*cool* at the annual spring fashion and culture fest — looks like Manhattan on the Bosporus, but the regions too have been transformed by a tidal flood of foreign investment. AK switched on the energising dynamo which escaped the notice of all their predecessors. Yet every step of the way, Washington sought to destabilise a government that it is not prepared to trust, entirely because it is Islamic, thereby making an absurdity of the much-proclaimed policy of transforming all Islamic countries into freedom-loving democratic societies.

AK was barely in power when the bombings started (Istanbul, 2003, 57 dead and 700 wounded, attributed to Al Qaeda). The toll mounted over the years to some 200 deaths and many more injured, with foreign holiday-makers among the victims. A judge of the high constitutional court was shot and killed by a 'Soldier of Allah' (a false-flag shooting by a known secularist thug) while the court was in public session. Hrant Dink, a prominent Turkish-Armenian writer arguing for rapprochement between Armenia and Turkey, despite the festering WW1 genocide issue, was gunned down in broad daylight. Vans piled with military-type explosives mysteriously materialised in the heavily-policed central districts of Ankara and Istanbul. One horrible incident which gained international notoriety featured the ritual disembowelling alive in April 2007 of three Turkish Christians employed by a bible publishing house at Malatya, a large city in eastern Anatolia. The government case against the accused killers alleges they were controlled by Ergenekon, but this has yet to be firmly proven.

Turks of an older generation recalled being here before, in the extended years of lead between 1960 and 1985, the unmistakeable image of counterfeit violence performed for political ends. Taksim Square is the hub of modern, bustling Istanbul, a constant ferment of traffic and blaring horns. On May Day, 1977, the crack of gunshots from high-rise blocks signalled a ruthless assault by Counter-Guerrilla secret army snipers on a huge throng, perhaps half a million, crammed into the square below. The largest mass demonstration by the Turkish Left came to a bloody end. At least 34 died and several hundreds more were struck by gunfire or trampled down in the general panic, worsened by repeated baton charges and water cannons. Twenty-one years later and again on May Day (2008), police were blamed for brutally laying into peaceful anti-AK demonstrators with clubs, gas and pepper bombs. The demonstration was composed mainly of troublemakers stirred up by the secularist, nominally Left-wing Cumhuriyet Halk Partisi (CHP) party. It was a blatant provocation, painting the Islamists as frightened of free expression. The truth is that every government since the 1977 massacre explicitly forbade any large group demonstrations in this sensitive location, and particularly on May Day. It was sealed off, the authorities accurately sniffing violence. Union officials prudently steered their members away.

The following riot was presented as the real face of AK behind a smiling mask, just as EU accession talks reached a critical juncture. CHP's curmudgeonly leadership will never forgive AK for hijacking the traditional rights and social privileges of the secular class, even less for transforming a floundering backward state into a humming world-class economy. CHP is an ultra-nationalist grouping whose interest in socialism is purely superficial. It is inherently insular and lukewarm, to say the least, to the ideas of linking hands with the EU. Its roots lie in Kemalist doctrines reflecting a Turkish version of social fascism, close to Francoism. Its support includes Turkey's nascent, rumbling extreme Right. The ongoing EU flirtation infuriated these disenfranchised élites, whose sole legacy was to render the country a permanent ward of the IMF. European political leaders beamed with approval on premier Erdoğan's and president Abdullah Gül's smart and effective reconciliation of pious Turks and market forces. Taksim Two was intended to smother this jolly honeymoon with a quickie divorce, and largely served those ends. It is quite true that Turkish police are scarcely renowned for their lightness of touch, but that was part of the clever calculation. The

government was instantly accused by EU officials of deploying disproportionate force against innocent demonstrators. Their rush to judgement
ignored both the deliberate breaching of the prudent historic standing ban on
demonstrations in such a sensitive quarter, and the street photographs
pointing clearly to *agents provocateurs* stoking a designer-label, pure Gladio
disaster.

It is an article of faith among AK's secular detractors that Ergenekon is a
mirage, a fiction controlled by the government itself, in short, a reverse coup.
This is a strident running theme of the Washington-based Middle East Media
Research Institute (MEMRI) whose presiding mastermind is Yigal Carmon, a
former colonel in Israeli military intelligence and personal security adviser to
premiers Shamir and Rabin. MEMRI poses as an independent research body
sifting through the Arabic media. But the real agenda, as *The Guardian's*
Middle East expert Brian Whitaker explained, is to act as a loudspeaker
projecting the distorted world view of Mossad/Shin Bet by means of heavily-
doctored translations. For all that, it pays not to be excessively dewy-eyed in
the Orient. The partial outing of Ergenekon is a ritual purging of just enough
of the structure to play on public nerves with drum rolls of the deep state's
continuing existence. From this perspective, AK is the true warden of
democracy, while steadily expanding its roots structure in the political and
economic landscape. The theme of creeping Islamisation flows from the
same narrative. AK's fiercest critics insist it is no more than a front for the
charismatic Islamic philosopher Fethullah Gülen, a Trojan Horse aiming to
establish a hard-line Islamist Turkish republic.

Rachel Sharon-Krespin, a senior MEMRI editor, darkly informed readers
of the arch-neoconservative *Middle East Quarterly* to beware the hidden
strategy of a 'shadowy Islamist sect led by the mysterious *hocaefendi*'
(roughly, master teacher). Observe the careful pepping of the sentence to
invoke chilling comparisons with bin Laden of the grotto. A pity, however,
that the real Gülen, with his sophisticated website, glossy worldwide
conferences and the 60 books he has authored, his conclaves with John Paul
II and the head of the Sephardic Jews, falls short of the man of mystery and
intrigue Sharon-Krespin writes him up to be. He is a rather plainly-dressed
resident of Pennsylvania, instead of a goggle-eyed fiend issuing fatwas on
picture postcards from some cavern deep in Afghanistan's Hindu Kush.

Gülen's problem for the US is the powerful allure of a theologically
conservative interpreter of Islam, a stout pro-business advocate preaching
non-violence and dialogue with other faiths. His post-modernist redefinition
of Islam runs specifically counter to powerful Zionist influence pressing on
every US administration. Israel's only foreign policy after all is to box in
Islamic power in any shape or form, at any price. What conspiratorial
evidence can be summoned against Gülen rests weakly on a rigged charge

levelled unsuccessfully by secular powers in 2000, alleging Gülen was scheming a coup. He won the case, and his acquittal was finally confirmed in 2008 by no less a body than the ultra-secular bench of the Constitutional Court. Yet, sympathisers with AK's ambitions on the secular side of the fence are worried at Gülen's burgeoning influence within the ranks of the public services, especially the police; at the proliferation of Gülen-supported religious colleges; and by the movement's conservative attitude to the role of women. Again we are confronted with Turkey's long-enduring national identity crisis, flowing directly from the deeply-ingrained Islamic character of the nation clashing with the cast-iron legacy of Mustafa Kemal Atatürk. It was the founder and liberator who confined backward, dogmatic religion, as he saw it, to the margins of the state. And Kemalism, in turn, is the source of the extraordinary power and the curse of the *derin devlet*, the secret state and all its mysterious subterranean machinery which served to torment Turks and their homeland for the past sixty years. Through the trapdoors and down the tunnels that lead to this Stygian world slipped those meddling agents of foreign powers, the intelligence services of the US and her NATO partners, responsible between them for maintaining Turkey on the sharp edge of the Strategy of Tension for so long and at such cruel cost to her people.

The exposure of Ergenekon revealed a working engine room packed with the vintage Gladio devices of targeted killings and false-flag terror. It possessed a deep-state structure connecting the military, Right-wing politicians and military officers, neofascist thugs, organised crime, and shady actors of the state. Like its Gladio predecessor Counter-Guerrilla, Ergenekon was shown to thrive by tithing narcotics flowing along the golden trail from the Far East and Afghanistan. As the lamps of history shone into the past, the clear outlines could be seen of Turkey's quarter-century-long dirty war on the Kurds, the military's lynching of premier Adnan Menderes in 1961, and the assassin's trail that led to St. Peter's Square in Rome one bright spring day in 1982.

II.
The Curse of the Two-Edged Sword

'You had to attack civilians, the people, women, children, unknown people far from any political game. The reason was quite simple — to force the people to turn to the state to ask for greater security.'
— Vincenzo Vinciguerra, convicted Italian terrorist.

One typically sweltering August morning in 1990, the Italian premier Giulio Andreotti — whose extraordinary survival capacities amid scores of scandals earned him the lasting epithet of 'the Divine Julius' — astonished the Italian public with an extremely rare personal confession. The six-times premier (a seventh mandate would follow) found himself summoned to a special commission of inquiry, hurriedly convened by the Senate to investigate the reports that a secret parallel state existed on Italian soil. Moreover it was apparently equipped with its own clandestine commando army, operating outside all established military structures. Andreotti was on his finest polished form, invariably the case when finding himself in a tight corner. Gently he soothed the listening senators by conceding that for many years Italy indeed hosted a clandestine army. It was however formally an element of the standing NATO structure. He calmly assured his listeners it was nothing more threatening than a prudent precaution to defend Italy in the event of invasion by the Soviets. When that threat appeared to abate, the secret soldiers were disbanded in 1971. It was only secret because the Russians were not supposed to know about the so-called 'stay behind' army. In any case, Italy was not alone, since all NATO countries had such forces. The performance was vintage Andreotti: the calm, downplayed manner in which he usually despatched any inconvenient political crisis that disturbed his meticulous tidiness of his desk.

Unfortunately, his carefully air-brushed account of volunteers standing firmly to arms against an incoming communist tide struck a discordant note with the Italian public at large, long accustomed to thinking the worst about their political classes. Nor were they entirely convinced that such a useful political instrument had been quite so easily waved away, especially when it became known that the secret army — named, as the Divine Julius admitted, Gladio — had well-stocked arms dumps in every corner of the land. Sensing a whirlwind political opportunity, the communist party ordered huge street protests which attracted many thousands, some dressed up as gladiators. Even by the standards of a country where spectacular political scandals are the everyday norm, the media enjoyed a classic field day.

Yet behind the great hubbub and blaring headlines, much of Italy's political class were only feigning their surprise — especially the Christian Democrats, eternal sun gods of Italian politics, and a few prominent fellow travelling 'lira socialists' (an allusion to endemic bribes). They had long known of '*lo stato parassitario*' (the parasitic state), and also precisely who were the owners of that valuable property. Their sacred number included Andreotti himself, a powerful shareholder in subterranean Italy for many years. Yet for the moment, he had every reason to believe he had defused the crisis, with Gladio safely back in the box. However, fresh alarm bells related directly to the Gladio crisis were sounding in other quarters of the state.

The alabaster-faced Andreotti was again unexpectedly jolted from his customary serenity by a warning from the attorney general. Investigating magistrates were about to expose the trail connecting the secret underground army to many acts of civil terror committed during the *anni di piombo*. The most dangerous and persistent of these — the stubborn Venetian campaigning magistrate Felice Casson, a constant bane of authorities trying to conceal the secrets of the deep state — delivered a monumental pile to the attorney general's office in Rome. As an additional precaution in the Italian political climate, the precious cargo was escorted by a well-armed *Carabinieri* detachment. Here was the ripened fruit of diligent investigations extending over a full decade, running to many thousands of damning words, ruthlessly exposing the Italian state as institutionally corrupted at every level. Casson's collaborators, rather too eagerly, gushed to reporters that clear evidence now existed to connect Gladio secret soldiers to specific acts of 'politico-military subversion.'[N1] They were certainly correct that the material amounted to an earthquake of such explosive power 'it could topple the government at any moment.'[N2][11]

Casson soon understood what sort of welcome his work was likely to receive from no less a totem than President Francesco Cossiga. In the course of a remarkable eulogy to Gladio, delivered before an audience of police and army cadets, the father of the nation praised the secret soldiers as 'patriots.' Meanwhile, in a devastating libel, he reviled the magistrate investigating

---

[11] Subsequently Senator Felice Casson, the man who bestowed on Thomas Mann's novel *Death in Venice* an entirely new meaning. His forensic skills exposed Italy's worst-ever eco-disaster responsible for the deaths of 157 workers employed by two firms in the industrial port of Venice called Porto Marghera. The men were contaminated with carcinogenic compounds during the manufacture of PVC. Porto Marghera has been described as 'the mother of all contamination' in Italy. This is mainly due to the discharge into the waters of the lagoon of vast quantities of highly toxic wastes. chiefly by chemical and petro-chemical industries. Casson is credited with the first definitive, independent exposure of Gladio. He has written and published extensively on the secret armies.

Gladio as inspired 'by the same subversive ideals' as those which fuelled Italy's Left-wing terrorists, the Brigate Rosse.[N3] Andreotti was now confronted with a fresh Vesuvian eruption of the Gladio affair.

Four months later, a string of revelations concerning the secret armies largely unstitched all his good work. In November, Guy Coëme, Belgian Minister of Defence, confessed to the Belgian units of sleeping soldiers, and was followed by his Greek counterpart, who admitted another troop known as 'Sheepskin.' Turkey shared with Italy the experience of decades-long, politically-skewed violence. On 3rd December 1990, General Kemal Yılmaz, chief of special forces in Turkey (the Special Warfare Department, or OHD), revealed the existence of Counter-Guerrilla. He was bound to be well informed, since the local stay-behind army reported directly to himself. It seemed there was a remarkable degree of co-ordination between these related announcements springing from a string of NATO countries, akin perhaps to a cleansing of the stables before uninvited guests turned up to inspect the premises. Unfortunately, in Turkey this exercise in limited disclosure was quickly undone.

The suspicion that Counter-Guerrilla operations ventured into torture and terrorism was confirmed by a retired general called Talat Turhan. He declared he had undergone excruciating abuse for several days at a villa in Istanbul's Erenköy district, at the hands of Eyüp Özalkuş, chief of the National Intelligence Organisation (MİT).[12] Almost immediately in the wake of the Italian revelations, veteran quasi-socialist statesman Bülent Ecevit informed the press that he was initiated into the existence of Counter-Guerrilla immediately after he began his first term as premier in 1974. Ecevit, who was locked up after General Evren's Counter-Guerrilla and CIA-backed coup in 1980 — and therefore had a quiver of reasons to fulminate revenge — was then indiscreet enough to imply that Counter-Guerrilla units might indeed have been involved in domestic terror. He specifically cited the stay-behind army's role in the bloody Taksim Square massacre in Istanbul on 1st May 1977. On hearing Ecevit's pronouncement, Defence Minister Safa Giray snapped: 'Ecevit had better keep his f***ing mouth shut!' *Or else*, one presumes.

Daniele Ganser posed the existential question concerning the motives of the secret soldiers. They were handsomely trained by Britain's SAS and the Pentagon's Green Berets, and a good many passed through an undercover training camp in wildest Sardinia. Yet when push came to shove, how many of these earnest volunteers would risk being caught by the Russians? It was

---

[12] One of the enduring pities of the ongoing Gladio exposure is how little of vital non-English-language material has made it into widespread translations, concerning this frontal assault on the civil liberties of millions of Europeans by their own governments. Turhan's clutch of books on Counter-Guerrilla and secret warfare in general offers an excellent example.

scarcely an edifying, life-enhancing prospect, in which contemplating infinity in a freezing gulag might be the featherbed option. In fact, as Ganser argued in his book, most of them expected to be plucked from such a fate in short order, seeing themselves foremost as soldiers rather than partisans. In 1940, expecting German invaders to cross the Channel at any moment, ministers doubted the stay-behind British Resistance Defence Organisation could hold on for more than a few weeks. The BRDO was the inspiration for Churchill's legendary 'we will fight them on the beaches' speech that year, and also inspired the long-running BBC TV sitcom of the 1970s called *Dad's Army*.

Even before the formal establishment of NATO in the spring of 1949, scouts from the Central Intelligence Agency toured Europe touting sweetheart deals with the commanders of wartime stay-behind outfits and local espionage organisations willing to sign on the dotted line, in return for substantial 'subsidies.' The CIA thus established important colonies in Greece and captured the whole of the intelligence establishment, as well as special forces units in Turkey, as soon as she joined NATO in 1952.[13] A decade would pass before an internal NATO briefing minute (dated 1st June 1959), slipped into the hands of a British newspaper, revealing the task of the stay-behind units had been formally switched to confronting 'internal subversion.' The secret armies were henceforth to play 'a determining role... not only on the general policy level of warfare, but also on the politics of emergency.'[N4] The document was the order of battle for the forthcoming *anni di piombo* which duly erupted across the European continent. All the more revealing to read it once again in the light of that other ground-breaking readjustment of NATO's role: the 1999 policy statement which firmly underscored the Alliance's future priorities in the field of asymmetrical warfare. It is unlikely, as we have seen, that during the intervening years NATO surrendered the counter-insurgency capabilities it so carefully assembled from 1950 onwards. The 1999 decision can be understood, like the one of forty years earlier, as a fresh order of battle to bring the 'politics of emergency' up to date, enhanced from now on with out-of-theatre capabilities. The notorious incident in the southern Iraq city of Basra on 17th January 2008 supplied concrete proof that Gladio tactics remain deeply rooted in British armed forces. Two SAS commandos were caught preparing a false-flag bombing on a police station. In June 2011 we find SAS units dressed as Arabs up to the same party tricks in Libya.

---

[13] The contract with the Greeks paved the way to genocide in Cyprus, the return of fascism to European soil in the guise of the Greek military putsch (1967), the destruction of the Greek monarchy, illegal heists of Gladio funds to pay the Watergate defence team as well as Nixon's re-election purse, and for good measure, a flourishing sideline in smuggling arms meant for the Greek army. Nice work, if one could get it.

The Stockholm connection provided an important insight to the prevailing mentality, the reliance on ex-Nazis and Right-wing extremists in general, as the backbone of the secret soldiers. In 1953 a notorious racist and ex-SS commander called Otto Hallberg fell into the hands of the Swedish police on suspicions of promoting terrorism. During interrogation he let slip that he was the leading light in the Swedish stay-behind army ('Sveaborg'). The relaxed and chatty Hallberg entertained his custodians with the remarkable tale of how he received his on-the-job training as far back as 1941, when he began assembling the nuts and bolts of a stay-behind army on behalf of the Germans, inside the Reich. This was called *Werwolf,* the Nazi *Doppelgänger* of the future Gladio, sustained in the same fashion by stores of food and munitions laid down in well-stocked hideaways. As Hallberg confidently expected, all police charges were quietly squashed on higher instructions. He was thus prevented from rattling many skeletons of the Swedish secret state in open court, such as the extent to which Swedish forces were under the direct sway of the CIA and NATO.

Sweden is classically one of those countries where things are never quite as placid as they appear to the surface. The murder in 1986 of the Swedish Prime Minister Olof Palme, a galvanising figure in world politics, rocked Scandinavia with an impact similar to the John and Robert Kennedy assassinations and ignited nearly as many conspiracy theories. Palme was premier of a country often described as the epitome of non-aggression and clammy omnipresent state paternalism. The revisionist view from John Ray, who writes about psychological forms of authoritarianism, regards Sweden as an example of 'fascism in slow motion.' In WW2, she leaned towards the Nazis, allowing war materials and troops to transit the country (to attack Norway), and fed the Germans with vital ores. The tightly organised *folkhemmet* (the Social Democratic people's state), developed from 1932 onwards, was a rigid form of corporatist society where high personal taxation — which paid for generous social and welfare benefits — functioned as a subtle means to exercise control over the population. Per Engdahl (1909-1994), charismatic leader of the Swedish far Right, was a great friend and ally of the British Blackshirt leader Sir Oswald Mosley. They worked together in the 1950s designing an anti-Semitic, pan-European fascist confederation. Engdahl always had strong support among the Swedish officer corps and the national *Polisen.* But his influence spread far wider. When he was in Stockholm setting up the Sveaborg unit, Bill Colby of the future watery grave — ever one to snap up a Nazi — recognised Engdahl's potential and quickly put him on the CIA's books. One of his first tasks was picking safe hands for the Swedish Gladio unit.

Swedes were fully aware of the technical nature of their neutrality in WW2. Many argued the country should join the Axis Powers. They hoped the Germans, Teutons like themselves, might win. Big business, raking in the profits on all sides, put a stop to talk of formally entering the war. When the Germans lost and the Soviet Union seemed to have won, Sweden continued a very similar strategy — neutrality with a bold face (or as President Theodore Roosevelt's favorite proverb had it, 'Speak softly and carry a big stick'). Jerker Widén, an analyst at the Swedish National Defence College, painted a picture of a highly militarised state enjoying most-favoured nation status with the US and NATO, ushered to the innermost corridors of power, and showered with the latest high-tech weaponry. Sweden was in truth a shadow member of the NATO joint command (as it is now) and in war would occupy a vital forward position. But Swedes at large did not share the knowledge possessed by Palme — that her western fjords bristled with American nuclear submarines, atom-tipped missiles trained on Moscow, until 1994.

Like JFK, Palme was a new-hope figure, rekindling the flames of social democracy then experiencing severe stress right across Europe. Palme — the globe-trotting peacemaker, fraterniser with the Palestine Liberation Organisation and Castro's Cuba, bold critic of US policy in Indochina and now UN umpire trying to stop the Iran-Iraq war — was not exactly the poster child of the Washington Big Top or the Swedish deep state. Palme was coldly realistic concerning US-NATO relations with Sweden, and he knew all about those giant silver whales submerged in Swedish waters. But he was walking a dangerous tightrope.

The brief facts about Palme's last moments to be stated with any certainty are the following. As a champion of open government, Palme spurned bodyguards, strolling freely about the streets like any private citizen. Close to midnight on 28th February 1986, as he was leaving the Grand Cinema in central Stockholm with his wife Lisbeth, a figure stepped from the shadows, drew a revolver and shot him once in the back, the barrel positioned to pierce the heart. The victim died instantly. A second round lightly wounded Mrs. Palme. The gunman's actions were performed at a leisurely pace. He displayed no signs of concern at committing cold-blooded murder in full view of witnesses, and then vanished calmly into the night without visible haste. Several observers commented his body movements seemed to indicate he knew to a second exactly when the premier would reach the spot where the execution would be performed.

The indications of a contract job, rather than a rash act performed by someone with a disordered mind, were compelling. Two years after the event, the obliging patsy duly made his appearance, a grubby petty criminal and drug runner called Christer Pettersson. His useful pedigree included a previous homicide and a tendency to brag that he wanted to kill Palme. The psychological urge to confess is not uncommon (as in Dostoevsky's *Crime and Punishment*), particularly if the individual is a wrong side of the track hankering for attention. Pettersson was well known to powerful Stockholm criminal clans, who probably served up his head on a plate. He was tried, convicted, and then cleared on appeal, which is how the matter stood until he too was murdered in 2004. Pettersson suddenly announced to the media that he had an 'important message' for Palme's son, Mårten, who agreed to a meeting — which in the event never took place. On 16th September, Pettersson was found lying in a coma at his home with devastating head injuries. Reports circulated in the media that he received a visit from the police on the 15th and was not seen outside his home thereafter. He never recovered consciousness. This crime is also unsolved. Like Jack Ruby, who struck down Lee Harvey Oswald, Christer Pettersson knew everything and nothing at the same time. A decayed and shattered personality was supplied with a sense of mission (again like Ruby) by the Palme slaying, which led him to claim responsibility even after he was cleared by the highest courts. As a serious candidate, he was perfectly incredible. We shall never know what he intended to tell Mårten Palme concerning the murder of his father on the eve of his own death in 2004. But it was sufficiently compromising for his skull to be smashed like an egg shell before he could open his mouth.

In that same year, Lawrence Redlinger and H. H. A. Cooper published *The Murder of Olof Palme: A Tale of Assassination, Deception and Intrigue*, in which they argued that Palme was 'a victim of a largely clandestine clash of forces.' Palme was certainly exposed as the UN mediator in the Iran-Iraq war, and an early end to it would not have been good for the health of Operation Iran-Contra.

Some years later, a retired police superintendent, who was a scene-of-crime officer on the night Palme died, began to talk about the peculiar behaviour of his colleagues. Despite the call for aid, it took a full seven minutes for the first police cars to reach the scene. There was no general alert and lockdown, as one might expect in these high-profile circumstances. Only selected cars got the alarm call anyway. One officer made the astonishing claim he 'wasn't sure' it was actually Palme lying in a pool of blood, although his was the best-known face in the country, after the king. The superintendent, Gösta Söderström, blew the whistle that police units in the capital were in thrall to Right-wing extremism and 'were lying about the murder.' His most serious charge was that 'they [police at the scene] helped him [the gunman] escape.' Many factual records of the night's events vanished.

The contradictions of the Swedish national personality extended to Palme himself. He was widely seen as anti-American. In truth, his attitudes to America were ambivalent. As a young man he thumbed his way coast to coast in a state of utter fascination. As a student he was courted by CIA talent scouts, who could see even at the age of 20 he might be groomed for stardom. The reputable daily *Dagens Nyheter* described a meeting at the US embassy in 1950, where propositions were put to Palme to spy for the CIA. It seems that during his travels behind the Iron Curtain, he did feed the CIA with interesting snippets, on a voluntary basis. At the end of 1950, Palme organised a conference in Stockholm which led to the creation of the International Students Conference. The CIA, secretly funding this organisation, wanted Palme to be the head, which he declined in favour of the diplomatic service. In 2009, Ingmar Engman — a former agent in Sweden's military intelligence — shed light in dark corners when he said 'Olof Palme's co-operation with the Americans and the CIA was well known throughout the military intelligence service.' Other sources described Palme as closely involved in setting up the Sveaborg stay-behind unit, which unquestionably would have placed him in close liaison with the secret soldier mastermind Bill Colby.

As Prime Minister, Palme hosted the May 1973 Bilderberg conclave in the Grand Hotel Saltsjöbaden close to Stockholm, alongside Marcus Wallenberg. The Wallenberg dynasty rules the largest family-owned company in Europe, a banking and industrial combine accounting for about one-third of Sweden's economy. It was a pivotal Bilderberg meeting, as documented by F. Wm. Engdahl in *A Century of War*. An American viceroy — probably Bilderberg regular Henry Kissinger — presented the vassals of Europe a daring strategy to rescue the dollar: an oil shock followed by petro-dollar recycling, and a long-term turn away from growth to 'greening' — controlling economies rather than growing them. A few months later, Kissinger instigated the Yom Kippur War, which gave the Saudis the pretext for the new oil price level, and for Israel to occupy more Palestinian territory.

Palme's trajectory steered close to another Swedish icon, Dag Hammarskjöld, second Secretary General of the young United Nations, once praised by JFK as 'the greatest statesman of our century.' Hammarskjöld died on 18th September 1961, when his official DC-6 came down in the Rhodesian veldt. He was on his way to investigate attacks on UN peacekeeping troops by American, Belgian and British-backed Katangese secessionist rebels in the sprawling Congo, newly independent from Belgium. His death, like that of Palme twenty-five years later, gave rise to claims of big power intrigues. All three countries were interested in keeping the vast Congolese reserves of copper firmly under western control, while officially the UN, under the auspices of Hammarskjöld, was opposed to independence for Katanga. Rescuers certainly dragged their feet getting to the scene of the crash, giving rise to the suspicion there were supposed to be no survivors to tell what really happened. The crash investigation conducted by the colonial Rhodesian authorities, heavily influenced by the British, was a sham. Every effort was made to quash witness statements describing a circling smaller plane that fired at the UN jet. The mystery is unlikely to be resolved. For certain Palme, like Hammarskjöld, always seemed too expansive a personality for one small country like Sweden to contain.

The nuclear subs assumed a growing significance as Palme the visionary detected the momentous political events that were about to change the world. As the decade of the '80s drew to a close, he believed that the huge eruptions tearing the Soviet fold apart would make possible his life-long dream of general disarmament. His hopes were dashed. The US had no intentions of cashing the blank cheque represented by the peace dividend, nor surrendering its influence over Sweden. In these matters Palme was an awkward obstacle, but he was also exposed on other treacherous ground. He was charged by the UN to negotiate between the parties engaged in the Iran-Iraq war, a dispute in which the United States had logistical interests on both sides. Scarcely a month after he was killed, a plane crashed in the Nicaraguan jungle; it was loaded with munitions, which led to the exposure of the Iran-Contra affair. If Palme had somehow intercepted the activities of the voluble Lt.-Col. Oliver North, then any man in possession of such knowledge was certainly walking a slender path between here and eternity.

The accumulation of evidence which points to a Gladio contract killing is compelling. Two CIA whistleblowers suggested the gunman was acting on orders from Gladio in Italy. They were Richard Brenneke and Gene 'Chips' Tatum, an Iran-Contra operations pilot who claimed Palme was victim of a hitherto unknown CIA secret assassination programme called Pegasus. In April 1992, *Dagens Nyheter* published a series of articles alleging a NATO-commissioned assassination, drawing on documents stating: 'planning local, technician imported.' (Full details in the endnote.[N5]) That same year, the Italian state television channel RAI broadcast a claim that CIA hit man Michael Townley visited Stockholm about a week before the shooting, supposedly on a reconnaissance exercise. In Rome, President (and former Gladio boss) Francesco Cossiga panicked himself into sending premier Giulio Andreotti an urgent letter pleading for advice what to do. Andreotti maintained his usual Olympian silence, and he had sound reasons. Townley was a close associate of the Italian neofascist Stefano Delle Chiaie, who crops up many times in these pages. Delle Chiaie moved in the inner circle of Gelli's P2 lodge. He was on warm terms with many intimates of Gladio, prelates and criminals, who were operating the secret finance conduits within the Vatican, and a secret outpost in Portugal acting as the command centre behind the *anni di piombo*. (See God's Terrorist: Yves Guérin-Sérac and the Press Gang, Chapter V).

Both Townley and Delle Chiaie were key figures in the Operation Condor terror and assassination programme set up by the Condor club of Latin American dictators. Some 60,000 deaths of Leftists and so-called revolutionaries would be laid against Western-backed death squads. Condor's operational tendrils ran through the Fort Bragg army black ops centre. Townley on your tail invariably indicated a dead man walking. In 1974, he exploded a radio-controlled car bomb in Buenos Aires which killed

General Carlos Prats Gonzalez, deputy to the assassinated Chilean president Salvador Allende. Two years later in Washington DC, he used the same technique to murder the exiled Orlando Letelier, another close confidant of Allende, who was making a considerable nuisance of himself by rallying political and public opinion against the Chilean regime of General Augusto Pinochet.[N6] The explosives were tucked beneath the driver's seat. The blast tore away the victim's entire lower trunk.[14]

A second figure with strong connections to Gladio contract assassination programmes now appears in the Stockholm frame, a shadowy Danish-Italian called Francesco Gullino, living in next-door Copenhagen. He is also the prime suspect in a spectacular and long-lasting mystery, the killing in September 1978 of Georgi Markov, a prominent Bulgarian émigré writer and anti-regime broadcaster living in London. Markov was struck by a tiny pellet apparently containing a lethal dose of ricin. The headline-seizing theory was circulated that the fatal dart could have been fired from an adapted umbrella functioning silently, similarly to an air gun. As we see in Chapter IX (Goodbye Piccadilly) such devices had recently been developed by American biological warfare experts and passed to the CIA. Traced to Budapest ten years after the murder of Palme, Gullino freely declared that one country where he would never dare show his face again was Sweden. The possibility that Townley was the set designer in Stockholm, and Gullino the imported stage technician, is persuasive.

There was a tragic sequel to the Palme affair on 11th September 2003, which played a significant role in replacing the traditional easy-going image of Sweden with the far darker one portrayed in the iconic Millenium series of crime novels by the late Stieg Larsson.[15] The Swedish foreign affairs minister — the young and popular Anna Lindh, rising star of the Social Democratic

---

[14] In the spring of 2010, it emerged that, shortly before these murders, Henry Kissinger quashed a telegram intended for all US ambassadors in Latin America, warning them of a forthcoming outbreak of political assassinations.

[15] Author of the iconic record-breaking *Millennium Trilogy*, starting with the *Girl with the Dragon Tattoo*. It has sold over 65 million copies, the greatest sensation in Swedish publishing history. A Hollywood version is in preparation, following on the galactic international success of the Swedish neo-noir ground-breaker. The books and films follow the adventures of a Swedish investigative journalist and his encounters with the Swedish deep state, the flourishing neo-Nazi movement and its links to Far Right politics. Larsson drew on his real-life experiences as editor of the Stockholm-based *Expo* magazine which operates in precisely the same territory. His last volume, *The Girl Who Kicked the Hornet's Nest*, alludes to a Gladio-style deep state organization, and Sweden's clandestine links with 'a foreign power' (Hint: the United States). Compelled to live a largely reclusive life because of constant death threats, Larsson eventually succumbed to a massive heart attack at the age of 50, on 9th November 2004.

Party, widely tipped as the next premier — was fatally stabbed in an apparently motiveless and frenzied attack while shopping in a busy Stockholm department store. Like Palme, she always shunned security details. The police pounced on a 25-year-old Swedish-born Serb, Mijailo Mijalovic, who appeared to hail from false-flag central casting. Mijalovic was rootless and dysfunctional, those excellent qualifications for the aspiring patsy. But difficulties immediately arose concerning conflicting descriptions of the alleged assassin, who to complicate matters kept referring to 'we' under interrogation. There was a reprise in Norway eight years later. The gunman Anders Behring Breivik, accused of a crazed solo massacre in July 2011 that claimed scores of victims, also spoke of accomplices.

Some witnesses (pointedly not called to court) who were present in the store that lunchtime insisted the knifeman was 'tall and powerfully built,' aged perhaps 35, with a hardened pock-marked face and a bulky military-style jacket. As Christopher Bollyn's superb investigation for the *American Free Press* later suggested, this image was completely incompatible with the widely-circulated fuzzy video snaps of the pathetic Mijalovic strolling into the store clad in a sweatshirt and baseball cap.

Mijalovic was duly sentenced to life. After legal arguments, the sentence was confirmed but the prisoner — diagnosed as mentally ill — was placed incommunicado in a closed psychiatric ward, where he remains. He spoke of presences in his head, especially Jesus, that egged him on to stab the minister. But other voices heard shortly after her death observed factually that Lindh was the fourth in a line of unremitting Swedish political champions of the Palestinian cause to meet a violent end. The chain commenced with Count Folke Bernadotte, the chief UN negotiator in Palestine, gunned down by Stern Gang terrorists in Jerusalem in 1948. Then came another famous UN peacemaker, Dag Hammarskjöld, in 1961. Lindh's political mentor Olof Palme, who was also a UN-appointed peacebroker and a prominent advocate of the Palestinian cause, had died seventeen years earlier. Lindh had accused the Israeli government of Ariel Sharon of ruthless war crimes, campaigned for a nuclear-free Middle East (not sparing Israel's atom silos) and insisted in 2003 that the EU sever all ties with Israel. This was scarcely likely to spare her from the long arms of Mossad or the CIA. Like the assassinated trio of Palme, Hammarskjöld and Count Bernadotte, Anna Lindh was another obstacle to big power machinations.

Lindh seems to have crossed a personal political Rubicon after surrendering to American political bullying to allow the CIA's snatching of an Egyptian citizen called Ahmed Agiza from a Stockholm street just before Christmas 2001 — with the help of Swedish intelligence. She subsequently told associates that she felt bitterly scarred by the experience, and the volume of her opposition to Israeli and American policies rose sharply afterwards. Eva Franchell, the minister's press officer, who was at her side during the ill-fated shopping expedition, published a memoir in 2009 which almost in passing suggested that her boss was not alone in the Ahmed Agiza affair. This was widely interpreted as a jab at the then justice minister, a controversial libertarian figure in the Swedish political landscape called Thomas Lennart Bodström (whose father had been Palme's foreign minister).

The rushed trial just four months after her death was a charade right from the opening statement, which declared that the only business of the court was to convict Mijalovic. The evidence presented many problems: the extent of the wounds the victim suffered; why Lindh was thought likely to survive and then died after a protracted operation; serious contradictions in witness statements; the absence of fingerprints on the knife the alleged assassin tossed away. The authorities did nothing to dispel suspicion by insisting on the old chestnut that much of what they knew must remain secret 'in the interests of the state.' This includes the absence of any credible explanation why the in-store video cameras covering the main escalator and the second and third floors, where the fatal action occurred, were conveniently switched off or otherwise inoperative that day — all the classic signs of a cover-up in motion. But even more remarkable was the amazingly swift arrival of the ambulance, in about one minute from the emergency call (the police required ten), as though it had been waiting around the corner with the engine running. By surely more than mortal co-incidence, the vehicle arrived containing one of Lindh's most senior advisers at her own ministry.

Bollyn concluded Lindh was taken out by an expert hit squad of at least four trained killers who were on her tail that morning. The one sure and certain fact emerging from this fog of confusion is this: a striking and outspoken communicator bearing a stubborn attachment to the Palestinian cause was eliminated, exactly like Palme, as a source of conflict with the ruling pro-Zionist stance of the western camp.

Our spotlight shifts to Belgium, a contrived and tormented state that arose from the shotgun marriage in 1830 between disharmonious French and Flemish speakers (that 'hated construction' derided by Flemish nationalists). Belgium's favourite Surrealist artist, René Magritte, is famous for his painting of a pipe on which he inscribed: 'This is not a pipe.' Today he might aptly produce a map of his native land and write on it: 'This is not a country.' It was the fate of this Kosovo by the North Sea, renowned for delights such as *moules et frites*, death-by-chocolate gateau and exquisite fruity beers brewed by monks, to find itself smashed by the Gladio bulldozer. Investigations by parliamentary authorities during the 1990s uncorked the immensely careful planning that went into constructing the secret military network which eventually ran amok so disastrously it may have terminally unhinged Europe's most conditional state. These revealed that in Belgium (in common practice with all NATO countries) the first step was the post-war establishment of a tri-partite committee linking the secret intelligence services of the host country, Britain and America. Diligent journalists delving for the explanations to Belgium's own devastating years of lead supported this conclusion.

So far, the standard Gladio compact. However, in Belgium, the Strategy of Tension underwent a genetic mutation, thanks to the 'Belgian Paradox,' which supplied two sets of secret armies in one country. A brief sketch will help explain how the paradox works. A large part of French-speaking Wallonia consists of deep forests (the Ardennes) flanked by a rustbelt, in times gone by Belgium's important industrial spine, scarred now with decomposing relics of coal pits and skeletons of abandoned factories. Flanders, on the other hand, sees itself as a well-organised nation state in waiting, with a humming modern economy. Swanky Antwerp with its diamond vaults, twin tourist gems Bruges and Ghent, and the proximity to bustling Holland, pack a powerful economic punch. Meanwhile sad, broken-down Wallonia is Belgium's Cinderella province, lacking access to the sea and natural resources of any great importance. Accidents of geography are not enough however to prevent the Flemings from complaining bitterly about the burden of supporting what they coldly dismiss as feckless Francophone Walloons. Both sides squabble endlessly concerning the linguistic fringes of Brussels, which is really an internationalised canton. The Belgian capital swarms with bureaucrats, military types and stateless corporate drones, a playground for narcotics smugglers and international arms traffickers (and far worse in that line, as we discover later).

Rupture has always beckoned in Belgium, which — in the course of interminable divorce proceedings — ended up with a bad case of double vision. There was a pair of everything: media, governments, political parties (even of the same stripe), languages, and (for neatness) secret armies and espionage outfits, one for each side of the language rift. As with Brussel/Bruxelles, all the main town names have two spellings (sometimes a third for the tiny German minority). The newly-arrived NATO (evicted unceremoniously from France by President Charles de Gaulle) desired this bastard state to hang together, since it was now in effect the 'Principality of NATO,' which could not be allowed to entertain seditious moles with a hotline to Moscow.

In WW2, Belgium contributed a modest number of volunteers for the German war machine from both sides of the national language divide, although the total strength amounted to not much more than two brigades. Some Flemings were attracted to the swastika out of the conviction that Hitler was inclined to concede long-cherished sovereignty, albeit within a Nazi-bossed empire. There is no evidence he had any such plans in concrete form, but the idea worked as a powerful recruiting poster. In contrast,

Walloons joined their own SS volunteer division out of sympathies with Vichy France. The pull of Nazi pagan symbolism proved long-lasting, scarcely ruffled by a few show trials of selected collaborators at the war's end. As in Italy and Germany, Belgian secret army and intelligence services, encouraged by the CIA, provided welcome berths for many trusty and reliable not-so-very-ex-Nazis. Before long, the familiar process of fusion attracted Belgian crime syndicates, corrupted politicians and soldiers — all the traditional ingredients that are so often found in a secret parallel state. But there was an additional rogue gene. Namely, the arrival of huge numbers of free-spending newcomers clustering around NATO, the burgeoning European integration institutions and the international corporatocracy. These new arrivals vastly multiplied the power of Belgian criminal networks, which turned this small country into the European cockpit of everything from arms and drug trafficking to horrific trade in human flesh. Belgians reeled from the paedophile scandals of the closing century not just because they were unspeakable and vile: they also reported something about the vestigial national personality that appeared to be badly unstuck.

In the 1970s and well into the '80s, the country witnessed its own *années de plomb*. Pitiless gangs roamed around committing random, seemingly purposeless crimes. In one grisly instance, shoppers queuing at a supermarket check-out till were coldly mown down with machine guns. Others were killed packing their groceries in supermarket parking lots. Investigations by the national parliament connected these atrocities to a secret state, dramatising a synthetic breakdown of law and order for political ends.[N7] The official inquiry into what became known as the infamous Brabant Massacres, after the province where most of them were committed, was published in 1990, appearing just before the public acknowledgement of Gladio in Rome. One conclusion of the panel declared with eerie percipience: 'The killers were cited as members or former members of the security forces — extreme Right-wingers who enjoyed high-level protection and were preparing a Right-wing coup.' The inquiry concluded the attacks were intended to send Belgians flocking to a strong central power. However, they obstinately rushed in the opposite direction. They connected the attacks and murders to the organs of a thoroughly-diseased public state, the infiltration of high public offices by organised crime, which led to the sheltering of criminals committing abominable deeds. When stories appeared of paedophile gangs operating in brazen contempt of the forces of law and order, it seemed that beneath the surface of a model civilised modern European state was a descent into a nightmare world of inhumanity.

The infamous Marc Dutroux — serial child abductor and murderer, the 'Monster of Charleroi' — pursued his horrific career secure in the apparent belief that he was safe from persecution by the authorities. The shocking truth gradually emerged that Dutroux's web of connections in the underground

Belgian state linked him to a cavern inhabited by powerful people — lawyers, judges, politicians, businessmen, secret policemen, criminals and members of the Belgian secret armies. They could do literally as they pleased, especially in the sordid shades of vice involving women and young children, by leaning on the official security services and protective espionage agencies. The vice rackets unleashed an orgy of blackmailing, in which the Dutroux network excelled. Be it said, however, that for all his appalling infamy, the Monster Dutroux was a comparatively minor foot-soldier in the service of others. That this creature from the depths reported to a higher command reveals the true extent of depravity which had taken hold of the state.

Long-simmering frustration provoked by the Dutroux affair finally burst into the open. In October 1996, two months after Dutroux was arrested, 300,000 Belgians poured into the streets of the capital to protest lethargic courts and cynical disinterest of government ministers. Many in this eerie ghostlike procession dressed entirely in white and carried white lilies, white roses and white balloons to symbolise the innocence of children. *La Marche Blanche* was of a size not seen since the campaigns for detachment from The Netherlands in 1830. It was a display of cynical official hand-wringing for public consumption. Its chief purpose was to defuse anger, which led to suspicions, well-grounded, of official hands behind an exercise in distraction.

The chronic story of the disintegration of this patchwork country, thanks in no small degree to the activities of paramilitary outfits owing allegiance to NATO, earns a chapter to itself (Something Rotten in the State of Belgium, Chapter XIII). For now we can say the long political crisis which began in summer 2007 dramatised the intrinsic ungovernability of Belgium against a creeping barrage of propaganda intended to encourage and dignify the full independence of Flanders. Such a state would of course prove the perfect safe haven for the North Atlantic Alliance, the armed camp manipulating the country's direction for almost 40 years. It was no coincidence that this electoral impasse occurred against a background of rising unrest and violence centring on Belgium's 500,000 strong Muslim community. The explosive growth of the Islamic population, which far outstrips the ethnic Belgian birth rate, raised to American and thus NATO minds the spectre of fabled Eurabia as successor to the lapsed communist bogey. Eruptions of street violence — especially in Antwerp with its fast-swelling immigrant Arabic population, all credulously reported by the media as the work of Islamic troublemakers.[N8] In June 2003, Donald Rumsfeld, then the US defense secretary, threatened to withdraw NATO HQ from Belgium unless the government revoked legislation granting Belgian courts the right to try US military personnel for war crimes committed anywhere in the world. Denouncing 'harassment by a pack of Left-wing lawyers,' Rumsfeld's threats — empty, if anyone thought seriously about it — nonetheless neatly encapsulated the contemptuous regard the US authorities hold towards a sovereign allied state and its government. This was exactly the attitude that resulted in NATO's eviction from France by President de Gaulle. The Belgians caved in, which left few doubts concerning the nature of the real power in the land.

To mention the name of Aldo Moro to most Italians is to awaken a pain at the heart of a nation. Did the man who dominated Italian politics for twenty years really perish at the hands of a fanatical cell of Left-wing extremists calling themselves the Brigate Rosse? Within the unfinished work known as Italy, broadly 30 per cent or so consider themselves on the modern liberal centre-Left, and they continue to doubt the official account. Italy is the consummate paradise of illusions. While an Assisi-like afterglow bathes the saintly Moro, he curiously shares a pantheon with the strutting and boastful Benito Mussolini. Together with his beautiful young mistress Clara ('Claretta') Petacci, the Italian dictator was shot by a pair of partisans near Lake Como in the Italian Alps in April 1945, while attempting to flee approaching Allied forces. The circumstances have never been properly explained. Suspicion points to a bungled attempt at blackmail in return for the pair's lives. The subsequent display of Mussolini and Petacci hanging upside down from the roof beam of a garage in Milan strikes Italians to this day as repellent. These two figures, Moro and Mussolini, representing as they do contrasting sides of the political gulf, are widely seen as victims of immoral and cowardly killers — and the country's endless political tragedy.[16]

When Andreotti confessed to the existence of Gladio, perhaps the disturbed spirit of the murdered former premier Aldo Moro flickered in his mind, like the visions that tormented Shakespeare's Richard III the night before his final battle on the field of Bosworth. The similarities between these ruthless social climbers, Andreotti and the Last Plantagenet, are eerily compelling, not least their common habit of eliminating obstructions. When Moro was violently abducted on 16th March 1978, the communists were a shadow force in the background of Andreotti's administration, voting

---

[16] On the 27th anniversary of Moro's death, Andreotti offered a strikingly equivocal, if not actually callous, personal account of the tragedy. 'Is it true that the liberation of just one member of the Brigades would have been sufficient to save Moro, and that President Leone was ready to pardon [Paola] Besuschio who was in prison after sentence? No, is the answer, because even if pardoned, she was on remand for another crime, *involving a mandate of obligatory arrest*, and hence it would have been a useless provocation to *pretend* to free her.' He finished with the dismissive line: 'Without Moro, the shrewd political project worked out by him was in any case impracticable.' One could sniff the vitriol singing the page, intellectual arrogance of a very high register, even by Andreotti's elastic standards — an Olympian detachment from a deed which served its ends. [Quotes extracted from *30 Days*, Andreotti's personal website, June 2005.]

obediently to keep it alive, in the hope of further preferment. But the Divine Julius did not intend to stare at communist faces sitting around his own cabinet table. The multi-layered case of Moro is complicated by the convenient elimination of important witnesses close to the event, who might have told important stories. Held incommunicado for fifty-five days, the wretched captive was permitted in this bleak *teatro nero* to send almost one hundred letters to his family and politicians, which magnetised the massive sense of national crisis in every Italian mind. Posed images before the Red Brigades banner which dominated newspaper front pages and TV newscasts for nearly two months conveyed a plain message: this is what you can expect from trading with double-crossing communists. In March 2008, Francesco Cossiga, who had been President (and thus reigning Gladio commander) during the Moro drama 30 years before, made two striking admissions. First, he falsely authorised a public announcement that the Brigate Rosse had killed Moro, when the ruling Christian Democrat hierarchy knew perfectly well that the president of their party was still alive. Secondly, that Moro was sacrificed for the sake of the 'stability of the state.' It was tantamount to admitting that the state sentenced Moro to death.

There was strong supporting evidence. Moro had barely been seized when President Jimmy Carter despatched the US government's chief expert in conflict resolution, the Cuban-born, Harvard and French-educated PhD Steve Pieczenik, hot foot to Rome. He was no conventional Ivory Towers publicity-shunning boffin. Pieczenik was close enough to the inner secrets of successive US governments to earn the political equivalent of Grammy awards for his psychological insights delivered to four secretaries of state — Henry Kissinger, Cyrus Vance, George Shultz and James Baker. According to his personal website, it appears scarcely any conflict failed to invite his attention.[17] And that was just his day job. He doubled all of this with writing racy psycho-political bodice rippers for the thriller factory run by Tom

---

[17] This Indiana Jones of 'psycho-political dynamics and conflict mediation strategies' enjoyed the high-powered title of assistant deputy secretary of state. He was the man whispering in ears during many terrorist episodes, including the Hanafi Moslem siege of Washington DC City Hall (1977), the TWA Croatian hijacking (1976) and the PLO hijacking of an El Al jet (1968). He advised Washington how to handle the assorted cast of Ugandan dictator Idi Amin, Mu'ammar Gaddafi, Carlos the Jackal and his co-terrorist Abu Nidal, plus for good measure Saddam Hussein — quite the royal flush of the terror pack. He dreamed up the scheme to either drive Panama's General Manuel Noriega insane or surrender, with giant loudspeakers parked outside his refuge, booming loud music around the clock. Where, we might ask, is the overdue Hollywood blockbuster devoted to this backroom shrink, who also developed negotiation strategies for the U.S.-Soviet arms control summits during the Reagan administration, Jimmy Carter's Camp David Israeli-Arab peace accords, not to mention the Cambodian Peace Conference in Paris?

Clancy. For good measure, he had a sideline advising the arch-neocon Council for Foreign Relations. In Rome, the famous psycho-warrior joined a crisis committee composed of Christian Democrat luminaries. Ostensibly, Pieczenik was despatched by Carter as a supporting negotiator charged with extracting the former premier alive. Whether this was ever really the intention is open to serious doubt.

The crisis cabinet was chaired by the ever-mercurial Cossiga — a brawler rather than quiet and patient deliberator — whose tendency to shoot from the hip could nonetheless prove useful in generating diversions. Cossiga, as chief lieutenant of Andreotti, had no intention of securing the release of Moro. The 'shrewd political project worked out by Moro' was intended to perish with its author. The catalyst in despatching Pieczenik was Zbigniew Brzezinski, Carter's Polish-born National Security Advisor. Coming as he did from a country which had suffered the brunt of Soviet aggression, Brzezinski viewed the Moro project of soft accommodation with the communists with great disdain. Pieczenik has offered conflicting accounts of his own role. He knew from long experience that if the intention really was to secure Moro's freedom, the political price would be relatively modest. Publicly, this was supposed to be the release of an incarcerated minor female brigadier, Paola Besuschio, confined in jail since 1975. Quite why the Brigate Rosse should be tempted by such a trifling morsel, supposedly having such an important bargaining chip in their possession, is inexplicable. Pieczenik insisted that he gave up on the case because the emergency committee was 'riddled with informers,' and by the end amounted to just Cossiga and himself staring at each other. So he raised his hands with exasperation, boarded a plane and went home. But in 2006, he gave an interview to French TV in a different light. Subsequently expanded in a book called *We Killed Aldo Moro* (2008), Pieczenik said that ultimately Moro was abandoned to his fate because he was giving his captors vital secrets of the state, in particular the hints of a 'NATO guerrilla army.' Of course the implication is that Moro believed himself to be a captive of a force other than the Red Brigades.

The food chain of this nugget is interesting. The Gladio units and their significance were of course known to Brzezinski and President Carter, between them representing the largest shareholder in NATO. It is unlikely that Pieczenik, confidant of presidents, flew to Rome in complete ignorance of Gladio. The begging question is this: if Moro was being indiscreet about Gladio, how did the council of Christian Democrat elders, stiff and dumb as Easter Island statues, actually know unless they had an inside track to the captive? Pieczenik then wrote: 'We had to sacrifice Aldo Moro to maintain the stability of Italy.' This was the identical refrain of Andreotti and Cossiga. It meant Moro's fate turned solely on keeping communists out of government in Rome — Carter's chief objective and that of every president before and since. If freed, Moro might start his bothersome campaign all over again. In

1997, when Senator Giovanni Pellegrino convened his parliamentary committee of inquiry into the *anni di piombo*, he summoned Pieczenik as a star witness. Pieczenik at first agreed and then begged off, under pressure from the State Department and probably the CIA. There were bound to be many difficult questions. In his 2008 book, Pieczenik let slip an important clue, that in the fourth week of Moro's captivity the 'US had to instrumentalise the Red Brigades.' It could be taken to mean goading them to action, or having Moro killed (as we see in a moment), with the blame then thrown upon the Brigades. But the book implied that the ultimate decision on Moro's fate was made as much in Washington as Rome.

The ruling political centre of gravity lay with the anti-Communist Right, the state intelligence services, the Mafia, big business and the Catholic Church, precisely the coalition mirrored by Licio Gelli's P2 secret government. The 61-year-old former premier was snatched on Rome's Via Mario Fani by a swarm of machine gunners, while on his way to parliament to commit the ultimate heresy — to bless an historic accommodation with the communists. Five of his guards were killed. In such a context, the petty demands of the Brigate Rosse were insubstantial and incredible. It followed that everything that transfixed Italians saw on their television sets was a manufactured illusion. Giuseppe De Lutiis' excellent book, *Il Golpe di Via Fani (Coup d'état on Via Fani)*, set out the case that the state, and not Marxist revolutionaries, had the most to gain from Moro's early departure from the scene. He constructed his case around the many 'disturbing inconsistencies' that he found with the official account.

> *The location where the members of the Brigades claimed to have held Moro prisoner is in a quarter of Rome [Magliana] that, at the time, was under the absolute control of a criminal gang with ties to the Mafia. The prosecutor's office ran into insurmountable difficulties trying to investigate Swiss bank accounts linked to one of the Brigades' commanders. The autopsy on Moro's corpse showed a muscle tone in the legs and a level of personal hygiene incompatible with a 55-day detention in a cellar like that described by the terrorists.*

The Brigate Rosse arose as a response from students and Left-wing radicals to the Italian state's violent suppression of labour unrest in Italy during the 1970s. Their style lay in selecting guaranteed headline-making targets, which the Moro affair might have fitted, but for the preference for prominent symbols of the abhorred capitalist order. Moro was glorified as an idol by organised labour (the natural Red Brigades constituency), Leftist intellectuals and the working classes in general. Within these ranks could be found sympathisers who saw the *Brigate* as urban heroes attacking a rotten system. This support was now burnt off as if by a flame-thrower. The incensed trades unions, whom the *Brigate* set out to defend, responded by calling a general strike. Some imprisoned *brigatisti* begged for Moro's release. Pope John Paul offered a ransom or even himself as a swap. The ghastly spectacle was, if anything, uniting the country, which ran utterly counter to the whole philosophy of the movement and broke the first objective of political terrorism, namely to achieve a result favourable to the perpetrators. The kidnapping was curiously spare of ideological dogma, decidedly unusual for these pen-wielding guerrillas. From another perspective, the kidnapping and murder yielded additional important political revenues. Hypnotised Italians observing the nightly death-by-newsreel stopped thinking of their increasing *depressione* at the sagging economy, with economic performance numbers like from the Third World, the last gasp of the post-war 'Italian Miracle.' Before Moro, the Andreotti government floundered in a sea of economic woes, while the Communists, flushed by the photo finish in 1976, looked muscular and set for a final heave.

Moro was shot with two weapons, both of some curiosity. The initial attempt was made purportedly by Mario Moretti using a German-designed 9mm Walther PPK, manufactured in France. The gun is often described as a spies' favourite, and fictionally carried as such by James 007 Bond. Adolf Hitler used an earlier model the PPK 76 to shoot himself in the Berlin bunker on 30th April 1945. The weapon is frequently found in the hands of the law enforcement agencies and the military. The Walther PPK apparently jammed after a single shot to Moro's chest, which failed to kill him, so the kidnappers finished their grisly task with a decidedly unusual alternative, a 7.65 mm Czech-made Škorpion vz. 61. This is an exceptionally lethal rapid-fire miniature sub-machine gun, capable of firing a thousand rounds a minute. It is highly compact and light enough to be easily concealed and carried. What is very unusual about this gun is the appeal that it has always held for counter-insurrection forces in third world countries. It is strange that such an unusual high-powered weapon boasting a massive rate of fire — and certainly not designed for a close-up assassination — was the only alternative available to the killers, instead of another pistol. The Škorpion is really designed to create a fan-like spread of fire in crowded environments, such as streets, or moving targets in the open at medium range. Used at close range the miniature cartridges would chop the body up as effectively as a machete. And why did the perpetrators in any event aim at Moro's chest, rather than a quick clean shot delivered to the temple or the back of the head, in the customary manner of executioners? Used in that manner, Moretti's first and obviously clumsy attempt with the Walther PPK would have killed Moro instantly. A weapon like the powerful and deadly Škorpion would create a huge amount of collateral damage to surrounding structures — furniture, walls, etc. — as the bullets passed through Moro. It can be silenced and smaller magazines fitted to restrict the fire rate to ten shots. But even so, it is far more likely that Moro was shot not in an apartment, but instead in a closed environment such as a sound-proofed basement.

Moreover, the Škorpion does not — from the ninety or so recovered cartridges — appear to have been among the weapons used in the original blood-soaked snatch on the Via Mario Fani, even though it would be well-suited to that kind of mass assault. Whatever the means used to kill him, and precisely where, Moro's bullet-riddled body was bundled into the trunk of a red Renault 4 fourgon, then motored undetected on the morning of 9th May 1978 to the heart of the locked-down capital, close to the River Tiber and the respective headquarters of the PCI (Italian Communist Party) and the DC (Christian Democrats, *Democrazia Cristiana*). The politically loaded signposts — the red delivery van, the location between the two rival political camps — spelt the message of a marriage postponed. Permanently. The subsequent post-mortem undermined the already confused picture of where Moro had been held. It seemed from the autopsy that his corpse had been transported a curiously short distance, little more than a kilometre. (A calculation helped by measuring the loss of blood and the degree to which rigor mortis had set in). Moro had also been in contact with asbestos, from the traces which clung to his clothing. This is rather difficult to square with the captors' inference that he was confined in a cave. He was unlikely to attract asbestos in any of the apartments where he was held. The explanation may well be, as I have suggested, that he was finally taken to an execution site with vault-like qualities. For example some kind of store (containing building materials for example) where asbestos might be found would supply an explanation. Stacks of building materials would also conveniently absorb the Škorpion-fired cartridges. It is evident that Moro was passed around like a parcel between different confinements, probably at least three, one of which, as we see in a moment, had exceptionally interesting associations. But for his last moments, I conclude that this exceptionally brave man was the live target in a shooting gallery. The nation went into mourning. But on the political scene, Moro was still very much alive.

The spotlight now falls upon a man who hovered for years in the dangerous everglades between State secrets, terrorism and organized crime, until his luck ran out. Antonio 'Toni' Chichiarelli appears to have modeled himself on the central figure of Marcello Rubini in Federico Fellini's iconic *La Dolce Vita,* the social-climbing journalist who becomes friend and confidant of the rich, famous and powerful. 'Toni' greeted the daylight as an impresario of the art world, a dealer in expensive pictures. These accomplishments concealed the darker side of his life. He was also a master forger and art smuggler whose services were widely sought around the world. He moved freely in the underworld inhabited by the arch neofascists of the Nuclei Armati Rivoluzionari (NAR), linked to the Bologna station atrocity of August 1980 and the bombing of the Banca Nazionale dell'Agricoltura in Milan in 1969.

Both organizations moved in the same orbit as the Banda della Magliana (for whom the ubiquitous 'Toni' acted as official forger). Chichiarelli had many connections that were certain to land him in serious trouble. This guardian of a thousand secrets typified the subliminal knots tying together the Italian underworld élite composed of Licio Gelli's P2 lodge, intelligence circles, the Christian Democrat oligarchy, criminal gangs and the Vatican. He knew of the ultra-secret accords that connected Mario Moretti, de facto leader of the Brigate Rosse at the time of the Moro tragedy, to the Italian state. Among his closest friends he counted the French gangster Albert Bergamelli, who ran the vast dope-smuggling racket in the port of Marseilles for the CIA; and Aldo Semerari, the strange psychiatrist run wild who was the Mob aristocracy's favorite shrink. His couch was their comforting retreat in coping with the tumultuous conflicts in the underworld of organized crime. This was a dangerous world where an excess of knowledge slips into risky compromise. Semerari was beheaded (the code for silencing tongues) by the *Camorra* in Naples on 1st April 1981 (All Fool's Day) shortly after he made a panic phone call to SISMI director General Giuseppe Santovito pleading that his life was in danger.

At the peak of the Moro crisis, Chichiarelli personally circulated the famous forged 'seventh directive' of the Brigate Rosse, purportedly ordering the leadership to liquidate Moro. This was an essential element of the plan to affix the responsibility for the kidnapping and murder on the *Brigate*. 'Toni' knew perfectly well that Moro's kidnappers were the Banda, assisted with back-up from the Calabrian criminal clan known as the '*Ndrangheta*. In this contorted environment, where the real and unreal bumped shoulders, there now appeared a Carabinieri secret service agent called Antonio Labruna. He devoted his professional life to disinfecting the Carabinieri SID special investigations unit to frustrate neofascist infiltrators. He suddenly received a strange tip-off from a Vatican informant at the height of the crisis that Moro was being held at number 96, Via Gradoli, an apartment block in a well-to-do central district of the capital. It transpired that this building with its 26 apartments was owned by the state secret services. In the circumstances an especially interesting tenant was none other than Mario Moretti, reigning commandant of the Brigate Rosse, the man who was ultimately convicted for the killing of Moro. Co-incidence leans rather heavily. It is clearly of more than passing interest that the leader of Italy's notorious political bandits rented his flat in a block used by the secret services, at the peak of a state emergency attributed to Moretti himself. Moreover, there are strong claims that Moro actually was held in this same block at one point during captivity. The evidence accumulates that Moretti (the so-called second stage commander following the elimination of the original leadership) was 'steering' the

Brigate into performing deeds favourable to the political machinations of the state, according to the classic precepts set out by the French terrorist mastermind, Yves Guérin-Sérac. [God's Terrorist, chapter V].

On 20th March 1979, fifty-year-old independent gadfly journalist Carmine Pecorelli, plain 'Mino' to his friends, was gunned down in a drive-by shooting near his office in the Prati district of Rome, roughly a year after the murder of Moro. Mino had intimate links to the underground state and secret services, a speciality of his craft. He was sufficiently trusted to enter Gelli's enchanted circle. Like his British *Doppelgänger*, the veteran journalist-snooper Chapman Pincher, Mino would be fed valuable scoops bubbling up from the underground state, and in return pass confidential materials in the opposite direction. It was the game of two masters that eventually cost the Mafia psychiatrist Aldo Semerari his head. Pecorelli was amenable to bribes for the privilege of keeping quiet. After Moro's death, Pecorelli published some of Moro's letters to his family, giving rise to considerable curiosity how he came to get them. When Pecorelli published in his news-sheet *Osservatore Politico* a story claiming that Moro's kidnapping was organised by a 'lucid superpower' (an oblique reference to the United States and its overlordship of NATO) he wrote his own death certificate. In a cryptic article in the *Osservatore* in May 1978, Pecorelli implied a connection between Gladio and Moro's death. Of course this was sensational because of the claims which disturbed Pieczenik: namely that during captivity, Moro obliquely referred to 'NATO guerrilla activities' on Italian soil. The source was a highly equivocal figure, the strikingly handsome senior Carabinieri general, Carlo Alberto Dalla Chiesa, whose sinuous, serpentine course through the Moro affair suggests intimate knowledge of every twist and turn. Searching an apartment in Magliana (another location named by Giuseppe De Lutiis as Moro's place of detention), while supposedly on different Carabinieri business altogether, he claimed to stumble on the famous 'Gladio letter' allegedly written by Moro. This he quietly tucked into a pocket of his crisply-pressed khaki uniform. There were well-grounded suspicions it was actually the apartment where Moro was really held (or one of the locations), exactly as Giuseppe De Lutiis implied.

Rome is really a very large village whose chief industry is gossip and plots that never seem to end. High state officials like Dalla Chiesa, operating in the hazy borderlands between the formal demands of the state and the aims and ambitions of the political caste, are required, ultimately, to operate within the system. It is probable, certain even, that Pecorelli brushed against General Dalla Chiesa in P2 gatherings. That may be why he always referred to him as 'General Amen,' possibly a cover since Dalla Chiesa was not on Gelli's regular dance card. Yet it is unthinkable in the incestuous Italian climate that such an important officer of the national military police was in the dark concerning P2 and the secret army machine. He is the most obvious source of

Pecorelli's information concerning the Gladio note and quite probably the treasure trove of Moro's private letters too. It is quite possible that Dalla Chiesa was the postman so to speak and that he also got possession of the highly incriminating *memoriale* that Moro composed during captivity. The general's peculiar performance during the crisis included a sudden call on President Cossiga, bearing the address of a mysterious 'cave' where Moro was purportedly held. Machiavelli might have swooned with admiration. Cossiga did not want Moro to be freed. General Dalla Chiesa, knowing the real location, covered his tracks since he knew that Cossiga would do nothing serious with this disingenuous red herring. Quite simply, Cossiga had always known the identity of the kidnappers who snatched Moro from the Via Fani and where he was being held, since he was himself responsible for placing the contract.

Magliana began as an illegal settlement populated by Sicilians pouring north in search of work. It is close to the Tiber in the southwest quarter of the city. By the '60s the district was controlled by the *Banda della Magliana*. Their violent and ruthless (but efficient) methods, organised around Soviet-like cells, forced most of their rivals out of the city. The Pellegrino Commission of Inquiry established that the Banda had close connections during the *anni di piombo t*o important props of the Gladio organisation: the Nuclei Armati Rivoluzionari (NAR) and SISMI. Contract jobs came naturally to the *Banda*. The bullets used to kill Pecorelli were of an unusual military calibre, 7.62 mm, manufactured by the Fabrique Gévelot, of Paris. This type of ammunition was commonly used by the Marseilles gangster clan associated with the *Banda*. It was also found after the murder of Pecorelli in a basement of the Health Ministry, of all unlikely places, which seems to have been the Gladio/Banda/NAR arms dump in central Rome.

Magliana had one other significant advantage. It was scarcely a kilometre — 'the short distance' — from the location where Moro's body was found. The famous 'crisis resolution committee' also included SISMI director General Giuseppe Santovito, another close acolyte of Licio Gelli and a member of P2. Santovito's fingerprints were found on many events during the years of lead, and the Moro affair was no exception. He was cynically nominated by Francesco Cossiga to represent the secret services on the crisis committee, and seems to have come to this task with curious diffidence, as though the outcome scarcely mattered. He mentioned almost in passing that Francesco Fonti, a prominent functionary (and future *pentito*) of the Calabrian 'Ndrangheta, informed him where Moro was held and by whom. Fonti named the Banda della Magliana. They had kidnapped Moro and were holding him awaiting further orders. Fonti said that he knew this because of the intimate fraternity between 'Ndrangheta and the *Banda*. Santovito casually took the information to the crisis committee, where he was told to keep it to himself because 'the politicians had changed their minds.' It was a classic example of *capolavoro,* the Italian expression for a masterpiece of sublime deception.

Through the fog, it became clear Pecorelli had sound reasons for predicting 'General Amen' would be assassinated, given his privy knowledge of the Moro affair. Indeed, four years later, in September 1982, General Dalla Chiesa and his wife were mown down by machine guns while driving in the Sicilian capital, Palermo. The general had recently been appointed as the new Prefect on Andreotti's personal orders to neuter the Mafia. This was another exercise in *capolavoro.* One door that led to the truth concerning Aldo Moro banged shut. Another was shortly to do the same, by similar means.

On 24th March 1984 a gang impersonating the Red Brigades raided the Brinks Securmark safe deposit centre in Rome. It was at the time the largest robbery in Italian history. The raiders stole $21.8 million in cash and valuables (about 35 billion *lire* in pre-Euro days). But this was no Brigate Rosse operation. The heist was led by none other than 'Toni' Chichiarelli, together with members of the Banda della Magliana and others who spoke with Piedmontese accents. Chichiarelli later told his wife, Chiara Zossolo, that he was 'allowed' to keep twenty billion lire from the overall haul, which he claimed actually netted between 50 and 55 billion lire. The story of the Brinks Securmark hit belongs in the much wider context of the financial scandals which rocked Italy and the Vatican in the mid '80s. These are famously recalled by the body of the man who was known as God's Banker, Roberto Calvi, discovered swinging from the parapet of London's Blackfriars Bridge on 17th June 1982. The Brinks robbery was essentially political in motive. Aside from the valuables, Chichiarelli carefully removed highly sensitive confidential documents relating to Calvi's dealings with the Vatican's private bank, Pope John Paul II and the Sicilian money launderer and Vatican insider, Michele Sindona. Both were close affiliates of Licio Gelli and members of P2. As we shall see in Chapter X (The Eye of the Serpent) the robbery was really a cover for a far wider conspiracy which led to every niche of the Italian secret state, including the Gladio secret army.

Chichiarelli had little time to enjoy his new-found wealth. On 28th September 1984, he was shot dead, a day after supposedly forgetting a *borsello* that he left in a Roman taxicab. This little gift parcel contained incriminating evidence concerning the murders of Mino Pecorelli and Aldo Moro. It included nine cartridges of the unusual French 7.62 mm type commonly used by the Magliana gang and traced to the body of Pecorelli, forged documents incriminating the Brigate Rosse and medicine identical to the type used by Moro. The story is curious. While 'Toni' Chichiarelli certainly knew the truth about Moro and Pecorelli, how were these articles instantly associated with him, and with such alacrity that he was immediately 'rubbed out,' in Mafioso parlance? It is more probable this little bag of treasures was planted by the secret services with the connivance of their underground connections. In any event Chichiarelli's usefulness had expired. Though only 36, he became careless and foolishly talkative. For this keeper of too many secrets, the grave yawned.

Now it was Andreotti's turn, by a splendid Machiavellian twist, to find himself mired in the Moro affair. As the century turned, the Divine Julius was arraigned on a string of charges including murders. One of these was Mino Pecorelli's. In 1993, Mafioso turncoat Tommaso Buscetta told the Sicilian Mafia Commission that his boss, Don Gaetano Badalamenti,[18] 'rubbed out' Pecorelli as a favour to Andreotti, who feared damaging new revelations concerning Aldo Moro. In 1999, Italians were stunned as the hitherto immortal Andreotti stood trial for Mafia associations alongside Badalamenti. The famous see-saw motion of Italian justice now began its customary wild gyrations. *Il Divo* (the title of Paolo Sorrentino's splendid 2008 prize-winning film about Andreotti's crimes and Mafioso associations) was acquitted, only to be pronounced guilty at the state's appeal in 2002, and sentenced — at the age of 83 — to 24 years in prison. A year later the sentences were quashed, but the accusation of Mafia ties continued to dog the circus master. He escaped a full-blown mob conviction in Sicily purely because constitutional time limits expired (an old Italian story). But that same Palermo court left the statement lying on the charge sheet that until 1980, Andreotti used the mob to further his political career to such an extent as to be considered 'a component of the Mafia.'

By the time of Moro's liquidation, the leadership of the Red Brigades (the so-called 'stage one' commanders) realised during long hours of reflection in confinement that their ranks were thoroughly riddled by traitors to the cause. The comrades poured venom on the alleged killer of Moro, Mario Moretti, as a stooge and agent of Italian intelligence. Senator Sergio Flamigni, who wrote a dozen works about Moro over the course of a decade, concurred in his book published in 2004, *La sfinge delle Brigate Rosse: delitti, segreti e bugie del capo terrorista Mario Moretti* (*The Sphinx of the Red Brigades: Crimes, Secrets and Lies of Terrorist Chief Mario Moretti*). Moretti received six life sentences for the murder, but served only 15 years before he was paroled. In all his works Flamigni stressed the elimination of Moro as a consequence of 'parallel convergence' between the Brigate Rosse and Italy's secret intelligence services. The comfortable apartment in Rome's Via Gradoli springs immediately to mind.

---

[18] Badalamenti, a grisly figure but criminal genius, became notorious masterminding a vast takeaway operation selling hard drugs from a chain of pizza parlours across the US. It lasted almost ten years. In 1987, he was sentenced to 47 years in federal prison. There he died, peacefully, in 2004.

Vincenzo Vinciguerra, whose explanation for the black years of Italian terrorism begins this chapter, was imprisoned in 1972 for blowing up three Carabinieri officers with a booby-trapped car. Judge Felice Casson's investigations revealed the bombing was carried out with C4 explosive, much favoured by the military and known in popular lore as *plastique.* Behind bars Vinciguerra underwent a Paulinian conversion. He turned *pentito,* the repentant one who so often sings the key solo part in scores of Mafia trials in Italy. The explosive came, he said, from a NATO-supplied Gladio munitions dump hidden in the main city cemetery at Verona. Casson named the neo-fascist organisation *Ordine Nuovo,*[19] to which Vinciguerra belonged, as collaborating closely with SISMI. Together they engineered the murders carried out by Vinciguerra and transferred the blame to the Red Brigades.

Vinciguerra testified he was backed by a network of sympathisers in Italy and abroad with the means to guarantee escape after each incident (subsequently identified as the fake press bureau in Lisbon run by the French master terrorist Yves Guérin-Sérac, of whom much more in Chapter V). 'A whole mechanism came into action,' Vinciguerra recalled in his talk with a *Guardian* journalist, 'that is, the Carabinieri, the Minister of the Interior, the customs services and the military and civilian intelligence services accepted the ideological reasoning behind the attack.' The explosion reverberated for years afterwards, because it marked the beginning of the trail followed by bloodhound magistrate Casson ending in Andreotti's reluctant exposure of Gladio. Vinciguerra's revealing comments to *The Guardian* included the electrifying information that he and his friends were sub-contractors to a

> *super-organisation which lacking a Soviet military invasion, which might not happen, took up the task, on NATO's behalf, of preventing a slip to the Left in the political balance of the country...*
>
> *The terrorist line was followed by camouflaged people, people belonging to the security apparatus, or those linked to the state apparatus through rapport or collaboration. I say that every single outrage that followed from 1969 fitted into a single, organised matrix.*[N9]

Daniele Ganser pointed to the same strategy, with certain refinements. To steer a group from within was a crafty ruse, 'beautiful,' since the duped gang members would respond to orders conceived somewhere else. An alternative

---

[19] A neo-fascist paramilitary grouping (meaning New Order) bearing blatant occult overtones. It was founded by Giuseppe 'Pino' Rauti, who later ran the *Movimento Sociale Italiano*, a party chiefly dedicated to the flame of Mussolini. Detractors debunked the initials as standing for 'Mussolini you are immortal' (*Mussolini sei immortale*). In 1961, Rauti gave a lecture at the US Marine College in Annapolis on 'Techniques and Possibilities of a coup d'état in Europe.'

in the smoke and mirrors game lay in counterfeit operations which resembled the urban guerrillas, a task for which Gladio was perfectly suited. In terms of psy-ops, first plant informers who anticipate terrorist plans, and then 'just let it happen' — JLIH (or LIHOP, 'let it happen on purpose'). The presence of genuine articles as distinct from counterfeit terror was an essential ingredient in this maze, to supply the necessary signs of credibility.

In 2004, the Right-wing government of Silvio Berlusconi showed every sign of toppling, fallen prey to factional infighting, scoring poorly in regional and European elections. At this trying moment, the anti-terrorist squad was directed to a huge weapons cache found at an apartment in a posh district of Rome. Ownership was immediately attributed, without a jot of evidence, to a reconstituted faction of the Brigate Rosse. Now the *Brigate* rarely dabbled in bombings, but here were several hundred kilograms of explosives and another two hundred detonators. The haul included grenades, mint Carabinieri uniforms, a small M12 machine gun, and equipment to make fake identity cards. Part of the story made the necessary headlines, but not this one the one that follows: The facts are that the flat was actually one of a clutch in the same block used by espionage agencies with special off-radar tasks, such as massive wire tapping of suspect journalists, politicians and businessman on the orders of the paranoiac Berlusconi.

As a novice, still in his political short pants, Berlusconi was in Gelli's who's who of the far Right (membership number 1816 on the list found in the Abruzzi villa). There was never much doubt whence the man derided by his critics as 'Pinocchio in platform shoes' drew his inspiration. In *Berlusconi's Shadow* (Allen Lane, 2004), David Lane wrote: 'Berlusconi claimed to be a man of action and so too had Mussolini. Both men showed no understanding of the limits to what they were allowed to do. Both said they worked very long hours and paid attention to precision and detail. Both hated criticism and considered they were beyond it. Both believed the world was divided into enemies and friends.'

Early in November 2011, Berlusconi finally discovered that his numerous enemies far outnumbered his shrinking coterie of friends. His limpet-like qualities of sticking to the premiership in the face of all odds collapsed in the space of a weekend.

On 13th December 2011, the accustomed calm of Firenze (Florence), Italy's treasured capital of the arts, was shattered by the murder of two Senegalese street vendors. A man named as an alleged supporter of the far right, one Gianlucca Casseri, aged 50, shot both men, injured three more, then killed himself when cornered by the police in a car park. The supposed far-right connections of the assassin were vague. His sin if any deems to be that he flirted with a band who keep the flame of Mussolini alive, centred on the Casa Pound ('Pound House') in Rome. The American-born poet Ezra

Pound, who died in Venice in 1957, is remembered as one of the leading intellectual progenitors of Mussolini's 'social realism.' But the Casa people have no record of violence, or inciting it, even if their tense attitude to immigration is broadly as acerbic as the views most Italians take on that same subject. British newspapers became very excited over Casseri's job at a magazine specialising in horror and fantasy stories. This is only important as component of the posthumous character profiling typically associated with the customary patsy or stooge steered by his minders to commit some act of violence. He certainly took the usual permanent exit. If Casseri did commit suicide, or he was shot by the police, is unresolved. By any standards judged by the Strategy of Tension, the outrage directed attention yet again at Italy's discomfort with mass immigration, chiefly from Africa.

March 2012 was a vintage month for Gladio greenshoots. In Greece a full scale coup plot code-named 'Pythias' was exposed. The plan dated to 2008. It was designed, like the NATO Operation Prometheus which installed the military government in 1967, to overthrow a civilian government judged altogether too friendly to the former Soviet Union. Pythias and Prometheus are figures taken from Greek mythology, one the symbol of true friendship, the other the hurler of burning spears. The government of the conservative New Democracy leader Constantine Karamanlis was the intended target. He would be deposed and possibly killed. His sins lay in the warm relations he cultivated between Athens and Moscow and his intentions to grant Russia wayleaves for the South Stream gas pipeline across Greek territory, a rival to the US-backed Nabucco scheme. The exposure of Pythias was traced to ex-premier Karamanlis, the secret services and unnamed Russian sources, who remained strangely quiet for practically four years, until the great austerity crisis struck the country. Like Prometheus its origins lay with a 'superpower' which indicated the United States and NATO. Then, in the Belgian city of Anderlecht a mosque was attacked and burnt down in an apparent squabble between rival and Sunni and Shiite factions. The resident imam smothered in the thick fumes. The attack served to focus attention yet again on the cleavage between Belgium's half a million Muslims and the native population. France was rocked on the eve of a tight presidential election by a gunman on a motor scooter who killed a teacher, his two children and another infant outside a Jewish school in Toulouse, in the country's south west. Three servicemen of north African origin were killed and a fourth wounded in separate attacks. The affair punctuated Nicholas Sarkozy's xenophobic rhetoric heaped on France's Muslim minority as he struggled to outpace his socialist challenger in the upcoming election, as we see in a later chapter (XVI, The Return of Gladio: In The Shadow of The Minaret). Sarkozy, who brought France back into NATO, has a record of winning elections with dramatic, perfectly-timed post-terror interventions.[N10] We see the clear outlines of the Strategy of Tension, Era Two.

III.
May the Force Be With You

'Psychological warfare is probably man's oldest weapon, aside from bare hands. In using it in today's dirty, secretive wars, or in the future, the important thing to remember is that it is a weapon and that a weapon has its own unique use and its own effect.' — Colonel Edward Lansdale, US Air Force

---

Towards the end of 2006, John Bolton, short-lived United States ambassador to the United Nations, a feisty, walrus-moustached antidote to conventional diplomacy, dropped one of his famous verbal grenades into a respectful audience of visiting European journalists. 'You must understand,' he declared, fixing them with a look reserved for moments of intimate candour, 'that the United States never acts except in its own interests.' To Bolton, there was nothing intrinsically intimidating in this remark. He was simply expressing the deeply-held opinion of many patriotic Americans, the concept of American Exceptionalism. Bolton's reputation as a neocon cyborg bent on castrating the United Nations obscured the fact that he simply paraphrased Lord Palmerston's famous dictum that 'nations have no permanent friends or allies, they only have permanent interests.'

The United States is a serial trespasser in her own neighbourhood. Large chunks of real estate were lopped from Mexico. The independence and stunning Eden-like innocence of the Hawaiian kingdom was ruthlessly crushed. Spain — a 'decadent and corrupt' empire but also an unfortunate European blemish on the American hemisphere, a bad case of 'the others' — was tricked into a phoney war. She lost what remained of her empire, including the crown jewel, Cuba. That 'splendid little war,' as the boisterous Teddy Roosevelt delightedly called it, subsequently characterised the behaviour of the United States on the world stage. A brief and highly-successful romp was the first in modern times to qualify for the label of a liberal intervention, thus fixing it firmly in the linear trail of unilateral corrections to the internal affairs of other countries deemed of crucial strategic interest to the United States. The Spanish-American war was certainly splendid enough to vault the triumphant Roosevelt to the White House, once a vacancy was declared following President McKinley's convenient assassination in 1901. In 1904, the unfinished works of the Panama Canal were taken over and fenced off with a client safety strip, the Canal Zone. In 1915 Woodrow Wilson — 'the great peacemaker' — exploited riots and instability as an excuse to send marines ashore in Haiti. They stayed for nearly 20 years, until Haiti's debts to American banks were paid off. Canada might have gone the same way, but for the deterrent of an ensuing struggle with the British Empire. British cabinets of the Edwardian era were prudently advised by their generals and admirals that war with the United States was at least as likely as with Germany or France.

Cuba was among the first modern engagements (along with the Boer War) in which the mass media were shamelessly drafted to drumbeat jingoism and black propaganda. The charge was led by the Hearst and Pulitzer newspaper chains, who wielded the influence in those days of Rupert Murdoch's Fox News today. Spain was ceaselessly castigated as a bad master and cruel tyrant in her colonies. In truth she was hopelessly outgunned, her strength long decayed, in no fit state to stand up to the harassments and bullying of young America. Trouble between the Spanish authorities and a simmering independence movement formed the pretext to send the battle cruiser USS *Maine* steaming into Havana harbour, supposedly to protect American nationals. When the *Maine* spectacularly blew up with the loss of 274 lives, it offered the instant excuse to provoke a conflict which, by the merest coincidence, future president Theodore Roosevelt — de facto first lord of the US admiralty — had meticulously planned for just such an eventuality, down to the last detail. Queasy liberals resisting chest-beating empire builders were flailed into submission by mass circulation newspapers ruthlessly dealing the patriot card. In a little more than a hundred days it was all over. Roosevelt, the last president to worship the great outdoors (rancher Bush Junior robotically dicing sticks is a non-starter) led his private troop, the Rough Riders, into the fray. The United States immediately matriculated as a junior world power.

Spain took the full rap for the *Maine.* The explosion provoked the rallying cry 'Remember the *Maine*! To hell with Spain!'[20] Investigations revealed that five tons of powder charges obliterated the forward third of the ship where most of the crew were resting or sleeping. The following day Roosevelt made the cryptically under-stated remark: 'We shall never find out definitely the cause of the disaster.' A clutch of official inquires debated a Spanish mine or spontaneous combustion in the coal bunker. False-flag sabotage was firmly quashed, despite the compromising Roosevelt Plan. The political riddle of what Spain might expect to gain from provoking the United States was never answered. In any event, the important question was always *who* sunk the *Maine*, not the infinitely lesser one of *how* it was done.

Cuba was destined henceforth to exercise an immense magnetic pull on the American imagination. Neither an American state nor a colony, but an in-

---

[20] Serendipity. The eagle-eyed who may happen to catch up with the biopic *Butch Cassidy and the Sundance Kid* may briefly spot the clarion call "Remember the Maine!" scrawled with lipstick on a bedsheet in the bordello where the pair seek sanctuary after a botched train robbery. They fantasize joining up to fight in Cuba and so escape prison for their crimes.

between protectorate expected to cleave unswervingly to American wishes. The arrangement operated tolerably well as long as the US could reliably manipulate the political order. Castro succeeded because he won the support of Cubans angered by the corruption of the ruling regime and its Mafioso allies behind the brothels and gaming parlour rackets. Castro's Cuba remained chronically poor and backward, dependent on Soviet aid, a strategic pawn of the Great Powers. When the Russians planted rockets, in retaliation for Honest John missiles rolled out in Turkey, the world came close to the ultimate brink. The shots that rang out in Dallas one bright November day in 1963 echoed over Cuba. The spectre of the sunken *Maine* lingered, too, in strange ways. In 1997, decommissioning of secret documents relating to the JFK assassination revealed the inner court of the American military, the five great chiefs who head the high command, coolly hatching a plan to wreak mayhem across America. Using hired snipers to shoot at citizens walking about the streets, they would then pin the blame on saboteurs spirited to American shores by Fidel Castro. It was perfectly simple. Pentagonia planned to attack the United States.

It is an axiom of American life that all actions of men and women in military uniform are virtually beyond reproach. Hate the war, love the warrior. Yet here, in cold print, were detailed plans for acts of terror to be performed under the American flag on the orders of the highest military commanders in the land. This deadly project, code-named Northwoods and dated March 1962, was aimed at garnering international support to justify a full-scale US invasion of Cuba, fostering the illusion the regime in Havana had descended into diabolical lunacy. One proposal — blowing up an American vessel in Guantánamo Bay and then blaming it on Cuba — slipped straight from the *Maine* playbook. While perfectly happy to gun down civilians, the navy's top brass cavilled at blowing up an American ship at sea, as that would entail killing the crew. So the fallback plan called for destruction of an unmanned ship and staging of simulated funerals.[N1]

Like items on a shopping list, the denizens of the War Palace calmly ticked off the downing of airliners and the real or simulated sinking of boatloads of Cuban refugees. There would be attacks by carbon copies of Cuban MiG fighters on neighbouring countries. Not the least grim aspect of the brazen campaign to fabricate a reign of red terror throughout Florida, and even down the wide avenues of the capital itself, was the cynical targeting of Cubans who risked their lives escaping to freedom in ramshackle boats. In his book *Body of Secrets,* on the ultra-secret US National Security Agency (NSA), James Bamford derided a virtual war 'in which many patriotic Americans and innocent Cubans would die senseless deaths, all to satisfy the egos of twisted generals back in Washington, safe in their taxpayer-financed homes and limousines.'

One plan offered an eerie premonition — and perhaps even some clues — concerning the events on 9/11. It called for the hijacking of a US passenger jet by special forces disguised as Cuban agents. The plane would slip below radar observation and then be replaced by a pilotless aircraft. This would crash, purportedly killing all the passengers and crew. The decoy plane would then land safely somewhere in the US, leaving the question open as to how all those on board could be relied upon to keep silent concerning their adventure. There was not a single item in the Northwoods manual that did not amount to a blatant act of treason, yet the high and mighty of the entire US military establishment despatched 'Top Secret — Justification for US military Intervention in Cuba' straight to the desk of Secretary of Defense Robert McNamara, for onward transmission to President John Fitzgerald Kennedy.[N2] Whether his carefully slicked trademark hair stood on end, or he was anticipating the incoming missile, is not known. Suffice it to say, within three days it returned from the Oval Office out-tray, paper-clipped to a presidential rejection slip.

The general staff had not been transformed into madmen, as Bamford suspected. Morality had nothing to do with it. The logic of Northwoods was the stripe of Gladio. The general staff inclined towards prefabricated violence because they believed benefits gained by the state count more than injustice against individuals. The only important criterion is success in reaching an objective. Kennedy's thoughts as he leafed through the Cuban project can only be guessed, but perhaps he detected the icy hint of a scythe passing over the nape of his neck. The president was too subtle to suspect his most senior commanders had collectively departed their rockers. They were 'mad' only in the sense of functioning in a deeply flawed environment contaminated with the egotistical warrior nationalism soaking the country.

Kennedy was as much cloaked in Old Glory as any of those Promethean princes brooding on the Virginian bank of the Potomac. Yet America's history of violent and unpredictable behaviour towards her leaders suggested a president with a touchy relationship with his military should tread warily around the accursed siren of Cuba. Kennedy observed with considerable reservation the Crown Prince of the Pentagon, the taut-framed chairman of the Joint Chiefs of Staff, General Lyman Lemnitzer. From the moment he arrived in the White House, the president understood he was pitched against an alternative government, concealed in the dark pool containing the military élites, secret services and the arms business. It was precisely that camp of which Eisenhower warned Americans to be eternally vigilant. The atmosphere of bad karma that clung to the Kennedy interregnum was unmistakeable, along with its source. Arthur Schlesinger, JFK's intellectual guru, was asked in 1978 whether the president enjoyed a full grasp of his administration. He replied: 'Well, we certainly weren't in control of the joint chiefs.' The Kennedy presidency cut a confusing zigzag making up its mind what to do about Cuba. The ideas file was virtually bare on how to expunge Castro without dragging the US into confrontation with his benefactors in Moscow. Into this breach stepped Lemnitzer with a parcel of schemes from a Pentagonian book of magic tricks. In a highly-competitive shopping mall of conspiracies, he was up against rival attractions offered by the CIA.

Lemnitzer soldiered his way from a frugal upbringing in a deeply conservative colony of German Lutherans in Honesdale, Pennsylvania. Second of three sons of pious and industrious parents, he shone at nothing in particular in school, leading to the sobriquet 'So who he?' which followed him around for much of his early career. He got his first job clerking in a main street tailoring store and seemed destined to follow his father's footsteps into the family boot-making business. Instead, he opted for army boots. He was a lacklustre performer at West Point, graduating well down the class of 1920. Few among his peers thought he possessed the savvy to rise above a backroom brigadier general. This clinical judgement seemed confirmed by the fifteen years he spent becalmed as an obscure junior officer, before his career received a high-octane boost, thanks entirely to Dwight Eisenhower's diagnosis of hitherto well-concealed talents. So the unpromising chrysalis hatched into the most powerful and highly political soldier the US army produced since the Civil War, barring certain claims by Eisenhower himself, with the proviso that Ike never aspired to be a politician. The comparison to an American Generalissimo Franco in waiting, rather than the vain and erratic prince of mischief General Douglas MacArthur, was not misplaced.

Eisenhower hovered over Lemnitzer like a guardian angel. The early middle-aged officer with the ramrod bearing and piercing eyes caught his attention as promising staff material. He was soon put to work planning Allied landings in North Africa and Sicily. Eisenhower's hunch was rewarded by the accomplished manner in which Lemnitzer deployed carefully nuanced diplomacy and his sound inkling for German ways in a top secret mission of the highest delicacy, which Eisenhower believed vital to the outcome of the war. This was to persuade German forces trudging out of Italy to surrender outright. Eisenhower was mesmerised by the notion these hardened troops with all their munitions would connect with others falling back from the west to make a last stand around Hitler's fortress in Berchtesgaden, thus imperilling thousands of Allied lives.

In the service of this chimera he provoked a rift with Churchill and his pet general Bernard Montgomery, with far-reaching consequences for post-war Europe. The 'national redoubt,' the myth of an impregnable fortress, was a Soviet hoax designed to allow Stalin an unchallenged lunge at Berlin. It succeeded brilliantly, thanks largely to Hitler's audacity and the shock he administered to the Allies with the famous boomerang known as the Battle of the Bulge (16th December 1944 - 25th January 1945). German tanks suddenly burst out of the Belgian Ardennes forests and gave the advancing allies very sore black eyes. Eisenhower, that rarest of supreme commanders — one who never in his entire career saw men die in action at the front line — took this as a clear warning that the Germans were far from exhausted or defeated. In the background, *Time* flailed generals for 'idling' while the Germans dug in.[N3]

Lemnitzer played a neat hand. He was up with the masters of the universe alongside Allen Dulles, looking across the table at the immaculately presented enemy negotiators, at whose side he might have found himself in only marginally adjusted historical circumstances. The Germans bought the counterfeit line that standing down would amount to a pause until the war resumed, this time against the Soviets. Lemnitzer thus demonstrated he was already a magician in the art of deception, the Platonic noble porky spoken in service of a higher cause, hallmark of early neo-conservatives boarding Eisenhower's administration in significant numbers.

The Lutheranism that Lemnitzer imbibed as a child made him an excellent fit with the bitterly anti-communist Prussian mindset which overtook American military leadership after World War Two. Many in the US officer corps (like the priestly infantry in the Vatican) scarcely bothered to conceal their admiration for Hitler's punishment of godless Russia, the stunning innovations like the *Blitzkrieg* ('shock and awe' in the modern US military manual), and the sheer stubborn belligerence of the German fighting soldier against all odds. Add to this the dazzling futuristic pioneering rocket science, which Lemnitzer eyed as a prize for the army, over the rival claims of air force commanders. Lemnitzer interpreted the clash of titans as an ongoing Manichean struggle between light and darkness: God's own elect, the Chosen People of the United States, pitched against the malignant and inherently evil Soviet Empire. Hardly by coincidence, this was exactly the driving force of fascist terrorists with strong ties to the Catholic Church who volunteered for Gladio armed struggles.

Once Eisenhower arrived in the White House, Lemnitzer's prospects assumed vertical liftoff. First, commander of US forces in the Far East, then army chief of staff and finally top gun in the Pentagonian war cabinet, all in the space of five years. He was an almost unprecedented shooting star, save for the iconic war hero Eisenhower himself. When he joined the Joint Chiefs of Staff, freshly blooded by command of UN troops in Korea, Lemnitzer took care to associate himself with all the most hawkish schemes. A shrewd Machiavellian element lay behind the power structure. The joint chiefs would operate most effectively when steered by a strong pair of hands. Eisenhower — with his own family roots in Germany's Rhineland Palatine country ('Eisenhauer – hewer of iron') – if a less-than-fully-paid-up Prussian —

presided over what was in effect a military government, spending more time with his chiefs of staff and playing their war games, than ever he did dealing with civil distractions of state. The Pentagon was always his real command bunker and spiritual home, rather than the modest mansion at 1600 Pennsylvania Avenue.

Thanks to Eisenhower, the council of war chiefs matured into a permanent around-the-clock war cabinet, a metamorphosis posing awful perils. It happened because Eisenhower's national security policy — the 'New Look,' which replaced the discarded strategy of limited war — was based on the unstoppable nuclear striking power of Strategic Air Command. It was straight back to the chimera of the national redoubt which formerly obsessed Eisenhower in Europe, transposed this time to represent America herself. The New Look invoked a psychological shift of profound consequences in American minds: henceforth the country was geared to a strategy of peace through the waging of perpetual war.

Eisenhower's generous patronage of Lemnitzer arose at least partly because he recognised in his protégé a strong likeness of himself, another young man who got off to an indifferent start in his military career. Their lives seemed to march in a pre-destined lock step. Eisenhower, too, plodded in the rearguard of the army until the US joined the war in 1941. After that, his rise was meteoric. He soared from a mere brigadier general to finish the war as supreme commander of all Allied forces in Europe, despite having no combat experience. Their common backgrounds brought up by plain, God-fearing parents in white-on-white Anglo-Saxon communities — the Lutheran Lemnitzer, Eisenhower in a closeted community of Jehovah's Witnesses — led them to share virtually identical religious and political chemistry. Their shared rabid anti-communism came at the font. Eisenhower, far from the benign uncle figure so often portrayed, was a closet admirer of Senator Joe McCarthy's red-baiting sentiments, if not his histrionics. He and Lemnitzer reeled from the unspeakable horror of homosexuality which they ranked with moral perversion and communism. Lemnitzer deeply approved when the president launched an executive witch hunt to root out 'sexual perverts' lurking in the federal government's employ, especially in the military and right down to the defence contracting industries. So, when in 1960 Eisenhower crowned his protégé chairman of the Joint Chiefs of Staff, it seemed as though he was raising up his own son in his stead. The paternal skew towards Lemnitzer may well have arisen from such an emotion. Eisenhower was haunted all his life by the ghost of his eldest son Doud, who died aged just six from scarlet fever.

Lemnitzer deduced Americans were indeed living through dangerous times. The enemy was within and without the gates. America required the smack of firm government that owed its first allegiance to the only reliable guardian of her liberties, the country's armed forces. The constitutional order, in Lemnitzer's eyes, was subordinate at all times to national security. Yet there was one key difference between these two men. Eisenhower had greatness thrust upon him, mostly as a consequence of the rudderless Truman government's erratic course. Lemnitzer, on the other hand, entertained few qualms about thrusting greatness upon himself, in true Bonapartean fashion, when the moment was ripe. Foremost a soldier, Ike gave the impression when he got to the White House of striving to float above partisan conflicts, a strong element of his essentially neutral appeal to the voters. His chief campaign promise had been to do 'something' about the festering Korean morass, though exactly what he had in mind was never very clear, except somehow to stop it. He always fell back on 'cheerful certainty' in the face of any odds, and the perpetual yearning for unity and tranquillity. This offset the unsettled mood of the American public in the new H-bomb world — but it also encouraged extremist military thinkers and deranged actors in the CIA to run wild.

As Ike took a long nap through the civilian obligations of his presidency, Pentagonia evolved into a full-blown state within a state, contemptuous of Congress and vacillating politicians across the board. Yet, inside the kingdom lurked quarrelling pocket states. The army and air force plunged into a turf war over control of the nuclear strike force. Eisenhower's reluctance to instil discipline grew largely from West Point *esprit de corps* and his typically diffident attitude to decision taking. So he idled as the rivalries became increasingly bitter. That in turn led to the unprecedented 1956 mutiny, known as the Revolt of the Colonels, the army versus the ultimately triumphant air force.

There had never been such commotion inside the military establishment since the Civil War. It got to the stage where the navy's chief representative, Admiral Arleigh Burke — a salty old ensign and Pacific War veteran teased behind his back as 'Steamboat Willie' — accused 'smart and ruthless' air force leaders of using techniques borrowed from Leninist textbooks to subvert authority from within. In fact, it was Lemnitzer who incited the rocket wars with the air force. As WW2 closed, he toured the defeated Reich shopping for promising ex-Nazis who worked on Hitler's secret weapons programmes, some of them glaring candidates for a one-way excursion to the Nuremberg war crimes trials. Lemnitzer foresaw with considerable percipience the silos of the future, Hitler's Peenemunde rocket ranges re-invented to catapult American missiles bristling with nuclear warheads over vast distances. He dreamed of nothing less than releasing the army from its earthbound shackles by aiming for the stars.

Lemnitzer's prize catch was Wernher von Braun. The Führer's rocketman, designer of the first projectile to achieve sub-orbital flight, was quietly spirited to Fort Bragg, North Carolina, and there kitted out with all his needs to fashion weapons of mass destruction. But to Lemnitzer's huge chagrin, rocket science left successive US governments stone cold until they woke up one October morning in 1957 to the alarming *bleep-bleep-bleep* of Sputnik, Russia's unexpected face-pull from space. According to the US embassy in Moscow, scrambling together a hasty excuse to cover its embarrassingly exposed sensitive parts, the Soviet Union had been drained of strategic resources to boot this insulting tin football upstairs. US intelligence was again exposed as no match for the Russians, but that was a domestic business. What thoroughly rattled Washington, at last, was the fact that Sputnik rose to the heavens atop a prototype Soviet missile with intercontinental range. Within a year, a von Braun spear hurtled aloft as the pilot for America's crushing response. In this game of ballistic one-upmanship, Moscow unwittingly scored a sensational own goal. The army may have emerged from the Pentagonian rocket wars the ultimate loser. But its appetite for absolute power remained undimmed.

The synchronised precision ballet of the National Socialist state exerted a powerful magnetism over Lemnitzer. He believed Germany's brilliant, original and courageous generals should have earned the plaudits of all civilised peoples for the pursuit of a selfless crusade against communism. The future chief of all Allied armed forces in Europe learned from his encounters with Nazi creeds that war was pointless, unless waged with total ruthlessness. The race that intended to survive and dominate should never flinch from the final solution. Thus the crypto-theology of exterminating an entire civilisation, deranged eugenics pursued to the final logical conclusion, passed from the Nazi code of war to the American one, enthusiastically endorsed by General Lemnitzer. He was at the forefront of a cadre of Right-wing officers in league with an influential cabal of Washington think-tank mavens preaching not only that nuclear weapons were fully usable in a general sense, but also that nuclear war was actually winnable. They clustered around the fanatical atomic zealot Herman Kahn, Kubrick's inspiration for *Dr. Strangelove*. Kahn argued the United States would always need the capability to destroy opponents with a pre-emptive strike so enormous that target nations would be wiped from the face of the earth — the 'more is always better' fantasia.[21] Kahn and his friends cheerfully argued

---

[21] Kahn (1922-1983) regarded nuclear war as the ultimate expression of freedom. As director of the Right-wing Rand Corporation, Kahn lowered the pole of nuclear war, probably irreversibly. He discarded the moral dimension as irrelevant to the debate. He also marked a watershed, in which policy wonks like him encouraged the military leadership to view with contempt the elected political class as lacking in courage to push the button, out of fear that the planet would vanish in a puff of smoke. The portly, owlish Kahn did not intend himself to be found after the apocalypse scraping the barren soil for scraps of food, eating the radioactive crops that he suggested could

that far from the ultimate Doomsday, life would go on, as it had after the Black Death of the 14th century. In the White House, and under Lemnitzer's influence, Eisenhower too surrendered to the braying of the nuclear hawks.[N4] Kahn has been dead for 25 years, but his penumbra clings to our collective consciousness. He remains the inspirational guru to a whole new chorus line of contemporary disciples bent to the task of rebuilding and expanding America's already enormous nuclear armoury.

The ascendancy of Lemnitzer marked the steady glide of the top officer corps into the everglades of McCarthyist madness. A strange, politically-charged mood swept the broad boulevards of Washington, which implied an unfolding standoff between the High Command and the Commander in Chief. JFK's bedtime reading quite probably included the political thriller *Seven Days in May*, which appeared in 1961. The sensational plotline featured a fictional president (called with scarcely-concealed finger pointing, 'Lyman') who becomes the target of a Right-wing coup staged by the Joint Chiefs of Staff.[22] A distinct whiff of mutiny drifted across the Potomac, to the extent an alarmed Congress ordered an inquiry into exactly what was going on inside the military. When some Democrats articulated their fears that JFK might awake one morning to hear the crunch of large army boots and growling tanks coming down Pennsylvania Avenue, as Franklin Roosevelt almost did back in 1933 (the stymied White House plot), the brooding presence of General Lyman Lemnitzer was not far from their minds. In their 1963 book, *The Far Right,* Donald Janson of the *New York Times* and CBS reporter Bernard Eismann were certainly not dealing in fiction when they wrote:

> *Concern had grown that a belligerent and free-wheeling military could conceivably become as dangerous to the stability of the United States as the mixture of rebelliousness and politics had in nations forced to succumb to juntas or fascism.*

The Senate Foreign Relations Committee agreed. In a lengthy report on Right-wing extremism flourishing in the armed forces, the committee warned

---

be fed to the elderly because they were going to die anyway. He would be maintained in a comfortably appointed bunker. His bleak testament is *On Thermonuclear War,* Princeton, 1960.

[22] *Seven Days in May*, by Fletcher Knebel and Charles Bailey, Harper & Row, 1962. The novel was filmed a year later, featuring Hollywood megastars Burt Lancaster and Kirk Douglas, screenplay by John Sterling, director John Frankenheimer. The book was a runaway seller, topping the *New York Times* list for a year. There was probably a well-thumbed copy in the Pentagon library (and the White House, for that matter). The neat role reversal is to dress 'President Lyman' as the softie on the communists, which is precisely what the real Lyman (Lemnitzer) thought about JFK. Inside track, obviously.

there was 'considerable danger' in the 'education and propaganda activities of military personnel' they uncovered. 'Running through all of them is a central theme that the primary, if not exclusive, danger to this country is internal Communist infiltration.'

According to one briefing prepared by a member of Secretary of Defense McNamara's staff, not even the élite National War College in Washington was immune. Dominated by extremist mentors, it was turning into a politicised bawdy house, where tutorials were systematically reduced to a rag bag of 'witch-hunting, mudslinging revivals' littered with 'bigoted, one-sided presentations advocating that the danger to our security is internal only.' This would be the creed of Gladio. Moreover, Fort Bragg units were already hard at work in Sardinia steeping the European secret soldiers in the mystical lore of psychological warcraft. They were treated to uplifting lectures by visiting American colonels, who passed around large doses of indoctrination inflating the 'internal threat' posed by communist fifth columns. For bedtime reading there were manuals and other stimulating literature dealing with subversion.

Since WW2, the record cruelly suggested American armed forces proved better at losing wars than winning them, which transformed senior commanders into agonising knots of pathological self-questioning. Korea was a messy, brokered draw; Vietnam got off to a wavering start, then sank into quagmire. The bearded Hannibal in Cuba was making the empire look a fool. Pentagonia believed the Kremlin Politburo were beside themselves with glee at America's discomfiture. In the circumstances, the stiff-backed Spartans in the Pentagon intended to pass the buck. Lemnitzer persistently displayed little respect at any point in his career for the political class to whom he theoretically reported. Its members were guilty of 'arrogance arising from failure to recognise its own limitations' (Kahn's strictures of 'political cowardice' ringing in his ears). He steadfastly refused to genuflect to plain 'Mr.' Kennedy as legal commander in chief of America's armed forces. In talks recorded for Pentagon archives in 1972, he consistently venerated 'general' rather than 'president' Eisenhower, as though his civilian credentials were inferior. In open defiance of the big rule book called the Constitution, which subordinates the military to the strict supervision of the civilian hierarchy, Lemnitzer waved his alternative: that the political caste, crippled by inexperience in military affairs, should leave such important decisions to the generals.

James Bamford wrote: 'In Lemnitzer's view, the country would be far better off if the generals could take over.'[N5] This disturbing notion registered with the Senate committee, which responded by pointing the finger of suspicion directly at General Lemnitzer, calling for an examination of the relationships between him, his fellow chiefs of staff, and extreme Right-wing Junker-like officer groups proliferating throughout the military. It veered extremely close to an astonishing and unprecedented indictment of plotting treachery or even insurrection, a remarkable confession from a body normally reluctant to cast more than a frown at the Pentagon. Bamford believed that cooking up the Northwoods scheme demonstrated the top brass had 'quietly slipped over the edge.' In fact, it perfectly encapsulated the profound distaste of the senior military caste for Left-leaning intellectuals in the ivory towers of the 'new Camelot' who, unless brought to their senses or stopped, would lead the country into the embrace of communism.

Lemnitzer viewed every act of the administration as shackling the military, from minor pin-pricks to a general tendency to interfere in military affairs. He scorned Kennedy's practice of dealing with big-ticket strategic issues in separated policy groups — actually a clever defensive ploy JFK devised to isolate Lemnitzer from seizing control of the initiative. The ever-suppurating wound remained Cuba. The popular imagination remains stuck firmly in the long-playing groove of the villainous usurper Fidel Castro tossing aside the legitimate government. In truth, it was the Biscayne Boulevard boys in Miami who backed a coup by their puppet stooge *El Presidente* Fulgencio Batista, when it became clear he was facing a rout in the upcoming general election. It took Castro another seven years to wear down the Floridian Mafioso and their CIA backers. When he finally came to power in 1959, there was an instant coalition of the losers. The drug trade ground to a halt, the boards went up at casinos run by mobsters, foreign corporations were unceremoniously booted out, the military stopped buying American weapons and thousands of Vatican priests were hustled off the island. The response, a little over two years later, was so expertly botched it could not be written off as a hapless example of mischance.

The CIA's Bay of Pigs misadventure of April 1961 was a perfect catastrophe from start to inglorious finish. Operation Zapata, as it was formally and more accurately named, referred to the peninsula in the area of the landing zone with that name. Much was later made of the similarity with the Zapata Oil Corporation — founded in 1953 by Texan petroleum baron and future president George H. W. Bush. A precursor Halliburton type of petro-industry services operation, Zapata entertained hopes of breaking up the global extraction cartel exerted by the Seven Sisters, by pushing into exploration and production in America's near-abroad waters in its own right. The company found itself cheated of potentially ripe drilling prospects, particularly in the region of the Zapata peninsula, when Castro took over. They clearly hoped to regain them in the wake of a successful invasion. There is a quite strong hint of private enterprise funding of the expedition, at least in some part, given the company's interesting political connections. In passing it should be noted that Cuba remains an attractive proposition for prospecting as-yet unexplored reserves, just seventy sea miles from Florida. The present offshore economic development zone is thought to contain at least twenty billion barrels of recoverable reserves, which raises the expectation of some new Libyan-style lunge based on the new crime of 'resource nationalism' invented by the State Department.

As Bamford has demonstrated, Lemnitzer had more than a shrewd idea Zapata was doomed, but did nothing to halt it even though he had enough opportunities. Lemnitzer's priceless experience gained in Allied invasions of North Africa and Southern Europe expertly placed him to judge just how haywire the CIA's plans were. Years later, Lemnitzer handwrote a detailed 52-page appraisal of the affair titled the 'The Cuban Debacle,' which he kept locked away at home. This secret confession described the opinion of the joint chiefs that the CIA, force-fed with worthless intelligence peddled by the Florida mob hankering after their bordellos, had no sensible grasp of the risks involved in putting ashore an inexperienced bunch of mercenaries against toughened defenders. He wrote: 'In view of the rapid build-up of the Castro Government's military and militia capability and the lack of predictable future mass discontent, the possible success of the paramilitary plan appears very doubtful.' Since that was the kernel of the plan, it was obviously foredoomed. How then to explain the cheerful opinion that Lemnitzer delivered to Robert McNamara declaring the joint chiefs reached a 'favourable assessment... of the likelihood of achieving initial military success.' Lemnitzer's motives were political and cunning. He was determined to prevent the upstart CIA getting above themselves and doing the Pentagon's work of running successful invasions. And he confidently anticipated the Kennedy government dissolving (naively, since it was a constitutional impossibility) as the direct consequence of a shambolic public relations disaster. Lemnitzer's silence was a psychological act of deception in which he revelled. The purpose was to butterfly the president's wings to an either-way disaster, damned if the invasion collapsed through faulty conception, equally damned if ground forces were denied crucial air support.

After years under the tightest of wraps — and even half-witted claims from po-faced Pentagon spokesmen that junior filing clerks somehow mislaid it — doctored extracts of the commission of inquiry ordered by JFK in the wake of the debacle finally surfaced in 1998. The inquest was chaired by General Maxwell Taylor, a hugely incendiary provocation to push under Lemnitzer's nose. Taylor was himself a former army chief of staff, and thus a member of the Pentagonian war court. There he made himself an avowed enemy of almost everything Lemnitzer stood for, especially what he saw as crackpot delusions with secret armies and subversive plotting. All of that would be quite sufficient to earn a threatening glower from Lemnitzer, but JFK rubbed salt in wounds: he hired Taylor, veteran clansman of the Kennedy's, as his personal military representative, the perfect alter ego of Lemnitzer. The reigning chief of staff was officially grand military vizier to the sitting president. So the burning question now was the identity of the *real* chief of staff, especially as Taylor frequently insinuated himself into gatherings of the Pentagonian magic circle. Lemnitzer would signal his fury at the presence of this interloper by pointedly absenting himself from the room. One should never underestimate the potential of this embarrassing rebuke to Lemnitzer's exalted status in cultivating future mischief by the Pentagonian chief of staff towards the president of the United States. Now, adding to his discomfiture, Lemnitzer found himself hauled as a star witness to a kangaroo court rigged, as he saw it, to protect Kennedy and the jelly-kneed, soft-shoed intellectuals surrounding him.

Still, the record reveals Lemnitzer weaselling miserably, claiming he had only seen the Zapata blueprints for evaluation and never formally approved them, which was untrue. As the story dribbled out under withering questioning from the chief prosecutor, none other than Attorney General Robert Kennedy, Zapata was exposed as littered with false-flag scams the CIA was addicted to. To make the escapade look like an all-*émigré* show, a few antique B62's repainted in Cuban colours were flown from Nicaragua to wallop Castro's airfields. Giving away his intimacy with every nut and bolt of the disastrous project, Lemnitzer admitted: 'They were never intended to accomplish the destruction of the Castro air force. They were to lend plausibility to the story that the D-Day [landing] strikes had been launched from within Cuba.' So brilliantly successful was this ruse, the Cuban ambassador denounced it the very same day at UN headquarters in New York as 'a dastardly act of the Americans.' Most of the planes landed in Miami without firing their guns, although a few managed to drop some bombs and make a limited nuisance of themselves.

Although it never came out in the Taylor laundry, the full operational details were known to Castro via the Russian embassy in New York at least a week before the landings. This nugget, which surfaced in the 21st century, explained the timely lurking of Castro's men amid a rich profusion of crocodiles and other unfriendly reptiles. Castro was certainly milking this heaven-sent just-let-it-happen opportunity. Lemnitzer gave himself good cover. Adopting the role of honest broker, he joined the chiefs of staff scooting to the White House as the grim scale of the disaster predictably unfolded. There, one of Jackie Kennedy's glistening soirees was in full sway. If they expected to rouse the president's fighting Irish temper in the face of deepening national humiliation, they misjudged their man. Kennedy stepped out of the ballroom cool and resplendent in white tie and tails, as the orchestra soared away in the background. He listened briefly, then curtly dismissed all pleas for air strikes to aid the brave heroes floundering in Cuban swamps.[23]

---

[23] Lemnitzer was not entirely sure he was immune from having his collar felt by inquisitorial Congressmen. Following the Bay of Pigs debacle he instructed

Kennedy honourably shouldered full responsibility, but there was no backlash of public indignation to force his resignation. JFK's unexpected resilience, and the failure of public trust to evaporate, left both top brass and the secret services exposed to allegations of sedition. Another significant factor was the distinct feel of a watershed in the social mood of the nation. Through to the Cuban crisis and beyond, the military failed to tune in to Kennedy's brand of social magnetism, 'patriotism with a human face,' fast on its way to capturing the soul of young America. Student power was on the move. It was hip to hang out with civil rights activists. The close-cropped officer corps recoiled at the sudden sprouting of long manes of knotted hair. The first perfumed wafts of flower power scented the breeze. Hallucinogenic boosters began their journey into the mainstream of American life, opening the way for Timothy Leary, high priest of psychedelic counter-culture to strike the keynote for the new generation: 'Turn on, tune in, drop out.' Gays — raising Lemnitzer's dread spectacle of unbridled licensed sodomy in the ranks — began flaunting themselves. College football heroes, formerly cheerleaders for enlistment press gangs, found themselves preaching to empty chairs. John Kenneth Galbraith set off a social and political earthquake with books (notably *The Affluent Society*, 1958) that undermined the moral rationale of America's helter-skelter pursuit of a winners-takes-all materialist culture, placing rampant militarism in an awkward spotlight. This was the unpromising backdrop to entrapment in Vietnam.

Kennedy's people quickly discovered Eisenhower had lost control of operations in Indo-China, while the civil war between the CIA and the Pentagon broke out anew. Roswell Gilpatric, deputy defence minister, a polished eastern intellectual whose gongs (Phi Beta Kappa, Yale) made him as popular at the Pentagon wigwam as an implant from the Kremlin, was put in charge of the first Vietnam task force. Kennedy simply did not believe the line he was getting from his generals. It was Gilpatric who raised a new issue altogether, warning the president how far the CIA was really operating as a quasi-military organisation beyond political remits or restraints. 'That's the first time I knew they were running Meos in Laos and Montagnards [local tribes] in South Vietnam. And as I got further into it, I found that we were not being told anywhere in the Defence Department very much about what was happening.' One could see why Gilpatric was scratching his head. The more he lifted the stones and peered under them, the more he came to suspect that what was going on in the jungles of Indo-China was something closely akin to black magic.

Brigadier General David Gray, chief aide responsible for Cuba, to destroy all his personal diaries recording the joint chiefs' actions and discussions during the lead-up to the landings. Gray's meticulous notes formed the only detailed official records. Destruction of these papers was a gross felony under federal law.

One of those primarily responsible was air force colonel and later general Edward Lansdale, who devoted his career to the madlands of macabre counter-insurgency and destabilisation plots. He earned his laurels practicing counter-insurrection in the Philippines and later Indo-China, before he was let loose on the world. Lansdale seemed to have stepped straight out of a surreal retake on James Bond, and the claim has been made he was the role model for Alden Pyle in Graham Greene's *The Quiet American*. But Pyle was much too sanctimonious.[24] Lansdale, on the other hand, decidedly was unquiet and quite possibly pathologically unbalanced. He was industrially mischievous, self-promoting and intelligent, and responsible for this gifted insight on black warfare: 'In using it in today's dirty, secretive wars, or in the future, the important thing to remember is that it is a *weapon* and that a weapon has its own unique use and its own effect.' Wary sceptics denounced him as susceptible to any 'nutty ideas that seemed to him plausible.' Yet he wrote with considerable perception: 'Psychological warfare is probably man's oldest weapon, aside from bare hands.' He developed an amateur grasp for the anthropology of myriad indigenous tribes, and soon began to convert their customs and superstitions into tools of war. One day he cheerfully had his men swoop down from the trees and impersonate blood-sucking vampires to terrify members of a particularly rebellious Filipino tribe. Colonel Walter Kurtz, who in Francis Ford Coppola's *Apocalypse Now* goes crazy on drugs and mutates into a depraved warlord surrounded by grisly tribal fetishes, is eerily close to a newsreel of Lansdale-inspired adventures carried out amid the lush vegetation of Asia. Lansdale's comrades, who wrote him off as a fantasist living out an extended practical joke in the blistering jungle heat, failed to see that beneath his affinity for eccentric and peculiar methods lay the deeply-held conviction that he was a political warrior employing the best local materials that came to hand.

As soon as he became army chief of staff in 1957, Lemnitzer had this clown prince of skulduggery plucked from Saigon and installed at a desk in Deputy Defense Secretary Gilpatric's office in the Pentagon. If the surroundings were less exotic than Asia, the scope for diabolical plotting was no less fertile. Kennedy still laboured with the Sisyphean burden of coming to office pledged to 'do something' about Castro (not least from his own latent pain over the loss of a Catholic heartland). Lansdale was put in charge of Operation Mongoose, a ragbag of burlesques under direct Lemnitzer patronage with the main object to eliminate Castro, in direct defiance of

---

[24] Lansdale (1908-1987) called his autobiography (1988) *The Unquiet American* as a reverse compliment to Greene. For a while he lodged with the ill-fated South Vietnamese president Ngô Đình Diệm. He tried vainly to prevent his friend's assassination by rebel officers of the South Vietnamese army, with the complicity of Washington, on 2nd November 1963.

federal law prohibiting political assassinations. Over the next four years, the great conjuror Lansdale would quietly participate in many covert operations, including raids and bombings in Cuba and other targets all over Latin America. Nor did he desert his penchant for exploiting superstitious natives. Playing on the primitive Catholicism of many Cubans, Lansdale planned to flood the island with rumours Christ had selected Cuba to stage his Second Coming, but had passed a precautionary word to his earthly sponsors that he wished to see Cuba purged of Castro first. On the night foretold, a US submarine would surface off the coast and set the night sky ablaze with thousands of exploding star shells, suggesting the heavenly chariot was indeed descending. One can imagine the wry smile on the lips of *El Comandante en Jefe* had he caught wind of his human powers to ward off the Saviour himself. But it was no less exotic than the 300 or so schemes hatched to bump him off — none of which panned out, obviously — that included exploding fountain pens, and seeding his favourite scuba diving site with booby-trapped clams. Lansdale's role in dreaming up similar thrillers for Europe had a profound influence on Lemnitzer. But altogether, it was rather like having a full-time witch doctor on the defence department payroll.

Lemnitzer was a prime motivating force in setting up the Special Forces Group in 1952 at Fort Bragg, where commandos were trained in the arts of guerrilla insurgency in the event of a Soviet invasion of Europe. Much of the expertise was borrowed from French guerrilla commandos fighting communist rebels in the Asian jungles, who in turn drew on the tactics of the insurgents themselves. A psychological warfare unit appeared on the same base at the same time; they were really two components joined as a tandem. Before long the men who proudly wore distinctive green berets were co-operating discreetly with the armed forces of a string of European countries and participating in direct military operations, some of them extremely sensitive and of highly dubious legality.

The Pentagon and the CIA got along like the odd couple, supposedly wedded to the same objective but frequently disagreeing on the tactics to follow, and at worst practising serious infidelities behind each other's backs. Lemnitzer was able to boast to Kennedy's advisers that deep involvement of the US military departments in many undercover aspects of the struggles in Laos and Vietnam 'have thus served as an excellent training laboratory.' But JFK had another idea. He decided to assume responsibility for insight of all special forces, a calculated affront to Lemnitzer and his fellow Pentagonians. Their hands were now to be tied. The despised General Taylor was placed in charge of a dedicated committee supposed to exercise close oversight. It was a strategic organ transplant foredoomed to failure. Allen Dulles, chief sommelier at the CIA, was invited along out of *politesse*, and spent his time reading unconnected documents or nodding inexpressively. Dulles had no intention of surrendering the CIA's valuable independence of initiative to a bureaucratic ad hoc committee of uncertain durability.

Lemnitzer held to the unshakeable conviction JFK would gamble away the huge advantage the US held over Russia's struggling ICBM (Intercontinental Ballistic Missile) programme. It was Cuba which supplied all the proof that he needed. As soon as he came to power in 1961, Kennedy ordered the immediate scrapping of ageing Jupiter medium-range, nuclear-tipped missiles scattered around Europe, including some on Turkish soil aimed directly at Moscow. Two years on, it would be these same Turkish Jupiter missiles that sparked off the literally earth-stopping collision between the United States and the Soviets over Cuba, yet by the time they came into play as bargaining tools, they were not supposed to be there at all. They were still tucked up in their silos because the Air Force took an unconscionable time obeying instructions from the president, which raises the intriguing question as to whether they ever intended to comply during the Kennedy incumbency. In the aftermath of the settlement with the Russians, Lemnitzer raged that JFK 'had no right' to trade off the Jupiters because they had been 'given to NATO.' This was another ploy in being imaginative with the actuality that all nuclear warheads stationed in Europe, apart from the independent French arsenal, were kept under firm US lock and key.

Yet the eerie sense of the Pentagon watching an egg timer on the Kennedy presidency was strongly reinforced when the joint chiefs discarded the earlier Northwoods false-flags camouflage to go straight for the jugular. They demanded the right to take over the island without further delay. This time there would be huge amphibious landings and a massive air assault, with no apologies for civilian casualties certain to be in many thousands. What happened now was very close to a 'step into line or take the consequences' ultimatum to the American president from his military commanders. Lemnitzer sent a fresh Pentagonian note intended for JFK's eyes via Defence Secretary McNamara.

The Joint Chiefs of Staff believe that the Cuban problem must be solved in the near future. Further, they see no prospect of early success in overthrowing the present communist regime either as a result of internal uprising or external political, economic or psychological pressures. Accordingly they believe that military intervention by the United States will be required to overthrow the present communist regime.

Unprecedented in the history of relations between the US military and the White House, the memorandum was couched in uncompromising language that implied a meltdown in relations between the Pentagon and the Commander in Chief. 'The Joint Chiefs of Staff believe that the United States can undertake military intervention in Cuba without risk of general war,' Lemnitzer continued. 'They also believe that the intervention can be accomplished rapidly enough to minimise communist opportunities for solicitation of UN action.' The tightened leverage was extraordinary in the sense that the chiefs made no attempt to hide the impression they considered their political nuance and judgement overrode the elected president. Lemnitzer did not intend to free the Cuban people, who were largely in support of Castro, but shut them up in a US prison colony. 'Forces would assure rapid essential military control of Cuba,' the president was told. However, 'continued police action would be required.'

By now Lemnitzer knew from his listening posts in the White House that Kennedy was intending to end the US presence in Indo-China altogether. He suspected that in good time, he would follow up by indulging in the ultimate heresy of *détente* with Castro. Some fitful contacts with Havana were indeed already under way, and Lemnitzer knew this. And so of course did the CIA. The Pentagon and the CIA finished licking their wounds over the Cuban disaster and started to think what to do with a president who seemed bent on high treason.

JFK was thinking along similar lines — about his chief of the general staff. A short while after the latest Cuban salvo — in another unprecedented tipping point in US history — the top commanders met secretly in a Pentagonian summit with the full Medici of the US military-industrial complex. The sole agenda was their mutual alarm at the seemingly imminent abandonment of America's war posture around the globe. The military were constructing a wider coalition. If Kennedy was under no illusions of the dangers posed by a rogue Pentagon, then equally he was constrained by the realities of political life in America in bringing this dangerously independent-minded officer to heel. To dismiss a highly-decorated war hero, commander-in-chief of the US army and chief of staff, might set off a chain reaction leading directly to the White House. Lemnitzer was certainly guilty of outright insolence and insubordination towards a president he regarded as incapable of carrying out his duties to safeguard America's security, but he believed the best cards were in his own hands. Kennedy, he was sure, would be stripped of all credibility on the world stage if he fired America's top warrior on grounds of plotting some kind of military *coup d'état*. He would also, or so Lemnitzer believed, suffer serious loss of political capital in the eyes of an American public accustomed to venerating their military without question. Lemnitzer's calculations had some grounding, but he gravely under-estimated JFK's determination to take all those risks and deal him out of the game. It was eyeball to eyeball across the Potomac, from the Oval Office to Lemnitzer's suite in the Pentagonal mother ship.

Between March — when Lemnitzer sent his invasion-or-bust projectile to Robert McNamara — and early autumn, a festering political crisis in the

Kremlin witnessed General Secretary Nikita Khrushchev fighting for his life against backstabbers in the Soviet Politburo. He urgently needed a political knockout blow, and fast. The old standby of an international crisis was thus fabricated, with the aim of forcing American Jupiter missiles out of Turkey. The stage was set for Red October 1962, when Khrushchev's gamble led to Russian missiles sprouting in Cuba. The world trembled at the brink.

JFK emerged from the crisis with his prestige vastly enhanced, everywhere, that is except Pentagonia. Kennedy's refusal to snuff out Castro and worse, permitting the United States to be humbled in the world arena by the Soviet Union, united them once again under Lemnitzer's authority. The danger to the head of state returned with renewed intensity. Barely had the heat of the immediate emergency cooled than Kennedy struck with an iron fist. He decided on a clever 'constructive dismissal' of his troublesome commander. Lemnitzer would be denied his due right of a second term of office as chief of the staff, effectively cashiered, and given his marching orders right away. A humiliating demotion would be disguised, somewhat at any rate, by secondment to the top NATO command in France. If it was a signal that Kennedy intended to stop the rot in the military, then his decision to install his court favourite, General Maxwell Taylor, in Lemnitzer's stead, could only be seen as another calculated insult. It was a Solomonic judgement in which Kennedy excelled, like his calm resolution of the Missile Crisis. Sending Lemnitzer into quarantine on the other side of the Atlantic, in charge of America's frontline with the Russians, his mischievous hands would be too preoccupied to plot trouble on the home front. Deprived of Lemnitzer's presence in Washington, trouble in the ranks would gutter out. Kennedy miscalculated, badly, on both counts.

Of all the juries that have probed the deaths of John and Robert Kennedy, official and informal, none have expressly pointed the finger of suspicion at General Lemnitzer. Yet if one man had the motive and desire to see the brothers off the scene, commencing with the president, then it was a soldier in the grip of hatred so powerful that any lengths were acceptable. Northwoods and its offshoots demonstrated that he regarded morality in the defence of American interests as a distraction. Here was a man who would enlist Mafia hoodlums in the service of his objectives. He cheerfully waved volunteers off to certain death in the Bay of Pigs fiasco. He planned to unleash terror on innocent Americans going about their everyday business so that he could get his way over Cuba. He contemplated extinction of a quarter of the human race — and very possibly life itself — with magnanimity. He hired Nazi war criminals with equanimity. He was not alone in that, but gave every impression of complete disinterest in their crimes against humanity, which he brushed off like dandruff.

When he got to Europe, this highly political animal in uniform found at his disposal a vast military apparatus — almost as big as any such plaything at home. Moreover, he had the splendid bonus of the secret armies — with which he could wreak havoc all over the continent, and did. The Lemnitzer years in Europe were warped by the descent into institutionalised state violence wrought against sovereign governments and their citizens. Lemnitzer shamelessly hoisted the black flag of terror over Europe. True it was already furled and waiting for him, but no other commander in chief of the Allied forces in Europe would find a better purpose for it than the most supremely ideological general the United States has produced. So far. The jury is out on General David Petraeus, ominously the first soldier to head the CIA. To a cynical eye, the appointment rather suggests a merger between Pentagonia and CIA, with disturbing prospects for the future of American democracy, badly frayed as that already is.

John Kennedy miscalculated an enemy who proved stronger than he. His elimination that November 1963 day in Dallas, followed not long afterwards by his brother Robert, fitted the purposes of Lemnitzer exactly. The mission to purify Asia went ahead with refreshed zeal under Lyndon Baines Johnson. The Cold War intensified, with Lemnitzer in precisely the right location to make sure that it did. The military industrial complex hummed as never before. Only defiant Cuba spoiled this blissful prospect.

Unwittingly, JFK provided Lemnitzer with safe conduct to finish his plan. The necessary accommodations were made with the CIA, who were of the same mind and willing to bury the hatchet in this greater cause. The agency's secret purse would prove extremely useful in funding the operation. Even before he was safely ensconced in his NATO day job, Lemnitzer was behind the schemes to murder President Charles de Gaulle, with the aid of disaffected Algerian veterans, Hungarian dissidents and Gladio guerrillas.

Dealey Plaza bore the template of a ready-made Gladio-style assassination project. Among the items which have long teased investigators is a photograph depicting the so-called 'three tramps' being led off by a rather unruffled cop, who looks as though he has been assigned a mundane chore. One of these scruffy individuals was later identified as Charles Harrelson, a contract killer with the Red Squads — undercover police intelligence units operating in the 1920s to infiltrate, harass and gather intelligence on suspicious political and social groups. Another of the tramps is reputed to be Chauncey Holt, supposedly the 'figure on the grassy knoll' appearing in the famous grainy footage, apparently taking aim at the JFK cavalcade. Holt was a brilliant counterfeiter with a curious sideline in painting celebrity portraits. Clint Eastwood was among those who sat before his easel. Holt never denied he was one of the tramps. Both were accustomed to working for the CIA and organised crime at the same time. They had also become enmeshed in the so-called 'International Rescue Committee,' the secret slush fund created by the CIA to launder money the agency earned from its freelance drug rackets. Holt explained his role was to drive into town one of the most feared terminators in the mob world, Chicago hitman Charles 'Chuckie' Nicoletti, who had at least twenty scalps to his belt. Nicoletti, it was said, never missed. The third is said to be Charles Rogers, a Houston resident accused in 1965 of chopping up his parents and freezing their remains in the family refrigerator. He has never been seen again, which may explain the swirl of rumours he left behind claiming he was a CIA sub-contractor. Lois Gibson — world-renowned 'woman of a thousand faces,' for her extraordinary expertise in facial profiling and pathology of photographic images — has stated unequivocally that all three tramps are correctly identified as Holt, Harrelson and Rogers.

As investigators began to pore over the identity of everyone in this strange snap, there were those who felt able to identify with some certainty a furtive figure creeping alongside a fence behind the three so-called tramps. According to his peers, this was none other than Edward Lansdale, not long before sacked by Robert McNamara for refusing to co-operate in the killing of Lansdale's long-time friend and best buddy housemate, South Vietnamese strongman General Diệm. Another account tendered requiring settlement. Lansdale was seen in Dallas that day by associates who swore they recognised him. As Henry Thoreau once wrote, 'some circumstantial evidence is very strong, as when you find a trout in the milk.'

The 'three tramps' were the perfect identikit of hoodlums Lemnitzer intended to hire for his Northwoods lunacies. Lemnitzer despatched his own man, Lansdale, as Master of Ceremonies. Out of sight and out of mind on the far side of the Atlantic, simmering with anger, the humiliated soldier wrote and settled the score. Lemnitzer smarted at altogether too many slights at the hands of a man who'd bobbed about in some kind of motor launch in the South Pacific while he, as Brigadier General, had swept from one triumph to another across Europe. There was the insulting imposition of shadow chief-of-staff General Maxwell Taylor as JFK's personal sheriff, prowling around the Pentagon, putting his nose where it was not wanted; the president's decision to supervise unorthodox warfare in-house; his backing off in the missile crisis; the removal of frontline missiles from Turkey; undermining and scheming to end the war in Asia; reversing America to peacetime footing when it was perfectly obvious to Pentagonia the threat from the Soviets and the Chinese had never been greater. And the ultimate insult: the first chief of staff to be fired and packed off to exile.

Lemnitzer's exceptionally long life — he was well on the way to his century when he died — was foremost about turning false purposes into a major tool of the US military and its political opponents. Like his protégé

Lansdale, he thrived in the fevered jungle of conspiracies and plotting. NATO turned out to be an impressive sunset to a career of infamy. When he finally hung up his uniform after 51 years, he went on to become a prominent fraterniser with the neocons and especially their schemes to deceive western publics over the scale of the Soviet threat. He sat on neocon-packed CIA-baiting committees whose objective was to trash all intelligence which suggested Russia was probably collapsing economically and politically, as indeed it was.

Lemnitzer died in 1988. He lies in Arlington National Cemetery, where all America's heroes rest, in a plot not far from the murdered Kennedy brothers. Ronald Reagan gave him the Presidential Medal of Freedom. Edward Lansdale died a year before Lemnitzer, although at 79 much younger. He, too, is sleeping in the arboreal national shrine, along with General Maxwell Taylor, who succumbed to motor neuron disease about the same time. There must be oft-unquiet spirits in those leafy glades by the Potomac. The three tramps slipped quietly away. On 29th May 1977, the man who never missed, Charles Nicoletti, found his match: he was himself finished off sitting in his car in Northlake, Illinois, by three neat 9 mm holes drilled in the back of his head.

Early in 2012 we learnt that the Pentagon was assembling a vast Doomsday Machine called Social Radar, composed of a vast array of sensors and technologies. The intention is supposed to be a battlefield weapon, to read the minds of the enemy. But now that President Obama has declared the whole of the United States to be the front line of the war on terror, we can understand the real purpose of this menacing development. It is nothing less than an Orwellian-Huxleyan-Bradburyesque spectroscope to inspect the daily thoughts, passions, hopes and fears of Americans themselves. Lyman Lemnitzer believed to his last breath that only the generals were equipped with the necessary skills to run America. Well, now they are.

IV.
The Propaganda of the Deed

'At his trial, Pisciotta boasted: "We were a single body — bandits, police, and Mafia, like the Father, the Son, and the Holy Ghost."' — Testimony after the massacre in Palermo, May Day 1947.

The Strategy of Tension was honed and perfected in Italy, perhaps unsurprisingly, albeit under quite a different label. One hundred and forty years ago, a virtually forgotten anarchist called Errico Malatesta (which translated reads ironically as 'sick in the head') enthusiastically adopted a creed that became known among its advocates as the 'propaganda of the deed.' A spiky bundle of energy with an unruly mop of hair, born in 1853, who lived long enough to watch Mussolini seize power, he was variously an ice cream salesman, mechanic, guerrilla and international roving prophet of anarchism. He travelled the globe spreading his message, and was especially influential in South America. On and off he spent ten years in prison. The intellectual mastermind of Gladio, Yves Guérin-Sérac, paid much attention to Malatesta's work and adopted many of his ideas. Malatesta described his theory of Propaganda of the Deed as 'violent communal uprisings to inspire revolutionary acts.' The reasoning went that people would see that governments were their real oppressors, and turn to liberators like himself to sweep them away.

Anarchists all over Europe and as far away as America eagerly plunged headlong into techniques with the appeal of operating almost invisibly, requiring a lone bomber or *agent provocateur* to create mayhem or bring off a high-profile assassination, of which there were many. The cliché image of the sinister cloaked figure leaping from the shadows to hurl a nail bomb, or strike down some crowned head or representative of the political élites, dates from a period which in retrospect uncannily resembled a trailer for the 20th century years of lead. It also struck a close chime with the forthcoming suicide bomber filtering unnoticed into a dense crowd.

Malatesta himself staged a short insurrection in the small city of Benevento, near Naples, in April 1877. Strategically, it backfired badly. What the perpetrators overlooked, and the government realised, was the attractive prospect of turning the tables. Thus Malatesta's followers found themselves accused of staging a number of failed assaults on the Italian monarch, the stiff and vain Umberto I, that were actually orchestrated by royal agents. Nobody believed fierce protestations of innocence from

Malatesta, and in any event the damage had been done. But the authorities now over-reached themselves in a spectacular fashion.

As the 19th century closed, Italy was slipping into a distinctly revolutionary frame of mind. Unity had not brought prosperity except for the already well-heeled minority. Chronic mismanagement of feudal farming estates pushed the country's poorest classes close to famine. The remoteness of the aristocracy and gentry — an ancient Italian grievance — served to unify forces of dissent. The unpopular House of Savoy represented by Umberto was preoccupied with imperial glory in North Africa. In May 1898 a general strike broke out in Milan which threatened to engulf the nation. Panic seized the government, which over-reacted to peaceful demonstrations against increases in the price of bread by declaring a stage of siege. Umberto summoned a ruthless old general named Fiorenzo Bava Beccaris, who seemed to think he was back in the North African colonial foreign wars, machine-gunning the local 'savages.' He roared into action against unarmed civilians with a regiment of infantry, and cavalry supported by artillery. In the ensuing massacre at the very gates of the royal palace in Milan, hundreds were slaughtered, including women and children. Estimates range between 250 and 400 dead, while some 2,000 more were carried from the scene in various states of injury.

The usual official line of protestors inciting the riot travelled the rounds of the newspapers. The propaganda of this deed was aimed at a broader audience who must be the shown the revolting nature of the masses and the threat they posed to sacred institutions such as religion and property. What really alarmed Umberto and his court was an unmistakable drift by the middle classes towards the protesting workers, especially in Milan, a bellwether that might favour the forces of republicanism. It was time to raise the spectre of the red peril over Christian Italy and the naturally ordained order of things. The gentle pacifist Filippo Turati, soul of the Italian socialist party — a man whose entire life was committed to the path of peaceful constitutional change — was thrown into prison on ludicrous charges of fomenting riots and trying to overthrow the state. General Beccaris had another medal pinned to his already overcrowded chest by the grateful monarch. The affair reaped a deadly blowback. In early summer 1900, an old friend of Malatesta's called Gaetano Bresci — described by his friends in America as one of the most tolerant men anyone could find, if they spent ten years searching for him — sailed back across the Atlantic. He made his way to Monza, in the province of Lombardy, where Umberto was expected on a state visit. There on 29th July, Bresci struck Umberto down, with four finely-judged bullets from a point 32 pistol.

Propaganda by deed sprang from the desperation many anarchists felt at the lack of motivation among working classes to bind themselves into organised opposition to the state. It was the state that was always their true enemy in any form. The exciting energy raised by the brief Springtime of the Nations of 1848 quickly collapsed, but the revolutionary pulse was still beating. However, important divides split the anti-establishment cause. Whereas socialists inspired by Marx wanted to capture the state and remake it to fit the aspirations of the proletariat, the anarchist dream was to do away with it altogether, the ultimate adventure in human liberty. The Bavarian Johann Most (1846-1906), a wild-eyed German advocate of this line living in America, placed himself at the cutting edge of the trend to violence. He disseminated an exciting tract entitled: 'The Science of Revolutionary Warfare: a manual of instruction in the use and preparation of Nitro-Glycerine, Dynamite, Gun Cotton, Fulminating Mercury, Bombs, Fuses, Poisons, etc, etc.' In the introduction to his explosive cookbook, he wrote: 'In giving dynamite to the downtrodden millions of the globe, science has done its best work. A pound of this stuff beats a bushel of ballots all hollow.'[25]

Errico Malatesta held firmly that successful revolution 'consists more of deeds than words,' and deeds would always be the most effective form of propaganda. So the last dazzling years of *La Belle Époque* were overshadowed by lurid violence. The short-lived revolutionary government of Paris in early 1871 — a brilliant shower of sparks, the aftershock of the French Revolution known to history as the Commune — ran like cold water into an abysmal sump of catastrophe. The Paris Commune exposed the intellectual chasm between anarchists and socialists, although the experiment was in any event foredoomed. In May 1878 a plumber called Emil Hödel almost killed Emperor Wilhelm, as he was riding in his open carriage along Berlin's leafy Unter den Linden. The reformist Russian Tsar Alexander II fell to an assassin's bomb in March 1881. In 1891, twenty-two people were killed in a Barcelona theatre by the bomb thrown by one Santiago Salvador (garrotted in 1894). A nail bomb was tossed into the French Chamber of Deputies in session just before Christmas, 1893. The perpetrator Auguste Vaillant's rallying words before the blade fell were: 'Death to the *bourgeoisie*. Long live anarchy.' In Paris a year later, Émile Henry (guillotined May 1894) hurled another infernal device at diners supping in

---

[25] Grotesquely disfigured by frostbite and botched surgery, Most was a gadfly who veered between primitive socialism and anarchism. His outspokenness frequently landed him in trouble with the authorities in Germany and Austria. His exciting tract on bombing led to him to flee to America. One of the early exponents of the Propaganda of the Deed: 'The existing system will be quickest and most radically overthrown by the annihilation of its exponents. Therefore, massacres of the enemies of the people must be set in motion.' These were exactly the future precepts of God's Terrorist, Yves Guérin-Sérac (Chapter V).

the Café Terminus at the Gare St. Lazare, killing one and injuring twenty, on the grounds that *bourgeois* found relaxing in such places were legitimate targets. His final address to the jury was a rousing call to anarchism and the propaganda of the deed: 'Its roots go deep. It spouts from the bosom of a rotten society that is falling apart. It is a violent backlash against the established order. It stands for the aspirations to equality and liberty which have entered the lists against the current authoritarianism.' In June that same year, the Italian anarchist Sante Caserio stabbed and killed the popular French president Marie-François Sadi Carnot during a public banquet in Lyon, an act which provoked widespread shock and revulsion. Not even the Greenwich Observatory was immune from its fair share of fragments and splinters. US President William McKinley died on 14th September 1901, having been felled ten days earlier in Buffalo, New York State, by a pistol shot fired by the anarchist Leon Czolgosz, the son of Polish immigrants.

As with the Strategy of Tension yet to come, self-proclaimed populist action groups and individuals with unknown or obscure attachments, clamoured for the blame or offered themselves as martyrs. Conventional wisdom declares that propaganda by deed inherently failed in its stated purpose of achieving a massive shift to people power. It frightened and antagonised the bourgeoisie with a reign of apparently senseless violence and terror performed by murderous fanatics, who for all anyone knew were completely insane. These acts were easily exploited by the authorities to bolster the existing order organised around the cardinal principles of Nation, Family, Authority and Property. The Greenwich case, which Joseph Conrad dramatised in his novel *The Secret Agent,* seems to be the classic instance of setting up a psychologically-confused patsy. The horrible murder of Tsar Alexander — who was distinctly ahead of his times in proposing sweeping social reforms, especially his far-reaching emancipation designed to raise up the serfs — delighted the ultra-conservatives in the Russian establishment. The Tsarist secret police were assiduous at intercepting plots. This exceptional overkill operation, calling for three actual or back-up bombers, was either a classic instance of 'just let it happen' or a state false-flag assassination. Alexander's successor, his dullard younger brother, instantly crushed reform. He promoted anti-Semitism and the interests of the landed gentry.

Anarchism itself ran out of steam, colliding head-on with the great buffer stops of early 20th century history: the First World War, the successful Russian communist revolution and the ascendancy of totalitarian systems of the far Right. The great hope of the anarchist cause was the working classes, but they cried out for more state involvement in their lives, and not the dream of a free, self-regulating society the anarchists yearned for. Yet the basic precepts of propaganda by deed remained intact, even as the anarchist dream faded. They passed into the hands of more sinister figures. This is how Adolf Hitler greeted the burning of the Reichstag on 27th February 1933:

> *This is the beginning of the Communist revolution! We must not wait a minute. We will show no mercy. Every Communist official must be shot, where he is found. Every Communist deputy must this very day be strung up!*

So how could Hitler be certain the fire had been set by communist terrorists, as the starting signal for a sweeping communist revolution right across Germany? As flames licked around the building, police stumbled on a befuddled young Dutch Jew who was instantly accused of starting the blaze. Marinus van der Lubbe was a mentally feeble drifter in the European communist movement. He wandered into the German resistance to Hitler largely by happenstance, scarcely a likely individual to carry out such an audacious and well-prepared attack on the highest symbol of the German state. The destruction of such a monumental pile requires considerable forethought and assistance. The Nazi propaganda mastermind Joseph Goebbels, however, was certainly well-qualified to commission such an exercise, given the full apparatus of the state in his hands.

The day after the fire, and six days before the scheduled general election, Hitler persuaded the elderly and confused president Feldmarschall von Hindenburg (the icon of WW1) that the crisis was of such profound gravity it could only be met by complete abolition of all personal liberties. In 1933, Hitler's grip on power was still extremely tenuous. Chiefly, he was seeking an excuse for a putsch cloaked in the guise of constitutional respectability. The poll on 5th March returned the National Socialists as the largest party with 43.9% of the popular vote. Yet with 288 seats in the Riechstag, Hitler faced massed opposition ranks of 359. He could count on less than half the votes of the assembly. Clearly no way to run a successful revolution.

The 'Reichstag Fire Law' conferred by Hindenburg gave Hitler many of the instruments that he required for a total seizure of power. Within two weeks parliamentary democracy was also reduced to the smoking embers of history. Reichs Chancellor Hitler convened a kangaroo gathering of mostly tame MP's. Those opposed to the Nazi seizure of power were mostly in hiding, or fled abroad. The infamous Enabling Act formally suspended the remnants of German democracy. The German people saw what remained of their rights to free assembly and freedom of speech (already well pruned during the Weimar years) snatched away. Their homes were prey to police raids; mail and phone calls were routinely pried into. Judges were turned into stuffed effigies of the Nazi state. Germany's 27/2 was the counterpart and uncanny precursor of the war on terror launched in the 21st century on 9/11, the same empty claim that to preserve a few basic liberties, the populace must surrender all others—the same Big Lie.

Hitler resorted with enthusiasm to the opportunities the Propaganda of the Deed presented. Perhaps the most infamous was the event that sparked WW2. SS units forced a small group of concentration camp victims, 'released' from Buchenwald and disguised in Polish uniforms, to stage a false-flag mock attack on the main radio tower in the Nazi-controlled free state of Danzig. Citing provocation by the Poles, the German invasion of Poland followed. Even Stalin fell victim, so terrified by the vertical rise of German power that he was tricked into signing the 1940 peace pact with Berlin. In some respects, Hitler won more victories by resorting to propaganda by deed than he did by *Blitzkrieg* shock and awe.

Sicily is the perfect theatre of the mysterious, where words convey confusing meanings and reality is commonly over-ruled by the indistinct boundaries between what is true and false, or right and wrong. We can never be sure therefore how far the island's legendary *bandito* Salvatore Giuliano was under the spell of Robin Hood, but he typified for Italy's poorest society how exhilarating it might be to live in a spirit of carefree independence. However, the accounts of Giuliano's adoption of the island's poor and repressed peasantry and his medieval gallantry to women, obscure his real pattern of loyalties towards the everlasting trinity of power in Sicily, the church, feudalism and Cosa Nostra.

Giuliano regarded himself as a bandit-politician, again like the legendary Robin Hood. He signed up for the grandly-sounding *Esercito Volontario per l'Indipendenza della Sicilia* (the Sicilian volunteer army), apparently in the hopes of some important preferment, should the Sicilian football finally spring free from the looming Italian boot. The legendary Sicilian Mafioso Don Calò Vizzini (the 'boss of bosses') was another supporter in the early days. He pragmatically changed his mind when the Americans arrived. Yet, the volunteers left one small scratch on history: they were an early genesis of Italy's Gladio, along with Giuliano himself.

Giuliano was born in 1922 in the small hillside town of Montelepre, not far from Palermo on Sicily's northern coastline. Fortune awarded him striking good looks equal to some future dramatic role (as it transpired, classically tragic and tailor-made for the Sicilian climate). Carefully-staged sepia photographs, that might have been produced by a professional theatrical agent, depict a classic figure in the mould of Rudolf Valentino, staring lantern-jawed at the camera through searing dark eyes, resting on pistol. Giuliano saw himself as an honourable rogue, except that he robbed for his own ends rather than the island's peasants. The stuff of legends inevitably sprouts from a handsome poetry-reading highwayman. Among many probably apocryphal stories is an encounter with the Duchess of Pratameno. He went off with all her jewels except her wedding ring. He 'borrowed' the book of poetry she was reading, so legend tells, and later returned it with a few scribbled page notes of his own.

Giuliano was purportedly gunned down by his cousin Gaspare Pisciotta (although the truth is still a mystery) at the ripe old age of 28. Yet in a grand finale worthy of the drum and cymbal peals of Giuseppe Verdi, Giuliano succeeded in fostering such an enduring legend about his life and times that he remains an indelible feature of the Sicilian and indeed Italian popular landscape. This perfect example of romantic southern banditry is the subject of several films, including one magnificent exercise in neo-realism (Francesco Rosi's wonderfully spare masterpiece of 1962) plus a clutch of serious academic essays and books, and for good measure, an opera. Rosi's grainy black and white tribute is enhanced in realism by the use of mainly amateur performers belonging to the intimate community where the events occurred. He brilliantly snares the harmony of primitive political yearnings in this wretchedly poor landscape, and the endlessly smouldering drama of Sicilian society, personified by the omnipresent Mafia.

At his lair deep in the Sagana mountains west of Palermo, a rugged and stony version of Sherwood Forest, Giuliano assembled a gang which at times numbered several hundreds, composed of criminals, army deserters and homeless vagabonds. He transformed this ragbag of misfits into a disciplined raiding force, thanks to military-style training in precision marksmanship. The island's Carabinieri soon learnt to pay due respect to a band that chased off intruders with a hot rain of deadly accurate machine gun fire.

Like any Wild West stereotypes, Giuliano's men resourced themselves in food and weapons by robbing notoriously snail-like Sicilian trains, holding up banks and drawing on the Robin Hood element of the fantasy, pretending he stole from the rich to redistribute their illicit wealth to the poor. During the war, Giuliano diversified his thieving skills to manipulating the black market. Responsible during this period for several brutal murders, including the shooting of a Carabinieri officer, he was the self-idolising criminal yearning to be legitimised by a cause. This was the notion that his poverty-stricken backwater — lacking any natural resources except fish and fruit and rugged mountain goats — could somehow summon the means to become an independent state. Like Emiliano Zapata finding himself in remarkably similar circumstances in Mexico, Giuliano's fame and fortunes rested with the political and economic realities of the hour. (The two men also met similar fates.) The mirage of independence scarcely held Sicily's masses in spellbound anticipation. Most of all they prayed for release from grinding poverty. In any event, the great liberator's moment had passed. In July 1943, American, British and Canadian troops began the liberation of Italy. Through the designs of — among others — Lyman Lemnitzer, leading officer in General George Patton's invading 8th army staff, together with the OSS, the

Allies made common cause with the Cosa Nostra even before they established beachheads. As the late unofficial CIA historian Chalmers Johnson wrote, 'the black flag flew over the advancing host.' The stated intention was to draw on the Mafia's strengths, to prevent Mussolini's forces sabotaging the island's east coast ports before Allied troops splashed ashore.

At this early stage the US was determined to prevent post-war Italy falling into the clutches of the Soviets, at any cost, and if this involved a pact with organised crime, it was figured to be a price worth paying. Roosevelt, the ultimate pragmatist, harboured deep misgivings concerning the future ambitions of the OSS, and regarded many of its chief actors as unpredictable, if not actually deranged (Frank Wisner a leading candidate). He stubbornly opposed continuance of the OSS after the war, guessing correctly that given the manic instability of some of its godparents, it would rapidly lurch into criminality and conspiracy. Yet in the urgency of the hour, even FDR was compelled to see the ironical logic of recruiting the man once demonised as America's Public Enemy Number One in the cause of conquering Europe, even if the individual concerned was still behind bars.

So it was that the long arm of the US government dipped into the heart of the New York State correctional system to pluck the 'first among equals' in America's crime syndicates. This was the legendary Sicilian-born Charles 'Lucky' Luciano, the most powerful and successful gangster in American history. This colourful bird of prey was already cosseted in a commodious private cell, hands free to manage the affairs of a sprawling criminal kingdom constructed largely out of dope trafficking. He was promised his eventual liberty in return for delivering the southern Italian Mafia as the fifth column backing the Allied cause. The seed had been sown that flowered into the role of the Mafia families of southern Italy, acting as a praetorian guard within the stay-behind armies.

Once the Allied generals George S. Patton and Bernard Montgomery settled their immediate private feuds and conquered Sicily, the Mafia immediately crammed every town hall and every post in the island's government with their own supporters and Christian Democratic lackeys. Luciano was finally thrown out of the US in 1946, much to his chagrin, since he considered himself a glowing example of the self-made American immigrant-patriot. He was immediately consoled with a glittering consolation prize, the chance to seize a share of the emerging global post-war heroin empire, that grew over time to stretch from the Chinese mobsters who controlled vast swathes of poppy production funnelled through Asia's golden triangle, to the streets of Europe and America. Afghanistan, Turkey, Lebanon and Bulgaria were sucked irrevocably into the vortex. The pipeline's terminals lay in Sicily, home to the main dope-processing laboratories servicing the exploding markets of Europe and North America.

The virus of the Lucky Luciano touch infected and institutionally criminalised the Italian political landscape for decades to come. These shocks carried a deep resonance, because throughout its short history as a unitary state, a wide gulf separated Italy's political and administrative classes from a mistrustful and suspicious electorate. Now the crucial step had been taken which rendered Italy virtually ungovernable in any practical fashion. This was the final presentation of account for the American government's courtship of the Italo-American Mafioso. The Italian Mafia's influence over wide tracts of the state and public life in general has never been greater than it is today.

Giuliano's famous letter to President Harry Truman in 1946, suggesting the US should annex the island as a full-blown American state, underlined his own waning sense of purpose. He lacked the inspirational energy to incite a popular revolt, falling back as always on the brute voice of the gun. The high-water mark came in January 1946, at Montedoro, in the wintry snow-powdered mountains south of Palermo. Giuliano and a small army that may have numbered a Garibaldian thousand engaged in pitched battle with the police and the army, and momentarily seized worldwide attention. Spectacular and pointless, the affair achieved no more than to dramatise 'the landscape of violence, this cruelty of climate, this continual tension in everything' epitomised brilliantly by Giuseppe Tomasi di Lampedusa in his Sicilian masterpiece, *The Leopard*.

No sooner was Luciano sprung than the moment was primed for Salvatore Giuliano to appear in an infamous act bearing the clear stripe of Gladio atrocities yet to come. Long-simmering forces pent up by the Blackshirt regime broke asunder. The Left was finally on the march across an island awash with searing social grievances. These waves broke against the dykes of the Mafia, whom Mussolini had suppressed because they offered keen competition to rival criminal confederacies within his own ranks. With *Il Duce* banished from the scene, old forces quickly resumed their former roles. The 'honourable society' (as the Mafia often styled themselves), the church and affiliated political parties, born-again fascists and criminal sub-classes gradually evolving into political terrorists, these welded the new alliance of the Right destined to torment Italy for years to come. The result, as immensely popular anti-establishment Italian satirist Beppe Grillo often says, is the curse of 'pretend democracy,' a society of rising tensions locked up in a pressure cooker.

In April 1947, after fitful explosions, Sicily's brooding political volcano finally erupted, leading to street fighting between communists and Mafia gunmen over the issue of a separate Sicilian republic. The Mafia hankered for independence as a way of finally cementing their power, while the Left opposed it as an affront to Italian unity and the historic legacy of Garibaldi rooted in Sicily. Organised crime ran into a formidable opponent, the charismatic Girolamo Li Causi, a Sicilian-born communist. He returned to the island from years of exile with orders to stir up a mild revolution, centring mainly on redistribution of feudal land holdings. His words, 'we plan no Soviet rule here,' cut no ice with the mob and the propertied classes, but revitalised the deep longings of the landless poor for social justice. A rather astounding reverse now occurred. The Left, never previously strong in the Sicilian fold, rocketed out of nowhere to the seat of power. All Italy was stunned by provincial elections which saw the popular front of communists and socialists win a resounding victory, pushing the Mafia-backed Christian Democrats into humiliating second place. Reverberations echoed from Sicily to Rome and across the Atlantic. With national elections scheduled for the following year, the Left's triumph in Sicily beckoned the American nightmare of a coalition coming to power led by Palmiro Togliatti, the communist leader who sat out the war under the hospitality of the Kremlin.

The Sicilian result jolted the bedrock of the Italian political system, the power of the Catholic Church, the Vatican's political allies and their acolytes in the honourable society. Moreover, it was a direct affront to the American campaign to ensure that Italians who did not fully share the ideology of the United States would not be allowed to elect a government. The reckoning was not long in coming. As May Day dawned a few days after these electoral convulsions, Salvatore Giuliano performed the first authentic prototype of the forthcoming Gladio atrocities (aside from the Syntagma Square massacre, Athens, in December 1944: see Chapter VII). Prominent Left wingers led by Li Causi were due to address an ecstatic crowd of supporters gathering in a mountain pasture, the Portella della Ginestra near Palermo, a customary location for May Day gatherings. Giuliano, accompanied by his second in command, his diminutive cousin Gaspare Pisciotta, purportedly opened fire at around ten o'clock in the morning. In the ensuing bloodbath, eleven people were killed, including four children. Two of them were small boys, just seven years old. Another thirty-three were wounded, including a little girl whose jaw was blown off. But other accounts pointed to other shots fired by expert marksmen from surrounding hills. In this scenario, Giuliano is the unwitting patsy, the fall guy, who in any case insisted his men 'obeyed instructions' by firing into the air. So who gave the order to shoot at the gathering throng?

The finger of suspicion pointed to another Sicilian, the pugnacious interior minister Mario Scelba, whose insistence there was no political motive behind the massacre provoked a huge brawl involving two hundred members of the Chamber of Deputies in Rome. Giuliano accused a coalition of leading monarchists, fascists and of course the always-honourable family, of putting him up to it. The only element missing was military intelligence, whose presence in the background Giuliano did not understand. A listless trial took place of some of these alleged conspirators. All the charges were thrown out. Giuliano was isolated, having served his purpose.

He quickly discovered his own carefully-cultivated image blasted to fragments. The alliance of fascists, the Mafia and powerful Christian Democrats like Scelba who led him on, now turned their backs. He was reduced to a shunned outlaw, trying vainly to keep his spirits up by taunting the Carabinieri with boastful letters, or dining around Palermo leaving cheeky notes about his presence, the quality of the food and his culinary advice to the chefs. But his men were drifting away. In the summer of 1949, remnants of the dwindling gang were blamed for a purposeless ambush on a police convoy just outside Palermo, in which seven officers died. This could have been a false-flag attack carried out (or allowed to happen) by Italian military intelligence. A year later, Giuliano himself was dead, allegedly shot on 5th July 1950 by his cousin Gaspare Pisciotta for a generous contract payment. Pisciotta (a slightly vulgar-sounding name in Italian) had little time to enjoy his reward. He too was betrayed, imprisoned for the Palermo massacre, and four years later quietly liquidated in his prison cell with a dose of strychnine in his morning coffee. At fresh elections for the island government in the wake of the bloodbath, the Christian Democratic Party scored a thumping victory. Yet, smarting at the presence of communist and socialist ministers in the provisional national government voted in a year before, the US froze all loans to the war-torn country, while pumping millions of dollars into the coffers of the Christian Democrats. American diplomats in Rome whispered to sympathetic reporters that the communists were funded by 'black bags' of money doled out from the back doors of the Soviet embassy, while privately the CIA would boast for years to come it bought every election in Italy since the war.

The Left's near triumph in Sicily tipped the US into paranoia. In the closing weeks of the 1948 election campaign, *Time* magazine inflated a Leftist victory as the 'the brink of catastrophe.' 'It was primarily this fear,' Bill Colby was to later admit, 'that had led to the creation of the Office of Policy Coordination, which gave the CIA the capability to undertake covert political, propaganda, and paramilitary operations in the first place.' 'Wild Bill' Donovan, legendary trench charger of WW1 and wartime head of the OSS — dismissed by the late FDR as a wild loose cannon — solemnly warned Italians that 'under a communist dictatorship in Italy, the nation's industrial plants would be dismantled and shipped off to Russia along with millions of Italian workers who would be turned into slave labourers.' President Truman, baited by Republicans for going soft on communism, accused the USSR, America's late wartime ally, of plotting the total subjugation of Western Europe. *Time* echoed the media war-drums from the run-up to the Spanish American War, demanding universal military training and resumption of military conscription to forestall 'threatened communist control and police-state rule.' An edition widely circulated in Italy shortly before the 1948 election raised the temperature: The 'US should make it clear that it will use force, if necessary, to prevent Italy from going communist.' American and British warships were already anchored in all the chief ports. Washington cynically promised Italians the recovery of their lost colonies in Ethiopia and Libya, when their liberation had been one of the Allies' proclaimed war aims. The bulk of Italians were concerned about work, poverty and hungry children. To hell with rotting dreams of empire.

The barrage of cynical deception rolled on. President Truman chose a month before election day to make a 'gift' of 29 merchant ships to the Italian government as a 'gesture of friendship and confidence in a democratic Italy,' failing to mention they were actually Italian vessels seized by the United States during the war. Trains decked out in Italian colours chuffed around the country, showering 'gifts of the American people' at every station. It was left to the agnostic CBS reporter Howard K. Smith to observe that the virtually-bankrupt Soviets had little in the way of spare resources to compete with such a tidal wave of largesse. Their hands were, in any event, more than full holding down the Eastern European colonies they were so freely granted by Churchill and Roosevelt at Yalta and Tehran. Moscow tendered a few feeble gestures — a handful of Italian war prisoners were released — but to all intents the Kremlin had no stomach or resources for this struggle, and largely abandoned the Italian communist party to its own devices.

The Sicilian episodes are insufficiently remarked by students of the Cold War as an important composition in a wider web of deception. The electoral threat, to the largest extent, did not exist, but the fear of insidious subversion ate like acid at minds in Washington. America was inexperienced in the European political cosmos, which invariably required coalitions and governments of compromise, quite unfathomable in the American context. In Sicily, even if he had been left in peace to govern, Girolamo Li Causi controlled only a third of the seats in the provincial parliament. It is true that in the 1948 nationwide elections, the communist vote actually shot up as a result of mass defections from orthodox socialists. Yet Togliatti, had he become prime minister, would have found his arms roughly twisted behind his back by the Christian Democrats. The May Day massacre in Palermo achieved its strategic purpose of turning back the red tide and returning political power in Sicily to those who saw themselves as the rightful owners. In the black pantheon of Gladio, Giuliano stands out as the figure identified with the very first shots in the years of lead. Propaganda of the Deed had spoken with exquisite precision.

As for Salvatore Giuliano, his restless unquiet spirit continues to roam his old haunts. The romantics like to insist that the bullet-riddled body found one morning in a yard in the dusty poor city of Castelvetrano, in the far south west of Sicily, was not his at all. Instead, it was said that he fled in heavy disguise to Tunisia and then made his way to America. There he purportedly basked in the mists of obscurity, which scarcely matches the outsize reputation and legacy of the Sicilian Robin Hood. It is certainly true that the circumstances of Giuliano's death are clouded with confusion and mystery. No precise account of how he came to be murdered and by whom has yet been tendered. In some ways, it seems a curiously appropriate epitaph.

V.
God's Terrorist: Yves Guérin-Sérac and the Press Gang

'We acted against the communists and against the bourgeois state, against the democracy which deprived us from our liberty, and thus we had to use violence.'
—Yves Guérin-Sérac[26]

If any man could be fairly described as a perverted philosophical terrorist, the claim surely rests with a man of extraordinary devotion to the revival of modern fascism. Lean, wiry veteran of France's Indo-Chinese wars, icy-minded and gifted organiser, brutal and ruthless terrorist, Yves Guérin-Sérac believed in his personal direct line to God. He obediently bowed his head to the chalice at Sunday Mass, secure in the conviction the Almighty perfectly understood why he just blew up a bank full of Italians performing their modest daily transactions. It was all part of the Creator's Great Plan. He was at war with the vacuous, bourgeois state, and could therefore deploy the same logic and arguments as Vladimir Ilyich Lenin, Leon Trotsky and scores of anarchists from bygone days. In 1962, the NATO-inspired plots to kill de Gaulle failing one after another, and his own role in them only too obvious, Guérin-Sérac was left with no alternative except to beat a sharp exit.

> *After the OAS I fled to Portugal to carry on the fight and expand it to its proper dimensions, which is to say a planetary dimension. During this period we systematically established close contacts with like-minded groups emerging in Italy, Belgium, Germany, Spain and Portugal, for the purpose of forming the kernel of a truly western league of struggle against Marxism.*[NI]

Taken together, it was the primacy of 'order and tradition' which composed the sole love interest in his life. As a captive on the couch, Guérin-Sérac might offer intriguing insights into the mind of the Christian terrorist. He spent his life in thrall to a new Black Empire, which he dreamed would combine the universal divinity of the Roman church with the United States and Europe, as successor to the Holy Roman Empire. Not quite the image of James Burnham, but rather close. Such precepts are often attributed to clerical or Christian fascism. Guérin-Sérac foreshadowed modern neo-conservatives, with his firm defence of property rights and inheritance, of public order and tradition, and his insistence on religion — the absolute

---

[26] One of his several *noms de plume*, or *noms de guerre*. He was born plain Yves Galliou, in the province of Brittany on the French Atlantic coast in 1926.

infallibility of the Catholic church — as the ordained arbiter of all public morals and wisdom. He could brush aside his associations and everyday dealings with gangsters and thugs, in the same terms as Richard Holbrooke's glorious compact with Lucifer. Yet there is something strangely curious to his make-up, a certain other-worldliness, essential quality as that may be to a dedicated and professional killer like himself. He appears to be exactly what the Russian-born libertarian writer and thinker Ayn Rand had in mind when she idolised serial killers as the 'ideal man,' a superior form of humanity refusing to be bound by the constraints and dull mores of society. Rand, who was particularly fascinated by one legendary American multiple murderer, wrote: 'Other people do not exist for him, and he does not see why they should.' It seems a fitting memoriam transferred to Guérin-Sérac.

His extraordinary career reads like an entry in the Black Who's Who: war hero, Algerian rebel, agent provocateur, assassin, bomber, intelligence agent, Messianic Catholic and intellectual grandmaster behind the Strategy of Tension. He belonged to several old gangs, including the first generation of ex-Nazis and fascists seeking refuge in Spain, Portugal and Latin America. Another was the veteran clan of French officers blooded in the Indo-Chinese and Korean struggles. This ferociously daring and aggressive officer, fanatical anti-communist hero of the French Army's 11th specialist shock parachute brigade in Indo-China, later arrived in Algeria. The French colony was in the throes of the violent struggle for independence from France. He joined the CIA-sponsored OAS (*L'Organisation armée secrète*) composed of disaffected French officers, with bonds to units of the French secret army organisations. The Algerian episode and its consequences for de Gaulle belong in the following chapter. But here is an appropriate point to remark that Christian Fascism exerted a powerful influence on the Algerian plotters, and also those who resorted to bomb and gun against de Gaulle.

The Christian Fascists in whose circles Guérin-Sérac moved boasted their own chaplain, Father Georges Grasset, an inspiration for the Vatican's ratlines smuggling refugees from the Algerian rising to Portugal and Spain. He was a prominent acolyte of Jean Ousset (1919-1994), the Portuguese-born founder of his own Christian Fascist sect known as *La Cité Catholique*. Guérin-Sérac was an early recruit, and in due course had pressing need of the reverend father's specialised travel agency. Ousset specialised in a distinctly unusual catechism, which combined fierce emotional piety with counter-revolutionary warfare techniques and trusty methods of torture to extract confessions. Portugal, Guérin-Sérac's chosen bolt-hole, was the sole dictatorship formally admitted to an alliance dedicated to the spread and defence of democracy. (Spain was not admitted to NATO until 1982, seven years after Franco died, while Portugal was a founding member in 1949). Moreover, the ease and facility of working with his NATO secret army counterparts led him to Lisbon rather than Madrid, as the base point for the next stage of his relentless crusade against communism. That Portugal's coastal flanks overlooked Atlantic and Mediterranean sea lanes spoke far louder than the absence of free elections and civil liberties, or jails filled with opponents of the fascist regime, at home and among scattered Portuguese dominions overseas. The determination of long-standing dictator António de Oliveira Salazar to cling to the empire, despite the historic 'winds of change' detected by the British prime minister Harold Macmillan during his historic visit to Afrikaner-ruled South Africa in 1960, struck a firm supportive chord with the CIA. The wave of African national liberation fronts proclaiming a socialist platform dismayed the United States, which viewed the huge continent as an important new front of the Cold War. There were increasing fears in Washington about Portugal itself. Despite lavish CIA bankrolling of the counter-insurgency programmes of PIDE, the Portuguese secret service, simmering opposition was starting to make Europe's oldest dictatorship (established 1933) look decidedly shaky. Nagging problems with President de Gaulle in France and the communists in Italy might all too easily infect this crucial NATO dependency.

Guérin-Sérac arrived in Lisbon early in 1966 with an inspirational blueprint for the next stage of the struggle against godless liberalism. He proposed to exploit the hospitality of the Portuguese authorities by establishing an organisation that would act as nothing less than an international travel agency for terrorists. The principal funding was supplied by the CIA, according to the Pellegrino Commission, established in 1995 by the Italian Senate to investigate the *anni di piombo*. Guido Salvini was the magistrate appointed to examine the 1969 bombing of the agricultural bank in Milan's Piazza Fontana. He pinned the blame firmly on Guérin-Sérac's Aginter Press. Salvini told the senators that Aginter operatives were active in Italy from 1967 onwards, instructing local militant neo-fascist organisations in the use of explosives.[N2] From this nugget, the CIA is positively connected to the Gladio wave of terrorism sweeping Europe.

On the surface, Aginter Press was a straightforward media co-operative, although its motto 'order and tradition' seemed rather odd to those who were not in the know concerning the real nature of its activities. Behind the plain business shopfront lay an invisible network designed to shuttle terrorists around Europe, Latin America and Africa, providing false documents and passports for killers posing as reporters and photographers, including Guérin-Sérac. He took it upon himself to modernise and redefine the precepts of Propaganda of the Deed, which of course connects him directly to the great lions of anarchism in the 19th century, notably Errico Malatesta and Johann Most. For all his religiosity, Guérin-Sérac was foremost an inspired clerical anarchist bent on demolishing and thus purifying the state. In what might aptly be described as his 'First Commandment,' he wrote:

Our belief is that the first phase of political activity ought to be to create the conditions favouring the installation of chaos in all of the regime's structures. In our view the first move we should make is to destroy the structure of the democratic state under the cover of Communist and pro-Chinese activities... at the same time we must raise up a defender of the citizenry against the disintegration brought about by terrorism and subversion.

Obviously we will have to tailor our actions to the ethos of the milieu — propaganda and action of a sort which will seem to have emanated from our Communist adversaries. [These operations] will create a feeling of hostility towards those who threaten the peace of each and every nation. [i.e. the Left].[N3]

Many innocents were destined to suffer or perish in the name of the subsequent 'western struggle against Marxism.' The states on which he proposed to unleash his ruthless brand of synthetic terror were not perceivably under any substantive communist threat, nor likely to be. But here was the fate of those who flirted with forces of the Left.

In the first phase of our political activity we must create chaos in all structures of the regime. Two forms of terrorism can provoke such a situation: the blind terrorism (committing massacres indiscriminately which cause a large number of victims), and the selective terrorism (eliminate chosen persons).

This destruction of the state must be carried out as much as possible under the cover of 'communist activities.' After that, we must intervene at the heart of the military, the juridical power and the church, in order to influence popular opinion, suggest a solution, and clearly demonstrate the weakness of the present legal apparatus. Popular opinion must be polarised in such a way, that we are being presented as the only instrument capable of saving the nation.[N4]

An analysis picked out in such brutally cold and emotionless language permits us to understand what kind of world 'God's Terrorist' was striving for. It was his perfect idealism in which anarchic and random violence unhinges the state to the extent it cannot survive, thus bringing about a new global authoritarian order. Just as the wild Johann Most was closer to Marx than he wished to admit, so in turn Guérin-Sérac owed much to Most and Malatesta and for that matter, Robespierre, Trotsky and Lenin. Guérin-Sérac regarded terror as an instrument of cleansing, a Trotsky-Leninist means to an end, which also made him a kind of terrorist in the image of Robespierre.[27]

---

[27] I might enter another claim of association, with his countryman the notorious Marquis de Sade (1740-1815). The Marquis is best known for his hyper-erotic sexual fantasies, which were intended to shock ossified French society. His hyper-erotic

Thus, when he led a small band to blow up the Banca Nazionale dell'Agricoltura in Milan's Piazza di Fontana on 12th December 1969, he was committing a revolutionary act of precisely the kind that Ayn Rand so freely eulogised. Quite simply, for Guérin-Sérac the dead and injured of that infamous day did not exist in any meaningful way. He clinically defined terrorism as a system of brutal social conditioning. There his shadow is long. Every terrorist act in the modern cycle since 9/11 has been exploited as an excuse for draconian reductions of personal liberties and freedoms. Where Guérin-Sérac's thinking obviously breaks company with the evolutionary line of anarchism and inverted socialism is the erection of a Christian Fascist state on the ruins of a despised bourgeois liberal order.

Aginter had other specialised departments under its roof. It was a Gladio finishing school, where recruits to the secret armies from all over Europe were trained in the arts of bomb making, assassination, psychological operations, destabilisation and counter-insurgency. Much of this was borrowed from the textbooks of the US Army's centre for covert warfare at Ford Bragg. Guest instructors from time to time included members of Britain's SAS, the Green Berets and figures in the mould of Guérin-Sérac himself, French Army officers turned mercenaries. Its graduates read like scrolls from the Gladio hall of fame, featuring the most illustrious members of the Italian Gladio/P2 establishment, and notably that ubiquitous Italian who crops up in so many episodes of the *anni di piombo*. Stefano Delle Chiaie was accused of complicity in the Piazza di Fontana atrocity, hauled back from self-imposed exile in South America, and put on trial. His legendary Houdini-like qualities when it came to brushes with the courts ensured that he was acquitted after the usual convoluted Italian legal proceedings. For all that, he was now indelibly associated with an act generally regarded as the Gladio declaration of war, the beginning of the years of lead. At any rate, if Guérin-Sérac was the driving intellect behind Gladio, then 'Shorty' (in reference to his stature) Delle Chiaie was the chief operations officer. He explained his duties and responsibilities in the following terms, leaving little space for the humblest kinship with humanity:

> *We acted against the communists and against the bourgeois state, against the democracy which deprived us of our liberty, and thus we had to use violence. We were considered to be criminals but we were victims of a militant anti-fascist liberal movement.*[N5]

As though he were a busy consultant called in to routinely advise on fixing up the railways or make the telephones work properly, Guérin-Sérac was blithely summoned to next-door Spain to organise the death squads

---

works disguised his commitment to revolution and change. Guérin-Sérac's appetite for violence is de Sade's pornography transposed.

crushing resistance to the Franco regime. Aginter activities have been traced to all those countries where the Strategy of Tension operated at peak volume: Turkey, Greece, Cyprus, Italy, Germany and Belgium. In Belgium, Aginter wore a cloak of respectability, co-operating with a local news magazine to smuggle agents into the country, by no co-incidence as the country exploded with its own violent years of lead.[N6]

It was two-way traffic. A curious insight occurred in 1977, in the twilight years following the collapse of the Salazar and Franco regimes and the eviction of Aginter from Portugal. Spanish police picked up Jorge Cesarsky of Argentina's Right-wing terror organisation Triple A, and Carlos Perez, a Miami-based Cuban exile. They were wanted for a string of murders of young Spanish Leftists in a campaign bearing a strong resemblance to the Strategy of Tension. According to the Spanish daily *El País,* this export trade of Cuban exiles pointed to the significance of a terrorist hub established in Miami, home, as the newspaper explained, of the 'newly created Fascist International.' It requires no stretch of the imagination to regard Miami as the new base headquarters of the re-located Aginter operation. Firm evidence supporting that conclusion will appear in a moment.

The establishment of a global fascist network was Guérin-Sérac's keenest, most burning ambition, to which Aginter was the springboard. Around the world, at different times and locations, other elements of the structure were dropping into place, amounting to an evolving 'ring of containment' that even George Frost Kennan might have admired at one stage of his life. In 1966, a significant (and lasting) development occurred, namely the establishment in Taiwan — following on plans laid earlier in the South Korean capital, Seoul — of the CIA-sponsored World Anti-Communist League (WACL). The organisation arose from a previous regional effort, the Asian Peoples' Anti-Bolshevik League, sponsored by the Chinese Nationalist Kuomintang regime. Financial backers of the new anti-communist world ring included ravenous cash-hungry Korean cult tycoon Sun Myung Moon, whose recruitment methods and renowned mass nuptials uncannily mirrored certain CIA experiments in brainwashing. The tentacles of this sprawling octopus eventually extended to all corners of the planet. This was visibly the Fascist International, the huge global Gladio, for which Guérin-Sérac's heart yearned. It was charged with the pure Guérin-Sérac brief to 'overcome and eliminate' any governments or forces considered sympathetic to communism. The means were not precisely specified, save for talking about warfare in psychologically political terms. Yet WACL was tracked to Operation Condor, death squads in Latin America and the Iberian Peninsula, the twin Kennedy assassinations and general oiling of Iran-Contra in life-after-death mode. So, it would not be surprising to discover WACL fingerprints thickly plastered all over The Enterprise of drug and arms dealing in its latter-day formation. In Europe, WACL was tied up with various neo-fascist fronts, particularly Licio Gelli's P2/Gladio activities, in Italy as well as South America. The 'liquidations' of both Aldo Moro (communist fraterniser) and Olof Palme (Iran-Iraq meddler, irritating Palestine interloper) have been cited as promoted in some degree by WACL.

The WACL was an excellent vehicle for having a great deal of important work performed for the CIA by remote control and off the balance sheet by an organisation which raised its own funds, presenting itself to the world as a charitable body dedicated to freedom and democracy. (The name was changed to World League for Freedom and Democracy after the fall of communism.) Borrowing an earlier cue from Ganser, we can say 'beautiful,' if morally disturbing. WACL was the hub with spokes leading to many important subsidiary operations. Not the least of these was the Paladin Group, a CIA guns-for-hire outfit initiated by the former *Waffen-SS Obersturmbannführer* Otto Skorzeny in 1970. By now he occupied an eyrie in Madrid, working alongside one of Guérin-Sérac's chief sidekicks, his old OAS compatriot Jean-Denis Raingeard. Paladin had ties from the outset to Aginter and the World Anti-Communist League.

Daredevil Viennese-born Skorzeny, holder of the Iron Cross and extremely proud of his obligatory duelling scar, sleek mane and flashy film star looks, led the glider team which plucked the imprisoned Mussolini from a hotel close to the summit of the almost three-kilometre-high Gran Sasso ('the great stone') in the Italian Apennines. He also confabulated a vastly exaggerated legend about himself as mastermind of the Odessa first-aid club for fugitive Nazis. Skorzeny's proneness to self-inflation led the French news magazine *Le Nouvel Observateur* to describe his activities in September 1974 as a 'strange temporary work agency of mercenaries' belonging in the same vein as Aginter. So, the skeletal form of Aginter appears yet again. Skorzeny was also the brains behind another misty syndicate, loosely grouped under a house front called Arms Co, in close alliance with Franco's secret service organisations and the CIA. It facilitated the illegal shipment of weapons, notably to countries such as Gaddafi's Libya, that were supposedly under international interdiction.

Without doubt, some of the finest insights into this fathomless dark universe were captured by a certain Danish investigative journalist who dedicated years to the task. Henrik Krüger is not a name prominently associated with the CIA's history of conspiracies and black ops around the world, and yet he should be up in bright lights. Krüger, globe-trotting international correspondent for the Copenhagen daily *Politiken*, published an extraordinary book in 1980, exposing CIA-sponsored international fascism as a vital conduit of the CIA's various private empires spiriting drugs around the globe.[N7] He fixed its nerve centre in the sunshine state of Florida. Miami was an international junction and all-purpose clearing house for the agency's hugely lucrative narcotics rackets and much else besides, including international terrorism. The tireless Krüger was the first to expose the wiring connecting political terrorists, crime dons and US espionage, 'yet the significance of Miami in the netherworld of international fascism remains one of America's better kept secrets.' Its tendrils stretched across the Atlantic to the Aginter operation, originally in Lisbon, and Skorzeny quietly sitting in Madrid at the centre of his arms smuggling web. To Krüger, the Miami-Lisbon-Madrid-Rome axis was the logical continuation of the CIA's record in forging alliances with high Nazi officials, notably General Reinhard Gehlen, Hitler's spy chief on the Russian Front, who became West Germany's first intelligence chief in 1947. American historian Carl Oglesby wrote: 'Everything after this [Gehlen] was just a consequence of this merger.'[N8] He could have said exactly the same of the North Atlantic Treaty Organisation, which by now had been led by the nose into the same network of black alliances. Paladin was located in a plain Madrid office block shared with the Spanish intelligence agency CESID and the CIA. Before Skorzeny died in 1975, he willed Paladin to its chief operations director, former right hand of Goebbels (and one of Gehlen's important SS refugees) Gerhard Hartmut von Schubert, who proudly boasted 'we have many qualified experts in many missions all over the world.' Paladin's bureau in Zurich was the contact point for undercover deals with Swiss arms firms. Conveniently, there was office space for the CIA-sponsored corporate twins, Permindex and the World Trading Centre (aka *Centro Mondiale Commerciale*). Both, as we shall see, were linked to assassination attempts on de Gaulle.

From Miami, that trail swung south to Latin America, and then eastwards across the Atlantic to Africa. Another vital prop of the Aginter operation was the Gauloises-chain-smoking mercenary and OAS adventurer Jean-Eugene Paul Kay, whose glamorous magnetism over women belied the fact he also held the keys to the French Connection. The 'pirate with a heart,' as he was once described by *Paris Match,* worked closely to the instructions of the man known as 'Monsieur Afrique' — Jacques Foccart, chief administrator of French West Africa — scooting around the former colonies staging a series of coups-to-order. He was also featured in other post-colonial struggles including the first Yemeni civil war, the attempt to prise oil-rich Biafra from Nigeria, and the long, drawn-out miseries of Lebanon. These were all CIA sideshows. Some called him the Right's answer to Che Guevara who, in later years, Kay peculiarly grew to resemble.

The Portuguese dictator, the ageing António de Oliveira Salazar, turned up his collar against the 'wind of change' because, like the CIA, he feared a surge tide of communism. Guérin-Sérac's press gang was behind the assassination of the renegade Portuguese General Humberto Delgado, gunned down in the border town of Olivenza on 13th February 1965. Next to go was Eduardo Mondlane, charismatic leader of the Frelimo independence movement, because he posed an increasing threat to Portuguese rule in the east African colony of Mozambique. He was a beacon for millions of young Africans all over the continent, drawn to liberation and empowerment. The tall and handsome scholar loved the bookish academic world he gave up just six years before. What followed proved that his enemies knew their man all too well. He was killed on 3rd February 1969, probably by an Aginter-devised booby trap mailed in a book, which exploded in his face at an American friend's villa in the Tanzanian capital of Dar-es-Salaam. The bomb set off another explosion, a brutal civil war from which the country has never recovered, while the CIA stealthily constructed a massive surveillance and espionage operation covering the whole of East Africa. The 'last enemy' Amilcar Cabral, mulatto leader of the freedom movement in the strategically interesting archipelago of Guinea-Bissau and Cape Verde, probably signed his own death sentence in Havana in 1966 when he declared:

We the peoples of the countries of Africa, still completely dominated by Portuguese colonialism, are prepared to send to Cuba as many men and women as may be needed to compensate for the departure of those who for reasons of class or of inability to adapt have interests or attitudes which are incompatible with the interests of the Cuban people.

Cabral could not be trusted with a clutch of gale-battered islands that happened to offer an almost-perfect haven for submarines cruising the Atlantic. He was assassinated, allegedly by PIDE agents (but quite probably by Guérin-Sérac's death squad) on 20th January 1973, just before his movement unilaterally declared independence.

Across the African continent — turbulent, teeming and undisciplined, a babble of a thousand confusing tongues — the disastrous unwinding of colonialism was a sideshow compared to America's problems in its own Latinised south. There Aginter was destined to play a command performance. In 1963, the CIA provoked a series of three revolutions, in Honduras, the Dominican Republic, and Guatemala. The Guatemalan business was grisly, involving the deaths of some 50,000 civilians in the tiny banana republic. Aginter people were involved in all these operations, but especially Guatemala, where a laconic, drawling American called Jay Sablonsky came to prominence. He was sometimes just plain Jay Salby, or Hugh C. Franklin (on his Aginter-forged Guatemalan passport). Supposedly a businessman hailing from Philadelphia, he was actually the third member of the triumvirate who controlled Aginter. The Scottish anarchist Stuart Christie, renowned for attempting while yet a teenager in 1964 to blow up Generalissimo Franco, believes he may have crossed paths with Sablonsky, when the two found themselves in the same Spanish hospital. But there was something else rather curious about this middle 30s, stubble-chinned Clint

Eastwood look-alike. A string of loyalties at various times connected this roaming hero of Gladio to the US Army's infamous School of the Americas at Fort Benning, Georgia, the Bay Biscayne waterfront boys in Miami, the CIA and the OAS.

By 1973, the goal of nailing down Latin America seemed tantalisingly close. Guérin-Sérac's Fascist International iron circle acquired additional tangible form in 1975, when an exclusive club of six Latin American dictators met in conclave, and created Operation Condor with the aim of crushing all resistance. Some key facilities, such as the radio communications hub at the US Army's Southern Command HQ in Miami, were lent out to tyrannical secret police units who ran the Condor death machine on a day-to-day basis. Condor was stiffened with OAS survivors. Reinforcements arrived in the early '70s, among them P2 puppet master Licio Gelli, who laid the foundations for long-running connections between P2 and the South American clique of grisly fascist dictators.

In 2004, the award-winning French investigative journalist and Latin America veteran Marie-Monique Robin wrote a book, supported by a television documentary, based on previously-unknown archives in the Quai D'Orsay (the French foreign ministry). These told the story that virtually all French experience gained in the Algerian war — torture, brutalities of every merciless kind, ruthless repression of civilians and agitators — was transferred intact to Latin America. Moreover, a permanent French military colony of officers schooled and hardened in Algeria was secretly housed in the Argentine version of the Pentagon. Almost to a man they were ex-OAS veterans. Grasset, 'chaplain of the OAS,' led an advance party to Buenos Aires in 1962, where he immediately established a local chapter of La Cité Catholique, ministering to the souls of the exiled OAS fugitives, while receiving a warm welcome from the local ecclesiastical nobility. Grasset enjoyed some impeccable connections. These featured Jean Gardes — the French army's psychological warfare expert so greatly admired by General Lemnitzer, and backbone of the French Gladio operation — and Bertrand Renouvin (another *cher ami* of Guérin-Sérac), who relaunched the old Far Right front called Action Française after WW2.

Once this public airing began, some important questions were answered, and even more intriguing ones arose. Robinexplained where many old OAS people had gone. Their banishment effectively ceased with the death of de Gaulle, and the French army welcomed home its own, so to speak. This certainly included Captain Yves Guérin-Sérac, whose enthusiastic attachment to the dirty war in South America began with his effective expulsion from Lisbon after the fall of the Salazar regime in 1974. Aginter's services as a valuable counterfeit press agency could no longer operate from the old address, but remained available to assist the trans-Atlantic 'executives of terror' from a new location. Robin's ferreting traced the links to the morbid La Cité Catholique, whose advocacy of torture and brainwashing were bound to go down well in the South American climate. Robin laid bare the longevity of OAS influence over the French state, and how it was capable of successive transformations. And she added another layer of confirmation to Henrik Krüger's 'third leg of the stool' resting in Miami. Krüger questioned if it was a coincidence so many known European fascists and their assorted criminal *confrères* were paying homage in Miami, either before or just after some major operations. The guest list included Kay, Raingeard, Guérin-Sérac, the diminutive Stefano Delle Chiaie, and many more, but significantly most of them with some bearing on Aginter or Skorzeny's Spanish tango. Krüger's brilliantly-aimed dart was the revelation that Miami acted as 'a milieu for many fraternising interests' with a larger objective. A hard-nosed foreign correspondent roaming the globe's hottest spots for some ten years unearthed far more than any of his American (or European) counterparts. He drew into his narrative the Bay of Pigs disaster, numerous conspiracies to assassinate Castro and the JFK murder, plus the terror campaign waged against Cuban exiles in Florida that uncannily mimicked Lemnitzer's infamous Northwoods lunacy. In a wealth of rich and masterly detail, he connected French intelligence, the OAS, the Corsican Mafia controlling the port of Marseilles on behalf of the CIA, the murder of the Moroccan so-called 'Third World travelling salesman' Ben Barka in Paris, the Nixon family and their links to fugitive fraudster Robert Lee Vesco, not leaving out the extraordinary story of how the CIA infiltrated and subsumed the Drugs Enforcement Administration (DEA) right across Latin America.

Krüger, whose work demands serious re-examination, diagnosed the existence of a 'European fascist network' steeped in terrorism to swing public opinion towards forces of the Right. He placed his finger squarely on Gladio a good ten years before it was exposed to the world. He also placed Aginter at the heart of the entire operation, as well as tracking the movements of its operatives around the globe. He spotted and described 'narco-terrorism' a full decade before the term was in common usage. *The Great Heroin Coup* is a stunning work largely ignored by mainstream media and commentators because the book was one of a kind, raising issues difficult to grasp. There was widespread unwillingness to row against established orthodoxies. Coming from a small off-radar country and producing the first edition in Danish were further obstacles to gaining wider recognition. But the fact remains: *The Great Heroin Coup* has withstood the test of time as a Rosetta Stone decoding a massive international conspiracy. It was the era dominated by Reagan's Evil Empire speech and Star Wars, the peak of the Cold War itself. Against that unpromising background, Krüger's finest achievement was to understand the real threat to democratic order lay in the renaissance of international fascism in cohorts with organised crime, at the behest of the United States and her allies in the western world.

In 1981, after so many years of plotting and struggles with his great rival Charles de Gaulle, François Mitterrand, the inscrutable Sphinx of French politics, rose to his life's ambition. He at last received the keys of the Élysée Palace, and naturally began to shower favours on all the good people who helped him on his way. One of these was the grand veteran mercenary Yves Guérin-Sérac. The services he rendered to the complex conspirator Mitterrand may only be guessed. But they were quite sufficient, during the fourteen years this fifth son of a provincial stationmaster occupied the presidency, to gain promotion to colonel, with enhanced pension. The following chapter describes Mitterrand's enduring enmity for Charles de Gaulle, who responded with equal quantities of vitriol. The honours received suggest, at the very least, that Guérin-Sérac was involved in plots to kill the president, either as planner or direct participant. Certainly he is the only known survivor from the ranks of L'Organisation armée secrète to receive what amounts to a presidential pardon. Colonel Yves Guérin-Sérac finally retired to his native Brittany, and would now be in his mid-eighties, if still alive. Enquiries indicate that he is, but maintains a diplomatic Trappist silence. After all, what is there to say? His acts have all been vindicated. He must survey the world scene with quiet satisfaction, now that the Black Global Order for which he plotted, bombed and killed is at last at hand.

VI.
One Last French Kiss

'President François Mitterrand travelled to central France today to attend the funeral of an old friend and long-time aide who shot himself in the Élysée Palace last week, but the mystery of what prompted François de Grossouvre to take his life remains unresolved.' — New York Times, April 1994

The death — or murder — within the precincts of the presidential palace set off a political earthquake around the tottering regime of François Mitterrand, the renowned escapologist of French politics. François de Grossouvre, 76-year-old aristocrat found slumped at his desk on 7th April 1994, with two bullet holes drilled in his temple, was a fading old retainer in the Gothic court of France's nominally socialist president. He was long celebrated as 'the man in the shadows' for his links to the French military-espionage complex, and guardian of uncomfortable truths concerning Mitterrand's much air-brushed past as collaborator and sympathiser with the extremist pre-war Far Right. He was also the man who knew too much about the sitting president's role in serial attempts to kill Général Charles André Joseph Pierre-Marie de Gaulle some thirty years before.

Grossouvre was estranged from his old boss Mitterrand, whose inscrutable visage was known to everyone in France as *Le Sphinx*. The media obligingly spun the cover story that he committed suicide from an 'aching sense of loss.' The small difficulty was that slugs fired by the pistol which sent him to eternity appeared not to perfectly match the revolver, a point 357 Magnum he was still gripping in one hand. Another curiosity was exactly how he managed to score two shots to his own head. There was talk, gulped down by the newspapers, of an 'indecipherable message,' manic depression, signs of weariness and yearning to leave this world. When he did — voluntarily or otherwise — he carried off many useful secrets. The man of the shadows was former commandant in chief of the French stay-behind army, who began his secret military career as officer in charge of *Arc-en-Ciel* — the Rainbow — based in Lyon. He was privy to Mitterrand's personal decision to sink the Greenpeace yacht *Rainbow Warrior* in Auckland harbour, New Zealand, on 10th July 1985. And he knew exactly why Mitterrand sanctified Yves Guérin-Sérac, the most fanatical terrorist in contemporary French history. In the course of a long life as a wealthy businessman, media magnate, counsellor of state, agent for French external intelligence SDECE and the CIA, the lean-framed, bearded aristocrat managed to find time to father six children. But he was really married to his lifelong *muse en chef*, François Mitterrand.

In the course of his confusing wandering through the landscape of French politics, Mitterrand earned many enemies, but none so powerful or enduring as Charles de Gaulle. Today, Mitterrand is regarded by turns as an unscrupulous Machiavellian schemer, or as de Gaulle's natural successor. Both are equally defensible. The general however regarded the little man from Charente (in south-western France) as a shabby turncoat stained by his confusing behaviour under the Pétain regime, not to mention a serial confabulator concerning his true role in the wartime resistance to the German invaders. For his part Mitterrand could never shake off visceral jealousy of de Gaulle's political ascendancy, nor his bitterness at de Gaulle's constant sniping at his doubtful past. The result was a lasting personal enmity in which Mitterrand — he who would be king but for the legacy of his foggy political background — aligned himself with dark forces bent on violently terminating the pestilential general.

When de Gaulle returned to power in May 1958, amid massive clashes of political cymbals, as the Fourth Republic collapsed about his ears, there was no telling how long he would last. Mitterrand saw correctly that if de Gaulle was not stopped more or less immediately, he would legitimise his rule for years to come. The only hope appeared to lie with Algeria and the disaffections of the officer class, deeply embittered by defeat in Indo-China and the prospect of a looming sequel in Algeria. Well to the fore of these smouldering forces was the visceral clandestine state that took a grip on France, known as the L'Organisation armée secrète (OAS). The turmoil delighted Mitterrand, who viewed with equanimity the rising tensions consuming the Fourth Republic, which he vigorously stoked by openly opposing de Gaulle's return from self-imposed exile.

The prospect of de Gaulle cementing himself in power as a kind of popular nationalist dictator equally unnerved Pentagonia, given the general's famously frosty regard for the Atlantic military alliance and the US in general. Awkwardly in the circumstances, its headquarters at that time sat on French soil. Few in the commanding heights of power in the United States understood the seat of de Gaulle's distrust. It lay less with the refrigerated treatment he received during WW2 exile in London than with Roosevelt's indecent haste in recognising Marshal Philippe Pétain's collaborationist Vichy government in 1940. Henry Kissinger once remarked that the Framers of the US constitution had difficulty in envisioning anything other than an isolationist America which kept its distant reserve from other powers. When the United States did begin to place a footprint on the world, some of her actions were excessively clumsy. Americans relations with France offered a classic example. Roosevelt harboured a deep-seated dislike of de Gaulle. He dismissed him once as a 'nut.' With the US finally in the war in 1942, Washington policy was based on the extraordinarily inept strategy of grooming Pétain as the 'most reliable person we could look for help in rallying the French.' Roosevelt made up his mind that when the day came to liberate France, the detested de Gaulle would be denied a walk-on role or even an observer's seat at the D-Day landings. It was a collective insult denying the Free French a vanguard role in the liberation of their own country. The business with Lafayette — who sprung the trap at Yorktown in 1781, thus delivering Washington victory over the British — was a page of history that Roosevelt apparently rarely turned.

Instead, he turned the screw. In March 1941, he despatched a secret message via an intermediary to Vichy, asking Pétain to step down and wait patiently for the Americans to arrive. Pétain, draped in the glory of Verdun, refused because it meant abandoning his sacred duty to France. FDR lacked a grip on the French psyche, the shame of defeat and the embarrassment of the Vichy collaborationist stain. De Gaulle was not exactly revered in all quarters of French society, it is true. But it was an incredible miscalculation to believe that Paris would erupt with frantic joy at the prospect of Pétain, the traitor who sold out to the Nazis, as the nation's liberator. Over the years, de Gaulle derived immense satisfaction by returning all these compliments with compound interest, beginning with a home-grown strategic defence policy that sharply diverged from the concept of mutually-assured defence enshrined in the NATO charter. The decision to establish the headquarters of SHAPE (Supreme Headquarters Allied Powers Europe) near Paris, flowed from a colonialist attitude to keep the French in line, with de Gaulle himself presently off the political stage, awaiting the summons of destiny in the depths of the French countryside.

Marcel van Herpen has written that Gaullism boiled down to a 'deep belief in the specific historical role of France' — or put another way 'French Exceptionalism.' By no mere irony it was a young French aristocrat, Alexis de Tocqueville[28] — often called the first modern political scientist — who coined the lasting phrase 'American Exceptionalism' on his return home, intellectually intoxicated, from touring the brash new state of America in the 1830s. De Gaulle's return to power unquestionably delivered an immense sense of urgency of France standing out for herself, which came to be

---

[28] 1805-1859. De Tocqueville's *Democracy in America* is considered a landmark pre-modern work in the field of political science, published in 1835 and still a best seller. He contrasted Americans favourably to 'vulgar and crass' old élites of Europe vainly parading their wealth in front of the poor, whereas in the New World workers learnt that hard work would deliver all manner of boons. He also feared the infectious mood of liberty might slip into authoritarianism. What might he say of America today? De Tocqueville is credited as a pioneer who understood the American fixation with private property effectively prevented socialism from taking root. 'Exceptionalism' he suspected was probably unique to America. Charles de Gaulle believed otherwise.

understood as the plain uncompromising creed of Gaullism; the general understood it as the recovery of sovereignty. When the decision was made in 1960 to build an independent medium-range nuclear striking force, friction was inevitable with NATO's mutual-defence charter. From the perspective of French Exceptionalism, de Gaulle intended France herself to be the head of a new *directoire*, extending a nuclear umbrella over the European continent. Roosevelt's blunders in dealing with de Gaulle came at a heavy price. A European deterrent, based purely on medium-range weapons, did make considerable logistical sense and — de Gaulle believed with considerable justice — would make war less likely. Insuperable difficulties arose when he made clear that the *force de frappe* (nuclear striking force) was to be kept firmly outside the NATO structure. So deep were these frictions that France left the alliance integrated command structure in 1960, the first step on the road to resuming full military independence. Under the heading of lessons gone unheeded in previous dealings with the prickly French, the Pentagon, the CIA and NATO between them proceeded to repeat the same mistakes all over again. Gains in strategic rewards: nil. Instead of diplomacy, the alliance for peace conspired to murder the French head of state, support a fascist coup in Algeria and overthrow the French state itself. To borrow from Talleyrand, the net result was a mistakenly-conceived policy followed by a series of grotesque blunders.

Following his return to power in the soft putsch of 1st June 1958, de Gaulle's relentless pursuit of French nationalism and independence in foreign and military policies was clearly incompatible with the North Atlantic charter. He openly proclaimed his belief that if France were to remain secure, she must rely on her own powers of deterrence, rather than distant guarantees that might not be honoured, as in the past. There were strong political reasons to doubt in the early '60s whether the Alliance had planted enduring roots. If France were to continue to cavil at American dominance of NATO — or possibly desert the Alliance altogether — the prospect of further defections (notably Italy or Greece) thus arose. The spirit of French imperialism — or the fabled exceptionalism — had clearly not run out of steam. De Gaulle made it quite clear that France would not be automatically dragged into a shooting war between NATO and the Warsaw Pact. It scarcely mattered if he demanded a formal written opt-out from the famous stone tablet called Clause V. There was no longer any automatic guarantee the French would be there on the day.

All these affairs were intricately entwined with the secret soldiers. The French corps, known as *Plan Bleu*, was assembled by Grossouvre on de Gaulle's orders as soon as France was liberated. From the outset, the secret soldiers' loyalties were equivocal. In 1947, they were called to arms to support a short-lived putsch by Pétainist sympathisers against a weak and strife-torn radical government clinging to power. The revolving-door politics of the Fourth Republic were underway. Like the units established in other member states, Plan Bleu fell under the responsibility of NATO when the organisation was established. But there is much evidence the stay-behind commandos had been re-assigned specific domestic political duties, under the control of French secret services closely connected to far-Right elements not especially warm to de Gaulle. There had been a period of serenity in Franco-American relations before his return to power on 1ˢᵗ June 1958. America had encouraged the French stand in Indo-China, until the war ended in their defeat in 1954. Goaded by the White House and the Pentagon, the CIA meddled continuously in the Algerian maelstrom, intending to keep Algeria firmly in French hands. An independent socialist Algeria would — in Washington's eyes, and by natural extension those of NATO — usher in the nightmare prospect of a huge Soviet battle fleet ranging the Mediterranean from safe anchorage in Algerian ports.

As the final crisis of the staggering Fourth Republic approached, disaffected officers in Algeria began scheming a Franco-like swoop on the mainland. Commandos seized Corsica as a bridgehead. They enjoyed the support of significant elements of the stay-behind soldiers, as the French authorities were ultimately compelled to admit, and behind the scenes, the covert backing of the CIA and powerful supporters within NATO. The coup fizzled out when the most famous French general since Napoleon took the helm of state. But the crisis in the affairs of Algeria and the danger they posed to order on the mainland, did not.

When de Gaulle returned to power, his principal pledge was to stop the war.[N1] This, as it turned out, was not to mean continuing the struggle to victory, as he loosely implied, but the unthinkable apostasy of Algerian independence. On 22ⁿᵈ April 1961, a fresh attempt by the OAS to eradicate de Gaulle swung into action. On that day, four disaffected generals known as the 'ultra group' staged a coup in Algiers. The civil caucus in Washington, the Pentagon and NATO headquarters in France were all implicated in the plot to eliminate the president and secure Algeria for the West. The coup leader, air force general Maurice Challe, was formerly commander of NATO's forces in Central Europe. His chief co-conspirator General Raoul Salan previously commanded all French forces fighting in the Far East, where he earned the admiration of American observers. The renegade US State Department officer William Blum related in his book on CIA machinations, *Killing Hope*, how in his senior NATO post, Challe was continually enticed by American officers that if he got rid of de Gaulle, 'he would do the free world a great service.'[N2] Salan's counter-revolutionary skills were such that he managed to utterly demoralise Algerian FLN independence fighters and bring them to the point of defeat. He was a power to be reckoned with, or so it appeared.

Challe's forces in Algeria were secretly primed with finance using channels closely connected to the French Gladio that we shall come to in a moment. Challe *et amis* were certainly going to need a lot of money, not least as bribes. On the eve of the coup, Richard Bissell, deputy head of the CIA's covert operations wing, bore glad tidings to a secret pow-wow with Challe held in Algiers. Challe was told that if he could get the country under control inside 48 hours, then the US government would formally recognise his regime. The CIA had every reason to expect their well-chosen candidate would succeed, and moreover, subsequently export his revolution to the mainland. They were blind to the fact that de Gaulle's intelligence eyes and ears had penetrated the entire plot.

Fiasco it certainly was, all over in six days. The great bulk of French forces in Algeria, and in metropolitan France, stood loyal to de Gaulle. Trying to galvanise the French, General Challe almost screamed in one pirate radio broadcast: 'Do you want Mers-el-Kébir turned into a Soviet base?' (This was the 'great harbour' where the Royal Navy sank the French fleet riding at anchor in 1940.) A few weeks later, the weekly magazine *L'Express* published one of the earliest exposés of the sweeping reach of the plot. Their Algerian expert Claude Krief wrote that 'both in Washington and Paris the facts are known, though they will never be publicly admitted.'

The CIA leaned heavily on General Challe to start his putsch. Krief revealed the countdown. The first outlines of the coup were agreed in the summer of 1960, when the former governor of Algeria, Jacques Soustelle, had a secret tête-à-tête with Bissell. In the same year, Challe stage-managed his resignation from NATO. In January 1961, perhaps the most extraordinary event in the whole story occurred. The main plotters, together with a group of sympathetic Right-wing politicians, assembled for a colloquy in the safe quarters of Franco's Madrid. The chief item on the agenda was to form the OAS as an alternative government, to follow de Gaulle once he had been toppled. Key figures in Plan Bleu were all present, including François de Grossouvre. His specific task was to report directly back to Mitterrand, who expected to gain a senior position — *the* senior position — in a post-de Gaulle administration, but for the moment followed his customary practice of never leaving his fingerprints on any skulduggery in which he was involved.

One can imagine how keenly *Le Sphinx* hung on news from Africa, preening himself for his arrival at the long-anticipated pinnacles of public life. The melodramatic Mitterrand, whose socialism was not even skin-deep, schooled himself in a pre-war nursery of political parties that skidded to a halt a hairsbreadth short of full-blown fascism. As Europe drifted to war in the mid-1930s, he belonged to the National Volunteers, a paramilitary group associated with far-Right movements, including the *Croix de Feu* (the Cross of Fire) which toppled a sickly, Left-leaning government in 1934. He wrote for *L'Echo de Paris*, mouthpiece of the Far Right, and was regularly seen at mass demonstrations with a strong xenophobic flavour. He had close friends in *La Cagoule* (The Cowl), extremists who made a considerable nuisance of themselves. Formally titled the *Comité secret d'action révolutionnaire*, or plain CSAR, La Cagoule had a fondness for causing terrorist explosions which were then blamed on the Left — the standard Gladio tactic. It was tightly organised on military lines, with cell structures later identified with the NATO secret armies. Prominent *Cagoulards* included Eugène Schueller, founder of the L'Oréal cosmetics empire; Jean Filliol, international assassin and leading officer of the Vichy military police; and General Henri Giraud, commander of the Free French forces in Algeria, who prepared the way for the Allied landings there in 1944. Lifting the stones from La Cagoule is to uncover a network of connections leading to the Jesuits, the Knights of Malta and ephemeral conspiracies like the Synarchists, usually dismissed as a paranoid fantasy of a big business plot to rule the world.[29] Keeping such exotic company as this, Mitterrand might be excused as a young man searching for a cause. What he definitely never found was socialism — even as ultimately the leader, nominally, of the French socialist party. Mitterrand's fluid political personality meant he suffered no discomfort in the company of men like the Gladio mastermind Yves Guérin-Sérac, and of course, his lifetime aide François de Grossouvre. Their willingness to employ any means to meet the ends suited his aims perfectly.

Despite the setback in Algiers, or perhaps actually because of it, the OAS continued to pose a threat, albeit a steadily decreasing one, for two more years. To describe this tense and unsettled period as a simmering civil war would be a step too far. While the president himself was the subject of a sporadic guerrilla threat, the French stood aside *en masse* and there was no expectation of a popular rising. Only the Paris Massacre of 17th October 1961, in which Parisian police crushed a peaceful demonstration of Algerians with dreadful brutality, upset the prevailing sense of public calm. The OAS decidedly did not succeed in its endeavour to become a real political power, because it was a one-trick pony for blood-soaked Algeria, a struggle which the metropolitan French could see was sapping the nation's physical, economic and moral reserves. There was a national mood to move on with stable political structures, after the endless see-sawing of the Fourth Republic; particularly with signs the German economic miracle then

---

[29] The word means a united set of actions, the polar opposite of anarchism, which was so intriguingly retrieved from the dustbins of history to fan the contemporary riots that are supposed to threaten law and order. Anarchists are promoted these days as the leading force opposing globalism, a threat to centralised government and civil order. Most and Malatesta might be delighted.

beginning to unfold would place an old enemy once more in the leadership of Europe. An unconscionable thought.

On 8th September 1961, an assassination attempt that came perilously close to succeeding yielded some interesting clues to all the designs on de Gaulle's life. This one occurred less than a year after he abruptly ordered all foreign nuclear weapons — meaning American ones — off French soil, and eight months after the Algiers putsch. De Gaulle was travelling as night fell, returning to his country retreat in Colombey-les-Deux-Églises, about 200 kilometres north-east from Paris. As his favourite transport, a smart Citroen DS-19, approached the sleepy medieval village of Pont-sur-Seine, it was scheduled to encounter a bomb made from a propane cylinder stuffed with *plastique* — familiar in NATO hands — planted in an innocent-looking pile of winter road sand. Nestling alongside the bomb was another canister filled with fifteen litres of napalm. The vehicle was intended to trigger a huge explosion by slicing through trigger wires strung from roadside telegraph poles. The bomb did explode, but the general's prompt command to his chauffeur to stamp on the accelerator regardless saved his life. Allowing for the passage of other traffic, the booby trap must have been rigged at the last moment, indicating a very precise intelligence operation. The episode never threw up a culprit, beyond the usual blame heaped by the media on the OAS.

There is no definitive means of proving who planned the attack, but a few pointers undermine the story which quickly circulated of an OAS strike. The thrust of current OAS tactics was a massive blitzkrieg in Algeria itself, intended to provoke the FLN to abandon the ceasefire and resume the war, with the hopeless aim of re-igniting French opposition to independence. The national referendum (the first of two) eight months earlier in any event effectively erased the issue of *L'Algérie française* from the French political scene permanently. The president was in no doubt that the real threat to his life came from the secret soldiers gathered under the umbrella of NATO.

Scarcely had the dust settled from the Pont-sur-Seine ambush than NATO HQ received a furious diplomatic protest from de Gaulle himself, ordering Alliance officials to cease 'manipulating' the French underground army forthwith. The president was clearly referring to the recent attempt on his life. De Gaulle's source was his personal supervisor of intelligence services, Jacques Foccart, an ambiguous figure always ready to work both sides of the tracks. He will shortly make a worthy bow in greater detail. Mention of Foccart at once conjures up a fourth, dimly-visible figure in the frame of Pont-sur-Seine. François de Grossouvre was the alter ego of Foccart in the murky world of scheming and plotting. His well-thumbed rolodex read like a Who's Who of the French deep state. In fact, the pair were in a duel of the rolodexes, except when — in the usual manner of *le souterrain politique français* — they found common ground.

Grossouvre, like his boss Mitterrand, was a figure of the Right but inclined to cross-dress politically when the incentive arose. So was Foccart, and they worked comfortably together setting up the extreme nationalist leader Jean-Marie Le Pen's personal militia. The explanation was simple, at least in France. Le Pen controlled a large reservoir of electoral support which could be swung in either direction of the political pendulum. It was also the natural gravitational sump for the half million or so ex-Algerian colonist *pieds-noirs* who fled to France. Le Pen's presence and importance in the French political landscape was sufficient to have an intelligence source planted close to him, and the support he controlled nourished against the day when it might be needed. These were still very young days of the infant Fifth Republic, when anything might happen, or could be made to happen. For de Gaulle, an axis of Foccart and Grossouvre presented the risk of *liaisons dangereuses*. Foccart's intuition that Gaullism might not be a passing phenomenon was a prominent factor in the assassination attempt at Pont-sur-Seine. If natural evolution of the political succession in France required a good shove now and again, then Foccart was the man to see to it. Bald and bespectacled, so rarely photographed he was known as 'the invisible man,' he was just as effective at mustering delinquents as he was bringing them to heel. For this reason he earned another title: 'master of infidelities.'

Foccart was truly the man for all seasons, the French Machiavelli and *noble de robe* to a succession of presidents. He might have been found whispering close to the throne in any Bourbon court, the image of the Cardinal-Duc de Richelieu, or perhaps better still, the French-Italian master intriguer but highly competent administrator, Cardinal Mazarin. Flexibility was Foccart's chief speciality. In that guise he created the *Service d'action civique* (SAC), ostensibly a Gaullist loyalist militia. In reality it acted as a lure to a host of ruffians and fantasists operating at the hazy borders between espionage, old Vichy police networks, street fighters and organised crime, and a hiding place for renegade stay-behind commandos. Foccart thought in very long seasons. If Gaullist power was bound up in the personality of the general himself, then what could be more important than controlling the order of succession? To Grossouvre, the natural candidate was Mitterrand. Foccart, for reasons explored below, was inclined to agree. SAC functioned in practical terms as Foccart's personal intelligence machine. In a much later, rare TV appearance discussing his career, he also admitted exercising effective supervision over SDECE, the French MI6. SAC unsurprisingly swapped or supported covert sabotage and mercenary operations of the stay-behind army. Anyone holding these keys was the most powerful man in France, next to the president himself.[N3]

Foccart was the time-honoured specialist in playing both ends against the middle, so long as it served the prime cause of his life — *La Belle France*. De Gaulle's rupture with the United States disturbed him, because he saw it as a distraction from the first priority — the preservation of French power and influence in the minerals-rich *Communauté Française*. This *Doppelgänger* of the British Commonwealth was the vehicle de Gaulle created in 1958, on the eve of granting francophone Africa the delusion of independence in 1960. As the Secretary General, Foccart was a mighty potentate in his own right, equivalent to a head of state. Nor did he desire France to leave NATO, another backward step as he saw it, that would weaken French influence over Europe. He was also one of two men in France that could, with the ease of smoke, arrange access to materials such as *plastique* and napalm, and place them in the hands of those who could make best use of them. The second was naturally enough de Grossouvre. As the figure closest to the court of de Gaulle, Foccart also possessed the most intimate knowledge of the president's movements. The split-second timing of Pont-sur-Seine depended on it. Mitterrand must have wept when he heard the news that de Gaulle survived without a singe.

Over the decade he was in power, there were more than two dozen attempts of varying severity on de Gaulle's life. The excuse, that the OAS were behind most if not all of them, was wearing rather thin. The tragic Algerian maelstrom was at last drifting to its conclusion. The timeline was this: official cease-fire by both sides effective from 19th March 1962. The Evian Accords with the FLN independence movement led to a second referendum in war-weary France in June the same year, which over-whelmingly approved Algerian independence, confirmed when Algerians themselves voted on 1st July 1962. Algeria was declared fully independent on 5th July 1962, and admitted to the UN virtually immediately. As for the OAS, the remnants in the field had already signed their own truce. The leadership was decapitated, with commander in chief Raoul Salan, serving life imprisonment for treason. All of these events drained what little purpose there remained in stubborn OAS resistance. Algeria was gone; there could be no return to the past, even if de Gaulle had been finally despatched by the fates to a solemn requiem in Notre Dame cathedral. Yet a little over a month after Algeria's independence, on 22nd August 1962, the president brushed with death once again.

Accompanied by Madame de Gaulle and his son-in-law, Alain de Boissieu, *le Général* was again travelling back to Colombey-les-Deux-Églises in his favourite Citroen DS-19, just as dusk fell on a warm summer night. The car was shadowed only by a small patrol van containing a few security officers; de Gaulle refused to be chaperoned like a dictator in his homeland. As it swept into the leafy Paris suburb of Petit Clamart, the party encountered an assault which appeared to verge on overkill, leaving nothing to chance. According to accounts circulated at the Élysée, the avenue was lined with cars loaded with sharpshooters armed with submachine guns, a few grenades and (so it was said) Molotov cocktails. In these auspicious circumstances, the small army of assailants ought to have made short work of the president. It was said they failed because the 'night was dark' — although it was only around nine o'clock on a lingering midsummer evening — so they failed to see the fast-moving mini-convoy soon enough. Word was later put around that the marksmen were restricted to firing at the Citroen as it passed alongside. It is inexplicable, then, that the unarmoured *voiture* was not peppered with holes, along with its four occupants. In fact, the fire came chiefly from the rear. With two tyres and its rear window shot out, de Gaulle's car skidded out of control and almost collided with an oncoming vehicle. His quick-witted chauffeur regained control and bolted to safety on two flat tyres. One slug passed between the president and Madame de Gaulle and narrowly missed the general's son-in-law sitting in the front passenger seat. It was, as the Duke of Wellington reputedly declared at Waterloo, 'a near run thing.' The scale of the assault could be judged from scores of spent casings collected from the street and even inside a small café. 'OAS' was whispered in the newspapers and TV channels, yet in the wake of the affair it became clear the president did not believe 'those idiots playing *boules* [bowls] in Tulle prison' had any significant role. He suspected a far more dangerous threat, which goes far in explaining his subsequent curiously soft behaviour to all the would-be assassins, bar one.

The alleged mastermind was an unlikely candidate. As with all the assassination events discussed in this book, he appeared to hail from the central casting list of convenient dupes. Lieutenant-Colonel Jean-Marie Bastien-Thiry was a 35-year-old air force engineer accustomed to crouching over designs for rockets, wholly lacking combat or similar experience that might fit him for command of such an operation. He was a military civil servant, if also a rather dreamy-minded member of an aristocratic family with old Vichy roots. He was intensely pious, devoted to his wife and three daughters. And he was passionate too about his work, which he viewed as a sacred duty dedicated to Christian civilisation.

The discordant note was Bastien-Thiry's fascination with the charismatic Portuguese-born Jean Ousset of earlier mention. Ousset developed a mystical philosophy he described as National Catholicism, with the aim of staging a Christian renaissance in France. It was intellectually close to the Spanish Falange but more intensely spiritual, with unmistakable authoritarian overtones. The uncompromising anti-communism of Ousset and his followers naturally exercised a strong appeal to officers of the French army like Bastien-Thiry, to whom Ousset appeared as a kind of saint, complete with shining halo. Ousset's La Cité Catholique was the inspirational and practicing arm of militant National Catholicism. The Vatican kept a discreet distance, but did nothing to discourage its activities.

When it came to his trial, Bastien-Thiry spun his story of an intended kidnap with unshaken conviction. De Gaulle would be seized and put up before a kangaroo court. Susceptible and spell-bound by Ousset, Bastien-Thiry was selected and effectively brainwashed by the master to play the role of the stooge, the hypnotised Manchurian Candidate. His role model was scarcely Charlotte Corday pouncing on the Jacobin revolutionary Jean-Paul Marat soaking his painful sores quietly in the bathtub. Just before the trial, President De Gaulle informed his Cabinet that he was minded to grant clemency to Bastien-Thiry, dismissing him as an 'idiot.' 'He will get off with twenty years and in five years I'll free him.' The usually unflappable de Gaulle then suddenly switched to a mysterious display of martial rage, for once losing his traditional cool, thundering aloud that 'if the French needed martyrs,' he would let them have one. De Gaulle's abrupt switch in mood is explained by the reports from interrogators the holy fool was in league with forces like the Ousset movements, linked in turn to the extremist military camp and the secret state manipulated by NATO. When he spat out the word 'martyr,' the president was playing the game back on the organisers of National Catholicism, in unholy alliance with *les étrangers* who sought the extinction of the defiant occupant of the Élysée Palace.

De Gaulle's additional justification accused Bastien-Thiry of bringing 'three Hungarians' into the plot. These were the three individuals listed on the charge sheet, including the young Varga László, who fought bravely in the Budapest insurrection at the age of fourteen. Unravelling the riddle of how this unusual trio came to be in the Avenue Petit Clamart leads to the dagger hidden beneath the cloak, clutched by a Hungarian CIA asset called Ferenc Nagy. He was briefly premier of Hungary, until the communists took over and then forced him from office at the end of May 1947. They allowed him safe conduct to Switzerland, to rejoin his son who had been kidnapped, as part of the persuasion exercise to get him to resign and leave the country. Nagy was granted asylum by the US and emigrated to the Washington DC area in 1948, where he went to work for the FBI. He then became an intimate of Frank Wisner, the CIA's Deputy Director of Special Plans. Given this warm relationship, it is quite likely that Nagy was the power behind the scenes in the CIA's widely-suspected clandestine backing for the doomed Hungarian rising in 1956. The CIA shopfront Permindex [Permanent Industrial Expositions] was incorporated in Basel with Nagy as president in 1956, on the eve of the Hungarian uprising. Nagy was also a director of the World Trading Centre (aka CMC or Centro Mondiale Commerciale) in Rome, and president of its American board. Both outfits were conduits for the CIA's covert worldwide commercial activities, including arms and dope trafficking, white-washing money, lubricating extremist organisations close to Gladio and running deals with European gangsters. Permindex had an offshoot in Italy, where P2's puppet master Licio Gelli sat on the board. New Orleans businessman Clay Shaw, arrested and questioned in connection with the JFK assassination, was for a time on the Permindex American board.

These companies had the curious distinction of seeming very well oiled, while never actually engaging in any visible commercial transactions. As was observed by the Italian campaigning newspaper *Paese Sera*, which in the '60s mounted detailed investigations of WTC's activities in Rome, 'It is a fact that the CMC [Centro Mondiale Commerciale] is the point of contact for a number of persons who, in certain respects, have somewhat equivocal ties whose common denominator is anti-communism.'

The same journal alleged that Ferenc Nagy funded the OAS through WTC and Permindex. OAS founders included de Gaulle's great wartime comrade, the noted anthropologist Jacques Soustelle. He was among the first to rally to de Gaulle's side when he broadcast from London urging total resistance to the Vichy authorities. He sat in the first government after the war as minister of information. He was governor too of Algeria, popular with the French settlers — the *pieds-noirs* — to whom he eventually switched his support. When de Gaulle changed his mind about *Algérie française*, the old comrades were instantly estranged; the pain felt by de Gaulle, intense. It was not eased by the insight filtered into his ears (by Foccart, naturally) concerning the source of OAS funding, namely the CIA, via Nagy's Permindex and WTC pipelines.

The Avenue Petit Clamart episode appeared to feature two men who were 'available for hire' (*disponible* in French, also connoting 'disposable') — Bastien-Thiry and Jacques Prévost, 32. Prévost was a former paratrooper and survivor of the massive French defeat at Dien Bien Phu, that indefensible pit into which the French decanted the flower of their army and then completely lost it in an act of suicidal vanity. He travelled in the same orbit as his fellow Asian hero, Guérin-Sérac, and may have been the stay-behind representative that day. Provost was a credible manager, so to speak, which the wispy 'idiot' Bastien-Thiry was not. We can be certain Guérin-Sérac — as a committed member of La Cité Catholique — played an important role in guiding Bastien-Thiry to the circles of Ousset's mystical brotherhood.

The freelance air to the operation suggested some hurried assembly. What can be stated for certain was the absence of any identifiable ideological content, except for Bastien-Thiry, the dummy leader in thrall to a Fascist Christian renaissance. He was so much in the loop he had no idea the intention was assassination, rather than the snatch and mock trial he later talked about. Bastien-Thiry was not the type to tell lies, even with his life hanging by a thread. The three Hungarians, refugees from their homeland, included at least one — László — with real shooting experience, which made him valuable. For the rest of it, they were figures moving in the gray zone between crime and subcontracting. Refugee groups from behind the Iron Curtain were always of considerable interest to the CIA, either as possible Soviet agents, or sources for potential activists behind the lines.

Communities like the Hungarian one in France were infiltrated as a matter of course. The figures on the Avenue Petit Clamart were there solely on the business of putting an end to de Gaulle, the CIA's most urgent priority, and thus that of the agency's top Hungarian recruiter, Ferenc Nagy. They were spared their lives, but they bore much of the responsibility, along with Nagy, for the patsy Bastien-Thiry losing his.

Of Ousset there is more to be said. The CIA has a long history of dabbling in esoteric cults that may prove malleable to its mischievous ends. They form a useful pool of often obsessive figures who can be persuaded (tricked, mesmerised, drugged) into black operations. So the rabidly anti-communist National Catholic movement appeared to the CIA bureau in Paris as a perfect opportunity. De Gaulle was a devout churchman, although not to Jacques Ousset, for whom he was traitor who handed part of the sacred body of France — Algeria — to godless infidels. He could not be a 'real Catholic' either, because he fought against Pétain and Vichy, from whom National Catholicism derived its inspiration. The fanatical Catholic and the CIA's secular desire to eliminate the president fitted like tailored gloves.

In Washington, General Lyman Lemnitzer was preparing to take up the reins of all Allied forces based in Europe, in January 1963, close to General de Gaulle's front doorstep. As chief of the general staff, he already pulled all the strings that mattered in any event. Now, as some consolation for his summary exile, there was at least the chance to supervise the elimination of the rogue general at close quarters. Petit Clamart was, of course, the direct continuation of Pont-sur-Seine, and before that the 'ultra' putsch in Algeria. It was François Mitterrand who was again biting his nails for news he (and Grossouvre) desperately wanted to hear. The Pentagon and the CIA hovered, waiting for the happy tidings that de Gaulle had been 'assassinated by the OAS.' *Monsieur Afrique* had some urgent cleaning work to do, once it became clear providence had intervened once again. Just as Foccart alerted de Gaulle to the role of NATO and the CIA at the bridge on the river Seine, it was Foccart who now informed de Gaulle of the Permindex/WTC connection with the OAS and Soustelle following the attack in Paris. Accustomed to tossing a scrap here and another there in the pursuit of his complex plots, he omitted to add he had known the workings of this chain for many years, and indeed dipped his own hand in its affairs from time to time, particularly in the service of his personal African empire.

After Petit Clamart, Foccart had Permindex and WTC operations on Swiss soil shut down. De Gaulle threatened the Swiss government with dire retaliation if they were not. This was a marginal blow to the CIA, which soon fabricated replacement shopfronts. The psychological impact was far more important. It was clear de Gaulle knew the extent of continuing NATO and CIA-inspired plotting against him. The divorce from the Atlantic Alliance accelerated in a mood of bad tempers all around. The French Mediterranean fleet had already been pulled from the NATO order of battle. In the autumn of 1962 (almost immediately following Petit Clamart), the Atlantic and Channel fleets were withdrawn as well, completing the French Navy's effective departure from the Alliance. Soon the president would turn to the air force. If this was the president in a playful, teasing mood, there was much more in terms of serious intent yet to come.

The NATO/CIA coalition had now sponsored at least two attempts to eliminate this obstinate Frenchman. Lemnitzer, supreme commander designate, was among the key agitators. Yet he was a firm admirer of French military strategists, who used Indo-China as a laboratory to brew up a new kind of unorthodox warfare. Chief among these was Colonel Roger Trinquier, who designed an 'interlocking system of actions — political, economic, psychological, military — that aims at the overthrow of the established authority in a country and its replacement by another regime.' His book *Modern Warfare* remains standard fare at military academies around the world, and in every American training school where officers are taught the arts of counter-insurgency. It was the template of regime change yet to come, including small and highly-mobile commando teams, liberal resort to torture, as well as copious psychological black warfare. Each one of these items on Trinquier's menu chimed with the check list in Lemnitzer's dark mind. Future OAS men admired by the Pentagon and the CIA also included Colonel Jean Gardes, French psy-ops expert in the Far East, and General Raoul Salan himself, with eight years of priceless experience combating insurrection everywhere in French Indo-China.

If Lemnitzer admired and enthusiastically adopted French tactics such as these, then he reserved nothing but scorn for de Gaulle. He dismissed him as the bolter who scooted off to the comforts of London instead of rallying his men and standing firm like a true soldier. He distrusted JFK's attempts to intercede directly with de Gaulle, using the hated General Maxwell Taylor — the president's personal military adviser and a sound French linguist — as the intermediary. France, it appeared to Lemnitzer, was swarming with communists and socialists. The nightmare prospect of the *force de frappe* plopping into outheld Soviet arms via some future communist government in Paris brought a cold sweat to the brows of the imperial high command.

Some 20 years later, by now president, Mitterrand tried to shift the blame for sinking the Rainbow Warrior on a freelance action by the French Navy. Admiral Pierre Lacoste paid him back by inferring that the sleeping soldiers had in the past been awakened to kill de Gaulle, slyly implying that Mitterrand expected substantial personal political bounty if they succeeded. There was a general belief in France — and Foccart shared it, with Lemnitzer — that if the head were cut off, then Gaullism would die with it. Some curious nuance from the admiral suggested the commandos of the stay-behind army were posturing as a 'Gaullist militia,' that same organisation called into being by the politically bi-focal Jacques Foccart.

In 1965, de Gaulle learned of yet another NATO-inspired conspiracy to have him shot. It was the final straw. All French soldiers were placed under national command, then all non-French soldiers ordered out of France altogether. Finally, that same year, like an angry landlord, de Gaulle gave NATO headquarters — the last remnant of Alliance authority in France — immediate notice to quit altogether within six months. A semi-mothballed Belgian army base near Mons was hurriedly resuscitated to receive the retreating forces, which duly arrived, puffing and out of breath, as the deadline neared. General Lyman Lemnitzer had received summary orders to quit, for the second time in his illustrious career.

The man who never pulled a trigger — Jean-Marie Bastien-Thiry — made his final journey on 11th March 1963, to the Fort d'Ivry on the banks of the River Seine, in a convoy of 25 armoured vehicles intended to deter any attempt to free him. It was a compliment to his importance he did not deserve. He died in the manner reserved for traitors, before a firing squad. He refused a blindfold, clutching his favourite rosary. Foccart lived for another 34 years. When his protégé, Jacques Chirac, finally clawed his way to the Élysée in 1995, he instantly summoned *Monsieur Afrique* from retirement, at the age of 81. He secured Chirac's second term by stage-managing the fake election shoot-out with Jean-Marie Le Pen of the National Front, in April 2002. *En route*, Foccart served Georges Pompidou and François Mitterrand. He wounded the vain and snobbish toff Valéry Giscard d'Estaing, who foolishly shunned him, by means of the Emperor Bokassa Diamonds Scandal. Possibly the most powerful man in France of modern times, Foccart died in harness in 1997. François de Grossouvre — the man who knew too much — was to become deeply implicated in the CIA's manoeuvres to manipulate and exploit mystical cults as a key weapon of the Strategy of Tension, before the final settlement — his death — in the Élysée Palace.

There remains Mitterand's pardon extended to Yves Guérin-Sérac, and of course the handsome promotion. There is much more we do not know or can readily confirm about the *cohabitation* — the French term for a political accommodation of opposed forces — between these two men. The unscrupulous sphinx Mitterrand certainly had scores of skeletons to conceal. But Guérin-Sérac was never the sort to fall for a bribe. In his bizarre, distorted fashion, he was too 'principled.' No, that service at which we can only guess was a token of some particular favour. *L'avenue Petit-Clamart*? On this, as with all else, *l'ancien mercenaire* Yves Guérin-Sérac preserves his own sphinx-like silence.

VII.
The Devil in the Deep Blue Sea

'F*** your parliament and your constitution. America is an elephant. Cyprus is a flea...' — President Lyndon Johnson to the Greek ambassador, in Washington, 1964

Early one dank October evening in 1971, an elderly couple scavenging for edible snails in a patch of seaside scrubland, about fifteen kilometres from Athens, chanced upon the body of a young woman, half naked, battered and strangled. The Greek authorities later pinned the killing of the 25-year-old radio reporter from London on a hapless peeping tom (a typical patsy). But the case of Ann Dorothy Chapman was very far from closed, and became a *cause célèbre* that stretched all the way to a full inquiry ordered by the European Parliament in Strasbourg, fifteen years after she died. The investigation was assigned to myself, as *rapporteur,* literally 'the reporter.' This is the Member designated on behalf of the appropriate committee (in this instance the one that considers grievances against public authorities, filed by individual citizens). He or she assumes responsibility for investigating the facts, reaching conclusions and then setting a report before the full house.

Ann's father, Edward, a retired engineer, was the petitioner on the grounds the Greek authorities had consistently denied him a truthful explanation of how his daughter died. My report, stating she was murdered by domestic and foreign secret services during the reign of the infamous Greek military junta, was adopted virtually unanimously. Within days, the chosen patsy, a poor retarded labourer, was released from prison. I was then approached to write an expanded version for a book. The result was *Blood on Their Hands* (1987). I expanded my original conclusions by taking into account the complex geopolitical storms raging in the Eastern Mediterranean, instigated by the United States and NATO, at the time that Ann Chapman was killed. It was clear from these inquiries that she fell victim of the complex labyrinth of treachery and betrayal ruling Athens in the early 1970s, inextricably connected to the activities of western secret services and their activities — akin to civil war — in Greece.

Ann Chapman worked for MI6, and in one of the saddest side acts of the Cold War, was caught in the cross-hairs of a feud between her secret bosses in London and the CIA station in Athens. The reporter-at-large is a popular disguise in the intelligence game (think of the famous British turncoat Kim Philby). She was ostensibly in Greece to record puff pieces on the tourist industry for the BBC's Radio London, where she had a cover as a freelance stringer. Her real brief was to sniff out a suspected Soviet sleeper either in

MI6 ranks directly (a hoary old ruse, that one) or among the various counterparties with whom MI6 dealt among Greek underground resistance cells. It was her fate to die as the very Soviet suspect she was sent to unfrock. She was kidnapped, tortured and then strangled by officers of ESA — the Greek military intelligence agency, which bore close links to the Greek Gladio unit — with CIA co-interrogators looking on. It was shades of clandestine detention centres yet to come — Abu Ghraib and others scattered around Iraq and Afghanistan. But she may have possessed some nugget of intelligence so threatening that it remains under lock and key to this day. When Ann's father persuaded Scotland Yard to make some cursory inquiries, he was told that making such a fuss about his murdered daughter might provoke an 'international incident.' The gentle intellectual and wartime resistance veteran, Georgios Mangakis — justice minister in the government of the socialist premier Andreas Papandreou — met me many times in the course of my parliamentary inquiries, and later while I was writing the book. He told me the truth was buried in the Cyprus File, which was unlikely ever to be opened 'due to the interests of the state.'

In the 180 years since the Greeks seized their independence from the Ottoman Empire, this small country of some ten million inhabitants, lacking few natural resources to speak of beyond sunshine, blue waters and olive oil, has known little else but chronic instability. The fiscal crisis which erupted in 2010 was merely the latest instalment of rolling chaos. The failure to evolve deep-rooted political structures — or resort to 'calm habits' in place of 'incurable political incompetence' — was a favourite theme of the late Right-wing prime minister Constantine Karamanlis. He continually chided his fellow citizens for their part in the endless national drama of instability. It is certainly true that Greece throughout her independent existence has reeled between plots, revolutions, constitutional upheavals, dictatorships, civil wars and perpetual meddling by foreign powers. So it was that the tiny Hellenic nation, a mere fragment of the glory that once was Greece, shared the fate of Italy, her people denied the pleasure of selecting their own form of government should that fly in the face of other and larger interests.

To understand the mood of Greece leading up to the fascist seizure of power in 1967, we must spin back the wheel of time nearly thirty years to the Churchill-Stalin pact, the latest of a long line of occupations decided over the heads of the Greek people. In 1943, Greece was allocated like a piece of choice real estate to the British sphere of influence, in return for the Soviets getting the keys to Eastern Europe. At the root of the unfolding tragedy was the Cypriot fantasia yet to come: the Soviets stoking communist partisans to stage an insurrection, and thus choke the empire's lifeline — the Suez Canal.

While Greece descended into mayhem, Stalin remained passive and inscrutable, thoroughly enjoying the unfolding spectacle. Perhaps he had an inkling of what might happen next, which explains why he surrendered this poisoned chalice so willingly. Greece was freed from the Nazis by the Leftist-leaning National Liberation Front (EAM). It was the largest mass political organisation in Greek history, with a membership of two million, about a quarter of the entire population at the time, and passive support probably from another two million. Winston Churchill, needled by Washington, persisted in seeing EAM as a Trojan Horse for the communist bloc. It was actually a genuine, deeply-rooted multi-party popular movement, although the communist rudder was quite obviously significant. That cast the entire organisation in the light of a threat to the new 'British protectorate.' A match was set to the tinder on a bright, cold Sunday, 3rd December 1944, a day of infamy in Greek history. One hundred thousand people demanding Greece for the Greeks crammed into the spacious Syntagma (Constitution) Square, the heart of Athens. The events that followed have never been clearly explained, but they resemble the Strategy of Tension pursued under false-flag cover far too strongly to be explained in any other way.

Panic ensued when unidentified marksmen aiming from tall buildings surrounding the square began to shoot at random into the crowd. They seemed to target women. After the first round of shots, more followed as help was rushed to the dying and wounded. Twenty-three were killed instantly and 140 injured. Athens erupted. The story was allowed to filter throughout the city that partisans fired the fatal shots. Another version blamed British army snipers. Like the forthcoming Portella della Ginestra atrocity in Palermo, the intention was to create a mood in favour of strong authority. Instead, the powder keg exploded and Greeks fell with great cruelty upon each other.

The Greek Civil War lasted until 1949, with an interval for an uneasy truce, fought between the Greek government army on one side — backed and armed by the British and the US — and the Democratic Army of Greece, the military branch of the Greek Communist Party (KKE), on the other. As the surrounding Balkan states turned progressively Red, former partisan brigades involved in the brunt of the fighting did receive supplies from Bulgaria, Tito's Yugoslavia and Albania. This extremely bloody conflict, involving horrific atrocities on both sides, aroused violent passions similar to the Spanish Civil War. With a few international brigades and a scattering of Hemingways and Orwells tossed in, it might have generated the same aura. This colossal after-tremor of WW2 should not be underestimated in terms of its shocking impact on such a small country. The war dead numbered at least 150,000 (three times those who perished during the German occupation). The Greek mainland lay in ruins, its economy and infrastructure in far worse shape than when the Germans left. Thousands languished in prison for years, or found themselves shut up in gulags on isolated Aegean islands. The wounds suffered by the Greek state never fully healed. To place the casualties in perspective, a similar war fought in the United Kingdom at that time would have claimed between 900,000 and one million lives, pro rata.

Britain's socialist government which followed Winston Churchill's wartime all-party coalition, spent the equivalent of £1.5 billion in modern money on this pointless colonial escapade, when the country had practically no reserves of foreign exchange. At home, British people were living in conditions of severe austerity, including widespread rationing of food and other essentials such as fuel and clothing. Politically, the war aroused heated passions similar to those the United States encountered over Vietnam. Greece was an albatross hung around the neck of a nation that won the war, but seemed to be rapidly losing the peace. Socialist premier Clement Attlee disposed of this unwanted inheritance to the Americans in 1949, wishing them every good fortune with this poisoned chalice. Greece was henceforth an American protectorate in the latest episode of pass the parcel.

When Ann Chapman was battered and choked to death in the dungeons of the ESA, a stone's throw from the American embassy in Athens, she was really the victim of a conflict which officially finished a quarter of a century before. Ann was attractive and perceptive, a loner by nature with no close personal entanglements, those qualities so endearing to the espionage industry. She had a good degree in psychology, another sound plus. After first rejecting advances from MI6 at university, she eventually succumbed, lured to a career offering mystery and adventure in foreign parts. She was already a seasoned solo traveller, including a solo hike across Afghanistan — hardly the naive lass the British media portrayed at the prompting of her former intelligence employers. Arriving in Greece in the autumn of 1971, she stepped into the latest aftershocks of the unfinished civil war. Even before leaving London, she was denounced to the authorities in Athens, by a senior official of the Greek embassy, as a possible Soviet double agent. The mood in Athens was thick with plotting, resentment of the military regime building like a pressure cooker. The imperial regent Spiro Agnew, Greek-American vice president of the United States, was due at any moment on a mission of immense sensitivity. The protectorate was more than restless. It was about to erupt.

With Greece swept into the American sphere of influence in 1950, the US effectively bought up the National Intelligence Service, KYP, and its military counterpart, ESA, with all the incalculable consequences for corruption of the Greek armed forces. Special attention was reserved for the 'mountain men,' veterans of a special wartime unit called LOK, from *loxos oreinon katadromon*, meaning in Greek 'fire hurled from a hidden cave.' LOK guerrillas formed highly effective wartime raiding parties swooping down from mountain eyries, wreaking havoc on columns of invading Germans and Italians. In short, stay-behind guerrillas. In the civil war, a few of these skilled fighters joined the communist side. But the great majority were more at home with British and US-backed forces and later the new stay-behind organisation codenamed Sheepskin, created by the CIA even before Greece joined the NATO alliance in 1951.

LOK was the foundation stone of Sheepskin. The Greek army of this period was riddled with closet officer clubs sold on the mystical conviction its initiates were latter-day successors of spear throwing, bare-chested Olympian warriors of old. These cabals had names like 'the Sacred Warriors of Thebes,' and membership was confined, largely, to middle-ranking officers. Sheepskin somewhat organically volunteered itself for these mystical unions. Relationships were cemented by secret bonding ceremonies which over-rode conventional military discipline, with grave consequences for the future. There were many other kindred loyalties. To the CIA, the arrangement was delightful. Most, if not all, of Sheepskin's officers were on the CIA payroll, held in reserve for some future perturbations in the Greek state. These might be real, or manufactured to order.

Barely ensconced in his new command in NATO, General Lyman Lemnitzer became obsessed again with a new Cuban-style conspiracy. This time he pictured the sunny island of Cyprus as the 'Cuba of the Med.' Without a scrap of hard evidence — but a good deal of disinformation spun by Israeli secret services — Lemnitzer fell to the belief that the island, bristling with NATO electronic intelligence beamed on the volcanic Middle East, was poised to fall like a ripe plum into the hands of the Russians. After Operation Zapata (April 1961), Northwoods (March 1962), the bitter clash with President Kennedy during the Cuban Missile Crisis in October the same year, and finally the renegade Chief of Staff's abrupt dismissal in November 1963, JFK was certain to adopt an agnostic stance to Lemnitzer's latest mania. This obstacle was eliminated, in Dallas, on 22nd November, 1963. Lyndon Baines Johnson was a different animal altogether, susceptible to ideas of Soviet encroachment in US zones of influence, even where the evidence was plainly too absurd to be taken seriously.

Lemnitzer fantastically believed that Archbishop Makarios — the island's deeply conservative Greek Orthodox head of state — was beneath his ecclesiastical trappings nothing less than a 'clerical Castro' bent on declaring a pro-Arab socialist republic. As with Northwoods, the general had lost control of his wits. The Archbishop, a wily, thickly-bearded figure with a strong dash of cutting humour, tweaked Allied nerves by signing up to the international non-aligned movement. At home he was in the centre ground of Cypriot politics, courting good relations with Greeks and Turks uneasily co-habiting together. Cyprus was only an isolated problem of ethnic quarrels, without the great power itch to meddle. Makarios understood this. He was firmly committed to the unitary Greek-Turkish state created on independence from the British Empire in August 1960, after a protracted and bitter struggle for self-determination. To any rational mind, Makarios appeared a figure of stability. However to the Washington-NATO axis, the 'solution' was to invent the necessary excuse for an intervention. Lemnitzer coolly advised LBJ to take the sovereign independent state of Cyprus, a member of the United Nations, and then chop it in two, like a prime Texas rump steak. The largest and juiciest slice, containing all the NATO facilities and air bases, would be handed to the Greeks, to be further rewarded by *Enosis,* the old dream of fusion with the Greek mainland. The Turkish population, the minority, would get their own morsel, a self-ruling canton in the north, as compensation. There were two obvious roadblocks: Makarios in Cyprus and Georgios Papandreou, the veteran centrist politician in Athens with strong — and to NATO, worrisome — inclinations to Greek neutrality.

In December 1963, one year into Lemnitzer's European reign, the first of a series of Cyprus crises erupted (the second came in 1967, the third in 1974-75, a sixth is on the horizon). Turks and Greeks began flooding the small island with all kinds of weapons, including bazookas and heavy mortars — reputedly a thousand boat-loads from the Turks alone. This NATO-inspired provocation led to pitched air and sea battles between Greek and Turkish forces, falling just short of inciting a major regional conflict. Turkish jets strafed Greek Cypriot villages and sprayed them with napalm. The human rights violations committed by both sides were to be expected in the circumstances of long-stewing ethnic strife. Yet it was the hidden hand of political plotting in high places that told the real story. Documents captured by the Greek Cypriot side revealed that well-armed Turkish-Cypriot irregulars were working to a preconceived plan to seize a significant northern strip of the island, including a natural beachhead close to Kyrenia, where heavier reinforcements from the Turkish mainland could then be placed ashore. This was precisely the blueprint, down to the exact location, that Turkish forces employed during the forcible rupture of the island eleven years later. As war fever raged across the eastern Aegean, the evidence of external meddling was exposed by RAF Lightning fighters swooping on Greek warplanes, while ignoring the much larger Turkish presence roaming Cypriot air space unchallenged. The Greeks, caught off balance, handicapped as they were by inferior equipment, had been ruthlessly double-crossed in the expectation it would be a short, if somewhat dirty, little scrap to sort out the Cyprus Question once and for all. For Cyprus, read Cuba. Lemnitzer's hurried, Zapata-like lunge to achieve a quick solution had not only gone badly awry, but veered extremely close to igniting a full-scale hot war between two NATO member states. By commission of the fates, here was his personal Bay of Pigs. Debacle it was, yet there were useful propaganda gains, for all that, in terms of imposing a final solution.

In 1964, Johnson despatched his peacemaker, Dean Acheson, on a crisis mission, using the cover story that inter-communal fighting had broken out once again between Turkish and Greek Cypriots. Unable to resist gnawing at the same old bone, the subsequent Acheson Plan predictably opted for partition. Naturally, Acheson did not inform the world that the US, through NATO, had been actively conniving behind the scenes to impose a division of the island by force. Earlier the same year, there was another visitor bearing important messages concerning the future of Cyprus. He was Brigadier Dimitrios Ioannidis, the future dictator, with a well-deserved sadistic reputation as head of ESA. He appeared in Nicosia for an appointment with President Makarios, bringing with him his equally unscrupulous henchman, the former Greek Cypriot guerrilla Nikos Samson. Both were feeding quietly from the CIA trough. Makarios listened expressionless while they coldly prescribed instant *Enosis* by the grisly means of exterminating every Turkish Cypriot man, woman and child in a mass pogrom. The president sent this grim pair packing without a word of encouragement. But they would return in good time, with fatal consequences for the Turkish Cypriot minority, and nearly so for Makarios himself. In Washington, the knives were out. Johnson was incandescent at Greek stonewalling of a key imperial project, as the premier discovered when he called in at the White House. Never the timorous sort, Georgios Papandreou calmly informed the president that if he increased the pressure to divide Cyprus by cutting off US aid to Greece, then he might be tempted to pull Greece out of NATO. As it was, the president could be assured that 'the Greek Parliament would never submit to the Acheson Plan.' Johnson imperiously slapped him down: 'Maybe Greece should rethink the value of a parliament which could not take the right decision.' A few days later, the Greek Ambassador in Washington, Alexander Matsas, was summoned for a formal dressing down by LBJ:

> *America is an elephant and Cyprus a flea. If these two fellows continue itching the elephant they may just get whacked by the elephant's trunk, whacked good. If your prime minister gives me talk about democracy, parliament and constitution, he, his parliament and his constitution may not last very long.*[N1]

Matters were not greatly assisted with the British behaving in an infuriatingly obstructive fashion concerning the partition plan. Cyprus held a special place in British affections, the last staging post before the leisurely glide through Suez Canal en route for the Orient and the Raj, or the first hint of home on the return voyage. Sentiment aside, it was also the gateway to Egypt and the Canal—precisely what made Greece such an alluring attraction to the Axis powers in WW2. Now, having fought *Enosis* guerrillas to a standstill and organised a shared home for all Cypriots, Greeks and Turks alike, here were the Americans with meddlesome plans to stir up trouble in order to enforce partition. The Royal Navy, including its highly capable intelligence division, dismissed 'Med Red Cuba' as a fantasy cooked up by Americans who, dangerously, understood practically nothing about the complicated rifts of the Eastern Mediterranean. The commander-in-chief in Malta, Admiral Sir John Hamilton, roared: 'We are not having those bloody Americans here.' The Sea Lords in London, looking at the disturbing incoming dispatches, dithered and worried about a breach with the United States. MI6 however was attracted to the idea of a palace coup, like the successful partnership with the CIA in Iran a decade before.

LBJ was more susceptible to swallowing Lemnitzer's never-ending schemes and plots than John F. Kennedy. Yet, as it transpired, Papandreou's instincts in playing the Greek veto were correct. The old sage was gifted with a shrewd instinct for the foibles of his countrymen. One of these was yearning for a neutral Greece freed from obligations to take sides in squabbles between the great powers. Another was the strong lure of hard-line authoritarianism dating to the pre-war regime of General Ioannis Metaxas.[30] Yet a third, unhealed wounds from the civil war. Papandreou saw clearly how these accumulating tensions had the capacity to rip the Greek state apart all over again.

Aside from the unlanced boil of Cyprus, there were other nagging issues rippling NATO's power in the Mediterranean lake. The US Sixth Fleet desperately sought the important Greek seaport of Piraeus, close to Athens, as a crucial mooring station. The fiery Maltese premier Dom Mintoff was already well into his campaign to demilitarise the tiny island state and its great natural haven at Valletta. He would finally achieve the permanent eviction of NATO vessels in 1979. The US navy fretted over the long-term security of anchorages in Turkey and Naples. Papandreou's leaning to Greek neutrality in the event the US continued to press for the division of Cyprus, was complicated by the mercurial behaviour of his American-born son, Andreas, who was acting like a loose cannon on the political foredeck. *Père et fils* confused absolutely everything by falling into a public slanging match. Andreas lashed out at his father for cutting political deals behind his back with the royal palace and the Americans. US embassy staff lost sleep over the nightmare prospect of the bombastic son succeeding his elderly, infirm father. Instead of calm diplomacy, the Washington response was to further destabilise two small nations already dangerously unsettled by external provocation. In his 1987 review of my book about these events, *Blood on Their Hands,* the late Christopher Hitchens agreed that I correctly stressed

---

[30] Ioannis Metaxas (1871-1941) the country's senior soldier, who appointed himself 'the national father' during a typically convoluted phase in pre-war Greek politics. He evolved into a Mussolini-style corporate fascist before Italian troops invaded the country in 1940. He died prematurely of a toxic throat infection, having successfully stalled and hugely embarrassed the Italians. In modern Greece, Metaxas is an idol of the far Right, reinvigorated by the EU imposed austerity crisis.

Cyprus as 'central to everything... to American foreign policy the counterpart, in timing and character, of Watergate in domestic policy.'

The King of the Hellenes, Constantine II, was a quixotic figure, with a clipped fuse and a marked reluctance to think before acting. In his early 30's, he had never displayed any signs of statecraft. He was thoroughly overawed by his German mother, Princess Frederica of Hanover, who never bothered to hide her strident authoritarian views. Since 1950, the United States largely controlled the political succession in Greece, paying little attention to an imported German monarchy with shallow roots in Greek soil. The king was, if anything, a pawn to be shuffled around now and again, fished out as a ceremonial decoration when absolutely essential. This included posing in full dress uniform alongside the usurping Colonels. In the closing days of his reign, Constantine pathetically misunderstood just about everything around him, believing himself a central figure instead of the pliant stooge he actually was. Just to be sure, the CIA planted one of its men, the mysterious Colonel Lipczyk (a pseudonym) in the royal circle. The British responded with their own man, Lieutenant Commander Martin Packard, a handsome and intuitive young naval intelligence officer, married to a Greek, a personal friend and regular squash partner of the king. Packard might have slipped from one of John Buchan's Greenmantle novels. He was by turns intelligence officer, peacemaker and negotiator in Cyprus, eyes and ears to Constantine, and then active underground resistance leader during the Junta years. Under cover of providing English language lessons, Packard lectured the infant Democratic Defence movement on secret codes and passing messages between underground cells. He then began to ship explosives and weapons from the UK. Packard sued, successfully, for libel when a Greek journalist claimed he ran his own network inside the resistance movement, Group C, that was really no more than a front for British intelligence. Group C did exist but Packard was carefully not mixed up in it.

A fluent Greek speaker with great reserves of diplomatic charm and patience and a strong attachment to the Cypriot unitary state, he was taken on by the UN as a bridge builder between the two Cypriot communities. One day, he found himself escorting an important visitor from the United States, Assistant Secretary of State George Ball. Tall and heavily built with a thick, wavy mane of silver hair, Ball, a lifelong Bilderberger, was an anti-escalationist dove on Vietnam. This was because he believed the European front against the Soviets should be the main priority. In the Eastern Mediterranean, Ball was a hawk, as Packard swiftly discovered.

Together the pair set off on a round tour of the island while the enthusiastic conciliator Packard eagerly explained how stability was gradually ebbing back. Placing his arm around Packard's shoulder, Ball came out with the astounding revelation: 'That's all very fine, son, but hasn't anyone told you we intend to divide this island?' But that was a mild example of the cynical depths of American policy, compared to future developments. Ball later wrote a self-pleading memoir to dress up a personal mission of big power intrigue in the parody of a humanitarian mission. The demonising of Makarios, which featured in all his telegrams to Washington, somewhat undermined the depth of American sincerity in looking for a genuine solution to a bulging crisis. This is an entertaining clip.

After the traditional tiresome pleasantries, the Archbishop led us to his study, where he went through an astonishing striptease, removing his gold chain, his head covering, and his robes until reduced to shirt sleeves. Newspaper pictures of the Archbishop, with his beard and clerical trappings, had given me an impression of a venerable ecclesiastic. Now I found myself facing a tough, cynical man of fifty-one, far more suited to temporal command than spiritual inspiration.[N2]

As they parted on one occasion, Makarios mused to his visitor through a wry smile: 'Who do you think should kill me, Mr. Ball, the Greek Cypriots or the Turks? The Greeks I think, don't you?' Shortly after Ball's visit, Major General Michael Carver, deputy chief of UN forces in Cyprus, ordered the return of Packard to his own unit, on the bizarre grounds it was 'inadvisable that British officers should carry out liaison duties on both sides.'[N3] This was precisely the mission specified by the UN itself. Of course, Ball had got at the general's back. Packard remains convinced that his undoing lay in a plan he evolved to re-integrate ethnically-mixed Cypriot communities, starting with a handful of villages in June 1964. The plan was unscrambled as soon as he left. Packard was left with no doubts of American intentions to sabotage anything tainted by the spirit of an integrated island republic. He was consoled that same year with an MBE in the Queen's Birthday Honours List. Interestingly, the favour was granted for precisely those 'inadvisable duties' on both sides of the line which the citation declared he had performed with the 'required tact and patience.'

Still on the Navy List, with an offer of permanent secondment to the UN, Packard often found himself in Athens in the period leading up to the Colonels' putsch. He and the king often played tennis and squash, exchanging gossip and theories arising from the increasingly heated political temperature. By 1967, as the final crisis approached, Packard was thus in an excellent position to keep an eye on Constantine, who was visibly falling apart under the constant pressure. The city was in a state of feverish turmoil, every coffee bar sizzling with reports and rumours of plots. The king's diminishing usefulness lay in his titular office and little else. He found himself tugged this way and that between the rival nests of plotters. The British Embassy and MI6 remained convinced — even in the face of the misgivings of on-the-spot naval intelligence officers — that the king could be brought into play to stage a personal coup, to blunt a crude putsch. So sure in fact that when Packard dashed to London to warn the Admiralty Sea Lords that he had just left an isolated and miserable Constantine, alone and brooding in his empty palace, expecting a CIA *coup d'état* at any moment, he was roughly sent packing. He caught the first plane to Athens with their Lordships' parting words, 'This does not square with our understanding of the situation,' ringing in his ears.[N4]

As dawn broke on 21st April, Greeks woke to find themselves subjects of a gaggle of hitherto unknown middle-ranking army officers. They rubbed their eyes with disbelief at three portly figures bulging from ill-fitting uniforms, smirking like fat cats who found the cream dish unguarded. This comparison is not altogether inapt. During the previous night, the conspirators tipped the Greek army's top brass unceremoniously from their beds, virtually imprisoned them, then bullied and harassed the confused young monarch into legitimising the putsch and, for good measure, set rival factions inside the US embassy at furious odds with each other. The Junta moved with deadly precision, thanks to Operation Prometheus, the script written by NATO to frustrate a communist insurrection, so there was no opportunity to mount resistance. The king was humiliatingly paraded in the token ceremonial uniform of a field marshal, along with ministers of the former government, as helpless in the present circumstances as he. He was photographed smiling stiffly alongside the grinning usurpers, his face drained white by popping flash bulbs. The royal figure resembled a lifeless china ornament in fancy dress. The impression was broadly correct.

The baton of power was jointly grasped by the triumvirate from the Greek Pentagon — Brigadier Stylianos Pattakos alongside a pair of one-pip colonels, Georgios Papadopoulos and Nikolaos Makarezos. Their joint dictatorship would last seven years, finally destroyed by the NATO-inspired invasion of Cyprus and the western change of heart that restored Greek democracy (albeit in a carefully managed form). The trio were all Sheepskin/Gladio men, soaked in Theban fantasies which they solemnly believed granted them alone the sacred honour of 'saving' Greece from godless Leftists. The repressive elements of the coup machine crunched into action. Thousands of potential opponents were pitched into prisons and military jails, where the torturing began. The solid and stubborn old statesman Georgios Papandreou, almost 80, was detained and held incommunicado, and denied vital medicines that he needed for his heart condition. The instruction was said to come from the CIA. He died under house arrest a year later. The persecution and tragedy of this gentle and wise old Greek patriot falls only marginally short of crude political assassination.

Greek citizens were not the only ones rubbing their eyes. The US embassy was gripped by enormous confusion after the night's hectic events, trapped between rival camps of the diplomatic service and the CIA, and even as we shall see, between internal factions of the CIA itself. Adding to the general air of chaos, the British embassy and British secret intelligence concluded they had been thoroughly double-crossed by the Americans. But, confusing the already highly confused picture even further, precisely *which* Americans? In London, *Evening Standard* news-stand placards were shouting 'King's men seize power,' which implied some pre-arranged briefing to Fleet Street editors by MI6. But this was certainly not the royal putsch which US Ambassador Phillips Talbot had anticipated and which the British supported. The official embassy policy was a 'soft,' carefully-crafted velvet-and-ermine coup, placing senior Greek commanders in the seats of power, should Papandreou's Centre Union win the forthcoming general election.

An inspirational, if ruthless, Greek-American CIA thug called Gustav 'Gust' Avrakotos then rudely gatecrashed the party. The former high school dropout turned CIA action man hijacked the slow-motion coup with his own daring freelance strike. It was Avrakotos who selected lowly Gladio officers to be the new rulers of Greece. Avrakotos always loved to describe how he joined the CIA. 'Do you like to play in dark alleys?' a recruiting officer supposedly asked the ex-bartender when he turned up for an interview at Langley. He got the reply, 'Sure. I love it.' Avrakotos boasted forever afterwards that his sympathetic questioner 'recognised my real talent — that I was a f***ing street guy.' He certainly stood out as a lone wolf among the Ivy League suits, who gave him a wide berth. The drawling, shock-haired, chain-smoking hard boozer with a ballistic temper bore scant respect for his superiors and always preferred to work alone. His main stripe was independence of mind, followed inevitably by precipitate action. In 1964 he was posted to Athens, possibly to clear the poisonous mood swirling around him in Washington. He plunged with glee into the complexities of the situation, tailor-made for his brand of dark skills. He quickly concluded his station colleagues were pussy-footing around the chief problem, which was Cyprus. Teamwork was not his strongest suit. He once showed a photograph of a colleague who crossed him to an old Greek woman reputed to be a witch, and solemnly instructed her to lay the worst imaginable curse on the victim. Pursuing matters in his usual freelance fashion, he looked up Colonel Georgios Grivas, hero of the *Eoka* rebellion against the British in Cyprus. With never more than about a hundred men, Grivas tied down an army of ten thousand. Mocking clumsy British over-kill tactics, Grivas wrote this sally: 'One does not use a tank to catch field mice. A cat would do the job much better.' Grivas was the perfect cat for Avrakotos. He marked his card for future reference.

Just as 'Gust' dismissed Constantine as an irrelevant bauble, so he typically sneered at the projected ermine coup. He much preferred those jackals who would 'do what it takes.' Blissfully unaware of the counter-plotting, taking their own good time, the complacent senior officer corps of the armed forces foolishly began to transfer seditious middle-ranking key officers — nearly all members of the Sheepskin stay-behind unit — to the immediate environs of Athens. These were precisely the cat-and-mouse tactics in which 'Gust' revelled. The three key plotters assembled at the home of Brigadier Pattakos on the night of 18th April. Over the ouzo they decided to execute the Prometheus blueprint forthwith. But there was a fourth figure present. Avrakotos was to be known for the remainder of his tenure in Greece as the 'fourth dictator.' His rough tactics forgiven, he was to remain the power manipulating the junta with unseen hands until finally outed by CIA renegade Philip Agee, author of the whistle-blowing epic *Beyond Hope.*

Avrakotos was already well acquainted with Brigadier Dimitrios Ioannidis, sadistic chief of the much-feared Greek military secret police, ESA. Its busy torture chambers, with their long post-coup waiting lists, were situated close to the US embassy. Unfortunates dragged to these dungeons would be coldly informed that nothing could spare them, since the 'United States and NATO backed the military government.' Ioannidis had a framed notice precisely to this effect placed on the wall behind his desk, lest there should be any doubt. Crude, greedily ambitious, known for an acidic sense of humour, Ioannidis was nonetheless hampered by intellectual blinkers. So he failed to interpret the warning signs of the role he was destined to play, in the final tragedy of the sundering of Cyprus, the destruction of the Junta, and the ultimate personal irony of the pitiless jailer confined behind prison bars for life.

Agee was among those privy to the chaos in the embassy, where Ambassador Talbot was reduced to desperately trying to discover who the new masters of Greece actually were. One can imagine 'Gust' smirking maliciously in the background. He had pulled off, quite literally, the biggest coup of his life to that point.[31] (He would enjoy even bigger excitements during NATO's Afghan War). The business on everyone's lips in the

---

[31] Posthumously, tough guy Gust became a Tinseltown star. His real-life role as the organizer of a mule train ferrying weapons to the Afghan Mujahideen featured prominently in the Hollywood movie *Charlie Wilson's War* (adapted from George Crile's 2003 book of the same name). Avrakotos was played inimitably by Philip Seymour Hoffman. The drama is based on Texas congressman Wilson's covert dealings in Afghanistan, and how his private-enterprise efforts to aid rebels fighting Russian invaders turned into the classic blowback, with unforeseen and long-reaching effects. Much of this was again due to Avrakotos. Officially off the CIA's books, he was later up to his neck in the hiring of Mujahideen volunteers to fight in the Balkans.

embassy was now the fate of George Ball's Cyprus Project. Agee saw telegrams from Athens which, if they reflected the general air of confusion, suggested the usurpers were 'sensitive' to American interests. The triumvirate appeared at the embassy, where they offered consoling reassurances. The sense of crisis began to fade. Greece would remain firmly anchored in the NATO camp, with the Sixth Fleet free to operate from important ports like Piraeus. The regime received a gentle tap on the wrist for the sake of American public opinion. The ambassador was withdrawn for a token year. In London, the socialist Prime Minister Harold Wilson for once stepped alongside US policy and quickly recognised the regime. When Constantine flew to Washington to plead for American ships to restore him to the throne (he had placed himself in exile) Lyndon Johnson all but yawned in the royal face. The West turned a blind eye to the blatant re-imposition of fascism on the European continent, even as Salazar faltered in Portugal, and Franco in Spain approached the departure lounge. There remained, though, the unfinished business in Cyprus, the centrality of all American strategic policy in the region.

We return to the Acheson and Ball plans to apply the carving knife to Cyprus, an integral element in promoting the Greek coup. On another of his missions to the island, Ball turned to an aide with the startling insight that since Makarios was the most important road block to these designs, it was better to get him out of the picture altogether. Ball explained that US intelligence was in touch with a 'force' on the island willing to eliminate this ecclesiastical pest. He was referring to the wily Colonel Grivas, agile and tough as a mountain goat, freshly returned to his former scenes of glory in command of the Greek Cypriot militia. His enmity with Makarios, once an ally, then an enemy in the struggle for the *Enosis* union with Greece, seemed to mark him as the natural choice to settle scores. Digenis — his *nom de guerre* — was still the unchallenged expert in concealing bands of fighters deep in the island's northern Troodos Mountains. Soon he was back to the old recipe of swooping on unsuspecting Turkish settlements and shooting at Left-wing politicians bitterly opposed to partition. When Grivas attacked a strongly-armed group of Turkish resistance fighters, the Turks threatened the 'heaviest retaliation.' The junta panicked, ordering Digenis and his band home immediately. Back in Athens, he set about organising underground cells with the aim of toppling the junta, ostensibly because they had become unpalatable with their sadistic manners, but really because he correctly suspected them of planning to double-cross the Americans over partition.

It was true. The fat cats had begun to revel in the ripe fruits of power. They dropped the scruffy uniforms in favour of smartly tailored suits. Papadopoulos, savviest of the trio, viewed the Cypriot imbroglio as a potential death trap, whose consequences might provoke open war across the region. Papadopoulos also strained relations with his colleagues by preening himself as a natural ruler. His carefully-posed image, featuring the pointedly raised eyebrows, the fixed glare at far horizons, beamed down in many a humble home in the rural conservative heartlands and the islands, where he was regarded as a saviour. To say this egregious self-promotion grated on his fellow dictators' nerves was an understatement. They decided to get rid of him. Waiting in the wings: the pathological Ioannidis.

There was a new president in Washington now, Richard Nixon. The Israelis badgered him to eliminate the troublesome priest in Nicosia before he had the chance to establish a Cuban-style Soviet client state, which would then pose a running threat to every sea route and air lane in the region. Utterly taken in by this excitable and absurd hyperbole, Nixon dispatched his winged Mercury in the form of Spiro Agnew, in October 1971. His clear instructions were to shake the junta to their senses over Cyprus, and honour their obligations. The omens were scarcely encouraging. There were gaping rents in the political fabric of the junta, steadily eaten away by the acid of personal jealousies. The obedient Nixon crony Henry Tasca,[32] whose long pedigree in Greek corporate crime offered useful potential in his new guise as US ambassador, cabled Washington with growing alarm at the developing power struggle. This he reported was mostly at the expense of Papadopoulos, the central figure but regarded by the military establishment as getting far too big for his fine imported shoes. Tensions were growing among the populace too, especially among restless radical students in the capital. The longer Greece remained susceptible to American pressure, the easier it would be to impose a solution in Cyprus, but that hold was looking more tenuous by the day. In the meantime other eyes eagerly scrutinised the activities of the imperial envoy for clues to American intentions.

Russian diplomats in Athens continually taunted the western partners with splendidly accurate inside knowledge of their every twist and turn in Greece. The Soviet embassy's most enjoyable prank was to summon prominent Greek journalists for drinks and a chat, then regale them with the latest snippets of salacious gossip. The Americans and the British, still in a mood of discomfort with each other, began to suspect a mole somewhere in the works — all too plausible in the light of former embarrassments. These notably included the double agents Guy Burgess and Donald MacLean, who were exposed in 1956, and the legendary case of Kim Philby, who fled to Russia in 1963. If the Americans doubted British reliability over Cyprus, the stuffy British for their part never forgave 'those bloody Americans' for

---

[32] A Nixon crony appointed ambassador in 1969. Diverted Greek Gladio funds to Nixon's re-election campaign and defence of the Watergate burglars. Reputedly involved in smuggling arms intended for the Greek army on behalf of the CIA. He knew Jack Ruby from way back. Fired when the junta fell in 1974. Died in 1979, in an unexplained car smash in Switzerland which involved no other vehicles.

misappropriating the royal coup. Under these strains, the famous special relationship wallowed in very heavy weather. Friction rose to the point where direct speaking between the two embassies posed difficulties. Ironically, there actually was a Soviet agent in the picture, a young Norwegian called Arne Treholt, but he was far away in Sweden, spying on the bunker containing the restless exiled Andreas Papandreou and his cohorts.[33]

Into this fractious landscape stepped Ann Chapman, travelling incognito with a posse of travel agents on a freebie, inspecting hotels for the following season. The party was led by a 30-year-old Greek, Aristotelis ('Tellis') Kotsias, a senior figure in MI6's special Greek squad, behind his cover as a local representative for the Olympic Holidays tour firm in London. Ann occasionally popped in on the travel agents for a social chat, but otherwise devoted her days to mysterious tasks she never described. Once, she let slip she was followed everywhere, but did not infer why. Progressively her mood began to darken, to the point where she was almost totally self-absorbed and barely communicative. Only with Kotsias did she seem fully at ease. I suspect that they were in love and that he was a key figure in her mission. Ann had arranged to meet contacts in Greece that were not involved with tourism. She had also been spotted in London talking to others who were on different sides of the Greek fence. She was regularly seen at the Troubador, a popular bar in Kensington that acted as a social gathering scene for members of the expatriate resistance movement. She met with senior officials of the Greek embassy, one of whom later went to great lengths to avoid discussing their talks. Ann called on the American Express manager in Athens, controller of a network of important underground cells. Tellingly, he was arrested hours after her death was officially reported, then thrown into the same ESA dungeons where she had been murdered.[(N5)]

The mission was compromised from the outset. In order to protect the mission's secrecy, the MI6 post in Athens had not been informed of Chapman's arrival. In any event, she operated under deep cover in all her service assignments. In a separate complication, MI6 and the CIA were still at cross purposes in the fallout from the coup. Thanks to the tip-off from a senior figure in the London embassy, exceedingly dangerous eyes and ears — KYP and its military counterpart ESA — were also on her tail. Chapman's activities, accidentally rather than deliberately, also became inextricably caught up in the tensions surrounding the visit of Spiro Agnew, the first such high-level dignitary to grace the military regime.

---

[33] Norway's most famous spy. A former journalist and later a high-flying member of the Norwegian foreign service, he was sentenced in 1985 to 20 years for high treason. He was freed after serving only eight. He is now a director of a Russian-owned business in southern Cyprus.

He arrived with an early Christmas present, the promise of a squadron of jet fighters for the air force, whose loyalty to the regime was considered highly suspect. Theoretically this was a breach of the international arms embargo against the junta. It was also a warning to the Soviets that America did not intend to weaken her strategic footing in the region. Ironically, it was a much-decorated air force brigadier who arranged a pyrotechnic salute to the imperial visitor by exploding a cluster of bombs near the airport. In the course of the visit, a helicopter joyride around the Aegean, hosted by Papadopoulos himself, intended to demonstrate the serenity of public opinion, was abruptly cut short because, reporters were told, of 'sudden bad weather.' There was not a single cloud in the azure sky, but curiously the entire Greek air force was officially grounded, instantly. The parish pump in Athens circulated stories of a projected air force attack on Agnew's helicopter, which later acquired substance when it became known that Andreas Papandreou, brooding and fretting in Stockholm, had called for an incident of some spectacular nature to re-galvanise drifting international opinion against the Junta.[N6] Conjecture perhaps, but nonetheless the plain technical fact is that only the air force possessed the capability to mount such a daring assault during Agnew's visit. Perhaps the airport bombs had not been such a sideshow after all, but a forewarning.

The junta preened themselves in the regal presence, explaining in a deluded fashion how they were planning a return to constitutional politics. The special US counsellor in the Athens embassy, Rodger Davies, prattled on about 'the proof of America's patient efforts to restore democracy.' This was solely for public consumption. Behind the scenes, Agnew railed at the lack of progress on the partition of Cyprus, which ironically was to cost Davies his life. The colonels muttered assurances, noticeably weak in respect of Papadopoulos. Ioannidis, watching and brooding, resolved to bide his time.

Chapman's disappearance from the cheap seaside hotel in Kavouri, the 'dirty business' which afterwards Kotsias could never bear to discuss again, set the British authorities off on a trail of deception which still has no clear end. Her father Edward, a retired engineer, exhausted every penny of his lifetime savings commuting to and from the country where his daughter died, hounding governments, ministers, embassies, courts and policemen to tell him the truth. The official account, accepted in a rigged junta court, was that Ann popped over a fence for impromptu sex (unfazed by her monthly period) with a minor pervert well known to the police, in order to pass a few moments waiting to catch a bus into the city.

The many mysteries around her fate included the victim's miraculous powers to transport herself from several locations to the field where she was finally found. The Peeping Tom managed to tie her ankles and wrists behind her back with barbed wire, torn with unscarred bare hands from a fence bordering the field. Moreover, my investigations for *Blood on Their Hands* suggested that the British embassy knew exactly how Chapman died, and at whose hands. Not for the first time in its chequered history, MI6 emerged from the affair scented with something other than violets. Not only did the MI6 station in Athens at first fail to understand she was one of theirs, but when their suspicions were finally aroused, they fell for the black confidence trick, planted by the US embassy, that she was possibly a traitor. The autopsy conducted by Dr. Dimitrios Kapsaskis left no doubts concerning Ann's treatment once she was inside Ioannidis' chamber of horrors.

The bruises on either side of her arms are marks made by the fingers of hands which violently grabbed the person by the arms in order to immobilise her, probably from behind as indicated by the thumb marks on the backs of the arms. There were multiple bruises to the centre and right of the forehead and across the bridge of the nose and around the left eye, all caused by a blunt instrument. A fractured rib probably caused by the downward pressure of a knee. Bruise marks caused by fingers on the throat, the result of strangulation applied with such force the victim began to inhale blood from her nose and pharynx during the violent constriction of the neck by means of the hand.[N7]

Having completed his exemplary forensic examination and specified precisely the causes of death, Kapsaskis then behaved very oddly. He butchered her features with his scalpel, for no evident scientific purpose, but clearly on orders of higher authority. No eyes were allowed to see evidence that compromised the forthcoming account of a peeping tom. Not one qualified individual identified her corpse in Athens, or when it arrived in London — not even her parents. They were kept at bay by Radio London's padre, the Reverend Eric Blennerhassett, whose brother worked for MI5. Blennerhassett's explanation to me at his retirement bungalow in Southsea, that he 'popped in to the undertakers' in West London, and saw Ann's profile 'going slightly yellow, like a banana going off' was, coming from a clergyman, something he may by now have accounted for to a higher power. The undertakers in any event firmly insisted his reverence had never been anywhere near their premises. The Home Secretary of the day, the scandal-mired Reginald Maudling, had the remains hustled into the Putney cremation chamber with indecent haste, to head off pressure for an inquest. The crematorium paperwork for Ann included special Home Office Order LA 071166.[34] The entire procedure was illegal. To round it off, the BBC issued a

---

[34] The document was destroyed early in 2009. According to crematorium staff – one of whom by extraordinary co-incidence once lived next door to the Chapman family and knew Ann well – this was normal practice after a certain interval. The certificate was still extant when I telephoned that year to check some details. When I called again a few days later concerning a different matter, it no longer existed. Staff were

unique and unprecedented diktat to all employees to refrain from connecting the dead woman to the corporation in any manner whatsoever.

The British embassy coldly ordered Edward Chapman to 'stop badgering' their officials with his demands. There was a gleam of motive some years later, when a kindly Home Office bureaucrat (a unique being, in Edward Chapman's bitter experience) wrote to say there was no lack of sympathy, only 'certain constraints we have no choice but no respect.' I was given a somewhat firmer explanation, partially at least, by the Justice Minister, Georgios Mangakis. When we parted for the last time, he escorted me to a chamber in the basement of the ministry, windowless, as he explained, 'a place for private conversations without an audience.' He repeated the problem of the Cyprus File, but added that if the truth were to emerge, then it would 'compromise the special relations between the British and Americans.' And upon that subject, he could say no more.

Agnew hurried back to Washington, convinced he had in his luggage the main souvenir he was sent to secure: the division of Cyprus. Their arms sore from the thorough socket wrenching, the junta created an offshoot of the Greek Gladio secret army, which they called Eoka-B, under the command of Giorgios Grivas. These guerrillas were armed and financed by the CIA through secret army channels, and primed to be ready for action in Cyprus. But for the time being, apart from some fitful actions, they largely cooled their heels, waiting for concrete orders.

The excuse to dispose of Papadopoulos presented itself with his bungled handling of the massive student uprising at the Athens Polytechnic — another day of infamy destined to ring down the years — 17th November 1973. He first made the mistake of sending emissaries to negotiate with the students, and when that failed to produce results, resorted to threats. The mood of the crowd changed to angry defiance. The police began firing shots, not in the air as they afterwards claimed, but straight into the mass confronting them. By dawn the following day, 43 bodies were counted. Ten days after the near-rising, a convoy of armoured vehicles grumbled up to the self-promoted general's residence, around midnight. He was smartly saluted by an officer who handed him his neatly-typed resignation statement. During his long years of prison confinement, the Doubting Thomas of the Junta would find at least some partial consolation in the knowledge that his agnostic stance on Cyprus had been right all along.

---

not able to explain how and by whom the body was transferred from an airtight cask to a coffin suitable for cremation, except that the personnel at Putney would not have been responsible.

The power vacuum within the Junta was filled by Ioannidis, who effectively became the sole dictator. The Americans judged correctly that this swaggering braggart could be easily be duped. Washington had already decided the military regime had outlived its usefulness; the sack of the Polytechnic had seen to that. However the important work of Cyprus lay unfinished, demanding that the Junta's life-support systems should be extended a little longer. In Turkey, Bülent Ecevit, a figure convivial to the 'double Enosis' partition project, was eased into the premiership with a helping hand from the CIA. He brought two happy blessings with him. First, he had studied Greek at university. Second, he had once been taught by Henry Kissinger at Harvard. Kissinger was now the American Secretary of State, up to his ears in the Cyprus conspiracy. Using the forum of NATO meetings in Brussels, a plan was concocted to stage a diversion that would allow Turkish troops to land in the north of the island. Legally, this would not be classified as an invasion. This was because Turkey was among the signatories to a four-power pact — the others being Greece, the UK and the US — that allowed each of the parties to intervene unilaterally in the event of an emergency. Ioannidis was just the man to set the ball rolling. Nikos Samson (not his real name; he thought it would make him sound heroic) of the earlier encounter with Archbishop Makarios was quickly co-opted to prepare himself for action — and promotion. Samson, who published his own hate-filled newspaper specialising in gory pictures of pogrom victims, had been responsible for some of the worst atrocities involving Turkish Cypriots, so the task he was now given was a natural extension. The old war horse Grivas conveniently died, quite probably poisoned, at his retreat in Cyprus as invasion day approached, out of fear he would subvert anything but full *enosis*. Throughout the early months of 1974, the grand design moved to its conclusion. Samson, the pathological terrorist who thought all Turkish-Cypriots should have their throats cut as a matter of course, was inflated to president-in-waiting. A great deal of posturing and bluffing occupied the international stage for the purposes of gearing up an artificial crisis, the renowned process of elaborate deception known as *skevoria*.

On 15th July, fresh reinforcements of Gladio cohorts were fired up by an enlivening personal mission statement from the deluded Ioannidis, basking in the glow of destiny. A small Greek naval flotilla landed the party on the western coast. They dashed straight to the presidential palace in Nicosia, where Makarios was entertaining a visiting group of schoolchildren. A scene of black theatre then ensued as the president-prelate, bullets whistling around his episcopal raiment, played cat and mouse with Samson all over Cyprus. He eventually claimed sanctuary in RAF Akrotiri, a British sovereign territory air base. From there Makarios was rushed by air force plane to London and then onwards with a government air ticket to New York and the UN, howling all the way at the duplicity of the Americans and their Greek stooges. The special relationship took another hammering, since the episode clearly indicated to American intelligence the scale of British deceit in foiling the liquidation of the despised archbishop. The rank smell of betrayal wafted around CIA nostrils, with lasting consequences.

Samson's reign of terror lasted only a week, during which he carried out the orders from Ioannidis to launch a terrifying pogrom. Villages were put to the torch, their inhabitants — men, women and children — mercilessly slain. Then by pre-arrangement, he too was duped, as a massive force of Turkish paratroopers and seaborne commandos landed in the north, in a near bloodless invasion. It was all over, and despite the wailing, hand-wringing and liberal helpings of *skevoria*, Cyprus had been slashed with the imperial cutlass. In Athens, Ioannidis screamed at American diplomats: 'You fooled us.' A few days later, he too was led away. The junta imploded and the chief stars of the resistance packed their bags for home. For all these calumnies, Greeks underwent the shattering of their frail democracy, their civil rights ground under the boots of commonplace officers, who under foreign orders mutinied against their superiors. Thousands were snatched from their homes on the vaguest pretext, abused and terrorised by pitiless thugs. Cyprus, an independent European state, recognised by the United Nations, was dismantled against a background of state-inspired genocide — one more country denied the right to have a government that ran against the grain of western geo-political interests. It was the recurrent theme of Gladio everywhere.

James Callaghan, the wartime naval lieutenant now on watch as British prime minister, was all at sea throughout the entire affair, appearing to have no clear grip as to what was going on. He even toyed with sending the Royal Navy to intercept the Turkish armada. If only for an instant, this raised the intriguing spectacle of two NATO battle fleets engaged in open combat, with Russian admirals sipping vodka around the radar screens in delighted wonderment.

The days of reckoning were not long in coming. Rodger Davies, the leading State Department apologist in the face of rising congressional sentiment against the Greek regime, was an acutely insensitive choice as the new ambassador to Cyprus. He arrived to prepare the ground about a month before the enforced partition. Not long after that he was dead, killed in a remarkable fashion as the embassy came under a sudden and violent siege. A sniper with a deadly aim, and a very accurate picture of the ground plan of the building, fired a single bullet. This travelled through the open doors of several rooms and the full length of a connecting corridor, before finding its target sitting at his desk directing the defence of the embassy. As his Cypriot secretary Antoinette Varnava bent over the stricken diplomat, her head was expertly lopped off by a repeat shot. Marksmen of that expertise were to be found by the score in the ranks of the stay-behind armies.

The death of Rodger Davies indicated a distinct swing of the pendulum. Despite pleadings from officials, Cypriot police made no attempt to quell the riot, or aid the besieged diplomats, thus allowing the gunmen free range. The shot that killed Davies came from a high velocity rifle fitted with uncommonly powerful sights, standard NATO kit. It was precisely the weaponry issued to Gladio Sheepskin commandos recently ordered to the island to assassinate Makarios. Davies's death was part revenge by bitter men who believed themselves thrown to the wolves by the Americans, and part the beginning of a process which would lead to the appearance of the November 17 death squad, together with its many clones, as guns for hire on the streets of Athens for decades to come.

Ann Chapman's friend and probable lover 'Tellis' Kotsias drowned in March 1980 in the River Thames, near a popular waterside pub. Following reports of some kind of incident involving a car, police frogmen discovered a Volvo saloon caught on the river bed, the body of a woman trapped in the rear seat and clinging outside, a man with his fingers caught in the driver's door. Martin Packard remained an articulate advocate of the rights of small countries and their peoples to choose their own solutions. Brigadier Dimitrios Ioannidis was convicted of high treason and accessory to killings during the Polytechnic rising. He died in jail in August 2010, aged 87. Georgios Papadopoulos died in prison, in 1999. He remains the idol of the Far Right, which recently made a dramatic return to the Greek political spectrum. Cypriot President-for-a-week Nikos Samson escaped any serious retribution, aside from token jail terms. He died of cancer in April 2001, aged 66. Having renounced the Greek throne, ex-King Constantine II lives reclusively in the swish Mayfair quarter of London, occasionally hawking the family silver at Sotheby's to make ends meet. Archbishop Makarios died of a heart attack in 1977. A quarter of a million mourners and 200 political dignitaries from around the world followed his bier to the graveside. Edward Chapman's remains lie with those of his beloved daughter, in a glade at Putney Crematorium in South London, re-united at last. Yet I have never been able to settle in my own mind that it actually was Ann's body that travelled to London in the hold of a British airliner. The confusing events in Athens, the bizarre disfigurement of her corpse, the antics in London and Athens to frustrate formal identification, and the question of how and by whom her corpse was transferred from an airtight transit casket to a wooden coffin suitable for cremation, all leave considerable room for doubt.

All attempts to reverse the Acheson Chop have so far failed. Northern Cyprus is a pariah state, recognised by no one save mainland Turks, who pick up the orphan's bills. The sundered island is half in the EU (the Greek side) and half out (the Turkish rump). 'November 17' lived on as the band name of an urban guerrilla faction who would be active in the Greek years of lead for the next three decades (another grand exercise in the Greek theatre of *skevoria* that we explore in the next chapter). And Greece is under foreign occupation once again, mugged by the global bankocracy and the EU.

Echoes from Syntagma Square.

Der Spiegel, 30th June 2011:

At the moment when the largest austerity package in Greek history was being passed, it was relatively quiet on Athens' Syntagma Square. Demonstrators sat on the ground, their shoulders slumped and heads down, smoking, chatting and drinking water from plastic bottles. They looked resigned, even while their leaders were still calling for an uprising.

Then all hell broke loose.

The Greek riot police hurled tear gas grenades into the crowd from left and right. Rubbing their eyes, people started moving — running, stumbling, unsure which way to go, but only wanting to get out and reach safety. Many started shouting. Others, gasping for air, looked for their friends. A young woman yelled: 'Help me!' Meanwhile, the rain of stones, bottles and tear gas grenades continued amid the chaos.

VIII.
Behind the Mask of the Red Death

'We believe the attack was carried out either by those members of Revolutionary Struggle who are still at large or by other active groups like the Conspiracy of Fire Nuclei or the Revolutionary Sect.' — Athens gendarmerie spokesman following anti-austerity protests in Athens, May 2010.

One bright summer morning in 2002, the accustomed sleepy calm of Leipsoi, a popular holiday gem in the sparkling Dodecanese necklace strung across the southern Aegean, was shattered by strange events. For years the island was the summer home of a scholarly lecturer from Athens and his French wife. Suddenly this tall, if rather stout figure, known for his love of good food and genial courtesy, was seen fleeing headlong towards the quays of the island's small port. He was apparently pursued by a fire-fighter's helicopter. The most wanted man in Greece was snared before he could board a hydrofoil that would take him to the safe refuge of Turkish shores.

The astonished islanders would shortly learn Alexandros Giotopoulos was none other than the mastermind and chief theoretician responsible for the wave of cold-blooded terror rocking Athens since the 1980s. Police boasted they had finally captured the head of the famously elusive gang of Marxist urban guerrillas known as November 17, inspired — their members insisted — by the brutally-crushed 1973 Athens Polytechnic uprising against the military junta. The arrest of this silvery-haired academic, now almost 60, provoked equal surprise among his neighbours in Athens. They cooed to reporters of his love of culture and literature, his sensitivity, politeness, and their envy at his success rate with young women at such a venerable age. The snatching and subsequent trial of Giotopoulos together with fifteen members of his gang — who were largely drawn together by blood ties — raised many curious questions. Giotopoulos, or Ekonomou, his alias in Greece, could claim noble lineage in an old Marxist-Leninist dynasty. He was born in France, where his father Dimitris had been personal secretary to Leon Trotsky, before the great splitter was forced to discharge his acolyte for preaching his own unsound private theology. Dimitris responded by forming his own breakaway movement called the Archeo-Marxists, who then distinguished themselves by turning their guns against the communists during the Greek civil war.

With such a background, his son was never likely to be a shrinking violet. His endowments included a well-furnished brain, his father's rich talent for plotting, and a debonair *ambiance* that ignited great passion among droves of female consorts. The young Alexandros also inherited his father's attraction to independence of mind and direct action. He was spotted briefly at a finishing school for guerrillas in Castro's Cuba. Then he turned up in Athens to make unholy war on the colonels. The underground cell he founded soon became one of those most feared by the junta for daring attacks and ability to fade seamlessly into the background, the stripe of 'November 17' yet to come. From faraway Stockholm, the career of this young revolutionary was observed approvingly by Andreas Papandreou, his own visions crowded with scenes of carnage and bloodshed that might raise the world against the Junta. Sensing the germ of the guerrilla resistance army for which he yearned, Papandreou saw to it that his socialist wing of the resistance helped Giotopoulos in any way that it could. But eventually things became too hot. Denounced, as he certainly was, by jealous factions among the ill-fitting jigsaw pieces of the resistance, Giotopoulos fled to exile in Paris. But first he made a detour to call on Papandreou, vengeful and side-lined, brooding in his Swedish bunker.

This episode is critical to unravelling the real identity of November 17 and its clones because of two important factors. The first puzzle was how the gang of bandit-guerrillas operating in a very small country evaded the police for 27 years, without the police detecting a hint as to their hideaway, still less making a single arrest. This was despite the abundance of obvious clues, many of which appeared to be scattered deliberately. The second was the throbbing question as to what extent November 17 may have been acting beneath a blanket of official blessing. Even that is a simplification. In this distorted underworld hall of mirrors, what reflection could be safely taken as real? When Giotopoulos was eventually sentenced, he railed at the forces of 'western intelligence' that he blamed for deceiving and betraying him and his followers.

One man who has provided important clues to the meaning of that outcry is the Thessaloniki-based investigatory psychiatrist, neurologist, sociologist, professional revisionist and prolific libertarian author, Dr. Kleanthis Grivas. In the course of half a century, Grivas set himself against authority of every pigment, particularly in the field of humanitarian shortcomings of the Greek state. Terrorism was unlikely to escape his attention. In 2005, he made the startling claim that high-profile assassinations attributed to November 17 — including the killing of CIA station boss Richard Welch in Athens in 1975, and the murder of the British military attaché Brigadier Stephen Saunders as recently as 2000 — were false-flag counterfeit operations by the Greek Gladio outfit codenamed Sheepskin. In a further twist, the killings were sub-contracted out by foreign intelligence services, in cohorts with the domestic espionage services. He further asserted that Saunders's fate was connected to NATO's Balkan Wars, in which he was a prominent figure.[N1] Some clear evidence that Greek authorities were old and experienced hands at prefabricating terrorist acts can be traced back to my book *Blood on Their Hands,* in which I described the fate of one of the country's most respected newspapermen.

The hunting down of an old lion of the Greek liberal media offers some light on the many cases in the gray zone, never formally claimed by November 17, but attributed to designer-label revolutionary cells of nominal substance. Georgios Athanasiadis, untiring scourge of all political chicanery and outspoken editor of the prestigious *Vradini* — a newspaper with a long and unfettered reputation for acerbic comment on public matters — made scores of enemies in high places. He fearlessly championed deep investigative writing, particularly concerning the Chapman maze and clandestine activities of foreign powers in Greece. But he tempted the fates to the limits with a series of articles calling into question the official line that November 17 was responsible for all terrorism in Greece. The paper's investigations suggested that the infamous terror gang might well be a glove for the hand of the government. If ever a man wrote his own death certificate, it was Athanasiadis. One day in March 1983, he was sitting in his office quietly chatting to a well-known Athenian businessman, Constantine Courcoubines, when a message was passed that a young man was standing downstairs in reception with 'a story he knew would interest the editor.' Running as he did an open house and never able to resist enticing tit-bits, the venerable editor invited him up. Courcoubines saw through a gap in the door 'the visitor whispering something in the editor's ear.'

> *Whatever he said shocked and alarmed Athanasiadis. 'This cannot be,' he cried out. Seconds later shots were heard. Athanasiadis was felled by two bullets from a small pistol, once in the back of the head and twice in the shoulder. Courcoubines was also shot three times as the assassin fled.*[N2]

The career of Athanasiadis, stubborn needle of authority, drained away in a pool of blood around his own desk, at the age of seventy-one. His audacious killer made not the slightest attempt to disguise himself. He strolled out, quickly swallowed by the raucous streets of Athens. He was seen by at least half a dozen qualified witnesses, one of them Courcoubines, who miraculously survived. The killer appeared arrogant in the knowledge that he was immune from detection. The Athens constabulary later claimed to have found leaflets claiming responsibility by an anarchist terrorist cell calling itself the Anti-Military Struggle. The furious anarchists for once broke surface and denounced the so-called 'evidence' as blatant official forgeries. The trail went cold, setting the pattern for the next three decades.

Grivas followed *Vradini* by suggesting that November 17 was housed in the fathomless depths of the Greek secret state. His claims were predictably dismissed by the authorities. Yet given the deformed pathology of the Greek political order and its vengeful history of settling scores, he was extremely courageous to raise them. When we discussed Ann Chapman, he agreed the murder formed part of the 'disturbed psychosis' of the country, trapped in a constant scrum between rival intelligence interests — domestic and foreign. During my research for the parliamentary inquiry and later for my book on the affair, I was often referred to secret forces in the subterranean state to whom Andreas Papandreou, then prime minister, could turn in the service of 'enforcement.' Georgios Trangas, a probing reporter working for *Vradini,* wrote articles tracing the origin of these forces back to the Civil War. Andreas Papandreou, the consummate Greek Macbeth, trusted no one, certainly not his own ministers. He installed his personal secret policemen, the so-called 'green men,' to spy on all of them, a theme taken up by Grivas, who wrote another revealing book on that subject: *Papandreism: A Dark Green Authoritarianism* (1994).

The celebrated humanist poet and Junta resistance hero turned politician, Justice Minister Georgios Mangakis, reviled Papandreou, and saw his main task as restraining the premier's many excesses. In 1984 he set his face against the prime minister by appointing an independent arbiter to sift through all the known papers concerning Chapman. Papandreou, who considered all discussion on the matter firmly closed, was enraged by such obvious defiance. Mangakis went ahead, sensing correctly that his political life was probably over in any event. A retired state prosecutor, who would otherwise have slipped back into the obscurity of a quiet law practice, was summoned to review everything which had not been shredded or conveniently 'lost.' Mangakis tried to protect Georgios Thefanopoulos, his old law school friend, by tucking into the brief several more 'unsettled' cases. In the finality, there was no independent investigation of anyone's files. Thefanopoulos was murdered shortly afterwards, driving to his office in broad daylight. Witnesses spoke of a young man on a motorcycle firing several shots at point-blank range through the car window. This method of drive-by execution was the hallmark of November 17. The gunman sped off, casting down a scrap of paper boasting about a revenge attack by the hitherto-unknown Democratic Anarchist Front. My prophetic words in *Blood on Their Hands* were the following:

> *In Athens the cynical view quickly developed — based on the gloomy experience of the past — that agents of the state were loose on the streets with a licence to kill, concealing their activities beneath the cloak of an imaginary anarchist threat to the nation. It was certainly curious how the frequency of attacks and threats to prominent citizens accelerated as the general election approached, together with solemn warnings from the governing party over the dangers by 'anarchists and dissidents' working against democracy.*

> *The similarity in favoured styles of execution and choice of victims was not lost upon those who were studying the outbreak of gun law in*

Athens. Neither was the strange inability of the police to get to grips with this supposed threat to the democratic stability.

The legal brain called in by Mangakis met a premature end before his work might acquire dangerous value. No successor to the murdered advocate was appointed, and Mangakis himself was abruptly sacked. The wider aims of the Strategy of Tension were however handsomely rewarded. In the general election of 1985, featuring the usual clash of the dynasties in Greek politics, Papandreou's Panhellenic Socialist Movement (PASOK) romped home against his old resistance foe Constantine Karamanlis. Greek voters opted for the devil they knew.

When Giotopoulos arrived in Stockholm fourteen years earlier in 1971 for a secret conclave with Andreas Papandreou, he received his personal benediction for all the pain he had inflicted on the Junta. Papandreou implied that work in a similar vein might be available once the hated regime fell. He once bawled at Karamanlis during a gloomy Wiesbaden gathering of resistance leaders at Christmas 1970: 'God intended *me* to save Greece.' It was an oblique reference to his conviction that the Almighty was on his side in dealing with the duplicitous Americans who foisted the Colonels on the Greek people. Papandreou anticipated more American double-crossing. He was not disappointed. Over his head, the US embassy staged a kind of pseudo-constitutional coup, in which Karamanlis, self-appointed tribune of the Right, was whisked back from his comfortable CIA-subsidised Parisian exile and awarded a fast-track political coronation.[N3] Papandreou exploded in futile rage. The years of settling scores beckoned.

Richard Skeffington Welch, Harvard-educated scholar still on the learning ropes as the rookie-in-post CIA chief, appeared to drop from the catalogue of classic assassination candidates. He was shot right outside his home, in full view of his horrified family, as they returned from the ambassador's traditional Christmas party in 1975. In a standard token of November 17, a teasing note was dropped detailing his personal schedule for his last hours. Welch had certainly been sacrificed, but by whom? *Cui bono?* We move to centre stage in Washington for the clues.

There the Gerald Ford White House swung into action. The air force plane carrying Welch's body obligingly circled the presidential Air Force One landing field for nearly an hour to make sure it touched down live before mass-audience TV shows. Ford waived aside all formalities, allowing a non-combatant to be interred in Arlington National Cemetery alongside the nation's fallen heroes. Was it pure co-incidence these obsequies chimed with the CIA's rising alarm over the powerful congressional committee, chaired by one of the agency's most vocal critics, Democratic senator Frank Church. His inquisition was digging ever deeper into CIA skulduggery and illegal activities in the wake of the Watergate saga. The state within a state had for once encountered a powerful counter-force. Church wanted the CIA yoked to strict civilian scrutiny instead of acting as a law unto itself. He proposed a new statute, a 'code of responsible behaviour,' to override all the top secret codicils granted to The Firm over the years. Ford cavilled as much as the CIA's top ranks at this insulting imposition. In the wake of the Welch murder, the Church Committee collapsed like a house of cards. A *Washington Star* headline struck close to the mark: 'Here was one CIA effort that worked.'

Welch's funeral, on 7th January 1976, was described by the *Washington Post* as 'an extraordinary show of pomp usually reserved for the nation's most renowned military hero.' Orchestrated theatre it was, replete with full military honours granted to a normally faceless functionary. In a rather grim parody that bordered on the mawkish, but stacked with unmistakable symbolism, the murdered spy was borne to his repose on the same funeral pallet that had carried the body of the slain President Kennedy. By the time the show was over, TV anchors had wrung the sponge dry. Anthony Lewis of the *New York Times* sniffed 'a political device' in this prime-time martyrdom, just short of a full state funeral manipulated 'solely to arouse a political backlash against legitimate criticism of the CIA' then underway in Congress. The *Washington Star* noticed some curious signs of premeditated events in Athens. Scarcely hours after Welch was gunned down, the CIA swung into a highly sophisticated media campaign, bearing all the indications of something cooked much earlier, designed to persuade Americans that Welch's death was a direct consequence of Congressional investigations of the CIA then under way.

The choreographer of these heart-rending rites was Dick Cheney, chief of staff to the president, which — even in the adolescence of a career devoted to elliptical management of the truth — should have set the geese squawking. The master of spin also whispered to the media that Senator Church and his infernal committee bore the brunt for Welch's fate, even though the senator's committee never mentioned his name at any point in their proceedings. But it was the loose lips of Bill Colby, grandfather of the stay-behind armies, that inadvertently challenged the official version of events. Colby ignited Cheney's nitroglycerin temper when he gushed that Welch was actually killed because he was outed in the tell-tale spookworld magazine *CounterSpy*. Colby was immediately ordered to step into line, and backed off 24 hours later, pleading 'a more general climate of hysteria regarding the CIA's activities around the world' was responsible for the assassination. All he did was compound his earlier felony with this clumsy change of stories. Colby certainly paid the price; he was unceremoniously fired at the end of the month, and died in suspicious circumstances in 1996. Colby was perhaps the most interesting and unusual director of the CIA, with a penchant for honest pronouncements that brought rare blasts of fresh air to the agency's activities. Yet, even the *CounterSpy* leak was a provocation, a red rag to a bull, as *Eleftherotypia,* among several influential Greek newspapers, concluded.

Who outed Welch is important but not the backbone of the story, if indeed he was sacrificed by his own government, as argued by Kleanthis Grivas. The usual suspect, the late Philip Agee, got the blame (again), but the leak may have been contrived as a prop for a highly publicised and emotional piece of theatre, easily attributable to the outfit calling themselves November 17. Critically, the daily *Eleftherotypia* noted that since Welch's cover was thoroughly blown, he was already under starter's orders to leave post early in the New Year, in line with usual CIA policy to protect its operatives. In any event, Colby's backtracking over the 'climate of hysteria' revolving round CIA activities had the unintended impact in Greece of confirming US involvement in the military coup. On the ground in Athens, it was a sorry mess. The suspicious Greek media had found the right button. Welch was on the point of leaving, so a revenge killing by a Marxist terrorist gang seemed a thin excuse for retribution. The cold truth lay in the unfortunate fact he was now dispensable, except in the circumstances that his death could be milked for all its worth to head off a frontal attack on the secret mandates and powers of the CIA. Back in the States, the story played to packed national TV galleries, plucking at the heartstrings of millions of Americans in the emotionally-charged Christmas season.

Dr. Webster Griffin Tarpley, Fulbright scholar and revisionist historian, a prominent 9/11 Truther among other garlands, is convinced that practically all terrorism is synthetically devised as a tool to skew public opinion to accept establishment authority, war and dictatorship. Tarpley travelled somewhat beyond Kleanthas Grivas in suggesting that November 17 was from the outset nothing but a death squad acting under direct CIA orders to further NATO strategic aims. To reflect the complexities of the Greek secret state's complex hall of mirrors, we may add the subtlety introduced by Grivas. This is to understand November 17 as a general cloak for all terrorism in Greece, some or much of which was performed by rival gangs involved in classic cloak-and-dagger deceptions. There are supporting clues connected to the shooting of Richard Welch. When the grand November 17 show trial dribbled to its conclusion in 2003, Giotopoulos left the court shouting that he and his confederates were the victims of 'treachery' at the hands of western secret services.

In the immediate wake of the shooting, the police described three masked gunmen, one of whom went up to Welch — who had no security protection, despite his recent public unfrocking in a country overflowing with anti-American bile — and asked for his name. This was an unusual precaution given the famous abilities of Greek terrorists to select and identify their targets with absolute precision. Twenty-seven years later, at the grand show trial staged in Athens, another version appeared featuring a younger man, an older one and a woman saying something in French — a convenient photo fit of Giotopoulos, his wife and an accomplice. Why anyone should start muttering in French in the crammed seconds of an assassination has no rational explanation. But it was sufficient to have Giotopoulos convicted of killing Welch (though not formally sentenced, due to the statute of limitations). Of course, the conviction usefully wiped the Welch slate clean.

As the 1985 Greek general election approached, amid a rash of attacks attributed to radicals trying to pry loose the hinges of state, Georgios Trangas gave me this explanation of who was responsible. Political terrorism in Greece arose not from a bunch of disaffected anarchists, but unseen forces working to a 'specific programme intended to maintain the alignment of Greek politics on a preconceived course.' He judged his words prudently, bearing in mind the fate of his editor Athanasiadis. Decoded, it meant that on one hand, the Karamanlis clan could be counted on to keep Greece lashed to the western defence system, while on the other no such reliance could be placed with the Papandreou faction. It was certainly obvious that the seeds of terror blew on the winds from many directions. Gunmen and bombers aped each other's deadly tactics, claiming allegiance to November 17, or to other bands of vengeful killers with scanty pedigrees or even none at all. Athenians schooled in the ways of Balkan vendettas traced the evident immunity of the killers to protection in high places, especially in the quarters of Andreas Papandreou's socialist party.

Papandreou had another game: to terrorise opponents of his draconian economic reforms and the steady drift to dictatorship. When these irreconcilable forces collided head on, it led to the infamous 'battles of the bulge' — the years between 1980 and 1993 dominated by Papandreou, when the Greek reign of terror reached its peak. As Trangas implied, here was the clear explanation for the impotence of the police, lounging around hands stuck in pockets, while terrorists wrought havoc in the shadow of the Parthenon. As the years rolled by and the deadly toll mounted, Greece was awarded the unwanted Olympian laurels of the European nation which took no prisoners, no matter how heinous the terrorist crimes committed on its soil.

The chief attraction of being a policeman in Greece is to benefit from lucrative side activities such as blackmail, bribery and collecting a percentage on lucrative dope rackets, while otherwise enjoying a life of ease and the warm sunset of a comfortable pension. Anyone unfortunate enough to be dragged inside a Greek police station is likely to rue the day, as a young self-confessed heroin addict from my constituency discovered when she was picked up in Piraeus. She was tortured for some days, including the favourite standby, an excruciating whacking on the soles of the feet, until she told her persecutors where they could find more drugs, for their personal salary enhancements. I won her release, but the psychological damage the poor girl experienced wrecked her mentally. There are good cops too, as in any force no matter how woeful its training and motivation, the handful of good apples among the bad, who for their efforts will always be passed over for promotion, assigned menial tasks or simply ignored. That is what happened to the officer assigned to maintain the so-called 'active file' on the mayhem in the capital throughout the 80's and 90's. As the files bulged and yellowed, no one ever came near him, his reports going straight to the small round filing cabinets belonging to his superiors. The lonesome sleuth begged for release, even demotion, anything to escape the mind-numbing drudgery. His unfortunate successor fared no better.

Greece was unique in failing to establish a specific anti-terrorist unit, despite enduring the longest-running urban terror campaign anywhere in Europe, except Ulster, until the turn of the century. Only in 2002, as Greek chests puffed with pride on winning the emotionally-charged bidding to stage the 2004 Olympics, did the slothful politicians drag themselves to approve a specific anti-terrorism law. The new legislation specifically defined a terrorist act for the first time. In the interim, any advice volunteered by counter-terrorism experts — from Scotland Yard and the French *Sécurité,* among others — was rudely tossed aside. No more than rudimentary forensic examinations were conducted at crime scenes, even allowing for the primitive facilities in the hands of the Greek police.

The perpetrators seemed to revel in the brightest possible limelight, an unusual trait in urban guerrillas who generally flourish behind the shades of anonymity. The police were openly taunted by young men roaring unmasked around the capital on motorcycles (number plates often jotted down by sharp-eyed and responsible citizens), gleefully brandishing heavy assault rifles looted from army weapons stores. Occasionally, wordy dialectical epistles on behalf of the proletarian downtrodden were hurled into the porches of the leading newspapers. The air of a charade — a piece of street *skevoria* — was everywhere. Assassins often brazenly dared to show their faces. Detailed descriptions of suspects went to the same circular filing cabinets which received the careful notes of licence plates. Over the course of almost three decades, gang members seemed to pilfer army munitions at will, picking up their necessities like the weekend shopping.

A peculiar incident typical of the entire *anni di piombo* years involved an anonymous tip-off to the police in the autumn of 1986, that armed men were planning to open fire on strollers in a popular Athenian piazza as dusk fell. For once, a small force of gendarmes duly hurried to the scene where they found a parked van and no occupants, but a stack of NATO-issue weapons and ammunition. Word reached the ears of a few newsmen, who were brushed off and away with an impromptu story of off-duty policemen 'stopping off for a coffee.' But a few witnesses who had spoken to reporters described the clear markings of an army truck, and not the familiar police wagon.

Giotopoulos himself was hardly shy with respect to his resistance record. In 1971, he was tried and convicted in absentia over a spectacular bombing in Thessaloniki, a case which generated many headlines. It was subsequently forgotten in the general grip of amnesia that gripped the police. So was the fact that few eyewitness scene-of-crime accounts tallied with the man they were now seeing on nightly television. The authorities came up with the bald excuse they ignored these clues because of a slight difference in the spelling of his name. After returning to Greece, Giotopoulos travelled again through the hands of the police. His fingerprints were taken and kept on record for some non-criminal infraction, without arousing suspicion. It was common knowledge among the media community that the mysterious godhead guiding November 17 was an academic with strong connections to France. Moreover, in the wake of some attacks, it was Leftish periodicals in Paris that received boastful claims of responsibility, almost as though someone were pointing a signpost.

In the congested, over-heated village of gossip and innuendo that is Athens, the fluently French-speaking Giotopoulos-Ekonomou with his French wife Marie-Thérèse, both possessing French and Greek citizenship, ought to have stood out as the Eiffel Tower of suspects. In 2007, I was informed by a reputable Greek source close to American diplomatic circles that certain embassy officials (a hint suggesting the local CIA post) had known his whereabouts all along. By some miracle, his fingerprints materialised in the instant a failed bombing of a shipping line office in Piraeus led to the entire gang, on the run for almost 30 years, now plopping like overripe plums into the outstretched hands of the gendarmerie in a matter of days. Another remarkable account was served up to the media in the rush of events triggered by the shooting of the British military attaché in Greece, Brigadier Stephen Saunders, on 8th June 2000. A bustling young conservative-minded PASOK minister called Michalis Chrisochoidis was instantly handed the brief, despite lacking a shred of ground experience in criminal detection. He purportedly experienced a sudden Eureka moment and shot off to pay a call on the counter-terrorism division of the French police, the first person in 24 years to think of that, despite all the evidence scattered along the trail that led there.

Chrisochoidis claimed that he was met by beaming officers and improbable words to the effect 'we've been waiting for you!' Public opinion was asked to swallow a line that the powers of a friendly state had been sitting on the fact they had known all about Giotopoulos aka Ekonomou' and the waves of terrorism rocking Greece for decades — yet failed to communicate with the Greek authorities. It is hard to believe that the advice tendered to successive Greek administrations by the French counter-terrorism authorities during the years of lead did not include looking for a tall, graying academic philanderer with a known ultra-revolutionary tilt. Another formidable question mark hung around the precise number of victims attributed to the activities of November 17. The tally that was presented to the show trial in 2004 was 23. But this was at least twenty, and probably more, short of all the recorded shootings and bombings over the same period of three decades rated as terrorist acts, leaving aside the scores more where there were no fatalities, and others that for various reasons, turned out to be damp squibs.

Like the lunar tug on the tides, terrorism in Greece ebbed and flowed around the pull of elections, chiefly influenced by the immensely polarising figure of Andreas Papandreou and his bespoke political vehicle, PASOK. The most prominent bulge in the frequency of shootings, bombings, bank robberies and assorted raids on the offices of foreign companies, occurred between 1980 and 1993, the period in which PASOK twice triumphed at the polls. Even though he toned down his fiery anti-western rhetoric and tore up pledges to order foreign troops out of the country, American and NATO policy makers continued to view this mercurial personality — steeped in populist nationalism — with considerable alarm. Certainly some of Papandreou's tendencies were acutely disturbing. He ruthlessly gerry-mandered the electoral system in search of a permanent PASOK majority, and not satisfied with that, stripped the *Vouli* (the Greek parliament) of many powers. He reduced the presidency to a rubber stamp. One by one he chipped away at the checks and balances of the post-Junta constitution, corralling virtually all power in his own hands. Small wonder that to the outside world he appeared to be set on the path towards that old NATO bogey — a neutralist Left-wing state lapped by the blue waters of the Mediterranean.

Papandreou's persistent meddling with the apparatus of state alarmed the middle classes and above them the *tzakia* — the wealthy upper crust, named after the hearths they could afford to warm their lush homes in the bitter Balkan winters. He packed every high office in the military, courts and state industries with PASOK cronies. Nor was the private sector entirely immune. Any businessmen who offered resistance might be blackmailed and bullied, or denied access to lucrative government contracts. Five prominent industrialists perished, each one an outspoken critic of Papandreou's attempts to ball and chain the private sector to PASOK's will. Nikos Momferatos, publisher of the now-defunct conservative anti-Papandreou newspaper *Apogevmatini*, was shot dead while driving to his office on 21st February 1985. In more than one sense Papandreou was running an enormous protection racket with the aim of levering the rival Karamanlis clan out of government permanently. Papandreou was not solely responsible for institutionally corrupting the country. This was a Greek pastime acquired over many years. But he took advantage of fertile soil to expand state power beyond all previous limits. Yet, this erstwhile Harvard professor was adored as the champion of the workers, the elderly and all who felt brushed aside in Greek society, even as his voodoo economics ratcheted unemployment and inflation skywards.

To Papandreou's mind, he was at last the vindicated chieftain of the resistance. No one dare scorn him now. The spectre of violence that haunted Papandreou in Swedish exile never left his waking thoughts, nor did his acolyte Alexandros Giotopoulos. When the attacks of the 'battle of the bulge' are forensically sifted, what appears is the clear outline of two dominant terrorist waves washing against each other in the same epoch. It is possible to deduce with some clarity whose fingers were on the triggers. The 1980-1993 wave shaped the bridge between socialist victories. A smaller one, though no less bloody, was the apparently separate 'anti-PASOK war,' conducted between 1980 and a pair of deadlocked general elections held in 1990. One envelope of time contained at least two, possibly even three, overlapping guerrilla campaigns. These could be summarised as: November 17 gunslingers, with conflicting loyalties; Gladio warriors following orders, including the impersonation or manipulation of other gangs; and Papandreou's hand-picked 'green men' pursuing the prime minister's personal agenda. During the battle of the bulge, three US embassy officials belonging to various tiers of American intelligence networks were attacked. They included another military attaché, Captain William E. Nordeen of the US Navy, who was killed on 28th June 1988, by a powerful, remotely controlled bomb which almost destroyed his armour-plated sedan. More than two dozen American soldiers were wounded in bombings. There were scores of attacks on US-owned properties, a sustained assault on American power and interests without peer in Europe, all of it attributed to November 17.

The assortment of 'deadly brigands' who eventually fell into the hands of the police were found to include a sad-eyed icon painter, and an absent-minded bee keeper who went around with the keys of the gang's safe house chinking in his workmans' overalls. Papandreou was not so foolish to be caught with blood on his own hands. But he hinted quiet approval by repealing legislation designed to deny terrorists the oxygen of publicity, which until then forbade the media to print or publicise the usual garrulous post-attack communiqués. One former Karamanlis minister narrowly escaped assassination. But Pavlos Bakoyannis — a prominent MP of the conservatives' liberal wing, son of a priest and the subject of many tributes for his genial character — paid the ultimate price, as prickly thorn in the prime minister's side. Bakoyannis was the leading inquisitor on behalf of a parliamentary committee investigating Papandreou's alleged direct involvement in the Bank of Crete loan-stuffing scandal. For his consummate incisive grilling, which threatened altogether too many important figures, apart from the prime minister, Bakoyannis was gunned down in the lobby of his Athens law office on 26th September 1989.

During Papandreou's reign, organised rackets flourished as never before. Orders went out to leave the local crime dons to their devices. Soon they penetrated previously virgin territories spanning the private sector, while creaming a percentage from the flood of subsidies sent by the paternal EU in Brussels to shake up Greece's agriculture and deplorable public infrastructure. Piraeus turned into one of the hottest crack cocaine portholes of the Mediterranean, thanks to lax policing and official blindness. Business was so lucrative there was plenty to spare for the pockets of PASOK officials and party funds. In return, crime bosses lent out guns for hire, all too obvious when assassins took no precautions to hide their identities. As terror swept the streets of Athens, the customary emblems of the state such as tax bureaux and police stations received their fair share of attention, but there was an unmistakable impression of window-dressing, a diverting sideshow to the main drama.

They never knew from whence their orders came and as contract killers, cared less. They were useful too for teasing acts of street theatre, such as young hoodlums enjoying a lark tearing around downtown Athens on motor cycles, sporting heavy weaponry. There was another bonus. The mob was permitted the choicest pick of banks to rob all over the country, each raid blamed on this, that or the other terrorist gang. The anti-American vendetta largely froze in the moment Papandreou's power temporarily fizzled out in the twin dead-heat elections of 1990, which halted PASOK in its tracks. Was it any co-incidence, however, that attacks on anti-Papandreou targets guttered out at the same time, while November 17 appeared to slip into a state of suspended hibernation, awakening only for a burst of short-lived activity during the first Gulf War? Then came the final brutal encore, the murder of British military attaché Stephen Saunders. Exactly how and why did all that pent-up anger suddenly dissipate? Terrorism in Greece displayed the curious facility of being connected to the electricity mains, switched on or off according to demand, lights alternatively brightened or dimmed, suggesting an ideological drift according to who among the rival family clans — Karamanlis and Papandreou — gripped the reigns of power.

As the new millennium dawned, Saunders — to the world the British military legate in Athens, but covertly military intelligence overseer for the southern Balkans region — was shot on the sunny morning of 8th June 2000, heading for work in the usual boisterous Athens traffic. He was hit four times at close range in the chest and head while his official car paused at traffic lights on a congested avenue in central Athens. On the surface, it was a classic November 17 drive-by shooting, performed by a marksman firing from a motorcycle. Saunders, 58 and approaching retirement, died from his wounds a few hours later. Richard Welch and Stephen Saunders represented a pair of book ends enclosing a generation of violence, their deaths open to interpretations differing markedly from the official version of events.

The sum of likenesses in these two cases was impressive. Each was a significant figure in the foreign intelligence community. Both men oversaw an espionage territory of broadly overlapping geography. November 17 invited the rap for both murders, the signature note describing all Saunders' movement plans for the day matching the one for Welch. When Dr. Grivas made his claim that Saunders — like Welch — was the victim of a Sheepskin designer job, the US Government seemed lost for convincing words. Grivas was wrong but only because 'the Greek government wound up the organisation in 1988.'[N4]

Brigadier Saunders was central to the arraignment of this strange cast of miscreants branded as some of the most evil men of modern times. The scribe who wrote his six-page obituary notice delivered to the Athens press, chest beating an act by November 17, was not far out by insisting that Saunders was no 'simple routine defence attaché' but actually 'the number one at the embassy.' After the usual ritual cursing of imperialist interventions around the world, the core was reached when the dead man was exposed as one of the key architects of NATO's bombing campaign to subdue Serbia. When senior government ministers turn publicly incandescent at such claims, as Foreign Minister Robin Cook duly did in the House of Commons, it is a safe rule of thumb that something close to the truth has escaped.

The story of American foreign policy as an ongoing exercise steeped in collective amnesia is fertile territory, as can be confirmed by a quick glance at snapshots of the young, beaming Donald Rumsfeld warmly shaking hands with a cordial Saddam Hussein back in the early '80s. Saunders was an insider to the poisonous turf war that broke out in the Balkans between British intelligence and the Pentagon/CIA complex. Despite public displays of glorious harmony they were not infrequently on opposite sides of the wire, shunting aid and munitions to warring Christian and Muslim ethnic groups. But even more remarkable was the evidence that some of the Afghan recruits were put to work on dirty tricks operations which, the British military subsequently claimed, directly imperilled the lives of their own soldiers.

Sir Michael Rose, senior British commander in the Balkans, was not the first among his ilk to find his communications routinely bugged by US intelligence. Yet as British protests intensified, the Americans responded by virtually shutting Britain out of the intelligence loop. The same punishment was inflicted on another NATO ally, the Greeks. The Athens journalist and war correspondent Takis Michas informed readers of the *Wall Street Journal* that Greek sins in the Balkans included direct military help to the Serbs, busting the oil embargo, supplying weapons, harbouring secret bank accounts, wholesale money-laundering, and sharing NATO intelligence with the accused Serbian war criminal General Ratko Mladić. When besieged Srebrenica finally tumbled to the Serbs in July 1995, Michas explained how the Greek flag was hoisted amidst great rejoicing among the captors.

The State Department did begin to fret early in 2000 that Muslim 'guests' might become a long-term potential Fifth Column on European soil. It was already far too late for such qualms. As the Clinton presidency faded, new powers edged forward, aggressive neo-conservatives with an unremitting anti-Islamic agenda. The abrupt lurch in American foreign policy that led to 9/11 and the NATO invasion of Afghanistan was underway. Brigadier Saunders was privy to the many inconvenient truths concerning the Pentagon's imported mercenaries and their origins in Al Qaeda, in which the Kosovo business formed a fragment of a much wider picture.

When Saunders went to Athens, it must have been in the clear knowledge he was taking a risky assignment, given his explicit knowledge of America's trading with unusual allies in the Balkans. Moreover, despite Robin Cook's furious Commons outburst, Saunders may have been involved in the oversight of NATO's aerial blitzkrieg aimed at Serbia in 1999, which seriously unsettled Greece as a closet Serbian ally. He was the keeper of many potentially compromising secrets, since he was privy to the tensions between western intelligence services in the Balkans. Yet he was allowed to travel about the streets of a notoriously dangerous city — legendary nest of motorcycle assassins with a penchant for cutting down diplomats — in an unarmoured car, minus security detail. From another perspective, Saunders was a sacrificial victim of crossfire in the espionage world, traceable to rancorous feuds thrown up during the Balkan wars. The fractures between British and American intelligence stretch back to the 1967-74 junta period, the invasion and division of Cyprus and the death of British agent Ann Chapman in a Greek secret service dungeon. Of that episode, it is worth recalling the Scotland Yard officer's question to her father: 'Do you want an international incident?'[N5]

In a racy memoir published in 2010 entitled *The Reluctant Spy*, John Kiriakou, the Greek-American former CIA station officer in Athens, claimed a case of mistaken identity: that he and not Saunders was the intended target of November 17.[N6] Kiriakou's version of the six-page missive that immediately followed the murder declared:

We saw the big guy but he was in an armoured car and we knew that he was armed. So we elected to kill the war criminal Saunders.

This is very different from the previously published versions of November 17's claim of responsibility. That, as we saw earlier, was extremely detailed, compared to a somewhat rough freehand sketch that we read above. But yet another alleged N17 proclamation published in the daily *Eleftherotypia* on 13th December 2000 was significantly different again:

> *[In] the moment of the operation, bottled up at the traffic light immediately in front was an American armed mega-spy of the CIA, while about 100 meters back was [wealthy shipowner] Vardinogiannis with his armed escort.*

The first version above is rather clumsy and imprecise, and implies the attackers changed their minds because the 'mega spy' they were tailing was so well-protected (despite their coming well-prepared with a heavy armour-piercing assault weapon). Such confusion was not a noticeable November 17 trait. Their track record pointed to highly accurate, detailed intelligence concerning their targets and their protection arrangements. Saunders was anyway travelling in his plain unarmoured official embassy Rover. Such attacks are always carefully rehearsed days in advance. On what grounds did supposedly professional assassins think that Saunders was travelling that day in an armoured vehicle? One can only say they appeared to have received unusually weak intelligence. Moreover, were they really unaware that prime targets like CIA station chiefs in Athens always travelled in an armoured vehicle, after the Welch affair? The 'big spy' is another puzzle because although Kiriakou insists he was in the vicinity, and drove past Saunders' blood-spattered car, he was himself 'some way back.' The first version serves the useful purpose of introducing Saunders by name, while the second makes no mention of him at all. The second version is closer to Kiriakou's eye-witness account, yet mysteries abound. How (and for what purpose) did *Eleftherotypia* come to print their account six months after the murder and four months after John Kiriakou left his post for home? Who was the grand 'American armed mega-spy of the CIA' if it was not Kiriakou, who seemed to fit the description? Why is such an elliptical roundabout account employed instead of specifically naming him?

Both accounts appear contrived and purposeless. I think Kiriakou is quite mistaken in thinking that he was the intended target. Were that indeed the case, his employers would not have hesitated four months before he left station. I am equally sure that Stephen Saunders, trapped in the usual grotesque traffic chaos, was indeed selected to die that day. But whether by the usual suspects known as November 17, remains seriously in doubt, exactly as Dr. Kleanthis Grivas proposed. The excess of conflicting communiqués definitely suggests a desire to blame disorganised gunmen making on the spot decisions, rather than cool, calculating assassins. This was never the style of November 17.[35]

Bestirred as never before, the authorities used television and the media to urge witnesses to come forward. The politician-sleuth Michalis Chrisochoidis gushed how a river of information poured into the hands of police after 'years of drought.' Following a telephone tip-off, an arms warehouse was miraculously uncovered in a private apartment, stuffed with grenades, military explosives including *plastique*, guns of all types and calibre, and limitless ammunition. It bore a marked resemblance to Gladio war chests uncovered all over Europe. Yet as scarcely anyone noted, nothing substantial in terms of tracking down Saunders' killers flowed from all this volcanic activity. The tipping point was the botched bombing at Piraeus in July 2002, leaving a badly injured man who could not stop talking once safely secured in police custody. He obligingly dished the entire November 17 clan, or so it appeared. The wounded canary's tidings reached the ears of Giotopoulos with considerable haste, which accounts for his sudden flight on receiving a timely tip from some trusted source. Logically, suspicion points to a mole in the secret state.

Independent intelligence experts did not believe the simplistic explanation of murder by some crackpot fringe group. They argued the assassins were expertly briefed with sophisticated knowledge on the movements of super-spies, which was not readily available; it could only come from well-informed insiders. These suspicious sources argued it did not stand to reason that Greek anarcho-Marxists could readily come by such information. The quality was such it had to be traced to trans-national sources. Unless November 17 were actually an arm of an espionage network with insider knowledge, this was rather unlikely. They advised careful consideration of the possibility that the veteran leaders of the 30-year old group — derided on the Internet as the 'Zimmer frame guerrillas' — were sacrificed as a public relations exercise just as the eyes of the world turned to Greece in advance of

---

[35] As the New Year 2012 dawned, Kiriakou was caught up in an extraordinary imbroglio over the water-boarding of terrorist suspects, which seems to cast doubt on his credibility. In 2002 he participated in the capture of the suspected Al Qaeda commander called Abu Zubaydah in Pakistan. Ten years later he was charged by the FBI with betraying CIA secrets of the event, including the use of the waterboarding torture technique to which Abu Zubaydah was subjected. Yet Kiriakou was not present at the interrogation sessions, and all his information was second-hand from CIA cables. To cap it all, he had become a prominent advocate of water-boarding on Right-wing TV shows. Kiriakou asserted that Abu Zubaydah was tortured only once by this method; it is no longer disputed that it was in fact 83 times. Kiriakou's claim that the victim co-operated after just one experience of waterboarding was taken on board by all the usual celebrity talk show mavens as proof that 'torture works.'

the Olympics. The subsequent media circus could then be relied on to drown out disquieting alternative versions of Saunders' death.

Beneath the headline 'Greek Terror Defendants Don't Look the Part,' Frank Bruni of the *New York Times* pronounced himself distinctly underwhelmed by the motley crew paraded on live TV, as the biggest trial in Greek history got under way in March 2003. Even by the standards of the labyrinthine maze that is the world of espionage, they seemed peculiar figures to earn such a deadly reputation. One man the police hunted hid himself for weeks in a tent on a nudist beach. Two others explained how they had to walk home after one attack, having left their car radio switched on so the battery ran down. The mood of being in some surreal wonderland of terrorism was typified by the start of the proceedings, when the presiding judge peered into the specially constructed glass cage and inquired, 'which one of you is the beekeeper?' He, it transpired, eked out a living on EU handouts to honey producers when he was not shooting people. None appeared to possess any definable political convictions, despite all the windy epistles of the working class struggle. The only figure with a look of stature and a steely eye was Giotopoulos. If he was, as the prosecution insisted, spiritual mentor of November 17 over so many years, then a mission to such unpromising material must have proved a deeply frustrating experience.

Even as the November 17 crew prepared for a lifetime under lock and key, a replacement band of avenging mutant Ninja turtles sprang from the underground pipe work of Athens to wage hostilities on the usual alien invaders, capitalists and their American overlords. But the avenging sword was blunted by rust. November 17 was an exceptionally brilliant and inspirational market brand, because it evoked the image of the just war of correction. The mordant sequel, drearily christened Revolutionary Struggle, seemed to be plucked from a fusty reliquary of utilitarian names for 19th century cloak-and-dagger anarchists. The creature that was, or was not, November 17, effectively expired after the battle of the bulge, its purposes virtually exhausted. The brief resurrection in the Saunders affair had a distinctly bespoke feel. Giotopoulos was much too shrewd not to realise his little greenwood band had stowaways on board, but he was sure he had little reason to care one way or the other. After all, as Trangas, Kleanthis Grivas and many others implied, November 17 was enjoying safe conduct beneath a blanket of official protection. When Sheepskin in disguise attacked November 17's type of targets, it was impossible to discern where the boundaries lay. Giotopoulos himself supplied the answer, in his telling cry when led away at Christmas 2003 to start 21 life sentences, that he was 'framed by American and British intelligence.' It was the only remark of significance during a long, drawn-out parody, a magnificent exercise in the old spell of *skevoria*.

Much the same was true of the riots which inflamed the Greek capital in the spring of 2010 and over the following months, while Greece fell into long-gestating economic paralysis. Successive Greek governments have been gaily falsifying the levels of public debt and GDP for many years, if not forever. They were aided by the global counting houses based in Wall Street, specifically those famous grave robbers Goldman Sachs and Morgan Stanley. The mandarins in Brussels turned a Nelsonian blind eye for fear of Greece, dropping out of the sacred fiction known as the euro. This is not the appropriate podium to explain the ingrained nepotism practised by the two family dynasties, Karamanlis and Papandreou, that vie for mastery of this small country, or the entrenched corruption which follows as a natural consequence. Save to say that the usual tactics of *skevoria* were invoked to misrepresent a genuine and popular outpouring of anger by the Greek people as the work of anarchists and communists, akin to the incarcerated November 17 stooges.

Greeks found themselves revisiting former years of lead, the same prominent symbols of Western capitalism. Banks and offices of well-known foreign corporations were selected for random bombings and arson. As always, the blame was attached to anarchists and other radicals working to unhinge the state. Looking back to my earlier words in *Blood on Their Hands*, the 'gloomy view' again developed among Athenians that shadowy agents of the state were the chief actors in this new eruption of violence. The CIA obligingly suggested that a military coup might restore order. Seeing their own country forcibly hawked to foreign carpet-baggers was the force driving Greeks into the streets in massive numbers. Once there, planted infiltrators worked the script as before. The dummy Western media dutifully followed the approved script, branding the protestors as hoodlums out for violent thrills. Street theatre provided all the necessary stage scenery.

Typical of this spoon-fed hyperbole are reports like this choice example appearing in the *Daily Mail* in March 2011, describing 'hundreds of masked and hooded youths punching and kicking motorcycle police, knocking several off their bikes....the violence spread to a nearby square ... where police faced off with stone-throwing anarchists, and suffocating clouds of tear gas sent patrons scurrying from open-air cafes.' Aside from the usual portrayal of the police as saint-like figures, which in Greece attracts hoots of derision among all classes and circles, these are the standard *agent provocateur* tactics of Sheepskin/Gladio in full cry. Greek investment in 'security' would do justice to a state ten times its size. Special forces include the greatly feared MAT public order squads and the EKAM riot suppression units. The DIS motorcycle SWAT teams are renowned for rough tactics such as running down demonstrators. Like their counterparts in the civil police, uniformed special forces are replete with under-cover agents, replicas of the hooded figures you always see in pictures of demonstrations all around the world. Recruits are poorly schooled, with a tendency for sudden acts of motiveless brutality. One especially dismal episode was the shooting of a fifteen-year-old boy, Alexandros Grigoropoulos, in the downtown Athens district of Exarcheia on 6th December 2008. It sparked the biggest riots Greece had witnessed since the student uprising against the military Junta in November 1974. The evidence — subsequently confirmed in court — pointed clearly to a deliberate provocation by a squad of MAT officers on routine patrol. They shot the boy, then left him bleeding to death in the street.

Turbulent and perpetually restless, the Exarcheia quarter is symbolic of the seething discontent between the emerging contemporary Greek generation and the self-renewing clans who dominate the country's public life and politics. That the state is totally unwelcome in this neighborhood of central Athens is made perfectly obvious by the graffiti leaping from almost every wall declaring 'A.C.A.B' (All Cops Are Bastards) mixed with cartoon mockery of Greek leaders and complex murals deriding the foreign vultures and parasites fighting over the meagre spoils.

The murder of Alexandros Grigoropoulos may have been a designer killing, according to reports circulating after the exposure of the Pythias coup plot in March 2012. The violence was intended to provoke riots that would invite a military crack-down. This is is likely to be a major theme in the full inquiry ordered by the country's highest court to identify the conspirators. Most Greeks in any event suspect that the usual suspects, NATO and its main shareholder, the United States, were simply repeating the old theme to keep the country on a tight leash to the western camp. The more interesting question is why the plot was exposed after so many years under wraps. I suspect that Pythias was in fact far from defunct. It was simply resting, and ready to swing into action should Greeks rebel against the globalist-imposed austerity strait-jacket. Practically as much was implied by the former French premier Michel Rocard that very same month. In this scenario, Karamanlis arranged a timely historical exposure in advance of the scheduled general election, with two intents in mind. First, to frustrate a physical coup, and second, to steer the electorate towards the safe arms of New Democracy, which remains a fiefdom of his family. In brief, nothing less than the Strategy of Tension in new clothes.

The rash of new radical movements springing forth to claim responsibility for bombings and general stirring of violence will not surprise the members of November 17. Those experts in terrorism manufactured to order, Alexandros Giotopoulos and his band of honey farmers and icon painters, are shut up for life at the grim central prison in the Athens suburb of Korydalos. In the silence of their specially-built high security monastic sepulcher, they must be reflecting with bitter irony how very little has changed in the politics and motives of Greek street violence.

IX.
Goodbye Piccadilly

'Its [sic] a very long time that I believed in the 'freedom of speech' which on both sides [of the Iron Curtain] boils down to the freedom to shout out loud what you think at home or in front of a few friends. But go and try to express your views in the 'independent Times' or the independent BBC — a fat lot of good the tattered democracy here will do you.' — Georgi Markov, letter to a friend, 18th February 1977

'The post-communist governments are accomplices in a crime. They had the opportunity to come out clean, instead they hid all information. All governments, all parliamentary majority groups, and chief prosecutors after 1989 have become accomplices in concealing the traces of Georgi Markov's assassination' — Richard Kamings, Radio Free Europe

The dense thickets of myths and disinformation which surround the Georgi Markov legend deify his character with saintliness to such an extent that objective truth or just plain inquiry tends to provoke harsh reactions. This is a tribute not only to the gullibility of the western media, but the grossly distorted picture presented concerning his life in Bulgaria, and of Bulgaria itself. The saddest victim is Markov. Presenting himself in London at one of the peak cycles in the Cold War, he was the perfect caricature for western — and particularly, British — exploitation. He became a packaged, manufactured personality. I will present the evidence in this chapter that although happily married with his new English family, he was deeply disillusioned and genuinely unhappy with his life as a reluctant émigré and western propagandist. Probably the most outstanding novelist and literary thinker of his generation in Bulgaria has gone down in history solely because of the eccentric circumstances in which he was supposedly killed by an umbrella. The gifted writer is transformed into a Cold War loudhailer, and served up as a media extravaganza. Such a mundane conclusion not only cheapens his genuine legacy, but frustrates the inquiries which are essential to explain his death in the setting of the times, and the circumstances of quite the most peculiar member of the Soviet Bloc.

Bulgarian television journalist Vladimir Bereanu and his colleague Kalin Todorov brought out a new exposé on the affair in 1991, *Who Killed Georgi Markov?* It contained the revelation that Markov was discreetly enrolled in Bulgaria's *Darzhavna Sigurnost* secret police, which opened an entirely new dimension to the affair. An English version of the book called *The Umbrella Murder* met a peculiar fate of its own, being effectively suppressed. A Cambridge publishing executive called Jane Tienne, who took up the cause when the Bulgarians could not find an English language publisher, spent her own private funds, with the help of a friend, to get the book printed. She was literally ruined by the experience, telling friends she was hounded with threats from telephone callers, who made her very frightened. Tienne now refuses to discuss the affair at all. The book was effectively killed by a court order, brought by Markov's English widow, Annabelle, who apparently objected to the secret agent claims concerning her husband; but others detected the hidden hands of British intelligence. [36]

When the fugitive Russian secret agent Alexander Litvinenko expired in a London hospital in November 2006, suffering from a high dosage of super-radioactive polonium-210, long memories flashed back thirty years to the apparently similar death of another East European exile on British soil. On 7th September 1978, Georgi Ivanov Markov, émigré and prolific broadcaster with the BBC World Service, the German international network *Deutsche Welle* and the CIA's *Radio Free Europe*, was heading for his usual shift. He followed his regular pattern of parking on the south side of Waterloo Bridge before boarding his usual bus for the short hop to Bush House studios in Aldwych. Scarcely had he strolled to the stop when he felt a sharp pricking sensation in his upper right thigh. Markov described a man who brushed against him, muttered he was sorry in a foreign accent, and picked up the umbrella in question, which Markov thought he dropped. At 49 years old, Markov was about to step into history as the first recorded victim of a lethal umbrella. What followed was a wild media frenzy stoked by rumour-mongering, distortions, half-truths and prefabricated falsehoods pouring from official sources. The sole aim was to fix responsibility for Markov's death on a sinister foreign power.

Both murders exhibited flashy James Bond appeal, bound to set the media frothing with exotic headlines, especially when the authorities swiftly spun that both were the victims of Soviet bloc secret services. Markov was exploited as the classic victim of the old Cold War, Litvinenko, who was probably contaminated by his activities in a polonium smuggling ring, as the new one under Vladimir Putin. London headlines at first screamed the story of a revenge killing contracted out to the KGB, until later a subtly amended version emerged, pointing the finger at the Bulgarian Committee for State Security (CSS) — generally known as *Durzhavna Sigurnost,* DS for short. They were supposed to have despatched one of their own men to London, armed with an umbrella adapted to fire miniature projectiles coated with the deadly poison ricin, with weapon and potion both supplied by the KGB.

---

[36] Somewhat ironically Vladimir Bereanu was himself named by the State Files Commission in August 2009 as one of 109 journalists who collaborated with the DS.

Markov was instantly mythologised by the media in stark black and white, the intellectual dissident bravely using the airwaves to pour ridicule on 'the most Stalinist of all the regimes in the Soviet Bloc,' in particular on the party strongman, Todor Živkov. So, the official version went, the grim stone faces in the Bulgarian capital Sofia and particularly the offended Živkov decided to silence this annoying chatterbox, and chose an extremely unusual but highly effective way of going about it. The Myth of the Umbrella Murder was born.

The source was the bureau known in Fleet Street as the soup kitchen, the information unit buried in the bowels of the Foreign Office, where reporters went to be spoon-fed the latest official spin concocted by the Information Operations Planning System (IOPS), a division of MI6. In fact, the identity of the villain was already known where it mattered, among the intimates of British intelligence: MI5/MI6 and Scotland Yard.[37] He was neither Russian nor Bulgarian, but a 32-year-old Danish-Italian, Francesco Gullino, under suspicion as the hitman who cut down Swedish premier Olof Palme in Stockholm five months earlier. He may also have been in St. Peter's Square three years later when Pope John Paul II almost died. Gullino was certainly not the standard model of a secret agent on any score. It is clear that he took orders from DS on contract jobs, and he lived in Bulgaria much of the time. He was 'Agent Piccadilly' on DS books, a curious reference to a famous London landmark.[38] He was also affiliated with British, Turkish and American intelligence. Gullino was deeply enmeshed in the criminal gang structures of Turkey and Italy, working the Golden Trail and all their connections with western intelligence operations. He was on intimate terms with Bulgarian party bosses and DS people taking their generous cut from the torrent of contraband goods pouring through the country. He was hand-in-glove with the Party bigwigs looting Bulgaria's cultural heritage under the cover of the secret services, the military and well-placed bureaucrats. No mean icon fancier himself, with professional knowledge on the subject, he was their marketing director, shipping the stolen goods to buyers abroad.

---

[37] On 18th August, 1983, the London *Observer* reported the existence of a retired army brigadier sitting with an office at the BBC, vetting job candidates. The newspaper also disclosed that certain key BBC personnel, including the heads of foreign sections, were required to sign the Official Secrets Act, whereupon they were duly invited to receive exclusive briefings from the Foreign Office and MI6.

[38] Indeed a puzzle — why choose a famous London landmark for a Bulgarian agent's code name? There are some interesting possibilities by adding the additional word 'circus.' At the western end of the busy London thoroughfare called Piccadilly sits the 'rondo' featuring the statue of Eros. Piccadilly Circus is an adaption of a circle, the Latin to describe some large round space containing bustling activities. MI5 was colloquially known as The Circus. The best seller of that name by Rupert Allason (alias Nigel West, the spy world's unofficial historian) covered MI5 operations from 1945 to 1972. So is 'Piccadilly' an oblique crossword-puzzle clue of the sort spies love?

And, if all that were not enough, he was an 'idealistic and convinced fascist,' belonging to the inner core group of such figures underpinning the Gladio network. Scarcely fitting the description of the 'small-time art dealer and criminal' that eventually appeared from the usual MI6 fact-crunching mill when his name leaked out. Gullino's story is so darkly complex and many-faceted it might have come from the hands of John le Carré.

The motive of a revenge killing put about in London, interwoven with the intriguing fascination of the fatal umbrella, was of course the perfect propaganda barrage to demonise the Russians and their Bulgarian consorts. Yet revisiting Markov's case suggests neat explanations are nearly always the least plausible, with the consequence his unquiet skeleton rattles to this day. Markov was never the emblem or national saint of Bulgaria under the Stalinist heel, nor did he flee to the West to escape persecution at home. Nor, in the terms generally understood, was he really a dissident. On the contrary, he cohabited with the regime at the highest level. His rise in the ranks of the cultural élites was helped by the patronage of the ruling authorities, in particular Lyudmila Živkova, the powerful and charismatic daughter of his former benefactor, dictator Todor Živkov. His fate was marginal to most Bulgarians, despite his bombastic attacks on the General Secretary, who in any case never took them seriously. Georgi Markov and his story are a fly-in-amber testament to a small country at the crossroads of the Cold War, swirling in a complex interplay of dual loyalties, ambitions, petty jealousies, treachery, big power politics, espionage and not least, the internationalised smuggling of weapons and narcotics which ignored political boundaries.

Markov died four days after feeling that sharp stinging sensation in his upper thigh. The official diagnosis was heart failure due to chronic septicaemia. This usually occurs when some infection entering the bloodstream causes the immune system to go haywire, eating away at the body it is supposed to protect. The survival rate is reasonable, but in the most serious cases victims may expire from severe toxic shock and renal failure. The strange rash and spot on Markov's thigh may have led his doctors to the conclusion of blood poisoning, or septic anaemia, which in medical terms amounts to death from natural causes. His body then left the hospital for Westminster public morgue, where an X-ray apparently indicated the presence of a microscopic metal object. This is where the government laboratories came in, as the drama moved into over-drive. By now, Scotland Yard was on the case, with MI5 and MI6 in hot pursuit, as the theory of a political assassination took hold, which of course demanded the customary news management for maximum effect. The corpse was transferred again, this time for autopsy at the top-secret chemical warfare establishment operated by the Ministry of Defence at Porton Down, on the edge of Salisbury Plain. The talents assembled there included, remarkably, Dr. Christopher C. Green, fresh in from Washington, one of America's leading forensic scientists and toxicologists, whose brief included reporting personally to the future US president George H. W. Bush, then director of the CIA. He was joined by Porton Down's chief toxicologist, the late Dr. David Gall. Markov and the scintillating umbrella mystery were being groomed for posthumous star billing.

The team at Porton Down extracted from the reddened spot on Markov's upper leg a minuscule iridium-tipped platinum pellet, 1.52 mm in diameter, the size of a pinhead. With ingenious precision, it was micro-drilled with two V-shaped channels leading to a sump or well, which it was presumed contained some kind of poison. Green and Gall surmised the fatal dose was contained by a soft wax or possibly sugared cap, which melted in the body heat of the victim, slowly releasing the deadly draught into Markov's bloodstream. The ricin story now moved centre stage. Ricin (*ricinus communis*) is derived by distilling the seeds of castor beans, which in benign form are also the source of castor oil, a common flavouring and additive to medicines. The impact of ricin poisoning is devastating. Liver, kidney and spleen collapse, the victim runs a high fever, can hardly breathe, may suffer from massive bleeding in the stomach and intestines, while blood pressure drops to perilous levels. Markov displayed at least some of these symptoms. Death is likely to be agonisingly slow, which allows the perpetrator to be far away before suspicions are aroused. It requires so little ricin to kill one human being that its use can be undetectable, the poisoner's perfect poison.

There was no trace of ricin in Markov's body, but such extensive damage to his internal organs appeared to point in that direction. As little as 500 micrograms (half a milligram, or the two-thousandth part of a gram) of the toxin can kill an adult, depending on the circumstances, whether it is inhaled, swallowed or enters the bloodstream by injection. The latter, fitting the story of a projectile, is the most effective method. A single ricin molecule is quite enough to kill a living cell, so in theory just three micrograms, amounting however to tens of trillions of molecules, would be sufficient to poison every cell in the human body. What is extremely curious about this part of the affair is why there was apparently no X-ray examination conducted at the hospital, which might have led to removing the pellet? How was it possible to ignore the indications of some kind of poisoning, accidental or otherwise, especially as word had it Markov was telling doctors he thought he may have been pricked and poisoned?

Septicaemia does reflect some symptoms of poisoning by ricin, which works in the same fashion by wrecking the immune system. The mysterious pellet was the X factor. Dr. Green declared in a subsequent declaration: 'We knew that the material used to kill him, ricin, had been under development by a foreign service,' finger-pointing which suggested the culprits would be traced to the Evil Empire lurking behind the Iron Curtain. An essential feature of the disinformation exercise was the constant pretence of ignorance among western authorities of the dangerous functions of ricin. Dr. Gall, as the chief Porton Down toxicologist, and in that position party to all Britain's chemical warfare secrets, certainly knew otherwise. Dr. Green was carefully selective in what he left out. He did not say that the United States and United Kingdom were pioneers investigating ricin as a chemical weapon during WW1, and tested practical applications — sprays and cluster bombs — during WW2. It was found unsuitable for mass destruction, such as mustard gas employed in WW1, but potentially useful for more selective work. Nor did he reveal that the US Army's Fort Detrick chemical warfare centre in Maryland had patented a range of small weapons — including adapted umbrellas — to fire toxic pellets specifically intended for targeted assassinations. These devices, after extensive testing, had already been supplied to his employers, the CIA, and disclosed to the US Congress. (The details, including the inventor, follow shortly.) The spin machine claimed Markov had been warned by a mysterious caller he would be killed by a poison 'that the West knew nothing about and would not be able to trace.' This was pejorative case-building after the event. The 'West' had known all about the castor oil plant and the fearsome properties of its beans for many centuries. Way back in Roman times, farmers knew to steer their cattle away from the bush and its deadly fruit. In 1888, the German chemist Peter Hermann Stillmark wrote his famous benchmark doctoral thesis on ricin as a toxin, which led in turn to the new field of biochemical science called lectinology.

The details then emerged of a supporting act, a similar incident in Paris about ten days earlier (although according to the victim's wife, three days *after* Markov died, which as we see is rather important). In any event, Vladimir Kostov, paraded as another émigré victim of the poisoned pellet, was judged lucky to survive an attack in the Étoile metro station, near the Arc de Triomphe. He was struck in the back, although the thick jacket he was wearing supposedly blunted the missile. This episode is very puzzling, not only because of the discrepancies with the timing. It appears some kind of metal object was extracted from Kostov's back: but it could never have contained the merest trace of ricin. It would require more than a miracle to survive a direct injection of the tiniest peck. Inhalation, perhaps. It cannot be diluted and, once in the bloodstream, will prove fatal. Yet Kostov seems to have bounced back as though he had suffered no more than the flu. (There was no ricin antidote then: this is a recent experimental development.)

The subsequent 'rehearsal' line duly did the rounds. The Paris experience was supposed to demonstrate Markov's killer was on the loose there too, and finding his aim rather wanting after Kostov survived, decided to perfect his act. Leaving aside the rather important confusion over the dates, the assassin would attack through the thin protection offered by his trousers, the umbrella dropped as a diversion, to bend and get a clear shot at Markov's upper thigh.

Kostov described his assailant as taking the probable weapon from a small container. So, we understand he got a look at the man who tried to kill him, but never, as far as I can trace, gave a clear description of his assailant, which an individual brushing with death would surely be unlikely to forget. Kostov's account at least disposes of the fatal rainshield, but leaves us wondering about his entire story, not least because Markov, a casual dresser, was wearing his customary stout pair of jeans, not thin trousers. The evidence I show later demonstrates how the American development work at Fort Detrick included copious tests using clothed tailors' dummies to finely judge the velocities required. So was the Paris business a real attack, or a rehearsal? Or even just a piece of street theatre, a warm-up act?

The waters around Kostov became steadily murkier. Unlike Markov's acerbic blasts, he kept his head down, steering a softer line in his broadcasts for Radio Free Europe, which in general were not controversial at all. He never resorted to personal attacks on strongman Živkov. On his own admission, he was a colonel in the DS before he eloped to France with his wife in 1977. His alleged defection was the excuse to have him sentenced to death, the perfect cover to cloak an émigré agent. A man on the inside of an organisation with many dangerous secrets of its own — an antiques thieving racket, along with narcotics — might have expected a bullet at any time. Yet he walked about the city with airy, untroubled nonchalance. A widely-circulated story suggested he was working for French intelligence on the side. The French Connection swirled around another Bulgarian, self-styled businessman Dinyo Dinev, living in France for more than twelve years. Dinev was the main suspect in trying to kill Kostov, but nothing was proved. It may have been a red herring to justify unfrocking him, which duly occurred. The French authorities put him in jail for three years for espionage, and thereafter he fades from the narrative, a strange loose end. Dinev's entrepreneurial activities were never clearly explained. But almost certainly he was the point man at the French end of the looted Bulgarian antiques chain, in which the secret services were up to their necks, Paris being of course the perfect market for that kind of goods.

In 1975, three years before these incidents, CIA director Bill Colby told an interesting story to the Church Committee (the US Congressional Committee of Inquiry investigating covert agency CIA activities, headed by the pronounced CIA agnostic Senator Frank Church). Colby admitted the CIA possessed a top-secret assassination kit in the form of a .45 caliber pistol, powered by batteries concealed in the butt, which silently fired miniaturised darts, or 'flechettes' as Colby called them. These could be tipped with toxic poisons. Colby admitted the idea was to kill people with a highly portable, silent weapon, which could thus be used in quite open public spaces. The senators then heard evidence from a biological weapons designer, Charles Senseney, that he manufactured to CIA instructions precisely such a lethal toy. Furthermore, the disguises to conceal the firing device ranged from walking sticks, fountain pens, drinking straws — even an umbrella. All of this had been put together at the Fort Detrick biological and chemical weapons site in Maryland. Coming to the crucial issue of penetrating clothing, Senseney said tests were done with 'various dogs.' But when it came to the impact on humans, the labs used tailors' dummies with various thicknesses of clothing to assess the velocities required to penetrate different garments. So the Kostov 'rehearsal' story takes another knock.

Years later, when the Bulgarian regime imploded, the London *Guardian* and *Times* disgraced themselves by repeating the tired old chestnut of the basement in the interior ministry in Sofia crammed with primed umbrellas, ready for action. It would have been better to pay an inspection call on Fort Detrick, where Senseney developed his miniature missiles to exact CIA specifications. And of course, tucked away in this corner of Maryland operating under complete secrecy, everything that could be known about ricin was known. (In June 2011, these same Fort Detrick labs were under suspicion of manufacturing the deadly, hysteria-provoking strain of *E.coli* bug, unknown in nature, strangely immune to the full pack of antibiotics, that curiously wandered into the raw vegetable chain all over the States and Europe.)

In the space of about a month, the DS seems to have woken up from a long sleep to deal with its troublesome dissidents abroad — in Markov's high-profile example, a nap of no less than seven years. The timing, as we shall see, had more to do with the pressing Cold War agenda, and particularly the controversial Pershing cruise missile roll out, than with some annoying characters on the run in the West. The Markov affair overshadowed the peculiar fate three weeks later of yet another Bulgarian working at Bush House Studios. Vladimir Bobchev (also known as Simeonov) ran an innocuous youth programme, steering well clear of courting controversy. Bobchev was first hauled in for an exhausting grilling lasting almost two days at Scotland Yard. In his last days, colleagues declared he looked 'mortally scared.' When he failed to turn up for his regular slot, his worried producer despatched a secretary to his Essex home. She found Bobchev's crumpled body on the stairs. There were signs from two tumblers of alcohol in the kitchen that he had recently received a visitor (odd, because Bobchev was a firm teetotaller). Ignoring the red-hot Markov connection, the coroner concluded he stumbled and drowned in his own blood... This same coroner, Gavin Thurston, was no stranger to muddying high-profile cases with compromising political overtones. In 1971, he refused to conduct an inquest on MI6 agent Ann Chapman's body (if it really was hers), then lying within his legal precincts in West London. In 1981, the writer Sterling Seagrave suggested in his book, *The Yellow Rain: A Journey Through the Terror of Chemical Warfare,* that Bobchev/Simeonov might have been a fairly low-grade operative liquidated because he knew too much about who really killed Markov. Quite probably. Wherever one looks, all the threads in some fashion link up with the pivotal figure of Georgi Markov.

The Bobchev business is significant for another reason. The death of Markov having become prominent in Bulgaria, the authorities there volunteered to assist the inquiries of Scotland Yard. They were rudely brushed off, on the bizarre grounds that such co-operation would only assist the regime in Sofia to destroy vital information. As the story unfolds, we see this extraordinary attitude was to prove the stripe of the Yard's peculiar behaviour over the years to come. Markov's well-hidden private life was veiled by the media portrayal of a talented outcast cut down. He was bitter, disappointed, and frustrated by a constant duel with his immediate superior in the *BBC World Service*, where he began working in 1971. The provocateur was Petar Uvaliev, a former diplomat who defected in 1947. He was another respected writer who produced highly-praised film scripts. The pair rubbed against each other so abrasively that Markov considered packing his wife and daughter off to Germany, or near the end of his life, to Paris, where he would set up a boutique publishing house.

It was far more than a personality feud. The confined space of the studio was a mare's nest of loyalties. Uvaliev was moonlighting for MI6, and viewed Markov as an agent for the Bulgarian secret services. Although I have not seen concrete proof, Uvaliev actually volunteers himself as a rather obvious two-timing candidate. At a personal level, he seethed over the generous time Markov was permitted to preen before the studio microphone, the famous 'steel daffodil' of the talk universe, compared to the compressed sessions Uvaliev was allowed to beam at the homeland, based on his eclectic personal mix of philosophy, art, psychology, and psychoanalysis. A former diplomat trained as a lawyer, master of at least seven tongues, Uvaliev was the perfect self-worshipping intellectual with an outsize chip. But, like Markov, the undercurrents of his life were complicated. In the mid '70s, Uvaliev occasionally relieved his banishment by returning home to deliver long-winded guest performances before selected audiences of eggheads assembled in the restaurant of the Hotel Sofia. When another exiled Bulgarian spoke of 'divine providence' behind this extraordinary degree of latitude extended to a notable defector, it was judged, correctly, as a coded reference to some guardian angel within the regime. The Markov affair belongs in exactly the same frame as Uvaliev's charmed powers to materialise in his homeland at will, together with the privileged existence Markov enjoyed before he fled to the West, concerning which Petar Uvaliev was very well informed.

Markov himself alluded to this in the letter that he wrote much later, in September 1977, to a friend also working as an émigré broadcaster, in Germany. Discussing his lifestyle at home, he wrote:

When I came to the West I was very surprised to find that almost all the people I met, both the locals and the immigrants, were dreaming and struggling for things I threw away when I left Bulgaria — money, a secure position, fame. Most everyone thought I had been mad, and that there was nothing morally wrong in taking it easy at the expense of a whole nation and living like a spoilt brat.[N1]

Had it been known to the invertebrate media obsessed by the fatal umbrella, Markov's pampered lifestyle at home in Bulgaria would rub much of the gloss from the martyr. Markov was a man of dual personality, undoubtedly like the doomed Russian defector Alexander Litvinenko. He steeped himself in the good life, thanks to the personal patronage of Živkov's iconoclastic daughter, Lyudmila Živkova, the future culture commissar destined for her own Politburo seat. Despite her youth, she was already an emerging power figure in her own right. Lyudmila was the guardian angel whose finger could beckon Uvaliev. Her presence in Markov's life was somewhat more intimate. His first choice of career was industrial chemistry, which he studied at the Sofia Polytechnic, but the romantic and poetic side of his immensely restless nature won out. So it was that he wrote himself into the national pantheon as one of the most brilliant young writers and social commentators of his generation. His work was crowned in 1962 when his novel *Men* won the prestigious prize of the Union of Bulgarian Writers. This was the key to the flattered innermost circles of the literati — and of course the young and attractive Queen of the Pride, the dictator's pampered 20-year-old daughter. Markov, in his early 30's, enjoyed a cultivated reputation as a heart-throb in a raffish *neo-bourgeois* set — one of the bulbs that flowered in the so-called Bulgarian Spring. Something like the famous pre-war café society blossomed once again in Sofia and a few other large cities. There were decadent literary soirées at Lyudmila's private apartments, the exciting atmosphere helped along with plenty of imported drinks and other nourishing stimulants, siphoned from the international narcotics trail passing through the country. Although the Comrade Princess was herself an ascetic, she knew how to throw a party. When she introduced Markov into the family circle, her father reacted with delight at having such a brilliant entertainer around him, his own son Vladimir being a rather sullen dullard.

In her early twenties, which she later described as the ripest years of her life, brimming with restless energy, Comrade Lyudmila overflowed with ideas to enlist the arts and culture into her personal mystical hotch-potch of truth and beauty worship, lifted from the Orient and flavoured with additional zest by her inspirational avatar, the Russian mystic Georgi

Gurdjieff (1877-1949). To indicate an idea of its curious flavour, in one famous oration about education in 1979 she mentioned 'Endlessness, the Infinite, the Eternal' on 38 occasions, the occult 33 times and 'celestial light' again no less than 33 times. Hardly, then, the staple fare of the class struggle. She called this eclectic mélange 'the harmonious development of Man' — Gurdjieff's old motto. Exactly what her hearers thought can probably be imagined but, as I was often told by many people who knew her, she genuinely believed she had found the means to re-charge the batteries of stale and out-moded socialist dogma. The neo-modern stump of concrete called the Palace of Culture in downtown Sofia remains a testament to her endeavours and skills at attracting foreign writers and artists, while packaging local culture as a home-grown Bulgarian cultural industry, belying Markov's subsequent claims the country was trapped in an intellectual and cultural gulag. Here is a curious indicator of Markov's attitudes to Lyudmila's ramblings. In that 1977 letter to his pal in Munich 'Zhoro' (familiar for Georgi), he described the rat race in London as having nothing to do with the 'improvement and betterment of mankind, or love and beauty.' These were exactly the oft-stated aims and language of the Crown Princess.

Another side of her busy activities involved nurturing and promoting artists she considered as fit for her fine agenda to 'imbue public life with beauty.' Georgi Markov fell into that class. She was fascinated by Thracian death cults — a rather interesting indication of some inward Gnostic yearning for the esoteric ancients, although there may have been more basic instincts at work, as we see in a moment. Yet it is doubtful if the cults were the foremost topic in their private moments. Markov was a frequent guest at the grace and favour villas dotted around Boyana, the exclusive suburb reserved for party nabobs, perched on the cool slopes of the extinct Vitosha volcano, whose brooding presence dominates the capital. He was indeed something close to dictator Živkov's favourite son, a highly flattered member of his nepotistic circle: rewarded by hunting trips with the Great Leader himself, and a silver BMW, snatched to order from the streets of Brussels by secret agents at the Bulgarian embassy. He was allowed considerable free rein to publish works that did not always stick closely to the politically correct party line, courtesy of Lyudmila. Markov was also permitted freedom to come and go broadly as he pleased, with generous access to hard currencies, thanks to an exclusive passport available only to the most favoured élite who were not actually in government jobs. Such a man in such a country, warming his hands at the hearth of the ruling cabal, privy to all the most exclusive gossip, commands an obvious appeal.

The 'spoilt brat' period of Markov's life at home ensured he was a great and even remorseless flatterer and conqueror of women. The investigative writers Bereanu and Todorov talked to some of his associates, one of whom painted the picture of the rake who settled a dispute with a rival for the favours of a particular Sofian beauty by playing cards for her. Markov won. Twice. In a similar account, he won a legendary game of high-stakes poker which seems to have been organised as a kind of sting. I heard many such tales, no doubt some apocryphal, others with a grain or essence of truth, but mostly factual. Markov — like many intense and gifted artists — was complex, a Jekyll and Hyde as he was often described, poised between various polarities. But he was certainly not in these years the gilded Galahad, brandishing his sword at the cruel and corrupt regime: he made his necessary accommodations, or compromises as he called them. It was the same everywhere in the Soviet Empire. He was Prince Charming with an incisive magic pen he was determined to use.

Certainly Georgi Markov enjoyed the benefit of royal patronage, but his literary achievements were unquestionably his alone. Comfortably secure, with a day job at a state publishing house in Sofia, and an open door to the court of the First Secretary, he produced insightful prose rightly judged today as highly important contributions to the modern realist genre. Mischievous and witty, Markov's love of light relief and strong sense of humour attracted him to writing scripts for Bulgaria's first mass attention-grabbing television series, *'We are at every Kilometer.'* The series was originally conceived as a plain hagiography, dedicated to the feats of communist partisans in the wartime underground. Markov and other good writers inserted a brilliant and uncensored interplay between the two main characters, a police detective and a resistance fighter, which seized the popular imagination by exploring sensitive zones not generally touched in the television arena. It was a smart coup for the regime and Lyudmila's semi-detached, hard-drinking playboy husband, Ivan Slavkov, who was given the run of Bulgarian TV as a private fiefdom. Slavkov (who died in 2011, bequeathing a huge football politics bribery scandal) is still remembered as the most inspirational director in the channel's history. Thus Slavkov got 'promoted' in Lyudmila's usual fashion, even though they led largely separate lives. Markov was a darling of the intellectual circuit without a doubt, but the television series made him a popular idol too, and this is the crucial point to keep in mind as we explore his subsequent fate.

Freedom of expression by the cultural élites was extensively promoted in Bulgaria, because Živkov saw it as a useful opiate to distract attention from obvious failings of the system, such as drastic shortages of food due to the huge quantities siphoned off by the Comecon system. The popular television series was a very important element of this project. Živkov rarely missed an episode, and kept a library of private recordings. In their fireside chats together he sometimes discussed the plots of Markov's books or suggested script lines for the popular television series. This is Markov's own assessment of the Great Leader (I am quoting from Bereanu and Todorov).

The whole country was full of jokes about Todor Živkov. He was always depicted as a cunning, primitive man of limited intellect [but] he was better than these popular evaluations gave him credit for and he was at least in my opinion superior to any of the other party leaders. He lacked in aesthetic sensibility.... nevertheless behind all this stood a powerful, natural intellect with quick reactions and an excellent memory.

There was no fixed ideological polarity to Živkov's constantly fluxing personality. If generally trimming before the prevailing breeze blowing from Moscow (although strongly resisting any significant direct Soviet interference) he was also a constant experimenter, dabbling in a Bulgarian version of Mao's Great Leap Forward, before swinging 180 degrees to home-grown *perestroika* before Gorbachev. Živkov's revulsion for Stalin was deep and well-known. Privately he often insisted that Mao (occasionally swapped for Khrushchev) was his 'real inspiration.' As soon as he gained full control of the Party in 1960, he immediately switched course from the brutal excesses committed by his predecessor, Georgi Dimitrov. This ghastly tyrant had ordered a huge and bloody purge in the late 1940s — teachers, priests, civil servants and former government officials, were all condemned and sent to their deaths as closet fascists. Živkov swept away all the labour camps scattered around the country. Bulgaria was no carbon-copy GDR, even with all the industrialised snooping, curtain-twitching and incestuous file-keeping. Nor was it exactly a liberal paradise either, but there was a certain flexibility which set it aside from the other satellites in the Bloc. In his rise to power, Živkov crushed the Stalinist wing of the party and refused to entertain Stalinists anywhere in his administration, making so many enemies he was forced to beat down a putsch from that direction in 1965. Throughout his career he tracked steadily to the Right, so that by the end he counted as one of Gorbachev's closest confidants outside Russia. The one serious blot on his record was the revival of enforced Bulgarianisation of the country's significant Turkish minority, reflecting a cycle of pogroms, intimidations and expulsions dating back to Bulgaria's independence from the Turkish empire in 1877. These persecutions of varying intensity and violence persisted throughout the communist period, reflecting the deep stripe of anti-Turkish culture in the national personality. Živkov's interpretation, the so-called 'revival process' — a kind of back-to-basics Bulgarianism — struck a highly popular chord, and a general silence on the issue by the broad mass of Bulgarians. The expulsion of 320,000 Turkic people just before the regime fell was broadly welcomed as 'taking back Bulgaria.'

Živkov otherwise pursued policies of moderate tolerance: if people were pushed out of the system, or caused offence, they would henceforth find themselves quietly elbowed to the margins. They might lose many of their privileges, be denied access to the Forex stores stuffed with western goods —

an especially dreaded punishment — but their heads were in the main safe on their shoulders. 'Tasho,' the Bulgarian colloquial for the head man, was rarely bothered by dissidents who poked fun at him. He especially relished the darts of satire aimed by the famously cheeky poet Radoy Ralin, a Bulgarian wild-maned version of the anarchic British comedian Spike Milligan. Indeed, as Markov the insider observed, Živkov often entertained his guests by reveling in self-parody. An execution ordered out of wounded pride and vanity does not fit the bill. The absence of the truly vengeful in his character really knocks away one of the most important props that Živkov connived the cold-blooded murder of Georgi Markov.

Chiefly, Živkov strove to rekindle the sense of empire in this much-shrunken country, seeking to restore Bulgaria to her old role as dominant ring holder in the Balkans. He was above all else a stout Bulgarian nationalist who regarded the Party as an instrument, a means to an end. When the regime fell in 1981, he was spared prison and lived comfortably under house arrest in one of his former country retreats. The new government wiped the slate of all the crimes of which he was directly accused. Significantly, none of them involved killings or murderous conspiracies of any kind. The charge sheet listed mismanagement of state money, embezzlement and so forth. He was not accused by the post-communist authorities of giving orders to have Markov, or indeed any Bulgarian émigrés, assassinated. The passing of a genuine patriot was expressed by the many thousands who followed his funeral casket when he died in August 1988, at the age of 86. In my travels around the country it was rare to hear a harsh word about Živkov. Bulgarians considered that while they had rather done entirely without the communist interlude, they were at least spared the crushing Soviet hand in much of their lives. Markov was intentionally distorting facts and history when his broadcasts continually castigated Živkov as an unrepentant hard-line Stalinist, which he knew him not to be. Markov was understandably expressing his intense bitterness, as he saw it, locked out of his own country which he greatly missed.

In the early 1990s, I was often collected at Sofia's scruffy airport by a taxi driver who had driven Živkov's official limousine. He told me how Tasho asked for transcripts of Markov's shows to read on long car journeys, and was known to laugh uproariously at the bald cheek of 'the little tramp.' Nor, intriguingly, did the regime routinely jam Markov's outpourings, as they did others, including some originating in other Soviet bloc states. It was perfectly simple to shut him up with the flick of a switch. The impression of Markov the angry and bitter barn-burner of the communist regime at home is in any event difficult to square with the pleasures and comforts that he enjoyed as a cosseted visitor at the Živkov hearth. The story of the clenched fist reaching out from Sofia starts to look threadbare. Strip that away, and what is left is one of the more extraordinary stories of the Cold War.

It was Tasho who began the deep criminalisation of the Bulgarian state, thanks to his flirtations with a pastiche form of private enterprise — the 'socialist market' — which turned many factory bosses into oligarchs, or 'free racketeers' as they came to be derided. The privatisation component was, to a large degree, organised crime profiting from Bulgaria's position as a way station along the ancient and exotic trail winding from the Orient, through Turkey and finally to Mafia counterparts in western Europe, notably the Sicilian Cosa Nostra. From these activities emerged the sprawling Teksim trading conglomerate, which worked on the power structure of Bulgaria like a jet engine fitted to a child's perambulator. But Teksim's managers were too greedy and arrogant. Foolishly they muscled in on territory belonging to powerful rivals, especially those in the intelligence services working the Bulgarian Trail in cohorts with their secret western partners. Živkov was reluctantly forced to cull this flagship of his great reforms and purge its top personnel on trumped-up charges of embezzlement and smuggling, a bitter irony considering these were pastimes of every apparatchik who could squeeze in on the act.[39]

Bulgaria was on the Axis side in WW2, in the hope of making territorial conquests, particularly the Aegean coastline seized by the Greeks in 1919. In the unsettled interwar years, Right-wing governments pursued the 'war of white terror' against communists and peasants, leaving permanent scars and a deep pool of Right-wing extremists. The secret services and much of the communist bureaucracy were laden with ideological baggage drawing on those times. They did not alter their views that much, and regarded the post-war party structure as a useful vehicle. Many among the upper ranks already sniffed the wind of change approaching Eastern Europe. Nest eggs were in order. Bulgaria was a very large business enterprise intimately bound up with local crime gangs and corrupt party officials, involved in cross-border trafficking of huge quantities of narcotics and weapons of all kinds, which involved face-to-face contacts with dealers in the West. Through this kink in the Iron Curtain slipped Francesco Gullino, the forthcoming man of destiny whom Markov encountered on Waterloo Bridge.

The simple word Kintex now appears centre frame. Kintex was a DS family enterprise, manufacturer and general weapons handler, but also a conduit for many more secretive activities, including the dope trade and

---

[39] In 1972, Angel Solakov, Minister of the Interior and ex-DS counter-intelligence chief, fell from grace after one famous Politburo scrap. Tasho suspected him of eyeing the top job. Namely, his own. So in classic Tasho style, he shoved him aside by flashing a letter around proving Solakov sold the CIA three million dollars-worth of Teksim guns intended for 'an Arab country.'[(N2)] Aside from Solakov's implied personal nest-feathering, this was the perfect illustration of the arms carousel in which party nabobs were up to their necks.

contraband arms dealings that made a nonsense of rigid Cold War political geography. Because of the country's reputation for secrecy, the Bulgarian Trail acted as a magnet to espionage agents on both sides of the ideological chasm, drawn like horse flies on a hot day to this rich feast. Kintex was a vital intermediary in the grand East-West arms and drugs bazaar. The PLO was a regular customer and paid for consignments with drugs. The firm interlocked seamlessly with a Turkish-owned front company in Italy — Stibam Ltd — and between them shared ownership of a heroin processing plant with the legendary Corleonesi clan in Sicily (role models for *The Godfather*). Stibam's chief proprietors (and protectors) were the Turkish mafia and deep state intelligence cells, but the firm also had strong ties to the Italian underground world, via Licio Gelli's Propaganda Due lodge and onwards to the Gladio secret army. It was also used as a front by Mossad, Bulgaria being the only country in the East Bloc with which Israel held genuinely fraternal and long-lasting ties (a tribute to the amazingly successful wartime efforts to rescue the country's Jewish minority from the death camps). Kintex was a highly successful operation, a vital cog in the illicitly-controlled, government-conspired contraband chains.[40] As we shall discover in due course, its partner Stiban would figure in the attempted assassination of John Paul II.

Western intelligence stuck their hooks deep into the Bulgarian Connection, not just because it was highly lucrative, but could also be used to disguise the most highly sensitive operations. At the height of the Cold War, these included the CIA's use of Kintex to channel weapons to Right-wing Nicaraguan paramilitaries in the Iran-Contra scandal, a subsidiary ring around Saturn of the vastly larger arms-for-narcotics roundabout known as The Enterprise. Some inklings that western intelligence were operating through Bulgaria were intercepted by a few persistent Italian journalists, notably the murdered Mino Pecorelli. Neighbouring Romania was also implicated, thus explaining why the pro-western dictator Nicolae Ceauşescu and his wife were summarily executed by firing squad on Christmas Day 1989.

Twenty-six years after Markov died, more detail emerged of the extra-ordinary power of MI6 and western intelligence in Bulgaria, in the substantial shape of Robert Maxwell — media tycoon, patron saint of money launderers

---

[40] In one typical Kintex export deal, 459 rocket launchers and 10,000 missiles were shipped in May 1977 from the Black Sea port of Bourgas in a Kintex vessel under Cypriot colours, skippered by a Greek captain. The provenance of the munitions is not known, but the implication is clear they could have been could well have been sourced from NATO stores. Probable customer: Israel. Source: Uğur Mumcu, pioneering Turkish investigative reporter, murdered in 1993 while probing 100,000 Turkish guns shipped to the Kurdish province of Iraq. Mumcu's insight concerning the attack on Pope John Paul comes later.[N3]

and criminal conspiracies, and vintage asset of a clutch of spy outfits including, to keep the list short, Mossad, the KGB, MI6 and the CIA. In 2004, American investigative writers Gordon Thomas and Martin Dillon published *The Assassination of Robert Maxwell*, exposing him as a ruthless predator responsible for institutionally corrupting Bulgaria, particularly its banks:

> *Under communism, there were no oversights in place and in the Maxwell case, you had high level officials involved in the deceit, including members of the intelligence community... our investigations were directed at Maxwell's links with the Bulgarian élite and other senior communist officials, especially in the period before November 1989, and how those links had a detrimental effect on the country after that period and post Maxwell's assassination.*

In truth, Bulgaria was institutionally corrupted long before Robert Maxwellarrived there. But the cavalier tycoon certainly found the thriving atmosphere of 'anything goes' attractive to his unorthodox business methods, not to mention the pressing needs of his various espionage clients. Dillon explained how Maxwell grabbed control of the Foreign Trade Bank, thanks to highly-placed stooges among the *nomenklatura* with political backing at the highest levels. The bank was then opened to business as the centrepiece of a vast centrifugal money-laundering operation, spraying the proceeds in all directions. Dillon's most explosive charge was not centred on Maxwell; it was his insistence that among the bank's customers were front organisations sheltering the CIA, ever on the lookout for invisible ink to mask its global contraband chains.

Into this contentious frame steps Anatoliy 'Andre' Lukanov, a Russian-born Jew and millionaire 'businessman' (lynchpin of the fabulous narcotics and arms pipeline) who held a number of senior jobs in the Bulgarian oligarchy, and eventually the premiership. Lukanov was Maxwell's chief point man in Bulgaria and equally one of his most important conduits to Moscow. They were natural companions in arms, both Ashkenazi Jews from Eastern Europe, masters of shady dealings and tricks of light, with pliable attachments. Maxwell's western intelligence connections, notably MI6, extended to Lukanov, who by no co-incidence at all was the most powerful figure in Bulgaria after Živkov and the First Lady, Lyudmila. So powerful, that he staged the palace coup which finally brought Tasho crashing down in 1990. Just before Maxwell 'fell off his yacht' in 1991, Lukanov came to see him, bearing a package of highly confidential and compromising documents. These were high secrets of the state concerning the arms and drug trafficking and the money laundering in Maxwell's stooge-ridden Foreign Trade Bank. Whether by carelessness, cleaning the files in a hurry or by design, they also dealt with Markov — and the strange death of Comrade Lyudmila. It is these materials which it was later suggested certain nocturnal visitors boarding Maxwell's cruiser were keen to acquire. Five years after Maxwell's death,

Lukanov was gunned down outside his home in Sofia. The usual suspects in this unruly and violent Chicago-style crime citadel of the East slipped away into the shadows.

General Kurov, chief of the National Intelligence Service (the post-communist successor to DS), was interrogated concerning the refusal of Bulgarian authorities to open up communist-era files, particularly those concerning Markov. The general blithely declared: 'I am a supporter of a radical approach, which was adopted in Greece and in Spain. All their archival documents, without being disclosed, and regardless of the names within, have been burned by a decision of the [parliamentary] organisations.'[41] In 1991, according to the journalist Hristo Hristov, cleaners went to work on all the files held in Sofia on Markov (and other Bulgarian émigrés) to remove any traces suggesting their involvement with foreign intelligence. But of course, Lukanov got the choice pickings first. One by one, these revelations began to peel away the onion skins surrounding the real Markov personality and the complex interplay of espionage agencies, East and West, inside this strange hall of mirrors parked on the Cold War frontier.

In 1969, Markov used his privileged passport to stroll gently out of the country, first to Italy, where he stayed for a while with his brother Nikola. Then he arrived in London in 1970, but without any stated intention of remaining there or setting up shop as the standard defector ranting against the regime. Because of the precious travel document and his high connections — and this cannot be stressed too often — he was not stopped from leaving the country. Nor did he seem to think he was facing any kind of penalty. On the contrary, he was shortly going to stroll into the Bulgarian embassy in London in the confident expectation his special passport, which was about to expire, would be calmly renewed. When this was refused, Georgi found himself in the awkward quandary of the suddenly stateless person. This was clearly the knees-bend or no-going-back tipping point, underlined by a scarcely-veiled hint that it was time to come home. Next, there was a carefully-orchestrated show trial, which resulted in a token sentence *in absentia*. Worldliness was not one of Markov's principal qualities at this time, finding himself washed up on foreign shores, virtually cashless. Bear in mind however that his exceptional status in Bulgaria had also allowed him to leave with substantial quantities of hard currency to support himself. Yet there was succour at hand, for none other than his old flame Lyudmila Živkova herself was an hour's train ride away from central London, researching her doctoral thesis among

---

[41] As the general knew perfectly well, some were. Arson at the party headquarters in central Sofia destroyed many important records. There was another fire about the same time at the Foreign Trade Bank. A retired official informed me that soldiers appeared with 'some foreigners' (she thought at least three nationalities) and made a huge bonfire of many papers documenting international transactions.

the dreaming spires of Oxford University. Whether this could count as a pure co-incidence is rather unlikely. Lyudmila's interlude in England possessed other important features that we address in a moment. But for now, we have the developing picture of Markov, the largely accidental dissident exile.

Leading up to London, Markov had busily criss-crossed the Continent pursuing his singular passion: to find a market that would publish translations of his books. It was a depressing experience, and yielded no firm offers. Markov did not so much flee Bulgaria; he drifted away, disillusioned. In one of his letters to a friend, quoted by Hristo Hristov, he wrote: 'the recent years for Bulgarian literature have been the most difficult of the period since the war, and in some ways even more difficult than the Stalinist period.' With that remark, Markov demonstrated the stripe of occasional naiveté that went with his character. It was also ungenerous. After all, he sheltered in the bosom of the dictator's family, and enjoyed rare freedoms denied other artists. And he knew perfectly well his fragrant patron Lyudmila had prevailed on her father to throw open the gates of the Iron Curtain to the global cultural milieu, and break down the rigid grip of the state on the arts at home. Aside from his fiction, Markov was an incisive social and political essayist, with considerable freedom to explore fields of his choosing, again a remarkable novelty. In any event, his literary success stood testament to Bulgaria's unique mood of cultural *glasnost* within the Soviet Bloc.

The matter of his unperformed plays — one ironically titled *Assassination in the Cul-de-Sac* — naturally rankled. So did the censor's refusal to print his book *The Roof*, an allegory of a catastrophic accident caused by bureaucratic incompetence at the sprawling Lenin steel *kombinat* just outside Sofia. But his feelings ran much deeper: he no longer wanted to be the big ambitious fish confined in a small tank. This was the real motive that drove him to fix on fame and fortune elsewhere. That fame he tragically found in awful measure, posthumously.

The decisive issue that focused his mind seems to be the refusal of the authorities to renew his VIP passport. His private mood darkened because he was in simple terms, homesick. He especially missed his ex-wife, Zdravka Lekova, among his various romantic attachments. So the important question is what exactly led Markov to such a sudden fall from grace. The answer is straightforward: at home, Markov was an indulged and privileged member of the royal circle, a personal favourite of the reigning monarch, permitted to make amorous approaches to his daughter. Živkov's feelings may be described as close to those of a jilted parent. Given the great deal that is known of his character, the absence of towering rages and furies or harboured grudges, it seems that he regarded Markov, Bulgaria's literary lion, sorrowfully as his own prodigal son. In any event, Markov was always telling people that despite the highly critical tone of his broadcasts, he did not fear his old patron reaching out from Sofia to terminate his earthly existence. Even when the Bulgarian shock jock punched the invective button — hard:

> *Not for a single moment did he have the illusion that he might go against the will of the leaders of the Kremlin. Even in the most serious and, I admit, sincere feelings of patriotism, he never forgot that the USSR comes first and only then — Bulgaria... He was the strongest, most reliable and most practical and above all the most loyal. It might be said of him that he served the Soviet Union more zealously than the Soviet leaders themselves.*

This clip is actually a perfect example of Markov painting a landscape that was a very shaky representation of actuality. It is clinical, rhetorical propaganda. Markov was intentionally distorting the facts and history when his broadcasts continually castigated Živkov as an unrepentant hard-line Stalinist, which he knew him not to be. He was driven by his intense pain and bitterness, locked out as he saw it from his homeland, which he blamed directly on Živkov. It was a way of venting his anger, and of course this kind of heated fury perfectly suited custodians of the various radio channels for whom he worked. In this department, Georgi was in a class of his own.

For his part, Živkov's antennae were too cleverly tuned to indulge in some folly sure to earn universal disfavour, not to mention alienating the important intellectual constituency at home. Lyudmila would never have forgiven him. The killing of a revered national icon, the man of the hugely popular *Kilometer* TV series, could only be a grotesque blunder. Many Bulgarians, and especially the arts community, knew the story being circulated in the West, of Živkov's Revenge. Sitting in the Ministry of the Interior in Sofia is a brief file (number 45, 4th July 1976) passed to the Politburo, remarking on some aspects of 'Georgi Markov's activities.'[N4] It contains a cursory account of his doings in London assembled by the embassy there. Even allowing for the scores of files that went missing, this one really suggests that the regime had a fairly relaxed view of the fiery émigré. It was one thing to keep an eye on Markov, quite another to kill him. News always filtered in from visitors passing to and fro, and from foreign broadcasts. But very few conceived the regime was genuinely responsible. Živkov, earthily calculating in his peasant fashion, saw perfectly well the inherent dangers of elevating his opponents to the status of martyrs. *Cui bono* yet again.

Not long after Markov left for Italy in 1969, the Sixth Directorate of the DS, whose duties included watching over the intelligentsia, began to suspect he was a British double agent. Yet, that may have amounted to no more than a precautionary seat belt for such a radical intellectual, the equivalent of taking out insurance. The catty writers' union anyway overflowed with sneaks gaily tattling on each other. But the Bereanu/Todorov book does suggest that Markov's desire for fame and advancement led him into what he himself called the 'great game.' This explains his driving around in the only BMW in the country, with enough ready cash to pursue his gambling addiction. (Many of Markov's works are autobiographical, hence the fast and loose central figure of *The Gambler*.) In fact it was Markov himself who stirred up the double-agent mud by his very obvious associations with MI5, who found him a job, as the service always ran out the standard welcome mat for interesting new arrivals. This could not be hidden from eyes and ears at the Bulgarian legation. Markov's former insider status at the dictator's court held a certain allure for British intelligence, but time quickly drains the value of such accounts.

Sofia was home to a little menagerie of potential informants roosting around the English Language School, whose notable patrons included the Comrade Princess. In 2000, Gordon Logan, a genial rough diamond of the mould often washed up in backwater expat communities, used the website of the controversial MI5 renegade David Shayler to accuse Marcia MacDermott, a teacher at the school, of working for MI6, while also doing a number with DS. MacDermott was doyen of the tiny English community, and well known for her encyclopaedic knowledge of Bulgarian history and culture. She was often likened to Agatha Christie's fussy lady detective, Miss Marple. And she did indeed have a standing invitation to the Živkov court, so it would have been neglectful if British intelligence did not avail itself of this useful channel, and just as surprising if the Bulgarian cultural police, the Sixth Directorate of DS, were in ignorance of it. Logan implied that British intelligence enticed Miss Marple to pour enough poison into Bulgarian ears to get them to terminate Markov. This is an interesting chink of light. Although Logan probably had no idea of its existence, an unorthodox channel did indeed connect MI6 and Bulgarian intelligence, and indeed other facets of East-West secret services, the so-called 'red on black' game of the spy world. Both, after all, had connections to the great arms and narcotics trade sweeping through the country. Petar Uvaliev's animosity at Bush House might appear in sharper focus, too. Logan's claim of a British intelligence pull-by-wire contract killing ran full counter to the official story, but he was certainly on to something, even with the undoubtedly quite innocent Miss Marple permitted to gracefully exit the stage, and reflect on these heady excitements in the Sussex seaside watering hole of Worthing.

Logan darts in and out of the story, shooting insights and claims in all directions. His wife, who once worked for the secret services, was apparently a former mistress of Tasho. So Logan had an ear to the strange goings-on within a court that frequently resembled the machinations of a medieval kingdom. Not content with making his explosive charges of the contract job, Logan went very public by pursuing senior figures at Westminster to re-open the Markov case and finally pin down the truth. Some — like the feisty red-haired Robin Cook, the former Foreign Secretary who resigned about the same time because he disagreed with Blair's invasion of Iraq — seemed to be taking Logan seriously. (Cook would in any event know the facts. Just weeks before he died of a heart attack while climbing a Scottish mountain, he declared openly that Al Qaeda was a creation of western intelligence. There was no exhumation of the Markov case.)

It is time now to revert to Lyudmila, whom we left comfortably ensconced in 1971 in the prestigious St. Antony's College at Oxford, a highly respected cloister devoted to an impressive internationalist graduate studies programme, where she was doing research on Turkish and British relations for her doctoral thesis on the subject. Between studies she lectured on early Bulgarian history, and by all accounts she was popular and gregarious. But she explored other interests during her sojourn in England. She formed a close personal relationship with her designated official minder, an equivocal figure called Krysto Mutafchiev, who joined her roll call of lovers. Mutafchiev is the leading candidate as the British intelligence double agent, the much-speculated Third Man, at the Bulgarian embassy in London. Responsible as he was for all the embassy's finance and admin (effectively number three in the official ranking, with access to all official cables) he enjoyed the highest security clearance. Mutafchiev's second string was pulled by the ultra-secret First Central Secret Service Bureau, a shadowy division within DS. He was a natural target for MI6. There is a more explosive charge, namely that in this capacity he 'talked in' Lyudmila on behalf of MI6, while enjoying the benefit of sharing her pillow. It was a ploy sufficiently deft to be worthy of le Carré's George Smiley. So now we have these three figures within the 'Oxford frame,' each entwined with an intimate bond: Lyudmila herself, Markov and Krysto Mutafchiev, the probable super-spy at the London embassy. Two of these — Lyudmila and Markov — will meet premature ends. The third man will be charged with crimes against the state.

Shortly before the killing of Markov in 1978, Mutafchiev returned to Sofia, where he gave up the life of a diplomat altogether. He was installed as the effective managing director of Lyudmila's great passion, her Cultural Heritage programme. Ostensibly, his first big job was to organize her pet project, the 1,300 Years of Bulgaria Foundation. This splendid body was supposed to round up all the treasures of Bulgarian arts and culture stretching back over the centuries, and then stage a grand display in Sofia. As it transpired, there would be an orgy of plundering of these precious articles by the so-called 'Lyudmila Circle,' controlled by Mutafchiev himself. What he and his band actually did was illegally export Bulgarian artefacts, or simply forge them, for black market customers abroad. The ringleaders were mostly First Secret Bureau people like Mutafchiev himself. They clearly believed they were immune from persecution, thanks to the blessing of the Princess Comrade herself, who was probably too naive to know what was going on. All were to find themselves sent for a spectacular show trial just before she died. One remarkable story chimed with *Raiders of the Lost Ark*, telling of clandestine expeditions with trucks, soldiers and digging equipment to the mountain massif of Strandzha. Deep in the southeast of the country, it was an archaeologist's paradise, known for hundreds of Thracian tombs and occasional spectacular finds. The dramatic stories of buried treasure, of armed convoys arriving in the dead of night by the light of flaming torches, grew into a great mythology. Without doubt they were charged by Lyudmila's fixation on everything Thracian but clearly, that was much less significant than the mysterious raiding parties looking for precious objects that might command a huge reward on the world market. Was Lyudmila party to the apparent orgy of grave robbing? She never gave that impression, but then, she was dead before anyone could find out.

For many years there was speculation of a highly-placed insider answering to British intelligence close to the dictator's throne. In 1992, I was told by a former DS counter-intelligence officer turned money-laundering ferret that Lyudmila was strongly suspected of liaisons with the British or the Americans, or even both. By early 1981, he claimed this was positively known. The source was apparently one of her colleagues at her own private fiefdom, the Heritage Foundation, currently plunged into turmoil because of the great smuggling scandal. A *pentito* was apparently proffering keep-out-of-jail titbits. Many years afterwards, the finger of suspicion was directed at her old flame, Mutafchiev, who did get off with a fairly light sentence. During an intriguing extended supper in a small Sofia restaurant owned by a friend, my informant stated the files on the business had been expertly cleaned. In any event, nothing was done because she was seriously ill and probably going to die, of cancer it was said. Her death came on 21st July 1981, a few weeks short of her 40th birthday, in circumstances which have still not been properly explained. Moreover, it was just before the great antiques ring show trial began. Whether by natural causes or design, the potentially serious problem of succession within the Politburo was for the moment solved. The whole of Bulgaria believed up to this point that Lyudmila was to be the first female leader of a Soviet state. This left two candidates. One was the subsequently assassinated 'Andrei' Lukanov, Maxwell sidekick, brilliant orator and pro-western thinker strongly favoured as an advocate of the reformist line. The other was Alexander Lilov, the ideology commissar and yet another in Lyudmila's extended chain of lovers.

According to Gordon Logan's version, the Comrade Princess was poisoned after a bungled grab at her father's throne while he was out of the country. As unlikely as this may be, she certainly did not drown in her bath (the official story). Another version said she died of an overdose of drugs such as sedatives for sleeplessness and injuries received in two unexplained car crashes. In one of these, her official sedan was a rammed by a huge truck. Still others pointed to her weird holistic medicines and diet. In an eerie echo of the Markov business, stories circulated that she was poisoned with doctored French perfume, a gift from her rejected love-mate, ideology commissar Lilov. All who saw Lyudmila in her last days remarked on her frightful haggard appearance, which indeed might be explained by some wasting disease.

What is certain is that her death in 1981 extinguished an extraordinary comet, the Eva Perón of the Soviet camp, whizzing around the world, clasped in a warm embrace with Brezhnev one moment, then Castro, Jimmy Carter, Indira Gandhi, the podium at the UN next, a combine harvester of pure high-grade intelligence. In 1970, all this promise of high potential was yet to be revealed, although her steady ascent of the political ladder ensured her cards were already well marked by hidden hands. In the next four years, she steadily progressed up all the important rungs of the Committee for Art and Culture, flowering as the president (commissar) and a member of the Politburo in 1975. Long before this majestic ascent, everyone in Bulgaria believed she was the real power behind her father's throne, with a writ that ran far beyond her beloved immersion in music, books and history.

When the regime collapsed along with the Berlin Wall, there were strange events concerning the nation's most famous exile. The instant desire to erase everything concerning Markov resembled panic. Most of the documents about him held by DS, several thousand pages each, packed in seventeen files, vanished instantly. And so did many more held on Comrade Princess Lyudmila. Much later, in 1994, General Vlado Todorov, former number two at DS, announced that Markov signed on to the agency in the late 1950s, and was certainly still in their employ when he left for the West in 1969. In 1992, Todorov was sentenced to sixteen months in prison by a military court for destroying secret files. The day before his show trial began, the corpse of his immediate superior — General Stoyan Savov, former deputy interior minister fingered as the brains of the Markov assassination — was found in an overgrown cemetery just outside Sofia. It was said that he despatched himself with his own pistol, which was found at his side. No fingerprints were taken.

We now begin to study the history of Francesco Gullino, who arrived in Bulgaria probably in 1968. He was still a young man in his early twenties, clearly with sufficient credentials to make him a welcome visitor. There was no hint of an ideological tug to the Left. On the contrary, from what became known later, he fixed his political polarity on the extreme Right. The idea of a wandering chancer smuggling icons having his arm twisted by Bulgarian secret police, as some claims insisted, is hardly likely. Since he scarcely replied to a want ad, the only possible conclusion is that he was hooked in some other way. In any event, Gullino was taken on board as a courier working the 'Bulgarian Trail,' chiefly narcotics, on behalf of his paymasters in DS. Under the cover of his Italian and Danish passports, he moved with ease around the main centres of the operation in Belgium, Italy and Turkey, all strongholds of mob connections to the Gladio secret armies — and of course the famous Enterprise. He appears to have been an efficient organiser, which drew him quickly to the attention of underworld gangs in various countries he visited, as trustworthy and reliable. During these peregrinations, he made other friends too, which revealed the twilight world where criminals, NATO secret armies and espionage outfits of all persuasions flirted freely. In 2007, when Gullino bolted to the headlines as the shadowy figure possibly wielding the lethal umbrella, the news was treated as a dramatic revelation. It was actually *déjà vu*. In 1993, two Scotland Yard detectives travelled to Copenhagen to interview him alongside their counterparts in the Danish security police and one official sent from Bulgaria. His fingerprints were taken and he was rather listlessly questioned. He denied murdering Markov but — significantly — confessed to espionage. That is the missing key to his amazing longstanding immunity. The prime suspect in a riveting murder mystery was then allowed to slip back into the shadows. Gullino did not linger after his encounter with the Yard and their Danish counterparts — but nor did he go to any great lengths to disappear in undue haste. He signed off, as one must in Denmark, with the registration authorities and left a phone number in Budapest.

With that clue, a patient sleuth — Bulgarian publishing entrepreneur Anthony Georgieff — tracked him down, again in 1993, for an investigative story in his magazine *Vagabond*. Gullino was polite, but in the course of a short telephone conversation pleaded he had nothing substantial to say because it 'was all such a long time ago.' But he did admit that in the course of his present travels, he feared to set foot in the UK, Italy or Sweden, three countries which featured high-profile assassinations or attempted ones. At that point, Gullino vanished from the narrative. But his associates were still talking.

One of these, a man who declined to be named for fear of reprisals, described himself to Georgieff as a professed 'non-violent anarchist' living in Denmark since before the war. He shattered all the assumptions of the Cold War divide by confirming co-operation between communist authorities and 'terrorist and fascist organisations' in the West that were far more explicit than otherwise revealed or even suspected, 'red mingled with black.' And the game they played was 'very dirty.' He added the telling words that Gullino was an 'idealistic and convinced fascist' and belonged to an 'organised international fascist movement.' According to Georgieff's source, the Markov murder was only a fragment of the Cold War spy puzzle as 'there were much bigger things involved.' Furthermore, Markov was 'not a clean man, and neither was Kostov.' These claims gained further traction from Kostov's statement he was sent to Paris as a correspondent for the Bulgarian

Communist party newspaper, conducting himself with such aplomb he was promoted to colonel in the secret service. According to the source, most of the people involved in such operations, both east and west, were still very much active with illegal arms sales and trafficking in drugs. Georgieff's informant connected Gullino to the attack on Pope John Paul II and the murders of Aldo Moro and Olof Palme.

The only organisation in Europe which fitted the description of an organised international fascist movement was the 'western struggle against communism' started by those earnest fascists and cold-blooded political mercenaries, Yves Guérin-Sérac and Stefano Delle Chiaie. Was it Guérin-Sérac, with all his Aginter Press-acquired counterfeiting expertise, who supplied false documents that Gullino would need when travelling on 'official business?' It later emerged that Scotland Yard detectives tracked a 'Bulgarian diplomat' flying into London three days before Markov was killed and then flying out after the attack, via Rome. It stretches credulity that a contract killer engaged on a hit job would be reckless enough to travel under his true identity. And how and from whom did the Yard learn of his name — and possibly his alias — and possible connection to the Markov murder? Why did the Yard admit they had always known of Gullino's whereabouts, but indulge in no more than perfunctory inquiries when armed with such important evidence? Twenty years ago, Bereanu and Todorov claimed they traced a likely candidate, whom they called Woodpecker, but this lead soon fizzled out.

Yet *The Umbrella Murder* contains one very significant episode: the walk-on appearance of General Oleg Kalugin, former head of the KGB foreign counter-intelligence branch. Kalugin, regarded by his detractors as a fantasist and in his former homeland, a traitor and a double agent, was duly wheeled out by the CIA to push the KGB-DS plot to kill Markov. He was the star turn at a press conference held in Sofia in 1991, during a fitful Bulgarian investigation of the case. The affair dissolved into farce, the reporters present holding their sides as the much trumpeted supergrass lurched from one improbable position to another. He even claimed that he was personally responsible for designing the 'air pistol' used to kill Markov. Kalugin was patently bored by the entire burlesque, failed to stick to his script and got into a frightful muddle. Clearly he knew nothing of the affair at all. He betook his flapping tongue back to America to peddle exciting tales of the Russian secret weapon to destroy the United States with massive earthquakes and tidal waves. But of course he was privy to the one important fact about Markov's killing: there was no connection whatsoever to the KGB or Bulgarian secret services.

The Markov affair had one important and lasting purpose: it was the classic Cold War horror story of vengeance perpetrated by a pitiless Soviet regime. Very few readers gulping down the spine-chilling stories cooked up by 'official sources' and then spoonfed to Fleet Street had a clue about life in Bulgaria, beyond the fact that according to reporters it was 'secretive and impenetrable' (not though by hordes of tourists bound for the Golden Sands of the Black Sea) and therefore by implication clearly capable of monstrous infamies. My former colleague in the European Parliament, the late Lord Bethell, knew the Markovs personally. He made a common practice of befriending eastern bloc émigrés, acting as a benevolent house warmer. The Foreign Office drafted him to bolster claims of the unsavoury nature of the Bulgarian regime.[42]

In 2005, it seemed the ice surrounding the Markov case was finally breaking up. *Dnevnik,* Bulgaria's most widely-read newspaper, began to publish a series of articles based on long years of tunnelling into secret service files by Sofia-based investigator Hristo Hristov. The only element that approached sensational was a new le Carré twist, naming Gullino as operating under the code name 'Piccadilly.' But the documents that Hristov examined did not take the story much further forward confirming Bulgarian complicity. The nearest they go is a vague reference to Markov being 'killed in London,' which appears to be the usual bureaucratic tidiness in keeping the records up to date. Any documents that might conclusively prove Bulgarian complicity disappeared in the earlier purging of the files, in any event.

We can assume that Gullino did not drop into Rome on the way home for a pizza and a spot of sight-seeing. Rome was the traditional junction for fascist and criminal sub-contractors hovering around Gladio. Gullino probably dropped in for the pay-off. Nor was it any real surprise that men like Gullino — for all his fantasies about the coming fascist planetary Reich — found it straightforward to co-exist with Bulgaria's Reds, and they with him. Every man should have a satisfying hobby. Bulgaria was the perfect location for Gullino to develop his private under-the-counter deals such as looting art and especially valuable icons. 'Piccadilly' remained on quiet and comfortable tick-over in this bizarre but crucial outpost of the Gladio empire, waiting for instructions. The well worn cliché 'have gun will travel' fits perfectly.

---

[42] Bethell had mixed form in spooky affairs. He was suspected of feeding on a rich diet of undercover activities for MI6, the KGB and the CIA, for which no concrete proof ever surfaced. He had a great row with Solzhenitsyn over claims of unauthorised translations. In one episode of serendipity that makes life rewarding, the late James Scott-Hopkins, one-time chairman of the Tory political group in Brussels, hauled me in as an East German mole. Eric Forth, late and much missed uncompromising Right-wing Tory MP, was an MEP at the time and shared the encounter. Later he told me Bethell had given Scott-Hopkins, a wartime intelligence officer, the tip-off. It was due apparently to my personal relationship to the family of a prominent director of a large US corporation, who had once been a journalist in East Berlin, and smartly bolted with his wife and baby daughter as the Wall was going up.

Serious investigators (Georgieff included) have puzzled over the apparent disparity. Scotland Yard, a palace of detectives engaged in a murder manhunt, sent only a couple of quite minor cops to Copenhagen, while the Danes let their secret intelligence organisation PET take the lead. The body language between these two sets of investigators was poor from the start and eventually ended in stalemate. PET were not so much interested in Markov as they were anxious to persuade Gullino to divulge his intimate knowledge of neofascist networks operating in Denmark, including some in PET itself and the national police force. They also wanted to know what role the Danish secret army, code-named Absalom, may have played in Gullino's recruitment to the Bulgarian secret service.

Gullino was blessed at his crib by the black fairy who bestowed the gift of near invisibility. His fellow-travelling neo-Nazis, figures such as Stefano Delle Chiaie, Yves Guérin-Sérac, Germany's Heinz Lembka and Karl-Heinz Hoffman, the Turkish criminal mastermind Abdullah Çatlı (of whom we shall learn much more) — all of them fine ornaments of Gladio — were well-organised, quietly methodical undertakers. All often passed through the Bulgarian hub on their way to or from some engagement. So did Çatlı's great friend, Mehmet Ali Ağca, the Turkish patsy set up for shooting Pope John Paul. But that is a story we delve into in a moment.

Early in 2008, Scotland Yard awoke from its long doze through the Markov business to announce his file was again 'active.' Detectives scurried off to Sofia, and after some cursory diggings in this 'highly political case' announced that Gullino — formally confirmed as Agent Piccadilly — was back on the charge books as knowing something serious about the murder. But not, the carefully couched official language made clear, the actual killing itself. Not a single British newspaper reported that Gullino passed through the Yard's hands as a prime suspect fifteen years before, and was then allowed to walk free. The Yard did not send a detective to Budapest, his last known place of residence. Nor did Interpol receive a request to apprehend Gullino, despite his jaunting around Europe, barring those sensitive countries he skirts. As recently as 2009, British Channel Five TV screened a documentary stating the suspected killer was just an ordinary traveller.

We are left to adjudicate on the motives for killing Georgi Markov — and begin by stating the most important question. *Cui bono?* Without any solid information, the Russian-Bulgarian axis was tried and convicted, out of nothing more than innuendo and flimsy concoctions. Thirty-three months later the attempted murder of the Pope brought together the same combination, I suspect because it worked so brilliantly with Markov. But the mud did not stick so well in Rome, and was effectively washed away altogether, not least by John Paul himself. The murder of Georgi Markov and the attempt on the Pope's life belonged to the identical frame of political conspiracy, the build-up pitch to Reagan's and Thatcher's brutal Evil Empire hell-and-damnation rhetoric. Both crimes distracted attention from the swirling stews of poisonous scandals enveloping the Vatican and Italian establishments, posing serious and potentially disastrous consequences for the credibility of the US and NATO. Across Europe, tensions were steadily accumulating concerning NATO's intention to ratchet up the Cold War by rolling out a new range of medium-range atomic missiles. The Soviet deployment of new SS20 short-range rockets invited a powerful Alliance response, but all the countries selected to host the new weapons — especially Germany and Belgium — witnessed widespread popular and increasing political opposition. Huge civil resistance, led in the UK by the Campaign for Nuclear Disarmament (CND), supplied NATO with its worst-ever crisis of public confidence. The spirit everywhere in Europe expressed a palpable and growing sense of general Cold War exhaustion.

The murder of Georgi Markov, like the attack on Pope John Paul II, was thus transformed into a violent political cartoon to dramatise the evil intent of the Soviet Bloc. In 1978, Markov's murder and especially the callous manner of it rang around the world like a blow on a massive anvil. It was a bleak and dismal triumph of black propaganda and sacrifice. The story that spread was the absolute need to ring-fence — 'contain' in the old terms coined by George Kennan — a criminal regime which had proved its powers to commission such a wicked deed, and surely would not stop there. The Markov case remains politically radioactive, which Scotland Yard has the small decency to concede, because the official will to resolve it remains non-existent. Occasional flurries of activity by the Yard are window dressing to keep this ghost of the Cold War on sentry duty. We will regretfully pass over the cruelty this represents to Markov's family, the raising of hopes and then dashing them again for crude political convenience, once the flashy headlines fade away. The KGB/Bulgarian plot, virtually identical in many significant features to the St. Petersgate drama yet to come, was a chimera designed to cloak another game altogether.

With the information we now have, is it possible that Markov was indeed a pilot target for the deadly miniature darts described by Charles Senseney at Senator Frank Church's show trial of the CIA three years earlier, along with Kostov in Paris? The awful possibility exists, the probability even, given the timeline. The evidence he was on DS books is too strong to be dismissed, but should not be inflated beyond the milieu of the times. It is a diversion from the real story. Markov was elegant and intelligent, a literary craftsman wafted by cynical minds into the sterile insanity of the Cold War. His murder was a classic episode of the Strategy of Tension and the mindset of Gladio.

As for Agent Piccadilly, he roams free, the truly untouchable man.

X.
The Eye of the Serpent

'In Italy, there is always a common denominator in politics, whether they be centre-left or centre-right: it takes its orders from foreign powers. The first of these is the Vatican and the second is the United States. The former dictates our laws, while the latter sets up military bases in Italy and enrols this country in wars, just like the mercenaries of old.' — Beppe Grillo, 'the comic who shook Italy'

Early one March morning in 1981, surprising events disturbed the citizens of Arezzo, an ancient Etruscan hill fortress renowned for its perfect falcon's prospect of the rolling Tuscan plains. The rising sun had just begun to disperse the early spring mists, as a large posse of Carabinieri descended on a luxurious villa. Few of the local people knew too much about the owner, except that he was wealthy and seemed to have many important friends who continually came and went in smart limousines. But the P2 grand master, Licio Gelli, was not at home that morning. Forewarned by a tip-off from Rome, the falcon had prudently flown the perch. Perhaps, in the urgency of the moment, Gelli neglected to switch off the red-eyed, automatically swivelling serpent's head that was said to scan visitors approaching the temple of Propaganda Due. The scramble was so frantic the normally diligent Gelli left behind the script of Italy's most astonishing political plot since the rise of Mussolini.[43] The dawn raiders found exactly what they were searching for. Among the hundreds of files scattered around the lavishly-appointed 30-room palace was the now infamous list of almost a thousand prominent Italians. These were the *intoccabile*, the untouchables of the secret alternative state, above the law. They included the bosses of all the intelligence services, fifty MP's and ministers, scores of industrialists and financiers, militant neo-fascists, journalists and shady figures connected to the world of gangsterism. Counting among the ambitious men riding the wave was the future premier, media magnate Silvio Berlusconi. The list was crowned, so to speak, by the

---

[43] The Bilderberg and Trilateral Commission overthrow of Silvio Berlusconi during 13th-14th November 2011 deserves a mention in the same context. The installation of a techno-government under the supervision of the prominent economist and chairman of the European branch of the Trilateralists, Mario Monti, was effectively an EU-sponsored coup d'état. Berlusconi returned to Rome from the G20 Euro crisis summit, blissfully unaware that the Belgian Bilderberger, Herman von Rompuy, president of the EU Council, had won the support of all the participants to remove him from power. A softer coup with the same effect installed another Bilderberger, the ex-US and European central banker Loukas (Lucas) Papademos, to impose the direct rule of Brussels over the Greeks.

demi-monde Vittorio Emanuele, pretender to the throne of the House of Savoy. These were the gentlemen planning to seize power and install a fascist republic.

They had a blueprint. In his hurried flight, Gelli behind left behind another stick of dynamite called the *il piano di rinascita democratica* — the Plan of Democratic Renewal — describing in detail every step of the intended NATO-backed Gladio putsch. The chief architect was Gelli himself. Its genesis lay in the turmoil and confusion which followed the fall of Mussolini and the rise of the Italian deep state as an American — and subsequently NATO — protectorate. This process rapidly escalated throughout 1944-46, as Anglo-American espionage services began to reconstruct Italy's military and civilian secret services and the Carabinieri. Many of the key individuals which they installed or sponsored later turned up as stooges of the CIA and members of P2. Gelli himself was an early volunteer. Despite a sordid wartime reputation, another of these rejuvenated figures was Federico Umberto D'Amato, Mussolini's former chief of police. He was once described as the J. Edgar Hoover of Italy. D'Amato's chief responsibility was a secret Carabinieri nucleus located inside the Interior Ministry, under his personal control. This was the Office of Reserved Affairs, also known as the 'Protective Service UR.' This shadowy body was a bedfellow with the OSS (later the CIA) in a well-disguised bureau on Rome's swish Via Sicilia. Many years later, in 1995, documents retrieved from the former office of D'Amato described as succinctly as any investigator might wish the functions and power of the *stato segreto*. It was the extraordinary revelation of *gli intoccabili* exercising control 'over administrative, judicial and also the political character, over the most delicate activities of the state.' By scarcely any co-incidence one can see the outline shape of Licio Gelli's forthcoming Propaganda Due. Furthermore, the 'Protective Service' was clearly the early genesis of Gladio.

D'Amato's name is not familiar with many Italians in these times. Yet he was one of the most important figures of the ex-Blackshirt state who were resurrected and promoted to high positions in the new Italy. Or should one say, the continuation of the former one? Just as the first act of the US in Germany was to re-Nazify the state, so the identical process took place in Italy. American interests in Italy did not bother themselves with promoting stable democratic structures that would enable the Italians to place the Blackshirt era firmly behind them. On the contrary, the US selected and cosseted scions of the former regime, like Licio Gelli and Federico D'Amato, to captain important interests and offices that were wholly undemocratic in nature. D'Amato, for example, was the hand-picked delegate who negotiated the Atlantic Pact, a forerunner of NATO, on behalf of Italy. Gelli was financed with generous funds by the US to go around institutionally corrupting the fledgling Christian Democrat party. Nor should it be forgotten, in terms of continuity, that it was Gelli the great talent spotter who started Silvio Berlusconi on the ladder to political fame. So there is a generational span which extends from *Il Duce* to his contemporary pupil, the black hand of Licio Gelli working the levers all the way.

P2 was another reaction to the rampant industrial unrest that erupted across Italy in the late '60s and early '70s, attended by the most serious wave of strikes since the war. The perpetually-ruling Christian Democrats blocked their minds to natural causes such as low wages, soaring inflation, or deteriorating conditions of work. They preferred — or pretended — to lay the blame on cells of intellectual radicals proselytising on factory floors. A sense of deep crisis arose once the flagship Fiat factories in Turin appeared to be infected by agitators taking orders from Moscow, yet there was nothing of substance to justify the fear of a nationwide workers' revolution swirling around Rome. Nevertheless, the country was soon gripped in a full-blown political crisis that was, at its roots, largely artificial. The huge blast in the Banca Nazionale dell'Agricola at Milan's Piazza Fontana on 12th December 1969 marked the commencement of hostilities that came to be known as the years of lead. The bank was chosen as an ideal citadel of capitalism in Italy's financial power house. Precisely the target to attract a gang of radicalised Left-wing militants in the game of deception and confusion, the basic superstructure of the Strategy of Tension. The blame was instantly pinned on the same Leftist radicals accused of provoking unrest in the Italian industrial heartlands. All the rules concerning scene-of-crime evidence were disregarded, clues immediately hosepiped and brushed away. But arrests followed with alacrity to reap what at first promised to be attractive propaganda rewards.

According to the terrorist Vincenzo Vinciguerra's subsequent confessions, the aim of *gli anni di piombo* was to create a climate of fear that would 'push the Italian state to proclaim a state of emergency.' This would be a soft coup, enabling the authorities to end the wave of strikes by means of a draconian clampdown, while permanently marginalising the Left. It was above all necessary to discredit, through guilt by association, the charismatic communist champion, Enrico Berlinguer, father of Eurocommunism. His swelling electoral appeal horrified the Christian Democrats. Scapegoats were the order of the day. Among those snared in the dragnet was 40-year-old self-educated railway fitter Giuseppe Pinelli, a quiet and gentle anarchist and committed pacifist. His unfortunate role in Italian history was to be canonised in radical circles as the first political martyr of the *anni di piombo*. Pinelli was hauled off to the police headquarters in Milan and questioned — or threatened — interminably, well beyond the legally permitted limits, clearly to extract a confession. Just before midnight on 15th December he tumbled to his death from a fourth-floor window.

The aftermath of these events was manifestly Kafkaesque. Years of protracted hearings eventually concluded Pinelli had nothing to do with the bombing or stirring violent unrest, so his name was posthumously cleared. However, he was not tossed out of the window nor did he commit suicide, according to the surreal, fatuous ruling that he 'fainted himself out of the window.'[44] His chief interrogator was an intimate of *gli intoccabili,* Chief Police Commissioner Luigi Calabresa. It was Calabresa, not Pinelli, who met a formal martyrdom. He was felled with two revolver shots in a Milan street on his way to work, on 17th May 1972. He may be formally beatified by the Vatican. He is on the heavenly ascent already, given that Pius VI made him a 'Servant of God.' The murder was purportedly commissioned as an act of revenge by Adriano Sofri, a leading figure in *Lotta Continua* (Continual Struggle), a small cell of young Left-wing activists touring factories around Milan. Sofri indignantly refuted the charge, which rested chiefly on the evidence of a doubtful *pentito*, one Leonardo Marino, the killer of Calabresi. Forty years later, Sofri is still adamant, although he relented to the extent of admitting some 'moral culpability.' The affair is a marvellous example of serpentine Italian justice, beset with confusing and mysteriously disappearing evidence at every turn. An iconic episode in the *anni di piombo* that drew the attention of the Italian intellectual Carlo Ginzburg, it is almost certainly best understood as a classic example of 'steering' a violent act from within, Gladio style. As for Sofri, he became one of Italy's best known political commentators, permitted free range in the country's media, albeit from behind prison bars.

The investigating magistrate. Guido Salvina, decided that the bomb at the agricultural bank was an operation planned between Yves Guérin-Sérac's Aginter Press and two prominent Italian neo-fascist outfits, *Ordine Nuova* and *Avanguardia Nazionale* (Advance National Guard). The hands of Stefano Delle Chiaie were steeped in both organisations. Salvina determined that Guérin-Sérac had travelled to Rome to meet with Italian military intelligence. The discussions concerned the selection of targets, and training neofascist militants in the use of explosives. On the evidence of a CIA informant, Carlo Digilio, who turned witness for the state and received immunity from prosecution, Salvina further concluded that Aginter Press was directly linked to American intelligence. The exposure of Gladio was fifteen years away, but one determined magistrate sailed very close to mapping the web of connections that led to the Italian secret army.

Historically, a fundamental shift had occurred in Italy's political and social fabric, with far-reaching consequences across the European continent. The tensions compressed into this short interlude enclosed the bombing of

---

[44] Dario Fo, who won the Nobel Prize for Literature in the same year, wrote a play about Pinelli's fate entitled *The Accidental Death of an Anarchist.*

the bank in Milan, Italy's worst labour unrest for years, the aborted coup and the murder of Giuseppe Pinelli. These events released the forces of protest which threw up the Brigate Rosse. In August 1970, Renato Curcio, a drop-out from Trento University in the Alpine region of Italy, together with his girlfriend Margherita 'Mara' Cagol, formed the pilot cell of the Red Brigades from like-minded activists gathering in Milan. In one of those strange parallel tracks of history, Andreas Baader and his girlfriend Gudrun Ensslin, together with Ulrike Meinhof and Horst Mahler, were turning their initial pin-pricks against the German state into the fabulous career of the *Rote Armee Fraktion* — the Red Army Faction. Italy had spawned not only Gladio but its alter ego, the child of rage which became the angry brigades of Europe.

The Plan of Democratic Renewal discovered in Gelli's Tuscan villa had already experienced a trial run. Almost exactly a year after the bombing in Milan, on the night of 7th December 1970, commandos loyal to the famous 'Black Prince' Junio Valerio Borghese, prepared to seize key points and prominent figures in Rome. It was to be the prelude to a full neo-fascist putsch. Borghese, modest icon of an ancient Sienese family, renowned for daring wartime exploits with pocket submarines, had been an intimate collaborator and flatterer of *Il Duce*. He planned to arrest the socialist president Giuseppe Saragat, assassinate the unreliable police chief Angelo Vicari, and then occupy the broadcasting stations and key ministries.[45] The interior ministry would be seized first, because within its walls lay the vital command post belonging to D'Amato's ultra-secret unit and its communications system, the basic sinews of the Gladio network right across Italy. Though the Black Prince himself was not personally present to direct the proceedings, his lieutenant was: namely, the ubiquitous Stefano Delle Chiaie, chief of the neo-Nazi front Avanguardia Nazionale. Some reports later claimed that American and British warships stood by ready to enter Italian ports, on the understanding that Borghese would be rewarded with the full support of the Right-wing establishment. According to the plan, the Carabinieri should have joined the coup and begun rounding up Left-wing politicians, union leaders and unsympathetic military officers in the usual pre-dawn swoops. When Borghese received word that powerful factions he thought would back him had deserted the cause, the comic opera fiasco

---

[45] The Black Prince commanded the legendary *Decima Flottiglia Mezzi d'Assalt*, usually known as Decima MAS. He made a great deal of trouble for the Royal Navy in the Mediterranean with his agile frogmen, midget submarines and small craft (*barchini*) packed with explosives. In his greatest exploit, he sank the British cruiser *HMS York* at Souda Bay, in Crete, on 26th March 1941. In 1943 he was forced to repaired to Mussolini's rump state at Lake Garda, where his followers earned a reputation for cruel oppression. See Endnote.[N1]

fizzled out. At midnight, Borghese's men glumly shuffled out of the interior ministry. They loaded up a pair of waiting army trucks with their weapons and then quietly went home.

Betrayed, Borghese fled. He died in General Franco's Spain in 1974. Suspicions fell on a contract job by Otto Skorzeny's Paladin mercenaries, to keep his talkative mouth permanently shut. Louche, alcoholic and long gone to seed, the former deadly corsair and scourge of the Royal Navy clearly experienced a certain amount of self-delusion in the affair. The usual endless Italian verbal post-mortem revealed that he did enjoy substantial support among the ranks of latter-day *Duce* worshippers, including Licio Gelli. Who then gave the countermanding instructions, leaving Borghese completely exposed, is a matter of speculation. In any matter touching convoluted conspiracies in Italian affairs during these times, the finger of suspicion invariably points unerringly to Giulio Andreotti. Resting temporarily from the never-ending parlour game of musical chairs for the seats of power, the Divine Julius had sound reasons to ensure no *Duce Due* would arise on his watch. Adriano Monti, a CIA asset who thought he was going to be foreign minister in the new regime, pointed in that direction. Andreotti was not inclined to be levered into power. He would perform any necessary levering perfectly well by himself. When he sacrificed Borghese, he sent a clear warning to the United States that he did not intend to be raised to office by a foreign power. Andreotti measured out enough rope for Borghese to hang himself.

Eleven years later, the message was repeated. In 1981 the carousel of plotting came around once more. The projected putsch rested more firmly this time on the shoulders of Gelli himself. There were limits to Gelli's intuition, as is often the case with serial conspirators, owing to a strong tendency to navel gazing. His fortunes were about to collapse. Some have pointed yet again in the probable direction of Andreotti, who kept a respectful distance from P2, which he regarded as a conveniently invisible instrument of state. He was attracted by the novelty of a below-radar organisation that could manipulate the political system, whereas Gelli's vision amounted to nothing less than the resurrection of full-blown fascist dictatorship to replace the entire parliamentary system. Andreotti's personal ambitions, viewed through this prism, might well be compromised. The endless turmoil in the Italian state was far more to his appetite, and if P2 served those ends, so much the better. When its usefulness faded, it was time to stop the music. I believe the equivocal Carabinieri general, Carlo Alberto Dalla Chiesa (whose serpentine course through the Aldo Moro tragedy we noticed in Chapter II) was instructed by Andreotti to organise the raid on Gelli's palazzo. Gelli fled via Switzerland to South America, where he made a great deal of mischief with the P2 offshoots established in support of the local dictators. He never regained his former powers. although he retained much of the secret wealth he had amassed with the aid of Michele Sindona, Roberto Calvi and the Vatican's Institute of Religious Works.

A body of an iconic Italian banker dangling from a Thames bridge displaying the signs of ritual Masonic murder. Looted banks. Scandals in the Holy See. Even by the customary standards of Byzantine intrigue generally raging in the Italian state, the country appeared to be losing its anchor. Revelations that began to seep from the recesses of the Vatican in the 1980s read like a far-fetched airport novel. But this was a true story, linking New York's mob princes, financial swindlers in the prelature, crooked deals in the pocket papal state's own central bank, money laundering, narcotics, the CIA and Gladio. There was strong suspicion that Pope John Paul I — the 'little sparrow' who reigned for just 33 days in the summer of 1978 — met a truly Borgian fate when he learnt of wrongdoings at the Vatican's bank, the Institute of Religious Works, and ordered the church bureaucracy to start cleaning up. This could never be allowed, because the Lateran state was a fiefdom of the P2 lodge and its own pope, the ubiquitous Licio Gelli.

To discover the roots of these events, we return to the same time frame of the Milan bank bombing in December 1969, and the subsequently aborted putsch in 1970. In that same year a lowly-born Sicilian mathematical prodigy called Michele Sindona made himself one of the most powerful men in Italy, in a triangle within the P2 structure completed by Andreotti and Gelli. An aspiring world-class banker with a second string minding the New York Gambino family's heroin rackets, Sindona wormed his way into the confidence of the gullible church bureaucrat Giovanni Battista Montini, Archbishop of Milan. Like God's Terrorist, Yves Guérin-Sérac, Sindona was assiduous at Mass, piously pursuing his fantastic project of converting the Vatican to the planet's largest money-laundering pin-ball machine. This enormously long shot, plus his own political skill for picking winners, paid off. In 1963, Montini became Pope Paul VI. In no time at all, Sindona was the man they called the organ grinder at the Holy See's formerly sleepy piggy bank, the IOR.

Sindona amassed banks like other greedy entrepreneurs salt away works of art. In every case they were corrupted the moment he laid hands on them. Soon the vaults of the holiest of holy banks were overflowing with the tainted heroin loot of the Gambino clan. His chief associates were Marcinkus and Calvi. Archbishop Paul Marcinkus, presiding officer of the Institute of Religious Works, a burly American prelate much feared as 'the gorilla' among Vatican insiders, once said 'you can't run a church on Hail Marys' (he never tried). The neatly moustached, debonair Roberto Calvi was the man who came to be known as God's Banker. He was the chief cashier at the venerable Banco Ambrosiano ('food of the gods'), a famously old-fashioned depository for old Catholic money, that is until Calvi got hold of it. Calvi's subsequently corrupted version was the main hideaway for Gelli's P2 dealings, as well as a branch of the Lateran money laundry run by Marcinkus and Sindona. Of Roberto Calvi, it can be confidently stated that at one point he was able to exercise almost complete control over the incestuous and wholly corrupted Catholic hierarchy of banking élites which dominated Italy — and the Vatican — in the late '70s and early '80s. In this position he exercised enormous power. He was at the apex of the pyramid touching on the Mafia in a number of countries, the Italian secret state represented by Gelli's P2 and western intelligence. He was privy to the activities of the Gladio secret army and the terrorism sweeping Italy. These were certainly prominent factors that led to the discovery of his body dangling beneath the Blackfriars bridge spanning the River Thames, on 17th June 1982.

There were prestigious customers queuing up to open accounts at both banks. Head of the queue: the CIA with its splendid global dope-smuggling rackets and other lucrative sidelines to hide from Capitol Hill. The Vatican bank and Calvi's Banco Ambrosiano were funnels employed to shuttle secret subsidies to P2's offshoots dotted around South America. In 1969, Marcinkus was elevated to secretary to the Roman Curia (the papal government). Effectively he was now disposing the powers of Vatican chief executive, a task to which he turned his hands and brain with consummate skill. The reigning occupant of St. Peter's Throne, Paul VI, consumed by his huge administrative reforms, had no business brain at all. But his great works needed money, and Marcinkus always seemed to be making plenty of it. As corrupt as any renaissance cardinal, this burly son of a Lithuanian window cleaner climbed to the summit of the church and the pinnacles of the Italian secular state. Marcinkus moved in the same intimate circles as Andreotti and Gelli. As he was an affiliate of P2, the workings and plotting of the secret state were everyday events to this purely nominal prelate. So, even as Pope Paul VI threw open the shutters to the first real draughts of fresh air the Roman church inhaled since the Middle Ages, his chief executive numbered among his personal sacred works wholesale perjury, theft and laundering money to support sadistic fascist dictators. To Marcinkus, it was just good business. But the stage was now set for an astonishing reversal of fortunes that would destroy Sindona and Calvi, shake the Italian and Vatican states to their very foundations and transform Marcinkus himself into the Prisoner of the Vatican.

For the moment, Sindona soared on top of the world. He owned a score of banks around Italy, which he proceeded to milk to build a personal fortune approaching $500 million. His collection fitted neatly with his humming cash register in the heart of the Vatican. He shipped at least $40 million in St. Peter's Pence through the IOR to his private accounts in Switzerland. Marcinkus creamed off millions in fees for the church poor box, P2 and of course, himself. Sindona now made the elementary mistake of many ambitious men who reach for the sky. This son of an impoverished Sicilian family yearned for a truly heavyweight American bank to command real respect. He duly got it in 1972, in the shape of Long Island's Franklin National. He was Icarus now, gradually feeling the heat. In April 1974, Franklin National plunged south in the worldwide stock market crunch and so did Sindona. In the autumn, Franklin National was declared insolvent. Sindona's vast network of swindles was thus revealed to the world. The lifeboat victims included, thanks to Marcinkus, the Holy See, to the tune of $30 million. Sindona was hung out to dry on a string of conspiracy charges in the United States and Italy. Like others finding themselves in similar difficulties (we remember Pisciotta, who purportedly killed his cousin Salvatore Giuliano back in Chapter IV) it would all end — as such matters are wont to do in Italy — with a morning sip of prison coffee.

On 16th March 1978, the harrowing tragedy of Aldo Moro began. A massive demonization of the Brigate Rosse was under way, an important preparatory exercise in cynical duplicity paving the way to the projected P2 coup d'état, the *piano di rinascita democratica*. It also served as a powerful distraction from waves of scandals breaking over the Vatican and the Italian state.

The principal highlights are as follows. By 1979, Sindona was under indictment in the US and looking at 25 years of solitude to think about his life and times without distractions. In July that year, Giorgio Ambrosoli, the lawyer charged with liquidating Sindona's Italian banking empire, was shot dead in Milan. It was a contract job organised by Sindona. A month later, Sindona vanished into thin air, by means of a bogus kidnapping. He resurfaced in Sicily three months later with a mysterious bullet hole in his leg — inflicted, so he claimed, by Left-wing Italian terrorists, from whose clutches he nonetheless managed to hobble. This implausible concoction concealed the real story. He was heavily sedated and then shot by Joseph Micili Crimi, an Italian-American doctor associated with P2. Sindona scuttled around the country with some notorious Sicilian thugs in tow, threatening former affiliates with dire consequences unless they helped him recover his banks. Above all he must recover the proceeds of dope trafficking stashed away by Cosa Nostra and the New York clans.

One of those who got the 'treatment' was Giulio Andreotti, presently taking a short rest from the cares of office. It was the worst mistake of what remained of Sindona's life. From that moment, he placed his fate in the hands of the FBI. He went down on 65 counts ranging from fraud to robbing his own banks. The Divine Julius patiently bided his time — and his turn.

On the sweltering morning of 2nd August 1980, the railway station at Bologna, packed with vacationers, was almost destroyed by a vast explosion. The atrocity was intended as a warm-up for the main event, the destruction of the Italian state itself. It was never to serve that end. A classic false flag, designed to throw blame on the Brigate Rosse, instead blew back on its real perpetrators, the Nuclei Armati Rivoluzionari owing homage to P2, Italian intelligence and Gladio. It was a setback. But the clock was still ticking towards Gelli's putsch. Then it stopped, suddenly, that March morning in 1981 when the raid on Gelli's villa threw up the Plan for Democratic Renewal and the Black List of a thousand members of Propaganda Due. Gladio remained, for the time being, under wraps.

In that same year, Calvi was arrested and handed a paltry four-year suspended sentence, and the lira equivalent of a $20 million fine for serious financial crimes. These included the transfer of $27 million out of the country, in violation of Italian currency laws. It was a slap on the wrist, Italian style, for a man with powerful connections. Incredibly, he was released on bail and kept his job as chairman of the supposedly staid conservative bank while branded a convicted swindler. In 1982, *Time* magazine latched on to P2 in an interview conducted with Sindona in his upstate New York confinement. There he began to receive a stream of reporters to whom he vouchsafed many interesting nuggets, which served to raise political temperatures in Rome to alarming levels. He prattled gaily to his visitors about the money laundering which surrounded the Vatican and key members of P2 like himself, Calvi and Gelli. *Time* reported:

Money was given to political parties. But money to dictators and generals was sometimes under the table. Calvi feared his trips to South America because the communists, the Cubans, knew that Calvi with Gelli were building rightist strength in South America. That was our goal.

When eyes in Rome fell upon these words, the calculation was made it might not be too long before Sindona started to babble about other creatures of the deep state. These might feature NATO's secret soldiers and their war against the Italian people, in collaboration with Mafia hoodlums and ruthless fascist terrorists. It was time for certain lips to be sealed.

Roberto Calvi's weird, ritualistic exit, displaying the signs of a carefully crafted Masonic execution, is generally attributed to the revenge of the Mafia and their friends in P2. In short, the ultimate punishment for losing a great deal of their money. But there is another explanation. On the eve of his death Calvi wrote to Pope John Paul II, seemingly pleading for his life. That he should involve the Supreme Vicar of the Catholic Church in this way is inexplicable, unless it was understood as a form of implied blackmail. The full story of Roberto Calvi has yet to be told. We shall better come to understand it by first regarding the John Paul II papacy as institutionally corrupted, and Calvi's role and influence within it as far larger than hitherto appreciated. Moreover, the clash of personalities between Calvi, the magician in the black arts of plundering banks on behalf of the Pope's political charities, and Licio Gelli, the master of political guile, may well have come very close to a bitter power struggle between them.

Calvi's letter dated June 5th 1982 to the Pope is rather more than a plea for papal intercession to save his life. Certainly he realises that he is in severe trouble. He also recognises that whatever protection may once have been extended by P2 and by Licio Gelli in particular is no longer available. He has also been cut loose by Marcinkus. Calvi began by warning the Pope that Banco Ambrosiano was about to collapse, which he said would be a disaster for the church. Then he turned to the 'millions of dollars' which he had devoted to Papal projects in South America and Eastern Europe. 'There are many of those who promised me help me on the condition that I would not talk about activities I conducted on the part of the church — and especially many of those who would like to know if I supplied arms and weapons to some South American regimes to help them combat our common enemies, and if I have supplied economical means to Solidarnosc and other financing to the countries of the East. Summing up, I asked that all the sums that I gave to the projects of serving political and economic expansion of the church, that the thousand of millions of dollars which I gave to Solidarnosc with the express will of the Vatican and the sums which I have employed to organise the financial centres (banks) and of political power in five South American countries, will be returned to me. These sums would amount to $1.75 billion.' Calvi concluded his epistle by saying that he was 'seeking serenity and merely to live in peace.' That sum that he mentioned as owing to him was close to the $1.3 billion shortfall investigators identified in the books of Banco Ambrosiano.

There are important clues to be found in a chain of high-end bank robberies that began in London on 25th November 1983. Each one could be related in some manner to Calvi. The robbery of the Brinks Mat high security warehouse at London's Heathrow Airport stunned the UK by its sheer audacity. In all, diamonds and precious metals worth £26 million were seized. Evidence presented in court insisted the thieves were shocked by three tonnes of gold (with strange elasticity, ten tonnes according to other accounts) which they found awaiting them. This is unlikely. What is quite certain is that a fencing operation on that scale would amount to a considerable challenge; but for the Italian Mafia, and particularly the master smuggler and fencer 'Toni' Chichiarelli, a fairly straightforward prospect. Kenneth Noye, a legendary South London criminal with affiliations to the US and Italian Mafioso, was sent down to serve fourteen years for handling the looted gold. He was released after serving only eight years (although later re-imprisoned for murder). The Brinks Mat investigation was confounded from the start by an internal civil war and rampant corruption raging within Scotland Yard. A significant number of well-placed officers had fallen under the sway of criminal gangs, to such an extent that inquiries like Brinks Mat were mostly conducted away from the Yard's premises. In one bizarre episode, Noye stabbed to death an undercover officer he found lurking in his back garden, yet he escaped scot-free on grounds of self-defence. The rather lame excuse was offered that most of the stolen bullion was buried somewhere, or melted down to make jewellery. Yet the political undertones connecting the London raid, and two more that followed, indicated a chain that led directly to Rome. Documents relating to Calvi, Banco Ambrosiano and the Institute of Religious Works were discovered missing when the investigators moved in.

Four months later the Brinks Securmark safe deposit centre in Rome was hit (on 24th March 1984) by the gang led by Chichiarelli, posing as members of the Red Brigades. Brinks is an international company of long standing, specialising in the transit of high-value cargoes and sensitive documents. Its general practice is to organise franchise partnerships in the countries where it operates. One of the founders of Securmark, precursor of the Brinks operation in Rome, was Mark Antinuci, a US citizen and partner of Michele Sindona in the *Daily American,* a chain of US-based local newspapers. A business partner of Archbishop Paul Marcinkus, a Yugoslav called Stefano Falez, was on the board of Brinks in the mid-seventies. Another figure connected with Brinks Securmark was Luigi Mennini, at one time executive director of the Vatican's private bank. Mennini was a member of P2. He was regarded as Calvi's general bag carrier within the IOR. In his quieter moments he fathered fourteen children. He died, peacefully, and doubtless exhausted, in 1997.

The firm's legendary watertight secrecy in shifting high value cargoes and sensitive documents exercised a natural appeal to Sindona. His private investment bank was among Brinks Securmark's first clients. So were the IOR and Banco Ambrosiano, forming with Sindona's private operations the troika of banks subsequently exposed as rotten to the core. Three days after this raid, Sindona — by now repatriated from the US — was sentenced to 25 years in an Italian jail for a string of banking frauds. So, was this the Mob's typical crossword puzzle signpost clue that by hook or by crook, they intended to recover everything that Michele Sindona, Roberto Calvi, and Paul Marcinkus had stolen from them? I suspect the answer is yes, with qualifications The real aim of the raid led by such a prominent neofascist, and Gladio affiliate to boot, was to recover a host of compromising documents relating to Calvi, his activities within the Vatican and the death of the journalist Mino Pecorelli. Equally, the 15 to 20 billion lire difference that Chichiarelli claimed to have pocketed was the reward money for pulling off the successful raid.

On 12th July 1987 the Knightsbridge safe deposit vaults in London were robbed by an Italian neofascist, Valerio Viccei. He was a colleague in Nuclei Armati Rivoluzionari with Roberto Fiore, who was busily assembling a business fortune in the UK at that time. Italian neofascists breaking into supposedly closely-guarded high security premises in the UK are a decidedly rare species, particularly when they are connected to figures such as Sergio Vaccari Agelli. He was an Italian art dealer based in London who enjoyed business and political contacts with Chichiarelli, Licio Gelli — and Roberto Calvi. Agelli was the last person to see Calvi alive, at the Chelsea Cloisters suites, where the disgraced banker was roosting. Agelli was also connected to the disappearance and murder of Jeanette May Bishop, the divorced socialite wife of Baron Evelyn Rothschild, a member of the iconic Jewish banking and investments clan. She and her local guide disappeared late on 29th November 1980, during a house-hunting expedition near Macerata, an ancient city on central Italy's Adriatic coast. Their well-hidden bodies were discovered by boar hunters two years later, entirely devoured by wild animals down to the bones. After the usual leisurely trawl of the evidence, the Italian authorities concluded the pair were murdered, by whom remains unsolved. A link was traced between Bishop and a robbery at Christie's auction rooms in Rome in 1980. It was organised jointly by that well-known pair of connoisseurs and art traffickers, Sergio Agelli and Chichiarelli. The story ran that some of the valuables found their way to Bishop, whether purloined or as a present from Agelli, with whom she evidently had become intimate in London. A middle-aged divorcee, she was often in desperate need of money. But there is an alternative explanation.

The Zurich branch of the Rothschilds became hopelessly entangled in a typically convoluted web of financial transactions devised by Calvi, on behalf of P2. The intention was to acquire the Rizzoli newspaper group. The bonus would be the control of Italy's most prestigious newspaper, the Milan-printed *Corriere Della Sera*. This was Calvi's last big throw of the dice, and undoubtedly formed a significant marker on the trail that led to Blackfriars Bridge. He created a magic carousel through which Ambrosiano lent $142 million to a Panamian shell company called Bellatrix SA, which then deposited the funds at Rothschilds in Zurich to pay for the shares. That was the straightforward part. Bellatrix were then to pay an inflated price for the Rizzoli shares — ten times market value — in order to generate a cash windfall for the real bidders, who were P2 represented by Gelli and Calvi. The dynamite element came from the claims circulating in Rome and Milan that the $142 million was in part the proceeds of the Christies robbery, and thus Mob property. The pack of cards came tumbling down when Italian regulators torpedoed the deal on a technicality. The bid was to be made through Ambrosiano's Luxembourg office, and that made it a foreign acquisition. The fatal torpedo was actually fired by the sitting premier, Arnaldo Forlani, a weak puppet standing in for the Divine Julius Andreotti.

Il Divo had decided that Licio Gelli had grown too big for his boots and it was time to cut him down to size. The Rizzoli deal would have given Gelli and P2 commanding influence in the event that *il piano di rinascita democratica* had succeeded. There was now a two-horse race between Gelli and Calvi to get at the hoard stashed in Zurich. With the whole scheme dropped on the floor, Calvi decided that the $142 million sitting in Zurich was his own private 'reserve fund.' His final destination was supposed to be Zurich, not London. Sergio Agelli knew every nut and bolt of this project. If he had divulged the details to Jeanette May Bishop, she might have been tempted to blackmail her former husband's family firm, given her appetite for money. This would be quite sufficient to earn the attention of Gladio subcontractors organised by Italian secret services.

This is a useful point to interject some observations concerning the man who towered over Italian politics for decades. Giulio Andreotti has rather eluded the full glare of the spotlight so far. Yet no man is more important in understanding the course of Italy since 1945. It is a great mistake to inspect the life and times of Andreotti as the standard Cold Warrior, a marionette of western interests. No, Andreotti's story is that of love of power for its own sake, of politics played as a grand game of chess. When he sentenced people to death — his colleague Aldo Moro, the renegade journalist Mino Pecorelli — or connived at the deaths of others such as General Della Chiesa, Sindona and Calvi, these were no more than moves on the board. Examined closely, his life and career display very few discernible signs of definable ideology. To Andreotti, the game was always the thing. He was disinterested in the dull administrative chores attached to the many offices of state that he held. There is no striking decision or principle that stands to his name, in all his years in politics. This tightly compressed little man, owlish, with his strange rodent-like pattering gait, possessed no head for economics and cared less. Politics was foremost concerned with manoeuvres. Everything else was a waste of his intellect. He was not personally greedy, but intellectually fascinated by the power structures and disconnection with morality practised by the Mafia. In so many ways they resembled his own. He came very close to Sigmund Freud's definition of the absolute Self. Licio Gelli's misfortune was to run his course of usefulness to Andreotti. So had all the endless mischief concocted by Propaganda Due, which Andreotti concluded had gone on for far too long. Along with its famous Black List of a thousand initiates, Andreotti saw P2 as reduced to a rather silly secret society containing a host of overgrown schoolboys. Like a headmaster, he abruptly dismissed the class. It was a perfect example of Andreotti's precision pragmatism.

After the raid on his villa, Gelli sharply bolted to Switzerland, keeping low until he attracted attention by trying to extract tens of millions of dollars from the famous Zurich account. He was arrested on 13th September 1982, confined to the modern, high-security Challon prison near Geneva, miraculously escaped (less miraculously by handsomely bribing his guards) and then fled to the shelter of South America. Three days after Gelli was arrested in Switzerland, Sergio Agelli was murdered, on 16th September

1982. This was roughly at the time the remains of Jeanette May Bishop and her companion were found by the hunters. The story of these affairs in Italy is invariably the use of signpost clues. Two months after the raid on Gelli's villa, Pope John Paul II was almost killed in an attack blamed on the KGB in cohorts with their associates in Bulgaria. Propaganda Due quietly slipped from the headlines.

The murky depths of Italian commerce were about to be exposed once again. Florio Fiorini, an Italian businessman and money launderer known as the 'pirate of high finance,' was dragged into last-minute capers concerning Ambrosiano. Calvi, whose rolodex was by now red hot, was tapping any contact he could to save the bank — and himself. He turned to Fiorini as a middleman in a last-minute bid to drag the notoriously corrupt government-owned ENI petroleum-industrial corporation into a rescue lifeboat. Guile being in somewhat short supply at this late hour, Calvi threatened to expose the secret channels the sprawling company was using to bribe prominent politicians and journalists. It was true that ENI's under-the-counter deals were being siphoned through Ambrosiano and the Vatican bank. It was too late. Sniffing a wounded stag, ENI's directors adopted a Trappist silence.

Calvi's zigzag escape route took in a private jet from Milan to Venice, thence a fast dash to Trieste by car, a brief respite in an Austrian ski chalet before turning up in Heathrow on a false passport. In Trieste, he picked up a pair of minders with gold carat mob connections. One was the widely feared gang boss Giuseppe 'Pippi' Calò, known as the Mob's Cashier, a man with a dedicated efficiency in settling overdue accounts. The last hours of Calvi's life were spent in the Chelsea Cloisters, frantically working the telephone. The by-now ex-chairman of Banco Ambrosiano was clearly facing an imminent deadline. Sometime during the evening of 17th June, he stepped out in his usual expensive top coat and favourite hand-made loafers. He was next seen suspended from an orange rope strung from builders' scaffolding beneath Blackfriars Bridge. As even the uninitiated generally know, orange is the keynote colour of the Masonic Craft. Calvi's body was loaded with ballast, about forty kilos of stones stuffed into his pockets and bizarrely, his trouser flies. His calves' leather wallet contained about £10,000 in sterling, Swiss francs and Italian lira notes. His expensive though unwaterproofed Swiss watch stopped at just before 2 a.m., the point at which it was dipped in the water by the rising river tide. After 2.30 am, the level of the water would not have been sufficiently high to reach Calvi's wrist.

But suicide would demand amazing agility from an overweight sixty-two year-old man suffering from poor eyesight and pronounced vertigo. In a statement of doubtless unintended irony, Superintendent John White of the London river police declared: 'The long and the short of it is that we do not know how he came to be at the end of that rope.' The scene of crime was drenched with mystical significance. The bridge lies in the area of London where the black-capped Dominican friars established themselves in the mid-1300's. Black is the colour most often associated with fascism.

The coroners' jury, under direction, returned a verdict of suicide. Calvi's son, Carlo, hired the well known American firm of Kroll Associates to make an independent assessment of his father's death. They suggested plausibly that Calvi was killed elsewhere. His body was then taken to the bridge in a small boat. The orange rope was tied to his neck, and then weighed down by bricks to prevent the corpse floating laterally. In 1991, a Mafia supergrass called Francesco Marino Mannoia (nicknamed Mozzarella, after the delicious soft Italian cheese made from buffalo milk) began to sing an interesting story. He informed the Rome public prosecution authorities that Calvi had been strangled by a certain Francesco Di Carlo on instructions of the mob cashier Pippo Calò. Kroll investigators had already discovered that $100,000 had been deposited in Mannoia's account at Barclay's Bank in London, on 16th June, the day before Calvi was murdered.

Twenty-three years later, in October 2005, when the murder trial finally commenced in Milan at the insistence of Calvi's family, *The Guardian*'s man in Italy, Peter Popham, listed the impressive obstacles Calvi would have had to overcome to take his own life:

> *In the pitch darkness he would have had to spot the scaffolding under the bridge, practically submerged in the high tide, stuff his pockets and trouser flies with bricks, clamber over a stone parapet and down a 12-foot-long vertical ladder, then edge his way eight feet along the scaffolding. He would then have had to gingerly lower himself to another scaffolding pole before putting his neck in the noose and throwing himself off.*

Save for the forthcoming arraignment of Ali Ağca, it was the most sensational political trial in modern Italian history. In 2003, prosecutors made sure of this with a preliminary conclusion that even if Cosa Nostra had sufficient motives to kill Calvi, they also acted to prevent his blackmailing 'politico-institutional figures.' This was an oblique pointer to high-ranking members of P2 and the Vatican Bank. Marcinkus had already taken precautionary vows of silence and self-imposed internal exile in the papal statelet. From this moment he was known as 'the Prisoner of the Vatican.' Gelli was placed under investigation but escaped formal indictment, though not before he made matters hot for the Papacy by suggesting looted funds controlled by Calvi had found their way to Polish Solidarity. This was an accusation with strong foundations, as we see in a subsequent chapter (St. Petersgate, XII). Five charges were laid against the grand cashier Calò and Flavio Carboni, the second of the mob's ushers who escorted Calvi to London. Carboni typified the extent of the unexposed iceberg beneath the case. He had a conviction for fraud at Banco Ambrosiano. He could be traced to associates with known connections to SISMI (military intelligence) and the Roman Magliana criminal gang implicated in the murder of Aldo Moro. Carboni's connections extended to General Giuseppe Santovito, the boss of SISMI military intelligence and a P2 affiliate bound up in so many political and terrorist scandals of the period.

After twenty months hearing reams of evidence, the presiding judge, Mario Lucio d'Andria, suddenly aborted the trial for lack of evidence. He also reversed the earlier London verdict of suicide to 'murder by persons unknown.' This patently confusing and contradictory ruling at least offered a crumb of comfort to Calvi's family. But it drew gasps of astonishment from the legal profession and the critical media. It can only be explained by interference at the highest level to halt the case before more damaging exposures rocked the Italian establishment. Italians composed a short list of suspects containing exactly two names: the P2 junior novitiate and serving prime minister Silvio Berlusconi, and the coiled asp, *Il Divo* Andreotti, senator for life since 1991.

Michele Sindona was not around to hear the final verdict on his old friend and ally. The serpent had long since struck his flapping tongue. Submitting to unrelenting pressure from Italian authorities, the US finally surrendered Sindona to the Italian judicial system for the crime of commissioning the murder of Georgio Ambrosoli, the lawyer investigating his bank frauds. He received a life sentence, which he proceeded to serve in the prison at Voghera in Lombardy, a peaceful small city renowned for its restoring sub-Alpine airs and fine lace. On the morning of 22nd March 1986, Sindona, now 66, portly and balding, drank his last cup of coffee, laced with potassium cyanide. In tribute, the satirical magazine *Cuore* (Heart) switched the last name of Italy's most iconic politician, Giulio Andreotti, to Giulio *Lavazza,* a popular brand of coffee.

The career of the Knightsbridge robber Valerio Viccei came to an inglorious end in April 2000. Veccei was attracted as a young man to the glamorous flirtation with danger associated with fascist youth banners. He graduated to an upper academy, Nuclei Armati Rivoluzionari, where he encountered, among others, Roberto Fiore. The self-professed lover of fast cars and equally fast women was responsible for scores of robberies in Italy, some of which inflated the balance sheet of NAR. He moved to London when the domestic temperature became too hot. Some say that he made off with money that he had 'collected' for NAR. He was caught after the Knightsbridge raid and sentenced to 22 years, quite possibly on a revenge tip-off. There is more than a hint that if he had misappropriated NAR funds, then the leadership duly paid him back. Thanks to a useful change in European human rights laws, he was transferred back to Italy to serve the remainder of his term. Viccei was allowed to treat his detention centre in the picturesque Adriatic fishing resort of Pescara as a kind of holiday rest home. He was given carte blanche to run his various business operations inside the prison, and stroll in and out as he pleased.

Viccei had gained these favours by turning *pentito*. This was his undoing. He planned to raid a bank delivery van near Ascoli Piceno, but unwisely discussed his intentions with another incarcerated whistle-blower, who obligingly tipped off the local Carabinieri. Some would call that rough justice. In the following ambush, Viccei died in a pool of his own blood on a dusty roadside verge.

On 25th June 1983, Antonio Bisaglia, chairman of the Christian Democrat organisation in Veneto (northern Italy) and a member of P2 took his turn with the fates. He was washed from his small boat in the bay of Santa Margherita Ligure, near Genoa, purportedly by a mysterious freak wave on an otherwise calm day. In a curious chime with the Calvi affair, his pockets were stuffed with stones and some items of correspondence. The post-mortem suggested he had been in the water for about 24 hours. He had been suffocated, not drowned. Bisaglia's manner of death suggested another Masonic style rite connected to P2. Bisaglia was a former minister of state in the governments of Moro, Andreotti and Cossiga. He was said to know the truth about Aldo Moro, Mino Pecorelli and the attack on Pope John Paul II. In 1992 his brother, a priest, drowned in a mountain lake near Belluno. He inevitably attracted trouble for himself by campaigning for a new inquiry into his brother Antonio's death. The cull continued. Bisaglia's personal secretary Gino Mazzolaio met a similar watery end while swimming in the River Adige in the Italian Tyrolean region a year later. The traditional Italian signposts, once again.

In January 2008, a mouse rustled in the attic of the Cold War. Official papers released in London under the 30-year rule inconveniently exposed the fact that in 1976, the western allies seriously considered deposing the Italian government, if the communists emerged on top in a closely-fought general election due that year. A top-secret Foreign Office memo circulated for key members of the cabinet must have sent some eyebrows vertical, if not those famously thatched ones belonging to Dennis Healey, the defence minister. As the guardian of the British Gladio organisation, he was on the inside track. The document was a combined briefing from the Foreign Office and the Ministry of Defence entitled 'Italy and the Communists: Options for the West,' proposing 'action in support of a coup d'état or other subversive action.' The authors admitted: 'By its nature, a coup d'état could lead to unpredictable developments.' But they added: 'In one way or another, the forces of the right could be counted on, with the support of the police and the army.'

XI.
Frolics in the Forest: A Very British Coup

'Wilson's departure was a political earthquake, wholly unexpected and assumed to have reshaped the national landscape. For Wilson had been at or close to the top of British politics for 12 years, spending all but four of them in Downing Street. For a large chunk of the '60s and '70s, the words 'prime minister' instantly evoked the face and flat Yorkshire vowels of Harold Wilson.' — Jonathan Friedland

On 20th August 1971, eight of Scotland Yard's finest burst through the door of a dingy flat in the north London suburb of Stoke Newington. They arrested four occupants and took away gelignite, a Sten gun, one Beretta pistol, explosive detonators, a duplicator and a cheap printing set of the sort children used to get for Christmas. They had nicked a key cell of the avowed anti-establishment Angry Brigade, accused of some 25 bombings. The subsequent trial lasted 109 days. There were over 200 witnesses for the prosecution, 688 exhibits and more than 1,000 pages of evidence — at the time, Britain's grandest-ever showpiece political conspiracy trial. As a convenient backdrop to the prosecution case, the spate of bombings attributed to the group continued even as the Old Bailey proceedings wore on. In his summing up of the case against the Angry Brigade, the judge aimed a glance at the press gallery and observed that political trials did not happen in Britain. He immediately disregarded his own words by informing jurors the Crown case did not have to prove the defendants had actually bombed anything — merely that they conspired to.

The 1970s marked an extremely odd interlude in which the British state appeared to break loose from its hinges. *The Times* solemnly ran an article discussing the appropriate conditions for a military coup. Scotland Yard's Special Branch, acting in concert with MI5 agents, staged a rash of Watergate-style raids on the homes of Labour Party aides. The Yard bugged their telephones. Crusty retired army intelligence officers huddled over tumblers of Scotch with the top military brass and plotted a coup d'état. They would seize Heathrow airport (for which there appears to have been a carefully choreographed rehearsal), they planned to occupy the BBC and assure Her Majesty the Queen's safety by surrounding Buckingham Palace. The script was co-ordinated by an underground force called GB75 (indicating the timing of the intended putsch). It was the brainchild of Colonel Archibald 'David' Stirling, wealthy Scottish laird, future corporate mercenary gun-for-hire and founder of the SAS, an important component of the British Gladio set-up. The conspirators included a useful offshore arms dealer, powerful figures in the media, retired army officers, some not-so-retired espionage agents and rich gamblers with extreme right-wing views. They frequented the exclusive Clermont Club in London's fashionable Mayfair district, hence their renown as the Clermont or Mayfair Set.

The next important step was to secure Royal patronage. To that end, press baron Cecil King, a veteran MI5 asset and publisher of the mass circulation *Daily Mirror*, gave a lunch for Earl Mountbatten — uncle of the Duke of Edinburgh, Prince Philip. King proposed the Earl might step in as caretaker prime minister, while the army went around 'restoring order.' Mountbatten then had a long talk with his nephew the Queen's consort. Three of Philip's sisters had married into German nobility with strong Nazi ties, and the Duke's own outspoken Right-wing views have often verged on notoriety. He once publicly mused that National Socialism was a 'welcome change' to the Weimar republic because it re-kindled hope, a quality apparently in short supply in the Britain of these times. (Philip also said that Hitler made the trains run on time, a legendary feat usually attributed to Mussolini; this may suggest the boundaries of the Duke's retentive faculties).

The episode had a strange aftermath. Mountbatten was murdered in mysterious and never clearly explained circumstances by an Irish terrorist in August 1979. Chapter XX, The Strange Tale of Two Earls, sheds fresh light on this royal assassination and the legendary vanishing act of the gambling peer Lord Lucan, a leading light in the Clermont Set, amid the prevailing neo-Weimar mood in the UK of the 1970's.

Beginning in 1964, a McCarthyist paranoia seized the British media, influential Right-wingers in parliament and noble peers of the realm, as well as the upper echelons of the army. It was triggered by the unexpected return of British socialism from the land of the dead.

The new prime minister, Harold Wilson, pipe-smoking Oxford-taught economist and philosopher fascinated by the power of statistics, hardly seemed cut in the revolutionary mould. But according to his secret intelligence files, Wilson bore what spooks call 'history.' Scarcely into his 30's, he was appointed trade minister in the post-war government of Clement Attlee, and was in that capacity a modest commuter to Moscow. Wilson found he liked Russians, and talked with senior figures in Moscow freely and with some candour about the ambitions of the Attlee government. Resting in Opposition after the 1951 election (which returned Churchill to power) he kept up some of these warm friendships, acting as a consultant middleman to various Left-wing businessmen looking for prospects in Russia. This was the sum of the ammunition concerning the Moscow connection subsequently levelled against him. He was always cool to Britain's 'independent' Polaris nuclear submarines, which he resented because they went to sea with American ropes attached. As premier he was reluctant to make regular cross-Atlantic treks to pay due imperial fealty in Washington, and looked wooden and awkward when he did. As an aspiring MP, ambitious, on the way up but not yet in office, he aligned himself with the firm Left Bevanite faction of the Labour Party, whose general anti-US stance was invariably interpreted as pro-Kremlin. As dirt, it was mild stuff, but enough to set pulses racing in intelligence circles. Wilson, who became premier in 1964 for the first time, could be a prize catch.

The United Kingdom was about to be on the receiving end of a classic Strategy of Tension sting. It was preceded by the usual creeping barrage of disinformation. To bolster their case for removing the democratically-elected prime minister of Britain, the secret services switched on the black warfare engine. MI6 conjured up the honey trap, a Russian lover for Wilson, and a compromising photograph of the pair supposedly canoodling on one of his long-past Moscow visits. They passed it to MI5, who made sure the photo was soon on the desk of every news editor in Fleet Street. Eyebrows rose at the unsuspected Lothario qualities of a man who seemed to have a greater passion for poring over pages of dry statistics. In the *lingua franca* of intelligence circles, this was fly-fishing. The purpose was steady sabotage of the Wilson public persona.

Wilson's government strayed across a number of thick red lines. If the prime minister was more of a conservative technician than an ideological purist, he was nonetheless obliged to tack continually to the Left, where the heart of the Labour Party's rank and file still throbbed. So he committed the blasphemy — in American eyes and among the Right-wing British officer corps — of flirting with disarmament as a main goal of the British government, just when the Soviet threat was alleged to be rising. Although the influence of the Campaign for Nuclear Disarmament (CND) was by now waning, especially after the Cuban missile crisis in 1962, some ministers and many back bench MP's remained strongly identified with the 'ban the bomb' movement, and frequently appeared at its mass demonstrations.

The years 1964-68, when Wilson's first government and the Democratic administration of Lyndon Johnson overlapped each other, witnessed extraordinary discords at the highest levels of Anglo-American bonds. These were provoked in the main by profound differences over America's wars in Asia. Wilson refused to even consider a token military contribution to a conflict deeply unpopular within the ranks of the Labour Party and British public opinion in general, despite unremitting pressure from Washington. In the absence of direct British participation, the Johnson administration responded by viewing Wilson's various attempts to umpire a political solution as unbidden meddling or even a downright insult. It was a tangled skein of issues — tensions over Vietnam, the many outspoken radicalised militants in Labour's ranks, Wilson's refusal to expel renegade CIA whistle-blower Philip Agee, his teetering around disarmament, and the abrupt withdrawal of the Royal Navy 'east of Suez.' Enough to ensure that the special relationship was the most threadbare involving any British prime minister and a US president in modern times.[N1]

Wilson had barely set foot in Downing Street when he became the target of a smear campaign orchestrated at the highest levels of the CIA. James Jesus Angleton, the CIA's legendary spy-catcher-in-chief, tipped off his opposite numbers in London that Wilson was a closet KGB agent. Some thought that Angleton was merely indulging in sour grapes, after being thoroughly duped by the urbane British defector Harold 'Kim' Philby, with whom he formed a close friendship during Philby's posting to the Washington embassy. When MI5 pressed for harder evidence, Angleton refused point-blank unless given a copper-bottomed guarantee — bluntly refused — that the British would not pass on the information. The stance reflected The Kingfisher's evident worries of more moles burrowing away in British intelligence circles. But his source, he believed, was impeccable, if still the cause of some nagging personal embarrassment.[N2] Angleton was on excellent terms with MI5's director of counter-intelligence and deputy controller, Sir Maurice Oldfield. Initially, Oldfield considered the Wilson claims vague and insubstantial, but to be on the safe side, he put a small team on the job, consisting of officers with strong anti-socialist leanings, even by the prevailing tilt of the service.

The information was extremely difficult for the Americans to ignore because it came from Anatoliy Golitsyn, a major working in the KGB's strategic planning department. His pedigree included the purported exposure of a veritable cuckoo's nest of household-name British double agents. These included Angleton's one-time best buddy in Washington, Kim Philby, then Donald MacLean, Guy Burgess and John Vassall. For good measure he pointed to the well-known gay Labour MP (and later peer) Tom Driberg as a KGB agent. The Allied crowing when Golitsyn eventually defected to the West in 1961 was almost deafening; it was unquestionably one of the greater espionage triumphs scored at the expense of the Russians during the entire Cold War. Many seasoned experts however continue to regard Golitsyn as a confabulist with a strong tendency to prodigious self-inflation.

Much of Golitsyn's material was mined from the famous secret archive assembled by Vasili Mitrokhin, who sat for thirty years like a spider in the central web of the KGB records department, diligently collating the details of hundreds of high-level western collaborators. Mitrokhin starred Wilson's information about British politics as 'especially highly rated' among the Kremlin audience. According to the FBI, the Mitrokhin treasure trove was 'the most complete and extensive intelligence ever received from any source.' After Mitrokhin defected to Britain in 1992, Home Secretary Jack Straw set MP's salivating with his revelations: 'Thousands of leads from Mr.

Mitrokhin's material have been followed up world wide. As a result, our intelligence and security agencies, in co-operation with allied governments, have been able to put a stop to many security threats. Many unsolved investigations have been closed; many earlier suspicions confirmed; and some names and reputations have been cleared. Our intelligence and security agencies have assessed the value of Mr. Mitrokhin's material world wide as immense.' Golitsyn received the accolade of an honorary Commander of the British Empire before clearing off altogether to become an American citizen.

Was Wilson's name included under the heading of 'earlier suspicions?' Or did he simply provide a succinct synopsis of British political trends, as he saw them, relevant to Russian interests? It sounds much more like the crisp and analytical Wilson, who never once during his long political career gave a hint of gullibility, except when it came to his questionable judgement in choosing some of his closest personal acquaintances. He was a consummate political operator, an unprecedented four-time winner of elections. He knew that in the Labour Party of his times, a turned back was likely to empty a cutlery drawer of the sharpest carving knives in seconds. In 1964, British intelligence had no inkling of the Mitrokhin Archive. It was, after all, exactly those precious leads that 'Kingfisher' Angleton was understandably keen to protect, given the already gaping rents in the fabric of the British security curtain.

Years later, the former deputy director of MI5, Peter Wright, wrote a kiss-and-tell book called *Spycatcher* exposing the deficiencies of the agency. It gained enormous notoriety and vastly-enhanced sales when Margaret Thatcher tried to ban it. Wright's book gave credence to Wilson's persistent claims that he was the target of a conspiracy against him by a cabal consisting of at least thirty extremist MI5 officers. Wright did not say that he was suspected within the service of being one of them.

Wright was extremely close to Angleton. Both shared a similar obsessive passion for hunting Reds in, let alone under, the bed. The two spent many hours playing chess together, rehearsing the moves in a much wider game. Angleton played one in which the pawns assumed an unusually fierce role, a striking insight into his own personality and spy craft. He is still considered by many within the intelligence profession as the single most polarising (yet gifted) spymaster of his generation, even if at the end of a career pock-marked with controversies, he drifted into a drink-laced black and moody paranoia of almost everyone around him. Even the KGB studied the tools of this master of the spy trade. Mossad and Shin Bet stand forever in his debt. Yet his deepest genius lay in the manufacture of complex deceptions and false-flag operations, which his first boss Allen Dulles recognised to such an extent he made him 'master of ceremonies,' co-ordinator of all allied intelligence agencies. In this role, he was a key manipulator and strategic designer in the operations and co-ordination of the Gladio secret armies all over Europe.

Given he was under such a black cloud of suspicion from the start of his premiership, it seems probable that Wilson was never formally told of the existence of the British secret army, aside from the usual special forces, unlike other European leaders whose trustworthiness was not considered in doubt. There is some documentary proof of this from the miles of so-called Wilsongate tapes, compiled in the 1970s by two BBC investigative reporters, Barrie Penrose and Roger Courtiour. By this time, Wilson was brooding in retirement, with Alzheimer's gradually corroding his faculties, but his brain still lucid. He is revealed as continually pre-occupied with MI5 throughout his premierships, although he sometimes referred mysteriously to other 'dark forces threatening Britain.' Unlike their counterparts at the *Washington Post*, Bob Woodward and Carl Bernstein, the BBC pair were denied a Watergate-style Deep Throat inside the establishment, so they concluded the plot against Wilson was a one-dimensional affair hatched by the spooks, with the support of blimpish backwoods colonels and Right-wing active duty officers. Certainly the idea of an intensely cosmopolitan plot stretching to NATO and across the Atlantic was not in their narrative.

When Angleton began to warn London of Washington's fears about Wilson, the CIA was already ramping up its plans, through the Gladio structure, to push aside awkward governments in Greece and Turkey. It was also preparing with NATO the death warrant for the unitary state of Cyprus. In the very year of Wilson's election victory, 1964, Gladio was involved in a silent *coup d'état* in Rome, where Carabinieri *comandante* General Giovanni de Lorenzo forced socialist ministers to exit Aldo Moro's Christian Democrat coalition. Wilson had not been expected to end the long run of strong pro-US Tory governments in Britain. Indeed, on polling day in June 1964, voters were almost evenly divided, and the Conservatives forced a near dead heat. Labour's vote rose by a miniscule 0.2% which, allowing for the well-known quirks in the British electoral winner-takes-all electoral system, was just sufficient to send Wilson to Downing Street with a wafer-thin majority of four.

The United States intelligence community was instantly traumatised by this lurch to the Left in Britain, the most politically important NATO member state aside from the US itself. The fissiparous situation in Italy paled into a local trouble spot by comparison. Washington plunged into agonised self-questioning as to what to do next. From the perspective of the Alliance, and especially the new NATO Supremo, General Lyman Lemnitzer, the hawks wanted the Wilson government destabilised and hustled off stage as quickly as possible, before it could establish firm roots. The Pentagon for once saw eye-to-eye with the CIA. Angleton's alarm call was meant to set this process in motion. The trouble was that neither MI5 nor MI6 could themselves substantiate a credible link between Wilson and the KGB, despite having him secretly under full surveillance, the first time this had happened to a serving British prime minister.

Wilson had already been watched closely while in opposition, for clues as to how he might act over the worsening tribal rebellion in Northern Ireland. There, British armed forces were locked in a dirty war on their own soil. MI5 and its sister service MI6 (not always in unison) had been intervening actively on the side of the Loyalists, staging copycat atrocities — bombings, murders and assassinations — for which republican paramilitaries were blamed. MI5's specialists responsible for counter-surveillance and subversion are housed in a task force known as F-3 Group. It in turn enjoys close filial bonds with Scotland Yard's own undercover services and the British army's ultra-secret Force Research Unit, suspected of collusion with loyalist paramilitaries in Ulster. It is the same axis that remains the core of the British post-Gladio parallel state. Only the names have been shuffled around from the '60s. It was precisely this small group that watched and bugged Wilson, the nest of the 'thirty or so MI5 officers' he suspected of co-ordinating plots to blacken his character and destroy his position. He could never have known, but pop icon John Lennon was receiving exactly the same treatment, on suspicion of bankrolling the IRA. F-3 turned immediately to the standard Gladio Strategy of Tension in order to dramatise the quiet calm of the former years of Conservative rule, set against the unrest and political uncertainties shaking British society under the new Labour government.

A bewildering plethora of attention-beseeching activists of the far Right suddenly sprang up from nowhere. Newspapers overflowed with foaming gossip, vendettas and rumours about Wilson's private life, sniggering he was a serial adulterer, especially with his innermost political minder, Marcia Falkender.[46] The sharper edge was supplied by *Searchlight,* an originally amateurish *samizdat* broadsheet which began to appear in 1965, filled with lurid tales of neofascist and assorted paramilitary agitators romping around the fringes of the state. *Searchlight,* according to some lights, is or was a useful front for MI5, to the extent of attracting contributions from the alumni of the far Right and other figures in the loopier frames of British politics.

---

[46] A wronged woman, thanks to MI5/MI6 media smearing. 'Lady Forkbender,' as she was portrayed by the satirical weekly *Private Eye,* was a dignified and composed backroom politician who was bound to make enemies in her circumstances. Certainly as Daniel Finkelstein wrote in *The Times* (March 5, 2004) there was a good deal of 'feuding, incoherence and incomprehension' following Wilson's re-run in power. The Labour Party, a highly complex coalition, had always revelled in those qualities. As the Head Matron of Downing Street, Marcia Falkender was deeply resented by those who saw her as a power figure in her own right.

This kind of entryism is a standard tactic in intelligence circles and there are many examples of it. Anyone could see that the more coup fever raged, the more it helped to paint the picture of a disintegrating state.

By spring 1969, Wilson was fully alert to the churnings in the underworld. When he told a May Day party rally in London that year, 'I know what's going on — I'm going on,' most hearers thought it was a reaction to internal jockeying for power which had grabbed the headlines. In actuality, Wilson's words were intended as a warning shot across the bows of the secret services, demonstrating he had intercepted their plots. In every case, F-3 played on the peculiar law which always seems to operate with tiny 'revolutionary' groups: that their sense of their own importance is generally in inverse proportion to what they actually represent in power or numbers. Of course they generate good headlines. News editors could be relied on to report any fantastical nonsense about their activities as gospel. F-3's ranks had been dwindling. Now they suddenly exploded. More undercover agents were urgently needed, especially to promote radical dissidents like the Trotskyite Militant Tendency, which conveniently appeared on the scene in 1964, and the Socialist Workers Party, in order to crank up fears of extremism. Internal subversion, of the kind practised in Northern Ireland, was the order of the day.

British voters stubbornly refused to get the point. In 1966, they awarded Wilson a near-hundred majority. But this was to prove Labour's high watermark for many years to come. The government rapidly sagged under a series of economic disasters, while the rise of radical forces like Militant, with a little help and encouragement from MI5, at last began to register a disturbing note with public opinion. The appearance of the country as caught up in some kind of pre-revolutionary ferment was eagerly fanned by the media, with the aid of a top-secret MI6 propaganda mill grinding away in the bowels of the Foreign Office, unknown to all but a select few insiders within the political establishment.

This was the Orwellian-sounding Information Research Department, or IRD, which at its peak in the '60s and '70s had up to 400 people spinning away behind their desks at an anonymous office block in Millbank. Their aim was to subvert the British media by sowing black disinformation around Wilson and his government. Until its alleged demise in 1977, the IRD — the 'British Wurlitzer' — manipulated dozens of obliging Fleet Street journalists, some unsuspecting, others quietly pocketing the Queen's shilling. The Foreign Office simply changed the labels and moved the furniture around: the unit was much too valuable to be discarded, so it was instantly reconstituted as 'Information Operations.' In that guise it goes on blithely as before, mangling facts in the cause of the 'war on terror.' The technique was and remains fairly standard. To kick off a particular propaganda campaign,

IRD would start a constant drip of innuendo, dressed up as hard facts 'from expert sources' filtered through the most reliable contacts. With sufficient repetition, fiction alchemised into accepted truth. This was precisely the technique employed to destroy Harold Wilson.

IRD spoon feeding was also an extremely convenient and welcome research tool for notoriously diffident reporters looking for easy scoops (and that arrangement has not changed, either). Professor Roy Greenslade, who specialises in media at London's City University, has commented on the virtually unchanged climate of the war on terror: 'Most tabloid newspapers — or even newspapers in general — are playthings of MI5.' Jonathan Bloch and Patrick Fitzgerald, in their examination of covert UK warfare, report the editor of 'one of Britain's most distinguished journals' as believing that more than half its foreign correspondents were on the MI6 payroll. Thomas Jefferson wrote somewhere that he pitied the man who read newspapers and thought he then knew something about what was happening in the world. It is advice to be remembered. Among those regularly duped in this way was *Private Eye*, which in the 1970s was fed stories of a triangular link between Wilson, the Israeli secret service and the KGB. The former editor, Richard Ingrams, glumly admitted: 'Looking back on it, it's obvious that the *Eye* could have been used by MI5.' In any event, the print magnate Cecil King — nominally one of the pillars of the orthodox Left — obligingly informed MI5 spymaster Peter Wright that the *Daily Mirror*'s columns were always open to any anti-Wilson dirty laundry the intelligence services might need airing.

With the opinion poll forecasts set fair for victory, Wilson called a snap election in 1970. He lost by thirty-one seats to the virtually unknown Tory leader Edward Heath. The politics of the paranormal now moved into overdrive, for in truth Heath was no more acceptable to the secret policemen than Wilson. The unsound Heath government was stuffed with MI5 and MI6 placements (political appointees), to which he was oblivious. When Harold Macmillan resigned as Tory leader, there was an MI6 putsch in which they levered their long time princeling, the landed Scottish earl Alec Douglas-Home (pronounced 'Hume') into the Tory leadership. Heath was a shabby substitute and decidedly to the conservatives' Left, so the full force of a Wilson-brand smear campaign swivelled around 180 degrees to fix on the new target, with the notion of shaming him to resign in favour of a trustworthy Right-winger.

An important walk-on role was found for Captain Henry Kerby, an obscure backbench MP for the Sussex seaside seat of Arundel & Shoreham, whose chief task — aside from dodging suspicions he was two-timing on the KGB payroll — was to keep tabs on his colleagues on behalf of his principal paymasters in MI5. Kerby dutifully oiled around the bars and Westminster corridors whispering — as 'Red' Ken Livingstone later recounted in his controversial precedent-breaking Commons maiden speech in 1992 — that bachelor Heath 'was a homosexual who had had an affair with a Swedish diplomat.' The implication that Heath was ripe for a honey-trap enticement scarcely required underlining. His instinctive gullibility and blindness to plots seething around him were the chief curse of his tragic government. So he was easily tricked by Douglas-Home, his Foreign Secretary, into the Great Russian Spy Purge of 1971, in which 105 diplomats were ousted at a fell stroke. The news broke over the country like a thunderclap, suggesting that a Soviet coup had only just been nipped in the bud, moreover as the barometer of industrial tension rose towards bursting point. On the outermost fringes of parapolitics, a revolution was in the air.

The name 'Angry Brigade' surged to occupy the daily headlines. The general public was sold the insidious idea that a small cell of committed anarcho-communists was bombing its way mostly round the capital, attacking a range of choice targets — the Post Office tower, the home of a cabinet minister and even the Miss World contest. The Millbank rumour factory churned out the story of an urban guerrilla warfare organisation attacking these prominent symbols of capitalism, so tightly knit and cleverly organised it was difficult to detect. In the weeks after Home Secretary Robert Carr had his front door blown off, the élite of the Scotland Yard counter-terrorism squad raced all over London, raiding houses of so-called Left-wing extremists, a posse of well-briefed paparazzi and reporters following in hot pursuit.

The *Sunday Telegraph* painted a suitably alarming picture of an unknown enemy within, whose fate was to be ruthlessly hunted down by a special flying squad, headed by a 'rough and ready' commander who was incognito 'for his own protection.' IRD spinners nodded with approval over their hyper-ventilated press cuttings. 'The squad is taking a tough line. It will raid hippy communes, question avowed members of the underground and build up a complete file on the sub-culture that threatens the present social order.' The rippling of fresh newsprint over the breakfast toast of Middle England was sufficient to spark a hurricane.

Amid these comic capers of Keystone Kops and bombers, the aim (which became obvious from the haul of address books, magazines and letters seized in various raids) was to dramatise the looming menace of an extra-parliamentary Left with strong anarchist overtones. Behind all the frenetic dashing to and fro and childlike block-type communiqués littering Fleet Street like confetti ('We are after Heath now — we are getting close'), there were various brigades, rather than any one single group. Some passionately believed they really were '*über* anarchists.' But the trail of a hundred or so bombings also led directly to the intelligence services and Gladio-style special forces. They held more skills than all the pseudo-anarchists in Britain

246   *Gladio: NATO's Dagger at the Heart of Europe*

combined, in assembling explosive devices and sneaking close to publicity-charged targets. These included newspaper magnate Lord Beaverbrook's widow, who had a booby trap attached to her limousine.

One of the constant themes of Gladio operations anywhere they appeared was to take out a franchise on local terror organisations. The Angry Brigade, or more accurately Brigades, were no exception. Of the hundred or so attributed incidents, it was never possible to decipher how many might have been the work of a few woolly-jumpered libertines, or planned in the underworld of the secret state. No one went to jail specifically for planting bombs in a campaign which lasted the best part of half a decade. Forensic evidence was extremely weak and the number of acquittals significant. Where convictions were secured, the courts handed down a string of judgements for conspiracy. Protesting victims received suitably extended sentences until the heat died down and memories dimmed.

The essential moving parts of the MI5/Gladio psy-ops strategy at this stage were the following: to depose Heath and replace him with a strong Right-wing alternative; destroy the Labour Party for all time; and wreck the credibility of the Liberals, to prevent them from becoming the third force that might preserve the socialists in power. It was still a soft campaign that fell short of Greek or Turkish-style bloodletting, or the Italian Gladio direct-action dagger blow. But the time for that was fast approaching. Heath's government was by now locked in combat with the striking miners' union, bearing powerful pre-revolutionary overtones. The country lay under the gloom of the three-day working week, as power and supplies of all sorts ran short. Inflation topped double figures. Heath, cast as a modern political Tosca, was in extremely serious trouble, with no obvious escape route save to appeal to the electorate for judgement as to exactly who ran the country, the government or unelected union czars. In the depths of winter 1974, the British people returned a Solomonic judgement in this highly polarised climate of blackouts and flickering candles. Virtually, a hung parliament. The chalice narrowly passed to Wilson, and thus a first tick appeared on MI5's shopping list. Heath's political ambitions were at an end. Wilson tried again in October the same year. It was to be his last turn on the carousel of fate. He was awarded a paltry majority of three.

In the spring of 1974, I was sent by my TV channel to interview the British general who had been one of General Lyman Lemnitzer's most senior deputies at SHAPE HQ, and the officer specifically responsible for oversight of the total Gladio network. With his neat military moustache and clipped manners, General Sir Walter Walker was every inch the polished senior officer in genteel retirement. Yet according to the media, here was the British de Gaulle, recalled to arms to save Britain from a communist conspiracy that threatened to sweep the country.

As the crew set up the recording equipment on the well-manicured lawns of his creamy, honey-stoned Somerset cottage, General Walker explained that he did not see himself — in his own words — 'as some kind of British Franco.' Rather he was simply a patriot called upon to steer the country away from disaster. In the manner of having potential greatness thrust upon him, Walker became titular leader of the Unison Committee for Action. It was later renamed Civil Assistance, which chimed well with organisations in a similar political vein attached to the mainland European Gladio structure. The source of the funding was more important than the name. The only organisation in British political history to sanitise the idea of a coup was set up with money partly provided by MI5 and MI6.[N3]

Walker's interview made the lead story on ITV's flagship *News at Ten* that evening, following immediately on the famous gongs of Big Ben. He referred explicitly to the thousands of loyalists who could be relied on to man essential services in the event of the general strike, which viewers were solemnly warned would be the starting gun for a communist putsch. Over the gin-and-tonic cordialities which followed the recording, the general hinted at what he meant by this. Walker's home was close to the legendary site of Camelot, where King Arthur's knights are reputed to be dozing until the trump awakes them to national salvation. The ex-Gladio chief inferred Britain had its own 'sleeping army' of ever ready volunteers. They would prove 'more than a match' for those, as he put it, who yearned to 'raise the hammer and sickle over Buckingham Palace.'

The general's blimpish charm and Tonbridge Wells backwoods politics seem virtually ludicrous caricatures in retrospect. Yet as the future Tory rising star and serial prime ministerial hopeful William Waldegrave later commented, in Barrie Penrose's BBC exposé of the coup melodrama: 'There was a sense at the time of everything going wrong at once.' Not long after I interviewed General Walker, I was filming in Savernake forest, on the fringes of the army-ruled playground of Salisbury Plain. There, according to accounts in the media, proto-Nazi paramilitaries gambolled around most weekends, training with real guns to stem the red tide — along with a busy sideline bombing Left-wing bookshops.

The media overflowed with stories of 'Column 88' as a cog in a Europe-wide network of Nazi conspirators. However, the conspiracy investigator Paul Cox alleged it was a figment of the 'well-oiled disinformation machine' he called Searchlight Information Services, a wholly-owned subsidiary of *Searchlight*. Certainly it looked like a fantasy dreamed up by spooks, doodling away on a quiet afternoon in a parody world of their own trade. The '88' for example was a kind of schoolboy secret code for the eighth letter of the alphabet 'H' repeated twice to signify '*Heil Hitler*.' Just twenty or so miles away, the solid guardians of law and order in the headquarters of the

Wiltshire Constabulary intoned they would take 'any reports of men with guns at loose in the forest glades with utmost seriousness.'

General Walker and Column 88 were two sides of the same coin known as the Strategy of Tension, serving as distractions diverting potentially prying eyes from what was really going on in the volatile early '70s. Probably the only honest thing ever written about Column 88 — and in *Searchlight* magazine at that — came in a much later reference stating it was part of the Gladio network. Indeed it was, in the sense that its godparents could be traced to the army's Special Intelligence Wing, who provided the walk-on actors for those carefully stage-managed frolics in the glades of Savernake forest. Walker went along with the theatricals, not because he seriously believed tanks would soon be rumbling down Whitehall, but more from his willingness to act as a lightning conductor in the service of his country. He was a credible figure in every army mess, where belief in a communist conspiracy was the standard psalm of happy hour. When his hour had passed, the general quietly packed his bag and retreated to sleepy tranquillity among the cider apple orchards of South Somerset.

The image of a country under siege from extremist forces on the Left and Right, precisely the Gladio plague visited on Italy, Germany, Belgium, Turkey and Greece with devastating consequences, had certainly gained a grip on the popular imagination. Moreover, Britain did seem to be dissolving into chaos, urgently demanding the slap of firm government, as *The Times* argued in its now infamous editorial. This was possibly written or at the very least inspired by Peter Jay, son-in-law of future Labour premier James Callaghan, and at the time economics editor of the paper. He doubled as affiliate of the eloquently-named Congress of Cultural Freedom, a front for the CIA and its publishing activities, which included the egg-heads' magazine, *Encounter*. Jay was a prominent thinker in this centrepiece of the cultural cold war. His intelligence connections later extended to strange work as chief of staff to 'Captain Bob' Robert Maxwell, who needed especially careful minding due to his serial infidelities with a host of spy networks. These intelligence connections exercised significant influence over the subsequent decision by Callaghan to appoint his son-in-law with the unusually charmed life as ambassador to Washington.

The open season on Harold Wilson — when the coup plotting and rumours reached fever pitch — followed the second of the 1974 twin elections, and lasted until 11th February 1975. On that day Margaret Thatcher rocked the establishment and the pundits by defeating Heath in the contest for leadership of the Conservative Party. Behind the scenes, it was Gladio's triumph. Heath was destroyed by the libels revolving around his sexuality and his own loftiness, rooted in insecurity, which rendered him easy prey to ruthless secret service gossip mongers. He also had a specialist on his tail.

Maurice Oldfield, director general of MI6 until 1978, was gay. For her part, Thatcher was thought to be in the safe manipulative hands of her husband Dennis, whose pronounced Right-wing opinions were backed up by strong ties to the Bureau of State Security (BOSS) — the South African apartheid state's secret service. Dennis Thatcher's links to the spy world were heavily alluded to in the stage version of the long-running 'Dear Bill' spoof correspondence in *Private Eye*.

Wilson was now the wounded stag. The hounds moved in for the kill. Wilson himself later declared that in the last eight months of his premiership, he had no effective control over the secret services. Bunker-like shutters descended on Downing Street and, amid the gathering gloom, MI5 re-ignited a long-standing feud between the two key members of his kitchen cabinet — the old army warhorse George Wigg, who served as his eyes and ears on the world of spies and dirty dealings, and his trusted political secretary Marcia Falkender. She never forgave Wigg for calling her 'the typist' and refusing to discuss secret service matters when she was in the room.

Joe Haines, Wilson's press secretary, liked to refer to Wigg if he was crossed as 'a walking canister of Semtex,' forgetting that hell hath no fury like a woman scorned. The sexual peccadilloes of those in high places rarely go unreported to the secret services. Blackmail is a key weapon of spy craft. So the future Lady Falkender conveniently learnt of Wigg's private tastes for rough trade in the way of prostitutes. Wilson put a tail on Wigg, who was tracked one evening to a flat in north London, where his host was a young unmarried woman with a small child. The greatest of Wigg's sins in Falkender's eyes was the exposure by him of her own illegitimate twin boys, to a chorus of malicious cheers from the red top tabloid press. The implication that Wigg had fathered on the wrong side of the blanket was a delicious reprisal, aside from the fact that Wilson, who never suppressed his innate north country puritanical streak, sacked Wigg forthwith.

On 16th March 1976, Wilson suddenly resigned. It was an amazing act of high political drama, because he declined to give any reasons. Speculation over the years included the descending fog of Alzheimers, some dangerous amorous connections, even the truth of the old KGB chestnut. Everyone who had been around him in those times similarly kept mum, nor even stoked the speculation, a hard act among the political castes for whom gossip and rumours is the staff of life. The most likely explanation is that Wilson received visitors and, left in a room with a loaded pistol, pulled the metaphorical trigger. He wanted, like Blair in years to come, to go with his legacy intact, and indeed his was still warm from the recent historic 'Yes' vote in the referendum to remain in the European Common Market (the future European Union).[47]

Michael Cocks was the Labour chief whip known as 'the ambulance driver.' It came from his remarkable skills in keeping the majority-less Callaghan government afloat with the votes of ailing Labour's MPs brought to the House on hospital stretchers. He was among my closest friends in politics until his death in 2001. Cocks, a great foe of arch Left-wing millionaire Tony Wedgwood Benn, was never really a Wilson man either. But he may have been close to the mark when he intimated years later the mystery was connected to Wilson's inopportune promotion of an obscure Welsh businessman called John Brayley who was knighted, then raised to the peerage, and finally had a short, scandal-starred career as arms minister. Joe Haines later made unsubstantiated claims that at this time Wilson accepted a large brown parcel from Brayley to pay for the running of his private office. There was a hint that it may have been consigned by Mossad.

Cocks's version was several notches different, namely that Wilson was honey-trapped by MI5 and blackmailed by Brayley who, behind his front activities, enjoyed a remarkably grandiose lifestyle. He supported it by working with Wigg — with whom he shared a passion for horse racing — to earn undercover commissions by manipulating government arms contracts. Brayley's job at the Ministry of Defence was certainly unusual. Wilson himself once sniffed his protégé could neither make a speech nor read one written for him. When Wilson lost the general election in 1970, it was Brayley who lent the penniless Wilson his London home and chauffeur. Cocks told me: 'Brayley got his talons stuck into Harold. It's what it was all about. He was bloody hopeless choosing his friends and got sucked into a one-way street.' Cocks' second wife was a prominent Zionist lobbyist. So his remarks might indicate obliquely the possibility of some Mossad connection.

To whom Brayley owed his loyalties remains a mystery. But taking a closer look at Wilson's behaviour in the closing days of his premiership may supply better clues. In 1976, the future president George H. W. Bush had just been installed as the new Director of the CIA. Hardly was he settled into his suite at Langley, Virginia, when momentous developments began concerning Harold Wilson's future. Lord Weidenfield, the publisher and Wilson's most trusted confidante, was despatched on an urgent mission to the United States bearing a personal letter from Wilson addressed to Senator Hubert Humphrey. The letter was drawn up following a highly confidential

---

[47] Perhaps Wilson's finest hour. The British had never settled down to being Europeans after Edward Heath's fiat decision 'to take the country in' without a referendum. The Labour Party was largely opposed to membership. Wilson brilliantly played a long shot, claimed he had 'renegotiated' the terms of membership, and won a clear majority. But the issue rumbles on to this day. He always warned the matter had been settled only for one generation.

discussion between Wilson and Weidenfield early in February 1976. The contents were explosive. They listed the names of MI5 and MI6 officers whom Wilson suspected of complicity in the plot against him. Wilson's letter, which obviously could not travel through the customary diplomatic channels, requested that Humphrey go immediately to Bush and interrogate him as to what links the CIA had with these British intelligence officers. Wilson now knew of the Washington connection and wanted to signal his knowledge — and fury.

But the February meeting between Wiedenfield and Wilson was already common currency in Langley, because the CIA, through MI5, had bugged not only the front office of Downing Street but the prime minister's private quarters as well. Wilson may have had his suspicions. He was seeing flickering shapes everywhere by now. In any event, Bush panicked and got straight on a plane to London to deliver a fatuous hand-on-heart assurance to Wilson that no one in Washington would dream of wire-tapping or bugging the British prime minister. Not even, which Bush did not say, when all the names on the list were shared operatives in the British intelligence/Gladio operation. Within a few days of receiving this important American visitor, Wilson resigned.

Brayley's remarkably successful insinuation of himself into the Wilson camp, moreover in the acutely sensitive area of defence, belied his origins in the unpromising backwaters of Welsh provincial commerce. It sent wider ripples to the shore when his wartime career as a special forces behind-the-scenes operative — which earned him a Mention in Despatches — was revealed. A West of England Country businessman whom I knew well, and who once sat with Brayley on the board of the Phoenix Glass Company in Bristol, persistently derided him as 'the spy,' once he was made a minister. A little over a year from Wilson's departure, Brayley — who always maintained himself in the peak of health — was off the scene after a surprisingly 'short illness.' But in the brief interval between Wilson's departure and Brayley's death, there was no repeat of the earlier financial lifeboat operation for a prime minister who, as usual, left office without a grolt to his name.

For ten years, I sat in the Strasbourg EU parliament with the socialist (but closet conservative) icon Barbara Castle, who never shook off the odious view she adopted of Wilson, after his *Realpolitik* decision to torpedo her plans to shackle the unions. We found time to discuss Brayley on several occasions. 'I found him repugnant,' she once told me. 'He was forever coming down the stairs in Downing Street with an awful smirk, as though he was the bailiff who had just come to collect something from Harold.' Could he have been blackmailing the prime minister? On that she thought Marcia Falkender had the key to all Harold's closets, save possibly Brayley. Her verdict was simple. 'He was something very personal to Harold and it was impossible to escape the idea that he was in some ways afraid of him, that he was obliged to some creature that he couldn't in the end control.'

If Brayley was some kind of microphone man in Wilson's kitchen cabinet, some complicated conspiratorial material starts to add up.

A little while after one of these discussions, my parliamentary companion on a long flight back from a congress in Jakarta was an ebullient Dutch MEP, Janssen van Ray. Over the Sabena gin and tonics we were ruminating the famous Wilson remark (perhaps his finest *bon mot*) that 'a week is a long time in politics.' Van Ray, widely suspected of links to Dutch espionage, suddenly said: 'It was quite known in Dutch intelligence circles why Wilson really went in that sudden and abrupt fashion. It was because he had some relationship, I think it was supposed to be when he was a younger man, of a highly personal and secretive nature with one of his ministers, and the CIA were threatening to fish it out. He was appalled at the shock it would give to his wife.' Barbara Castle's only response to this when I put it to her was oblique. She pursed her lips and recalled that, 'Harold certainly tried like hell to help Jeremy [the charismatic Liberal leader Jeremy Thorpe destroyed by a homosexual scandal — more below] when he got into a pickle.'

There was another conspicuous footprint on the trail. When the small MI5/MI6 black ops team working up the Wilson and Heath plots got down to work in the early '70s, they made a subliminally curious choice of 'Clockwork Orange' as the in-house code name. Stanley Kubrick's disturbing and controversial film adaptation of Anthony Burgess's story of deranged misfits plaguing the streets was widely regarded at the time as a 'queer' exercise in sexual debauchery if not an actual motif, as many saw it, for blatant homosexuality. Was it merely a co-incidence that Heath was smeared all over London as a closet gay, or that the bombastic Ulster Protestant, the Rev. Ian Paisley, another victim on the same hit list, would be dragged into a scandal concerning paedophilia in the Kincaid children's home? The implication of a dirty tricks sting against Wilson on the grounds of sexual skeletons rattling in his cupboard could hardly have been more obvious to future investigators. If Wilson was going to be flirty-fished by the CIA and their friends in London, and he knew it, then we may have the explanation for so smartly clearing his desk. Equally, the descent of the veils of silence in the halls of the Labour party. The appearance of George H. W. Bush in Downing Street might have been akin to setting out the best bone china for the Grim Reaper.

The British people reacted as they might to the death of a well-loved public figure. And the strange thing was that despite his nasal Yorkshire vowels, his appalling taste in clothes (especially rain coats)[48] and lifelong habit of fixing his gaze on some obscure object far in the distance, Wilson registered widespread affection. I interviewed Harold many times, consistently struck by his sincerity and candour. He was one of the few prominent political figures who did not want questions written down in advance. He relished the one-liner trade with hecklers (some of them planted).

The rank and file of the Labour party were literally numbed. They almost took to black arm bands. There was an uncanny funereal sense that something special and unique had indeed passed permanently away. Not so in Spookland, where the champagne corks popped and the pink gins gushed. The check list now looked like this: Heath out and Thatcher — the future strong leader with a dependable husband — in. Wilson eliminated and weak, easily-manipulated place man Callaghan — in. (He was nicknamed 'Farmer Jim' after his arborial country retreat). The liberals, considered felonious traitors of the Lib-Lab pact, had been thoroughly stitched by the destruction of their own leader, the jaunty, trilby-hatted *Papageno,* Jeremy Thorpe. He was driven from parliament in the MI5-fabricated conspiracy to implicate him in a plot to murder his male lover.

It was indeed a rosy dawn, from certain perceptions. The secret intelligence services, in collusion with NATO, the CIA, a rapidly politicising Scotland Yard and the Right-wing establishment, succeeded in completely re-configuring the landscape of British politics to a slavish conformity with American and American-manufactured NATO policies, which remains indelible to this day.

And Brayley? The Man Who Knew Too Much seems to fit. That he was some kind of Jewish lobby bagman, not so well, but it cannot be ruled out. After all, Harold Wilson and money were always strangers. In the early spring of 2011, the British media scrambled aboard the bandwagon propelled by middle-class, vaguely Marxist-inspired radicals (no one could be quite sure about their pedigree) with an appetite for attacking the tax avoidance activities of big business cartels. When I first read about UK Uncut (inspired by the Coalition Government's death of a thousand cuts inflicted on everything from schools to the armed forces), I was tempted to think in terms

---

[48] Another perfect insight into Wilson's curious ways with old pals. In his 1970 resignation honours, he knighted the obscure Joseph Kagan, a fellow Yorkshireman and inventor of a waterproof cloth designed for raincoats called 'Gannex,' which ultimately became an emblematic symbol of the Wilson years. Kagan eventually clicked for a peerage too, before his fall. He was charged with theft and dodgy book-keeping, fined several hundred thousand pounds and served a jail sentence. On his eventual return to the House of Lords, his fervent advocacy of prison reform, based on his intimate experience, struck a political chord. Died, forgotten, in 1995.

of a British take on the US Tea Party. (The reverse occurred: a US Uncut copycat outfit duly emerged.) Then I realized I was missing the more likely progeniture lay with the Angry Brigades, the same uncanny resemblance to products of the MI5 psy-ops funny farm. As with the Angry Brigades, the same strong indications of counterfeit activities and *agents provocateurs* planted in the ranks. The writer and supporter of the Tax Justice Network, Nicholas Shaxon, gushed that its guiding lights should be congratulated on creating the most beautiful, well-organised street movement he had ever seen. But, did the timing and the brilliance of this phenomenon by perchance make a match?

There is no doubting that tax avoidance practices by the likes of globalist champions such as Vodaphone, Boots the giant drugstore company, the Tesco supermarket chain and various operations of billionaire businessman Sir Philip Green — all targets of UK Uncut — grate badly with the electorate. Better than all the books and pamphlets or learned oratory, how clever to ram home the facts about tax larceny with a Moonie-like fervor which cuts across the class structure and political boundaries alike.

Such a manifesto raises interesting questions. Is (or was) UK Uncut a sapling of Chartism, which had set 18th and 19th century England alight? Or grassroots populism that should unnerve the establishment parties? Or even break-out street socialism, taking on the tasks from which lame opposition Labor flinches? Conceptually there are two ways UK Uncut — or for that matter US Uncut and its sisters Anonymous and Occupy Wall Street — could come into being. Is this a purely natural, organic reaction against tax avoiders, when many thousands are about to lose their livelihoods thanks to the austerity cuts? Or is it at least in part a carefully-created designer outfit which, thanks to planted interlopers, will be tugged into the maelstrom of violence as the government's very future eventually takes centre stage.

No such organisation as this is ever spared infiltration by the intelligence services, in any event. Practically speaking, there is rarely any such event in political terminology as an accidental co-incidence. The entire spy-ops apparatus, as this book demonstrates, is predicated on infiltration of convenient protest movements. There is abundant evidence now of undercover agents regularly penetrating animal rights and environmental activist organisations in the UK, in order to spy and generally keep tabs. But there is another ploy straight from the Gladio operations manual: the use of infiltrators to provoke acts guaranteed to reap incriminating blowback.

It can explain incidentally the meticulous planning of the various operations, calculated of course to prove extremely photogenic, with the aim of capturing front pages and prime time television slots. Moulding public opinion by selective images is nothing new. Think back to Winston Churchill's bowler-hat-and-cigar tryst with dangerous thugs in the famous and brilliantly choreographed 'Siege of Sydney Street' early in January 1911. Just by breathing the cordite at close hand that winter London morning, the Home Secretary, rising star in the Liberal government, experienced a miraculous hoist in his chances of reaching for the premiership. Churchill's entire life was dotted with carefully crafted theatrical interludes such as this.

There was something peculiarly convenient — 'cue UK Uncut' — following closely on the violent events in London in late 2010. The London Riots provoked by the Coalition's savage hike in university tuition fees were heavily impregnated with black flag operations. Some of the hooded figures photographed and filmed indulging in window smashing and other incendiary actions were clearly provocateurs drawn from the ranks of the intelligence agencies and the secret state's psy-ops squads (whose existence surfaced in connection with the public execution on the London underground network of Brazilian electrician Jean Charles de Menezes, on 22nd July 2005). In one telling photograph which made many front pages, a careful eye can actually spot the mobile communications rod sticking out from the jacket as its owner was busily smashing a department store window. Of course, banks and other such symbols of despicable capitalism got the required attention from mysterious hibernating 'anarchists' on the rampage with students.

Faced with incontrovertible evidence assembled by peaceable protestors, the Yard admitted it had been fielding plainclothes undercover cover officers at public demonstrations and others in uniform without identification numbers. This is a clear breach of the Police Regulations. The evidence that some of these figures were under orders to indulge in provocative acts was overwhelming, but dismissed by the mainstream media. Their main duty was to portray the masses of protestors as incited by nihilist anarchists conveniently awakened (it seems) from yet another long hibernation.

The riots served their intended purpose of blunting opposition to the swinging increase in university tuition fees which hit, foremost, Tory and Liberal-voting middle classes. They also saved the Coalition's bacon, since minority Liberal Democrat dissenters lost any traction they might otherwise have had on the issue. In the halls of public opinion, it is hard to see what 'student anarchists' had to gain from staging an orgy of destruction. *Cui bono?*

For the struggling Coalition, it was a massive shot of adrenalin at precisely the right time to discredit opposition to a deeply unpopular imposition. If Middle England — the natural constituency of the centre-right Coalition, and the most sensitive to the fees issue — was naturally appalled by such graphic images, there was worse to come. Prince Charles and his consort, on their way to the theatre in the palace Rolls, were themselves set upon. The Duchess of Cornwall was said to have received the shock of her life when momentarily touched by an assailant. The episode reeks of 'just let it happen' taken to cynical extremes.

No attempt was made to divert the royal party from encountering the huge throng which had spread out from Parliament Square, engulfing Regent Street, along which the royal pair was sedately proceeding. Reciting more of their famous cross-my-heart and hope-to-die porkies, Scotland Yard spokespersons blamed 'misunderstandings' caused by officers using incompatible cell phones. The excuses were absurd and quickly forgotten. Whether sympathetic to the monarchy or not, the public got the intended message. Pampered and spoilt adolescents teamed up with violent anarchists were prepared to drag the ageing heir to the throne and his wife, dressed up for the evening out, into the streets and there humiliate them. On the decibel register of public outrage, this is-ear shattering.

The London rumpus out of the way, university fees duly scrubbed from the front pages, the squeaky-clean Angry-But-Very-Well-Behaved Brigades appear bang on cue to dramatise another pressing social issue, in collision with the government's massively unpopular austerity program. On the surface, this would appear to sail dangerously close to the Coalition government's incestuous links with City financial institutions, including substantial contributions to party funds in return for milk-and-water-treatment of the controversial gold-plated bonuses. Really, it is a tried and trusted psy-ops technique, which draws on over-exposure of an issue and the tendency of the public's attention span to exhaust itself in a mire of detail.

The slow-grinding cogs of the inquest proceedings concerning the London transport bombings of 7/7, to which we duly arrive in a moment, belong in precisely the same category of slow release of managed and carefully-textured information. These tried and trusted tactics exhaust public attention to the point of disinterest. Another member of the same family is the Chilcott Inquiry, chaired by the usual noble law lord, vested with investigating the credibility on which the Blair government — or more correctly, Blair alone — dragged Britain into the Iraq war. The well-rehearsed appearances of the star actor — by turns contrite or weightily delivering the verdict on himself as the man of history steered inevitably to the hour — was, frankly, a masterpiece in the annals of egregious, stomach-churning vanity.

The wreck of the USS *Maine*, Havana Harbour, 1898. Payback: A convenient war with Spain sparks the American Empire.

Photo # NH 46774 Diving on MAINE's wreck

The great late developer and future commander of Gladio, General Lyman Lemnitzer (seated far left), Chief of the US Imperial General Staff, Masters of the Universe, October 1960.
Fired by JFK two years later for insubordination, exiled to NATO.

Scene of crime, moments after Swedish premier Olof Palme was shot leaving a Stockholm cinema, 28th February 1986.
No conviction was secured.

Palme was Sweden's new hope JFK figure, but he rattled American nerves with his support for the Palestinians, and UN-sponsored attempts to broker a ceasefire in the Iran-Iraq war, in which the US was backing both sides.

Partners in a deadly destiny: Palme and Anna Lindh.

Salvatore Giuliano, psuedo-romantic Sicilian bandit and separatist, Gladio godfather, sacrificed patsy, in classic pose.

The Italian Years of Lead – the *Anni di Piombo* – begin on 12th December 1969, with the bombing of the bank at the Piazza di Fontana in Milan executed by Gladio technicians, organised by the French terrorist genius and Gladio mastermind, Yves Guérin-Sérac.

The final solution in Cyprus, NATO's aircraft carrier in Eastern Mediterranean waters. Turkish tanks encounter atrocities committed by Greek guerrillas with allegiance to the Greek Gladio organisation. The legendary island of Adonis, God of Love, was riven by ethnic strife, stirred by NATO to secure division of the island on the grounds that its president, a highly conservative Orthodox priest, might be a communist.

Fat cats lick the cream: Gladio-backed coup installs Greek fascist junta, 21st April 1967. The Greek years of lead will last a remarkable and unique three decades.

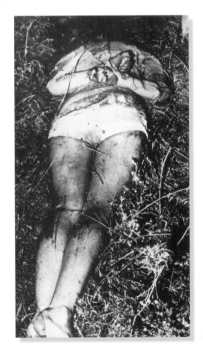

The death of a statesman. The crumpled body of ex-premier Aldo Moro, dumped in a van in central Rome, 9th May 1978. This was the ultimate penalty for compromise with the communists.

Fallen in the line of duty. British agent Ann Chapman was caught in the crossfire of rival intelligence services in Athens.

Psy-ops victim: British socialist premier Harold Wilson, posing uncomfortably with LBJ on a rare visit to Washington. Politically undermined as a closet Red, by a joint CIA-British secret intelligence sting answering to the CIA's psychotic Kingfisher, James Jesus Angleton.

The alleged assassin Ali Ağca (circled), central to the highly-touted KGB Connection, aims at Pope John Paul II. But Ağca was a long-time member of the Turkish Mafia and a neo-nazi mercenary gang allied to Turkish Gladio.

Pardoned by the Pope, repatriated to Turkey, Mehmet Ali Ağca is freed after completing a sentence for killing a newspaper editor. He told John Paul II who was behind the attempted assassination, and keeps the secret.

Marc Dutroux, serial paedophile, the only conviction secured in the horrific, long-running Belgian sex scandals touching high figures in the country's establishment, business and the Vatican, as well as the underground state, which lured victims to orgies involving children for blackmail.

Hanns-Martin Schleyer: stereotype ex-Nazi, chieftain of industry, victim of the Baader-Meinhof guerrillas and the German state, which milked the drama for pure Strategy of Tension political theatre. The drama ended with the disputed deaths in the Stammheim high security prison where the core of the RAF were held.

September 26, 1980. A blast blamed on neo-nazi Gladio sub-contractors kills thirteen and injures hundreds, at Germany's iconic Munich beer-swill *Oktoberfest*.

The Madrid 3/11 train bombings. The massive damage points unmistakeably to the use of high explosive.

Central to the London 7/7 prosecution case, the Luton Four arrive at the town's station to board a train for London. But the picture looks like a photoshopped composite, there are visible puddles on a warm dry summer morning, and the digital time stamp is out of sync with the time the trains actually ran that morning. Note the rear figure seems to be stepping through iron railings.

One of the bombed tube carriages in London, 7th July 2005. Note the signs of upward vertical thrust, suggesting explosives planted beneath the car. The leading French terrorism expert called in to advise, M. Chaboud, stated that military grade explosives had been employed.

Extra-judicial murder performed in a rush-hour London tube train, by unidentified secret state marksmen. The body of Jean Charles de Menezes, a Brazilian, wrongly identified as a terrorist suspect, tailed and shot to death. The mystery remains unexplained.

Bulgarian writer and broadcaster Georgi Markov, killed with a ricin-tipped pellet, supposedly fired from the famous doctored umbrella, London, 11th September, 1978. He was in the thick of a vast western intelligence conspiracy in his highly-criminalised homeland.

The high-flying Swedish UN chief Dag Hammarskjöld crashed to earth in Rhodesia, September 1961. With Count Folke Bernadotte (assassinated in Palestine, 1948), Olof Palme (murdered 1986), and Anna Lindh (killed 2003), four prominent pro-Palestinian Swedes left the stage of history by violent means.

Earl Mountbatten, last Viceroy of India, martyred by the IRA. His murder in Irish waters benefits the British cause in Northern Ireland.

Bologna station, wrecked in August 1980 by Italian neofascists (the *Nuclei Armati Revoluzionari* or NAR) in cahoots with Italian secret intelligence. A Gladio atrocity initially attributed to the Red Brigades soon blew back on the perpetrators instead with spectacular force, with life imprisonment for one of the NAR founders.

The Oslo bomb blast. If Breivik planted a car bomb, why is there no crater? Were explosives planted in the building? This would explain the damage to the upper floors (left), and the 'training exercises' which concluded 26 minutes before the explosion.

Anders Behring Breivik: Norway's mass killer lived next door to a special forces training camp.

Lord Richard Lucan, to the manner born. Was he to lord it over the British in a putsch?

Nordine Amrani, the 'Monster of Liege'– or the classic patsy 'suicide'? On parole, with no incentive nor funds to amass an arsenal. Was participation in a terror drill the price of a plea bargain?

Medals of the much-decorated terrorist mastermind, Yves Guérin-Sérac.

Mohamed Merah, an asset of French intelligence agency DCRI. Was he another entrapped patsy 'suicide,' framed for the Toulouse shootings?

The old gentleman next door. Licio Gelli, P2 grandmaster, in his ninth decade.

XII.
St. Petersgate

'"It was a true act of war in a time of peace." In those extraordinary terms, Italy's Defence Minister last week described new revelations concerning the attempt by a Turkish terrorist to assassinate Pope John Paul II 19 months ago. Lagorio was one of four ministers who, in the space of ten hours, appeared in Rome's ornate, 17th-century Parliament to accuse Bulgaria, and by implication the Soviet Union, of standing behind gunman Mehmet Ali Ağca's failed effort.' — Time, 1982

Pope John Paul II was shot at close range on 13th May 1981. His limousine was circling St. Peter's Square, just before the popular Wednesday general audience. A vast throng of 20,000 excited pilgrims clamoured around the papal cavalcade. Then, amid the jostling and cheering, and according to the reports of some witnesses — partially, at least, confirmed by one television recording — two sharp cracks rang out. These were attributed to a 9-mm Browning semi-automatic revolver fired at close quarters by a 23-year-old Turk, Mehmet Ali Ağca, a member of the (literally) howling Gray Wolves Turkish terror organisation. He was charged with attempted murder.

But the mystery of exactly how many shots and more precisely who fired them, with what type of weapon, and from what angle, now began to colour the many differing versions of events that day. There seemed to be a striking overlap with the confusion at Dallas almost thirty years earlier. There was confusion over the number of shots, whether fired by a single gunman or a task force. The chief suspicion fell on Ağca, a brainwashed patsy in the mould of Lee Harvey Oswald. And not least a mysterious grainy image, captured by a bystander, showing an unidentified figure hurrying from the *piazza* moments after the gunshots. According to his trial testimony, Ağca insisted he fired 'two or three shots in rapid succession.' Three struck John Paul. One slapped into his lower intestine, the others struck his left hand, passing through his abdomen, and his right arm. Two people in the dense crowd were injured, either collaterally by the same bullets, or by others aimed from a different direction.

Thousands packed into the crowded space burst into tears, or screamed and fell to their knees in disbelief. Ağca was grabbed and wrestled to the ground by onlookers, including a nun and Camillo Cibin, veteran chief of Vatican security renowned for his lightning karate chop. A small diversionary explosion was set off in a corner of the square. Significantly this crucial item was never properly addressed in the trial. Photographs depict Ağca holding a pistol with both hands, scarcely a meter or so from the Pope, who is standing and waving. He seemed to be aiming carefully, allowing for the crush around him, holding the pistol on the eye-line profile. Witnesses described the Turk as seemingly drugged and oddly unanimated. None apparently saw him whip out the concealed weapon and take aim, which is strange considering the closely packed crowd. Literally bleeding to death, John Paul was rushed to the Vatican hospital complex. In a gloomy prognosis his doctors quickly established he had lost almost two-thirds of his blood. The Pope's life flickered in the balance.

About the alleged weapon. This type of Belgian-made Browning double-action service revolver is known for lightness but uncertain accuracy. It is definitely a close-quarters weapon. It has long been supplied to police and armed forces around the world, particularly NATO forces, including the Turkish military. As an assassination weapon, this puny pistol seemed to many experts perfectly incredible, about as practical as using a starting pistol to shoot a deer. Its very lightness (an advantage in everyday police service for example) would make it difficult to control, taking a long time to aim accurately, especially in a heaving crowd. Francesco Bruno — the Italian state's secret service arms specialist between 1978-87 (therefore on duty during the Papal shooting) stated unequivocally that 'no serious assassin would have used the Browning pistol to mortally wound his victim.' Ağca 'did not target the thorax, neither shot the whole magazine, as any professional assassin would have done, nor wanted to use a precision rifle.' Bruno guessed that Ağca 'was the fall-guy, indoctrinated to believe he was supposed to fire warning shots, or at most create a diversion.' Bruno's expert conclusions were brushed aside.

The arrest warrant, signed by Rome's procurator general, Achille Gallucci, stated that Ağca attacked the Pope 'in collaboration with other persons whose identity remains unknown.' Luciano Infelisi, a renowned independent-minded crusading magistrate assigned to investigate the attack, concluded the following after his initial sifting of the evidence: 'There are documental proofs that Mehmet Ali Ağca didn't act alone.' This was a reference to the variety of casings found in the vicinity, subsequently suppressed in the following court proceedings. Infelisi was implying a conspiracy. For such impudence he was promptly shifted to other duties. The two most important officials immediately summoned to the case dismissed the lone gunman theory out of hand. Why, then, did the wind suddenly shift in a different direction?

The trail shifts to Paris, and the elegant figure of Count Alexandre de Marenches (1921-1995), chief executive of the Service of External Documentation and Counter-Espionage (SDECE) from 1970 to 1981. He was unquestionably one of the most extraordinary figures in the history of French espionage. This aristocratic Knight of Malta, thorough-going authoritarian and virulent anti-communist, managed to run the French equivalent of

MI6/CIA alongside his own private enterprise show at the same time. This was the Safari Club, a kind of shadow CIA established in the mid-70's with Saudi money and the backing of George H. W. Bush and the Shah of Iran. Kamal Adham, head of Saudi intelligence, directed the outfit alongside de Marenches. From 1979, a member of the inner court of the Saudi royal family, Prince Turki al-Faisal, shared the helm. The Safari Club was crowded with ex-CIA people who for one reason or another were fired or left for more exciting pastures. These included the legendary Theodore 'the blond ghost' Shackley, who was present in Rome the day the Pope was shot. The only aim of the Safari Club was to discredit communism, by any means. Its functionaries were also accustomed to performing contract jobs on behalf of the 'real' CIA. Its shadow in the underworld was now about to undertake its most spectacular operation: the assassination of Pope John Paul II.

The Knights of Malta are understandably a rather misty concept. They inspire comparisons with Dan Brown's mystical fantasies of Vatican conspiracies bordering on black magic. The Sovereign Military Order of Malta (an abbreviated title from a previously far grander and longer one) is an extremely ancient Catholic lay order of chivalry, dating from the First Crusade (1096-99). The Order's former territories (Rhodes and Malta) have long since melted away. To compensate, there is a world-wide network of medical missions operating in 120 countries. According to Wikipedia, the Knights are supported by some 12,000 active members who oversee and support 20,000 medical personnel. So much for the worthy field of good endeavours. However, the charitable functions are far overshadowed by the Order's status as a recognized sovereign state, complete with an observer's seat at the UN, and the full kitbag of diplomatic privileges. These include the precious facility of couriers passing borders without hindrance, which any espionage organization is bound to prize. But surely, even a subliminal state with exactly three registered citizens needs some kind of government? The Sovereign Order has one, the inner council of the Knights, which in turn responds to the absolute authority of the Vatican.

The American investigative journalist Seymour Hersh has argued that behind the cover of charitable functions, the Knights are waging a cultural war on behalf of Christianity. He claims their fertile recruiting grounds include the highest levels of the American state and related friendly powers, the secret services and the Pentagon. Speaking in Washington DC at Georgetown University's Foreign Policy School in January 2011, he said: 'They do see what they're doing.... it's a crusade, literally. They see themselves as the protectors of the Christians. They're protecting them from the Muslims [as in] the 13th century. And this is their function.' Of course Hersh got the full Dan Brown treatment from the eye-rolling US media. But Hersh's central theme is absolutely correct. The Vatican, aided by the sovereign Maltese Knights and secretive internal cults like Opus Dei, is an essential component of the totemic pathology that we recognise as the war on terror.

Licio Gelli, grand master of P2 and in passing, a devout agnostic, was ushered into this exclusive holy of holies by his close friend and P2 associate, Umberto Ortolani. He was a silver-tongued lawyer with a love of good wines and food, who exuded egregious self confidence. In WW2 he joined Mussolini's OVRA counter-espionage service. His career after the war was closely bound up with Gelli, who like Ortolani had a boundless appetite for money. Ortolani was helped by a shrewd brain for shady business deals, which naturally attracted Gelli and for good measure, Roberto Calvi and Michele Sindona. Ortolani was known as the 'holy ghost,' thanks to his skills in worming his way into the innermost councils of the Vatican. In 1972 he pulled off a particularly spectacular coup. He was the middleman who handled the sale of a majority interest in Banca Cattolica del Veneto (renowned for making loans on generous terms to hard-up clergy) to Calvi's already thoroughly corrupted Banco Ambrosiano. All the players, including Gelli, Ortolani and Archbishop Marcinkus, took a handsome cut for themselves.[49]

The Banca Cattolica affair is one of the lesser-known Vatican banking scandals, yet in many respects it was a pathfinder that led to Calvi's corpse hanging from a bridge in London exactly ten years later. In 1978 the journalist Carmine 'Mino' Pecorelli used his weekly *Osservatorio Politico* report to unfrock 121 Vatican insiders, including high clergy, named as taking Masonic vows in defiance of the strictest church ordinances. He was referring of course to members of P2. Ortolani was on that list. Pecorelli was murdered shortly afterwards, in March 1979. Many students of the period regard Ortolani as effectively second in command to Gelli within the P2 structure, which explains why he made a sudden bolt to South America when P2 was exposed in 1981. There he put his banking talents to work once again, making himself fabulously rich with a financial empire of his own. Ortolani is widely credited, with Sindona, in organising the elevation of Pope Paul VI. In return the new pope gave the trio of Gelli, Sindona and Ortolani

---

[49] Marcinkus has been cited by researchers in the mysterious affair of Emanuela Orlandi, a 15-year-old schoolgirl, Vatican resident and citizen. She disappeared on 6th June 1983 on her way to a music lesson. Reports of the archbishop's taste for young girls and procuring for vice parties held in his private apartments have circulated for years. The magistrate who undertook the first investigations concluded Orlandi was killed to silence her after she was raped at an orgy. The Italian authorities laid a trail of disinformation connecting her to Vatican political scandals, in order to disguise the more probable connections to rampant vice involving priests inside the Holy See. Given the running exposure of paedophilia within the Catholic church, this explanation bears credibility. Her body was never found.

the keys of the Vatican's Bank of Sacred Works. From this Pandora's Box flew great troubles.

About a month before the Pope was shot, Count de Marenches passed a warning to the Vatican's security services to anticipate an attack by an unspecified 'foreign power.' *M. le Comte* was clearly working from a short list of one. He was also building a case. This scarcely-disguised inference that the Soviets planned to kill the Pope formed the supporting platform for all the later claims to that effect. If the warning was passed to the Pope, as it probably was, then His Holiness almost certainly dismissed it with a scornful wave of the hand. He knew from his experiences in his homeland that he had nothing to fear from the Soviets. Marenches could not have known of the Pope's secret financial dealings with the Kremlin. Few did, except for the innermost members of his court. But Marenches did reflect the growing alarm among the western allies at the Vatican's dangerous foreign policies, especially the increasingly warm relations with Moscow. Alexandre de Marenches was a perfect trinity contained in a single being: he was a member of the ruling inner circle of the ultra Right-minded Maltese Knights; a top-drawer intelligence chief; and the joint proprietor of a private enterprise spook outfit accustomed to taking on dirty work for the CIA. Who better to sow a rich layer of confusion around the crime of the century?

The trial of Ağca was all over in three rushed days. Only one interesting nugget of evidence set the adrenalin flowing. The court was shown an interesting photograph taken by a tourist. It showed a young man apparently running from the square in great haste. That man, according to the investigating judge, Ilario Martella, was a second gunman, that he named as Oral Çelik. He was a leading figure in the Turkish Gray Wolves paramilitary organisation, and certainly one of Ağca's closest friends. But he was not, as the media fell over themselves to insist, the man who taught Ağca to enact his first crimes. Nor did he help him escape from jail in 1979, after shooting Abdi İpekçi, editor of the popular Istanbul daily *Milliyet*. Those honours belonged to another more sinister individual altogether, Abdullah Çatlı of earlier mention. The Running Man is the mysterious Grassy Knoll figure of St. Petersgate. Like his counterpart crouching behind a bush in Dallas, apparently taking aim as the Kennedy motorcade passes, the Running Man has never been formally identified. Yet he knows — or knew — most of the secrets of that spring morning. Çelik was indeed in Rome. So was Abdullah Çatlı. Both were professional killers on the Interpol most-wanted list. And both are credible candidates as the Running Man.

In any event, Ağca himself said nothing about any Bulgarian connection until five or six days after the shooting. By this time he was receiving a steady procession of important visitors to his prison cell at faraway Ascoli Piceno. Instead of more convenient confinement in Rome, Ağca finds himself in the distant province of Marche, close to Italy's Adriatic coast. Nor, significantly, has he mentioned up to that point that he had accomplices. At his trial he insisted that he acted alone. The presiding judge, Severino Santiapichi, was not convinced. He acknowledged there were 'grave questions referring to the possibility [that]… a high-level conspiracy [had] arisen.' Ağca had demonstrated a grasp of 'intricate phenomena, of intimate mechanisms, which he wouldn't be able to know without being involved in some manner in a criminal enterprise.'

The choice of this curious hideaway, almost two hundred kilometres from Rome, raises many questions. These suggest a web of connections linking the assassination attempt with the Italian secret state. Among the early callers on Ağca's cell was Francesco Pazienza, a P2 lodge member connected with the disappearance of funds from Roberto Calvi's stricken Banco Ambrosiano. From 1979 to late 1981, Pazienza was a SISMI agent, important enough to become adjutant to the director, General Giuseppe Santovito, a Maltese Knight and another close acolyte of Licio Gelli. Santovito was later traced directly to attempts to expunge the Turkish Mafia presence in St. Peter's Square. Pazienza was a close associate of another P2 clansman frequently recurring in these pages, the neo-fascist Stefano Delle Chiaie.

In September 1981, General Santovito resigned as general director of SISMI. His position was indefensible. He had been named as a P2 affiliate in the famous list discovered in Gelli's villa in Arezzo in the spring of that year. Santovito was the perfect example of the 'diseased culture' of the Italian secret services mentioned by the crusading magistrate, Carlo Palermo. He was under suspicion for complicity in the bombing of Bologna railway station in August 1981. He was deeply involved in the accelerating crash of Banco Ambrosiano. He perverted the course of justice in the papal investigation. His close friends included the murdered General of the Carabinieri, Carlo Alberto Dalla Chiesa, the equivocal figure closely connected to the murder of Aldo Moro. Fearing a similar fate, he fled to the United States. He returned the following year, and was promptly arrested for involvement in the Bologna station bombing. He died in 1982, the unresolved charges hanging over his head.

For all the official denials that Ağca was expertly coached to denounce his six alleged Bulgarian accomplices, the compelling evidence to that effect is overwhelming. Ağca received so many important visitors they were bound to excite attention in the confined quarters of a prison. They certainly did not elude a fellow incarcerate, the famous *Camorrista*, Giovanni Pandico. He was the legendary 'super-computer,' considered the most important *pentito* in the history of the battle against the Mafia. He denounced practically a full battalion of Neapolitan mobsters in 1983, based on his amazing total recall of all their names and infamies. Pandico confirmed that he frequently saw

Francesco Pazienza in Ağca's cell. Another VIP who paid his respects was General Giuseppe Santovito, DG (*Direttore Generale*) of SISMI. In the ancient manner of the Vatican, the prison chaplain, Father Pietro Santini, dutifully repeated these comings and goings to his Bishop, Msg. Marcello Morgante. He in turn sent regular reports to Archbishop Marcinkus, the brooding spider at the centre of the web in Rome.

Pazienza spent hours with Ağca, coaching him to memorise a dossier containing photos of the Bulgarian stooges. Ağca rapidly absorbed the smallest details — uneven teeth, facial tics and blemishes — it seemed hypnotically. Three months later, six new suspects — five Bulgarians and a single Turk — were suddenly named by Judge Martella and arrested. The recuperating Pontiff was fully informed about these curious tutorials, even as the fantasy of a Bulgarian/KGB plot gripped the public imagination.

Ağca was raised in the desperately poor central Anatolian province of Malatya, which offered little work except scratching the poor soil. But it was close to the golden dope triangle, and he fell naturally enough into the hands of criminal gangs. He grew up strikingly handsome, tall and bearded, with piercing dark eyes. In 2010, when he was finally released from a Turkish prison, he still cut an impressive figure, clean shaven, prominent jaw, the same penetrating stare. Ağca started on the Anatolian career ladder as a professional narcotics smuggler working the Orient-Turkish-Bulgaria-Italian axis. He was trusted with front office work, such as passing payments and messages between various branches of the enterprise. His counterparts could be found in New York, Caracas or Naples, anywhere the Mafia flourishes. His minders soon noticed he could be relied upon to repeat robotically what he was last told. As an executioner, he was primarily a back-of-the-head artist, which scarcely qualified him for St. Peter's Square. Indeed, after extensive ballistics tests, Judge Martella concluded that three shots had been fired at the Pope and that only the first two came from Ağca's Browning pistol. The third slug passed through the Pope's left hand and was never found. So on the sketchiest of evidence, Judge Martella concluded the 'running man' supposed to be Çelik was a second gunman firing from a different position.

The world was now plunged into turmoil over the sudden projection of a KGB plot behind the events in St. Peter's Square. The first claims broke in West Germany eight days after the shooting, from a source with long-standing associations to the Gray Wolves, and moreover to the Turkish Gladio organisation code named Counter-Guerrilla. As the Pope's life wavered in the balance, a hitherto unknown Turk called Musa Serdar Çelebi sprang to the headlines at a press conference in Hamburg. In the course of an excitable performance, Çelebi poured high-octane fuel on KGB conspiracy theories. The cynics noted that he failed to produce a shred of supporting evidence. But those who delved into his own murky past soon uncovered his reasons for trumpeting a Soviet plot, aside from revelling in five minutes of fame. For a start, Çelebi knew Ağca extremely well. He was also the head of the German *Gastarbeiter* ('guestworker') branch of the Gray Wolves' political wing, the National Action Party. The NAP enjoyed warm relations with West German intelligence, the BND. In 1982 Çelebi was suddenly arrested and charged with physically aiding Ağca with money and weapons to shoot the Pope. Unintended consequences followed when the police uncovered a web of connections leading to high officials of Germany's Christian Democratic party renowned for their extreme Right opinions. They in turn maintained close links to Turkey's far Right extreme nationalists.

Other strands examined by the court led to Colonel Alparslan Türkeş — the rascally Turkish Cypriot grand mufti known as Başbuğ or 'The Leader.' Turkes played a decisive role in creating the triumvirate of racist Right-wing forces responsible for the dirty war of the '60s and '70s on the Kurds. These included the influential anti-communist National Movement (MHS), their private paramilitaries the Gray Wolves, and for good measure the Counter-Guerrilla stay-behind force. As a high priest of Turkish racial purity, Türkeş was an outspoken advocate of Hitler during World War II. He was also devious and clever, an embezzler on an heroic scale. Despite all his calumnies, he served as deputy prime minister, a truly Italian-style outcome. German intelligence BND regarded him as one of their most important contacts with the four-million-strong resident Turkish community, and the narcotics and weapons smuggling rings run by the Turkish mafia. When he died in April 1997, his secret wealth stashed in foreign banks amounted to almost $1.5 million.

It is now necessary to take an important step back to 1959. In that year, a secret pact between the Turkish armed forces and the CIA shunted aside the civilian establishment in Ankara, whose flavour was not to the liking of NATO nor Turkey's politically restless military. The agreement shifted the emphasis of Turkey's stay-behind soldiers to the primary role of policing internal enemies of the state, such as Leftists and Kurdish secessionists. Here was the nursery of the future Ergenekon scandal. The German investigative writer Jürgen Roth — who specialises in gangster politics — supplied an additional international layer to these activities. In his 1994 book *Criminals Incorporated*, Roth observed that 'Gray Wolves like Abdullah Çatlı could act with immunity across Europe.' In Germany, Turkish immigrants with Right-wing backgrounds played a leading role alongside German intelligence in pushing against the phantom threat of 'red terror.' This was the classic definition that applied to Musa Serdar Çelebi.[N1]

But there were other temptations within the Turkish secret state. These included the enticing doors to the vastly lucrative heroin smuggling business

— said to be worth $3 million an hour — flowing through the ancient golden triangle connecting Turkey, Iraq and Afghanistan. The CIA was thus able to tap into the numerous pipelines controlled by the Turkish secret services, channelling huge quantities of heroin to the heart of Europe. Dennis Dayle, the late former chief of the élite DEA enforcement unit known as Centac, declared in 1985: 'In my 30-year history in the Drug Enforcement Administration and related agencies, the major targets of my investigations almost invariably turned out to be working for the CIA.' William Blum described how in 1947 CIA arms, money, and disinformation enabled Corsican criminal syndicates in Marseilles to wrest control over the docks. This created the 'perfect conditions for cementing a long-term partnership between the CIA and Mafioso drug syndicates, who between them turned Marseilles into the post-war heroin capital of the western world.'[N2]

The 1959 Ankara agreement was cut from the same deck of cards. The CIA dealt itself a smart hand by accelerating the criminalisation of the Turkish state, bagging a pivotal role in the internal drugs triangle linking the military, the Turkish mafia and extremist Right-wing political organisations. It was scarcely a co-incidence that only a year after the 1959 deal with the CIA, the Left-leaning premier Adnan Menderes was ousted from power and then murdered (a coup in which Başbuğ Türkeş was a leading actor). Menderes was victimised by his opponents, the military and the far Right, as 'soft' on Islam. In fact his government posed greater dangers to the traditional ruling establishment, by threatening to root out the criminalised elements of the state and their involvement in the lucrative narcotics smuggling trails. Menderes was overthrown by the army, using the sleeping soldier unit Counter-Guerrilla and its Mafioso allies. After a sham trial, which shocked humanitarian conscience around the world, he and two cabinet colleagues were lynched in a military jail, on the isolated island of Yassiada in the Sea of Marmara. To ensure there could be no last-minute reprieve, the High Command ordered the telephones to be cut off.

In the 1980s, the mood of *glasnost* sweeping over Turkey began to yield up a trickle of secrets that soon turned into a flood. Ignored for the most part by the western media, these revelations offered the keys to many Cold War mysteries. Besides the attempted assassination of John Paul II, they cast yet more unfavourable light concerning money laundering by drug barons and western intelligence services through the vaults of the Vatican's precious Institute of Religious Works. From there lay a direct connection to a story of such incendiary content, the espionage community hurried to have it under the blankets of secrecy without delay.

It was in many respects an iconic story of the dwindling Cold War age, so extraordinary and yet seemingly far fetched it might have come from the ranks of a best-selling thriller. Western citizens were socked with drugs by their own authorities, in collusion with organised crime. A huge international arms-for-narcotics go-round delivered top-of-the-range military hardware to the Middle East — siphoned from NATO stockpiles all over Europe — in exchange for heroin, which then flooded western markets.

As the 1980s opened, Judge Carlo Palermo — a former Italian MP, bustling lawyer and painstaking magistrate — was quietly sifting through a stack of reports at his chambers in the mountain city of Trento. He was searching for clues to the Sicilian Mafia's heroin-running activities in collusion with drug cartels in Eastern Europe. Powerful incriminating evidence had started to filter from the wreckage of Michele Sindona's banking and money laundering empire. About the same time, Uğur Mumcu — fearless investigator for the Istanbul daily *Cumhuriyet* — established in 1983 the facts of the vast east-west arms and drugs trafficking carousel, passing through a niche of the Soviet bloc:

And the interesting thing is that the weapons smuggled in Bulgaria are weapons produced in NATO countries. Don't the Bulgarian police know or see how all these arms from NATO nations clandestinely enter a Warsaw Pact member nation? They know — and see.

Uğur Mumcu would pay for this and other revelations surrounding the Turkish deep state, including the attack on the Pope, with his life. He was assassinated by a car bomb outside his home on 24th January 1993. Judge Palermo joined the ranks of diligent magistrates who took a great personal risk in exposing many dangerous secrets harboured by the Italian state. He almost paid the same price, narrowly escaping assassination in a booby-trapped car. Palermo's detective work confirmed a network which linked several eastern countries, including Bulgaria and Turkey, operating through a major junction in Italy. But, unwittingly at the time, he tripped on an even bigger stone: the sinews linking the narcotics racket, the massive NATO arms scam and the involvement of western intelligence in all of those activities.

On 24th November 1983, Palermo issued no less than two hundred arrest warrants in the great arms and drugs merry-go-round. In a later memoir he wrote: 'I was [informed] by Milan's Finance Office about the role carried out by an important Islamic credit institution, the Bank of Credit and Commerce International, a bank founded by the Pakistani mafia operating all around the world, entailed to the drugs and weapons traffic, and even to terrorism. That report also included some inculpating elements among those high level complicities, and some of our mysteries: that of the Banco Ambrosiano, the P2, Calvi's suicide in London, that of our deviated secret services, the most recent that of the attempt to kill the Pope.' In April 1985, a car bomb meant for Palermo tragically killed a mother and her twin sons, while the judge was following the narcotics trail in Sicily.

Palermo had a close friend and collaborator, none other than Ilario Martella, the investigating judge working on the Pope John Paul II inquiry. As the two men swapped notes, it became obvious they could be dealing with overlapping suspects. Some of the names on Martella's list were recognisable to Judge Palermo, one in particular. This was a Turk called Bekir Çelenk, who was indeed in Rome the day the Pope was shot. As a senior logistics manager in the Turkish mafia's narcotics operations, in which Turkish state intelligence (MIT) were deeply enmeshed, Çelenk visited Italy frequently. His main tasks were to ensure the continued smooth running of the drugs and arms-go-round. He had another line too, the final settlement of accounts considered 'overdue.' In 1997, *Le Monde Politique* reported the 'shadow of generals, hired killers and drug traffickers supporting Turkey's pivotal role in the international drug trade over many years.'

However, Judge Martella then abruptly abandoned the Turkish connection to chase the Bulgarian bandwagon. Five Bulgarians and one Turk were immediately singled out. Egged on by the disinformation machine, the media instantly convicted the accused before the court of public opinion. American newspapers especially made play with an especially tragic figure snared in the trap. He was Sergei Ivanov Antonov, manager of the Balkan Airlines office in Rome, who attracted much attention in the media because of his sinister Russian-sounding name. All the Bulgarians except Antonov, plus the lone Turk, Bekir Çelenk, quietly slipped away once the prosecutor general, Antonio Marini, announced in the early spring of 1988 there was no evidence to support the charges. Mehmet Ali Ağca was again the lone marksman. The identity of the Running Man no longer concerned the court or the Italian authorities.

Antonov was muddled with *Antony* Ivanov Antonov, a near namesake who lived in Turkey for years, a cog in the Sicilian dope smuggling ring. Who denounced him, while subordinates in Rome then mangled names? The wrong Antonov was also named as an East German double agent. Markus Wolf, head of the GDR General Intelligence Administration (*Hauptverwaltung Aufklärung*), took the unusual and possibly unprecedented step of speaking directly with Italian state intelligence SISDE. His message was simple: There is no agent by that name on my payroll. Please improve your homework.

Another man of mystery now comes to the surface, a certain Ruzi ('Ruzy') Nazar, an Uzbek who seems to have led many lives. He was in the Ukraine when WW2 broke out, and either hid from the Red Army, or more likely promptly deserted when the Germans arrived on their way to Moscow. He is written into one of the forgotten chapters of WW2, the decision by thousands of Muslims drafted in the Red Army to switch sides and fight for Hitler. Nazar volunteered for an SS Turkic-speaking unit, where he was quickly spotted as highly promising material. After a spell of grooming in officer training, he graduated to the staff of the German High Command. If the war had gone a different way, he might have found himself raised to *Obersturmbannführer* of the subject Turkic Union, which sparkled in Hitler's post-war visions. Instead, with the defeat of Germany, he was evacuated by the famous Nazi ratline run by General (and future West German intelligence chief) Reinhard Gehlen. The CIA were quick to spot his talents. Before long, he was an important figure in the American Committee for Liberation from Bolshevism — known for short as Amcomlib. On the surface it was a band of worthy patriot businessmen, writing checks to spread the gospel of democracy. Underneath, it was a CIA front to manage the propaganda-churning stations Radio Free Europe and Radio Liberty. From there he was drawn into the thick of CIA scheming and plotting in Turkey, which eventually dragged the country into the internal Turkish dirty war of the '60s and '70s. This is one of the darkest episodes of Turkish history. Thousands were killed, or thrown into jail and tortured horribly on the grounds they were Left-wing activists or sympathisers. The violence was the excuse for the CIA-backed coup d'état by the hard-liner General Kenan Evren in September 1980. Earlier he commanded Counter-Guerrilla, Turkey's Gladio secret army. Counter-Guerrilla and the Howling Wolves paramilitaries were chiefly responsible for provoking the reign of terror that brought Evren to power.

Under the new regime, 'Ruzi Bey' was a darling of the cocktail party circuit in Istanbul. Then came a transfer to Bonn, where he was instructed to nurse Right-wing elements among the masses of Turks living in Germany. The signs suggest that Nazar may have been a key mechanic of the Papal plot, with the task to stick the pin in the Bulgarians. He worked with the late Paul Henze, a serial confabulator of KGB conspiracies and former CIA station chief in Ankara. It was Nazar who introduced Çelebi to his flickering appearance before the footlights of history in Munich in the days after the Pope was shot. On or about 12th March 1983, Ruzi Bey vanished from CIA records, his cover blown.[50]

Ağca was now all that remained of the spoof KGB-Bulgarian plot. The French investigative journalist Jean-Marie Stoerkel said he had determined 'beyond any doubt' that Abdullah Çatlı, Bekir Çelenk and Oral Çelik (all Ağca's most likely accomplices in Rome) were 'active killers used by the western secret services.' Stoerkel had even hotter potatoes. He pointed to

---

[50] Interestingly, the always reliable Uğur Mumcu tracked Nazar to the former US embassy in Bonn. Mumcu stated that he was assigned to work with Gray Wolves units on behalf of the CIA, while retaining his close links to the great *Başbuğ* Colonel Turkes. He was therefore in post in Bonn during the run up to the attempted assassination and is therefore the key to the German Connection through BND.

specific instructions appearing from inside the Italian justice system and the secret intelligence services to ignore Ağca's Turkish accomplices. Pressure had been applied by the CIA in order to foster the myth of the Bulgarians obeying instructions from Moscow. The incriminating instructions appeared in a leaked communication signed by the SISMI director General Giuseppe Santovito. It was addressed to Domenico Sica, the assistant state prosecutor investigating the failed assassination. The document was dated 25th May 1981, just twelve days after the shooting. Here is the remarkable smoking gun of St. Petersgate. We understand now how it was possible for the Italian authorities to identify Turkish suspects with such amazing speed after the arrest of Ağca. He, after all, had always insisted that he acted as a lone gunman, until the phantom Bulgarian connection emerged. Never at any point in the story did he point the finger at other Turks. We learn from Santovito's actions that the prime suspects Çatlı, Çelenk and Çelik — and for that matter, Ağca himself — were well known to Italian intelligence as contract killers before those near-fatal shots were fired in St. Peter's Square.[51] Moreover, Santovito had been directly involved in the drugs and arms trafficking that centred on the same Turkish criminals.

As the story unravelled, it became inseparable from the hard evidence appearing from Judge Palermo's stunning paper trail. Large quantities of sophisticated NATO weaponry, including tanks and American-made Cobra helicopters, were routinely purloined from the Alliance and smuggled around the world throughout the 1970s and early 1980s. It was the world's most powerful clandestine arms trafficking organisation, eclipsing anything previously known. Moreover, it ignored the political barriers which divided Europe. I was told by several contacts, while involved in Bulgarian matters, that American accents were heard as cargoes were shifted between planes at the capital city's rundown airport. Anonymous-looking, white-painted aircraft usually recognized as part of the CIA's private fleet were said to be regular visitors. On 24th November 1982, Judge Palermo issued arrest warrants against two hundred suspects of a dozen nationalities implicated in the vast weapons and narcotics cycle 'which sent heroin to the West and weapons to the East.... dominating this traffic in both directions from Turkey and the Near East to all Western Europe and the United States.' Palermo

---

[51] Santovito was a protégé of Andreotti and his chief henchman, Francesco Cossiga. His web of connections extended to Giuseppe 'Pippo' Calò, the Sicilian mob's enforcer, Totò Riina, godfather of the Corleonesi clan, and Rome's Banda della Magliana. Judge Palermo named Santovito as a leading figure in the East-West arms and dope carousel, but the suspect died, strangely and quickly in 1982, after receiving a court summons. It was Domenico Sica who opened and promptly shut, permanently, the investigation into the snatching of Israeli nuclear weapons whistleblower Mordechai Vanunu from a BA jet at Rome on 29th September 1986.

named Bekir Çelenk as the leading figure on his list. The dogged magistrate put his finger on the real Bulgarian Connection, the overwhelming quantities of arms and drugs waved through Bulgaria under the unseeing eyes, as Uğur Mumcu described them, of the Bulgarian customs agents.

Italy was the hub. The heroin which paid for the arms was then marketed by American and European crime syndicates, most of that siphoned through Sindona's and Calvi's banks or the ones they controlled, including the Vatican's Institute of Religious Works. Propaganda Due brought together all the necessary political contacts and infrastructure needed to control the operation. More nuts and bolts were supplied by the usual services of Stibam International Transport. The Syrian (or Armenian) Henri Arsan, who ran the outfit, would sometimes boast he worked undercover for the US Drug Enforcement Administration. This was a rather provocative indication of his real connections. Arsan, alternatively Arsanaylan, was known as the 'playboy Mafioso,' out of his addiction to gaudy clothes and flamboyant gold jewellery. The playboy's big friend in the Turkish Mafia was none other than Çelenk, Palermo's chief smuggling suspect and the *baba* named in the plot to kill the Pope. Stibam's offices in Milan were conveniently situated right above Roberto Calvi's palatial suite in the Banco Ambrosiano building. But Arsan held other keys, as a confidante of Licio Gelli: namely, the crucial P2 connection.

Juan Arias — the Spanish philosopher and close intimate of John Paul — observed that 'the fact that the P2 in some way, directly or indirectly, participated in the papal attempt has always been a taboo that everyone wanted to avoid.' This is one of the most significant and revealing assertions in connection with St. Petersgate. Coming from such a trusted confidante, it demonstrated the Pope knew exactly whose hand was on the trigger. As much had been suspected by General Ambrogio Viviani, chief of SISMI's counter-intelligence division (1970-74). Before he turned *pentito*, Viviani was an affiliate of P2. Speaking to the Turin daily *La Stampa* in 1994, he suggested that to 'analyse the assassination of the century it is necessary to write the facts of what was happening by then in Poland, Ağca's movements and what was happening in Italy.' Readers will discover exactly such a template on a later page.

Vanni Nisticò, formerly the press officer of the Italian socialist party, and another P2 affiliate, circulated an odd tale around Rome that Licio Gelli once showed him some photographs of John Paul relaxing *au naturel* at his swimming pool at the Castel Gandolfo summer papal retreat. According to Nisticò, Gelli commented enigmatically: 'If it's possible to take these pictures of the Pope, imagine how easy it is to shoot him.' Put another way, as Nisticò obviously suspected, how easy it was for Gelli — whose personal rake from the Sindona scams has been estimated at $500 million — to pay his papal informers to snatch such intimate moments. These revealing holiday snaps, if anything more than apocryphal, confirm Judge Palermo's critique of 'our deviated secret services.'

Drenched by decades of unremitting propaganda, the well-fertilised public will to believe the worst of the Soviets and their allies overpowered the uncritical media. Soon the Soviet plot acquired the status of established fact, helped along by Paul Henze, and the professional CIA whitewasher Claire Sterling. She worked out of the CIA station in Rome, posing as a reporter, the classic espionage cloak. Her 1981 book, *The Terror Network*, which blamed the Soviets for causing all terrorist violence in the world, uncannily chimed with the forthcoming attack on the Pope. Retrospectively, it looks suspiciously like an overture. As Henze was the CIA's point man with Turkish intelligence MIT, he was naturally familiar with every nut and bolt of the narcotics and arms carousel. He was the chess master who knew the moves of every Turkish gangster roaming Europe. It was now the moment for one of the pair's closest friends, Michael Ledeen, to take centre stage.

Ledeen is a key wing nut of the arch neo-conservative American Enterprise Institute, functioning nerve centre of all US Republican governments, and no mean influence on Democrats. He was immediately a vocal proponent of the KGB red herring, wallpapering TV channels and the printed media around the world. Ledeen was also an ideally positioned insider within the Reagan White House, a Zionist Likudnik die-hard with strong ties to the CIA and Italian intelligence. Michael Ledeen's personal trajectory through Italy offers many important insights into the formation of a personality steeped in latter-day romantic fascism, and a penchant bordering on the pornographic for violence as the chief weapon of state. He arrived in Italy in 1974, and immediately set about soaking himself in worship of his idol, Benito Mussolini. He became a key tool on behalf of the CIA inside the complicated layers of the Italian intelligence fabric. He made ends meet writing for the Milan daily *Il Giornale Nuovo*, long suspected as a mouthpiece for the CIA. From 1976 he was active, alongside Sterling, in undermining Aldo Moro's concordat with the communists. Much of Ledeen's thinking amounts to addiction for military Viagra, not so much for conquest as the bloody glory of violence for its own sake. In a book that he published in 1999 (*Machiavelli on Modern Leadership*) he pleads the need for 'Machiavellian wisdom and leadership,' while ignoring Machiavelli's prudent injunctions never to get involved in wars where the local population are the invader's first enemies. This is a typical example of neocon commandeering of long-dead sages (Plato is another) to justify the state of eternal war. Ledeen eulogises the 'manly vigour of strong leaders,' who must be prepared 'to fight at all times,' while taking good care to personally steer well clear of the field of battle. It is enough for him to write that the 'great scholars who have studied the American character have come to the conclusion that we are a warlike people and that we love war.' The mainstream Right detects another explanation. Dr. John Laughland, himself an acerbic Right-wing British conservative, wrote in the June 2003 edition of the American Conservative that Ledeen 'drew more from fascism than the American Right.'[N3]

Deception — the 'noble Platonic lie' promoted by the German-Jewish philosopher Leo Strauss, high priest of the neocons — is stock in trade to Ledeen. Despite his denials, he is believed by his many critics to have inflated the Yellowcake Affair — the claim later exposed as utterly false — that Saddam Hussein bought nuclear enrichment materials from the West African republic of Niger. He was steeped in Iran-Contra, and famously claimed to have once said that 'every ten years or so, the United States needs to pick up some small crappy little country and throw it against the wall, just to show the world we mean business.' (Only once in ten years? The unending interventions against any number of countries go without mention, of course.) Incited by Ledeen, newspapers and writers in Italy with well-known CIA connections latched on to the KGB plot. *Il Giornale Nuovo* began touting the story about the same time as the West German revelations, picked up by the *New York Times*, thanks in no small measure to Claire Sterling.

The Reagan administration hurled itself onto the assassination bandwagon as a brilliant propaganda opportunity, the perfect theatrical diversion from the Gladio-backed Roman putsch. Behind it, however, lay the discernible signs of actors moving through a carefully scripted drama. Above the din, hardly anyone paused to consider why the Soviets might want to kill the Pope, a Slav like themselves. After all, should you kill one pope, another would instantly arise in his place. From the perspective of the Kremlin, locked in struggles to dam the flow of global forces running against the decaying empire, this was scarcely an alluring proposition. As we see in a moment, high-level private enterprise interests developing around the KGB had sound reasons to preserve His Holiness in rude good health. On 2nd July 1985, the CIA's working party investigating the attempted assassination filed a report which reached the same conclusion: 'Moscow had little to gain with his elimination... to kill the Pope would not have solved Moscow's Polish Solidarnosc problem, but on the contrary, it would have exacerbated it since it would cause more agitation.' This was not of course the script the neocons wanted the world to read.[N4]

Another figment was invented by the irrepressible Ledeen: that John Paul despatched a private communication to the Russian General Secretary, Leonid Brezhnev. Purportedly this contained a strong warning from the Pope that unless the Soviets desisted in the persecution of Solidarnosc, then he would be forced like some medieval prince of the church to lead a personal crusade against the infidel. Nothing could be less likely to spring from a mind trained to think in precise analytical values. The Vatican instantly dismissed the story as a preposterous fable, as indeed it was. But Ledeen, remember, was trying to re-heat a script which had been written for the world to read in the wake of a *successful* assassination. The Pope concluded the Bulgarians and Soviets were blameless, a conclusion that he confided to his old school companion, closest friend within the Vatican and personal confessor, Cardinal Andrzej Maria Deskur. The Pope was making powerful enemies, to be sure, but definitely not in Moscow. John Paul's most dangerous political sin was to severely challenge the mood and patience of the conservative establishment ruling the US administration, as well as NATO. Both set their faces against a negotiated compact that might let the USSR off the hook, without a psychologically crushing American victory.

The most serious crisis in the history of the Bulgarian socialist republic sent the regime reeling. First Secretary Todor Živkov ordered the Interior Ministry's counter-intelligence division to employ every one of their specialist contacts in foreign countries on an urgent investigation. Foremost, he wanted to know exactly who was behind the allegations. As the copious files which are still extant demonstrate, Markus Wolf, the GDR's consummate spymaster, characteristically provided solid information. The plotters were Turkish criminals known to his own agency over many years; Ağca was a simplistic, impressionable dupe; and the organisation of the plot could be traced to the United States, in the shape of the CIA. From agents in Rome, the Bulgarians also learnt at an early stage that the Vatican dismissed the whole idea of the Russo-Bulgarian plot as a decoy.

After the Second World War, the Vatican clamped itself to the massive global alliance composed of the United States, NATO and western intelligence. The common interest clearly lay in a great bulwark against the spread of communism, yet this is to understate the sheer scale of the power the Roman church invested in the great game. The Pope's battalions around the globe include (or so it is claimed) more than a billion committed worshippers, 400,000 clergy, an impressive global diplomatic service, highly-sophisticated espionage skills and cradle-to-the-grave mind conditioning systems aided by schools, universities and the media. Taken together they enable the Holy See to perform as a world power. When Paul VI died in August 1978, the western camp was deprived of its trusty rock of ages. In 1978 John Paul II succeeded to St. Peter's Throne following the 33-day interregnum of the tragic 'little sparrow' John Paul I. His sudden death has never been properly explained, and remains the source of many theories that he was murdered to block radical reforms of the Holy See's internal structures.

In fact Pope John Paul II, the first non-Italian to reign since Pope Adrian VI in the mid-fourteenth century, was to prove no less radical. He immediately broke with the long-standing post-war concordat that automatically bound the Catholic church to priorities set by Washington. He was determined to seek an accord with the Kremlin, to unfreeze the Vatican's relations with the millions of Catholics locked behind the Iron Curtain. Yet he was also prepared to turn the papal blind eye to the rackets within the sacred precincts (particularly as some of them were his own). John Paul's personality was deeply affected by the impact of Nazi tyranny, the Soviet invasion, and the subsequent occupation of his homeland. The young Karol Józef Wojtyła was forced to work in quarries and factories. There was never enough food, and political suppression was everywhere. He responded by adopting a very particular brand of Christian humanism, which also enabled him to deal with the communists on a pragmatic basis. Poland, his homeland, had been gift-wrapped by Churchill and Roosevelt at Yalta and Tehran and then presented as a war prize to Stalin in 1945. After an initial period of friction, the godless ones and the holy church slowly settled down under the same roof. Not exactly easy bedfellows, but uniquely in the Soviet camp, millions of the devout trooped to Sunday Mass.

As Archbishop of Krakow, the future Pope's conciliatory skills stood another serious test. This historic city retained a large Jewish population, despite the wartime pogroms. Anti-Semitism runs deep in the Polish character. It dates from the gradual settling of Jews expelled by pogroms in countries to the west, particularly Spain, subsequently encouraged in greater numbers at the controversial invitation of Kazimierz the Great (1310-1370). Kazimierz, or Casimir, whose court sat at Krakow, was determined to employ their legendary financial and administrative skills to radically reform his backward country, plagued by the tiresome and obstinate baronial caste. The ancient tensions between the two communities arose again when Christians turned against those Jews who elected to side with the communist authorities. Schooled as he was with tightrope skills in this difficult climate, John Paul's great reserves of diplomatic nuance stood him in great stead when he became head of the church. That he was alone among the West's powerful leaders in dealing on a daily first-hand terms with a communist leadership was obvious. To the great consternation of Washington, he now proposed to translate this experience to his dealings with the Kremlin. When whispers circulated that John Paul II had been Moscow's favoured candidate for St. Peter's throne, there was genuine substance. Many years later, this was duly acknowledged by Mikhail Gorbachev in the presence of the Pope himself. What the western leaders forgot was another of John Paul's qualities, the fact that he was a Slav, like the Russians, and therefore gifted with unique insights into the workings of the Soviet leaders' minds.

Such a tryst placed John Paul on a starkly divergent path from the one followed by the western alliance. By the time he was shot, John Paul II — old hand at playing poker with communists — was sure he had reached an accommodation with the Soviets to allow Solidarnosc to peacefully enter the government in Warsaw. Moreover, Solidarnosc was already operating as a fully-fledged and legally registered political movement, committed to negotiating a peaceful concordat with the communist authorities. Less than two years before, in June 1979, John Paul preached to vast throngs across his homeland, which the communist authorities did nothing to frustrate. But for the backdoor scheming in Washington and Brussels, the Iron Curtain might have collapsed some years earlier than it actually did.

Unfortunately, from the perspective of Ronald Reagan and more especially the neocons buzzing around him, the premature demise of the Soviet Union, the enemy image, was the last thing they wanted. Both Reagan and Britain's new prime minister, Margaret Thatcher, adopted the hottest rhetoric against the Soviet Union heard since the 1950s. When they jointly spoke of the 'evil empire,' the phrase resounded around the world.

During the period known as the Second Cold War, lasting until 1986, the Reagan administration spent $2.2 trillion on new weapons, not to mention fruitless experiments such as Star Wars. This Mars-like stance deepened the anti-war mood that began in the late 1970s against the rolling out of nuclear-tipped American Cruise Missiles. The fabulous Star Wars initiative, intended to focus vaporising rays on Russian missiles approaching from space, seemed to suggest the imminence of nuclear war. Far from making Europeans feel safer and better protected against the Soviets, this new twist of the arms race stirred suspicions of NATO as aggressive and looking for trouble. NATO was fast losing credibility, threatening its entire *raison d'être*. The Gladio Strategy of Tension switched into top gear.

The number of so-called terror attacks attributed to Leftist radicals rose dramatically. Especially in countries considered front-line states — Belgium, Italy, Germany and Greece — the years of lead returned with renewed force. Viewed from Washington and Brussels, the need was more acute than ever for headline-making distractions suggesting the beast behind the Iron Curtain had not changed its manners, the constant theme of the Strategy of Tension.

Pope John Paul II slipped into eternity in April 2005 with a portfolio of many secrets. We cannot be sure how close he may have been to the communist authorities in his formative years, or learn the intricate details of all the pacts that he subsequently made — or renewed — as Holy Father with western intelligence as well as Moscow. He certainly never flinched from making quite a number with crooks, such as Roberto Calvi and Michele Sindona. Unquestionably his papacy was driven by an exceptional appetite for money. When he sanctified Opus Dei — the cult-like 'church within a church' — with the unique honour of a 'personal prelature,' its role as a phenomenally successful (if highly questionable) fund raiser was surely granted equal heavenly credit next to godliness. For years, rumours drifted from the Vatican and around Italian corridors of power that John Paul II used the money from the Vatican's overflowing coffers to bring the Russians, borrowing a phrase of le Carré's, 'in from the cold.' It was the story of the 'Red Gold,' and inseparable in its mechanics from the P2-Gladio secret state.

As usual Marcinkus overshadowed this very strange affair with his customary aplomb. Late in 1980, he entertained a group of visiting CIA dignitaries for an excellent lunch followed by a bracing round of golf. Thus restored, they agreed the Vatican Bank would act as a conduit for a $200 million slush fund, with the theoretical intention to boost the fledging Solidarnosc movement. The money would enter the Vatican from forwarding banks in Panama and South Africa, together with Coutts, snooty London bankers to the British Royal Family, and the Sindona network. It was understood that profits from the CIA's off-radar activities would count among the proceeds. More would be sourced from various government agencies, Right-wing think tanks and the American AFL-CIO labour movement. There were many hands rubbing with glee at the prospect of a share in these gala proceedings. But Solidarnosc was just the cover story of a much grander drama.

The token archbishop himself sometimes mused in retirement over the Red Gold sifting through his fingers. A clue as to what he meant came from Elizabeth Wasiutynski, who ran the Solidarnosc office in Brussels in the early 1980s. She was adamant that she never saw such galactic sums passing through her hands. At most she handled about $200,000 petty cash every year. Moreover, what need had Solidarnosc of such amazing amounts, given its main financial pressures arose from the need to fork out meagre amounts of occasional strike pay? Richard Pipes, one of Reagan's key advisers, soon began to question exactly where the $200 million, which he suspected (rightly) was only the tip of the financial iceberg, actually went after it vanished down CIA plugholes. The ardent Zionist Pipes, like all Zionist-Likudnik neo-conservatives no bosom chum of the CIA, suspected its dirty tricks department working hand in hand with the notoriously corrupt Vatican on some grand smoke and mirrors deception. Indeed it was, in classic Italian fashion. Even as Reagan heaped fiery rhetoric on the evil empire, hands were moving behind the scenes to disable the Soviet Union with the most effective weapon of all: money.

It is time to resurrect again that grand master of duplicity and financial chicanery, Robert Maxwell, who above all knew how an intricate web of shell companies, operating under an anonymous group umbrella, could shuttle funds unseen around the globe. Maxwell was the key to the Red Gold and the

Pope's Kremlin Connection. By the end of the 1970s, intelligent realists in the KGB and in particular one man, the hard-line but coldly practical KGB boss and Politburo member Vladimir Kryuchkov, understood that the USSR was bankrupt politically and financially. It could only be repaired by importing the precepts of the West. Kryuchkov is of course remembered chiefly for his role in the short-lived 1981 coup against Gorbachev. This was a classic Russian-style false-flag operation, which effectively destroyed the last remnants of the rigid conservative base holding out against sweeping reforms of the Soviet system. As the future presidential candidate General Alexander Lebed said afterwards: 'There was no putsch as such. It was a provocation, planned with genius, carried out brilliantly, large-scale and unprecedented, where roles were set down for both the clever and the stupid.'[(N5)]

Gorbachev was a designated heir of the briefly-reigning, long-sighted Yuri Andropov, the only true intellectual ever to head the Politburo, although Kryuchkov, his former deputy at the KGB, was of the same stripe. With Andropov's encouragement, he set about the papal Noah's Ark project. It was to quietly escort the most senior inner party members to the safe haven of about 600 companies established on western lines, to secure a future in the inevitable transition from the command economy to western-style corporatist capitalism.[52] From the seed corn capital transmitted through the Vatican, giants such as Gazprom arose from the ashes of the communist party. The recipients of this secret nourishment were destined to flower as the all-powerful oligarchs who came to dominate post-communist Russia (and Poland too, where a similar project was bearing fruit). By weaving trading links with western companies and learning through their expertise, these KGB front companies would obtain access to the refreshing energies of capitalism.

Robert Maxwell, the American taxpayer, the Mafia and the Pope appeared as an unlikely quartet to get the wheels turning. Maxwell was an old Moscow hand. John Major turned to the man the London satirical magazine *Private Eye* dubbed 'Captain Bob,' rather than MI6 or the Moscow embassy, to understand what was really happening behind the scenes in the great flap that surrounded the manufactured coup against Mikhail Gorbachev in 1991. Giddy at the power and profits bound to flow from this veritable El Dorado opening up before him, Maxwell turned, in his customary way, to the underworld to help things along. His practised eye fell upon a Ukrainian-born Jew called Semion ('Simon') Mogilevich, the 'Brainy Don' of the Rising Sun mafia syndicate, one of Moscow's most powerful criminal clans. He was already a highly respected figure in the emerging Russian crime

---

[52] In the course of discussions with the British naval intelligence officer Martin Packard, concerning events in Greece, he alluded to the same knowledge.

scene, a shrewd operator capable of assembling complex international schemes, a perfect fit with Maxwell himself. Soon, thanks to Maxwell's good offices, he was equipped with an Israeli passport to develop the money laundering, weapons smuggling and narcotics trafficking that were his core activities. It was the Maxwell-Mogilevich channel that formed a vital artery in transmitting covert funds to the nascent oligarchs in the dying USSR, His Holiness cheerfully oiling the gears.[53]

Black clouds gathering on the horizon turned to thundering storms. In the months and weeks that led up to the assassination attempt in May 1981, the Italian state was successively rocked by the implosion of Michele Sindona's sprawling financial empire, the exposure of Propaganda Due and the fermenting plot for a Right-wing putsch in Rome. The final crisis at Calvi's Banco Ambrosiano drew closer by the day. An enormous financial and political pyramid started to totter and edge towards collapse, with highly fissionable consequences that could expose many other hidden players. Calvi, Sindona and Marcinkus had plunged themselves into a bitter tangle of narcotics trafficking, swindling, and arms smuggling. Hot money swirled in all directions — the slush funds sent to Moscow, plus their own industrial skimming activities. Panic spread to every corner of *lo stato parassita*. These disturbing circumstances called for a spectacular diversion, the old Gladio standby.

In the midst of this evolving crisis, the Holy Father appeared to be serenely preserving his head, while all around, others were dashing about in dread of losing theirs. His patient efforts to control the Solidarnosc situation are clearly visible from the mosaic of events over this tumultuous period. But the perfect storm, the one that almost swept him away, was fast approaching.

Now, taking up General Ambrogio Viviani's earlier cue to examine the envelope of events:

The trail that led to St. Petersgate: The Years of Tension 1979-1981

- 20th March 1979: Carmine 'Mino' Pecorelli, Italian journalist with close links to Italian intelligence, shot dead. Cited Gladio in the death of Aldo Moro. Intended to expose the NATO involvement in

---

[53] In January 2008, supposedly on the run and untraceable (thanks to his host of aliases), Mogilevich was grabbed off a Moscow street by 50 armed commandos and hustled into a top security jail, looking remarkably suave and unperturbed in the circumstances, as though for all the world expecting an appointment. It transpired he had been living openly in one of Moscow's largest Stalin-era hotels under the noses of the authorities for years, despite the FBI and Interpol having warrants out for his arrest. It strains credulity that the CIA station in Moscow did not know such a hot property was roaming about free as air. He was let off in 2009 because his crimes were dismissed as 'not particularly serious.'

the guns for narcotics ring, P2's connection and the links to the 'Divine Julius' Andreotti.

- 11th July 1979: Giorgio Ambrosoli, lawyer and liquidator of Michele Sindona's imploding banking operations, shot dead in Milan. Sindona eventually convicted of murder.

- 21st July 1979: Boris Giuliano, police superintendent investigating Mafia links to an arms and drugs ring, looking for connections to Sindona's operations, shot dead in Palermo.

- August 1979: Under indictment in the US, Sindona stages a bogus kidnapping to conceal a three-month trip to Italy. He tries to blackmail fellow P2 collaborators in high places.

- 25th November 1979: Ali Ağca sprung from military prison in Istanbul.

- 13th June 1980: Michele Sindona convicted of conspiracy, fraud, perjury, false bank statements and misappropriation of bank funds.

- 2nd August 1980: Blast attributed to the Red Brigades wrecks Bologna railway station. Neo-Fascists linked to intelligence circles and Gladio planted the device.

- 31st October 1980: Poland's communist authorities register Solidarnosc as a recognised trade union.

- 17th March 1981: Propaganda Due and the Putsch Plan exposed. Licio Gelli — the Grand Master — exposed as controller of P2. Carabinieri uncover a P2 plot to take over the country with the aid of Gladio.

- Spring 1981: Cruise missile protests erupt around Europe.

- 10th May 1981: Mehmet Ali Ağca arrives in Rome after criss-crossing Europe for weeks.

- 13th May 1981: Pope John Paul II seriously wounded in St. Peter's Square.

- July 1981: Roberto Calvi's Banco Ambrosiano, laundry to the arms-drugs carousel, collapses.

- 22nd July 1981: Ağca is sentenced to life imprisonment.

- 13th December 1981: Martial law declared in Poland, Solidarnosc outlawed.

- 17th June 1982: Roberto Calvi, God's Banker, discovered hanged beneath Blackfriars Bridge over the River Thames in London.

By May 1981 — with Solidarnosc finally recognised as an independent trade union by Polish courts — the Pope relaxed with quiet satisfaction. There would be no bloody rising in his homeland, and no Russian invasion either. Both objectives were handsomely achieved, as history confirms. That was part of the pact with the KGB. All the Politburo records of the period that I have seen demonstrate the KGB took the lead in squashing a potential Warsaw Pact invasion of Poland. With the Afghan situation lurching from bad to worse, this was scarcely surprising. The problem was in any event located in Warsaw, not Moscow. The Polish authorities went off on a tangent of their own, at the behest of the chief of the general staff, the extremely odd General Wojciech Jaruzelski. This complicated personality, a minor aristocrat, was kidnapped by the Russians while barely a teenager. He was forced to work digging coal in the Urals. He volunteered for the Red Army, and gradually underwent a conversion to a kind of quack military socialism. Jaruzelski was in the vanguard of the Russian forces as they approached Warsaw. The experience convinced him that he was ordained to rescue Poland from a repetition of the partisan rising in 1944, which had reduced the city to ruins. The signature dark glasses, which he wore even during his televised sermons, dated from a splinter received in the mines. It made him resemble a South American dictator, a comparison not altogether inapt. Jaruzelski convinced himself that the legions following the charismatic and generously whiskered Gdansk shipyard electrician Lech Walesa were bent on violent revolution. About a million of them were actually card-carrying communists, or foot battalions of fellow-travelling priests. Stalin once said that trying to convert the Poles to socialism was like fitting a saddle to a cow. By the time Jaruzelski staged what in effect was a personal military coup, the Kremlin had effectively abandoned this troublesome satellite to its own devices.[54]

The spotlight now returns to the alleged assassin. In August 1979, while serving a life sentence for murdering the newspaper editor Abdi Ipecki, Ağca made his quiet walk to freedom from the Istanbul military prison. He strolled out wearing an army uniform. He appears to have quietly sat out the six months he served of a life sentence, knowing full well he was too useful to moulder in jail. The sole alibi to blame the shooting on a

---

[54] Jaruzelski, who grabbed all the chief offices of state, invented the prospect of a Russian invasion as the motive for martial law. One of his first remarkable acts was to abolish the communist party's leading role in favour of a his own personality cult. Despite his pleas, the Kremlin turned down the usual Warsaw Pact intervention. Its hands were already full with the Afghan debacle. Jaruzelski's own aide de camp, Colonel Ryszard Kuklinski, spilled every detail of the forthcoming martial law crackdown to the State Department in Washington, which then pretended shock and surprise. In an egregious display of mawkishness, candles were lit in White House windows. [(N6)]

communist plot rested on Ağca's sojourns at different times in Bulgaria *en route* to Rome. But his shuttles around Europe had nothing to do with biding his time waiting for the summons to shoot the Pope. He was simply going about his principal day job of middling manager and fixer in the great narcotics ring. Given that Sofia was a vital hub of the network, and as Uğur Mumcu wrote, virtually the smuggling capital of Europe, Ağca's regular line of business had taken him in and out of the city for years.

His minder on the contrived escape from prison was the same Abdullah Çatlı who figures so often in these chronicles. Çatlı carefully nurtured his Elvis Presley looks for the magnetism they exercised over women. He also carried a long list of atrocities against his name. These included the Strategy of Tension murder of seven Left-wing students. Charges were laid, but he walked the streets untroubled nonetheless. He was an intimate welcomed in the high circles of the political élite, such as Prime Minister Tansu Çiller. He frequently worked to the orders of Mehmet Ağar, director-general of the national police. Under the Çiller regime (1993-1996), the future victim of the Susurluk Incident commanded a secret SWAT squad. This was responsible for a wave of targeted murders of Kurdish irredentists in southeast Anatolia.

Çatlı was also a key figure in the neo-fascist support network underpinning Gladio operations all around Europe, along with Guérin-Sérac and Stefano Delle Chiaie. Between them, the trio amounted to three of the most dangerous men on the loose in Europe — yet protected by an invisible hand of official immunity. If Delle Chiaie was merciless and cruel by nature, he was also, like many of his comrades, a calculating planner. These talents were put to good use by Franco, who hired him to organise Spanish death squads. He and Guérin-Sérac worked closely on this task, frequently visited by their mutual friend Abdullah Çatlı, who was again spotted meeting with Delle Chiaie in South America in 1982, less than a year after the papal shooting. The probability that Abdullah Çatlı was actually the Running Man of Turkish appearance dashing from St. Peter's Square moves from circumstantial to probable when the facts of his own death are considered. But before reaching that point, it is essential to pose our recurring question: *Cui bono?*

As several Italian newspapers were quick to observe, the attack on the Pope took place as the Vatican and the Soviet Union were moving toward diplomatic rapprochement on important issues: nuclear disarmament, diplomatic recognition of the PLO, and the Solidarnosc crisis. There the real difficulty was not Russian obstinacy but the ambitious General Jaruzelski, Poland's de facto military dictator. In the immediate aftermath, conspiracies flourished by the score. For their part the Russians seemed genuinely shocked and taken aback. Indeed they might well have been, given the steady payments of ransom money gushing from Rome, and the generally warm relations with the Lateran State. Within a few days of the attack, and still far from certain he would recover, the Pope revealed his own doubts. He issued a personal statement that he had forgiven 'our brother' Mehmet Ali Ağca.

These are the possible characters who formed the execution squad:

- Abdullah Çatlı: stage manager and director, bearing a diplomatic passport and official licence to kill, allowing him to cross frontiers without fear of Interpol. Principal candidate as the Running Man.

- Francesco Gullino: shadowy Danish-Italian suspected in a string of international slayings with a penchant for deadly accuracy, holding close connections to Çatlı and the Portuguese Aginter network. He was in Bulgaria at the time Ağca made periodic visits there. Admitted later that he now steers clear of Italy.

- Hot suspects: Oral Çelik and Bekir Çelenk.

- Theodore Shackley, representative of the Safari Club (and the CIA).

Abdullah Çatlı is often cited as having organised the escape from prison and flight to Europe of Mehmet Ali Ağça. In fact, Çatlı was simply an escort, given that the prison authorities acted on higher orders from the state to allow Ağça his special leave of absence. There was no 'flight;' Ağça simply went back to work. It is also reported that Çatlı organised the assassination attempt on the Pope at the request of Turkish mafia chief Bekir Çelenk, for a contract payment of three million West German marks. Again, his role has to be stressed as that of a technician or subcontractor, using his credentials as an international terrorist, to weave the necessary connections. The political responsibility lay elsewhere.

In 1998, *Le Monde Diplomatique* reported that Çatlı was seen in the company of Stefano Della Chiaie, who was then in exile in South America, and again when he and Della Chiaie were spotted on a visit to Miami in September 1982. The groundwork for this information came from the Danish journalist Henrik Krüger, the foreign correspondent of *Politiken* (Chapter V).

Questioned by a judge in Rome in 1985, Çatlı insisted he was contacted by the BND, and offered a 'good reward' of three million marks to organise the shooting of the Pope. This was so long as he implicated Russian and Bulgarian secret services. The link in this chain may have been Musa Sedar Çelebi, the Turk based in Germany who blew the whistle on the KGB-Bulgaria plot. Çelebi's connections to West German intelligence quickly surfaced during the police inquiries, which resulted in his arrest for acting as the pay-off man. Çelebi bleated that he in turn was paid by BND, whereupon the investigation ceased. He was quietly released from jail. The German connection was smothered. Çelebi slipped below the waves, eventually to re-surface two decades later as a genial, smiling front man for a fiercely anti-

Islamist nationalist movement reportedly promoted by the CIA. What Turkey and Germany have in common here is membership in NATO.[55]

The presence of two of the CIA's most experienced covert action and assassination experts in Rome at the same time could hardly be co-incidental. Theodore Shackley, who supposedly left the Agency under a cloud in 1979, remained on the books working quietly as an undercover consultant helping, with its arms and narcotics rackets. He was summoned to Rome by Alexandre de Marenches, to bring his renowned expertise to a high-profile targeted assassination. According to Webster Tarpley, Shackley may have been on station in Rome in the '60s, just as the *anni di piombo* got under way. Shackley's colleagues rated him businesslike and efficient, but 'cold and weird.' He was so averse throughout his career to being caught on camera he was called the Blond Ghost. Shackley would be a natural choice to head up a damage limitation exercise on behalf of 'The Firm' in the wake of the Sindona-P2 scandals. With so much at stake involving the CIA's precious arms and narcotics rings, not to mention the Vatican laundry, Shackley's legendary invisibility was priceless.

At his side was his old second in command, Tom Clines.[56] Clines was suspected in the murder of Chilean president Salvador Allende. Both were accused of organising death squads in various Latino republics. Shackley had been deeply immersed in plots such as Mongoose, the Cuban Zapata saga and many more capers to overthrow Castro. Tarpley's suggestion of a Roman attachment is significant because in their Latin American years, Shackley and

---

[55] In a commentary published in 1995, the Turkish secret state investigator Serdar Çelik described Turkish intelligence MIT as an integral branch of the CIA in collaboration with Mossad and BND: '...many operations of the Special Warfare Department [aka Counter-Guerrilla, the Turkish Gladio arm] and Mossad are carried out in collaboration with the MIT. A third of the MIT's functionaries are members of the armed forces and the rest are mostly retired military personnel.' Note the axis leading from MIT and its Gladio units to the CIA and potentially Mossad – not excluding the long-standing collusion between the Gray Wolves paramilitaries and Counter-Guerrilla – on the route to St. Peter's Square.

[56] Shackley was an old conspirator with Edwin 'Ted' Wilson, one of the most amazing tales in American spydom. Wilson amassed a fortune running CIA front companies, shipping arms around the world until things got too hot. In 1973 Wilson earned $500,000 alone for delivering a spy ship to Iran under the cover of the CIA ghost company World Marine. He was framed selling *plastique* to Libya, and spent 22 years in jail before he was freed after proving he was only obeying orders. Shackley did better: his shining performance in Indo-China brought promotion to associate deputy director for operations, the CIA's third most senior post (indicating the priority it assigns to dirty tricks). But his accession came just as the storm clouds were gathering in Congress. The extent of Shackley's involvement in illegal undercover ops saw him out of the door. He kept busy in retirement, just the same.

Clines worked with Stefano Delle Chiaie and the various Propaganda Due offshoots scattered around the Latin American continent. Clines was a key player too in the globe-spanning Enterprise outfit. Between them, they possessed ideal skills to carry out a perfect diversionary exercise from troubles crowding in on CIA interests in Rome, while landing a blow on Moscow at the same time. They were not in the Eternal City to admire Michelangelo's frescoes in the Sistine Chapel.

When he journeyed to Bulgaria in the spring of 2002, the Pope publicly announced that he had never believed in the 'Bulgarian connection.' He absolved all Bulgarians of complicity in the plot to kill him. He had long since forgiven Ağca, understanding very clearly his walk-on role in a much bigger plot. John Paul II was too steeped in the ways of detecting hidden hands, dating well back to his formative years in communist Poland, not to suspect that western intelligence might have been attracted to using him as a Cold War martyr. At Christmas 1983 a unique moment occurred in the history of the Catholic Church, a personal and intimate encounter between a Pope and his would-be assassin. The season of forgiveness was certainly in the Pope's mind, but so was the all-important question of who had given Ali Ağca his orders. Italian state television was permitted to record the extraordinary moment during the interview when the Pontiff leaned forward to listen carefully to Ağca's words. There was a pause, and the Pope seemed momentarily frozen. Then he covered his face with his hands. He appeared deeply moved but quickly calmed himself: 'What we have told each other, that will remain our secret.' Ağca kept his word — and the Pope his.

Much has been made tracing a link between the shooting and prophecies of an apocalyptic nature uttered by a floating image of the Virgin Mary appearing before some children near the small Portuguese town of Fatima in 1917. As he slowly recovered, the Pope remembered that the assassination attempt occurred at the same time and date as the Virgin first appeared. He sent for the envelope sealed deep in the Vatican vaults containing the third verse of the 'Three Secrets of Fatima.' It was long withheld by the Vatican authorities because of rumoured warnings from heaven concerning the fall of the faith. There, John Paul II read for the first time the portentous pronouncement by the Virgin that a Holy Father set in the future was destined to be 'killed by a group of soldiers who fired bullets and arrows at him.' In this moment, the spiritual personality meshed with the ever-pragmatic calculator.

John Paul II had long enough to reflect on the identity of his would-be assassins, to sort out a list of prominent candidates, or at least those behind them. Ağca confirmed what he already feared, namely that hands in Rome itself were behind the attempt to cut him down on the sacred apron of St. Peter's Basilica. The Pope was well acquainted with the political conspiracies seething in the capital and the Vatican itself. Calvi's famous last lament pointed clearly to the fact that the Pope knew all about illicit financial transactions and weapons trading in South America. Ağca probably did not, in those few moments, elaborate on the complicated confederation behind the assassination plot. But he knew enough from his close connections with the Gladio machine that his orders to kill the Pontiff came from the Italian state represented by P2 — and thus the Gladio command.

Actors in the drama: how the fates intervened.

- Roberto Calvi: 17th June 1982, discovered swaying at the end of a rope beneath Blackfriars Bridge, London. No convictions secured.

- Henri Arsan: Died suddenly in San Vittore prison, Milan, November 1983, allegedly of a heart attack.

- Michele Sindona: 22nd March 1986, died in prison after drinking poisoned coffee.

- Robert Maxwell: 5th November 1991, fell or was pushed overboard from his luxury yacht Lady Ghislaine while cruising off the Canary Islands.

- Abdullah Çatlı: 3rd November 1996, killed in a car crash with government officials, in possession of a Turkish diplomatic passport and documents allowing him to carry arms overseas.

- Bekir Çelenk: 1996, murdered in prison, Istanbul.

- Archbishop Paul 'the untouchable' Marcinkus, head of the Vatican bank for 17 years: 20th February 2006, died of undisclosed causes in Sun City, Arizona, aged 84. He was still protected by Vatican diplomatic immunity.

- Sergei Antonov: Accused as complicit in the assassination attempt, but acquitted for lack of evidence. Mentally and physically scarred from his spell in Italian jails, force-fed on mind-bending drugs, he spent the remainder of his life as a hermit. Died in Bulgaria August 2007.

- Mehmet Ali Ağca: Pardoned by Italian president Carlo Azeglio Ciampi at the personal insistence of John Paul II in June 2000. Extradited to Turkey, where he was imprisoned for the 1979 murder of the newspaper editor and two bank robberies. Released early in 2010.

In 2002, a red-herring parliamentary commission hand-picked by the stupendous opportunist Silvio Berlusconi purported to investigate the extent of KGB influence over prominent figures in Italy. No credible evidence on any count was ever adduced to the committee, which otherwise relied on innuendo, the standard instrument in black propaganda dating back to the Holy Inquisition. Its principal task was to slander the dreary dead-pan opposition leader Romano Prodi (an ex-Christian Democrat, former Goldman Sachs consultant and EU Commission chief) as Moscow's stooge in Rome, in advance of upcoming elections. Aside from the usual rumpus in the Italian kitchen, international headlines were seized when the commission's chairman, the shameless, mercurial opportunist Paolo Guzzanti (left, right or centre, on any given day) claimed to have 'proven' the KGB's hand in the shooting of the Pope. Guzzanti is a prominent editorial ornament in the former premier Berlusconi's media empire. He also happened to be on close terms with the commission's sole but well-paid adviser, one Mario Scaramella. He is a sometime Neapolitan lawyer and Walter Mitty figure, a self-appointed specialist in environmental matters who roams around continually insinuating himself into enticing scandals with the intention of generating publicity. It was therefore unsurprising to find him supping with Alexander Litvinenko at the poisoned chalice supposedly supplied in a London restaurant by the post-KGB Russian intelligence, the FSB. Scaramella's academic qualifications have been exposed as duds, by the London *Evening Standard*, among others. He fits the stereotype of CIA stooges who reveal themselves whenever there is a pressing need to distribute false evidence like so much confetti. The Vatican dismissed these theatrical intrusions as a further example of Berlusconi's endless and tasteless exercises in working political mischief.

John Paul II devoted his papacy until his death in 2005 to a worldwide crusade in the name of peace and reconciliation. In 1989, Solidarnosc negotiated a pact for the transition to democracy alongside the remnants of the Communist party and the Polish Catholic Church, at the proceedings known as the Round Table. On 1st December 1989, Mikhail Gorbachev paid the first official visit of any Soviet leader to the Vatican State. Gorbachev warmly greeted the Pope as 'Holy Father.' For his part, John Paul varied his routine in a significant way. Vatican watchers noticed some extremely rare diplomatic body language. Normally, the Pope chose to greet important visitors at the door of the library, one floor below his private apartment. To demonstrate his particular esteem, he stepped out to meet him in the Throne Room.

For the first five minutes, the pair were alone, speaking in Russian. According to accounts circulated by Vatican media, Gorbachev informed the Pontiff: 'Holy Father, we are aware that we are dealing with the highest religious authority in the world but also someone who is a Slav.' At the end of a remarkable encounter which sealed the long years of clandestine relations between the Holy See and the Kremlin, John Paul declared. 'I'm sure that Providence paved the way for this meeting.' No doubt the Pope's thoughts returned to the 'Komsomolsk Generation' who, in the stagnating years of the Brezhnev era, began the seismic shift towards a market-based economy. Millions of formerly imprisoned Catholics and Orthodox worshippers in the East began their walk to freedom.

An extraordinary Vicar of Rome, by any historical standards that you may choose to apply. With a little help from his friends Roberto Calvi, Michele Sindona and Licio Gelli.

A postscript.

The definitive history of the vast corruption which soaked Solidarnosc has yet to be written. Working in Washington in the early 1990s, I became acquainted with a wealthy Texan business woman called Amanda Hill. She owned a string of radio stations in the US, and was interested in exploiting business opportunities in the newly liberated territories of eastern Europe. She was also the lover of the Harlem-born Ron Brown, who went on to become Bill Clinton's Commerce Secretary. Through Hill's introduction, I learnt from Brown that he was involved in channelling AFL-CIO trade union funds to Solidarnosc. I had the clear impression that the money was going through the Vatican bank. Amanda Hill's first stop-over on her European tour was Warsaw. Brown was scheduled to join the expedition 'to call on old friends,' but called me to cancel at the last moment.

Hill was extremely agitated in Poland. She felt she was being followed everywhere. She was convinced the bedside radio in her room at the Marriott hotel was bugged. When I raised this with the management, they shrugged and openly admitted that it was. Clearly, Brown had been due for an eyes-and-ears reception committee. Enough is now known to state that much of the AFL-CIO funds supposedly sent to Solidarity were creamed off by local Polish oligarchs, nascent right-wing parties and Clinton's private political purse, not to mention the Italian mob.

Ron Brown died on 3rd April 1996 in a mysterious plane crash. He was killed along with the entire crew and a delegation of 34 American businessmen when his air force Boeing came down on approach to landing in Dubrovnik, in the Balkan state of Croatia. It appears the pilot made a terrain judgement error. This may have been due to the planting of a false radio beacon in the surrounding hills. There was a hint that Brown may have survived, briefly (as did one crew member) from the indications — afterwards suppressed — of a small-bore bullet hole in his cranium. Amanda Hill met her own fate. She was ruined by the Internal Revenue Service (IRS). Her flourishing broadcasting business was utterly destroyed.

XIII.
Something Rotten in the State of Belgium

'Imagine, everywhere you hear that story about a blackmail dossier in which organisations of the extreme right are in the possession of pictures and videos on which a number of prominent people in and around Brussels have sex with young girls; minors it is said. The existence of this dossier has always been vehemently denied, until it was proven that testimonies and videos of this affair indeed were in the possession of the police services.' — Senator Hugo Coveliers

---

On the misty and chilled autumn morning of Sunday, 20th October 1996, 350,000 Belgians, dressed in ghostly all-over white, flooded the boulevards of Brussels. The skies above the capital filled with clouds of white balloons. The host moved in a silent flow towards the centre of the city. The patience of a people had finally broken with the authorities of a cobbled-together state of convenience, which throughout its short history failed to acquire the stiffening backbones of genuine nationhood and social harmony between Flemish and French speakers. Now, the grisly affair of Marc Dutroux, the Monster of Charleroi, child abductor and torturer, laid bare a horrifying sickness at the heart of Belgium. The procession of sheeted figures filing quietly through the hushed city that autumn day knew perfectly well that a man guilty of the most terrible crimes had received the protection of the state at the highest levels.

These outrages occurred under the noses of the local gendarmes, who never managed to catch any culprits. Like Dutroux and the organised, politicised gang of paedophiles he belonged to, the killers had enjoyed a charmed immunity from detection. In 2006, the guns and the ammunition used in the Brabant massacres were finally traced, to the supposedly defunct branch of the Belgian stay-behind army called 'the Special Intervention Squadron' — the one known within the Gladio command structure as the 'Diana Organisation' (after the Huntress of Greek mythology).

The rush of changes sweeping Belgium after WW2, coupled with the arrival of powerful new organisations such as NATO and the emerging European Union, crushed any lingering faith in a viable Belgian state. Between them, these powerful institutions superseded and subverted what little there was holding this sorry state together. Crime and graft — much of it politically motivated — unhinged the government. The flow of hot money drawn to Brussels — Europe's very own Chicago — unleashed horrific forces, which undermined the moral bedrock of the country. There was a sense to many observers of this small nation slipping into a kind of mass lunacy, where hallucinations and nightmares unfortunately turned out to be events in real time. Sex trafficking, industrial paedophilia, the reports of snuff movies made for political and financial blackmail, or just for profit, were all entangled in a black cobweb of spies, officially connived drug running, the secret paramilitary network, and the constant meddling of NATO's high command in the internal affairs of the country.

Belgium and its eleven million inhabitants seemed predestined for such a tragic fate. The country is a cast-off from the old Spanish lowland provinces, a failed buffer state arising from Napoleon's sallies around the region. She finally staggered to a breach with the Netherlands, unilaterally seizing an uneasy form of independence in November 1830. The name was adapted from the tribes of the Belgae, who once inhabited roughly the same quarters in ancient history. Poor ersatz Belgium straddled a number of cultural divides, which made sure it was always an anachronism. This feeble creature had no common language or religion, an artificial capital wracked by gaping cultural divides and for good measure the imported (from Germany) Saxe-Coburg-Gotha monarchy, which immediately set about exploiting their new property as a private corporation. The atrocities committed in the vast Belgian Congo — originally not a colony but a private royal fiefdom, acquired as an early example of 'humanitarian intervention' — made the cross-Atlantic slave trade look like a travel agency. Belgium had the geographical misfortune to lie on every army's march to somewhere else. Crushed and trampled by rival forces in WW1, she found herself once again caught in the open at the start of WW2. The national ethnic divide between French and Flemish speakers was scarcely likely to heal in the circumstances. Many Flemings either openly or symbolically sided with the Germans, in hopes of Flemish nationhood — even within a Nazi commonwealth — doing away with Belgium altogether. Pétainist sympathisers from the Walloon province were also drawn to Nazi colours. The Germans recruited modest numbers from both sides of the ethnic divide to stiffen *Waffen-SS* brigades, but the numbers were less significant than the further damage to the split personality of Belgium itself.

These entrenched yearnings for the far Right were not extinguished by the close of hostilities. A residue from wartime fraternisation with the Germans led to Nazi-style paganistic symbolism and mystical blood bonding ceremonies within the Belgian stay-behind network and elements of the national armed forces, which in any event inclined to the Right. This mystical streak was set for a chilling significance in shaping many of the perversions yet to be wrought on Belgium. A taste for SS-style initiation rites shipped on board by Belgian wartime volunteers transposed itself to the fascist underground network, which had begun to acquire a stranglehold on so much of the country's public life. Much worse, they leached into the minds of criminal gangs, who began to organise diabolical ceremonies and activities centred on kidnapped children and other victims of sexual exploitation. When the nascent EU institutions began searching for a home, they selected Brussels precisely because of its neutral, small-country image as the 'cockpit of Europe.' The grandness of the compliment unfortunately disguised the truth that Belgium was hopelessly ill-equipped — in terms of civil infrastructure or mentality — to cope with what came next.

And what came next was NATO, evicted in insalubrious circumstances from France. The incoming warriors went about transforming this already schizophrenic state into the Kingdom of NATO. Hot on their heels came the rapid expansion of European federal institutions and the inward rush of huge corporations, eager to edge as close as possible to the councils of these two great caliphates, the most powerful military and economic alliances the world has seen since the Roman Empire. With them came the legions of camp followers: politicians, bankers, lawyers, think-tankers, the Pied Piper legions of PR guru Edward Bernays (nephew of Sigmund Freud), lobbyists, armies of spies and counter-spies, arms traders (straight and shady), drug lords, con-men and criminals. Plus, rivers of money in quantities never before experienced in this small country. Little Belgium soon had the second most powerful and intrusive crime cartels in Western Europe, so well-organised that even the market leaders, the Italian Mafiosi, fell back in admiration. In a very short time, Europe's cockpit was also its chief narcotics and illegal arms hub, with an even nastier sideline involving human flesh.

The weak fabric of the Belgian state was absolutely unfit to cope with this avalanche. The country staggered along with a decrepit legal system from the 1830's. Policemen went on taking orders from politicians, as of yore. What might have served as some kind of unifying factor — the huge infusion of new wealth — served to set Belgians against each other more than ever before. The centre imploded. Quarrelsome nationalities retreated behind their own zones of influence, leaving Brussels as a quasi-independent, internationalised canton. This virtually complete cleavage spelt the effective end to the 'national experiment.' By the spring of 2010, the 'war of the cantons' confirmed the *de facto* arrival of an apartheid 'separate development' state at the heart of Europe. It was fought over the incomprehensible linguistic contortions of the Halle-Vilvoorde suburbs on the outskirts of Brussels, fiercely Flemish, adamantly opposed to admitting French speakers (in Flemish eyes, settlers). The general election, in June that year, was the rubber stamp. Any shallow-rooted government planted in this unpromising soil has few prospects of long-term survival.

When General Lyman Lemnitzer arrived in Belgium to take charge of the new NATO mission control, the process of national disintegration was already well advanced. Belgium was to be denied a strong, centrally-minded government — if there had ever been a concerted ambition to entertain such a thing — that would persuade Flemish and French speakers to live in harmony. A Belgian nationalist is a contradiction in terms, whereas a Flemish nationalist qualifies as a patriot. The poor French-speaking Walloons were left wallowing on the margins. The CIA had long been dabbling in Belgian politics. It was recruiting Belgian Nazis — mostly, but not exclusively, Flemish — as soon as the war ended, prodding many of them into high offices at state and provincial levels, and protecting others from justice, or prising them out of jail. But no other country in Europe, not even Italy, experienced more bizarre, or tragic, circumstances than those which now began to unfold in Belgium.

Gladio's activities in Italy pointed to the power that a parallel state could amass, in no small measure due to the Vatican's willingness to steep itself in such ungodly activities as money laundering, and fraternising with organised crime and fascist political structures. But tiny Belgium was blessed with nothing less than a *pair* of Vaticans: the 'European Pentagon,' or NATO; and the 'New Rome,' the rapidly flowering institutions of the EU. Both were outside and above what passed for Belgian civil and criminal law. Once the furniture arriving from France had been uncrated, Lemnitzer assigned his political team the task of creating the strongest possible anti-communist front to shore up the defences of the new NATO principality. Lemnitzer sent for Frank Eaton, a shadowy DIA figure with known leanings to the extreme Right, who plunged into the exotic undergrowth of extremist Belgian politics with relish. He was soon on confidential terms with most of the key figures, and even devised a network to comfort neo-Nazis held in jail.

Lemnitzer looked sourly on the state of Belgian politics, and especially the clout of the powerful socialist unions. Nor could he easily forget that of all repulsive figures, Karl Marx hatched the *Communist Manifesto*, and effectively the Communist movement, between 1845 and 1848 in the sumptuous gilded surroundings of the 13th-century Grand-Place. By the early 1960s, Belgians were thinking of their country as the 'sick man of the common market.' The economy flagged, weakened further by shaky coalitions and mass strikes, which the unions threw at authority again and again. The establishment arm — big business, the military, intelligence, police and especially the royal family — feared a revolution in the making.

Nerves were thoroughly rattled when the prominent Left-winger Ernest Mandel, echoing the Fourth International, declared the only solution to the endless rolling crisis wracking Belgium was 'a worker's government based on the trade unions.'[N1] It sounded very much like a clarion call to insurrection. From that moment, NATO strategy was clear: namely to destabilise and knock the socialist movement out of politics altogether. What followed was the criminalisation of Belgian politics to such an extent the political apparatus never recovered — the infection of the state by vice, perversions and a campaign of state-inspired terror that finally broke the back of this thoroughly schizoid country. In classic Gladio fashion, it was first necessary to invent a threat that did not exist, then create the means to deal with it. As a result of NATO's machinations and the industrious efforts of Lemnitzer's imported experts in counter-insurgency, Belgium found itself with twin Ku Klux Klans operating on either side of the linguistic canyon. Belgian Gladio operations divided scrupulously along politically correct lines into SDRA-8 (French) and STC/Mob (Flemish) divisions.

According to journalist Manuel Abramowitz — a leading investigator of the far Right in Belgium — neo-Nazis were egged on to infiltrate all the mechanisms of the state, with special attention reserved for the police and the army. By the 1980s, this level of penetration had become so deep — thanks to fascist fronts such as the neo-Nazi militia Westland New Post and its French-speaking counterpart, *Front de la Jeunesse* — that Belgium's military forces could be said to have fallen almost entirely under extremist control. Not once, in the wake of the many false-flag operations over the coming decades, did convincing proof ever appear of a credible co-ordinated Left-wing subversive force operating on Belgian soil, while seditious organisations of the Far Right flourished openly. One prominent ex-gendarmerie commander Martial Lekeu — who was eventually given sanctuary in the US for crimes committed in Belgium — informed the Brussels daily *Le Soir*: 'When I joined the Gendarmerie I became a devout fascist. At the Diana Group I got to know people who had the same convictions as me. We greeted each other like the Nazis.'

Before long, the CIA purse was open to a cluster of Right-wing front organisations sprouting in the emerging Euro capital. Some overlapped with espionage networks, for which they were primarily a front. *Le Cercle*, for example, on the surface a respectable talking shop for big business heavyweights and politicians, had a much more important task collecting and feeding enticing tidbits to the CIA and the European intelligence network. It was a kind of private-enterprise spy network, working under US and NATO control and relying on a great many operatives who could supply useful information, even by unorthodox methods. It was hardly surprising that it took on such a twist, given that one of its founders was the French wartime collaborator and arch-Nazi, Jean Violet. Another was the former French premier Antoine Pinay, who belonged to the solid Pétainist Right.[N2]

Descriptions of the Propaganda Due lodge in Italy were heavily overlaid with reports of mystical ceremonies, the swearing of oaths of fealty and bonding vows. The secrecy of the Gladio structure everywhere invited isolation from ordinary structures and restraints of civil society. It was a provocative invitation to escape all moral boundaries. Belgium was lurching into madness. The links between NATO, organised crime and cultist-minded neo-Nazi organisations, started to become institutionalised. At the same time, the long-running rivalry between the CIA and the Pentagon continued to rage on this foreign turf. Lemnitzer found the ideal opportunity in his new seat of power to discriminate against the CIA in favour of his own creature, the Defence Intelligence Agency, which he elevated to a prominent position supervising the Gladio structure. The supremo's old penchant for working with criminals unencumbered by scruples was soon confirmed by the recruitment pattern to stiffen the ranks of Belgian Gladio.

One early DIA recruit was an idealistic fascist signed to the payroll at the tender age of seventeen. His name was Paul Latinus, and his chief qualifications were small-time car thief, street runner and general factotum to the Belgian criminal gangs. His absence of a moral compass qualified him for expensive NATO career training in secret warfare by the British SAS, plus a spell at the US Army's Fort Bragg black ops finishing school; he was then planted as a reserve lieutenant with the Royal Belgian Air Force. He sneaked on politicians and other public officials for state security. This was mainly to set them up for blackmail, which brought him into touch with underground sex channels involving minors. He joined the Front de la Jeunesse and then helped to found its Flemish counterpart, Westland New Post in the early eighties. Latinus reached the ranks of the *crème de la crème* when he was eventually installed as the head of Group G in the Belgian coup structure code-named F-4, which was maintained on permanent standby, and nearly activated once, in the 1974 crisis. This was the direct thread that led from NATO HQ, to the Belgian national gendarmerie, the Westland New Post militia and then finally to the street gangs who carried out many dirty tricks operations on the orders of higher interests.

Among his regular contacts was Jean-Michel Nihoul, mastermind of the rapidly expanding sex traffic and paedophile industries, and several of his corporals, including the Monster of Charleroi, Marc Dutroux. Latinus was discovered by his girl friend, roped up in the bathroom at his home on 24th April 1984. Post-mortem examinations were inconclusive. Whether he was murdered or killed himself remained unexplained, which the cursory investigations by the police did nothing to answer. Latinus always claimed that he kept a secret file as his life insurance policy. If so, it seems to have worked in reverse. An extremely inconvenient figure connecting the Belgian Gladio operation and the depravity soaking Belgium, was now off the stage.

Dutroux and Latinus knew each other from their common passion for stealing expensive cars. But Latinus' trade speciality was setting up targets for blackmail, which lends strong support to later allegations that child abuse networks had the prime objective of luring clientele into places where they would be secretly filmed with young girls and boys. The content of videos intended for the worldwide black market remains to this day a highly toxic and unresolved mystery, which the Belgian authorities have done all in their power to suppress. When the Dutroux time bomb finally exploded in all its horrific detail, some dozens of victims came forward with alarming stories of snuff movies involving torture, murders, ritual sacrifice, blood drinking and extreme psychological stress. They mentioned target practice involving child victims. The state's defence has always been that none of this incriminating evidence physically existed, while admitting that much of the material seized by police is concealed from prying eyes. The persistently dogged Belgian MP and subsequently Senator Hugo Coveliers, chairman of the special investigating committee probing gangsterism and terrorism in Belgium (1988-1990), tracked the presence of incriminating materials to a special unit called the 'judicial police.' Here is what Coveliers said on what became known as the 'scandal of the X-Dossiers.'

> *Imagine, everywhere you hear that story about a blackmail dossier in which organisations of the extreme right are in the possession of pictures and videos on which a number of prominent people in and around Brussels have sex with young girls; minors it is said. The existence of this dossier has always been vehemently denied. Until it was proven that testimonies and videos of this affair indeed were in the possession of the police services.*

> *The at first non-existing dossier turns out to exist. The videos without substance then turn out to be interesting enough after all to be handed over to the examining magistrate tasked with the investigation into the Gang of Nivelles [held responsible for some of the shop massacres]. But this person subsequently is afraid to testify about that! What do you think has been going on here!*

Incriminating pictures of high officials abusing children would be enough for the state to panic. But in a summary written by a trio of investigative Belgian journalists in 1999 — *The X-Dossiers* — there is powerful evidence, painstakingly accumulated, with all doubtful or unreliable claims discarded, that tapes which the police still hold in their possession — and insist are 'worthless' — do feature evidence of sadistic abuse connected with public officials.[N3] Moreover, they lend weight to two extremely dangerous avenues of exploration. One of these leads to an entrapment technique in which victims are lured into ever more perverse activities, and then effectively placed under political blackmail, with no line of retreat. The second points to the chilling possibility that some of the activities reputedly recorded on tape and retained in top secret files, were actually part of cultist initiation ceremonies. It was alleged these involved paganistic neo-Nazi traits such as blood rituals, practised by elements within the state's secret forces, as well as the orthodox military structure.

More disturbing questions were raised by an allegation from a former treasurer of the Parti Social-Chrétien (PSC) youth division called Jacques

Thoma. He is on public record as claiming he was once invited to mass orgies by his superior, an associate of Jean-Michel Nihoul and Marc Dutroux. They were explained to him as 'an Opus Dei initiation test.' Once again we find mystical currents seeping from neo-Nazis and the paedophile gangs, implying the possibility of seamless connections to the Vatican's so-called 'church within a church.' Opus Dei, which translates to 'Work of God,' has been accused by its detractors of various ungodly activities, featuring the intimidation of members, denigration of women, and infiltration of governments. The organisation's bonding practices are said by critics to involve self-mortification, with devotees obliged to wear spiked chains around their thighs, whip their buttocks and sleep on hard boards. For all its protestations to the contrary, it is certainly true that Opus Dei operates well below visible radar and venerates secrecy. When I undertook the European Parliament's high-profile probe into family-splitting cults, Opus Dei attracted by far the largest response in my mailbag, more even than high-profile organisations like the Moonies and Scientology. It was excluded from the report after heavy lobbying from the Vatican hierarchy and its powerful supporters in Strasbourg, including perhaps the most prominent Euro-MP, the late Austro-Hungarian archduke Otto von Habsburg.[57]

The sickness of institutionalised paedophilia in the Belgian church broke surface with a vengeance in June 2010. The Bishop of Bruges, Mgr. Roger Vangheluwe, resigned after admitting years-long abuse of a single victim; within days, police swooped on a sitting conclave of high church officials, looking for more incriminating materials, seizing computers and many documents. This unprecedented action, which provoked an outraged response from Pope Benedict himself, included the bizarre indulgence of drilling into the tombs of two dead prelates in search of incriminating files, clearly following a tip-off arising from within the church. In this light, the Opus Dei claims begin to carry some credibility. The tottering Belgian government, having quite sufficient problems on its hands already, waved the white flag. Police were ordered to drop all their inquiries and return all the seized materials. But this time the Vatican was itself check-mated. An independent investigator with access to the incriminating materials — which described organised and systematic paedophilia by the Belgian clergy stretching over many years — dumped the entire files in the public realm. It is impossible to avoid a straight connection between a corrupted state which has, effectively, condoned the worst cases of sexual abuse anywhere in Europe, and the

---

[57] My parliamentary inquiry was literally deluged with complainants concerning Opus Dei. Many who described themselves as victims also spoke of mental torture, forced tithing of their incomes and the threat of social isolation if they threatened to speak out. The Congregation of Other Faiths at the Vatican asked Members to vote in favour of my findings so long as Opus Dei was excluded.

Belgian church, which is itself an extended division of the Belgian establishment.

The man long suspected of being the real high priest of the grisly sex rings and drugs rackets was Nihoul, known to intimates — and his alleged victims — as 'Mich.' He was a familiar figure on the shady night-club circuit, who could be seen in the company of important figures from the Belgian upper crust. He was known as the man who could fix anything to suit particular tastes. He rose up from street gang territory and made good money on the bar and drugs scene to become the most powerful crime boss in the country. He would always talk himself down as a mere 'pub owner.' Those who knew him better understood that his network of alliances was respected by the most powerful élites. Dutroux acted as a pimp and sometimes master of ceremonies for Nihoul's orgies, that were alleged to attract prominent public notables. There was a certain irony when Mr. Big found himself dragged into the limelight concerning his underling. His smirking arrogance at his own court appearances was such that he bawled to reporters that he would never be convicted because he 'knew too much.' So, for that matter, did Latinus, but he was not available after 1984 to answer questions. 'Mich' had another line of defence. Like his corporal Dutroux, he was a police sneak on the side. Thus, a protection racket worked in reverse, even when Dutroux's trafficking, torture and murder of young girls and boys was known to senior officers of the gendarmerie.

There was another link between Nihoul, Latinus and the street gangs that could be highly compromising to both the Belgian state and the Gladio circuit, and which probably accounts for Latinus' sudden exit. He knew a good deal — and probably, far too much — concerning another important figure in Group G. This was Paul Vanden Boeynants ('PvB' for short), the paunchy and wealthy son of a pork butcher, who became defence minister and twice premier. Compared to the average dour prime minister of Belgium, he had an unusually colourful career. His 'Social Christian Party' was infiltrated by western intelligence, and was really little more than a vehicle for himself. He put his chubby hands to everything that offered profit, beginning with the national gendarmerie's National Bureau for Drugs, where he installed a pliant general who was on the CIA's payroll. His task was to make sure that regular shipments of marihuana and cocaine bound for the CIA crossed the border into Belgium without harassment. Boeynants, the made-good butcher's son, found time to open a meat processing factory in Malta as another cover to wash CIA dope funds.

The narco-traffic flooding Belgium belonged in large part to the CIA's long-established international drug circuits, with a certain amount creamed off by Nihoul and partners in return for co-operation on the marketing side. On his part, PvB's carefully articulated populist charms disguised his control over an enormous bundle of enterprises owing strong connections to the underworld and the CIA. When the time came for scores to be settled, the enemies that he made in the years of good fortune arranged his prosecution for tax evasion. Boeynants responded with threats to sing in no uncertain terms. He was let off with a slap on the wrist, even if his ambitions to become burgomaster (mayor) of Brussels travelled no further.

Then, early in 1989, Vanden Boeynants was kidnapped by members of the well-known Haemers gang, which, it later transpired, had close connections to both Belgian Gladio units and Dutroux's activities. The government tried to pretend he had been snatched by an unknown cell called the 'Socialist Revolutionary Organisation,' which strongly suggested Gladio fingerprints. PvB was held for a month, then released after payment of a whopping ransom. This being the surreal state of Belgium, there were further twists to the episode. First, the prominent gang boss Patrick Haemers — someone else who knew too much — joined the lines of convenient prison suicides. His two accomplices were luckier. One fine day in 1993 at the Brussels-St. Gilles prison, their guards left their cells unlocked. They quietly strolled away to freedom.

Behind such a carnival lay the revelations from a troop of witnesses that Vanden Boeynants frequently participated with judges, army officers, lawyers, businessmen and other élite figures, in orgies involving young children and acts of ghastly bestiality, including hunts where children were chased through the woods with Dobermans. PvB is dead, following a heart operation that went wrong. All that he knew about Belgium's depravities has usefully gone to the grave. Yet his legacy lives on, connecting him to almost every organisation spinning in the orbit of crime, neo-Nazi cults and the key figures in the secret army operations. In this domain we find the Public Information Office (PIO) which cropped up in 1974. In a sense, the name was an appropriate pun on its actual task, to act as a sponsored private army headed by one Major Jean-Marie Bougerol. He was a member of SDRA-8 — heart of the Belgian stay-behind network. He was also one of the chief suspects, alongside Vanden Boeynants, behind a projected Right-wing coup — the 'April Crisis' of 1973.

The intention was to evict the weak socialist government then in power. PIO was bidden to co-ordinate the coup and supervise all the hard work Gladio people would need to do. Vanden Boeynants was widely touted as NATO's choice as figurehead premier, and Bougerol as the brains. The plot was sufficiently advanced to have the country's armed forces standing on full alert, before the order came from the Ministry of Defence — and, some say, the royal palace — to pull back. It was a precipice moment. The government tottered on for another year before the matter was settled at the ballot box. In March 1974, the dependable and solidly pro-NATO Flemish Bilderberger

Leo Tindemanns emerged as premier, following the election that tilted the country firmly to the Right.

Bougerol seemed ideal for the task of masterminding the coup. He enjoyed high patronage, and he specialised in all kinds of sabotage and secret operations. From this scarcely veiled front for NATO, Bougerol gave orders to the head of the Front de la Jeunesse, one Francis Dossogne. Bougerol busied himself in other ways, turning up as an instructor at training camps deep in the Ardennes forests run by the French and Flemish neo-Nazi militias. He was assisted by commandos from regular Belgian army units. The major travelled around extensively with other members of the Gladio network, and was noted at various times conferring with his opposite numbers in Italy, Greece and Portugal, and especially in the Netherlands and France. He had the air of a senior staff officer or even an ambassador enjoying important responsibilities.

PIO also reached into the pockets of big business, including immensely secretive Belgian banks. Just as the Nihoul network washed its sex traffic and narcotics haul through numbered anonymous accounts in obliging Belgian banks, so the CIA — and Lemnitzer's ever-shadowing DIA — used the same route to clean up the funds collected from the dope industry. How much money travelled from the private commercial world to the secret subterranean state in these times will never be established. But there are important clues. The strange tale of the Wackenhut Corporation and its role in Belgium is one of these.

It was started as a private security operation in Florida in the 1950s by a rough diamond called George Wackenhut, whose personal opinions belonged so far to the Right he left Senator Joe McCarthy in the shade. The FBI took him on as a special agent to spy on suspected Left-wing subversives. Enshrined in his own business, he never gave up the habit. From the outset, it was stuffed with ex-FBI and CIA cronies, including one really big cheese, Frank Carlucci — former deputy director of the CIA, Reagan's adviser on national security and later defense secretary 1987-89. The Wackenhut outfit followed Lemnitzer to Belgium, where it was soon working for the local military and NATO. Wackenhut also drew for some of its employees on the Westland New Post paramilitaries. One of these was a known bomber and hit man, the Frenchman Jean-François Calmette, a notorious veteran of the OAS rebellion against de Gaulle and close conspirator of Yves Guérin-Sérac. He was director of the Belgian division of Wackenhut up until 1981, while doubling as senior Westland New Post commander. These were curious relationships for such a prominent businessman in the security business. Among his more exotic activities was looking after security for a lavish tinselled Christmas gala, the ultimate fantasy of a Gladio Ball staged in a swank Brussels hotel. The guests at what was officially a Vanden Boeynants party read like a VIP Who's Who of the Belgian secret state. Beneath the sparkling chandeliers, a Belgian industrialist's consort was as likely to take the floor with a member of a NATO-sponsored street gang as a high-flying army officer.

In 1982, Barbier was assigned as a Wackenhut security guard to the synagogue on the Rue de la Régence in Brussels. During his watch, it mysteriously blew up. The plans of the building were later found in Barbier's home. This same Marcel Barbier was later discovered to be a close personal associate of Paul Latinus, effectively his deputy. The plot thickened. Security duties agreed with the Belgian army involved the strange melting away of Wackenhut security patrols during a number of incidents in which these bases were supposedly 'attacked' by revolutionary forces. In every case, these Strategy of Tension assaults were mounted by paramilitary units, with Westland New Post to the fore. On occasion they were directly supported by US army units, as when a troop from US special forces flew in from Fort Bragg and parachuted into the Ardennes. They hid up for a few days, and then with the aid of local SDRA-8 people, shot up a gendarmerie post in the small town of Vielsalm, killing one officer. On another occasion, a similar US-led raid on an army barracks was supposedly pulled on 'higher orders' from Brussels. The Americans (DIA paramilitaries or perhaps members of some other ultra-secret Pentagon unit) continued to cruise the neighbourhood camouflaged in civilian clothes, and then went in on their own to attack the barracks, leaving two more fatalities and a dozen injured.

In the mid-1980s, Wackenhut closed down in Belgium, amid reports of marching orders from the Ministry of Defence. It may have been that things got too hot for comfort, and the chief clients wanted the show out of town. Judged in the light of later events, Wackenhut's activities in Belgium anticipated mercenary activities by trigger-happy private security contractors of several decades later, notably the infamous Blackwater outfit.

The supermarket massacres (rather a misnomer, since a wide range of shops and restaurants were attacked, including typically Jewish-owned targets such as jewellers) all occurred during the early '80s, during NATO's roll-out of manoeuvrable, nuclear-tipped American cruise missiles across Europe. NATO was taken aback by the strength of public opposition in Belgium. The socialists found themselves with such a strong and galvanising populist groundswell they began to tout the idea of leaving NATO. The Belgian parliament, which subsequently investigated the attacks, concluded with unusual cross-linguistic support that purely criminal explanations advanced by the gendarmerie were absurd. On one occasion, a sack of looted money was discovered tossed in a stream. Bank robbers are rarely so charitable.

No logical criminal purpose could ever be adduced. The special Paramilitary Inquiry concluded it was a false-flag exercise, controlled by the hand of the state to sow confusion and fear among the populace. Voters would be prompted to flock to a Right-wing, law-and-order orientated government which would muzzle opponents of the missile programme. In short, the classic Strategy of Tension ploy. Rumours of involvement in the Brabant/Nivelle imbroglio persistently swirled around the debonair figure of the part-Algerian secret policeman Madani Bouhouche, who worked for the national gendarmerie's BOB special investigations unit. He doubled these tasks with a closet role at Westland New Post. The X-File investigators believe that Madani Bouhouche belonged to a group of neo-Nazi officers in the gendarmerie who were responsible for 'a terror exortion campaign' connected to the *ballets roses,* the so-called 'pink ballet' juvenile sex orgies. Bouhouche drove a fast BMW which some of the victims claimed he used to take them to a factory just outside Brussels, where they were systematically abused, and some victims murdered. In 1982 he was arrested on a charge of murdering an Algerian gun-runner. Shortly afterwards Bouhouche's friend and fellow militant Jean Bultot shot off to Paraguay (that popular sanctuary for Nazis), where he informed a pursuing newshound from *Le Soir* that every single incident had taken place with the help of the state 'at the highest levels.' Bouhouche was eventually convicted for the murder of the Algerian arms salesman and the later killing of a diamond dealer. Released on parole, he rented a cottage in a remote part of the French Pyrenees. In November 2005 he managed to behead himself while cutting wood with a chain-saw.

On 29th May 1985, television pictures flashed around the world told the story of a bloody massacre at the Heysel football stadium in the Flemish-dominated outskirts of Brussels, long a dominion of neo-Nazi thugs and skinheads. An encounter between the European Cup titans Liverpool and Juventus finished in one of the worst riots in the history of the game, leaving the bodies of 39 Italian fans crushed to death on the terraces, and dozens more injured. What happened that day at Heysel bore all the signs of a deliberately incited, designer riot. But now as the football world mourned, it was time to beckon on the usual scapegoats. Knee-jerk reactions placed the blame squarely on Liverpool supporters. Margaret Thatcher, who intrinsically despised anything tainted by socialist Merseyside, led the charge. British football was instantly banished from Europe, while Liverpool FC found itself the subject of odium for years to come over the alleged behaviour of its supporters. There was some general muttering about the inadequacy of Belgian crowd control, but almost no one except Liverpool chief executive Peter Robinson noted the disturbing background to the catastrophe.

Robinson, an objective and thoughtful administrator, was puzzled how such a devastating riot could occur, when prior to kick-off, rival fans had been indulging in good-natured banter. His careful post-mortem included crucial evidence that nearly all the tickets had been sold by Belgian sources, in defiance of the usual rigid precautions. Over-concentration of ticket sales in the hands of the host state is often a contributory factor to violence. Moreover, the usual strong police contingent expected for such a high-profile clash had been downgraded to little more then a handful of men. It would have taken a more skilled eye to note that the officers on the scene were not the customary gendarmes but men from the *Rijkswacht,* the élite military police force under the direct control of the Minister of Defence, one of the main components in the Gladio structure.

Robinson and the Juventus management had protested over the choice of Heysel, a structure so obviously run down and decrepit it was unfit to stage any public event. They were coldly over-ruled by the Belgian authorities. When the managers jointly proposed a security zone with strong barriers to isolate Juventus and Liverpool supporters, that suggestion too was tossed aside. In the end, the only crush barrier was a flimsy fence, against which both groups of heaving fans pressed. And finally, large amounts of seditious material, in the form of Nazi-type banners and even BNP [British National Party] literature, had apparently been stored inside the stadium and scattered around well in advance.

The BBC radio station in my Bristol constituency rang my apartment and asked me to file an eye-witness account of the aftermath. Aside from the scene of expected devastation in the wake of the deadly stampede, the most remarkable reactions came from local people, who spoke of a large contingent of Belgian skinheads who entered the stadium as kick-off time approached. Locals were astonished to see Rijkswacht officers, whose duties were well known to be reserved for the highest matters of state security. They concluded prominent VIPs must be present. But other eyewitnesses noted how the senior commanders apparently not only expected the phalanx of skinheads, but were sufficiently acquainted with their leadership to get into 'smiling conversations.' One ordinary gendarme I found told me as he surveyed the shambles: 'This could only have been made to happen. Those people [the rival fans] were shunted so close together that it was like preparing a match for gunpowder. Then our skinheads were let into the ground and that was when the trouble started.' He shook his head and went on: 'It's like Brabant, Nivelles.' When the staff of my Brussels office tried to contact this same gendarmerie officer about a week later, giving the rank and serial number that I noted down, they were informed that no such person had ever served with the force.

Much was later made of the Juventus contingent taunting British fans with florid banners covered with Nazi insignia. There was some comment, however, in the Belgian media, that their design appeared to owe their cultural origins to paganistic Belgian skinhead gangs rather than Italian backgrounds. The one Italian connection that seemed clear involved a Juventus supporter who had been boasting to the home contingent he was 'with MSI' [the Italian post-fascist party]. He appeared shouting and firing a pistol at the height of the rioting. Despite being recognisably clear in the live TV coverage, that key figure was never arrested. MSI was an integral component of the Gladio and P2 structures in Italy. Nor was any official inquiry held into the 'spontaneous' Heysel riot. No authority in Belgium formally requested one. The British football authorities failed to demand an investigation, because they had been so utterly cowed by Thatcher for her own political ends. The searing shame, on the city as well as the club, was too great.

So how did the Strategy of Tension fit the Heysel disaster? The answer lay, as usual, in the national political geography. The unusually long-running government headed by Wilfried Martens, a dependable friend of NATO, was beginning to look susceptible to elections that could sweep in the socialists on the back of the missiles crisis. This was not the time, however, to lose such a strong ally in the home town of the alliance. What the country urgently needed was a good dose of unity, and it worked. Heysel fulfilled the answer. Here was an utterly cynical diversion designed to focus the country's voters away from the missiles affair, the growing pension crisis and accelerating economic woes, and of course, the rival attractions of the Left. Stupefied Belgians — preoccupied above all with the one uniting passion that holds this fragile country together, namely the national game — could think of nothing else but the tragedy. A semi-ruined soccer stadium, close to skinhead and neo-Nazi territory, skimmed of virtually any security precautions despite a high likelihood of friction between the protagonists, came straight out of Gladio central scripting. In a country where families were mown down while doing their shopping, children tortured to death in dark cellars or chased through the woods by ravenous dogs, Heysel fitted the black landscape of designer atrocities.

As the 1980's drew on, a series of storms erupted over kickbacks involving NATO defence contracts. A general who knew of links between huge US arms firms such as Lockheed Martin, leading Belgian politicians and the Royal family, was found dead in circumstances that pointed more to murder than the official claim of suicide. A really large head rolled when Willy Claes, former foreign minister and at the time Secretary General of NATO, was toppled in a kick-backs scandal involving Italian Augusta helicopters. The attention-diverting tactics of Gladio instantly swung into play. The country reeled at the spectacle of violent attacks on armoured cash trucks by raiders armed with military bazookas, assault rifles and battering rams and — echoes from the earlier Brabant/Nivelles Gang business — random murders committed in supermarkets and parking lots. Special attention was reserved for American business symbols and installations linked to NATO. Blame was pinned on a terror group, the *Cellules Communistes Combattantes* (CCC), whose chief architect — Pierre Carette, bearing all the credentials of a convenient patsy — was eventually jailed for attacking all these standard temples. The Strategy of Tension carpet was rolled out once again.

1991 was to prove another of those years when momentous events occurred in the Gladio calendar, pointing to something extremely sinister beneath the covers of the state. André Cools, a significant figure in the vastly corrupted Walloon socialist party, and an ex-deputy premier, suddenly threatened to blow the whistle on links to secret funding and worse, implicating people in high places. He was almost immediately assassinated, in a drive-by shooting in Liège in July that year. Cools was tainted by the Italian Agusta helicopter bribes affair, and implicated in the mysterious disappearance of millions of dollar bonds supposedly in safe transit at Brussels airport. Unquestionably, Cools — a characteristically corrupted and vain Belgian politician with much to hide — was being blackmailed, and decided that if he was going down with the ship, then he would take all hands with him. The newspapers were engrossed at precisely this moment with the widely suspected links between prominent Belgian politicians and the stories of sordid sex trafficking.[58]

The Flemish newspaper *De Standaard* pitched with delight on the Walloon socialist organisation. It was portrayed as the centre-piece of a sprawling web of corruption linking big business, major banks, insurance firms and construction companies, with many ties to crime networks. What the paper could not say was how much money the party (and its leaders individually) banked directly from NATO slush funds. Cools may have intended to discuss the matter *en plein air*. Witnesses who escaped the Nihoul sadistic orgy circuit often cited Cools as a regular participant, which adds force to his statements just before his death that he was about to make some 'shocking revelations' about the Belgian mafia, and their links to some of the most important people in Liège.

By early 1997, Dutroux was practically a footnote in the scandal tearing at the foundations of the rickety state. Besides a whole range of petty criminals, secret investigations were being opened up against an ever-lengthening list of politicians, bankers, police officers, magistrates and

---

[58] In 2003, criminal proceedings that finally started in Liège muddied the waters even further. Richard Taxquet (former chauffeur and secretary to Alain van der Biest, another Parti Socialiste minister) and an Italian gangster called Giuseppe 'Pino' di Mauro were both sent down for twenty years. From the evidence that emerged, it was a contract hit job. Van der Biest, who was himself briefly held on murder charges, was unavailable to enlarge the court's knowledge, having conveniently committed suicide a year earlier.

officials in the international agencies. It was only after a number of subtle changes in the chain of command that the important work could begin, of shutting down all these dangerous inquiries in the weeks and months after Dutroux was arrested. All the powers of the establishment were set loose, including state radio and television networks, to isolate Dutroux as a one-off, isolated pervert, demolish the stories of a national sex and sadism circuit, and not least clear Nihoul of all incriminating charges. In an especially despicable episode, a young woman called Regina Louf, who came forward to testify she had seen her closest girlfriend murdered at one of Nihoul's wretched parties, was traduced by official spinners and investigating magistrates as an insane liar.[59] The police interrogating team was sacked and replaced by another, which tossed out all her charges. Another side of the same force raided a decrepit mushroom farm specified by Louf and found the dead girl's remains in exactly the circumstances she described, roped and tied so that she asphyxiated herself during excruciating torture for the amusement of onlookers. It is hard to credit a political system with the slightest perception of civilisation when it refuses to bring the perpetrators of such a horror to justice, particularly when they are known to the authorities. The innocents of a misfit country drown in the ordure of its criminalised élites. Dutroux was also present at this ghastly spectacle, according to Louf. He remained a nagging problem — too visible to assassinate, the customary remedy. He returned to the headlines a second time, having first been arrested in February 1986 and convicted two years later for the gruesome kidnapping, photographing, torturing and raping of five girls between the age of 11 and 19. Due to his intimacy with the police and previous inquiries, Dutroux was known long before that as a manipulative psychopath, devoid of morality. However, in Belgium, well-behaved convicts often serve a third, sometimes less, of already low sentences, relative to other EU states. So he was soon back on the streets. Incredibly he managed to secure a handsome state pension by convincing a government psychiatrist that his prison sentence rendered him mentally unfit for work.[N4]

When he was in trouble once again in 1996, it transpired key police officers knew he was snatching young female victims to order, who were then subjected to sadistic horrors practised in the dungeons of his slum dwellings scattered around Charleroi, or dragged around the vice circuit. But no one moved against him. As many later reports clearly established, his

---

[59] Louf: 'They took the victim to a heavily guarded house and convinced her that it was 'her' party. There would then be a great performance with masks, candles, inverted crosses, swords and animals. The only aim of these rituals was to totally disorient the victims. They plagued these kids with a load of nonsense – 'Now you are the wife of Satan" – and also gave them coke, LSD or heroin.' *De Morgen,* 10th January 1998.

largely accidental exposure tipped the Belgian establishment into a tailspin. At all costs it was essential to divert the public gaze away from the paedophile network organised around Nihoul, the ringmaster, and beam the spotlight instead on Dutroux, who would act the sacrificial scapegoat. This much became blatantly obvious as the glacial Belgian legal system dragged its heels ever more slowly. The trial was a grotesque charade. Vital evidence, especially any that pointed to Nihoul, was lost or stifled before it came to court. The initial investigating magistrate, Jean-Marc Connerotte, was feted as a national hero when he personally rescued two more kidnapped victims from Dutroux's cellars. Then, on the specious grounds of taking an informal meal with some of the victims' families, he was dismissed from the case as 'biased.' When the trial finally began and Connerotte was summoned as a material witness, he railed against the bullet-proof cars required to protect him from the vengeance of the secret state.

Despite the worldwide outcry, for almost three years the state system lost virtually all interest in Dutroux and his crimes. It turned its main attention to discrediting the annoyingly persistent Connerotte and his legal career. This required instructions from the highest quarters of the state. The authorities were playing for time, gambling that the attention span of the public would fade away, once the case and its lurid claims disappeared from the headlines. To ensure national amnesia, no less than nine crucial witnesses met violent ends.

- *François Reyskens*: in July 1995, on his way to a police appointment to present evidence concerning two of Dutroux's victims, he fell under a train.

- *Bruno Tagliaferro,* an ironmonger in Charleroi and acquaintance of Dutroux, who declared he had a compromising list of names connected to Dutroux. In November 1995, he was found dead, supposedly from a stroke. Forensic evidence indicated poison.

- His wife *Fabienne Jaupart* demanded a fresh autopsy. A little while later, her charred body was discovered on a smouldering mattress, doused with inflammable liquid.

- In August 1995, *Guy Goebels,* a police inspector investigating the deaths of two young Dutroux victims, supposedly shot himself with his service revolver.

- *Simon Poncelet*, the police inspector investigating Dutroux's car swindles, was found shot in February 1996.

- In 1996, *Anne Konjevoda* called police to say she had crucial information linking the kidnappings and the stolen car racket in Charleroi. She was never interviewed. In April 1998, her body was fished from the canal in Liège. She had been strangled.

- *Brigitte Jennart*, Nihoul's friend and personal dentist, reportedly killed herself in April 1998. Jennart was arguably among the most important of the deceased witnesses, because she intended to reveal Nihoul's involvement in deals with African asylum seekers that involved child trafficking.

- *Jean-Marc Houdmont*, another acquaintance of Marc Dutroux, died in a car crash in February 1997 en route to testify in court against Dutroux.

- And finally, *Hubert Massa,* chief prosecuting attorney of the investigation into Dutroux and the lead investigator into the 1991 murder of André Cools, 'shot himself' on 12th July 1999.

In March 2004, the German state television channel ZDF suggested that as many as 27 people with important evidence concerning the vice, blackmail and extortion rings had been killed, committed suicide or disappeared in suspicious circumstances. At a trial crowded with hundreds of reporters, Dutroux was convicted for kidnapping, the murder of two victims and manslaughter of two more (who starved in his dungeons while he was absent). At an earlier hearing, the element of farce overwhelmed the grimness of events when Dutroux, supposedly heavily guarded, 'slipped' his handcuffs in a feat of ingenuity worthy of Houdini and briefly escaped. The impression some keys belonging to warders played a role in this miracle was not lost on the media. The trial was another farce. In an unprecedented development, the jury formally protested at the presiding judge Stéphane Goux's behaviour, particularly in rushing victims' testimonies, without sufficient time for the evidence to sink in or allow for examination. Nihoul was excused all the paedophile charges and jailed solely for unrelated drug running. He was proved correct when he bawled to reporters he would never be convicted for sex trafficking. It was already public knowledge that he enjoyed protection in high places. These extended to convenient relationships with the judge investigating the Regina Louf allegations. Belgians concluded this was the end of the business and quite possibly the state itself.

Many of the figures who shuffled through the streets clad in white sheets eight long years before were unwitting extras in an act of politically inspired drama. There were many families on parade that day whose breadwinners were in the military or belonged to the vast government bureaucracy, drafted in to swell the numbers. To encourage mass attendance, the authorities ensured that railway tickets to Brussels were made available at discount fares. The hand behind the event belonged to the Belgian government itself, to all intents the intended target. The logistics of marshalling such a host called for management and propaganda skills of a high order. The clouds of white balloons and shroud-like gowns, spirited apparently from nowhere, all pointed to an organising genius in the world of public events, not to mention the borrowed tactics of the Strategy of Tension. They bore witness to the theories of calculated 'swarming' created by American behavioural psy-ops expert Gene Sharp, long-time collaborator with American espionage services. The script was written to guarantee prime time worldwide TV material, a mass optical illusion whose sole purpose was to defuse a crisis. So it turned out. Ministers solemnly trooped before the cameras, wringing their hands, declaring 'we cannot ignore such a manifestation,' which nonetheless they did, once the great rally served its intended purpose of defusing public passions.

Belgians gave up with a weary sense of futility in trying to overcome the system. The Dutroux business guttered out like a dying candle, and many worried occupants of high places breathed a sigh of relief, after more than a decade of fearing the worst. No one else was called to account. The Belgian ship of state continued its steady passage towards the rocks.

Regina Louf's evidence strikes an eerie chord with the cluster of brainwashing and extreme drug experimentation programmes clustered around the CIA's top secret MK-Ultra program. Specifically, she points to the calculated de-humanising degradation employed to reduce a child victim like herself to abject obedience, no matter how horrific the acts she was ordered to perform or watch — including, she has claimed, human sacrifice. Drugs played a significant role, along with the satanic initiation ceremonies which the victims were encouraged to regard as a game — even a grim parody of a 'birthday party.' The techniques that Louf describes indicate sophisticated forms of mental programming — otherwise known as brainwashing. MK-Ultra supposedly folded in the late 1960s, and all the incriminating documentation of maddened pseudo-science around it destroyed. But the sheer scale of depravity that overwhelmed Belgium may indicate that MK-Ultra — or some grisly nuts and bolts of it at any rate — survived as a kind of controlled experiment in a nation-sized real-life laboratory. Incredible? What is more incredible than the evidence assembled in this chapter, which is necessarily but a brief précis of the whole damning, heart-rending story of a deranged nation? In this light, the determination to discredit and destroy Regina Louf as a credible witness might acquire a far larger significance. Like the renowned Gurkhas, Belgian gendarmes may be relied upon to take few prisoners.

XIV.
If You Go Down to the Woods Today, Be Sure of a Big Surprise

'If one sets a car on fire, that is a criminal offence; if one sets hundreds of cars on fire, that is political action.' — Ulrike Meinhof

---

In the autumn of 1952, history played what seemed to be a joke in rather poor taste on the people of Germany. A story tumbled from the pages of the 9th October morning newspapers, suggesting that the Hitler Youth were back in business. The headlines reported that a secretive organisation was armed and trained with American dollars to fight a guerrilla war on German soil. A little over a month earlier, a former SS officer called Hans Otto strolled into the state police headquarters in Frankfurt, apparently to unburden himself of an unendurable sense of guilt. He explained that he was involved in nurturing an extreme Right, totally secret but state-supported formation of commandos, under the guise of an innocent-sounding youth league. The story might have ended right there, with Otto being shown the doorstep and sent on his way with consoling advice to seek expert advice. But in the Germany of 1952 — lumbered with the ruins of war and thick with former Nazis, many of whom might have access to weapons and munitions — the most senior officers on duty decided to make prudent inquiries.

The next development was expressly political. When word reached the ears of the Hessian state Prime Minister, the upright anti-Nazi Georg August Zinn, he immediately detected whiffs of born-again National Socialism. This was enough to send him racing straight to Bonn, where he created a huge commotion in the Federal Chancery, occupied at the time by Konrad Adenauer, *Der Alte Fuchs* ('the old fox'). Adenauer's first reaction was to calm the furious Zinn down, before this explosive story got into the newspapers with devastating political consequences. Adenauer was at his foxy best, although acutely exposed because he knew all about these secret soldiers, and the ex-SS resources employed to set them up and supervise their training. Zinn bore in his briefcase the *coup de grâce*, an extremely dangerous cache of papers (supplied by Hans Otto) listing prominent Social Democrats to be 'liquidated' as potentially unreliable in any conflict with the Soviets. Fifteen sheets nominated communists, but the huge offence to Social Democrats was caused by no less than eighty pages which ticked off candidates on their side. It was tantamount to saying that Germany's main party of the Left overflowed with potential traitors.

Zinn refused to be silenced, despite enormous pressure exerted by Adenauer and the US authorities in Bonn. He listened in cold silence when the American ambassador assured him unconvincingly that no such plans to 'manipulate the political climate' existed. In any event, these were rogue gangs who deserved to be shut down. It was an extraordinarily insulting lecture delivered by a foreign plenipotentiary to an important politician, moreover one with such a stout record opposing fascism. The Hessian prime minister next went to the state parliament, where he delivered a public statement on the affair. In a calm and controlled voice, Zinn laid bare the dangers of resurgent Nazism: 'It is very important to realise that such secret organisations outside all German control are the starting base for illegal domestic activities. Our people had to make this sad experience already three decades ago, and these features were also manifest within this organisation.' As they heard the deadly roll call of names proposed for elimination, agitated members gasped, 'This means killed — incredible!' Zinn sat down to a standing ovation.

In the story of Gladio, this was an exceptional day by any standards. A full 38 years before premier Giulio Andreotti's famous admission to the Italian Senate concerning NATO's secret operations on Italian soil, the exact replica had been unveiled in the German Federal Republic. Of course the NATO connection was unknown, although almost all the MP's who heard Zinn's statement suspected American involvement. Yet the same far-Right connections, political motivation and secret sources of funding had been laid bare, as surely as an expert surgeon wielding a scalpel. Hans Otto certainly sliced at one especially raw nerve during his long hours in the Frankfurt police headquarters. Evoking the spectre of the *Hitler Jugend,* he revealed how a branch of the secret army was code-named 'Technical Service of the German Youth Federation' (*Technischer Dienst Bundesdeutscher Jugend*). In time this mouthful would be known by the much shorter handle 'TD BDJ.' Otto explained that Nazi credentials were not essential to join this exclusive club, 'but most members of the organisation featured them.' This was true of the main supervising body of the secret soldiers, the *Bundesnachrichten-dienst* (the Federal Intelligence Service, plain BND for easier digestion), which positively overflowed with SS refugees. Such was the dependence on ex-Nazi networks that the stay-behind group for a time worked under the initials ORG, standing for Organisation Gehlen, the new intelligence body established in 1946 by Hitler's former spy chief on the Eastern Front, run by Nazi spy chief General Reinhard Gehlen. This fine ornament of the Nazi state became the first director of national intelligence in West Germany, due to direct pressure applied by the United States government. The 'Org' lasted as the CIA's main intelligence operation operating behind the Iron Curtain well into the Cold War, while sheltering many Nazis into the bargain. [N1]

Wherever and whenever the secret armies were unfrocked, the response of political leaders was usually to extol the virtues of men pledged to give their all to the struggle behind enemy lines. The turmoil in Hesse exposed how this patriotic aim was pushed aside in favour of deadly paramilitary activity and state executions. Those are precisely the reasons Otto gave for turning informer. It was left to the TD BJD commandant — the wiry former *Luftwaffe* crack 'night hunter' wing commander Erhard Peters — to eviscerate what remained of 'staying behind.' He declared that his men intended to beat a smart retreat rather than face being overrun by the Soviets.

American diplomats found themselves trapped on the roasting spit. Despite the earlier blank denials by US diplomats stationed in Germany, nagging American journalists who followed up the German headlines extracted a partial confession which stood everything the saintly Zinn had been told on its head. The *New York Times* declared: 'Authoritative officials [code: Pentagon/CIA] privately confirmed today that the United States had sponsored and helped finance the secret training of young Germans, including many former soldiers, to become guerrilla fighters in the event of a war with the Soviet Union.' *The Times* was not taken in by this bald cover-up, informing its readers how many active socialists, including government ministers, were on the list of summary executions by the secret army in the event of hostilities. Even as headline power slowly waned, Zinn promised the Hessian deputies he would uproot this poisonous plant. But he deceived them, and regrettably himself. Greater forces than the premier of a modest German federal state were at work. Zinn's energies dissipated when the main leadership of TD BJD, rounded up by the Hessian state police, were detained for a short incarceration, then let off on direct instructions from the Chancellery in Bonn.

The picture of a secret state crawling with unreconstructed Nazis eager to usher Left-wing politicians in front of firing squads could not have appeared at a more inopportune moment. The United States had run into formidable headwinds with its flagship project to lever West Germany into NATO. Talk of successful de-Nazification was shattered by Otto's revelations, leading to the widespread conviction, particularly in countries which had felt the Nazi heel, that Germany needed a good deal more recovery time in the political sanatorium. Otto's exposures represented a major set-back in building the case for inclusion in NATO. Germany was revealed as honouring members of the former regime to such an extent that they were operating the levers of power in the highest places.

In May 1955, Germany was finally introduced as a paid-up member of the NATO camp. A high-level pact was immediately concluded between the German and US governments, in which it was agreed there would be no legal persecution of former Nazis connected with the secret armies. *Der Alte*

Fuchs signed it willingly enough. After all, Hans Globke — the prominent Nazi jurist who helped formulate the 1935 anti-Jewish 'German blood and honour' laws, was one of the most important ex-Nazis in the State Chancellery. He was sitting just along the corridor from Adenauer's personal suite as National Security Adviser. General Erich von Manstein, convicted war criminal and favoured poodle of NATO, was the Chancellor's chief political adviser. Yet the truly insidious aspect about this keep-out-of-jail contract was the blanket immunity it conferred for any act the German secret soldiers performed on behalf of their ultimate masters in the North Atlantic Alliance.

The ongoing re-militarisation of Germany, which followed hard on admission to NATO, led to a general sense of *Angst* among Germans of all social groups and persuasions. It was not merely the echoes of imperialism derived from Bismarck, Kaiser Wilhelm and Hitler. Seeing the ruins of war all around them, Germans felt they were being elbowed into the front line of a confrontation they would prefer to avoid. It was plain that America's obsession with securing German forces under NATO command was intended to disguise the conversion of Germany into a front-line armed camp. If this was supposed to mean peace and security, then a rising generation of young intellectuals profoundly disagreed. In 1966, the creation of the grand Left-Right ruling coalition reduced federal politics to a virtual one-party state. It reminded these increasingly angry youngsters of the years of drift during the Weimar Republic, that unsettled period which ended in usurpation by the Nazis. They decided to shock Germans out of their apathy.

In 1970, Andreas Baader and Ulrike Meinhof formed the *Rote Armee Fraktion* — the Red Army Faction — popularly better known as the Baader-Meinhof gang. The founders included Gudrun Ensslin and Horst Mahler, who between them composed the royal family of the RAF. Three years later, the *Revolutionäre Zellen* — Revolutionary Cells, or RZ — began a twenty-year campaign from a different position in the extra-parliamentary politics of protest. The Revolutionary Cells were markedly anti-Semitic and closer to anarchism, compared to the Bolshevik-type of underground structure favoured by the RAF. Both viewed post-war German corporatism as little more than an extension of National Socialism conducted beneath the Stars and Stripes. Curiously the RZ was far more active and more violent than the Red Army Faction. Yet its leaders never attracted — nor apparently sought — the glamorous worldwide rock star profile of the Baader-Meinhof Gang. However, RZ's actual orientation may not have been quite so straight-forward, as we discover later.

The extent to which the RAF connected to the anti-establishment *Angst* drenching Germany of the 1960s and '70s was underlined by the vast numbers of the ordinary public who thronged to their funerals. Perhaps few who thus paid their respects shared any close affinity with the 'armed struggle,' or for that matter Marxism. Setting aside the *verboten* allure that inevitably travels with foredoomed martyrdom, the underlying message dramatised the huge social gulf in German society. As Horst Mahler subsequently explained, the RAF adopted shock tactics precisely to invite a draconian response, because that would expose the German state's essentially unconstructed fascist nature. The ponderous Left, typified by its leader Helmut Schmidt, a dour and deeply conservative figure who dominated German politics between 1974 and 1982, had failed miserably in delivering promised social adjustments and reforms. Germany remained at heart the same largely unaltered corporate structure inherited from the National Socialist system. The middle classes, who in earlier times had flocked to Adolf Hitler, found themselves equally disappointed with the main party of the Right, the Christian Democrats. Prosperity was certainly returning to Germany. The motors of the economy were humming once again. Yet the new Germany seemed soulless and directionless, if anything a watered-down version of National Socialism. Across all social boundaries, West Germany's sensitivity about her recent past suggested the avoidance of militaristic, confrontationist foreign policies. Public resistance ensured there would be no German armed contribution to the Vietnam War, despite enormous political pressure from the United States. The prospect of German military forces under NATO command disturbed the public imagination. Germany had been routed in two mighty conflicts, emerging from both with an odorous reputation at the price of huge damage and massive population and territorial loss. Now she was back in the front line against a powerful recent adversary. In this landscape appeared intelligent and well-educated youngsters drawn to the bullet and the bomb. The RAF was in propitious territory. As one social commentary suggested:

> *Against the odds, there followed an impressive dynamic, whereby RAF prisoners' struggle for survival behind bars — resisting isolation torture, sensory deprivation, and legal attacks on their lawyers — would repeatedly succeed in rallying support on the outside, even inspiring new waves of activists to cross into the underground, and renew the organisation.*

The late Bernd Eichinger — producer of the Academy-nominated 2008 movie drama based on the book written by Stefan Aust, former editor-in-chief of *Der Spiegel* — pointed to the glamorous appeal of terrorist chic. 'Andreas Baader and Gudrun Ensslin had a real sense of style and pose — the fast cars, the clothes, the hair, the sunglasses... all that was very deliberate and it worked. They were like political rock stars. Apart from anything else, they had great sex appeal. We had to show that in order to convey why people were mesmerised by them.'

The psychological element lay with the duplicity of the authorities in milking the popular appeal of 'boutique terror chic' for their own ends. As we have seen, the mimicking of violent protest organisations was a common stripe of Gladio right across Europe. Germany's very own Red Army proved no exception. Yves Guérin-Sérac, the Frenchman who wrote the manuals of Gladio terrorism, laid special emphasis on infiltrating movements organised in the name of social protest, with the object to manipulate their direction and tactics. The RAF's leadership was acutely aware of the potential for stowaways. During a group sojourn by the founders at a PLO training camp in Jordan in 1970, suspicion fell on one participant, Peter Homann. He was threatened on the spot with a death sentence, accused as a spy. Homann drummed himself out of the RAF shortly afterwards.[N2]

Guérin-Sérac taught the clever ploy of intercepting plans for terrorist attacks and then allowing those events to happen. The authorities would then reap the propaganda benefits in terms of social persuasion. The destruction of the communist party in Italy in the wake of the Aldo Moro affair in 1978 was the classic example. But first Germany led the way with a remarkably similar demonstration that bore strange overtones of a rehearsal. The political prizes of a sensational episode were attractive. It ended with the elimination of the core RAF royal family. It also marked the steady slide of federal Germany into a reflection of the pre-war national security state.

During what became known as the 'Long Autumn' of 1977, the abduction and murder of a prominent symbol of German capitalism, and the virtual state of national siege that followed, marked the climax of the first RAF insurgency. The Schmidt government acted with iron resolve, imposing the first state of emergency since the war. Germans experienced a draconian crackdown on civil liberties, and news management techniques of *Nineteen Eighty-Four*. The trigger was the kidnapping on 5th September 1977 of Hanns-Martin Schleyer, beerishly corpulent doyen of post-war German capitalism, who stepped into his fateful role in history as the all-too perfect target for the RAF. The date, probably by no co-incidence, also marked the massacre of Israeli athletes and officials at the Munich Olympic Games five years earlier. The *New York Times* described this former middle-ranking SS officer who rose to the upper ranks of German big business, the Employers' Federation and the Federation of German Industry, as the exact 'caricature of an ugly capitalist.' Indeed, as the German media speculated, he was the No. 1 candidate likely to earn the attentions of the RAF.

The indicators leading up to the kidnap could not have been more obvious. Dr. Schleyer was under 24-hour security surveillance as an ideal RAF target. Yet no one appeared to notice that he was closely shadowed by the RAF's usual pre-strike reconnaissance squad. In one of his recordings, he pointed to the obvious by insisting that the authorities 'had made it very easy' for him to be kidnapped. This is one of the most important remarks that he made before he was shot to death in a French forest. Schleyer died with the conviction that his fate had been at least partially ordained by the state.

There was certainly an uncanny resemblance to a practice run for the Aldo Moro tragedy a year later. The distinctive shared features included a bloody assault on security guards, protracted manhunts, and regular parading of the victims before revolutionary banners (the staged Moro and Schleyer poses were, curiously, virtually identical). Ostensibly the snatch was staged in order to force the release of the RAF high command — Baader, his girl friend Gudrun Ensslin, Ulrike Meinhof, Irmgard Müller and Jan-Carl Rapse, all held in the fortress-like Stammheim maximum security jail near Stuttgart. During 44 days in captivity, the kidnap victim was shifted from one safe house to another in three different countries, Germany, Netherlands and Belgium. In itself this was a remarkable feat, despite all the heat of a great Interpol hunt. Schleyer was finally killed in a wood near Mulhouse in eastern France on the morning of 18th October 1977, with three execution shots to the back of his head. Aldo Moro had been shot ten times, after 54 days as a hostage. Both murders bore the same clear blueprint, exquisitely prolonged to cultivate maximum impact on public opinion and reap the desired political harvest. This was the standard feature of the Strategy of Tension.

In the 2008 revised introduction to his book, Stefan Aust — who knew Ulrike Meinhof well in her pre-RAF days — pointed to another curious parallel with Moro. Namely, 'how a massive failure of the police operation meant that Schleyer was not freed, despite the fact that less than 48 hours after the kidnapping there were concrete clues to his first hiding place.' What Aust described as a 'massive failure' was nothing of the kind. The authorities knew all along that Schleyer was to be kidnapped, and where. What followed was the deliberate dragging of feet. Schleyer was first taken to an apartment in the pretty riverside town of Erftstadt, which is about 20 kilometres from Cologne and close to the kidnap location.[60]

From the outset, Hanns-Martin Schleyer was a doomed sacrifice. In a few compressed hours, it became apparent how disinterested the authorities were in expert police work in order to locate and still less, release him. The local police had already intercepted reports of suspicious activity at an apartment building not far from the kidnap site. Witnesses later said they had given the

---

[60] Stefan Aust is regarded as a leading choreographer of the suicide pact proposition. Yet readers of the latest edition of his *The Baader-Meinhof Complex* may not feel the thesis of state murder has been entirely discredited. The bank of forensic evidence listed by Aust in support of the conspiracy explanation is more convincing than his own dismissals, which are rather weak and contrived, to this reader at any rate. RAF sympathisers attacked Aust's home with red paint to mark the first screening of Eichinger's film version of *The Baader-Meinhof Complex*.

police the numbers of vehicles that seemed strange in the neighbourhood. One resident even questioned one of the kidnappers, and described the blue child's perambulator that was used as a decoy device in the attack in Schleyer's Volkswagen limousine. The witness thought this strange, because there were no children in the apartment the new tenants had just rented. Surveillance of Dr. Schleyer by the terrorist planning team was never spotted by the authorities, least of all by his supposedly expert protection team.

Acting on an old-fashioned hunch, the local police superintendent fixed on the specific apartment block precisely because it was close to the location where Schleyer was snatched. Glancing through statements by local residents concerning suspicious activity, he pored over recent switches in tenancies. The customary precise German records indicated new people moving into the apartment where, it was later confirmed, Schleyer had been initially held. He concluded the kidnappers would avoid an immediate long-distance haul of their precious captive for fear of running into roadblocks. This unsung detective was right on all counts. At one point he even rang the bell of the very door behind which Schleyer held his breath, a gun pointed at his head by his sole nervous minder ('one noise and we both go together').

Conclusion: in the early hours of the kidnap, the authorities had all the information they required to storm the suspect apartment. Why, then, no swift action? The local police assumed that having passed their suspicions upstairs, either the BKA (federal investigation co-ordinators) or GSG-9, the select federal anti-terrorist squad, would immediately step in. Instead, the responsible authorities appeared to make haste at tortoise pace. 'Crisis groups' were assembled by the federal government, exactly like the crisis committee the Italian government formed in the wake of the Moro kidnap. The German government appeared paralysed or, more probably, self-paralysed in these early days. This was another striking parallel with the torment of Aldo Moro.

The objective, from the proclaimed perspective of the RAF, was to free the leadership held in the ominous grey block at Stammheim. The seventh floor contained a specially-built pen to contain political prisoners. Instead, the authorities played out the drama in an extended cat and mouse game, toying with Schleyer's captors on the terms of a swap for the incarcerated leadership. In retrospect, we can detect the Strategy of Tension in high profile, since the German government had another objective altogether in prolonging Schleyer's agony. The leadership of the RAF, the government's own toxic hostages, were dangerously iconic crowd pullers, rapidly evolving into folk heroes (as posthumously, they became and remain). The erotic chemistry of violence and explicit sensuality swirling around Baader, his lover the vampish Gudrun Ensslin and the sexually smouldering Ulrike Meinhof, ignited public opinion bordering on a passionate sense of drama and forbidden romance. A poll conducted in the spring of 1977 gauged that almost half the population regarded the gang's deeds as politically motivated rather than criminal. Unquestionably, the massed procession of hooded mourners who attended Meinhof's funeral, following her reported suicide in the Stammheim jail in May that year, thoroughly rattled the establishment power structure. Against this hypnotic allure, it appeared increasingly likely that long-term confinement and possibly even release of the core commanders at some future date was becoming unthinkable. The unfortunate Schleyer was now a pawn in this much wider drama. That is why his captors were allowed to quietly slip away from the apartment in Erftstadt. To cover their own tracks, the government virtually closed down the media. In the light of the extraordinary cover-up now in progress, this was perfectly logical.

Certainly, every German government then and since has maintained a strict wall of silence around all events in the early days and hours of the kidnap. The impression that Schleyer was intended all along as the sacrificial victim to provoke the final solution concerning the RAF leadership cadre is too strong to put aside. It is now known that inside their supposedly impenetrable maximum security penitentiary, Baader and Co clandestinely assembled an intricate internal communication system, which also tapped national broadcasting channels. They achieved this with the aid of materials smuggled under the noses, or with the connivance of their guards. Conveniently, they were in touch with external events. This would be turned against them.

Schmidt's government would later claim that a failed PLO rescue mission was a significant factor in the decision of the core commanders to kill themselves. In October 1977, PLO hijackers seized a Lufthansa airliner carrying German holidaymakers en route from Majorca to Frankfurt. The release of the imprisoned RAF leadership was the price of freeing the passengers. The plane eventually landed at Mogadishu in Somalia, after touching down in several Middle Eastern states for fuel and supplies. The captain, Jürgen Schumann, was murdered in Aden. The German government made a pretence at negotiations. Then, on the night of 17th-18th October the crack GSG-9 anti-terrorist squad, backed up by the British SAS, stormed the plane and freed the hostages. It was all over in a quarter of an hour. Mogadishu was notable as Germany's first overseas military mission since WW2. On 18th October, Hanns-Martin Schleyer was murdered. The German government later claimed that this time frame explained how the RAF leadership gave up all hope of rescue and decided to jointly end their lives. The prisoners in Stammheim learned on their smuggled radio equipment that the PLO mission had failed and that Schleyer was dead. They supposedly conferred through their secret internal communications network and arranged a suicide pact. This unlikely storyline was indignantly denied by the lone survivor, Irmgard Möller. She recovered from serious stab wounds that she furiously insisted were not self-inflicted, as alleged. On the contrary, at her own word, she was drugged and then attacked by infiltrators.

Cui bono? It was not a difficult calculation by the incumbent German government that keeping the RAF captives alive for the long term might prove excessively costly in terms of political capital. The same view could be adopted by politicians who in future might find themselves inheriting the problem. Helmut Schmidt's government had all the information that it needed — including the snooping of nosey neighbours in Erftstadt — to squash the Schleyer kidnap within hours. Likewise it is probable, although it cannot be proved, that the authorities had intercepted the Lufthansa hijacking before it happened. Be that as it may, the successful storming of the jet, the death of Hanns-Martin Schleyer and the suicide pact of the RAF commanders, all compressed into a few hours, seem to stretch the boundaries of co-incidence too far.

The rushed official investigations had no purpose other than to whitewash the night of the long knives at Stammheim. Crucial ballistic evidence assembled by Dr. Roland Hoffman — chief scientific adviser to the Federal Criminal Investigation Office — was either ignored or elbowed aside altogether. First by the investigation office itself and then by a 'commission of inquiry,' whose activities were distinguished only by indecent haste. Dr. Hoffman was unable to find any convincing proof that would support the official suicide account. Stefan Aust himself writes: 'The Public Prosecutor's report is all of sixteen pages long... it does not say a word about discrepancies in the findings.'[61] Not solely German but world public opinion recoiled from the pat explanation that Baader and his colleagues killed themselves. The finger of suspicion pointed to judicial murder.

The choreography of this 'war of six against sixty million' was unmistakable.[N3] Schmidt's solemn television sermons, millions of handbills with blurry, black-and-white mug shots of fugitive RAF terrorists, and streets crawling with police caused Germans in all walks to shudder at chilling memories from the past. The violence, to some extent, encouraged ordinary Germans to support the Schmidt government's 'drain the swamp' methods to crush the militants and their networks. But the mood turned to unease when the authorities were accused of widespread illegal wiretapping and abuse of prisoners, beset with rumours of murder.[62]

---

[61] A summary of the order of fatalities can be found at Endnote 5[N4] and difficulties raised by Dr. Hoffman concerning the exact proof of suicide, at Endnote 6.[N5]

[62] Yet at the same time Professor Zygmunt Bauman reminds us in his book *Liquid Times* (Polity Press, reprinted 2011) that worries over terrorism rose from 6% to more than 60% during the peak period of RAF activity. This is the natural

West Germany's frail democracy quaked at these unsettling images of police swoops on individuals and private homes with all the chilling overtones of a political vendetta. The comparison with the well-known Stasi police state in the eastern rump of the country was more than disturbing. The government's stated intention was to shut off oxygen supplies to the underground's support systems. But in practice, this took the form of a crackdown verging on the paranoid. SWAT teams pounced on anyone in public places sporting hippie stigmata like knotted hair or patched jeans, and picked up known radicals without charges. Strong-arm squads went about roughing up squatters, invading private gatherings and hassling people belonging to non-violent radical movements. There was a distasteful odour of social cleansing in a country with a difficult legacy on this subject. And it was the same blacklist mentality that enraged premier Zinn thirty years before, that *all* Leftists were potential enemies of the state.

This unconstitutional war on anyone or anything displaying a pink tinge sat uncomfortably with many Social Democrats, but such was the air of crisis few dared to speak up. If Schmidt expected to reap a harvest for his tough line, he was disappointed. At the 1980 election, the Social Democrats were hammered. They clung on, but the coalition with the Liberals disintegrated. There were those who spoke of the Revenge of Stammheim.

The notion that the RAF was nothing more than a creation of western intelligence is too trite to be taken seriously. That it was expertly infiltrated and manipulated, according to the manuals of Yves Guérin-Sérac, is another calculation altogether. The Schleyer affair is a perfect illustration. When Schmidt met Schleyer's widow, Waltrude, to solemnly commiserate on her husband's death, he did so knowing that the German state as much as the RAF had consigned her husband to his fate. It may also be argued that Stefan Aust isolates the RAF and especially the Baader-Meinhof component as a specific social phenomenon, choked with internal personality tangles. This leaves the essential wider issues of their original motivation largely unresolved. The one concise remark that came closest to answering the equation was made by the social protest analyst Dr. Raphael Schlembach: 'They were slightly mad, slightly cool — but the ideological conversion from lefty students to an armed struggle organisation remains an enigma.'

The violence and the political counter-assault punctuated a period of rising tensions with the Soviet Union, typified by the Soviet invasion of Afghanistan in December 1979. The sharp end of the anti-NATO coalition, which in essence the RAF represented, led to major protests against the stationing of ground-launched cruise missiles on German soil. Many

---

consequence of what the professor himself describes as 'the strategy of fear.' The German authorities duly reaped the harvest.

Germans of all shades of opinion did indeed share the view that as the principal, frontline state facing the Warsaw Pact countries, Germany was taking a dangerously provocative line. The sense of fear was dramatised by the draconian culls of civil liberties introduced by Schmidt during the Long Autumn of 1977. In retrospect we can recognise all the signs of forging a synthetic revolutionary mood. The naturally authoritarian Schmidt (in passing, a perfect daguerreotype of Tony Blair)[63] exploited the slaying of Schleyer to instil a psychological mood against compromise with the Soviets Union. This occurred amid a general shift on the mainstream German Left towards the Reagan-Thatcher axis, based on the rhetoric of the Evil Empire.

That the German secret state in all likelihood infiltrated the RAF and manipulated its activities is only remarkable in the context that it has been ignored for so long. In late September 1980, just a week before the country was due to go the polls to choose a new government, Germans were stunned by the worst atrocity since the murder of eleven Israeli athletes at the summer Olympics held in Munich eight years before. Again Munich was the chosen target. The victims were fun seekers at the annual Bacchanalian swill known as the *Oktoberfest*. The huge bomb, almost two kilos of high explosive, threw a ghastly pall over Germany's biggest annual party for years to come, a deadly blow at the psyche of a nation and one of its most sacred rites. Thirteen people died and 219 were injured; 70 were badly maimed. No claims were made by the usual suspects, the RAF. The assumption that Leftist radicals were behind this senseless act of savagery was simply allowed to take hold in the public mind as millions prepared to vote. There was an unmistakable symbolism of a massacre in the very city where the famous Beer Hall Putsch of November 1923 established Hitler on the ladder to power.

Munich was a classically engineered exercise in synthetic terror, planned in the deep state and carried out by neofascists, timed to influence the outcome of the approaching general election. But the real significance of the Oktoberfest blast was the trail which led through the dark undergrowth of unextinguished German fascism, to the secret army and onwards to NATO. The day after the bombing, police hauled in several members of a neo-Nazi club called *Wehrsportgruppe Hoffman*, who immediately began to sing an astonishing, if selectively correct, tale. The *plastique* used for the bomb was supplied from a secret arms dump concealed in a forest. There were sufficient weapons and munitions to arm several brigades. The canaries

---

[63] This is not the only curious co-incidence. Schmidt's re-orientation of the German socialist party on the Right flank of politics preceded Blair's designer movement called New Labour, which absorbed or consumed the old working-class socialist movement in the UK. This is a distinctly Hegelian manoeuvre, which is now being repeated as the United States moves inexorably towards a one-party system.

explained they were led to the wood by a forest ranger called Heinz Lembke, whom they pretended otherwise not to know. In a matter-of-fact fashion, so they claimed, this humble woodsman explained he was training 'volunteers' to shoot people and blow things up.

Lembke had an interesting career. He spent some years in the German Democratic Republic (GDR) and then joined the BVJ (*Bund Vaterländischer Jugend*), the born-again version of the Hitler Youth. The BVJ functioned as an arm of the German Gladio outfit. The industrious Herr Lembke was also a commander of the *Wehrsportübungen,* the label for about half a dozen Nazi groups hiding behind innocent-sounding sports clubs, whose gambols in the woods disguised paramilitary manoeuvres.[64] Lembke, a puffy-faced, chinless figure, another 'idealistic and fanatical fascist,' clearly belonged with his natural comrades like Yves Guérin-Sérac, Stefano Delle Chiaie and Francesco Gullino in the European neofascist galaxy.

A *Polizei* posse was duly despatched to the wood at Uelzen, a small town bordering the NATO training ground near Lüneburg Heath ('the biggest parade ground in Europe'), where fabulous stores of NATO-mint weaponry were found. These included such choice items as fifty anti-tank bazookas, 156 kilos of high explosive (of exactly the type used in the Oktoberfest bombing), hundreds of hand grenades and for the last resort, an impressive stockpile of ingredients to pack chemical weapons. The men of the *Wehrsportgruppe* indicated they were free to stroll in and select items from what was clearly a Gladio stay-behind arms dump, to which Lembke, among others, held the keys. Once again, the case was acutely political, the suspect parties falling within the ancient secret protocols to spare NATO's ex-Nazis from all persecutions. Lembke was a link in a chain that led to high places in Bonn.

Gundolf Köhler, the patsy who blew himself up in the Oktoberfest outrage, was a young student renowned for rather anti-social leanings. He was a member of the neo-Nazi *Wehrsportsgruppe Hoffman*, who presumably supplied him with the explosives that he purportedly dumped in a trash

---

[64] His 'commanding officer' in the Hoffman Brigade of the Sports Group was its chief patron, Karl-Heinz Hoffman, a known extremist who thought of himself as the reincarnation of Hitler. In January 1980, Gerhart Baum, the Federal Interior Minister, unhesitatingly banned the *Wehrsportgruppe Hoffmann* as anti-constitutional. Hoffman appealed to the Central Administrative Court in Berlin, which overturned the ban in December the same year, although the Hoffman unit was under suspicion for complicity in the Oktoberfest bombing. Clearly the famous Gladio immunity clause of yore was still in good working order.

basket.[65] Whether due to inexperience or design, the bomb exploded prematurely. The Hoffman connection was never pursued by the police. A scandal now existed of sufficient power to blow the Schmidt government to smithereens, like the unfortunates at the Theresienwiese fairground. The situation further deteriorated when Lembke was arrested and taken in for questioning. Here was an individual positively thrumming with radioactivity on the political Geiger counter. He knew exactly who gave the orders for the Oktoberfest bombing. This in turn led to the dangerous question of how much of the violence laid at the door of the Red Army Faction had its authorship in the secret German Gladio state. The indications of Guérin-Sérac style 'steering' emerged from the claims of another — although quite possibly equivocal — witness called Frank Lauterjung, who supplied the police with first-hand accounts of the devastation. However, he was subsequently revealed as holding senior positions in the *Bund Heimattreuer Jugend* (BHJ, otherwise *Der Freibund*), which is often accused of holding sympathies with the Far Right. According to the magazine *Der Spiegel*, Lauterjung — who died of heart failure in 1982 — was the movement's deputy commander. Some BHJ officials aired their suspicions that Lauterjung was an interloper working for the German state intelligence BND. Most of the evidence to posthumously convict Köhler rested on Lauterjung's statements. In 1997, the case was effectively closed, and all the evidence painstakingly assembled by a special inquiry department destroyed.

But there was a good deal more in terms of seismic threats. Should Lembke turn *pentito*, how much might he say about the secret tunnels between the West German state and the Eastern one, particularly in the crazily-paved world of espionage, the 'game of foxes'?

Forstmeister Lembke's earthly tenure ended shortly after his arrest. He was found hanged in his cell on the morning of 1st November 1981, the Day of the Dead. Thanks to yet another timely suicide, he was now the missing link in a necklace of dangerous connections. No one was convicted for the Oktoberfest massacre. The worst terrorist blast in post-war German history lay on the books unsolved, permanently. Schmidt picked up the tailwind of shock and rage blowing from Munich, and got the mandate he sought. Centre of the road liberals did well, too.

Both the Stasi and BND were thoroughly rooted in the same Gestapo background, and spooks on both sides of the east-west divide often shared common bonds from their pre-war Nazi heritage. When the former parachutist Norbert Juretzko revealed that the stay-behind network he created

---

[65] Other probably more accurate accounts state the explosives were packed into a fire extinguisher. This accounts for eye-witness accounts of a suspicious figure carrying a heavy, cylindrical object that he seemed to be manipulating.

for the BND in the late 1940s was immediately betrayed 'one hundred per cent' to the Stasi, few eyebrows were raised.[9] Then came the embarrassing episode of the late Otto John. He was a fervent anti-Nazi who famously tried to kill Hitler in July 1944. He was elevated to head of the 'Office for the Protection of the Constitution,' the *Bundesamt für Verfassungsschutz* or BfV. On 20th July 1954 — the anniversary of the Bomb Plot against Hitler — he vanished, surfacing two weeks later in the GDR. From there he railed at Konrad Adenauer's surrender to American militarism, and the incorporation of West Germany into NATO. The affair remains one of the most intriguing unresolved Cold War mysteries. John later insisted he was kidnapped by the KGB, but when he finally got home he was jailed for treason just the same. A tidy conclusion remains elusive. In 1944, after the Bomb Plot failed, John managed to escape to England, where he worked for the BBC German Language Service. Undoubtedly he was a prize catch for Allied intelligence; reputedly, Churchill once spent half the night talking to him. When he decamped he was written off as a worn-out alcoholic and womaniser. One is reminded of le Carré's anti-hero Peter Guillam, the central character in *The Spy Who Came in from the Cold*. He adopts the cloak of a worn-out rake to bait the trap for East Germany's most efficient superspy. Was Otto John cast in the same mould? When he re-surfaced in the Federal Republic, the spin machine set to work dismissing him as a confabulator under the strain of mental illness. What should never be forgotten is that in his role as chief of the BfV, he was the leading minder of the German Gladio set-up.

Nothing could be more dismissive than spywriter Erich Schmidt-Eenboom's description of the BfV all through the Cold War years as a 'kind of Disneyland-Gestapo operation riddled with moles.' Perhaps that might explain the ease with which prominent Red Army Faction members, including Baader and Meinhof, were able to flit in and out of the GDR, on at least one occasion flying from Schönefeld airport for a working sabbatical with the PLO. Some authorities such as the journalist Jens Mecklenburg offer a more sinister explanation. If the East Germans and the Stasi in particular were directly manipulating the RAF and its various proxy mimics, was the double-cross tactic known as 'just let it happen' in play — with a vengeance? The famous Entebbe Raid may well fit the picture, as we see in a moment.

The few voices raised against the red-baiting witch hunt were accused (as they are now) of being 'soft on terror.' In 1990, we find Hermann Scheer, defence spokesman for the opposition Social Democrats, talking as if he were the long-dead Zinn and the events in Hesse occurred the previous day. Scheer raised the spectre of a 'Ku Klux Klan,' a Right-wing political network bearing a deadly peacetime motivation. Then he really rattled the roof-timbers. He went on to demand German prosecutors should probe the existence of an 'armed secret military organisation....which must be prosecuted according to the criminal law.' But he fell instantly silent when taken aside and quietly informed that the socialists, when they were in government, were involved in the same 'cover-up that effaces the traces' which decorated his speeches. A few brave journalists nonetheless raised the stark parallels between this new Big Brother *Sicherheitsstaat* (security state) and the former one established by the Nazis. Scheer's Ku Klux Klan was, of course, the German Gladio operation, and dredging it up in connection with the Hanns-Martin Schleyer affair amounted to political provocation of a very high grade.

Schmidt, as so often before, was out of step with much of his party, siding with the increasingly strident anti-Russian tone of American policy. Anti-American foaming on the radical Left, throughout Europe and especially in Germany, was certainly growing more alarming in Washington and NATO. It seemed as though German public opinion was going soft just as the Cold War moved to a decisive phase. The need to retain a firm and dependable captain with a steely grip on the German tiller of state became increasingly urgent.

Professor Wolfgang Kraushaar of the Hamburg Institute for Social Research, one of the leading students of German protest movements, makes the telling point that active membership of the RAF was greatly over-estimated. In any event, matters were confused by its proxy function for other, ideologically aligned groups, or their imitators, to maintain the ever-present spectre of urban terror. When all the RAF soldiers of honour, as they saw themselves, were either under lock and key or silent in their graves, the violence, apparently subcontracted or franchised to other hands, went on.

The Red Army Faction, under different leaders, was officially still in the field. Jens Mecklenburg argues that the dark magic and theatrical power that magnetised the old Baader-Meinhof cell was curiously lacking under the replacement commanders. There was an impression of systematic deception of the public to keep the RAF phantom alive, as one great captain of industry after another went down in a hail of bullets. Icons of German business, supposedly granted the finest security protection, were murdered with impunity, even in their own homes, surrounded by swarms of armed guards. Killers and bombers enjoyed extraordinary immunity from arrest, even where they were under round-the-clock surveillance. The chief of the official prosecution office openly accused Helmut Schmidt and his government of blatant collusion with terrorists. In the stiff world of German bureaucracy, this is very hot talk indeed. Among the prominent victims in this so-called 'continuation period' was Detlev Karsten Rohwedder, a prominent social democrat and director of the controversial *Treuhandanstalt* agency, set up to sell former state assets in the ex-GDR. He was shot in April 1991 by a sniper as he stood at the window of his supposedly well-guarded house in Düsseldorf. The killer, who was positioned only 60 or so meters (approximately 190 feet) away, fired 7.62 rounds commonly employed by NATO armies. Wolfgang Grams, a fringe associate of the RAF leadership, was inconclusively blamed. He in turn was killed in 1993, in a mysterious shooting incident at a railway station in northern Germany. It was almost the end of the century when a faint whimper was eventually heard from the Rote Armee Fraktion, announcing its formal dissolution.

The important question is this. Who directed the mission in the 'continuation period' of the RAF, after the elimination of the Baader-Meinhof founders? Perhaps the best clue lies in political background of the times. The slow melting of the Cold Front between East and West was marked by the arrival of Mikhail Gorbachev, with his seductive messages of *perestroika* and *glasnost*. This soothing Pied Piper from the East was having a huge — and to Washington and NATO, wholly detrimental — impact on German and European public opinion. Cohabitation with a softer version of the USSR might pose the awkward question that NATO's sole task (to deter the Soviets from attacking the West) had fallen by the wayside. No bogey, no threat, *ergo* mission accomplished, the Alliance folds its tents. The bogus coup of August 1991 against Mikhail Gorbachev effectively drew a line under this period of uncertainty. So was it entirely co-coincidental that the armed struggle in Germany ended with an armistice, in the precise moment Gorbachev cemented his hold on power? Jan Mecklenburg's thesis is appealing: a public relations-propaganda war that reached a natural conclusion with the close of an epoch in the Soviet camp.

In August 1994, the Bavarian *Landeskriminalamt* (provincial investigative police) seized a suitcase belonging to a Colombian passenger off-loaded from Lufthansa Airline Flight 3369, just arrived from Moscow at Munich's Franz Jozef Strauss Airport. It was found to contain 363.4 grams of Plutonium-239, one of the major elements in the nuclear fuel cycle. German security authorities swiftly claimed smart detective work and careful co-ordination had uncovered an international criminal network of nuclear trafficking, drawing on suppliers in the CIS and potential buyers among terrorist networks and dictatorships from Asia to North Africa. Bernd Schmidbauer, minister in charge of coordinating intelligence services, raised the temperature higher by suggesting the materials might be destined for a North Korean bomb. The spectacular arrest of the Colombian and two Spanish accomplices waiting at the airport indeed appeared to be a triumph for the BND, the hand behind the scenes, except to suspicious reporters who soon began to nose out an alternative version. This suggested the entire operation was a false-flag sting performed by German intelligence, the materials supplied by the agency itself to three generously bribed patsies.

In March 1995, the weekly *Der Spiegel* charged the BND with 'abetting serious crime, endangering human lives, lying to the public and dangerously gambling with foreign policy.' SDP leader Rudolf Scharping told the magazine the Munich heist was probably intended to force the Federal Parliament to extend the legal powers of the BND. Almost exactly a year later, his words bore fruit. The BND was indeed granted unique powers to control crime inside German borders for the first time. The spooks were now on solid political ground. Two months after the Munich sting, the two Right-wing Christian parties — CDU and its sister in Bavaria, the CSU — swept to a triumph in the Federal and Bavarian state elections, campaigning on a law-and-order platform hitched to the nuclear smuggling episode. As for the accused, the authorities accepted they were enticed to commit the crime, while noting the absence of evidence demonstrating the involvement of any buyer other than the BND. In July 1995, the Munich District Court awarded minimal sentences to the three confessed smugglers. The trusty Gladio absolution dating back to Konrad Adenauer thrust to the fore again.[N6]

It remains to briefly examine the curious history of the Revolutionary Cells (RZ). Although they were held responsible for almost 200 bombings and shootings between 1973 and 1995, they were entirely overshadowed by the RAF, bar one spectacular incident which captured the imagination of the world, being milked for all it was worth by the Hollywood propaganda factory. On 4th July 1976 (the 200th anniversary of the American declaration of independence), an Air France Airbus en route from Tel Aviv to Paris was hijacked shortly after a stop-over in Athens, allegedly by two members of the Popular Front for the Liberation of Palestine (PFLO). It called to re-fuel in Benghazi, Libya, then diverted to Entebbe, capital of Idi Amin's Ugandan pariah state. Remarkably, two RZ founders were on board, Wilfried Böse and Brigitte Kuhlman. She was snapped talking to the Air France captain, who is sipping a coffee, looking remarkably composed in view of her waist belt festooned with hand grenades. The version which now follows is wholly at odds with subsequent glamorized Hollywood docudramas.

The dramatic Israeli rescue posse resulted in a shootout in which all the hijackers, including the two Germans, perished. Three passengers died in the cross-fire. At the height of the crisis a British diplomat, D. H. Colvin, based at the Paris Embassy, sent a note to London citing a usually trusted confidante in the Euro-Arab Parliamentary Association. He said the hijacking was a collaborative effort between Shin Bet and the PFLO, a false-flag operation designed to discredit the rival PLO headed by Yasser Arafat, with whom the US was becoming too warm for Israeli comfort. He might have thrown in West German intelligence, with a little more information.

Susan Sontag, who wrote about the distortions of image-making conducted through the one-dimensional photographic eye of the media, had a perfect instance in view. The Entebbe Raid, glorified as the most successful operation of its kind in Israeli history, bore every signs of orchestrated choreography from start to finish. The purpose of the two German underground commandos on board was never clear. The cover story of recruiting the hijackers and then acting as stage managers was obviously absurd. Arab terrorists generally managed perfectly well without tutors or chaperones. No one asked at the time why Flight 139, having re-fuelled at Benghazi, then made the long trek 2,300 miles south to Entebbe. As Justin Raimondo observed, the Israeli state frequently resorts to pure duplicity, shadow play, to achieve its propaganda goals. This one scored on all points. The former Israeli president Chaim Herzog wrote:

> *We are proud not only because we have saved the lives of over a hundred innocent people—men, women and children—but because of the significance of our act for the cause of human freedom.*

Herzog judged correctly the world would see the affair as brave little Israel seizing innocents from the grip of a monstrous African tyrant. He skirted the long-standing tryst between Uganda and Israel, the massive construction projects by Israeli firms (including, ironically but significantly, the airport), and the generous shipments of armaments to a valued ally. In the lead-up to the hijacking, Amin's Oliver Twist act of constantly asking the Israelis for more, especially fighters for his puny air force, became tiresome. It turned serious when he abruptly abandoned the Israeli camp, professed to be a devout Muslim and laid out the welcome carpet for King Faisal and a stream of Arab leaders. Amin was in debt to Israel to the tune of $20 million, which a convenient regime change might recover. So, already there is a sub-text to the raid which points to retribution and punishment of a former ally. The swing in Israeli relations away from black Africa to an alliance with South Africa was also moving into gear around this time.

Palestine Facts — an on-line tract which selectively interprets the 'military and political background to the on-going struggle between the State of Israel and the Arab Palestinians' — states:

> *The success also weakened the dictator Idi Amin by emboldening Amin's opponents. Sabotage and resistance increased and by 1979 he was deposed.*

Translation: Outstanding account settled.

At a glance it appears simple to explain the presence of the Germans, Böse and Kuhlman, as classical campaigners for Palestinian justice. In looking at the track record of RZ, however, this does not quite stand up to scrutiny. For a start the Cells appeared to operate in two distinct divisions. True, the internationalists kept tenuous links with the grossly over-deified Carlos the Jackal and a few fringe movements in the Palestinian resistance. At home it was a different story. Composed of individuals who led their lives in open society, and yet were supposedly responsible for scores of attacks, it was all the more remarkable the police never managed a single arrest. Quite a record considering such activity pursued on an industrial scale over two decades. Like November 17 in Greece, these clinical technicians of terror never left as much as a single smudged fingerprint. 'Homeland' RZ pursued an extremely elastic anarchist script and rarely indulged in ideological rhetoric. The handful of manifestos that did appear from the comrades without an obvious cause sounded contrived, vague and unconvincing, in short, cooked up. They largely mimicked the activities of other urban revolutionaries, but the protest ragbag of apartheid, NATO, the plight of the homeless, even the excessive cost of commuter train tickets, was glaringly short of a unifying theme, much less the designer label, rebels-with-a-cause glow of the RAF.

Carlos himself believed elements of RZ had connections to East German intelligence. The legendary spymaster Markus Wolf, chief of the *Hauptverwaltung Aufklärung* (HVA), the foreign intelligence arm of the GDR Ministry of State Security, was a mole planter *par excellence*. Yet Wolf, the alter-ego of George Smiley in le Carré's stories, would have seen RZ as no more difficult to penetrate than a Swiss cheese, and about as useful. Claims have long circulated that RZ was a 'parallel front' manufactured and exploited by elements of West German intelligence for the purpose of staging Strategy of Tension false-flag incidents, the recipe described earlier by Professor Kraushaar in connection with the RAF.

The interesting question in this whole affair concerns the true role of Böse and Kuhlman. The only possible answer is that they were they working to a pre-conceived plan. How else to explain a pair of fully-armed terrorists with two accomplices boarding an aircraft, without raising suspicion, in one of the most strictly supervised airports on earth? Did the Israelis really drop their guard to that extraordinary extent? As Justine Raimondo observed, it could only be achieved with the 'co-operation and collusion of Israeli intelligence.' Moreover, nothing in the past character of the pair, or the history of the movement they jointly founded, suggested an affinity with suicide missions. The international wing of RZ was fiercely anti-Zionist: yet Israeli officials cheerfully waved the pair through passport control (in and then out) without a blink, with Mossad apparently wearing a collective blindfold.

Böse and Kuhlman were either — at best — BND dupes, convinced their task was to ensure the safety of Jewish passengers until the winged rescuers arrived from Israel; or, as closet BND collaborators, were they duping their comrades from the start? Böse perhaps presented the best clue: He told one frightened passenger, who showed him his concentration camp tattoo — 'Don't worry, I am not anti-Semitic, I am an idealist.' For once, Markus Wolf, East German masterspy, probably envied the skills of the BND for pulling off a sublime deception.

In October 2011, the United States announced that it would dispatch a hundred military 'trainers' to Uganda. These would be deployed to assist the regime of the de facto dictator Yoweri Museveni, who is engaged in a long struggle with a rebellious force calling itself the Lords' Resistance Army. The LRA's mass abductions, industrial-scale rape and pillage, and wholesale kidnapping of children who are turned into monster killers, bear every sign of a CIA MK-Ultra derived programme to create robotic 'no questions asked' terrorists. The problem is that Joseph Kony, the self-appointed leader of the LRA, the ex-choir boy, brilliantly flexible break-dancer, the new US terrorist poster child, has worked for the CIA for years. So for that matter has Yoweri Museveni. This is the new great scramble for Africa. The aim is to destabilize the entire region so effectively that most of it can be effectively controlled under the disguise of the usual humanitarian mission. Thus the West will seize control of Central Africa's fabulous reserves of gold, uranium, copper and oil before the Russians — or the Chinese — get there first.

XV.
Ghost Trains: Madrid, London and the Template of Tension

The date 3/11 means a great deal to the people of Spain, but lacks the graven staying power which preserved the Twin Towers and the London bombs of 2005 in the public imagination worldwide. Yet the powerful blasts which ripped through four jam-packed commuter trains in the Spanish capital of Madrid, in the early morning of 11th March 2004, rank as the most devastating act of deliberate carnage any European country has witnessed in modern times. The passengers that died on the way to work or school that blighted morning numbered 192; another 1,100 were injured, more than 150 critically. Many have never fully recovered from their injuries, or the psychological shock.

Spaniards are accustomed to turning a stoic face to terrorist acts, after fifty years of violent agitation by separatist Basque nationalists. The civil war that raged from 1936 to 1939 witnessed grotesque savageries committed by both parties to the conflict, government forces and General Franco's Falangists alike. The election fixed for 14th March 2004 had all the signs of a close finish between the conservatives and the opposition socialists. The explosions on the morning of the 11th immediately altered the political landscape. The government of premier José Maria Aznar immediately attached the blame to ETA (*Euskadi Ta Askatasuna*), the Basque militant front. They appeared to exploit this massive act of terrorism for political returns — the old stripe of the Strategy of Tension. The outcome was a huge blowback delivered by public opinion. Instead of a sure return to power, as most observers expected, the ruling conservative Popular Party was roundly defeated by the opposition socialists, following massive protests which erupted across the country. Aznar — a cosseted favourite of George H. W. Bush — pounded the message of a strong line against terrorism throughout his campaign, as a way of countering huge opposition to Spanish troops serving in Iraq and Afghanistan. His decision in the immediate aftermath of the bombings to blame the Basques — which he backed with personal calls to the editors of Spain's leading media organs — appeared as a lame attempt to wriggle out of an embarrassing mistake of his own manufacture, namely to fight the campaign under the banner of fighting terrorism, only to find it exploding in his face. The police were already making short work of the prime minister's alibi, although their initial conclusions raised more problems than solutions. For the first time in the so-called war on terror (save the rather special case of the Norwegian bombings, examined later) Islamists and non-Muslims uniquely co-operated together. Two of the alleged perpetrators regularly grassed for the Guardia Civil (the national gendarmerie) and a third important figure actually was a policeman.

The Basques were astonished, bewildered and extremely angry. But who then did blow up the trains, since it was soon obvious that ETA militants were not the guilty parties?

The incoming socialist government immediately switched attention from rebel Basques to cells of Jihadist sympathisers, supposed to have secured access to supplies of dynamite, or Goma-2 ECO stolen by contacts from coal mines in the northern Asturias mountains. The theory held no more water than the discredited Basque claims. Diligent officers of the Madrid bomb squad, *Técnico Especialista en Desactivación de Artefactos Explosivos* (TEDAX), pointed to signs of military explosives from the 'composition' family such as C3 and C4 (*plastique*). Moreover, they accused their own colleagues of removing potentially incriminating evidence that compromised the official account. In any event, an Asturias explosive was not really man enough to account for the huge force of the blasts, which suggested a powerful shock wave of supersonic proportions, punching through the heavy metal in the range of 10,000 — 25,000 feet (3,000 — 7,500 meters) per second. The ferocity of the blast also accounts for the massive number of casualties, another significant feature in common with the bombs planted on the London Transport network a year later.

A famous decoy rucksack ('exhibit 13') loaded with the Asturias type of explosive was the sole evidence pointing in that direction, although the terminal wires had not been connected, and the exhibit itself was dismissed as a fake. The chief of police responsible for explosives removal declared, 'What I am totally convinced of is that after the search carried out by the Tedax.... there was not a single back pack containing an explosive device. And I can assure you of that.'[N1] The story circulated in the media that one backpack contained screws and nails intended to serve as shrapnel. However, autopsies proved that none of the train bombing victims had been struck by sharp metal projectiles, the equivalent of shrapnel. Moreover, Carmen Baladia, chief Guardia forensic officer, bluntly stated there were 'no nails, no nuts, no screws.'[N2] There were more such instances to follow, of different departments of the Guardia Civil working to conflicting scripts.

The image of a tightly-bound cell of dedicated extremists looked decidedly unpromising when the indictments were handed down, portraying a heterogeneous group of Islamic New Agers, heroin traffickers, police informers and an ex-Francoist hardliner. This strange and motley crew was alleged to be capable of military-scale precision and planning, smuggling explosives into the city centre without arousing the smallest suspicion.

The Guardia already had some of the alleged perpetrators, Moroccans living in Spain, under surveillance. After the bombings, when a group was supposedly taken by surprise in a safe apartment, they obligingly blew themselves up. The daily *El Mundo,* Spain's second-largest selling daily, which took a highly critical line of the official Jihadist accounts, duly commented: 'It would appear that Spain's 2004 elections were stolen by terrorists alright. But the terrorist operation that brought the socialists to power may have been an inside job — in effect, a coup perpetrated by some of the same authorities who are responsible for preventing terror.'

Luis Manuel del Pino, the well-known freelance investigator linked to the high-profile online *Libertad Digital*, author of several important works on 3/11, worked around the cracks in the official account to come up with the following hard conclusions. First and foremost, *ni ETA ni Al-Qaeda* (neither ETA nor Al-Qaeda). The bombs were 'ordered' just three days before the elections, but the planning for the operation may have started up to a year earlier. There were two different sets of bombs: ten loaded with high explosives, which wrought the carnage, and four more which posed little threat and did not explode, or even as some Guardia officers insisted, were not real bombs. Evidently one highly-sophisticated operation was superimposed on top of another, amateur effort. Del Pino has founded a movement — *Peones Negros* (The Black Pawns) — devoted to exposing the lies and the machinery 'moving in the shadows,' which squashed any prospect of an honest exposure from the very beginning. One editorial in *El Mundo* suggested the skills to pull off the operation could obviously be found in TEDAX, the specialist bomb squad, which clearly knew far more about the sequence of events than any of those subsequently swept into the police dragnet — in short, a Gladio-style deep state blueprint. Certainly the show trial of the 28 accused conspirators failed to produce a shred of evidence of Al Qaeda provenance. Seven of the men walked free from the courtroom. None of the questions disputing the type of explosives used or the meticulous planning were aired. The court case was written off by international observers as a cover-up and a farce. It was a rehearsal for virtually the same stage script with the London bombings, fifteen months later. The Spanish court elected to ignore all the basic rules of evidence in order to divert speculation — in the interests of 'social calm' — from the possibility of a conspiracy organised at the heart of the government.[N3]

When Judge Javier Gómez Bermudez handed down his judgements at the close of the record-breaking 21-month, chaotic trial, no one in Spain was any the wiser who was responsible for the most appalling episode of mass murder in Spain since the civil war of the late 1930's. Only one minnow, Jamal Zougham, was actually convicted of planting explosives, in a rucksack. Others went down for long sentences amounting to thought crimes. Much of the evidence was entirely circumstantial, which is conveniently permitted in Spanish courts. No effort was made to explain how a league of amateur conspirators with such diverse backgrounds gained the sophisticated ability to co-ordinate such a complex attack. To cap it all, the so-called emir of the entire enterprise, an Egyptian, left the court a free man, once it was proven the Guardia fabricated incriminating phone messages he purportedly made to other conspirators.

In such a case, the crucial element is understanding precisely what kind of explosives were used and how they came to be placed, the essential signature of the crime. Just two days after the bombings, the mangled coaches were broken up and melted down for scrap, a wanton destruction of crucial evidence. The issue of forensic traces drifted into unreality once the trial got under way. Expert witnesses complained the police had very few samples, or had lost them altogether. The court erupted in gales of laughter when another expert suddenly recited a list of chemical compounds of which she said there were traces, a document never revealed in the previous three years. Her excuse was 'no one had asked for it.'

The prosecution insisted the gang supplied themselves with material obtained from the Asturian coal mines. But the central issue of the explosives grew murkier when an expert in identifying munitions testified that such extensive ripping of substantially-constructed steel coaches was consistent with very high-powered explosives. It was the identical conflict between backpack bombs and high explosives that later arose in London. The judge complained the convoluted and conflicting evidence he heard from bomb squad officers was incomprehensible. Efforts to explain how the rucksack bombs reached the trains along with their handlers appeared to have been dreamed up on the back of an envelope. The story went that a stolen Renault van, packed with explosives and abandoned near the Alcalá metro station on the outskirts of Madrid, was left there by four men, who then calmly strolled to the ticket office, where one of them bought tickets. The usual hearsay evidence of men with 'scarves on their heads' was the essential pointer to Islamic terrorists, but the clerk at the booking office insisted that the man to whom he sold the tickets did not look Arab, was not wearing headgear and had no foreign accent. In another of the many fables that day, supposedly the truck contained a bomb due to explode as a train passed on the nearby Madrid to Barcelona high-speed track. Investigated as a suspicious vehicle, it received a thorough sniffing by trained hounds, who gave the all clear. All the more curious that after it was towed to a police yard, the required signs of 'substances' miraculously appeared. Fingerprints are generally the conclusive proof in crime detection. How odd that so many of them belonged to policemen or their confederates.

Two key suspects were Guardia informers. One, Rafa Zouhier, lined the conspirators up with an explosives trafficker. In the two days before the attack, cell phone records show he was called twice by his controllers. Did he omit a trifling conspiracy to terrorise the railway network? The second,

Emilio Trashorras, was the alleged middleman squaring the deal. He had conversations with his police contact the day before the bombings and the day after, but more significantly, spoke to his controllers immediately after he handed over the explosives. What else were these officers thinking about, if it was not the mass homicide in the capital city? As the *coup de grâce*, the mobile phones intended to trigger the bombs were unlocked at a shop belonging to a policeman of Syrian origin, Maussili Kalaji, whose duties were to spy on potential Islamist dissidents. Of course we are operating in a two-dimensional world where the patsies are the actors we see on the stage. The really important activity is taking place unseen in the wings. This, too, is a common chord with the subsequent London bombings. Taken altogether, the extraordinary sum of the over-lapping similarities in Madrid and London point strongly to an experienced organisational hand moving in the world of synthetic terror.

Even by the parameters of an investigation that frequently veered to the surreal, the story of a group suicide pact belonged in a separate universe. Three weeks after the train bombings, officers of the anti-terrorist squad GIA swooped on a flat in Leganés, a swollen over-spill city on the fringes of Madrid. The target was a cell of supposed bombers led by a bespectacled young Moroccan, a small-time property speculator and crack handler, married to a pretty Spanish wife; their young son was dutifully studying his catechism at the local Catholic school. Jamal Ahmidan, alias El Chino ('the Chinaman,' and the name of a legendary tango bar in Buenos Aires), scarcely seemed to fit the bill of a crazed Islamic zealot circulated by the media. In fact he and his friends were simply guilty of doing what they always did: running errands for the Madrid mafia. The *Guardia* supplied wildly differing accounts as to why they selected the apartment. In one, they talked of a street gun battle, but that soon faded away. Then, the public was told that intelligence intercepted calls on cell phones, in which El Chino and his two confederates bid sorrowful farewells to their loved ones. One man who actually received such a call did not recognise the voice as that of his brother and, highly alarmed, promptly telephoned the police emergency number.[N4] Clearly, cell-phone ventriloquy was a key element behind the psy-ops story line of an Islamic plot.

Remember, these young men had been sitting quietly for the best part of a month, while Madrid's finest turned the city inside out looking for them. Clearly they felt themselves in no particular danger, as underlings who played a minor role as general runners for the bombing operation. In another co-incidence too far, one of their neighbours was found to be an undercover agent for the security forces. The police account stated that 'a large force of officers' forced the door open and fired some shots before an explosion killed all the occupants and one of their own men. No bullet holes were found to substantiate the shoot-out story. Despite the great force of the explosion — which injured eleven officers — it was remarkable how artefacts found in the rubble had survived the blast. These included a magic heatproof stick of dynamite (the Asturias Connection) and a usefully unscathed tape of masked men confessing to the bombings.

Whether or not the victims were alive in the apartment when the bomb — or possibly a booby trap — went off can never be proven. Nor can we know for certain if they were actually there at all. One of the officers told Spain's most popular radio station: 'They call us heroes... we were fools to go where we did.'[N5] The 'suicide pact' had served its purpose of profiling fanatical extremists, flown to the arms of the virgins as a last desperate stab at authority. Unfortunately the prosecution case of radicalised extremists was thrown out of court even before the sentences were handed down. The investigating magistrate submitted his opinion that the accused were no more than 'vaguely influenced' by Al Qaeda. Even that was a desperate exercise to keep a myth alive. Many Spaniards, and significantly the volunteer support organisation set up to help the survivors and families, stuck firmly to a plot contrived by the state for political ends. *Cui bono?* The timing, just before a tense election, was paramount, although it is unlikely José Aznar, the outgoing premier, was privy to the plot. Many commentators suggested that Aznar's conservatives paid the largest price at the polls for misleading the public. Naturally, Aznar's socialist opponent, José Luis Zapatero, finding himself so unexpectedly summoned to kiss hands with the king, milked a whirlwind opportunity for all it was worth.

The official explanation, that Jihadist terrorists aimed at punishing Spaniards, rested on weak grounds, since over 90% strongly opposed Spain's embroilment in foreign wars. This being so, the Madrid bombings may belong to a rare category where ideology was not the ruling factor. Could there be a mysterious third force? The most compelling answer is organised crime and its tentacles extending into every aspect of Spanish life.

El Chino and his kinsmen sat tight in Leganés because they had sound reasons to believe they were under police protection, and the same is true of others in the motley rogues gallery paraded before the court. They were but small fry in the service of the country's largest industry, endemic across-the-board corruption, ranging from town hall planning bribes, cream-offs from public contracts, political payola, drugs and sex trafficking. Writer Michael M. Walsh, who lives in Spain, calculates the country has 77,429 professional politicians and hangers-on who, despite 184 million euros in generous annual subsidies, always seem to need a little extra. He calls them 'godfathers of the brown envelope.' Spain wallows in the troughs of the Transparency International league table between such champions of honesty and fair play as the United Arab Emirates and Dominica. Corruption ran amok under Felipe González's long reign as socialist prime minister. Despite all their hesitancy to vote for a party with Francoist sympathies, Spaniards — tired of the crime barons with claws stuck in every corner and cleft of society — voted in 1996 for Aznar and his pledge of clean government. Aznar's war on crime — especially in the lucrative field of building permits, and particularly in Marbella, the Spanish Las Vegas-on-the-Med — struck a popular chord. In 2004, another four years of brute Aznarism was something that the crime syndicates could well do without. A socialist government traditionally soft on crime presented a rosier prospect. When billions are involved, a certain price is worth paying.

The 11th March attacks were conducted — like 9/11 — on a size and scale to resemble an act of war. The exceptional skills required point to a Spanish Ergenekon/Gladio, a deep state weave of intelligence services, police cells, supportive factions of the military, and of course the gangster clans whose story is always inseparable from Gladio. An important question is whether the players with a walk-on role — for example El Chino and his pals — were themselves privy to the atrocity. The answer is that to some extent they were, albeit in minor roles and almost certainly 'steered,' once again by vintage Guérin-Sérac techniques. Suffering the classic fate of the patsy, El Chino and his collaborators had to be eliminated before they had the opportunity to talk.

Aznar's party travelled express to the political cleaners. Despite Right-wing voices like *El País* drumming away on the Jihadist plot, the mass of Spanish people were not taken in. Dismissing the trial as an irrelevant and insulting state theatrical, the Association of Madrid Bombing Victims (AVT) continues to insist with Luis del Pino that political interference at the highest levels obstructs a proper explanation of events on 3/11. As usual, the political élites closed ranks to block an open inquiry. How like London and 9/11. In Spain's bustling criminal quarters, business as usual.

There is a curious footnote, either by random co-incidence or perhaps some carefully devised subliminal message, to connect the World Trade Centre and the Madrid train attacks. They fell precisely 911 days — or 2.5 years — apart. I am not one to search for esoteric occultist messages and symbolism — I leave that to the talents of Dan Brown — but this one, to the surface at any rate, seems to stretch the point of accidental happenstance to curious limits. Sifting through the debris of Madrid and London bombings is close to inspecting a strange symbiotic relationship between the sum of events in two countries.[66] Consider the following, as a short list

- The clash of narratives between haversack bombs and something far more lethal originating from military sources.

[66] My publisher John-Paul Leonard observes: '7/7/2005 = 777. It's satanist numerology.'

- How such enormous damage to the trains could be explained by amateur bombs.

- The vagueness of any connections between the young men alleged as the bombers in both capitals, and allegiance to Al Qaeda.

- Suspects in Madrid and London under surveillance by the police and security services without gaining clues to bomb trains.

- The indecent haste to destroy important evidence, such as the wrecked train carriages.

- True, there were no worrisome elections on the horizon in the UK. But there was a pressing and urgent need to bolster support for Blair's faltering adventures in the Middle East and Spain's participation in America's unpopular wars.

The story of July 7, 2005, begins far from London, amid the sumptuous splendours of Scotland's famous Gleneagles Hotel. There prime minister Tony Blair was concluding a leisurely breakfast with fellow grandees of the G8 powers, before getting around to the scheduled morning chat on the plight of the world's starving poor. What finer gala setting for a major instalment of the war on terror, performed before a global audience? By the afternoon, the agenda switched abruptly from the advertised topic to Blair's grandstanding, promising in full-blown Churchillian rhetoric to root out the villains who attacked 'our way of life.' It may be a trifling detail, but at this early stage, conclusive evidence of an extremist Islamic plot was far from established. For now, the echo of the wartime blitz — 'Londoners can take it' — soaked the news stands and the air waves. The horrific blasts that day cost 52 lives and injured 784. Many who found themselves miraculously alive were permanently mutilated and traumatised.

That same bright summer morning, three young men of Pakistani origins, Mohammad Sidique Khan (30), Shehzad Tanweer (22) and Hasib Hussain (18), together with a friend born in Jamaica, Germaine Maurice Lindsay (aka Abdullah Shaheed Jamal, 19) met up at Luton railway station, about thirty miles from central London. There they boarded the 7.40 commuter train to Kings Cross, allegedly flushed with euphoria at the prospect of the delightful waiting virgins. The plan was to simultaneously explode a series of suicide bombs on the London tube network.

Exhibit A of that day is a grainy shot of the four young men captured by closed circuit camera number fourteen at Luton station at 7.21.54 am. They bought four return tickets at £22 ($34) each, having already purchased a pay and display car park ticket. Next they boarded the 7.40 to Kings Cross Thameslink. There, so we are told, Exhibit B snapped them leaving the main station platform at 8.26 am. The problem with this account is quite simple: it cannot possibly be true. The Thameslink railway company was having a bad hair day. The 7.40 never ran that morning. What followed was a bewildering trail of false statements and deceptions. The four bombers were now switched to the following 7.48, but that alibi collapsed too. That train was held up by problems with the overhead electrical wires, and did not get away from Luton until 7.56. It arrived at Kings Cross a full twelve minutes after the crucial snapshots were supposedly taken there, and just eight minutes before the first explosions.

The one remaining possibility was the earlier scheduled 7.30, again delayed, which eventually left at 7.42. But that did not reach London until 8.39, at least fourteen minutes after Exhibit B rolled for its moment of fame. It takes a spirited imagination to explain even young men with heavy backpacks sprinting through dense rush-hour throngs at the biggest interchange station on the underground network, in time to meet the scheduled 8.50 synchronised appointment with destiny. Yet almost a year later, in June 2006, John Reid, the Home Secretary, solemnly informed the House of Commons that an irritating minor civil service slip occurred while compiling the official narrative (prepared by civil servants to stem the public appetite for a full inquiry). The bombers were now aboard the 7.30, the third attempt to transport them to the capital. Later versions of the timetable were doctored to fit this new account, by pulling muscle on the train operators.

The pantomime at Luton is, plainly, incredible. But are these anything but minor quibbles about which train departed at what time? Would not any train suffice? Why the obsession with having synchronised explosions on three specific subway trains? What happened — or more accurately, did not happen — at Luton station early on 7th July 2005, is the key that unlocks the true story of the London bombings. Ironically, the most crucial nugget of evidence was supplied by Whitehall itself, thanks to the dogged persistence of 7/7 truth campaigner Bridget Dunne. Ms. Dunne had made herself a powerful nuisance concerning the 7.40 ghost train,[67] which had now found its way into the 'official narrative' which takes the place of the full, open inquiry that Blair contemptuously dismissed as a 'ludicrous diversion.' [N6]

Bridget Dunne demanded to know why, by January 2007, the record concerning the 7.40 had still not been amended in the official account. The unofficial answer was a huge amount of bureaucratic wriggling. The official response was, eventually, this: '*It has now become clear that the exact timing of the train's departure, given as 07.40, was based on what were later found*

---

[67] Dr. Nafeez Mosaddeq Ahmed, Executive Director of the London-based Institute for Policy Research and Development and author of the heavily redacted (by UK intelligence) *The London Bombings: An Independent Inquiry* (Duckworth, Overlook, 2006), and Nicholas Kollerstrom, author of *Terror on the Tube: Behind the Veil of 7/7, an Investigation* (Progressive Press, 3rd edition, 2012), overlapped with the same discovery of the train times confusion.

to be conflicting witness statements.' It is curious how anyone on the station platforms that morning might have witnessed a train that never existed. The reference to 'witnesses' is in any event another invention. The Luton story teetered on a slippery slope.

Building the case around four angry young men bent on blowing up the tube network demanded the bombers be seen at Luton with sufficient time to board the ghost train. This would require a good twenty minutes in hand as they amble into the station a shade after 7.22 a.m. Not any more. In an adjustment worthy of Orwell's Winston Smith, the most famous rewrite artist in dystopian literature, Dunne received this bland FOI reply from the Information Policy Unit (aka *Nineteen Eighty-Four*'s Ministry of Truth) at the Home Office, concerning changes to the fatuous official account.

Page 4. The time of 07.15 should be changed to 07.14.

Slipped innocuously into the public record with no explanation, the purpose was expressly political. The Secretary of State found himself awkwardly pinned down — and not exclusively by the earlier blunders concerning the ghost train. He allowed just three minutes for the bombing party to scoot to the platform, buy tickets and pass the barriers. The lie is risible. In fact, with the 7.30 running late, camera fourteen's original digital timing could have been left as it was, for all the difference it made.

Questions pile up. Why are we apparently looking at a wet pavement with puddles lying around, on a warm, dry sunny morning? For a rush-hour snap, the entrance to this very busy commuter station seems oddly deserted but for the four figures. But are they really there, or ectoplasmic figments like the witnesses who saw the ethereal 7.40 to Kings Cross? The strange halos around the images imply photo-shopped paste-ups, taking individual images and then stitching them into the frame to appear as a group. Magnified, there is a blurry appearance to each figure, so facial features are not properly recognisable. One figure, we are told it is Khan, seems to be stepping through metal bars. What might dispel the strong suspicion of forgery is a row of animated images showing the individuals physically interacting with each other. Or footage from other cameras distributed around the station. In their absence, the assumption of surveillance shots taken independently, and then merged, is overwhelming. The message spells: clumsy doctoring — and patsies.

Similar problems arise with Exhibit B at Kings Cross. It has never been independently verified for authenticity, which considering it represents a glaring hole in the official account, is not surprising. Likewise the thousand of hours of CCTV tape the police claim to possess confirming the guilt of the lone bombers. That, too, is under lock and key, away from prying eyes, barring a few carefully selected items that began to filter out when the inquest on the victims began in November 2010. Yet if the story of the young bombers is right, then a running visual account should record their every movement, every step of the way, presenting cast-iron proof of guilt, not merely selective highlights. Each time some new security scare is the excuse for even more cameras, we are told this will add to the safety of the travelling public. Yet on the summer day that London was bombed, there are just a few derisory images, and a strange visitation that conveniently blinded many crucially-located cameras. If the police have so many miles of tape shadowing their movements, as the former Assistant Metropolitan Police Commissioner for Special Operations Andy Hayman so often claimed, then organise a comprehensive screening. When governments and their agents keep such secrets, it amounts to nothing less than stealing the truth.[N7]

The first explosion on the eastbound Circle Line occurred at 8.51, eight minutes after the train left Kings Cross. The second, almost simultaneously, on the westbound Circle Line, eight minutes after leaving Kings Cross. The third, on the southbound Piccadilly Line, which has deep level tube access, again eight minutes after leaving Kings Cross. Whichever way the train puzzle is presented, it would require the winged Mercury to perform a remarkable miracle; in the brief time available, flash through the access barriers, hurtle along the maze of walkways and escalators, crammed tight with frantic morning commuters, and then find a train with doors open and waiting, ready to go. Conclusion: mission impossible. The story can only be made to fit the pre-designated story of the 7.40 actually running and arriving at Kings Cross at 8.26, bang on Exhibit B time. Few Londoners who cram aboard their daily rush hour underground trains have the faintest idea of the schedule (as they do with mainline trains) simply because the services are so condensed. Yet we are required to believe the bombers knew the schedule of the target subway trains precisely. An absurdity of course, until perhaps the most important and damning clue concerning 7th July comes into play.

Amid the shock felt by the stunned nation, a crisis management specialist called Peter Power suddenly sprang up on nationwide BBC television and radio. He stated that his security services company, Visor, was paid to run a crisis drill that very day on behalf of a prominent company based in the City of London. Moreover, by extraordinary co-incidence, the exercise involved precisely the same three trains and locations, and exactly the timings of simulated bombs, which then occurred in real time. It seemed that events had flipped in from a parallel universe. In the course of a peculiarly jocular BBC *5 Live* interview, Power tendered the 'just one of those things' explanation. He informed the interviewer Peter Allen in a laconic fashion that 'I still have the hairs on the back of my neck standing upright.' Shortly afterwards he flew off to Canada for a disaster management exercise, and told viewers on the Canadian Broadcasting System concerning the London bombs:

It's a coincidence, and it's a spooky coincidence. Our scenario was very similar — it wasn't totally identical, but it was based on bombs going off, to the time, the locations, all this sort of stuff.

At the *Prison Planet* website Alex Jones had actuaries calculate that the chance of co-incidence was 1:1 followed by 43 noughts. The sum of co-incidence does not end there. Up until 1990, Power was an officer with the Metropolitan Police anti-terrorist squad. This does not make him a conspirator or personally incriminated in the day's events, but invites a large degree of inevitable compromise. Almost exactly a year earlier, he was one of a select panel of experts selected to assist the BBC in preparing a distinctly Orwellian fictional preview of the 7/7 attacks. This was broadcast on the flagship *Panorama* current affairs programme as 'London Under Attack.' It might have been a documentary enticed from a parallel universe, because it featured the same script of bombed underground trains and solemn political denunciations of Al Qaeda. A chlorine tanker stood in for the red double-decker bus wrecked a year later in real time. The BBC's publicity department contributed this advance promotion, as events transpired, of an actual event; 'This fictional day of terror unfolds through the immediacy of rolling news bringing the catastrophic attack into our living rooms.' George Orwell, who was paid to broadcast wartime propaganda on the BBC, would instantly recognise the dangerous transition from news reporting to social manipulation. It was after all the ideological spinal chord of *Nineteen Eighty-Four*.

What we really learn is this: there was something magnetically enticing about those particular trains which made the invisible hand behind 7/7 guide those young men towards them. Now we have some explanations for the frantic scrambling with the Luton timetable, inventing witnesses, meddling with CCTV snaps, all to paint the suspects as being on board three specific ear-marked trains. As for the television interview, professional information managers (spinners) recognise this as the time-honoured technique of teasing out awkward information when public attention is focussed on the high drama of the event itself. To this day, the coincidence has been largely buried by the corporate media and ignored by the authorities. It is nowhere mentioned in the ludicrous official whitewash called the official narrative. The powder-puff television interview served its purpose: bury difficult news while the public is distracted by the horrors of a deadly Islamic raid on the capital.

Only three years later did Peter Power finally state that the FTSE 100 and FT Global 500 publishing, business and security services company Reed Elsevier was behind the commission. It can be safely stated that Power was well-placed to talk about infernos on the London underground network. On the evening of 23rd November 1984, he was the star turn as the Pied Piper who escorted passengers to safety when a train was involved in a fire near Oxford circus station. The ambitious off-duty Scotland Yard inspector took control of the train after barging into the driver's compartment and seizing the tannoy to broadcast instructions to passengers. When the driver protested at this rude invasion of London Transport property, Power responded by smartly knocking him out. Almost exactly three years later he was the Met duty officer at the devastating fire which broke out at Kings Cross station (18th November 1987) killing 31 passengers. By another of those strange intrusions of co-incidence that seem to follow Mr. Power around, a certain Ian Blair, his future superior as London's chief policeman, was also on duty during the deadly blaze. Reed Elsevier's designs in entertaining a catastrophe scenario on the London transport system, moreover beneath a blanket of tight secrecy, have never been publicly explained. The firm remains silent on the subject. The assumption is that it was intended as a contribution to the risk solutions side of the business. From the restricted information to date, the Visor simulation was attended by no more than about six senior management staff, using fairly basic PowerPoint. In which case, why did the talkative Mr. Power feel it necessary to burst on to the BBC's air waves with his dramatic announcement, at the height of the crisis? Was this in itself an element of the exercise?

A fourth bomb wrecked a Route 30 double-decker bus in Russell Square, close to Euston station, killing thirteen passengers. Among the many mysteries is again the timing — at 9.47, roughly an hour after the train bombs in the tube. Hasib Hussain, the tall, bulky eighteen-year-old touted as the youngest member of the deadly cell, is the subject of Exhibit C, the spotter camera which snapped him at 9 o'clock ambling gently out of the Boots drugstore on the main Euston station concourse. Despite his imminent summons to martyrdom, he stopped to purchase batteries, supposedly to explode his bomb. Are we really to believe he overlooked that vital detail? According to the 'official narrative' he was supposed to be dead by this hour.[68] Then he hung around for a hamburger before joining the Marble Arch

---

[68] The story of mobile telephone communications between the alleged bombers on the morning of the bombings ignores the simple and well-known fact that calls cannot be made from or directly received in London's underground stations and trains. Yet the tech-savvy youngster Hussein is supposed to have frantically tried to contact his partners when he found the Northern Line shut down. For the same reason, it would not be possible to use signals from cell phones to set off bombs below ground. Yet an unnamed police source told *The Times* (25th July, 2005) about Hussein's urgent messages demanding advice: 'I can't get on a train. What should I do ?' These phantom calls were — unsurprisingly — not mentioned at the inquest. The irony is that Scotland Yard knew perfectly well that the underground network is as yet out of bounds to cellphone technology, since their own equipment does not function there either. (See Death in the Underworld, Ch.XVII.)

–Hackney Wick bus line at Euston Square at 9.35, supposedly on a whim because the Northern Line, his intended target, or so the official account insisted, was shut down. Exactly how did he reveal that intention to the authorities from the farthest shades? Like everything connected with the London bombings, much of the script thrives on ESP. The unfolding story of No. 30 is nothing less than television drama viewed in real time:

- Number 30's normal route sweeps along Euston road, then makes a sharp loop around Euston Square. Why was this particular No. 30 not steered away from Euston Station altogether, instead of sending it on the detour? Why was it the *only* bus on route 30 diverted that morning, up to the point of the explosion?

- Why was it the only bus serving that particular route to undergo 20 hours of special CCTV maintenance in the previous days? How did this 'maintenance' come to be performed by a technician the garage managers did not recognise, and who was admitted in defiance of strict Health and Safety rules? No further need to inquire why none of the all-seeing eyes on board or on the street were working that day.

- Who gave the sudden order to switch routes, and why?

Native-born Londoner Daniel Adigwe, riding on the lower deck of the Number 30, was now to claim an experience that day that changed his life. He narrowly escaped death, only to find himself ignored as a key witness, and then plunged into a sinister cat-and-mouse pursuit by the police and intelligence services. He received the full 'no truther left behind' treatment. His account would seem to supply graphic evidence pointing to all the events of July 7 as a massive false-flag exercise in synthetic terrorism. Daniel found himself alive in a dreamlike landscape where fact and fiction crossed apparently seamless boundaries. The difficulty is that he has never supplied credible evidence that he was actually a passenger on the bus, though there seems to be no doubt that he was an eye-witness to the events immediately after the explosion.[N8]

Adigwe's account states that just another routine commute to work was abruptly wrenched into a horror story when No. 30 abruptly switched streets. Riding on the lower deck, Daniel stated that he had a good of view of a brief ballet in which two smart sedans, a BMW and a Mercedes, pulled in front of the bus. A police motorcyclist drew alongside and was shown some kind of pass. The bus driver was motioned to follow the cars. Moments later, bus No. 30 was practically destroyed, fortuitously near the offices of the British Medical Association. Finding himself stunned but unhurt, Daniel surveyed the appalling chaos of wreckage, bodies of the dead, dying and injured. He observed in close succession two figures who remained forever embedded in his memory. Even those like Nicholas Kollerstrom, who doubt that Adigwe was a passenger on the bus, agree that the scene which he then describes is accurate. The first, Camcorder Man, dressed in all-over black, minutely recording the casualties and wreckage as though he was a visitor from a parallel universe. Next, White Bandage, whose image was to flash around the world as the symbol of a ghastly atrocity. Problem. White Bandage was at least 50 yards in front of the bus, whereas it was obvious the full force of the explosion had blasted away the rear of the fifteen-tonne vehicle, and sheared the roof clean away. The thin gauze wrapped around his brow bore no indication of blood stains, and the few dabs on his chest resembled stage paint. He seemed like an actor fresh from make-up, as indeed he was, because seconds after the explosion there were obviously no medics at the scene to dress his 'wounds.' But for images preserved by Alex Jones at *Prison Planet*, White Bandage — sandy-haired, medium build, mid-30s — is an unperson who has vanished completely.

Daniel Adigwe had the distinct impression of wading in a film set soaked in real blood. Peter Power did not mention Russell Square as part of the Visor crisis drill. There is no evidence or proof of any kind that it was. But everything that Adigwe recorded in minute detail, such as 'foot soldiers' (as he described them) standing around and acting like spectators, the strange behaviour of other characters at the scene such as White Bandage and Camcorder Man, conveys an uncanny impression that it was another rehearsal that flipped into a real time atrocity.

We may add a few more noughts to Alex Jones' calculation by revisiting the underground explosions, which scores survived to describe in precise detail. They spoke of a sudden surge of power and a strange blue light in the tunnels, accompanied by an acrid smell, which can be associated with large and sudden voltage fluctuations (as we see in a moment). Then came the huge blasts which punched open the floors and lifted these solid subway cars, weighing around twenty-seven tonnes gross, vertically from the tracks. Such enormous force is inconsistent with home-made bombs either carried or dropped by suicide bombers, because the blast would then be lateral, not vertical. In any event they would be insufficient to account for terrible injuries, which were mostly to the lower part of the body. Nor could amateur kit account for such massive physical damage to the carriages. Yet it is possible that the blue flashes and apparent power surge can be prised apart from the actual explosions, albeit in terms of microseconds.

Many of the reports that made their way to the media that day spoke initially of a power 'surge' along the electric cables that serve the underground railway network. To a layman this means some sudden increase in voltage. This is correct, but the actualities are technically far more complex. For a critical analysis, I turned to one of the foremost experts on railway electrification in Europe. Given the sensitive nature of the subject, he has asked to remain anonymous. In everyday language, here is what he had to say. An induced surge is a standing procedure to test the effectiveness of high-voltage insulation systems. It allows engineers to inspect a diagram of electrical wave formation and spot weaknesses in the circuits. However a surge conducted in traffic conditions would be pointless — and probably harmless. This is because any excess voltage that reached the conductor rail (from which the train shoe collects power) would be absorbed and smoothed by the traction equipment of the train itself. So a surge conducted with a diagnostic purpose would be a waste of time while services were actually operating. Therefore surge was the wrong word to employ on the day, either in terms of the concurrent training exercise or the explosions themselves. There is however another and far more disturbing explanation. I quote in full from the report that I received:

In a situation where an electrical short circuit or fault occurs, high currents flow and on Direct Current systems [such as London Transport] this will be inevitavably be accompanied by bright blue light from the electrical arc that is initiated. It will also be accompanied by an acrid smell of burning, and arcs can be maintained for some time and could ignite other combustible material.

The significant words are 'other combustible material.' So, if we switch the redundant explanation of 'surge' to 'an electrical short circuit' we have a credible explanation for the many survivor accounts describing the bright blue lights illuminating the tunnels and the bitter, choking acrid fumes. These are precisely the symptoms of a short circuit, which could be the result of a fault — or human intervention. Either way, if there were explosive packages slung beneath the carriages or placed on the track (less likely), then as 'combustible material' they would ignite. If the hidden hands, so to speak, were expecting the trains to stop by inducing a surge, they were wasting their time. Nothing would happen. On the other hand, a deliberately induced electrical short circuit would have quite a definite physical consequence — the bright blue illuminations, acidic smoke and the electrical arcing that would continue for some time. They could well be convinced that a terrorist attack was in progress.

Many witnesses corroborated reports that the bombs went off beneath the carriages. Metal surrounding the blast holes twisted into a crown-shaped formation, and the holes were big enough to swallow victims while they were still alive, which happened in at least one case. Passengers bled to death from the force of injuries to the lower half of their bodies. There were ghastly descriptions of people staring in disbelief at the exposed stumps of their shattered legs. To those dissatisfied with the explanation of suicide bombers, suspicion focused on explosives placed on the track. Possible, but doubtful. During the overnight shutdown, cleaners and maintenance teams swarm through the tunnels. Unusual objects would be noticed or set off by scouring equipment. But not if the explosives packages were slung underneath carriage floors, then triggered by the short circuit or similar fault. For this, the perpetrators would require access to the service depots. We should remember the unrecognised technicians who secured entry to the depot where the doomed route 30 bus was garaged. Now the blasts and the surge can be reconnected.

A mass of contradictions collide in this compressed interstice.

- TfL's first accounts spoke of 'power surges.'

- Police and broadcasters at first followed the same line.

- Because of the inconsistencies in the travelog, it is extremely unlikely that Tanweer, Khan and Lindsay were actually aboard the subway trains.

- Were the Luton Four hired as extras in a simulation exercise, which might require Asian-looking actors playing parts in a terrorist attack? It would explain why they bought return tickets, an inexplicable nicety if they were fixing to blow themselves and a host of innocents to Kingdom Come.

- Could they have been secretly 'personality profiled' in advance to fit the subsequent claim they were the bombers, acting entirely alone?

- Like the Spanish general election, the *casus belli* was a big-ticket event, Blair's heroic preening before the G8 conclave in Scotland.

The issue of the explosives is soaked in political interference. There were indications grimly apparent to the first teams who crawled over the wreckage, broken bodies and remnants of charred clothing, that enormously powerful explosive had been used. The French anti-terrorist chief, Christophe Chaboud, who was urgently summoned to the scene from Paris, pointed to the signs of military-type explosive such as C4 *(plastique)* — possibly imported from the Balkans — which he described as 'highly disturbing.' Chaboud made himself unpopular in London by pointing to Iraq as the real fuel for the attack. Of course, his suspicion of the powerful munitions involved could not fit lone bombers high on inflammatory Jihadist fuel. Military-type bombs indicated sophisticated planning. Within two weeks, government officials began to insist that the bombs were made with basic household materials set off by primitive timers or by the bombers themselves. M. Chaboud returned to Paris, and was not asked for his unsettling opinions again.

The switch occurred after a secret bomb-making factory was conveniently unearthed at an anonymous terraced house in Leeds — number 18 Alexandra Terrace, situated in the quiet suburb of Burley. There were signs of someone mixing acetone peroxide — known as TATP (triacetone triperoxide, peroxyacetone) — in a bathtub. The usual ingredients of this compound are sulphuric acids, hydrogen peroxide (found in hair dyes) and acetone (a common solvent). The discovery was then propelled into a firm hold on the public imagination by the supine media acting on the usual anonymous 'briefings.' TATP is a chemical explosive, unlike the C4 detected in the London explosions. It is chiefly a gas-producing agent caused by the rapid shedding of the acetone content when ignited. What scientists call an entropic explosion is reminiscent of the swift reaction that — upon collision — produces gas in the safety airbags fitted to cars. There is considerable explosive force but tellingly, it does not generate heat or flames. TATP is highly volatile, susceptible to shocks from jolting or dropping, and needs to be constantly cooled. This makes it a challenge for lugging around in haversacks on moving, crowded trains, rushing through underground stations, or attaching it to moving, bumpy trains.

Practising this sort of cookery on a layman scale, for example in the much-touted Leeds devils' kitchen, requires fairly strong nerves. There would be a fair indication to a wide neighbourhood that something seriously smelly is going on. There is a further hitch. Hydrogen peroxide (H_2O_2) is enormously unstable, and simply exposing it to sunlight for short periods of time introduces enough energy to to start the process of decomposition to water and oxygen. This is why it is always sold in dark, opaque bottles. Boiling it supposedly to distill its explosive force can be exceedingly dangerous, because of the risk of ignition. The technical term is an 'exothermic reaction.' In the form of high-test peroxide, otherwise known as HTP, it has a long history as a propellant for submarines and rockets. We have to imagine that these young men were bent on concocting a lethal cocktail of hydrogen peroxide, plus H_2SO_4 (sulfuric acid) and acetone, known to every woman on earth as nail polish. Two major snags. The weak concentrations of 3 to 6% peroxide sold over the drugstore counter are of no use at all. Simply not up to the task. They need the highly concentrated form. Next they would require the sulfuric acid to be similarly highly concentrated, which would not be easy to obtain. Next, mix the H_2O_2 and H_2SO_4 to meld a strong oxidizer, and then finally lace it with the acetone as a reactant. This would indeed be a very explosive and lethal cocktail, as the mixers would discover if they had not taken due care to use dry ice in large packs to cool the mixing tank or bathtub to at least -78C. The most difficult part, aside from the cooling, is adding the last drops of acetone; this is a task calling for exquisite care and precision. And the final challenge, carrying this lethal mixture around. The allegorical bottles of chilled supermarket water or portable icepacks are an absurdity in the circumstances.

So it follows that high-concentration H_2O_2 can only be produced industrially or through a complex and tightly controlled synthesis in a professional lab. To attempt conversion in some kind of home laboratory would require a great deal of practical know-how, significant scientific knowledge and equipment way beyond saucepans — plus iron nerves.

The authorities wrestled with every kind of glass slipper to force the narrative of kitchen and bathroom organic chemical kits as the chief means to steer suspicion away from the high explosive which actually wrought the havoc on 7/7. There came a point at which the TATP version was no longer credible. So it was abruptly discarded to pursue an alternative story, which immediately ran into difficulties with forensic scientists. The new chief suspect was the explosive organic compound hexamethylene triperoxide diamine — HMTD for short — which is another powerful but also chronically unstable agent. The history of HMTD is quite long, stretching back to the late 19th century, when it found many applications in mines. One of its chief ingredients is again hydrogen peroxide, the ubiquitous bleach of the hair-dying process, that magic elixir to hold back ageing that gives off a powerful whiff from any ladies' hairdresser on Saturday mornings. If hydrogen peroxide of itself had explosive potential, then many customers would quite literally lose their heads the moment they popped them under the cocoon-like hairdryers. Wikipedia offers a neat description of the potentially lethal cocktail: 'HMTD may be prepared by the reaction of an aqueous solution of hydrogen peroxide and hexamine in the presence of citric acid or dilute sulfuric acid as the binding catalyst.' This is not something that rank amateurs may play about with on the kitchen stove.

Yet, hydrogen peroxide always plays to the public gallery because you can get it anywhere. Hearing of its apparent role in the bombings, the presiding coroner, Lady Justice Hallett, observed that anyone could walk in off the street and stock up with as much hydrogen peroxide as desired, but the same person would raise the chemist's eyebrows by demanding an excessive quantity of aspirin. Ergo: stroll down the nearest High Street and stock up with enough explosive materials to practically destroy underground railway carriages weighing twenty tonnes and more apiece.

Once HMTD has been assembled — something that would require rather more than A level chemistry — it is highly sensitive to shock, friction, and heat. This makes the substance extremely dangerous to manufacture. The new line now insisted that HMTD was triggered by a compound of black pepper, thus adhering to the anyone-can-buy-this-gear masking of military-type high explosive. There were two problems with the HMTD story. First it is long known as an agent whose volatility makes it a dodgy choice as the trigger to explode the main bomb materials. Second, its selection, combined with black pepper as the primary trigger, by an inexperienced crew of amateur bombers seemed strange to the point of incredible. Not to say that it could not be done, but if it was, then as a procession of forensic scientists testified, there appeared to be no record of anyone resorting to this unusual concoction before.

Kim Simpson, senior case officer at the government's own Fort Halstead forensics lab in Kent, veteran of Afghanistan, IRA terror attacks, Lockerbie and the Madrid train bombings, intimated that she was dealing with something she had never previously encountered in this context in her laboratories. A second expert, Dr. Clifford Todd of the Ministry of Defence Forensic Explosives Laboratory at Sevenoaks (see below) averred that some traces of HMTD did turn up. He too was surprised to find it, and overall the combination of materials was unique in the UK and worldwide. So there we have it. These four young men — none of them with any knowledge of chemistry — made bombs that were not just unusual; they were seemingly unique. Colonel Peter Mahoney, Professor of Anesthesia and Critical Care at the Royal Centre for Defence Medicine in Birmingham, was called to the stand to deliver his assessment. He tip-toed around the subject by pointing to the absence of post-mortem reports (see below) for corroboratory evidence. He said that photographs showing disfigured victims could not be relied upon. What Colonel Mahoney wanted to understand was the forensic evidence, and none had been produced.

If anything has seemed surreal and bizarre in this unfolding tale so far, now consider what the inquest was told in respect of the detonators of 'at least one' of the bombs. This was apparently a kitchen-table type of assembly, constructed from a charge of HMTD ignited by a light bulb wired to a nine-volt battery and wrapped up tidily in an aluminum foil bag. Entire tube carriages were thus blown up with huge force, 52 passengers died, hundreds were injured, and this flimsy contraption (or enough of it) survived to tell the tale?

The bombs on the Number 30 bus at Russell Square and the tube trains were alleged to contain at least 10kg of explosive manufactured from hydrogen peroxide and pepper. Note this explanation retreats from full-blown HMDT, as described above, a more complicated cocktail that also suffers from the chronic instability problem. We have to understand how the slurry mix concocted in the purported Leeds bomb factory was transported to London without the bombs exploding on the way, or even in the car on the journey to Luton station. Mixing the concentrated hydrogen peroxide cocktail with an organic substance like pepper might of itself invoke an instant chemical reaction, disposing of the conspirators there and then. The official narrative comes up with the explanation that the bombers kept the explosives cool with freezer bags. But this is missing the point altogether. These materials are not easily transportable, packs of ice or not. The risk of one kitbag exploding prematurely is high. On the probability scale, *all four* exploding prematurely, even higher. In the circumstances, it might have been better if the composers of the official narrative skipped over what kind of explosive charge was employed altogether. Some commentators cast further doubt by suggesting that the stains found in the bomb factory sink were nothing more than insecticides.

We still have no clear idea how the three subway bombers were supposed to synchronise the explosions so exactly, which is the kernel of the suicide plot theory. Timers activated by cell phones were out of the question because of the underground communications black-out. A purely random phenomenon is immediately in trouble with the laws of chance. Pre-arranged pulling the cords by stop-watch simply brings us back to the looming question of why it was so crucially important for the bombs to go off in this manner, and tangentially the Visor exercise running at the same time. As with the constant churning over the explosives, we are again re-visiting glass slipper syndrome.

A singular disturbing aspect of the bombings, which has received little coverage from British media busily spinning the official line, concerns the behaviour of police and other state performers in the immediate aftermath of the explosions. Any psychologist understands that part of the grieving/healing process is empathy with the physical remains of the deceased. Yet, in the wake of the bombings an extraordinary cover-up ensured that bereaved relatives were not allowed to see their loved ones for up to a fortnight. Some, like the family of 30-year-old Rome-born Benedetta Ciaccia, who died at Aldgate, were advised not to see her body — 'better to remember her as she was before.' Poignant, harrowing stories from that awful day abound.

- John Taylor, whose 24-year-old daughter Carrie also died at Aldgate, struggled with authorities for ten days to even confirm she had been killed.

- A week after 7/7, the distraught mother of Nigerian-born, 26-year-old Anthony Fatayi-Williams stood in Tavistock Square, to exclaim her public agony that she feared he was on the Number 30 bus, but still had no facts or information of any kind. 'He's missing and we fear he was in the bus explosion….we don't know.'[N9]

- Relatives of Samantha Badham could not make a formal identification until July 16th, nine days after she gave her full name to paramedics at Russell Square. She died shortly afterwards. Her parents say they were never invited to see her body or even know where it was.

- The Rev. Julie Nicholson, whose daughter Jenny died at Edgware Road, was given the extraordinary explanation by a police officer that delays in identification were occurring because hundreds of body parts had been dispatched for expert examination at a laboratory in Bosnia, of all places. Like other parents, Jenny's mother was discouraged from viewing her daughter's body. When finally she was allowed to, she could only be sure it was her 'because of her hands.'[N10]

Of all the stories of the London bombings, perhaps the Rev. Nicholson's is one of the most important in terms of clues. Jenny had clearly suffered terrible injuries as the consequence of a truly massive blast, with a signature pointing away from High Street DIY kit.

Organic compounds such as hydrogen peroxide laced or propelled by pepper generate intense thermal heat precisely because of the rapid oxidization of the pepper. So, the bodies recovered from the blast and the wounds of the injured should exhibit primarily, if not exclusively, exposure to intense heat — especially burns. Instead, the injuries — and especially those of victims who literally disintegrated — were consistent with the enormous upward pressure that lifted the heavy subway cars upwards off their tracks. The evidence points to military-type munitions capable of huge force, and not kitchen table ruck-sack bombs.

To be fair, a certain degree of bureaucratic confusion and muddle (not to say ineptitude) is certainly inevitable after such a calamity, as with the curious business of the London Ambulance Service deploying only half its available crews. Moreover, unlike an aviation disaster or one at sea, railway accidents have no convenient list of passengers to work from. Jenny Edkins, of the University of Wales, wrote an excellent study of relatives 'plunged into a world of disaster victim identification, forms, police liaison officers and stonewalling by officials,' which is obviously one element of the story. Yet I would be happier with this explanation were it not for a thunderbolt that emerged from the London inquest. There had never been any post mortems — in practical terms — conducted on the bodies of the 52 victims (or for that matter, the alleged remains of the bombers).

Under the laws of England, a full post mortem when deaths occur in suspicious circumstances must take place if ordered by the responsible coroner. We are now caught in the convolutions of the inquest procedure. For reasons never properly explained, it was delayed for five years, save for the formal opening. No qualified person — a coroner — ordered post mortems during this lengthy period, although it was in all respects a necessary safety procedure. The inquest authorities tried to fudge the issue by invoking 'non-invasive' procedures, quite unknown to legal statutes, whereas again every pathologist knows that assessing the state of internal injuries is a crucial element of the post-mortem process. This is essential to to assure the valid issue of a death certificate. And what did these strange 'non-invasive' post-mortems involve? Nothing more it seems than a fluoroscopy, an X-ray of a body bag to ascertain its contents. And that was it. There was trouble, too, concerning photographs of the victims. Lady Justice Hallett was at pains to confine these — which she described as 'of the utmost horror and gravity' — held in the possession of police, medical and fire brigade services, away from circulation. There was a legal argument about using the highly fire-walled extranet facility, which guarantees privacy, to frustrate cynical ghouls. As counsels for the relatives argued, as interested parties defined by the inquest rules, there were certain rights to view the material, distressing as it was certain to be.

The thread is unmistakably obvious, the necessity to mask any evidence which points to injuries inflicted by massive force, exerted by powerful high explosives rather than home-made cocktail bombs. In this cause relatives were steered away from seeing the bodies — another doubtful skirting of the laws concerning coroner procedure. (I was reminded once again of my investigation of the murder of the MI6 agent Ann Chapman — Chapter VII — hustled into Putney crematorium by illegal edict of the Home Secretary, her cadaver viewed only by a clergyman with family secret service connections. The same arguments of 'distressing to the family' were rolled out then.) It took up to two weeks for some grieving families to discover the whereabouts of their loved ones. They were initially not informed where the remains were being kept. In fact most if not all were taken to a mobile mortuary equipped with cryogenic suspension facilities, commissioned at short notice from a specialist supplier, which just happened to arrive at the barracks of the Royal Artillery Company in Moorgate only the day before the bombings. Here was the perfect location, minutes from the explosion sites, yet intended, it was said, as part of a London-wide programme of preparations for civil emergencies. Like the disaster rehearsals of the Visor company, some co-incidences in the London bombings story strain credibility to the outermost limits.

There were no formal — meaning invasive — post mortems. Even photographs had become a contentious issue. We are back to the ludicrous desk-top 'narrative' commissioned by another Home Secretary, Charles Clarke, which had no purpose other than to side-track demands for an open public inquiry. The only point of all this obfuscation is to conceal evidence which points to high explosives instead of home-made bombs cooked up by rank amateurs. Should that be exposed — or even sufficient doubts raised — the case against the Luton Four is in serious difficulty.

Nor can we convincingly answer the looming question — where are they now, if they died on the trains? Only Tanweer has at least a nominal resting place, near his family home back in Pakistan. Nagging media inquires eventually impelled Scotland Yard to confess (in *The Guardian*, 24th August 2005) that its forensic experts were involved, three months after the bombings, in a bizarre, Frankenstein-like exercise to re-assemble the bombers from the sum of their body parts. No explanation was tendered for this morbid procedure, or why the remains of Tanweer alone were released — assuming they were his. The casket was closely guarded during the air journey, and the grave site itself kept under surveillance for some days following interment, presumably to allow the heat to perform its gruesome work in what was basically an open grave. Given the advance of DNA as an effective means of identification, why did the Yard need to conjure Victor Frankenstein from the vast beyond with talk of reconstructing the corpses? I will revisit the DNA issue later on.

If the Luton Four were not blown up by their bombs, then how did they meet their ends? Death while in police custody is not unknown in the United Kingdom or the United States, or anywhere else. Suggestions they were executed by gunshots somewhere near the precincts of the humming Canary Wharf tower in London's Docklands seem difficult to square with such a high-profile location. Other more concrete suspicions point to Britain's very own Guantánamo Bay, the high security Belmarsh detention centre located near the wretched Thamesmead commuter development, which is practically as grim as the jail that it hosts. Belmarsh is situated about five miles east of Docklands, on the south bank of the River Thames. It would be difficult to find another such facility in the London area better equipped to keep the alleged bombers from prying eyes. But of course there is no corroborative evidence, and there never will be. The case of the Iraq whistle-blower, the chemical weapons expert Dr. David Kelly, refuses to fade into history because important parliamentarians and medical experts got behind the case. So far such figures have left 7/7 and the fate of four young men alone, because they have been largely convicted in the court of opinion, honed and perfected by the mainstream corporate media.

For all the horrid seriousness of the atrocity, the inquest proceedings frequently stumbled into the realms of burlesque, particularly when anonymous MI5 officers insisted they had no inkling deadly attacks were in the offing. This was allowed to stand in direct contradiction to contrary claims by MI5 of tailing Mohammad Sidique Khan as a possible threat, only to rule him out as a 'marginal figure.' How one ranks as a marginal figure and an important terrorist suspect at the same time is an interesting contradiction. Similarly, MI5 admitted it knew Tanweer and Khan spent three months in Pakistan before returning to Britain in February 2005, raising the suspicion they had undergone some kind of training in bombing tactics at a Jihadist training school. Even more incredibly, *The Independent* claimed that American authorities placed Germaine Lindsay on a terrorist watch list, which MI5 then passed off as a case of 'mistaken identity.' How to account too for snapshots of the alleged perpetrators in a supermarket loading up with trolley loads of water supposedly to cool their unstable bombs. These and other video pictures were subsequently circulated as proof of the Luton Four's culpability on 7/7. The material was scarcely startling, apparently oddments of the suspects going about their ordinary daily lives and family affairs. The public gallery may be forgiven as understandably confused that MI5 officers were subsequently taken aback by the explosions — caused by people they dismissed as credible terrorists — whom they nonetheless followed around with assiduous attention.

In 2008, the British government seemed to be gently testing the waters, to close down mounting speculation and conspiracy theories. In a unique instance of British justice, the Luton Four were put on surrogate trial, as was once the fashion when the dead were tried and convicted in medieval courts. Three young Pakistanis were arraigned for supplying back up to the bombers, including scouting the locations (would this require anything more elementary than an everyday map of the underground network?) But in essence they were simply the stooges, whose own convictions would secure the guilt of the prime accused, and sanctify the contrived work of fiction called the official narrative. The jurors at Kingston-upon-Thames were the very first to be called to offer a definitive judgement on the events of 7/7. What followed was a classic and wholly unexpected example of legal blow-back. The ultimate example of a trial conducted *in absentia* left the jury profoundly under-convinced. The government failed to prove its case and worse, succeeded in casting doubt on vital evidence concerning the purported bombers. It boiled down largely to the scattering of personal effects around the subway carriages, such as mobile phones and paper and plastic identifying materials. But, as the forensic expert Dr. Clifford Todd came forward to say, although they were 'damaged to some extent,' the damage was not such that might be expected if they were on the body of the bomber or in his rucksack. He added: 'In each case they had been deliberately separated by some distance from the actual explosion.' But by whom? Dr. Todd, whether intentionally or not, opened the jury's collective mind to the possibility the possessions were scattered by third parties *after* the event. Not a single surviving witness spoke of anyone behaving so oddly before the explosions. What was supposed to be a prime element of the prosecution case disintegrated. Then came the crushing verdict. To convict those who were physically on trial, it was necessary to prove their connections and assistance to the bombers, and by implication in turn, their guilt. The jury failed to agree, and the case collapsed.

The Kingston trial (the first of two, as we will see) remains an important benchmark because it was supposed to demonstrate, incontrovertibly, that the accused bombers were on the trains and set off their bombs to a pre-arranged schedule. Instead, the case backfired, reactivating long-expressed doubts as to how their personal property came to have such remarkable survival qualities, and what the bombers intended to achieve by some last moment scattering of their effects. Clearly, these artefacts had been 'discovered' at some convenient distance from the huge force of the explosions. The credibility gap is obvious. Why should suicide bombers bother to 'sign off' in this strange fashion? Was is to reap the status of glorious martyrs? Other evidence which might support that contention — such as the alleged last will and testament of one of the young men — has not been released (up to the point of writing). The authorities have not so far produced convincing proof that the Luton Four were on the trains or had anything to do with the bombs, such as viable residues of DNA abstracted from their remains. We manage with fudged pictures, ghost trains, the 'co-incidence' of the training exercise, the incredible helter-skelter through Kings Cross tube station — and the absolute necessity to prove young men incited by the troglodyte in the faraway grotto were behind a deadly act of destruction.

A year later, three of the Kingston accused found themselves back in the dock for another attempt by the authorities to win convictions that would point to the guilt of the Luton Four. The second trial effectively fizzled out as well. The trio never denied they knew the alleged bombers socially, but maintained they had no hand in preparing the attacks. They were acquitted again on that charge, though convicted on the lesser one of planning to attend a militant training camp in Pakistan. The prosecution rested solely on Soviet-style guilt by association, which strongly suggests the authorities skating on extremely thin ice. The latest incumbent to occupy the musical chair of Home Secretary, Jacqui Smith, was reduced to wet mutterings about Britain being 'tough on terrorists.' What became obvious at both Kingston trials, flops as they were, was the mesmerised fascination the authorities held for a Pakistani-American in his early thirties with an extremely chequered record. This was the man of mystery who became known as the terrorist supergrass *extraordinaire,* a certain Mohammed Junaid Babar. A rather classic example of a serial attention seeker, he was awarded Queen's Evidence star billing at both show trials. Babar is the cosseted darling of intelligence services in the United States and Canada, as well as Britain. So far as the UK is concerned, his impact on juries is a great deal smaller than his own inflated ego.

In February 2011, the remarkable story of the charmed life enjoyed by the self-promoting super-informant flashed across the Atlantic. Babar's boast he set up the training camp in the Pakistan wilderness at which one of the alleged 7/7 bombers — Sidique Khan — was taught bomb-making techniques, made him a hot property to British intelligence. Yet as we saw, his claims of inside knowledge on the Luton Four and their alleged affiliations had already been thrown out of court by the two Kingston juries. He had mixed form in yet another high-profile terrorist prosecution in the UK, the-called Crevice Affair in 2006, sometimes known as the Great Fertilizer Plot. He was again billed as the star turn as seven Pakistanis — all said to be known to Sidique Khan and Tanweer — went on trial. They were accused of plotting to explode home-made bombs constructed of very basic materials at targets such as the giant Bluewater shopping complex in Kent and the iconic Ministry of Sound nightclub in London. So once again it was a guilt-by-association trial, which earned five of the accused 40-year sentences for the fertilizer charges, their alleged intimacies with the Luton Four hovering in the background. Babar swept to the Old Bailey in an armoured police convoy chaperoned by a helicopter, a piece of pure *opera buffa* staged for the benefit of the media. But for the evidence of the fabled supergrass — journalese shorthand guaranteed to reduce the most cynical news editor to a quivering jellyfish — it is quite possible this trial would have suffered the same fate as the Kingston hearings. As it was, two men got off altogether. At the conclusion of a long and chaotic trial which cost more than £50 million, Babar was ringingly denounced by the leading defense attorney as as 'a liar, nothing more than a conceited fantasist.' This assessment, as we discover in a moment, is probably correct.

Crevice was essentially a political exercise in window dressing intended on the one hand to cultivate the atmosphere of constant fear, on which the war on terror depends. On the other, to secure by means of some spectacular convictions incriminating connections to the Luton Four, concerning which Babar so often boasted. Four years later, *The Guardian* spoilt the party with news of an interesting court case in New York. In December 2010, the self-confessed terrorist who ran his own bomb-making academy was set free by a kindly judge with a light tap on the wrist and a $500 fee for the costs of the hearing. It transpired that Babar had been hibernating in the American correctional system for more than four years — just one of those those served in high security quarters — and strolled around free as air for another two. Babar received kid-glove treatment thanks to what the benevolent judge called his 'exceptional co-operation' with US intelligence agencies, probably (as *The Guardian* suspected) before the 7/7 attacks. How came it otherwise that such a high-grade source went whither he pleased for at least two years, with a get-out-of-jail bail ticket stuffed in his pocket, a rare bounty granted to a man who publicly boasted that he wanted to murder American soldiers? The only plausible explanation is that so long as he kept the kettle whistling, he could look forward to a light rap. So it was that the original seventy-year sentence progressively shrivelled to four and a bit, and then clicked to 'time served.' A number of sources following Babar and his circus claim that the White House directly intervened to ensure he was spared a long jail term.

A surreal turn of events pointed to yet another episode of extraordinary panic and confusion emanating from MI5's wedding cake glass palace on the banks of the River Thames. A photograph was rushed before the ongoing 7/7 inquest proceedings supposedly depicting Khan and Tanweer together. They were snapped on a London station after a rendezvous with the fertilizer bomb plotters involved in the Crevice affair, in Kent. This was the photograph passed to Babar to support identification of the pair. It was actually the only tangible connection. If the fabulous supergrass actually did see this curious photograph, and that is not certain, then he must have scratched his head. The original color photograph had been copied in black and white and then cropped in such a crude fashion as to render Tanweer unrecognizable and remove Khan altogether. Hugo Keith, counsel to the inquests, said the clumsy edit had 'left Tanweer without even identifying marks on his hat, much of a nose and parts of his clothing,' adding for good measure that his own children could have done a better job.

We have been in this territory before, the case of the infamous Iraqi defector and precious CIA asset Rāfid Ahmad Alwān. Codenamed Curveball, he tricked former US Secretary of State Colin Powell into informing the UN in his famous set-piece speech that Saddam Hussein was fooling international weapons inspectors. Hand on heart, Powell declared that Saddam was churning out chemical weapons from mobile labs kept constantly on the move around the country. These lines of fiction clearly belong with the financially-pinched, part-time reluctant spy hero of Graham Greene's *Our Man in Havana*, set in pre-Castro Cuba. The hero excites his London paymasters with lurid tales of secret weapons, backed by sketches of spare parts for the vacuum cleaners he is hawking around the island.

Babar was an obscure trainee taxi driver until he caught the attention of the FBI with a bombastic interview broadcast on Canadian television, in which he boasted of setting off to Afghanistan, to attack American soldiers alongside the Taliban. Babar was entrapped by one of the Stasi provisions of the Patriot Act permitting federal officials to access a suspect's library record, in this case investigating Babar's visits to a public library to use its computer facilities. It was said that he was using these to share messages with fellow Al Qaeda sympathizers around the world. In custody and facing many years in a grilled cage, or worse, he began to trill about plots to blow up railway stations and pubs in London. It is my impression that Babar scooped up what little knowledge he had from gossip and rumours he read on the net. Thus, he was more an attention-seeking weed than a supergrass. Like Curveball, he boasted well-cultivated skills in telling his interrogators what they wanted to hear.

The treacherous Pakistani snakepit is no place for the unwary, given the onmipresent shadow of the Inter-Service Intelligence (ISI), the country's sprawling invisible government. If Babar is all he claims to be, then ISI is either manipulating him or playing a decoy; if neither, then he is a background noise, an irrelevant fame-seeker hyping fantastical associations and knowledge of dark plots. It implies that ISI is sitting back and enjoying the fun, regarding this great chump of western intelligence as nothing more than a charlatan. He may be wheeled out in due course for more star turns, at the inquests on the Luton Four (if they take place). Since there will be no one there who can contradict him, he will have a field day.

The London bombings enabled the British government to tar every member of the 1.6-million-strong Muslim community as secretly sympathetic to the 7/7 atrocity. These were Muslims going about their everyday lives promoted en masse to suspicious persons. A spectacular and utterly botched raid on a home of innocents that we visit in a moment came perilously close to a state execution.

At the Labour Party conference that autumn, Blair struck a Führer-like pose and pronounced 'we know we must be more strictly controlled.' (Hitler did use strikingly similar inferences after the Reichstag burnt down). The lack of definition concerning 'we' is open to many interpretations, but in general, we take it to mean reducing the mass of the population to slavish obedience. Catherine Austin Fitts, despite being a Washington Beltway insider, describes what is going on all around the world now as the 'harvesting' of live human beings to support intolerant and autocratic élites, like a vast nest of ants feeding the dominant majesty. So the list of 7/7 victims (like those of New York and Madrid) must be expanded to encompass every citizen subjected to the wholesale destruction of individual civil liberties, the loss of ancient rights, privacy and the priceless treasure of the right to anonymity.

The police in the UK have been slipping out of civilian control for the last thirty years, complaining they have insufficient powers to prevent terrorism, or simply concentrate on their main task of confronting crime. (Viz the heroic chaos — and corruption — in Scotland Yard over the Murdoch press phone-hacking affair in 2011). We will note in a moment how innocent people framed for the Guildford and Birmingham IRA pub bombings three decades ago wasted much of their lives in prison for crimes they did not commit. Such a deplorable record never stops the police from getting whatever they demand. So, in quick succession, they were given powers to stop and search at random, and to arrest and hold people without trial for the vaguest reasons. Britain was the only EU country to suspend Article 5 of the European Charter of Human Rights, which is supposed to guarantee that no one shall be subjected to 'torture or to cruel, inhuman or degrading treatment or punishment.' We have a chilling indicator of what may be happening inside the walls of detention centres like the infamous Belmarsh detention pen. In November 2009, a High Court judge agreed the government could hold special secret hearings concerning six former Guantánamo Bay prisoners. They sought damages from the UK government on grounds that British intelligence agencies were complicit in their detention and ill-treatment. The claimants and their lawyers would be locked out, and their interests represented by an appointed Special Advocate. He would be forbidden to discuss the proceedings or the materials presented — the usual timeworn excuse being the 'public interest.' Reversing the judgment six months later, the Master of the Rolls Lord Neuberger stated:

> *In our view, the principle that a litigant should be able to see and hear all the evidence which is seen and heard by a court determining his case is so fundamental, so embedded in the common law, that, in the absence of parliamentary authority, no judge should override it.*

Fine words, your Lordship, but the key ones here are 'parliamentary authority.' The Conservative-Liberal coalition, that found the recently-vacated authoritarian boots of New Labour such an excellent fit, will return for certain with another shot at jury-less, Star Chamber secret trials. There are portents. In October 2011, the British Government, under pressure from the CIA and the US State Department, agreed that any trial, inquest or other legal proceeding bearing on US intelligence interests would henceforth be held *in camera*. A handful of MP's were present in the Commons chamber when the legislation was introduced. The necessary enabling legislation for full-blown Star Chamber justice is unlikely to meet significant opposition in the House of Commons. The House of Lords — in the short time left before the forthcoming abolition of this ancient and independent-minded correcting chamber — may represent the last bastion of resistance.

Other insidious forces are already at work. The former prime minister's namesake at Scotland Yard, Sir Ian (later, Lord) Blair, personally rewrote the English criminal code when he declared there was really no distinction between crime and terrorism. Once this dangerous boundary was crossed, and thanks to the Terrorism Act (2000), people found themselves picked up and booked on anti-terrorism charges for cycling on walkways, throwing litter or daring to heckle the prime minister. It is useless to argue that these powers are a disproportionate response, now that throwing a policeman the 'wrong kind of look' or behaving in a 'cocky' fashion can land you in hot water or a roughing up there and then, at the least. Tourists taking snapshots of the Mother of Parliaments or Downing Street risk having their equipment seized. The criminalisation of innocents has changed the landscape of the British state forever. The London bombs made sure of it. British people of all walks will come to fear the legendary blue lamp of their local police station. Count on it.

One has to revert to an important article in the *Daily Telegraph* of 20th May 2009, by Duncan Gardham, to understand the contortions performed by the then Labour government, now aped in every significant respect by the Coalition, to prevent the 7/7 truth coming out. In a stunning example of calculated insensitivity, the Inner London coroner, Andrew Scott Reid, wrote a five-page letter to relatives of the 52 members of the public who perished, containing the bald statement that a 'full inquest' might not be required. He had no obvious legal grounds for frustrating a proper inquest. But he went on to make the astonishing assertion it was probably unnecessary since a verdict of unlawful killing was inevitable. As an exercise in pre-judgement, it served only to prove that, hidden from public gaze, certain authorities were turning on a spit.

In the circumstances, he argued, the inquest could be formally re-opened, the causes of death stated and then adjourned permanently. This is such a hideous parody of justice it made a perfect travesty of the ancient provisions of *habeas corpus*. To add insult to so many injuries, the obsequious Jack Straw, then occupying the post of Justice Secretary, was said to favour a High Court luminary to preside over any inquest that was held. Yet, in a country awash with High Court judges, he was having trouble finding a suitable candidate. One wonders how many otherwise estimable candidates passed the buck when proffered the poisoned chalice.

The relatives were chiefly determined to question the Intelligence and Security Committee, a quango then under Tony Blair's direct appointment — in itself, a wholly unsafe procedure. They demanded to know how it was that the purported bombers got through all the supposed security nets. This is a potentially dangerous cul-de-sac, which in event of untruthful or obfuscated responses, leads to 'just let it happen.' Or, other damaging revelations. The inquest, as eventually convened under Lady Justice Hallett, an establishment figurine and a judge of the Court of Appeal, surprised even legal insiders, given the obvious risk of conflict of interest arising from the wearing of two opposed wigs. Her Ladyship quickly announced she would sit juryless 'after hearing submissions from Interested Persons.' These shadowy parties include of course MI5/6 and the Metropolitan Police. Consider this perfect gem, appearing on the official HM Coroners web site under the heading, 'who can be called to give evidence in an inquest?'

> *The Coroner is solely responsible for deciding which witnesses will be heard and the legitimate scope of questions, although of course she intends to canvass her views on this with the Interested Persons in advance.*

So the Ministry of Truth got its way in the end. Before they wound up in May 2011, the inquests were a carefully orchestrated exercise in cultivation of guilt, with the establishment media acting as the loudspeakers. As a tone-setting warm-up act, a barrister solemnly asked the chief police officer attending the proceedings to dismiss any hint of conspiracy theory: that the authorities had spent five years cooking the evidence. Of course Inspector Knacker of the Yard was hardly going to reply: 'OK, it's a fair cop, guv. We did.' We are in the famous 'When did you stop beating your wife?' territory. The purpose of the inquest was to label anyone with the temerity to question the official account as a crank, even the heavyweight ballistics experts —

domestic and foreign — who cast doubt on the main plank of the government's case. This stated the explosions were caused by four young men who manufactured their bombs with over-the-counter chemicals mixed together at a suburban house in Leeds. Or how survivors witnessed deaths and savage injuries caused by massive explosions erupting *beneath* the carriages.

The United Kingdom displays the appearance of an embryo Stasi state where everyday e-mails, phone calls and faxes are intercepted and stored by faceless people tucked away in the GCHQ headquarters set in the leafy Cotswold Hills. The inquest followed highly questionable legislation pushed through by the outgoing Labour government, which reversed the ancient precautionary provision that a coroner conducting an inquest must sit with a jury. If this was thought an essential precaution in Saxon times, is it an accident that it is discarded now, when the power of government over the private citizen is already without limits? Of course this is a rhetorical question, because the sole aim is to frustrate inquiries in which the authorities are at risk of censure. These include deaths of servicemen in useless foreign wars, victims of brutality in police custody, or in this case, the narrative concerning the bombings ruthlessly massaged by politicians and their obedient servants in the Civil Service.

We have been here before, in Era One of the War on Terror, which wracked the British Isles during the troubles in Northern Ireland in the 1960s and '70s. There were two famous trials involving IRA suspects that made legal history, and exposed the treacherous grounds on which the authorities so often rely to secure convictions. These included planting false evidence, and a stampede by the police to find anyone for whom a conviction would hold up in court. The wider aim was of course to create the impression of pitiless Irish republican terrorism, that regarded any soft civilian target as fair game. The comparison with contemporary Islamophobic hysteria is uncanny.

The public memory vaults being as desolate as they are, a glance into history will refresh current events. In 1989, the so-called Guildford Four, found guilty of bombing two public houses popular with off-duty soldiers, were freed after serving fifteen years in prison. In 1990, the Birmingham Six, similarly convicted for pub bombings, were finally freed. Substantial sums were paid out in compensation for wrongful imprisonment. In both cases, convictions were secured by coercion, industrial framing of evidence by police officers, and complicity of the courts and the media to pre-judge the guilt of the accused.

There is no more depressing example of these times than Lord Denning, Master of the Rolls, second most senior judge of the realm, a brutal and crusty old system upholder. If the gallows had still been available, he would have had the Black Cap flying on and off his legal wig on auto pilot. He uttered the following infamous sentences when the Birmingham accused came up for one of their appeals. Read them, and weep:

> *If they won, it would mean that the police were guilty of perjury; that they were guilty of violence and threats; that the confessions were involuntary and improperly admitted in evidence; and that the convictions were erroneous.... that was such an appalling vista that every sensible person would say, 'It cannot be right that these actions should go any further.'*

Yet, that was exactly the vista. The innocents were in the dock where the police — who falsified incriminating documents and brutalised the accused — should have been. Denning, like any 18th century judge hanging a starving child for stealing a morsel of bread, or deporting the unfortunate to Australia, would not, in the end, accuse the system. The sole objective in this bleak legal mind was to convict victims of injustice in the Court of Public Opinion. We are brought directly back to the London inquests. But first, remember Denning's presumption. It was not that the state was incapable of doing wrong. No, quite the opposite: rather the state must not be *convicted* of doing wrong, or presumably, civilisation would fall. The fate of innocents was immaterial in this warped paradigm.

The successful appeals after so many years left exposed the vital over-hanging question: who then did bomb the pubs? After all, almost two decades of incarceration of the innocents, and two more decades since then, a great deal of thrashing around has produced no more than speculation as to the real perpetrators. The deep state itself is the obvious answer.

One may look for guidance to the very strange stories from the dirty war in Northern Ireland. The 'Poppy Day' bomb which exploded in Enniskillen on 8th November 1987 struck at the sensitive chord of the annual 'Remembrance Day' salute to those who fell in two world wars, and other conflicts in which the UK has been involved. Again, the bombing at Omagh eleven years later, on 15th August 1998, was blamed on a a splinter group of the Irish republican nationalist movement. This was perhaps the most appalling terrorist atrocity in all the Irish years of lead. There were 29 dead and more than 200 injured by a bomb left in a parked car. Enniskillen, branded as an IRA atrocity (which the IRA indignantly denied) failed to yield up a single suspect. Omagh was attributed to a disenchanted offshoot of the IRA. One man charged was convicted, then freed when it was revealed the Royal Ulster Constabulary offered perjured evidence. A second was found not guilty.

One important clue we do have is the dirty war waged in Ulster and on the UK mainland by British intelligence, replete with false flag atrocities, and the deliberate manufacture of a pattern of terror in the public mind. These are, of course, the well-tried tactics of Gladio, the throwing of guilt or suspicion in order to achieve political ends, using the ventriloquism of terror.

Omagh occurred at an extremely delicate point in the protracted Ulster peace negotiations. The IRA suffered severe collateral damage, which permanently undermined its image, even among the republican community. The BBC *Panorama* programme later alleged that police on both sides of the border had known the identities of the culprits even before the attack. This revelation arouses strong suspicions of 'just let it happen,' that familiar Gladio sleight of hand.

The Royal Ulster Constabulary certainly took an unconscionable time hauling in a slew of suspects, without in the end convicting anyone. Some of the relatives and victims started a civil action against those accused by BBC *Panorama*, and won £1.2 million in damages. There have been no further criminal proceedings.

I have devoted a few moments to these Irish examples because their similarity to Gladio terrorism strongly suggests they are out of the same stable. I mentioned the deplorable old curmudgeon Lord Denning, whose stock in trade was to absolve the state and its agents from all misdeeds. It is once again extraordinary how the public interest consistently fails to prevail, even as authority never fails to plead it as the excuse for demolishing civil rights and liberties. The self-gagging Strasbourg geese of the media, force-fed on a rich diet of government propaganda, bear a great weight of responsibility. If, to take one possible line, the London bombings occurred because the astral Interested Persons were compromised by their protection of sleepers among the members of the Londonistan Muslim community, then the public is entitled to have that information in front of them. After all, peaceful citizens going about their daily business were the victims of the tube and bus bombs, not legions of home secretaries, gold-braided grossly superannuated policemen and still less, pampered spies. Yet not only is the inquest into the fate of the victims thoroughly compromised by official strait-jackets, another (which might throw real light on many questions, an open and impartial inquest concerning the four alleged bombers) may never happen. At the time of writing, the arrangements for the last remaining fudge have yet to be settled.

The fates of Germaine Lindsay, Hasib Hussain, Sidique Khan and Shahzad Tanweer, represent the Black Hole of this story, into which all logic has disappeared. The advance of DNA as an essential item of the forensic tool-kit has so been so rapid we take it for granted that the mystery of identification is now solved. Each individual's DNA is identifiable with his or her next of kin, so all that is required is a matching snippet. Still, accurate profiling requires several days, sometimes weeks to get a positive fit. Remarkably, when bin Laden was allegedly killed in May 2011, the American authorities claimed within hours to have nailed the right man, thanks to some conveniently available tissue. Was it sitting there on board the carrier *Carl Vinsen*, along with a full rapid-response lab facility, waiting for the incoming corpse to arrive, like some bizarre take on MASH? (The story of the flu jabs to acquire samples from the local bin Laden clan was pure after-the-event theatre.) Either the age of miracles is not over, or scientific credulity is under considerable strain there. But not when it comes to the Luton Four. Their remains, we are told, have been in the morgue for five years (except Tanweer's, supposed to be back in Pakistan). Yet there is a shroud of silence around the obvious route of DNA typing to clear up the issues of identification once and for all. There are no reports of relatives ever being approached to supply the samples that would end all speculation, one way or the other.

Yet there is no scientific evidence of that kind to connect any of them to the bombings. Echoing the great detective Sherlock Holmes and the famous case of the Dog That Did Not Bark — there is not a scrap of convictable DNA which can be related to the four alleged dead bombers in existence. The 'proof,' in the form of personal identity materials scattered around seemingly at will, is not a viable substitute.

Since 1998 there have been 333 deaths of persons either in the custody of the British police or during police interventions. No officers of any force have been convicted.

XVI.
The Return of Gladio:
Death in the Underworld

'Mohammed Kahar said at the press conference: "I believe the only crime I had done was being Asian with a long beard."' — A victim speaks after the Forest Gate raid in June 2006, in which he was shot by a policeman.

'London is often cited as the most harmoniously multi-ethnic city in the world, and there's some truth in the boast. But that's no thanks whatsoever to its police, its newspapers or its politicians.' — Mike Marqusee, American expatriate author and activist in London

---

On 21st July 2005, four bombs again disrupted London's transport system. Small explosions occurred around lunchtime on that day aboard subway trains at Warren Street, Oval and Shepherd's Bush stations. A fourth incident occurred on a bus in the East London suburb of Shoreditch. Curiously, the bus came from the same depot in Stratford, East London, as the one blown up on 7/7. A co-incidence too far?

Coming only fourteen days after the savagery of 7/7, the heated propaganda impact in the media re-inforced the impression of the British capital under siege by Islamic fanatics. Excitable and untruthful hyperbole of devices packed with nails and other sharp objects, detonated by Chapati flour mixed with hair gel or hydrogen peroxide, seized the media; but how then to explain why the actual explosions had the force of little more then a noisy firework. In effect they were paltry smoke bombs. There were no injuries and the bombers fled unharmed.

In the service of stoking the agenda of fear, reporters were fed the utterly false account that one of the alleged bombers had tried to explode his package with a revolver. However, it is significant that shortly before these squibs went off, a number of passengers on board the three trains described the same noxious rubbery smell that was also reported by survivors of the 7th July explosions. Was this the consequence of another electrical voltage spike? If so, were the Chapati flour bombs really intended as a mask for another deadly assault? In that event, 21st July — and the still unexplained murder of the Brazilian jobbing electrician, Jean Charles de Menezes, aboard a busy rush-hour tube train at Stockwell station the following day — acquire a dramatically enlarged significance.

In the now familiar story of Gladio patsies and stooges, all four young men accused of causing the 21st July events were well known to the police and intelligence services as potential Islamic militants. They were secretly filmed at a so-called terrorist training camp in the English Lake District. One of the plotters was closely associated with the 54-year-old Egyptian-born cleric, Abu Hamza al-Masri. Known for his fiery rhetoric proclaimed at a mosque in North London, al-Masri was arrested in 2004 on charges of inciting terrorism. The self-appointed imam is known as 'The Hook' because of the prosthetic he wears in place of his missing right hand, which he lost in an explosion, along with one eye. Altogether, he makes for a somewhat unsettling composition, resembling an extra in the hit movie series *Pirates of the Caribbean*. He remains on the FBI's most-wanted list for allegedly abetting Al Qaeda activities in the United States. His extradition is so far blocked by the European human rights commission on the grounds that the US authorities might seek to execute him or subject him to inhumane detention procedures. A ten-man MI5 team followed Muktar Said Ibrahim, the alleged ringleader of the 21/7 bombers, on the night that he left Britain, supposedly heading for terrorist training in Pakistan. So, between them MI5 and Scotland Yard possessed a very complete picture of four inflamed activists working up to some kind of suspicious adventure. Yet they were left alone, with the specious explanation that there was no 'proof' of intent to undertake terrorist acts. In the aftermath of 21/7, and the brutal murder the following day of Jean Charles de Menezes, the British media collectively reveled in stories of bungling secret policemen tripping over their shoelaces. After soberly examining the facts, we are left with the conclusion that the events of 21/7 may be better explained as a thoroughly-infiltrated cell steered to commit offences which the state could then milk for political advantage in tribute to the war on terror. Moreover, an ultra-secret military unit honed during the long insurgency in Northern Ireland specifically to manipulate terrorist groups and convert activists into double agents, may well have been directly responsible for the death of Menezes.

At the subsequent trial of the 21/7 suspects, one of the most eminent experts in the field of explosive materials let off a different kind of bomb. Much of the evidence concerning the events that day seemed to owe more to alchemy than science and chemistry. For all the florid claims by the prosecution that only 'good fortune' had prevented many people dying in the attempted attacks, Hans Michels, the professor of safety engineering at Imperial College London, informed Woolwich Crown Court that the devices were intentionally put together to cause nothing more than a fright. (This was subsequently the court defence of the accused.) And there were definitely no nails or other such lethal shrapnel. Only the detonators exploded. The professor gave it as his expert opinion that the devices were of such an amateurish nature they were not actually capable of causing explosions. Predictably, his evidence was crushed by the juggernaut of a massive terrorist plot to repeat the horrific events of 7/7. Disreputably, the ITN television news network claimed to demonstrate how the bombers boiled hydrogen peroxide on a kitchen stove to increase its explosive strength. The simplest chemistry lesson demonstrates how the heating process removes oxygen (the essential propellant needed for an explosion), while the peroxide decomposes naturally as it becomes hotter. The prosecution relied on the average's layman's lack of scientific knowledge to present a case of deadly bombs, supposedly equal to those of 7/7. Most of all, the events on 21st July served to drive home the story that home-made bombs of the kind that the Luton Four supposedly cooked up in the famous Leeds bomb factory caused the deadly 7th July explosions, and not as well-qualified doubters insisted, high grade military explosive.

There are two potential suppositions here. The first is that 21st July was actually intended as a deadly repeat performance of 7th July, resulting in a similar scale of casualties. I find this explanation at least partly persuasive because of one very important clue. On 21/7, the day before the murder of Menezes at Stockwell tube station (which occurred at 10.06 am) there was a serious incident on the Victoria Line near Vauxhall, in south London. Vauxhall is the next stop immediately north of Stockwell. At approximately 9.10 a.m., an emergency was declared aboard a train heading in the northbound direction. It was sufficiently disturbing to call for a line of emergency vehicles on the nearby Thames-side Albert Embankment. There are some reports that this impressive convoy assembled *in advance* of the alert. This is the story of the phantom 21/7 bomb, which has until now eluded the serious attention that it so obviously merits. In short, was there an attempt to blow up an underground train near Vauxhall station that morning, an almost replica incident to the three explosions on the tube network two weeks earlier? The answer is almost certainly positive. The emergency began when a woman passenger noticed an unattended bag, panicked and activated the alarm to stop the train. In the moments before the incident, the passengers in this carriage noticed something very significant and familiar: the air in the compartment filled with choking, acrid fumes, and a bluish mist appeared in the tunnel. As we noticed in the descriptions of events in London on 7/7, this acrid rubbery smell accompanied by a strange blue illumination was described by many witnesses shortly before the deadly explosions that day. It is the tell-tale indicator of the over-heating of electrical circuiting that comes with accidental or deliberate voltage spikes. Subsequently TfL insisted that the fumes were provoked by the driver applying the brakes, which is entirely disingenuous because the passengers were aware of the fumes and the strange blue glow in the minutes *before* the driver applied an emergency stop procedure.

Here is what one traveler on the train told *The Antagonist* website, which in late 2005 ran an investigation into the Vauxhall incident:

I was also on the carriage between Stockwell and Vauxhall where the alarm was raised. Just wanted to add that I too could smell fumes and see a bluish mist that was unlike anything else I had seen or smelled on the tube [underground railway network]. I tried to remain skeptical for as long as possible, but it became overpowering, causing people to cough. At that point the 'oh my god' woman pulled the alarm... everyone around me was independently reacting to the fumes, covering their mouths and coughing.

And a second corroborating account appearing at the same web site:

Me and my girlfriend were both on the actual carriage in Vauxhall that filled with fumes after leaving Stockwell. The operation took over three hours — significantly longer than any of the recent 'false alarms.' The station was about to be reopened within about 20 minutes of the incident when police realised that the smell of the fumes was not the smell of the train's emergency brakes. They then mounted a very large security operation including bomb disposal units in contamination suits and masks.

We both stayed with the police in the cordon throughout, then were moved at one point, completely out of sight into the street behind. I can say, and several other witnesses will corroborate, that our carriage definitely filled with some kind of acrid chemical smelling haze.

The presence of such a strong force of police and emergency services in such a short time clearly points to a potential bomb incident foretold in advance. Moreover, quite unlike the fireworks on three other trains that day, there were no reports of anyone on board acting suspiciously. There were no sinister figures fiddling with potentially explosive devices, just the acrid choking fumes and mysterious blue glow. The appearance of bomb disposal units who remained on the scene, apparently working in complete secrecy for some three hours, leaves little doubt that some kind of device was aboard the train. The supposition must be that having failed to explode, it was then defused and removed behind a security screen. The episode passed into the media fog as a 'false alarm,' and there it rested. The question that immediately arises is why the authorities did not leap to instantly bang the drums of yet another seemingly tailor-made episode in the war on terror. Here was a rare blanket of silence. The answer can only be that the script had not been prepared for the eventuality of a plot that failed.

The second supposition is that the Brazilian-born electrician, who was hunted down the following day by Scotland Yard police and a top-secret military squad, may have been in possession of compromising information concerning an intended repeat performance of 7th July. The excuse that he was mistaken for someone that he did not remotely resemble is simply fantastic. There is no evidence that Menezes ever worked for the various

Gladio: NATO's Dagger at the Heart of Europe

companies operating the underground network, even as a sub-contractor. But it is not impossible that as a freelance electrician he might have made enough contacts to stumble on some compromising information concerning the malfunctioning of electrical circuits. This might explain that Menezes was selectively killed as a warning to possible collaborators who might share his knowledge. There is another explanation to be explored later: that Menezes was himself connected in some way to British intelligence, and eliminated on those grounds because of something immensely compromising that he knew concerning the failed attacks the previous day. What is absolutely certain is that in the final hours of his life, Menezes never displayed the slightest indications that he was a terrorist setting off single-mindedly to attack an underground train. All the posthumous claims that he was acting suspiciously, wearing a thick belt trailing wires, failed to stop when ordered by the police, were exposed as blatantly false. This means that the 'mistaken identity, we got the wrong guy' alibi trotted out in the wake of the shooting automatically collapses.[69]

The plain facts are the following. On the morning of 22nd July, just after ten o'clock, 27-year-old Menezes was shot seven times in the head on a rush-hour Northern Line underground train at Stockwell tube station. The media filled with reports that he was mistaken for a suicide bomber. By the law of unintended consequences, the grisly assassination of a man revealed subsequently as innocent of any wrong-doing whatsoever, raised the curtain on the apparently stupefying muddle and operational chaos among shadowy operational units inside Scotland Yard and deeper levels of the British secret state. The searchlight beam also identified a Scotland Yard SWAT squad with powers to carry out no-questions-asked killings. Its activities were code-named Kratos, after the Greek deity renowned for strength and power, and tellingly, the lead character in a fictional computer game which features the Spartan captain of a rapidly growing and powerful army.

At every point the fail-safe procedures that might have averted a tragic killing failed to save the victim's life. In a bizarre distortion of justice, the authorities instead invoked their own mistakes and incompetence as a kind of perverted justification for cold-blooded murder. The chief plank of this defence lay in misidentification of the target. Yet, as it later transpired, the light-skinned Menezes could not possibly have been mistaken for the dark-

---

[69] Scotland Yard was accused at the Old Bailey Health & Safety Executive trial in 2007 of manipulating a photo of Menezes so it could be compared to that of one of the 21/7 bomb plotters. The image had been 'stretched and sized' to form a composite image of the Brazilian and Hamdi Isaac aka Hussain Osman, to impress on the jury the difficulties of identification. This truly Orwellian exercise was the practice of deceit on a high scale, because leading officers of the Metropolitan Police had always known that the suspected bomber had fled the country.

skinned Ethiopian-born terrorist suspect involved in the previous day's alarms. That wanted man was in any event well on his way to Italy, the British government's massive electronic security apparatus tracking his mobile phone calls every step of the way.

With each twist and turn of the case, it became obvious that the authorities, Scotland Yard to the fore, were determined at any cost to avoid exposing either the teams involved or why they were ordered to murder an innocent man. Moreover, if Menezes, a devout Brazilian Catholic, really had taken the plunge into Islamic terrorism, this would amount to a strange alliance. In the subsequent stampede to convict the dead man, not one organ of the corporate mainstream media raised the singularly important question of his motive.

Instead, Menezes was described as making himself an object of suspicion and thus inviting his fate. He was said to be wearing a bulky jacket that may have concealed a waist bomb. He purportedly ran away when ordered by officers to stop, and then vaulted the ticket barrier at the tube station. The accounts of a passenger called Mark Whitby which appeared to incriminate Menezes were constantly relayed on the news channels over the next twenty-four hours. Menezes was 'an Asian-looking figure' wearing a thick coat and a baseball cap, who seemed suspicious from the moment that he entered the compartment. He behaved like a cornered animal before the officers sprang on him. The media swallowed Whitby's account that Menezes made himself an object of suspicion by wearing such bulky clothing on a typically mild English summer day (62 degrees Fahrenheit, 17 centigrade) which implied that he was concealing explosives. It was a tissue of lies. He was dressed for work in jeans and a light denim jacket. Nor was he wearing any kind of cap. The media similarly made great play with the alarming account of one Anthony Larkin, who famously fabricated the story that 'this guy… appeared to have a bomb belt and wires coming out.' BBC News 24 recorded an eyewitness who said; 'It looks like the guy that was shot had previously left a bag on a Victoria line train (the one I would have got this morning if I hadn't been running late), and got off the train at Stockwell. His bomb (in a back bag) then failed to explode.' All these stories were fictitious and circulated in the aftermath by the Scotland Yard spin machine and the gullible media fiction factory, with the intention of sketching the image of a pitiless fiend at loose on the underground. Of course there are always publicity-seekers who materialize right on cue after any dramatic incident. They are always ready with dramatic testimonies the instant they are fished up before the cameras for a moment of fame (as I can readily state from so many interviews as a former television reporter). Yet this does not seem to be the obvious explanation. One has the clear impression of stories prepared in advance for instant circulation in the wake of the event. The surreal impression to events at Stockwell that day also included the behavior of Menezes himself, who apparently displayed no significant reaction to arrival of the policemen. On the contrary he seems to have calmly stood up from his seat. Another passenger noted that Menezes appeared perfectly tranquil even as a gun was held to his head. Nick Kollerstrom (author of *Terror on the Tube*) reported on his 7/7 web site the rumours circulating in London that Menezes seemed to recognize the men who burst into the carriage. Menezes' behavior might be taken to suggest that he was an actor in a drama, who was not expecting to be shot dead there and then.

The revelation that two specialised operational teams were involved on the confusing trail of incidents that day caused few surprises. Chief of these was Specialist Firearms Command, formerly known as CO19 in long past days when hardly any British policemen carried weapons. Now it was the Kratos unit, licensed to kill. Alongside this team on 22nd July was the Special Branch CO12 surveillance squad, whose numbers had dramatically swollen on government orders, and at least one other covert force identified in a moment. At a subsequent judicial hearing, held under Health and Safety Executive laws to avoid the political dangers of a full-scale public inquiry, a senior officer was asked why the decision was taken to extra-judicially execute a man in a crowded railway carriage. He replied coldly, but also untruthfully, according to the statements of eye witnesses: 'It was the first available opportunity. It is not ideal, but in London there are very few places for an ideal intervention to occur.' An 'ideal termination' certainly takes some imagining. A tube compartment chock full of horrified morning rush-hour commuters scarcely fell into that category. Yet the subliminal impression was that the state murder of Menezes may have been 'ideal' if viewed in a different perspective, namely the conclusion of an exercise intended all along to end with his death. This raises another question. Was Jean Charles de Menezes actually 'steered' to meet his death in the compartment of a Northern Line train at Stockwell station?

Menezes lived with his cousin in a plain apartment block in Scotia Road, Tulse Hill, a rather undistinguished South London suburb. So however did a close friend of the man suspected as one of the bombers on the previous day. This was the Ethiopian, Hamdi Adus Isaac, who also called himself Hussein Osman. He became a prime suspect because a torn photograph of himself and his wife — rather oddly but conveniently bearing the address of the Scotia Road flat — was found in the abandoned haversack containing the Shepherd's Bush squib (the improbability factor being obvious, the story was swiftly superseded by his friend's sports gym card). Given that witnesses saw the man described as Isaac flee after his 'bomb' went off in a puff of smoke, it strains credulity that he slipped quietly away to sit things out in a friend's flat, knowing the entire Met and in all probability far worse were after his hide. What he really did was to bolt that very same day, heading for what he believed to be a safe house in the Italian capital, Rome, where his brother-in-law was living. He was arrested there by the Carabinieri eight days later. A cyber dragnet co-ordinated through the British government's GCHQ communications surveillance centre in Cheltenham stealthily tracked Isaac from the dozens of calls that he was making on his mobile phone.

On the morning in question, a small hand-picked anti-terrorist squad were staking out the Scotia Road block. Curiously, they made no attempt to barge into an apartment possibly containing a man suspected of trying to kill scores of subway passengers the previous day. Six people emerged during the stake-out, but Menezes was the only one they elected to follow. In one rather pantomime interval, the senior officer in charge of the squat was 'relieving himself' when a colleague asked him to video-record one individual emerging from the building. The presumption was allowed to take hold that it was Menezes. He was then permitted over the course of half an hour to leisurely board two buses before catching the tube train, the incognito posse trailing after him for a good two or three miles in a morning safari around South London. Menezes' journey was prolonged because when he arrived at his usual commuter station, Brixton, the southern terminus of the Victoria Line, he found that it was closed. The reason given was a security precaution in the aftermath of the emergency at Vauxhall the previous day. So the suspect phoned a colleague to say that he would be late for a job repairing a fire alarm at Kilburn, in north London, then hopped on another bus to Stockwell station, a mile or so away.[70] The Niagara Falls of spin which subsequently drenched the affair included the explanation that 'Gold Commander' sitting in Olympian judgment at Scotland Yard — on this occasion the Oxford-educated high flyer Assistant Commissioner Cressida Dick — ordered Menezes' pursuers to prevent him boarding an underground train. But not two buses, although a bus was targeted the previous day, and despite the bloody carnage on 7/7. Even so, there was trouble keeping to the script, a prominent feature of the entire affair. Gold Commander Dick's injunction was compromised by one of the undercover agents code-named Hotel Three. He admitted during the course of the subsequent inquest that he was specifically instructed by CD [Cressida Dick], the duty supervising officer at Scotland Yard, to allow Menezes enter the station, because he was not carrying anything. An unnamed officer advised her in a 'management

---

[70] Although the Victoria Line was temporarily closed purportedly on account of the Vauxhall incident the previous day, services on the Northern Line, London's busiest, were operating normally. The two lines intersect at Stockwell. The Northern Line was operating despite the fact that one of the dud bomb incidents the previous day occurred at a Northern Line station, Oval, and another at Warren Street, which is served by both the Victoria and Northern Lines. From this we read that the incident near Vauxhall was serious compared to the powder puff that went off at the Oval station.

discussion' that the decision was safe. There is only one plausible construction to this statement. The suspect suicide bomber was permitted to board a train in order to justify his execution. I am not convinced that Dick was a party to any such scenario. On the contrary, she appeared to be acting calmly in what were increasingly complicated and confusing circumstances.

It is more probable that different scenarios performed by the actors on the ground were not complementary to each other. This explains a good deal of the confusion on the day and during the subsequent scramble that became the grand cover-up. But it is obvious that Menezes could have been seized at any point during his half-hour journey to find a station that was open for business.

There is another factor concerning the magnetic allure of Stockwell station. It was from there on the previous day that the would-be train bombers purportedly set off for their various destinations on the underground network. So, in the collective consciousness it becomes possible to connect Menezes, a man living in the same apartment block where a terrorist was thought to be hiding, with a repetition of the previous day's events. In the space of twenty four hours, Stockwell station assumes the following unusual prominence.

- 21st July, around 9.30 a.m., a train proceeding north from Stockwell towards Vauxhall is involved in the strange emergency incident just described.

- 21st July, as mid-day approaches, the bombers board trains for their respective destinations.

- 22nd July, 10.06 am., Menezes is shot dead in the compartment of a Northern Line train.

- Mid-day: Sir Ian Blair refuses to open Stockwell station to investigators from the Independent Police Complaints Commission (IPCC). The dozens of CCTV cameras festooning the station and its platforms are alleged to be either faulty, or the tapes were not replaced after police investigators took them away in connection with events the previous day. Tube Lines, the station operator, furiously dismissed the claims.

- At 12.04 Scotland Yard issues a statement that a man was shot dead at Stockwell station 'after being challenged by officers.' This is one of the most important and oft-repeated falsehoods of the day.

- On the day of the shooting we find one Blair — the top London cop — urgently writing to another — the occupant of Downing Street — urging him to stop an inquiry by the Independent Police Complaints Commission (IPCC) on the grounds of 'unique circumstances.'

XVI. The Return of Gladio: Death in the Underworld   381

These are curious words. Of course the murder was obviously 'unique' in the sense that it should not have happened. But this was not sufficient of itself for such high political play to keep the spotlight away from the background to the events that day. Sir Ian Blair's attempt to silence the IPCC on the very day of the incident offers further proof that he knew perfectly well that Menezes was not a suicide bomber. There is a strong implication that the prime minister was already in possession of the same information.

It seems that it was a marksman belonging to a Gladio-style ultra-secret military unit rather than a Scotland Yard marksman who pumped seven shots into Menezes' head, another in his shoulder and fired two more that missed. A security agency source contacted by the *Scottish Sunday Herald* said: 'This take-out is the signature of a special forces operation. It is not the way the police usually do things. We know members of SO19 have been receiving training from the SAS, but even so, this has special forces written all over it.' In 2006, the BBC's *Panorama* programme alleged that 'Tango Ten' — the alleged terminator of Menezes — was a soldier from a hyper-secret unit, the Special Reconnaissance Regiment, spawned by the SAS. The SRR's speciality developed in Northern Ireland is infiltration and converting terrorists into double agents.

Tom Griffin is a London-based Irish freelance journalist who instantly concluded — based on gritty street-level experience gained in Ulster — that multiple shots to the head pointed to the standard modus operandi of SAS trained SWAT squads accustomed to taking no prisoners, just like the British Army's legendary Nepalese Ghurkha mercenaries. Griffin deduced the much-feared 14 Intelligence Group ('Det' for short), which honed its skills in the front line against the Irish Republican Army, was the backbone of the SRR. A freedom of information request earned Griffin the standard 'can't say, won't say' brush off.[N1] But as the *Sunday Times* reported in June 2006, press pictures taken in the immediate aftermath of the killing revealed to trained eyes a masked man carrying a modified version of a Heckler & Koch G3K rifle with a shortened barrel — standard issue to the SAS but not SO19, the Metropolitan Police armed response team. The authorities subsequently grudgingly admitted that 'special teams' had indeed been 'rendering assistance' at the scene. Suspicions concerning the official police account were hardly dispelled by the contorted official explanations and excuses submitted to the Health and Safety Executive inquiry and subsequently the long-delayed inquest (finally held in 2009, featuring the unusual spectacle of weeping policemen). The jury dismissed the evidence from a parade of secret policemen pleading an unfortunate blunder, arising from mistaken identity, as a tissue of lies. Gagged and bound by the coroner, Sir Michael Wright, from returning a verdict of unlawful killing — thus reducing the proceedings to a pointless farce — the jury unanimously responded with an open verdict.

Only the BBC's *Panorama* investigation, broadcast in 2006, broke with the ruling trend of parroting officialdom. The presenter, Peter Taylor, who specialises in investigating terrorism, pointed to the high risk factor that police communication equipment did not work underground, so officers were effectively 'blind' once they went below the surface. Nor were they required to be quite sure that a target was actually armed, or displaying other tell-tale signs such as dangling wires or a thick waist belt.

Sir Ian (now Lord) Blair, the Metropolitan Police Commissioner, responded to queries from the media with three famous assertions;

1) '… as I understand the situation, the man was challenged and refused to obey police instructions' (Menezes was never at any point challenged by the police).

2) 'The man emerged from a block of flats…. his clothing and behaviour added to their suspicions' (Clad in light summer clothing, Menezes walked calmly along the street to catch a bus).

3) That he personally 'didn't know of the dreadful mistake' concerning the shooting of an innocent man until 24 hours after it happened. Senior officers at Scotland Yard had already concluded shortly after the event that an innocent man had been shot dead.

Sir Ian Blair of course knew of the murder in the minutes after it happened, but throughout the day stuck to the line that his officers had killed a suspected SB (suicide bomber). In fact he knew perfectly well that the government's massive GCHQ apparatus at Cheltenham had already tracked the suspect Isaac to Italy. Was the head chef in or out of the kitchen at a time of high-profile public alarm? According to a whistleblower that we meet shortly, he was very much there, and moreover feeling the heat.

Scotland Yard spinners next sprang on Menezes as an illegal who had outstayed his visa. He was said to have forged a new visa when the first one granted on his arrival in 2002 expired. He was next smeared as a suspected rapist in a case some three years before. A woman who had apparently never made any previous complaint came forward to state that Menezes attacked her in a West End hotel. His innocence was settled by the ghoulish use of the dead man's DNA. The corporate media allowed the rapist slur to stand uncorrected. All the powers of police intimidation kicked in, confirming the impression of panic at a high level. The police insisted that spy cameras at Stockwell station were not working on the day that Menezes was shot. This was another blatant lie. In fact Canadian-born, 32-year-old Lana Vandenberghe, a secretary at the IPCC, viewed the 'non-existent' footage:

He [Menezes] wasn't a terrorist at all, he was just a normal guy, wearing normal jeans and a jacket, going to work. And when I saw the videos, then I saw the state after he was shot, my heart. I just thought, 'Oh my God, this could be my daughter.'

Vandenberghe photocopied and leaked documents calling into question police claims that Menezes had fled from officers and that he was wearing bulky clothing which could have concealed a bomb. She thus blew Sir Ian Blair's 'I was in the dark' alibi sky high. She destroyed the famous witness statement that Menezes 'had a baseball cap on and quite a sort of thickish coat — it was a coat you'd wear in winter, sort of like a padded jacket.' For this she had her front door kicked down in a dawn raid by ten burly, uniformed custodians of law an order. She found herself locked in a cell where she was denied visitors and compelled — in imitation of Stasi-like dehumanising practices — to use a lavatory scrutinised by CCTV. Vandenberghe had indeed committed a clear offence under the Official Secrets Act, for which others in like cases would have been brought to court. But this was not the Yard's game, since parading her in public would only lead to more uncomfortable exposures. This is the real explanation for that strange oblique reference to 'unique circumstances.'

Six months later, Independent Television (ITV) national news producer Neil Garrett was arrested, together with his pregnant girlfriend, on the grounds that Vandenberghe — an acquaintance — passed them incriminating evidence, including photographs, which proved that Menezes was not dressed in a fashion that would expose him to suspicion as a bomber. They, too, received the full-scale Stasi State treatment, tossed into cells and held for hours without food or drink or access to legal aid. No grace was shown to a pregnant woman. While he was incarcerated, Garrett's home in Leicestershire was smashed up and virtually wrecked by the local force, his laptop and computers confiscated. None of the trio was charged with committing any offence. They were intimidated by police state tactics with the intention of forcing them to admit they had stolen confidential documents for purely financial gain.

Not content, Scotland Yard next launched an unprecedented official assault on the verdict of the trial held by the Health and Safety Executive. This was a criminal prosecution that resulted in a conviction and a fine of £175,000 for failing to ensure the safety of Menezes. The London police were further ordered to meet legal bills amounting to a third of a million pounds. Using its official web site, an organisation devoted to law and order and upholding respect for the judicial system then launched a blistering attack on the alleged bias of the judge. The IPCC subsequently cleared all fifteen police officers directly involved in the affair from any further proceedings, erasing the Vandenberghe exposures as though they never existed. In *Nineteen Eighty-Four* George Orwell described such rewriting of events as 'historical revisionism.' Because the police are socially isolated from society at large, the result is quite often herd behaviour which shields members of the élite tribe from external persecution, in the ritual conviction they are incapable of wrong doing. In the United States the same phenomenon generally goes under the heading of 'silo culture.' The incestuous wiping of the slate by the 'Independent' Police Complaints Commission was nothing less than a wretched capitulation to dishonesty at the highest tiers of the Metropolitan Police.

To his credit, Peter Taylor's *Panorama* programme steered closest to the heart of the affair; was Kratos a shoot-to-kill policy and if so, who gave the termination order? Here is the key interchange between the investigator Peter Taylor and Scotland Yard Assistant Commissioner Steve House.

Taylor: When you strip everything else away, Operation Kratos, in the end, is about a shoot to kill policy, isn't it, because the point is, you've got to kill the suicide bomber.

Steve House: No, I can't agree with that. What we train our officers to do is what we call immediate incapacitation.

Taylor: Which is aiming for the head?

Steve House: Which is aiming for the head. I understand why it is that people say that's a shoot to kill policy but it is not a shoot to kill policy. We do not recruit and train our officers to shoot to kill, and that's not what police firearms officers do. They shoot to incapacitate.

This sublime example of undiluted Orwellian double-think was supposed to convince the audience into believing that pumping seven officially banned dum-dum bullets into a man's head was some kind of restraint procedure.[71] Certainly, Jean Charles de Menezes was 'incapacitated.' One shot to the temple with such devastating ammunition would be sufficient to achieve the desired state of permanency, given the victim's brain would be instantly liquefied. So why no less than seven, which supplies over-kill with an entirely new meaning? Once we are done with soothing words like 'incapacitation' to mask 'termination,' Inspector Tony Kalli, a Met firearms instructor, dispensed with semantics: 'We need to stop that person from doing that act, and the only thing we can guarantee is if we shoot someone in the head then their functions will cease and that person will fall.' The

---

[71] These hollowed out so called-frangible bullets burst inside the body without passing through to inflict collateral damage. They are specifically banned from use in warfare by the Geneva Convention, but are in common usage by police and secret services around the world. The police can avoid the Geneva interdict, because they are not considered as military forces. In 2011, Scotland Yard announced the ammunition would be issued 'in a commitment to making London safer.' The Health and Safety Executive had not seen the events concerning the death of Jean Charles de Menezes as much of an advertisement for keeping Londoners safe.

inspector has a sound point if the suspect really is clad in bulky clothes, bristling with wires, fidgeting, looking for all the world like the classic suicide bomber, about to blow up a carriage packed with commuters. But what if that same person is clad in light casual clothes, calmly pays for his ticket with his usual Oyster charge card, stops to pick up a free newspaper, strolls calmly to the platform and then casually picks a seat on the train to quietly read it?

What is missing is the clear explanation why a 'mobile surveillance *exercise*' suddenly switched to a deadly Kratos man-hunt. The excitement apparently began when a man with 'Mongolian looking eyes' (How many Mongolians are found in London? Are the capital's policemen trained to recognise Mongolian faces — or eyes?) who emerged from the block became the spur to sudden activity. The mystery man was the unfortunate Menezes, setting off for work, in his usual smart denim jacket. It is possible of course that in the general air of nervousness, hunter-quarry syndrome seized a small, closely-bonded social unit. This kind of group psychosis is often described as the 'canteen culture' ruling the British police service at all levels from the 1960s onwards. Canteen culture feeds on rumour, gossip and innuendo. But on this occasion the explanation does not fit. Hamdi Adus Isaac was nowhere near the block at Tulse Hill, which the entire security apparatus knew. So the only convincing explanation is that Menezes was himself the intended pre-selected target. There can be no other explanation for what now followed.

A London underground worker who caught the same ill-fated train that morning was surprised to find it held at the platform by a red stop light, the doors standing open. A lady witness supplied the significant clue that at least one of the assailants was already aboard the train, seated and looking around nervously before Menezes arrived. The victim himself was immediately grasped in a bear hug and at 10:06 a.m. shot dead. In a bizarre twist to the drama, the driver of the tube train, Quincy Oji, was then chased by an armed police gunman through the tube tunnels, narrowly escaping death as he leapt over the live conductor rails. No rational explanation was forthcoming for the incident, except from Mr. Oji himself: 'I heard gunshots, there were about fifteen of them. I saw one of the men [on the cab monitor] with a large gun shooting, and I thought they were fanatics and they were shooting at people in the carriage.' So he ran for his own life. His claim for compensation for post-traumatic stress disorder was initially thrown out by the Criminal Injuries Compensation Authority, on the grounds that he was not a witness of the murder. He appealed with the support of his union and was awarded a miserly £1,000.

As a regular London commuter, Menezes would have been accustomed to morning announcements broadcast on the capital's media concerning any changes or interruptions travellers might expect. But he was evidently unaware that Brixton underground station had been shut, in connection, so it was claimed, with events on the network the previous day and in particular, Vauxhall. Brixton is the southern terminal of the busy Victoria Line, which extends through London's West End to a final destination at Walthamstow in the north-east of the capital. Drawing on an immediate local population of some 67,000, Brixton is one of the busiest stations on the London network. It is also renowned for its immensely diverse racial mix, and occasional explosions of serious public violence in which the police were viewed in a poor light. Between 10th and 12th April 1981 Brixton witnessed a massive riot whose causes were rooted in general impoverishment and social exclusion. The unrest quickly developed into a wider full-scale confrontation between the local African-Caribbean community and the district police, who were immediately accused of intimidation and heavy-handed tactics. More fuel was poured on the flames of the great melee when police brutality was blamed for the death of a young black male, who died in hospital from a deep stab wound. Local gang warfare was the more likely explanation, but in this heated atmosphere it scarcely mattered. Four years later another outburst of violence erupted following the shooting by the police of a Jamaican woman lying in her own bed. She was thought to be hiding her son, who was wanted by the police on a firearms offence. Although the unfortunate victim was permanently paralyzed, the police officer who shot her was cleared of any misdemeanor. Yet another round of riots began on 13th December 1985, when a black 26-year-old man died of a heart attack while detained in custody at Brixton police station.   This is scarcely the best available backdrop against which to conduct an 'ideal intervention,' with the prospect of provoking yet another mass disturbance in this feverish territory. In the circumstances, shutting down the station that Menezes regularly used would conveniently move the scene of action to another less compromising location close by. When the inquest was eventually held, police witnesses implied that on the day, 'nothing went wrong.'

. Can such words be understood to mean that an operation undertaken (recalling Ian Blair's own words) in 'unique circumstances' was intended all along to finish with the assassination of Menezes in very public circumstances as a dangerous suicide bomber nipped in the bud? A Gladio-type targeted assassination, performed with brutal force before a traumatized audience, might be explained as a deliberate act to silence an individual man the authorities had certain reasons to fear. If Menezes had genuinely been mistaken for Hamdi Isaac/Hussein Osman, despite the absence of any likeness, then fifteen armed men were more than sufficient to overwhelm him in such a confined space. When it came to the inquest, the fact emerged that at least 45 individuals from the police or special forces had been involved, whether in mission control or at the scene of the crime. An operation of that magnitude would require careful assembly, not to say advance planning over a much longer period than the emergency circumstances supposedly ruling on the morning of 21st July. One explanation might be that one operation involving different participants was super-imposed on top of another, neither fully in gear with each other. Events then collided, so to speak. Or put another way, ran fatally out of control. But even given that possibility, we are left struggling to understand why Menezes was selected to be taken out. Some quite baseless speculation circulated (or was trolled) on the Net that perhaps he helped the 21/7 suspects assemble their bombs. Whichever way we choose to exit this complex maze, we encounter a dead end; the absence of any logical explanation why the man was killed in cold blood on his way to mend a fire alarm. I believe the best clue lies in the words of Sir Ian Blair concerning the 'unique circumstances' which caused him to communicate so urgently to his namesake in Downing Street on the morning of the shooting.

These were evidently so unique that they cannot be accounted for by Menezes having the 'wrong' face or simply caught up in a rolling snowball of events which overtook a machine system on over-drive. Was it some kind of perverted charade, a training exercise that went horribly wrong? The way that Menezes behaved in his last moments in the compartment of the underground train, that he may possibly have recognized his assailants, or perhaps was expecting them, points in that direction. The absence of fear on his face or in his reactions is indeed extremely strange. Now add the failure to stop a suspected suicide bomber as he trailed his way around South London, the clear impression of prefabricated witness statements to explain his death, then some kind of picture begins to emerge from the fog of mystery. The presence of heavy-weight special forces, including the recently created Special Reconnaissance Regiment, in support of what would usually be a pure Scotland Yard show, certainly comes under the heading of 'unique.' It is reasonable and prudent that keeping the prime minister informed of a violent incident on the London transport network, given the recent history of serious troubles, would be a natural reaction by the capital's chief constable. But Sir Ian Blair was patently less concerned with securing Tony Blair's understanding than begging the chief officer of state to frustrate an independent inquiry into the circumstances of Menezes' death. This, too, is 'unique.' However, two IPCC investigations did proceed, subsequently known as Stockwell 1 and Stockwell 2, but these added nothing of substance in explaining the murder of an innocent man. The second inquiry ritually criticized the police command structure and Scotland Yard's misleading communications to the media in general. But neither inquiry added to the pitifully inadequate sum of knowledge surrounding a public execution. In essence, both inquiries did little more then drowning the subject in words, in the hope that public attention would fade away. The refusal of the coroner, Sir Michael Wright, to allow a verdict of unlawful killing, effectively frustrated any further judicial inquiry. In rejecting Sir Michael's gag, the jury, by returning an open verdict, quite clearly implied that Menezes was indeed unlawfully killed. If we were to read of something similar in Russia, or China, then the western media would fall over themselves to point the finger of blame at a degenerate political system. Yet Prime Minister Blair famously dismissed an official inquiry into the events of 7/7 as a distraction. This is the mark of an undemocratic system, that relatives cannot discover why their loved ones were killed or maimed in such a senseless act, because the government of the day would not allow it. Above all when we look back at the Blair years we shall remember them for a passionate obsession with secrecy to disguise and obscure the acts of his government.

My conclusion in considering and analyzing all these 'unique' factors is that British intelligence knows a great deal about the purpose and motives behind the organized and deliberate murder of Jean Charles de Menezes. Should we be privileged to share that knowledge, then much more would be known about a far larger event, namely the bombings that cruelly decimated so many lives in London on 7th July 2005.

Scarcely twelve months later, on 2nd June 2006, another event occurred which bore disturbing similarities to the Menezes affair. Certainly it was clear from the outcome of 'Operation Volga' that the Metropolitan Police, for all the official crocodile tears wept over the murdered Brazilian, had gained little in practical experience. A huge force of 250 policeman reaped an unexpected overtime paycheque bonus when they stormed a four-room house in Forest Gate, North London. There a 'skilled marksman' shot and almost killed another innocent man, 25-year-old Mohammed Abdul Kahar, as he came down the stairs, half asleep and confused. Although he was struck in the shoulder, about an inch from his lung, he survived to tell another tale proving that nothing had been learnt from the culling of Menezes, save the necessity to maintain Londoners hovering in a state of permanent emergency. When it become obvious that Forest Gate was yet another grotesque mistake, Sir Ian Blair calmly refuted any criticism of the Metropolitan Police. His language implied that members of the Muslim community living in the United Kingdom should accustom themselves to such armed raids, in the interests of public safety.

The impression of a massive, overweening presence in the form of a dawn raid designed to shock and awe the entire population could hardly be avoided. Such an exercise must have taken days to organise, even down to the tea and sandwich refreshment wagons which conveniently rolled up bang on cue to succour the hungry policemen. Yet, the official pronouncements — including those emanating from Tony Blair's office — insisted that such an enormous display of force was vital given the suspects were believed to be sitting like hens in the coop on an arsenal of chemical weapons and suicide belts. Incredibly, a no-fly zone was enforced over the entire area.

It was pure Menezes *déjà vu*. Trial by media jury once again returned the verdicts. First, Kahar was shot because he impertinently struggled with hordes of masked men invading his home, then he was shot by his own brother (who had just applied to become a policeman). Finally, a clumsy officer wearing thick gloves pulled the trigger by accident. Official statements dismissed Kahar's shoulder wound as 'superficial,' as if that made it excusable. The only response from Scotland Yard was a gritted half apology for any 'hurt' that might have been caused, which presumably included hauling the elderly mother of the brothers from her bed, then dragging her off in handcuffs. The indignities made no sense at all, except to humiliate. Forced to account for their actions, the sense of authorities brushing off expendable sub-humans was inescapable.

The background was a Stasi-style denunciation by a mentally impaired enemy of the family, currently doing jail time and hoping to buy early release. Faced with a PR disaster, Scotland Yard bureaucrats started a whispering campaign against Downing Street, insisting that senior officers doubted the integrity of a tip from MI5 right from the outset. But Tony Blair's private office insisted on a maximum high-profile raid to underscore and propagate the war on terror. According to puzzled eyewitnesses, officers seemed to be milling around as the sun rose like actors on a set, desperately impatient for someone to ask them the time. Not a scrap of evidence emerged to justify an operation that set the taxpayer back a cool two million pounds and more. As with de Menezes, there was the usual outpouring of disinformation concerning the suspects, who were publicly branded as terrorists and even child pornographers before they were hustled to a five-star hotel in Kensington, since their home was by now completely wrecked. So, another disastrous episode in public relations? Not by the intended standards; namely, to pick on a district with a large Muslim population, and plant the seeds in the vaults of public memory that any one of those thickly bearded men strolling around clad in white bed sheets might be a potential bomber. The entire exercise fitted a drama performed in the Fourth Dimension, where unreality encounters the Strategy of Tension, perfectly. Not a single representative of the spineless mainstream media asked the leading question, namely that if a small regiment of policemen could attempt to barge into a miniature house on some vague suspicions, why were exactly the same tactics not employed at the Tulse Hill apartment block on the day that Menezes was murdered? The reporters who turned out to order at Forest Gate were themselves walk-on actors, as though they had dutifully returned their RSVP's to Scotland Yard's special events office. Of course they dutifully worked to the pre-rehearsed script, every word of the Yard's account the gospel of the day's events, while the shifty Arabs stepped straight from central casting. *The Observer* newspaper celebrated the death of English liberalism and the latest advance of the national police state with the words; 'Better a bungled raid than another terrorist outrage.' The Newham Project team who followed the affair closely, concluded; 'Much of the responsibility for the media strategy following the raids must rest with members of the senior management team in New Scotland Yard. Amongst this group of officers were personnel who had virtually total control of the operational information finding its way into the media and credited as police sources.' In short, blackwash, political propaganda. On 3rd August, following a rushed inquiry, the Independent Police Complaints Commission concluded with depressing familiarity that the shooting was yet another police accident, with no indication of reckless behaviour by the officer concerned.

The account sent to the taxpayer for the colossal blunder known as Operation Volga came to more than £1.2 million including these items: £860,000 ($1.32 million) expended on overtime payments, £90,000 ($140,000) on hotel bills for the family and not least £120,000 ($185,000) to repair damage to their home caused by the police. Notwithstanding these huge sums, Operation Volga was vaunted as a great success, another way stage in the war on terror. Scotland Yard eventually paid the family another £60,000 ($92,000) as personal compensation. Tony Blair's triumphalising of a brutal raid, based on nothing more than some vengeful remarks by a sneak with a personal grudge, took the line that any amount of mayhem was justifiable to 'keep London safe.'

In the two months after the 7th July bombings, 10,000 people were stopped and searched as they went about their daily business in London streets. About a third of them were Asians, who account for not much more than 12% of the capital's population. This sweeping dragnet worthy of the Nazi *Sicherheitspolizei* did not yield a single arrest nor lead to any concrete evidence of terrorist intent. Behind these cold statistics is the reality that the chief aim of the Strategy of Fear — the revamped and revitalized Strategy of Tension — is the need to divert public attention away from brutal armed invasions of oil-rich Islamic countries by governments of the United States, the UK and the NATO fold in general.

Sir Ian Blair's career as the United Kingdom's most senior policeman came to a grinding halt on 1st December 2008, when he admitted having lost the confidence of the Mayor of London, Boris Johnson. Blair took with him the abiding remark that Islamic terrorists posed a greater threat to civilians than the Second World War. In that conflict between 40 and 50 million non-combatants were killed. He now sits as a non-party crossbencher in the House of Lords. The other Blair, Tony, had earlier resigned as prime minister on 27th June 2007, almost exactly a year following the Forest Gate raid. On the same day he was dispatched on indefinite sabbatical as the high

XVI. The Return of Gladio: Death in the Underworld

representative of the Quartet (the UN, US, EU and Russia) charged with negotiating a solution to the Israeli-Palestine impasse.

The nation-wide riots which struck the UK like a massive thunderbolt in August 2011 were once again pinned on radicalised anarchists and black activists. For once the mainstream media failed to toe the official line. Both *The Guardian* and *The Daily Telegraph* suggested it was 'blowback'. Humiliating heavyweight policing suffered by minority social groups, the yawning social disconnect between upper and lower layers of society, the payback of long years of exposure to rampant consumerism in a society where education has ceased to matter, were posited as forces behind the explosion. London revealed the susceptibility of the English climate to the so-called 'colour' revolutions which exploded throughout the Arab world the same year, primed by the same social networking circuits which David Cameron moved instantly to censor. It was no co-incidence that the Metropolitan police were ordered to stand by as looters and pillagers stormed the battlements of high-street department stores stuffed with pricey electronics and must-have street savvy designer clothes. By happy chance, Cameron's personal embroilment in the phone-hacking scandal surrounding Rupert Murdoch's media empire immediately flew off the front pages and the airwaves. Long live the Strategy of Tension.

XVII.
The Return of Gladio:
In the Shadow of the Minaret

'Sibel Edmonds told this newspaper that members of the Turkish political and diplomatic community in the US had been actively acquiring nuclear secrets. She claimed corrupt government officials helped the network, and venues such as the American-Turkish Council (ATC) in Washington were used as drop-off points.' — The Sunday Times, 20th January 2008

Every picture, runs the old adage, tells a story. Consider the electrifying photographic scoop which flashed around the newsrooms and studios of the Turkish media in mid-February 2008. The composition is grainy but the message clear. It shows two men, both stocky, the older bespectacled one neatly dressed like a businessman in neat collar and tie, the younger dark-haired man to his left dressed casually in an open shirt. The caption might be 'the terrorist and the general' variation on the 'the vicar and the night club dancer.' The young man pictured in the white sports shirt is a fanatical Right-wing thug who will shortly burst into a sitting of the Turkish constitutional court, shoot one judge dead and wound four others, bawling he is a 'soldier of Allah.' The man with the stiff bank manager bearing is a retired high-ranking general called Veli Küçük, intimate confidant of the army commander in-chief, subsequently arrested for crimes related to the Ergenekon secret army scandal.

All Turks know these earthquakes occur with depressing frequency each time the country tilts the sociological compass to establish its true direction. If (to the perception of the secular élites) this fails to point to true ideological north, represented by the mausoleum of Atatürk located in Ankara, then a hurricane blows up. Ergun Babahan, columnist with the mass-market daily *Sabah,* wrote: 'Whenever there is an increase in demands for democracy, freedom and justice, the [deep state] signature is on acts designed to frighten people back into the authorities' arms.' Guérin-Sérac could not have put it better himself. Turks now had clear evidence the so called 'national front' — the quadruple alliance made up of the Istanbulese gin and tonic-tippling classes, secretive spook units, the stoutly secular army and fanatical Right-wing extremists — had resurfaced as a daily factor disturbing their lives after a decade of modest tranquillity.

Early in 2008, the country was transfixed by the 'headscarf spring,' the sudden relaxation by the incumbent Islamist rulers on rules forbidding female students to cover their heads in schools and universities. Predictably, out in the political jungle, old lions growled disapproval. Some went a lot further. Doğu Silahçıoğlu, a former senior general staff officer with a new pulpit at the popular *Cumhuriyet* pro-secular daily, openly called for insurrection:

> *Even if the [ruling, moderate Islamist] AK Party is banished from power, there is another condition that should be met in order for this method to succeed. And that is that proponents of the Atatürk republic should be able to seize political power in the elections and should develop methods for staying in power until a new generation grows up.*

The modern towers of capitalism probing Istanbul's skies, alongside the older ones called minarets, symbolise a country in a state of headlong and frequently wrenching transition. The latest trading at the high-tech bourse, perched on a magnificent parapet overlooking the silver-sheened, sewage-choked trench called the Bosporus, vies with the word of the Prophet rising from the heaving metropolis below. In the middle of this uncertain compromise sits another member of the cast, the third estate, the top drawer military élites, with a mendacious inclination to meddle in government, often violently. Against such a background, assassination of one of the country's most senior judges exposed the fault lines running through Turkish society. The affair also revealed the bizarre contortions that the inhabitants of the *derin devlet* will employ to throw the switches of instability.

The convicted killer, Alparslan Arslan, the young man rubbing shoulders with the seditious-minded general, boasted a reputation as a provocative lawyer with extreme Right-wing nationalist views, well known for trying to frame public figures for 'insults to Turkishness.' In short, a secularist down to his US-brand trainers. Yet here he was looping the loop in a giddy oxymoronic performance from one extremist polarity to another. As the trial continued, the Turkish media busily re-scribbled their portrait of Arslan as a man steeped in the violent world of ultra-Right extremism, since his days as a politically bilious Istanbul law student. In the run-up to the slaughter, Arslan was recorded making scores of calls to cell numbers traced to members of the military high command identified with the secretive Special Warfare Unit. This was the operation whose activities had already been connected to rogue and false-flag operations against Kurdish irredentists. Yet he stepped calmly off the street and took aim at a row of secularist judges (who had just delivered another tough anti-scarf ruling) posturing as a militant Islamic fundamentalist. Arslan was also accused of hurling grenades at the offices of *Cumhuriyet*, tablet of the mosque-despising secular establishment, and suspected of numerous other acts in similar vein. On the final day of his trial, he nonetheless smiled broadly at the judges and declared: 'I want Sharia law to be proclaimed in Turkey,' then stepped off cheerfully to serve a life sentence (without parole). Those with long memories nodded and recalled the often hotel-like qualities of the Turkish penal system, swarming with Right-wing sympathisers inclined to quietly wink when convicted killers check out when they feel like it — Mehmet Ali Ağca was the notable instance. Interestingly, Arslan is a protected witness in the Ergenekon imbroglio, which may well prove his get-out-of-jail ticket.

Scores of suspects including army officers, serving or allegedly retired, tumbled into the dragnet on suspicion of complicity in the Council of State attack, or in the dozens of bombings and killings that scarred the country following the elevation of the AK party to power in 2001. Others were shadowy figures in Turkey's Teflon-like criminal hierarchies with 'high patriotic connections' in military echelons and the secular oligarchy. Some of those named in a string of unfolding plots tip-toed abroad, with the benefit of the usual false papers. The highly secret gendarmerie intelligence cell called JITEM (*Jandarma İstihbarat ve Terörle Mücadele*: secret anti-terror police) turned out to be in virtual control of Turkey's largest port and its annual published revenues of some five billion euros a year. Ambarli sits on the northern shores of Istanbul's grossly polluted lagoon, the Marmara Sea, astride the key shipping lane through the Bosporus channel to the Black Sea and Russia's underbelly. In the early 1950s, the port fell under the control of Turkey's notorious narcotics smuggling clans, who in turn enjoyed the protection of the Turkish secret army Counter-Guerrilla, and other engines of the underworld. Its choice position makes Ambarli the El Dorado of cocaine transit to Europe and the former USSR, thus a source of much off-balance-sheet secret revenues of the CIA. What therefore could be less surprising in the Turkish climate than one of the chief suspects in the Ergenekon saga, none other than retired general Veli Küçük, supervising the security that kept prying eyes away from the port's deep-state smuggling traffic. A rent in the curtain appeared when the boss of the port operations co-operative — a prized creature of JITEM — was picked up on suspicion of arms trafficking to Hezbollah. He got a stiff sentence, but a few confessional letters from his cell concerning underhanded deeds at Ambarli settled the score. He was freed and comfortably re-instated in his old job. Very Turkish.

The complexity and sophistication of Ergenekon scarcely suggested an organisation hurriedly assembled to meet the needs of the hour. On the contrary, the detail and finesse of the set-up suggested a body with a great deal of accumulated experience acquired in the murky world of the *derin devlit*. On 22nd September 2008, Turkish newspapers published a detailed organogram demonstrating a cell-like structure broken down into six main compartments, each with its own commander: the Intelligence Department Command; Intelligence Analysis Command; Operations Department Command; Intra-organisation Research Department Command; and two tagged as 'civilian': the Financing Administration; and the Theory, Design and Planning Department. Here we are peering into history, for this is precisely the working Organisation & Management chart of every Gladio unit that ever existed, including of course Turkey's very own Counter-Guerrilla organisation. The incumbent Islamists sent an unmistakeable subliminal signal to watching powers, notably the United States and NATO, that in Turkey, secret states were not so secret any more.[72] Turks rubbed their eyes, seeing among the names of the alleged collaborators a renowned academic at a famous university; the chief columnist of a prominent secular newspaper (who it was claimed sponsored a classic false flag, the bombing of his own offices with hand grenades traced to a military dump); a scattering of politicians with extreme nationalist views; a clutch of retired officers; and a lawyer notorious for persecuting journalists who disagreed with state ideology on the Armenian genocide allegations. To cap it all, a pair of private eyes who operated a private intelligence net with close military links. This was the Special Intelligence Bureau, as eerie as its name suggested, for it was nothing less than a Stasi-Gestapo web of street informants.

But there was a crucial new ingredient, ramping up of the psychological impact of rumour, innuendo and disinformation which Bülent Etekin of the daily *Zaman* called 'an information war.' In a crisp editorial, he explained how an artificially generated climate of crisis fed on 'various types of paranoia... which ranges from constitutional institutions to the Ergenekon terrorist organisation on the one side and from out-and-out agitators who take refuge in fascist remarks to influential media plazas on the other.' In other words, the secret state was aided by modern technology to find new ways to infiltrate and manipulate the public arena. Moreover, strange alliances were appearing between monopolist media moguls with the important capability to sway public opinion, ultra-nationalists, and their obliging friends in the underworld, all to bring about a change in the management of the state.

In other countries, Gladio shamelessly dipped into the portfolio of clashing ideologies to provoke mayhem. As the assiduous sleuths in the Istanbul state prosecutor's office discovered, so it was with the Ergenekon leadership, which used the trusted equestrian Trojan Horse ploy (in the land of its pilot outing) to manipulate the Kurdistan Workers' Party (PKK). There were other strange fish swimming around Ergenekon, such as the Maoist Revolutionary People's Liberation Front, the ultra-shadowy Turkish Workers' and Peasants' Liberation Army and the Marxist-Leninist Communist Party. There too was the Turkish Revenge Army, the old Gray Wolves back on best howling form. The respected Turkish political

---

[72] In March 2012 Judge Felice Casson, who unearthed Gladio in Italy, was invited by the Zaman Group to visit Turkey and tender his advice in respect of Ergenekon. He confirmed that Ergenekon structures and networks conformed to the standard Gladio pattern.

Gladio: NATO's Dagger at the Heart of Europe

commentator Ali Bayramoğlu left little room for doubt, writing in *Zaman* as the scandal unfolded:

> *[Anyone] looking for Ergenekon need not go too far. This is the story of Ergenekon — the Turkish Gladio — from the assassination of Abdi Ipekçi [a journalist killed in 1979] to the massacre of March 16, 1978 [when seven students at Istanbul university died in a bombing], then peaking in Susurluk and possibly involved in the Council of State shooting [in 2006].*

We already know the secret Ankara Agreement with the CIA shifted the main task of the stay-behind units to policing internal enemies of the state. The question arises as to whether the modern day look-alike enjoys the same patronage — not just of the 'The Firm' but of NATO into the bargain. The broad answer lies in America's complex relationships with Turkey, which follow the same giddy oscillations as those with Pakistan, another front-line Islamic state in the fictitious war on terror. The Turkish military is now a regional powerhouse, yet cooling on the NATO connection, which it sees as a tie without two-way benefits. Turkey is rich in minerals, her territories are perfect for oil pipelines, and — alone in the region — she has a powerful weapon: water. Without flows from Turkish rivers, filtered through a massive bank of seventeen dams in her south-eastern quarter, Syria and Iraq are doomed to disappear into the sands. A further factor is the steady souring of the special relationship with Israel, another child of the Ankara Agreement. The tensions over Gaza have seen to that. Turkey's land borders with Iran, Syria and Iraq, her great population (sixty millions), powerful military forces and seething economy, suggest she is really a big power restraining herself. In the summer of 2011, premier Recep Tayyip Erdoğan answered the important question, namely: was Turkey an inferior regional power, a dwarf on the world stage, or an aspiring global player. The answer the world received was unmistakable. The sleeping giant of Ottoman power had snapped his chains. Turkey has challenged Israel and the Saudis as the predominant power in the Middle East and wider afield, established herself as the beacon of the Islamic world. The former grovelling to the paramount interests of the US and NATO is over. She may now decide that owning her own nuclear weapons is the only practical means of asserting her sovereignty and strength.

Into this contentious frame steps Valerie Plame, flaxen-haired beauty queen of the CIA's undercover squad supposedly probing breaches of the non-proliferation rules, popping in and out of Turkey on a season ticket. This straight-from-Ian-Fleming, real time spy-gal who swung open yet another Washington 'gate' was prospecting in promising territory. According to the report produced by the Center for Nonproliferation Studies in Monterey, California, between 1993 and 1999 there were scores of trafficking incidents through Turkish ports involving smuggled shipments of raw and low-enriched uranium, weapons-grade uranium-238, black mercury and plutonium. This was aside from key components to assemble centrifuges. The *New York Times,* drawing on sources at the Turkish Atomic Energy Authority, revealed that in the eight years up to September 2006 there have been 104 attempts to smuggle nuclear material into Turkey.[N1]

Most of the seepage originated at leaky and frequently pillaged sites in a scatter of former Soviet republics including Moldova, Azerbaijan, Kazakhstan, Uzbekistan, as well as Mother Russia herself. At the centre of this bazaar — like some plump, malignant troll — sat legendary Pakistani mastermind of nuclear proliferation and Father of the Islamic Bomb, one Dr. Abdul Qadeer Khan, to the world plain A. Q. Khan.

The German-trained, multi-millionaire metallurgist is deified as a national hero in his own country for producing a loud raspberry in response to the Hindu Bomb. Controversy rages over his wider reputation as a ruthless racketeer in the game for the health of his bank account. The Khan network's operations in Turkey leaned heavily on the following, in more or less equal priority: the Mafia's incomparable expertise in managing one of the most sophisticated narcotics smuggling operations on earth; cells of well-placed sympathisers in the military, to provide underground workshops; the ongoing protection cover extended by Turkish secret intelligence at all ports of entry and exit; compliant diplomats; and not least, the over-arching infrastructure of the Turkish Gladio operation to supervise, screen and liaise between the parties in total secrecy.[73]

Since nothing is ever really new, it was the logical continuation of ancient mercantile channels exploiting the latest popular demands. Khan's blue-chip client list featured all the usual suspects, with Pakistan and Libya at the top, Iran next, then strong evidence of materials finding their way to covert nuclear weapons programmes in North Korea, Argentina, India, Egypt, Saudi Arabia and for good measure Israel, of whose interests Turkey had been a long-term defender. Then, the destination that almost everyone overlooked, yet the key to the entire adventure: Turkey itself.

---

[73] Khan's partner-in-crime, the late Alfred Hempel, ex-Nazi with very close links to BND (German intelligence), enjoyed similar immunity from persecution by his own state authorities. He was able to run a vast worldwide nuclear black-market operation, specialising in shipments of heavy water and rare materials needed for bomb making. Hempel's private air force operated through European airports with ease, a feat only possible with official connivance. He held a powerful ace: he was good for German business. Khan is in a curious state of legal limbo, allowed to wander freely around Pakistan but nowhere else. The United States is not happy with this arrangement and, given the advance of drone technology, AQK should watch the skies very carefully.

It would be inconceivable that deep state agencies like JITEM — an integral motor of the Turkish Gladio, seamlessly welded to the criminal underworld — were blind to what was going on. How could they be, since they financed themselves away from the state balance sheet by creaming off a generous percentage on the proceeds of all the arms and narcotics smuggling scams originating anywhere in the country. Recall Ergenekon's finance department, exposed in the 2008 organisational chart. The Turkish mafia co-ordinates shipments in conjunction with MIT (the Turkish Intelligence Agency), the top military command and the national police. Some estimates put the trade as worth 15-20% of the nation's GDP if one employs that quaint phrase, earned income.

Turkey's weave of the visible state with the cavernous one meant the highest officers of the state could hardly make any practical pretence of a crackdown, which led some of the most liberal-minded reformers of the day into the baited trap. As Seymour Hersh has observed, no operation of this magnitude could go unnoticed by the US government, particularly since the CIA had been overlording Turkey's secret stay-behind operations for more than 50 years. Uncle Sam was again caught speaking with forked tongue in the course of all subsequent denials, since the US actually kicked off Turkey's nuclear ambitions in 1960 with the gift of a one-megawatt research reactor called TR-1. It was a key sweetener in a secret protocol to deploy Jupiter ballistic missiles aimed at Russia.

Between 1993-1996, when the Khan network was running its nuclear labs in Turkey at full tilt, the prime minister was the rather glamorous lady professor Tansu Çiller. It was she who let slip the government's harmonic relations with the *derin devlet*, when she eulogised have-gun-will-travel Abdullah Çatlı, killed in the legendary Susurluk car smash. Her funeral oration included these words: 'Those who fire bullets or suffer their wounds in the name of this country, this nation, and this state will always be respectfully remembered by us.' This was a clever chameleon act designed to impress the Turkish Pentagon. Çiller consciously imitated Margaret Thatcher. She saw herself as the burnished sword of Turkish nationalism. Some thought she strutted around like Joan of Arc, whose fate she more closely shared. Pragmatically she tried to square difficult political circles by throwing money at the Turkish army, which the alligator generals cheerfully swallowed. They then got rid of her — permanently — when she started preaching seditious sermons on how the deeply conservative, religiously observant Turkish folk in the Anatolian highlands could be brought into the secular national fold. About this time, Dutch spies informed the CIA they had enough evidence to arrest Khan for pilfering a uranium processing plant, onward shipped through Turkey. They were told to lay off because the Americans wanted their own people to follow the trail, like the white pebbles

Hansel scattered in the forest. This of course was pure double-speak. The CIA wanted the stones kicked away altogether.

The fragrant Plame has been spectacularly double-crossed twice in the practice of her trade. The most painful slap came at the hands of top-notch White House staffer Lewis 'Scooter' Libby, as a result of a vindictive spat between his choleric boss Dick Cheney, and Plame's husband, retired diplomat Joseph C. Wilson. The fluent French speaker was sent out to West Africa early in 2002 to follow up intelligence reports traceable to the serial confabulator Michael Ledeen, but possibly owing some mischievous origins inside French intelligence as well. Supposedly Saddam Hussein was sourcing enrichment materials — 'yellowcake,' or uranium oxide ore — to manufacture WMDs. Wilson reported back that the whole story was a preposterous fabrication, which seriously undermined or even shredded the case for invading Iraq.[N2] The picture of Cheney consumed by one of his towering vengeful rages, ordering his obedient chief of staff Libby to drip poison in a few selected media ears, outing Plame as an undercover CIA spook, seems very much in keeping. But it was more likely a very cleverly timed sham act to divert attention from menacing developments elsewhere.

When the Iranian-born, Turkish-American Oriental language expert Sibel Edmonds — almond-eyed, raven-haired tribute to her Caucasian roots — went to work as translator at the FBI late in 2001, she began to overhear astonishing conversations. These suggested her own employers, the State Department — at mantelpiece level — and the Pentagon were riddled with officials bribed by a joint Turkish-Israeli spy net to steal American nuclear technology. If true, then Edmonds' allegations of such a startling conspiracy might be tantamount to treason. Among her damaging allegations was her insistence that she overheard a prominent government official tipping off a senior Turkish contact to steer well clear of a CIA front company called Brewster Jennings and Associates. At the time it was soliciting for work with the Ankara government. The outfit had no existence at all except on paper. But it was Valerie Plame's cover — as a 'security consultant' — to investigate the enormous black-market trade in nuclear hardware and fissionable materials with its central roots in the Khan network. It was an important milestone on the trail that then led all the way to some really big names in Washington. Curiously all had forged strong Turkish connections in the interests of the American state.

Counter-Guerrilla-cum-Ergenekon was from the outset involved in supporting and underpinning an exercise in western-countenanced nuclear proliferation. Turkish workshops capable of sophisticated operations manufactured the centrifuges, including the motor and frequency converters used to drive the motor and spin a rotor to the necessary high speeds for enrichment. Do all this and you mostly have the doomsday weapon, bar some tidying up. With false end-user certificates, which easily passed under the noses of Turkish customs officials, the completed centrifuges were then shipped to Dubai and thence onwards to the waiting clients.

The British *Sunday Times* insight team outed one Marc Grossman, number three in the State Department politburo — and interestingly, ex-ambassador in Ankara — as the one who blew the whistle on Plame's disguise at Brewster Jennings. Thus Plamegate, turned on its head, has another and far more insidious purpose. Plame had to be levered out of the CIA altogether, with a good dose of smearing to boot, in order to stop her following those glistening pebbles. The other leading lady in this affair, Sibel Edmonds, was right when she sensed a conspiracy — with lots of proof to hand — ordained at the highest levels in Washington. We understand that high officials in the US government had long known of Khan's activities in Turkey, tacitly condoning them. At this delicate stage Plame might be dangerous. The stream of allegations from Sibel Edmonds and the black justice dealt out to Plame overlap so closely they logically belong to the same family. Edmonds was practically smothered by an avalanche of gagging orders under the Orwellian blanket called State Secrets Privilege. It amounted to a heavy-handed form of intellectual house arrest.

Edmonds had actually stumbled on the re-incarnation of The Enterprise, the long-running CIA-Pentagon-Mafia narcotics and arms network discussed in earlier chapters. The Enterprise had now turned its attention to a new market, trafficking in nuclear materials, a scandal that far eclipsed the Iran-Contra carousel. But she was walking on turf previously well-trodden by perhaps the most brilliant and dogged counter-proliferation analyst that any government agency in the United States has ever employed. It cost him his career, reputation, pension, marriage and all but his sanity. Richard Barlow, a lean and studious academic by background, but politically naive and utterly out of his depth in the complex filtering processes that dictate strategy in the higher counsels of government, found himself suddenly sacked by his employers, the CIA. His sin was to voice suspicions that Khan's Turkish network had made Pakistan capable of producing advanced tritium-boosted bombs. He was taken on by the Pentagon's anti-proliferation office, where he quickly ran afoul of Dick Cheney, Secretary of Defense in the closing Reagan years. Cheney's preoccupation, on the surface, was arming Pakistan with enormous US F-16 airpower intended as a deterrent to the Russians, then embroiled in Afghanistan. Barlow's sin, in too many eyes, was allowing Congress into these dark cloistered rooms, where the secrets of the Turkish Connection are kept, along with the truth concerning the Israeli nuclear deterrent.[N3]

Anyone who works in Washington for long understands the most sensitive departments are broken into provinces ruled by satraps in a state of permanent conflict. By the mid-1980s, neo-conservative hawks took advantage of this arrangement to adapt the old Kennanist policies of ring-fencing the USSR with the fiercest weapons of containment it was possible to devise. The high-risk blessing of Pakistani and Indian bombs fell into this category. When Barlow continued to report how far along the road the Pakistanis had gone, he was fired for circulating alarmist reports, hounded and trashed until he ended up eking a living from a trailer park as a consultant, even though officially rehabilitated. He was left with nothing, not even his wife, whom he had met at the CIA. Readers will note that the chief constable in all three of these affairs is Dick Cheney, whose private fiefdom — energy services supplier Halliburton — has a chequered record around the world for questionable practices, including trading with off-radar regimes (and a marked aversion to taxes). Back in 1996, the firm was fined $3.8 million for using subsidiaries to supply Libya with sensitive drills that could be made to trigger a nuclear weapon. The future US Vice President, whose baggage train so frequently calls at Conflict of Interest Central, was chief executive officer of Halliburton from 1995 through August 2000. United States laws are disposable trivia to Cheney. Two years after the fine — and three before being elected vice president — he blithely told the neocon Cato Institute meeting in Washington that sanctions 'don't work... I think it is important for us to recognise as a nation the enormous value of having American businesses engaged around the world.'

Western intelligence, led by the CIA, was able for many years to exert enormous influence over Turkish governments, thanks to effective control of the deep state. This long-standing arrangement has now largely collapsed. Dr. Nuri Ersoy, a professor at Boğaziçi University, who follows regional nuclear issues closely, filled in some spaces in the nuclear debate, as the latest of a line of tenders came to closing in the autumn of 2008:

Turkey is not only constructing a nuclear power plant. Turkey wants to have localisation of the entire fuel cycle, starting from production of fuel for the plant from local uranium and thorium reserves to the enrichment of uranium and the treatment of the waste. This cannot be explained only by the domestic demand for energy.

Turkey steadfastly refuses to be drawn into the embrace of the atoms-for-peace supervision umbrella touted by Washington. It is considered insulting in Ankara, on the grounds that Turkey has been hosting more nuclear-tipped weapons on her soil than any other NATO member save Italy. Turkey's rainy-day policy of pursuing nuclear weapons via peaceful reactors is underscored by the presence of substantial — if currently expensive to mine — uranium deposits. This small difficulty may be cancelled out by her large concentrations of thorium, a rare alternative in the nuclear fuel cycle, in which Turkey may be self-sufficient.

Turkey is moving through portentous times. Her convoluted politics are not easily understood by foreigners, but in essence there is now a broad national consensus that she must put into practice the principles of deterrence in dealing with Israel. That means possessing the bomb. The United States tried to prevent this — as it did the independent French deterrent 50 years ago — and identical issues of splitting NATO arise if Turkey goes it alone with her nuclear ambitions. Ergenekon falls into the picture because it was intended as a tool to undermine and remove the props supporting the Islamic forces which (depressingly to Washington and Brussels) swept to power on such a tidal wave of popular support. The United States and her NATO allies have always conspired to remove any Turkish government that wanders too far from the limits of independence set by the US-dominated Atlantic alliance, at any price in blood. Once again, they used the same tactics of waking up the sleeping soldiers and setting them to work to destabilise the country.

The attempt to manipulate the secret armies against Charles de Gaulle ended with the expulsion of NATO from French soil, and something close to that is the explanation for the sudden outing of Ergenekon, or more precisely, the *partial* outing of Ergenekon-Counter Guerrilla. The Islamic government salami-sliced a few chosen victims — who gave the public impression of being abandoned — to demonstrate its power over the network. But the cull does not run deep. No Turkish government that seriously intends to remain in power will isolate itself from such a priceless asset, still less give it into the hands of others.

What exists in Turkey now is an Islamic brand of Gaullist nationalism, which is gradually recovering what it sees as natural Turkish sovereignty. The intelligence networks of the West have essentially surrendered control of the deep state just at a time when enormous pressures are building up on a crucial front-line player. But the clumsy blundering goes on. Washington tried to throttle a new set of tenders for the initial power plants the AK Government decided to build. Suddenly, throngs of western nuclear lobbyists hanging around Ankara disappeared. Only the Russians entered the bidding. This transparent attempt to prevent Turkey from obtaining enriching uranium like her next door neighbour Iran was doomed to fail. In May 2010 the Turkish Government signed a deal with the Russian Government to construct four 1,200 megawatt VVER pressurized water units totalling 4,800 megawatts at Akkuyu, on the Aegean coast. The plant will be built, owned and operated by a Russian subsidiary of Rosatom, the state-owned nuclear company. The region suffers from regular earthquakes, but Erdoğan has dismissed fears of another Fukushima by insisting that the plant has enough fail-safe procedures to rule out any serious risk. There is a groundswell of opinion against the decision, on plausible safety fears. Yet, at the same time many Turks see it as a decisive move away from the system of alliances which are increasingly regarded as insultingly paternalistic.

In 2010, the US started to blame the Europeans for shutting Turkey out of Europe, as though EU membership were a gift for Washington to bestow. Loudhailers like *Time* started to bewail the 'loss' of Turkey (like China of yore) as though it were an American bauble which forgot the right way to vote, like the Italians, French, Greeks, Belgians and even the British. Turkey booms away with the seventeenth-largest economy in the world. Its back will not be so easy to break as in the past. The controlled smashing of Ergenekon is the beginning of a process of disengagement, but it may invite painful consequences.

For unfortunate Belgians, the secret war never ceased. In the late 1990s — and thus confirming its continuing existence — the veteran stay-behind structure code named Diana was completely reorganised. It was now the *Commandement territorial interforces* or CTI. This was a military intelligence agency organised by provinces, and composed of about a thousand carefully picked reserve officers with orders to infiltrate 'immigrant communities which represent a permanent clandestine threat.' Here was the classic Gladio stamp: first invent the threat, then fabricate the need for the public to fly to strong order. Before long the necessary circumstances would arrive, headline-making riots guaranteed to set public opinion against Belgium's ever-swelling community from the Islamic world.

In the wake of 9/11, conservative propagandists on both sides of the Atlantic began to dramatise the 'green peril' of Islamification. This was the awesome prospect of the Planet of the Arabs, a threat to western civilisation comparable to communism. That led to a prospect of Europe dominated by minarets, on the brink of cultural extinction in the face of a relentless and uncurbed tsunami of immigration, raising the spectre of the fabled state of 'Eurabia.' A strong source of this fantasy was a clutch of neocon policy think tanks, led by the Hudson Institute and the American Enterprise Institute, both of whom established well-heeled offshoots in Brussels. The city was not only the power nexus of NATO; perhaps more significantly, it was home to the increasingly ambitious and vocal parliament of the European Union. An elected assembly of more than 700 members, brought together from all 27 countries that make up the present EU, was evolving quickly into a centralised body of opinion rivalling the Congress of the United States. It therefore justified the same weight of expensive influence mongering. The result was a massive propaganda offensive to line up public opinion behind the war on terror. As Marshall McLuhan famously stated, the medium is invariably the message. Move the furniture around and change the labels and it was back to the 'enemy within' and the Strategy of Tension; instead of reds under the bed, it was now the long shadow of the minaret descending across

Christian Europe. Little Belgium, with half a million Muslims, or about 5% of her population owing allegiance to the Prophet, was a most promising sales territory to press home the perils of the green tide lapping literally at the doorstep of NATO.

Belgium, the unknown country, can sometimes provide clues to western strategic thinking, being in such close proximity as host to NATO's high command. In 1996, *Le Soir* provoked public uproar by publishing a classified document indicating a subtle shift in Belgium's defence policy. The contents were electrifying and amazingly prophetic. It was titled 'Base plan for the military defence of the country.' What it indicated — almost five years before 9/11 — was a subtle shift away from external threat towards a purely internal one posed by the presence of Belgium's large Islamic immigrant population. It was an insight to a clash of civilisations which had yet to appear on the global political radar, except in Samuel Huntington's book of the same name (and time), suggesting rifts on faith-based fault lines would reflect the Cold War. Huntington's work was sub-titled *The Remaking of the World Order*, to which *Le Monde Diplomatique* responded by suggesting the real intention was to legitimise western, US-led containment of China and the Islamic world. In other words, Kennanism fetched from the storage loft of history, dusted off, spruced up and set to work to wall in 'the arc of instability' represented by the Islamic world and its potential ally, China. What is there about human affairs that is in the end truly fresh and surprising?

Le Soir bluntly labelled the document as a racist plan, and quoted sections which stated: 'Many communities of immigrants have settled themselves in large agglomerations. If these population groups should reach a position of strong disagreement with Belgian politics, they could launch actions destined to counteract these policies or to make their concerns known.' Here was the ghost in the machine. 'Belgian' could be rubbed out and replaced by that of any Alliance member state. The re-organised and re-christened CIT, charged with infiltrating ethnic minorities (it could only mean Islamic), clicked neatly into an emerging pattern derived from the Base Plan scenario. More components were soon added. In 2006, federal elections looming less than a year off, a secret organisation known in Flemish as *Bloed, Bodem, Eer en Trouw* (Blood, Soil, Honour and Loyalty) tumbled into the public domain. BBET, on the surface a vigilante civic protection squad, was soon unfrocked as a branch of the secret state. Police investigators traced its roots to a string of military barracks and Belgium's equivalent of Sandhurst or West Point, the élite Royal Military School. Its known members — about two dozen in all, most of them active and specially trained service soldiers — enjoyed unlimited access to hidden stockpiles of NATO weaponry. It chimed with the élite Diana intervention SWAT squad responsible for Belgium's years of lead back in the 1980s.

Many Belgian minds flew back to the Brabant supermarket massacres, and other intriguing aspects of *déjà vu* invoked by this apparently accidental exposure. One was the strong linkage, in the ancestral Belgian manner, between BBET and a clutch of Flemish skinhead and neo-Nazi organisations, those same old marching companions in cahoots at the Heysel stadium atrocity. Ministers in the ruling centre-left administration predictably expressed shock at these revelations, rolling their eyes for public and media consumption at yet another plot to destabilise the country. Yet, given the glaring existence of the Base Plan, bearing the clear stamp of official sanction, was it possible for those same political élites to be in complete ignorance — or denial — of plans to stir up the Islamic community with false-flag incidents? — and other such black paraphernalia downloaded from God's Terrorist Yves Guérin-Sérac's standard Gladio instruction manual. The cell's chief task was to act as *agents provocateurs*, stoking unrest and trouble in areas with a large migrant presence, especially the celebrated Antwerp racial fault line. At virtually the same time, and to make sure there was no mistake about the threat, Belgians were fed the information that some 20,000 immigrants from Islamic countries were under perpetual surveillance by domestic espionage agencies, without any legal writ, on grounds of present danger they might pose to the state. The three legs of this stool — the re-commissioning of the Diana squad, the licensing of BBET, a branch of the secret state connected to the neo-right, and the Base Plan itself — all suggested a concrete and co-ordinated policy to ferment unrest and milk the consequences for purposes of propaganda.

On 1st December 2002, the primed bomb exploded. Antwerp, city of diamonds transformed into city of shattered glass, was struck by rioting on an unprecedented scale. The fury arose from the motiveless killing of one Mohamed Achrak, aged 27, an Islamic religious teacher of Moroccan origin, known for his retiring manners and disposition — allegedly by an elderly white and mentally disturbed neighbour. The events in Antwerp that dark winter morning in 2002 confirmed Islamophobic anti-terrorism as the new universal church. The words of the 1997 'base plan' hung over the scene like a pall of tear gas.

> *If these population groups should reach a position of strong disagreement with Belgian politics, they could launch actions destined to counteract these policies or to make their concerns known.*

In the commotion that followed, the martyred Achrak disappeared to the sidelines, swept away by the corporate media's picture of a race riot fanned by the country's most widely known, feared and admired Muslim activist. Dubbed by sensationalist reports as the Malcolm X of Belgium, Dyab Abou Jahjah, Lebanese-born president of a militant Muslim rights organisation called the Arab European League, certainly played a role that day. According to Flemish police, he was at the centre of the multitude holding forth to hundreds of Arab and Turkish teenagers and inciting them to violence. In fact the media-savvy Jahjah, recognising a public relations calamity, was actually trying to calm inflamed tempers, as later became clear.

Abou Jahjah was easily portrayed as the Eurabian nightmare personified. He was certainly an old thorn in the side of the Belgian establishment. He provoked outrage by demanding Arabic should be Belgium's fourth official language, alongside French, Flemish and German. Numerically at least, he had a point. He also denounced assimilation and integration as 'cultural rape.' (A delightful irony, as Jahjah must surely have intended, in the Janus-like land of shotgun marriage where two sectarian partners, French and Flemish, steadfastly refused to cohabit with each other, and discouraged the use of opposing languages within their respective territories). But the most explosive issue was the vigilante patrols — or Islamic Police as they were invidiously branded — patrolling the poorer quarters of Antwerp with video cameras to protect residents from the notoriously racist Flemish police. This helped fire up both the riot, and accusations against Jahjah of forming a private militia. Such a position of 'strong disagreement' justified firm intervention by the state. It conjured the prospect of Europe's major cities pock-marked by Fallujah style no-go ghettos where Sharia law held sway. The massed European media virtually turned Jahjah into a devil incarnate, while the Arab world beatified him as a hero.

In the heated aftermath of 9/11, some British reporters deserted informed journalism for demonising propaganda. *The Guardian*'s local representative, Andrew Osborne, wrote of shifty-looking 'muscular young men, many of whom wear traditional Arab headgear... filing into an unprepossessing internet café' before setting off on a 'night's shadow patrols.' In the bizarre hall of mirrors, is anything ever quite as it seems? Jahjah's most bitter critics — and there are plenty of those in his own ranks — pointed to his brilliance as an orator, his charisma and the film star cut of his looks. It was not sufficient, however, to prevent the reigning British home secretary, Jacqui Smith, banning him from the kingdom on grounds of preaching hate, whereas his main stock in trade is militancy against compulsory assimilation. If he is inflammatory, then who is not on the other side of the racial divide?

Yet there is much of the charm school about his behaviour. In the aftermath of Antwerp, Guy Verhofstadt, the Flemish-born federal premier, immediately accused Jahjah of starting the riot. He was taken into custody, and then in a strange parody of a criminal investigation, held in his own apartment in the city's largely Muslim quarter, not far from the centre of Brussels, in a kind of house arrest. From this eyrie he held free and open court for the Brussels press corps, enlightening them with his version of events and the Arab League's manifesto (somewhat easier than organising a press conference in jail). Then it was baldly announced there was not a scrap of evidence that might stand up in court. So, a show trial abandoned lest it should turn into a propaganda coup, or perhaps another explanation? The *Daily Telegraph*'s international business editor, Ambrose Evans-Pritchard, who was on the paper's Brussels beat at the time, suspected Jahjah was 'up to mischief,' and could well have ties to the intelligence world.

In 2011, only twelve days before Christmas, the people of Liège, Belgium's fourth largest city, fell into mourning following a seemingly motiveless shooting rampage in the Place Saint-Lambert, the heart of the city. In the space of a few minutes a frenzied attack with high-powered rifles and, it was claimed grenades, accounted for four deaths at the scene and another 125 injured; three more victims later died in hospital. The alleged perpetrator, a 33-year-old man of Moroccan origins, born in Belgium, was said to have run amok, firing at will on shoppers enjoying themselves at the city's annual Christmas fair. He selected his targets from the veranda of a *boulangerie* (or according to alternative accounts, the roof of a bus shelter, which strongly suggests the presence of other shooters), then climbed down and hurled hand grenades at people waiting for their buses. His bloody work accomplished, the gunman, one Nordine Amrani, then killed himself with a shot to the head from a .357 Magnum revolver. Within hours of the attack, the authorities circulated the perfect profile of an unbalanced loner with a passion for guns, including a special liking for heavy types of ordnance, which got him into trouble with the police and in jail for almost five years. This is the so-often perfect DNA of crazed individuals who suddenly loom from nowhere to perform violent acts, leaving entire communities and even nations in a state of numbed shock. The Amrani affair could be almost perfectly transposed to the shootings in Norway six months earlier, which we encounter in detail in a subsequent chapter (The Massacre at Pleasure Island). Again the blame is pinned upon a lone gunman who seems to be functioning out of sync with society at large, probably has undiagnosed mental problems, has fantasies about guns and then suddenly starts using them on live targets for no properly explained purpose.

Anders Behring Breivik, the purported Norwegian mass murderer responsible for blowing up a significant part of central Oslo, and then shooting at scores of people on the Norwegian socialist party's private holiday island close to the capital, insisted that he had 'friends' with him that day. Witnesses who survived the slaughter described shots coming from different directions, and other gunmen. They were ignored by the police, the government, the courts and of course, the lackey corporate media in their usual rush to convict the official stooge or patsy presented to them on the plate. This is another scenario that can be super-imposed on events in Liège. Witnesses in the Place Saint-Lambert spoke of other gunmen armed with powerful rifles, casually taking aim at their victims. As the shooting died away, one masked armed man was seen by a number of witnesses running off through a subway. The number of casualties accomplished in such a brief episode also raises serious questions. Amrani was said to have used a Belgian-manufactured FN-FAL self-loading repeating rifle, which is commonly used by NATO armies as a battlefield weapon. Considering that he was supposed to be under close police scrutiny, after his earlier conviction for holding illegal and dangerous weapons, it is strange that such a powerful gun associated with NATO came to his possession. The FN-FAL can fire off 600 rounds a minute, so for a mass killer it would be perfect. But the time frame enclosing the shootings definitely indicates the presence of more than one gunman to score so many hits, moreover from different directions. This is a significant conflict with the official account.

Amrani, a rather short, round-faced, bearded individual, was not the classic Islamic terrorist portrayed in the usual official identikits. He could not speak nor could he read Arabic, and gave the mosque a wide berth. He had no associations with militants of any description. He grew cannabis, but then who doesn't in Belgium. On the way to his shooting spree, a five-minute trip from his apartment, he apparently paused to kill a 45-year-old woman who kept house for a neighbor. The pretext for a murder conducted on the spur of the moment was never adjudged. There was talk of attempted rape, which went no further. Still less, why he decided to launch his onslaught in the Place Saint Lambert shortly after 12.30 pm that same day. The mystery seems irresolvable, unless we approach the possible solution from a fresh direction.

The description of other assailants in his company implies that Amrani genuinely believed he was taking part in some kind of exercise or security drill (another parallel with Anders Behring Breivik in Norway) for which he was carefully selected and coached. In October 2010, Amrani was released on parole for his weapons offences. Within almost no time at all, he acquired a fine new armory of assault weapons, including the FN-FAL assault gun and a sack of grenades. There was no explanation how a man working as a modest welder (when he was not serving time in prison) came by the money to acquire such an impressive arsenal. As some media accounts did notice, his police supervision was lax to the point of invisibility, despite his apartment supposedly bristling with dangerous weapons. We are beginning to sense the appearance right on cue of the standard cultivated patsy.

Just before the shootings, Amrani's parole was due to expire. He greatly feared returning to prison, as he frequently told his live-in girl friend. Given that he was allowed such a free hand to acquire his fabulous store of munitions, it would be a simple act of persuasion to strike a bargain concerning his parole, so long as he agreed to take part in a forthcoming short police training exercise in the city centre. I suspect that he believed he was firing blanks. Likewise, he believed that the grenades were dummies intended for effect, like a thunderflash, not to kill. And he did not commit suicide with the Magnum revolver. In this scenario, he was executed by a rifle shot fired at a distance, before he could tender some differing account. The fate of the housekeeper that he supposedly molested and then killed, belongs with other hands. As we have seen from our earlier studies of homicide in Belgium, this explanation is entirely coherent. Recall that lengthy list of key witnesses in the Dutroux affair who conveniently died, were murdered or had accidents before they could tell their stories in open court.

Cui bono? We are back to the 'Base Plan' concerning those members of minorities who might engage in a strong dissent with the Belgian politico-cultural system. Amrani might not have been the standard mosque militant, but he still filled the bill for the Strategy of Tension: he was a Muslim by birth, he played with deadly weapons, he was easily manipulated or controlled, and he came from nowhere in the sensitive Christmas season to wage horror on god-fearing innocent Christians. The similarities with the earlier atrocity in Norway are so striking that a strong suspicion arises that the design and organisation came from the same stable.

If you stopped anyone in Holland before the 'war on terror' and inquired what state they felt themselves to be in, the response would have been along the lines of laid-back, easy-going tolerance. Not any more. The Dutch find themselves on the frontiers of the frantic faith-based collision between East and West, inflamed by two shocking murders which stunned the sixteen million people crammed into another small country roughly half the size of Scotland or South Carolina.

Wilhelmus 'Pim' Fortuyn, the hedonistic, openly gay leader of his self-founded populist political force, the Pim Fortuyn List, was considered most likely to emerge as prime minister from the usual prolonged post-electoral haggling in the commotional world of Dutch politics. On 6th May 2002, he was gunned down by a vegan animal rights eco-campaigner as he left from an election interview at a radio station in Hilversum. He had no security protection, the subject of much critical comment later. The official account states that 32-year-old Volkert van der Graaf shot Fortuyn with a powerful semi-automatic pistol purchased at a well-known, under-the-counter weapons den, but his exact motives were another knotted and confusing matter altogether. At various times a very confused individual, suspected by psychiatrists of suffering from personality disorders, he claimed he killed Fortuyn so his 'pernicious policies' would die with him, although he understood the act was morally indefensible. He rambled vaguely of Fortuyn turning Muslims into scapegoats and generally attacking vulnerable elements of society. But interesting clues lead in quite another direction altogether.

The overawing power of the Industrial Agribusiness Complex in this small country is a force the political classes learn to treat with respect. As the election neared, a fierce controversy arose over the efforts of the incumbent environment minister — the greenish radical Laurens van Brinkhorst — to close down the mink-farming industry. The Netherlands is the world's third largest mink producer, after Denmark and China. Its 163 fur farmers produce 4.5 million pelts a year, almost one-tenth of the fifty million pelts produced globally. Fortuyn and Van der Graaf collided on this passionate issue. Fortuyn vowed to protect an industry important for the Dutch economy, while Van der Graaf was a determined opponent of 'animal concentration camps.' Allegations surfaced after the murder that the national secret service AIVD (*Algemene Inlichtingen- en Veiligheidsdienst*) — the Dutch equivalent of US Homeland Security and the FBI rolled into one — wire-tapped two animal cruelty campaigners discussing loosely whether Fortuyn should be killed because of the mink farm business. The call was supposedly made from Harderwijk, in central Holland where Van der Graaf happened to live, so the assumption is he was party to the death discussion. With that kind of information in their possession, the police might be expected to raise a strong cordon around the potential target, not to say detain individuals plotting ill towards a prominent public figure. Yet there is something ectoplasmic, insubstantial and folklorish about this wire-tap story, which seems too easily presentable as a supporting act in the framing of that rare creature, the white protestant who will kill in solidarity with Muslims.

Van der Graaf waited patiently outside the 3FM radio studio, on a bright early summer evening, and then calmly pumped all but one shell from his revolver's full chamber into the victim's back at point-blank range, having first circled him to be sure of the target (so we are told, but if that is true, why was no one in the party alarmed?) A prime minister-in-waiting minus a security detail is anyway a very strange affair, given the abundant death threats in preceding weeks, raising again the eternal Gladio ploy of 'just let it happen.' This is one explanation. But another suggests other actors may have been moving in the frame. Shooting people with a pistol is not as simple or accurate as it is usually portrayed by the gullible goose-chase media. Handguns, especially of the type allegedly used by Van der Graaf, have a tendency to be wildly jumpy and fly about in experienced hands, let alone those of complete amateurs. Do we assume Van der Graaf found some quiet place for target practice? His deadly professional accuracy was a classic shooting gallery performance, quite remarkable for a man who must have been under considerable emotional stress, undoubtedly shaking at the prospect of killing a man — and an eminent one at that — for the first time in his life. To a professional with a steady hand, firm eye and grim resolve, no more than the demands of his calling; for a rank amateur, an extraordinary feat of accuracy.

The wounds were inflicted by a single-action 9-mm gun he is supposed to have bought from an under-the-counter weapons source close to the Deelen air force base, not far from his home. The small community thereabouts also hosts an army barracks, quite a dense packing of the military. The tendency of small arms to 'leak' from such establishments is well documented. We must ask however why Van der Graaf was drawn to select a Firestar M-43, commonly encountered in the United States and often touted as the assassin's favorite, because of its vaunted 'concealed-carry' qualities. There is nothing in his background to suggest how the quiet ecologist knew anything at all about guns and the particular qualities of different types, still less how to select a bespoke weapon for the task in hand, unless he had some kind of professional advice. Or was this perfect assassination tool in other hands altogether? For now I am prepared to advance the proposition that there is space in this account for another actor (or actors) at the murder scene, which has not been explored by the Dutch authorities. The following background to the murder may explain why.

Fortuyn's political personality fluxed in the traditionally confused Dutch spectrum between Left and Right, but in essence he was Amsterdam Man: custodian of that libidinous pleasure dome, where anything gay is straight. There was never much ideological stuffing to the Fortuyn agenda, if one took away the populist immigrant-baiting. Here was the brightly plumed libertarian parakeet, the opportunist whose advocacy of mono-culturalism in the prevailing climate of Islamist hysteria played mainly to a gallery that resented many of the liberal reforms he was so closely identified with — euthanasia, gay marriage and legalised prostitution. This is the often-remarked peculiar paradox of Dutch politics.

The mish-mash of motives served up by his assassin, Van der Graaf, looks like another example plucked straight from the Lee Harvey Oswald/Jack Ruby/Sirhan Sirhan/Timothy McVeigh/Ali Ağca hall of fame. Ağca may be the closest relative. We noticed that after the Papal shooting he was whisked away to a distant prison far from Rome, where an obvious and sophisticated indoctrination exercise then took place. Van der Graaf was held in close confinement for several weeks, and then for some months afterwards — still in isolation — declined to explain why he killed Fortuyn. However, the award-winning Dutch thriller writer Tomas Ross did venture an explanation in his semi-fictional book *6/5* (*De zesde mei*, *The Sixth of May*). The plot depicts Dutch intelligence duping Van der Graaf into killing the maverick Fortuyn, who was grinding on the nerves of the entrenched political establishment, particularly over his equivocal stand on a controversial multi-billion-euro defence contract with the United States. Ross' friend Theodore van Gogh made the book into a film, with a mix of fact and fiction that is the common style nowadays. The important thing about it was the inflammatory gesture of publicly muddying the official line by fingering the secret services. *6/5* hit the internet and movie theatres early in 2004.[74] A few months later, Van Gogh was horribly murdered. With his invocation of the secret state in the Technicolor tragedy of Pim Fortuyn, did he then invite his own death, displaying every sign of a furious revenge killing, at the hands of a 26-year-old Dutch-Moroccan who belonged to a group thoroughly that was penetrated by the AIVD?

Van der Graaf was sent to a forensic psychiatric institute for assessment, where the government tried to have him kept under strict supervision 24 hours a day. The doctors at the Pieter Baan centre in Utrecht apparently resisted, arguing they would never be able to assess his true mental condition under such restrictions. He was judged fit to face trial, although diagnosed as suffering from obsessional disorders, which should have cried out as a disqualification. The assassin now begins to resemble the standard patsy, of which there is further convincing evidence to come. On 23rd November 2002, a full seven months after the shooting, the prosecution announced the prisoner had finally made a humble confession admitting his full guilt. The contents of this important document, or even its physical existence, remain secret. The evidence submitted to the court included the puzzling affair of Fortuyn's DNA, alleged to match traces found on Van der Graaf. How was this remarkable transmutation remotely possible, given there was never any opportunity for physical contact between the two men? Immediately after the shooting, Van der Graaf bolted, until he was cornered moments later by Fortuyn's chauffeur in a nearby petrol station. Ten years ago, the niceties of DNA procedure were not as popularly understood as they are now, so no piercing questions were asked about the magical properties of Fortuyn's DNA to disperse itself at will. The logical explanation is the determination of the authorities to pin the blame securely on the prisoner in the dock. Their anxiety seems more than curious, given the alleged confession still warm in their hands, and the statements of witnesses at the scene of the crime. We seem to be looking at a rather blatant example of over-egging the omelette.

The striking similarities with Ali Ağca accumulate. He, we remember, was seen by hundreds taking aim at the Pope and apparently shooting him. Van der Graaf performed a public execution in broad daylight, which appeared to leave not a scrap of doubt concerning his guilt. Yet he, like Ağca, was kept under wraps, in Van der Graaf's case for months on end, although he saw his lawyers. The suspicion that Van der Graaf was coached, or more precisely brought to understand by central authorities the required

---

[74] The Ross-Van Gogh script for the 6/5 film features a fictional photographer waiting to snap him leaving the studio. When he develops the pictures, he sees other figures acting suspiciously in the margins of the murder scene. We may read from this a suspicion in an acute observer's mind that the official account of the killing had alternative explanations.

version of why he shot Fortuyn, becomes persuasive the more one trawls through the facts and circumstances which surround that fateful day. Was the man known as the Green Robin Hood gradually steered away from a rambling animal rights grudge against Fortuyn — the fur farms and so forth mentioned in the alleged wire-tap — to something more theatrical, fitting the heated electoral climate? Or was he set up from the very beginning?

Van der Graaf had no connections with the Muslim debate searing the Netherlands, nor the vaguest hint of activism in that quarter. Nor, for that matter, any record of violence, although efforts were made to invent one. The police made much of a stash of high-street chemicals found in his home that could be combined to make explosives. They were exactly of the type animal rights activists often employ to make smoke bombs. Yet what need had he of these combustible chemicals, given his outstanding record of pursuing, with annoying success, entirely non-violent, patient litigation against environmental offenders in the field of animal rights, working through his own environmental protection agency? Intensive agri-business, responsible as it is for vast amounts of highly toxic groundwater pollution bespoiling Dutch poulders, is an extremely powerful political lobby, known to be in league more often than not with the very authorities supposed to monitor and curb their activities. Van der Graaf made few friends by breaking into this charmed and potentially vindictive circle. Its members were enraged by his constant run of successes in cases avoided by the competent authorities, with the results that culprits were forced to pay fines and step in line with environmental legislation.[75]

The bottom line, as usual, is *cui bono?*

Had Fortuyn lived to become premier, one of his first decisions would be the fate of Dutch participation in the highly contentious Joint Strike Fighter project promoted by the United States through the Lockheed Martin company. Fortuyn correctly sniffed another multi-billion dollar boondoggle with the built-in capacity for a massive cost over-run, yet was compelled out of *Realpolitik* to consider the jobs impact on big-payroll Dutch sub-contractors like the giant Philips electronics conglomerate. Lockheed Martin,

---

[75] A small country renowned for hosting global giants such as food megalomerate Uniliver, the Netherlands is one of the most intensively farmed and chemically saturated countries on earth. Dairy production alone from 1.69 million cows is only slightly behind the global leaders, the UK and USA. Such figures court a heavy price. Intensive farming practices are responsible for substantial aquatic run-off from pesticides and other toxic by-products. Mass farming dominates the industry, as the traditional mixed-crop small farmer is driven off the land by loan sharking banks, inadequate capital and industrially organized rivals. All this comes before animal welfare issues aroused by intensive farming, which Greenpeace and other such bodies oppose. This was the daily diet of Volkert van der Graaf.

one of the great bulldozers of the military-industrial complex, dragged the Dutch royal family through scandal dirt a quarter of a century earlier, throwing Queen Juliana's consort Prince Bernhard a $1.1 million dollar bribe to favour a Lockheed jet for the Dutch air force. He spent most of it feathering a nest in Paris for one of his many courtesans, weeping crocodile tears it should have gone to the World Wildlife Fund, where he was a prominent figure. Fortuyn's quibbles over the JSF — he was not a pacifist but wary of the over-weening military-industrial complex — ensured powerful enemies in the Dutch military establishment, and even within the ranks of his own list. I have identified at least one possible intelligence plant sprouting there, well known to myself, which suggests a certain naivety in Fortuyn's judgment in choosing his collaborators. Although his associates later claimed he toned down his anti-JSF line, his mind on that subject by the time he died was frankly not known. He was certainly having his arms roughly twisted.[76]

Willem Oltmans is a name well known in Holland as an acerbic critic of the Dutch establishment. In a quite extraordinary episode, which partly involved the Orange royal family, Oltmans was awarded eight million guilders compensation in 2000, when the Dutch government tacitly conceded trying to gag him for the past decade. Not long after that he was in trouble again, this time for claiming that the US Ambassador in The Hague, Clifford Sobel, secretly met with Fortuyn to resolve the fighter plane impasse. This might be seen as a perfectly acceptable instance of diplomatic lobbying to resolve a contentious issue. Why then did Oltmans claim shadowy figures from the Dutch deep state suddenly threatened to kill him (he died in 2004) or have him locked up in a mental home.

This mystery, like so many others, died with Fortuyn, but I am certain that the JSF controversy was connected directly to the murder. I suspect Sobel reported back to the State Department the stubborn premier-in-waiting would not budge, unless there were strict rules on cost over-runs. In which case, the encounter was sensitive, to say the least, given the embassy denied the meeting ever took place. The JSF express certainly gathered remarkable speed, not to say indecent haste, as soon as Fortuyn was out of the way. The faction's new leader, Mathieu Herben, formerly a long-serving staffer at the Defence Ministry, took over and sharply moved the party line in favour of the fighter project. Only thirty days after Fortuyn was slain, Edward Aldridge, Pentagon secretary responsible for defence acquisitions, flew in to

---

[76] Posthumously, Fortuyn was right about the monumental folly of the $318 billion F-35 project. The runaway cost for each fighter has risen from $50.2 million to the range of $80 to $95 million. The key element, the primary engine program, will itself come to at least $7.28 billion, almost double the original estimate of $4.8 billion. Needless to say there is not a single plane yet in squadron service.

the US Soesterberg air base near Utrecht, to sign the official documents of Dutch participation with defence secretary Henk van Hoof. The election returned a large party of Fortuynista at the price of complete chaos, even by the usual Dutch standards, in forming a coalition. The long years of 'poulder politics' — stability achieved by carefully gauged consensus — imploded, never to surface again. Van Hoof's own days were numbered. He was a hangover from the outgoing government of Wim Kok, a caretaker in office, yet was allowed to sign one of the most important international treaties of recent years, despite a complete power vacuum in government.

The *cui bono* score card looks like this. Eliminated: the gaudy but electorally spell-binding entryist Fortuyn, with his charismatic potential to undermine the traditional political establishment, agnostic to the Joint Strike Fighter, and potentially unreliable in other matters involving the United States. Behind bars: Volkert Van der Graaf, enviro-activist who went against the grain of the powerful Industrial Agribusiness Complex. Bereft of Fortuyn's guiding hand, the populist list collapses. And the authorities begin to prepare the wholesale slamming of civil liberties, including the passing of repressive laws reminiscent of the wartime Nazi occupation. But we must add one further profit from his demise. The age of licence, otherwise known as the permissive society, also died outside the radio station in Hilversum. Hollanders would progressively surrender their carefree rights to assemble and demonstrate for any cause that seized the public mood. Soon to go, those freedom-loving hash cafés, to the cheers of the Dutch Mafia, who had been out of pocket for years thanks to liberal drug policies. It was a grand victory for the Strategy of Tension, a triumph for extremism. For all his faults and glitzy flamboyance, Fortuyn would have fought against this with all his soul.

Exactly two and a half years later, the country was convulsed yet again, this time by the murder in Amsterdam of the archly eccentric film director Theo van Gogh (his great-grandfather was the ear-impaired painter's brother). In a sensational climax to a lifetime's public performance that might have come from one of his own scripts, he was repeatedly stabbed, virtually decapitated and for good measure shot by a bearded Islamic fundamentalist, a message from the killer pinned by a dagger to his chest. Renowned for his blustering attacks on Islamic policies to women and Technicolor racism, van Gogh instantly shifted from gadfly to martyr of free expression. Ostensibly, like Pim Fortuyn, this member of the iconic family line seemed to have fallen victim to the faith-driven tensions wracking the country. But there were clear pointers suggesting the assassin may have been another graduate of central casting. These we examine in a moment, but first a deeper understanding of the nature of terrorism in Holland is an important prerequisite.

Islam duly received the worldwide bad press from these events, each one playing on the fears of the 'enemy in the midst.' The killings proved a significant factor in fuelling the populist libertarian Party of Freedom, started by hard-line anti-immigrationist Geert Wilders, another controversial film producer specialising in shock tactics. Under the cultivated dishevelled appearance, the bullish Wilders is a decisive power broker in the Dutch political landscape. His platform is really no more than an endless reel of hate speech about the imminent collapse of Judeo-Christian civilisation. But his influence as a kind of counter-imam goes down well in neighbouring Flanders, where he is regarded as a folk hero by the influential Vlams Belaang nationalist bloc, and has crossed the Atlantic to the US. But is Wilders all that he seems? In turns out from interesting digging around his past by the anthropologist Lizzy van Leeuwen that his roots are traceable via his grandmother, Johanna Ording-Meijer, to a venerable Jewish-Indonesian colonial family. This placing the great ranter, by delicious irony, only several steps removed from an immigrant himself. Moreover, she contends, it is not mere vanity which is responsible for his thick, untamed wavy golden mop. No, just plain peroxide bleach, to achieve the necessary blond Nordic appearance over the swarthy Javan mane lurking beneath. In 2005, Wilders told the *Nieuw Israëlietisch Weekblad* that he lived in Israel in his late teens, and has subsequently visited there about 30 or 40 times in all. More recently, his Islam-bashing landed him in an Amsterdam court on charges of inciting hatred. He was cleared with a light slap on the wrist..

Sleepy, bourgeois Holland — sedated by centuries of humourless Calvinism, addicted to clogs, and footballs made of cheese, one large swimming pool should the dykes burst, a flatland where a slope counts as an alp, legendary home of the hairnet army — this is indeed the picture most people have of the place. In fact, there was a strong pro-Nazi party pre-WW2, and Dutch soccer terrace neo-Nazi skinhead hooligans have won a fearsome reputation around the stadiums of Europe. Latent neo-Nazi, anti-Semitic sentiments led to the banning of skinhead-linked Right-wing parties in the '90s. As recently as 2010, a holocaust memorial service at the former SS Vught concentration camp in southern Holland was disrupted by curiously unidentified gangs. In 2008, director Hanro Smitsman's controversial film *Skin* about the neo-Nazi skinhead movement, set against a background of increasing racial intolerance, underscored the reality that the Dutch were always far more likely to encounter skinhead hooligans than maddened Jihadists. Indeed, were it not for the two high-profile murders, Islamic terrorism could be said to scarcely exist. A *Handelsblad* headline in the winter of 2009 offered a concise summing up: 'In Dutch terror cases, many are arrested but only few convicted.' ('Many are called, but few are chosen' — Matthew 22:16). Since 9/11, 153 people have been arrested, of which twenty were convicted, 22 set free and all the rest released without charges. Take the killing of van Gogh: neither police nor AIVD could produce convincing evidence of a concerted conspiracy. As some international observers have noted — and Holland is not alone in this respect — the legal system seems bent on struggling to secure convictions based on thought terrorism, rather than actual practices or intent. In other words: proving the existence of terrorism in order to fight it — the pure Gladio-Strategy of Tension mantra.

Immediately after the London bombings, Tony Blair solemnly pronounced 'the end of multi-culturalism.' That great Social Darwinist, he of the uncontrollable itch to engineer and regiment human capital, really meant the banishment of pluralism, in favour of apartheid-style first and second-class camps. This was the same text underwriting the Dutch murders and, if anyone remembered, traceable to the ethos of the 'base plan for defence' the Belgian newspaper *Le Soir* exposed less than half a dozen years before. Next came the empire-building, a further step towards reducing government to police activity and control of the public squares. Sybrand van Hulst, boss of AIVD, demanded hundreds more agents and exceptional powers to confront the raging radicalisation of Muslims in Holland. Clearly unashamed by the miserable tally of convictions his activities had managed to secure in courts — themselves increasingly agnostic to the industrial scare-mongering — he insisted that even 'moderate' Turks living in the country were now infected, like some sort of virus. In fact, one social impact study after another suggests that Muslims are secularising in large numbers, leaving religion behind in the hope of finding local mates and settling in. The chief task *Mijnheer* van Hulst seems to have allotted himself is his devotion to the Strategy of Tension. Casting around for more fuel in 2011, he suggested a Fifth Column of ultra-radicals were quietly infiltrating the Dutch army to sabotage overseas operations. The question Van Hulst could or would not answer is where his minions were on the evening Pim Fortuyn was gunned down in Hilversum. And why Theo Van Gogh, cycling through the streets of Amsterdam on his way to work, died at the hands of an apparent fanatic who was under the constant scrutiny of his own spies.

Any facet of Islam was now under suspicion, the same paranoid Cold War fantasy of the fifth column formerly aimed at supporters of the Left. But there was another, much less publicised murder in this chain of events which failed to generate headlines outside Holland. On October 6, 2007, Louis Sévèke, 41 — studious human rights activist and secret-service watcher — was killed execution-style with two clean pistol shots to the head in the centre of Nijmegen, the second as he was stretched out on the ground. The following morning, a close friend and ally of Sévèke, the well-known investigative journalist and stone-turner Gerard Legebeke, informed listeners to Dutch national radio that all indications pointed to 'a political murder.' One of Sévèke's constant refrains was the land of windmills and gay pride evolving into a Stasi-style police state. Most people who followed his work agreed heartily. It emerged in the summer of 2010 that Dutch intelligence was installing secret 'listening posts' in town squares and railway stations, to eavesdrop on everyday chat and conversations. An arch-xenophobe minister actually previously suggested nothing but Dutch be legally spoken in the streets.

But Sévèke's most explosive charge concerned the gruesome deaths of the twin national celebrities, Pim Fortuyn and Theo Van Gogh. On the very eve of his death, he appeared on television accusing AIVD of deliberately fabricating its own fake Al Qaeda terror group called *Hofstadgroep*. Sévèke insisted the plainly unbalanced individual accused in the grisly Van Gogh murder was expressly linked to the same organisation, which was true. It would emerge he was the leader of it. 'That is their normal way of working,' Sévèke declared. When the AIVD boss predictably clamoured for more special powers and agents, he specifically identified *Hofstadgroep* as multiplying everywhere in the country, for which there was not a shred of proof, then or since. Sévèke then published and broadcast claims it was a cloak for *agents provocateurs* working in an underhand fashion — the same Gladio tactic of old — to supply hand grenades and weapons to 'a very dangerous group,' knowing full well the uses they would be put to. Such grenades wounded police officers in 2006, when they stormed a so-called Al Qaeda safe house in The Hague, after the usual tip-off from an unknown source.[77] The story of what is or is not *Hofstadgroep* now takes an interesting twist.

The Dutch authorities were forced into the great embarrassment of admitting the assassin of Theo Van Gogh, 26-year-old Mohammed Bayouri, was well-known to the secret services, and the subject of a bulging file. He was kept under round-the-clock surveillance, until the snooping was inexplicably dropped two weeks before the murder. The lame excuse was advanced that he knew only minor figures. Yet, as the story dripped out in court, he was the ringleader of this alleged tightly-knit terrorist cell, composed of at least thirteen alleged hard-line conspirators, who regularly trooped to his flat on the Antheunisstraat in The Hague. This was festooned from top to bottom with listening devices installed by AIVD, so the assumption must be that as these excitable young men cheerfully babbled away about their nefarious plots and schemes, all was automatically heard and jotted down. The tailing may have been called off, but the eavesdropping, not.

---

[77] Legebeke, the 'father of scoops' as he was known in the Dutch broadcasting community, died suddenly while on holiday in France on August 1, 2008.

Clearly, it is impossible to dissociate the security services from the acts of a small and apparently seditiously-minded group if they have them under the microscope night and day. This is not quite the claim of synthetic terrorism advanced by Sévèke, but it is close enough to accept his case as proven. The name The name *Hofstadgroep* — which means in Dutch the equivalent of a group at court, in the sense of the royal presence at The Hague — was never employed by the conspirators, but invented by AIVD as a code for the evil ones they were watching. This did not prevent the eye-rolling media from using the term as a generic label for all the terrorism in Holland, a classic instance of disinformation and mission creep in the same breath. The nebulous nature of this organization, if it really existed in any concerted form, was to become the subject of torturous legal debate akin to defining the sexual status of angels. Bar the single case of Mohammed Bayouri, the authorities were left with demanding convictions for hot air and generalities: heady talk of bumping off MPs, downing airliners, bombing a nuclear power station and so forth, for which they apparently lacked the necessary sophistication or the equipment. The picture which arose from the extended court proceedings suggested a lot of high-flown Jihadist rhetoric and little else. The highest court in the land thought so too. On 23rd January 2008, the national appeals court sitting in The Hague threw out certain earlier judgments of lower courts in cases that involved planning terrorist plots. The judges lightened the sentences or acquitted a number of suspects because they found no convincing evidence the Hofstad network really existed. In Holland, it is possible to appeal against appeals, so the legal roundabout continues to dizzily whirl, with prosecutors arguing that absence of a formal organization is no excuse for acquittals. Reading between the lines, the appeals court decided something different altogether. This was to question the central thesis of the prosecution case, namely the physical existence in Holland of an organized and directed terrorist cell, equipped with a clear programme and the necessary ongoing capabilities. Of course, the credibility of the ongoing Dutch war on terror demands there should be.

We are back in the familiar Gladio territory, the honey trap or false bait, the 'beauty' as Daniele Ganser put it, of steering a group from within, that classic device proposed by master terrorist Yves Guérin-Sérac. About two months before Van Gogh was murdered, a certain element of building a case was detectable, although of course not obvious at the time. A 34-year-old Moroccan called Othman Ben Amar, also living in Sévèke's hometown, Nijmigen, working for a specialised internal unit of AIVD, was peremptorily arrested and accused of circulating secret documents to people connected with the phantom *Hofstadgroep*. Prosecutor Annemieke Zwaneveld said Ben Amar was also suspected of passing a list of AIVD investigations to a group in the city of Utrecht, whose members were arrested on suspicion of possessing explosives. Ben Amar was described by neighbours as a passive sort of Muslim who went to the mosque as dutifully as nominal Christians attend church at Christmas. His three brothers, also living in Holland, were also government employees. At his earlier employment in the immigration service, he enjoyed virtually free licence to decide who should be allowed to stay. He was taken on at AIVD as a specialist translator of wiretaps, drawing on his encyclopaedic knowledge of Arabic dialects. As for this new work, he portrayed his daily tasks as arranged in such a chaotic, unsupervised fashion to make them largely useless in any intelligible form. He is quoted in his court files as saying: 'I had to determine for myself if a conversation was important. I noticed that only a quarter of all material was processed. This also happened with material of the other co-workers. It has occurred that when a co-worker was on sick leave, the wiretap conversations were not processed at all, not even at a later point in time.' These are the signs of a lazy, complacent bureaucracy, writ large. When he complained about overwork to his superiors, it was the equivalent of marking his own card.

Dutch alternative media aired another version — that Ben Amar was a sacrifice to the uncomfortable connections noted by Sévèke, between Dutch intelligence and radical groups which they penetrated or controlled. AIVD went about assiduously farming connections which suggested duplicity in Ben Amar's former job at the immigration service (consisting of precisely one disputed case involving a Turk), his sinister activities running a Moroccan travel agency, and a media-monitoring service which tried to promote more balanced reporting of Islamic life. When the case came to court, the contact to whom he allegedly passed the documents, Germaine Walters, was acquitted.

Sixteen months after Sévèke was shot in Nijmegen, the police apparently flailing in efforts to trace who shot one of their severest critics, a breakthrough came from a surprising direction. The Guardia Civil in Barcelona suddenly informed their Dutch counterparts that a Hollander called Martinus (aka Marcel) Teunissen was in their custody, claiming to have killed Sévèke. Teunissen had form as an activist of the global Earth Liberation Front, or Elves, a militant, anti-corporatist activist organisation with scores of cells or imitators around the globe. He was a suspect in the 1996 bombing of the factory owned by German chemicals giant BASF in Arnhem. Both he and Sévèke were mixed up in a protracted wrangle with the city authorities in Nijmegen, involving some old buildings occupied by squatters which developers were eager to knock down. This supposedly led to bad blood between them, so Teunissen shot Sévèke with the stylish élan of a professional executioner and jumped to Spain, where he squealed on himself. He was sent to the same psychological assessment unit centre in Utrecht in which Van der Graaf was confined, and diagnosed as unstable and irresponsible, sufficient to put him away under life imprisonment. In Holland, there is no parole for such a sentence. What did this affair prove?

Conveniently, it proved guilt by association, between an international terrorist and Sévèke the annoying Leftist whistleblower who rattled the nerves of the state, with his claims about secret service manipulation of *Hofstadgroep*.

So, another dog whose bark has been remarkably muffled. In this trio of assassins, Marcus Teunissen and Mohammed Bayouri are locked away under Dutch law until they die. Not so Volkert Van der Graaf. He is the odd man out who escaped the ultimate penalty. In 2003, he was sentenced to eighteen years in prison, which in theory at least qualifies him for parole in 2014. His crime was no less heinous than the atrocious murders of Sévèke and Theo van Gogh, politically at any rate far more radioactive. The implication of a plea bargain is unmistakeable. The Dutch people seem to be stunned into sleepwalking through their very own years of lead, too horrified and gripped by the paranoia of Islamophobia to question the authenticity of official accounts in a series of dramatic, politically-fuelled murders.

In 2006, the bare bones of Gladio redux *Hollandaise* broke surface, which may help to shed some light on the Dutch war on terror and possibly the disturbing events in this chapter. A Dutch Marine, 'Derik O' — accused of shooting an Iraqi man in the back as he ran away from a looting incident — was demonstrated in court to hold a 007-like licence to kill. Moreover he was exposed as a member of the Special Support Unit of the Royal Marines (now renamed the Marines Intervention Unit), specifically briefed to carry out operations in the name of anti-terrorism, with government approval to carry weapons that might cause fatalities. The existence of a shoot-to-kill squad (like the Belgian Diana sharpshooters and the British clandestine police and military marksmen) supplies further proof that Gladio-type tactics dating back to the classic episodes of the *anni di piombo* are all there, in full working order. So, too, are the tried and tested psychological weapons: infiltration and manipulation of radicalised cells. Attacks on high-profile public figures, designed to swing the public mood in a particular direction by a calculated combination of fear and anger. The strange melting away of security presence when trouble is brewing — never more glaring and obvious than the case of Pim Fortuyn. The constant whipping by police and intelligence services of the old hobby horse called the enemy within. These combined form the clearly visible outlines of the Strategy of Tension.

Across Europe there was a new connecting thread between the activities of the deep state. These were state-sponsored abductions, such as the snatch that lifted the imam Abou Omar from a quiet Milanese back street. They became known as 'renditions,' a new twist of the Gladio terror campaign, in which persons merely suspected of some links to terrorism were hijacked to countries bearing scant regard for human rights. Yet a scandal in Greece proved that some of the worst examples of abuse occurred in Europe itself.

From 2002 onwards, secret CIA flights were not only crossing European skies, but also touching down at airports such as Athens, to deposit their unwilling passengers for ill treatment at the hands of local secret services, police and military units. Poland, Bulgaria, Romania and Lithuania were also accused of hosting secret torture centres on behalf of the CIA, generally in out-of-the-way airfields.

The secret Greek military police have never lost their reputation for brutal mistreatment of the unfortunates who fall into their custody. This was confirmed again in 2004, when two dozen Pakistani residents of Greece were snatched from their homes and despatched to various torture centres, located in military bases scattered around the country. The story made sensational headlines when the men started a hunger strike, and thus lifted the curtain on complicity of Greek and NATO authorities in wholesale torture. The case was dramatically publicised by Dr. Kleanthis Grivas, the psychiatrist-detective whom we encountered in the earlier studies of Greece, who was himself harried and bullied by uniformed thugs. But there was more embarrassment to come. One of the mistreated men suspected that an Englishman present at one violent beating seemed to be a secret agent. He was unfrocked by a canny reporter as Nicholas Langman, head of the MI6 station in Athens, who was rapidly spirited out of the country, amid furious denials from London that Britain in any way endorsed torture. Yet the damage was done. (In passing, this same Langman was on duty in Paris the night that Princess Diana and Dodi Fayed died.)

It was the old story of the serious information hidden in the small print. About a month after the 9/11 attacks, a little-noticed report appeared in *The Guardian*, which suggested an extraordinary shift in policing arrangements for the capital. The snippet explained how Lord Harris — serving chairman of the Metropolitan Police Authority — had been to see one of the revolving home secretaries, David Blunkett. He was pleading for extra funding, in the wake of a remarkable decision to abandon many of the Met's crime-fighting functions in order to concentrate on Islamic terrorist threats, which at that point had made no appearance in Britain, and in fact did not do so for almost another four years. A chink of light had appeared on the existence and reshaping of the Gladio structure in the United Kingdom, moreover at a time when British consent to join the 'coalition of the willing' in Iraq was still, officially, far from any radar screen. This obscure item of reporting also laid bare the authorities' expectation that a terror campaign would reach British streets, and moreover, the job of fighting it was to be primarily Scotland Yard's. The report was sensational in one important respect: it revealed the gradual dissolution of boundaries between the civilian police force and the military. Scotland Yard had long been slipping under the ken of the politicians currently on watch, as we saw in the previous chapter. In the next chapter, we see that it was stealthily being militarised in the bargain.

The attacks which stunned France in March 2012 dramatised once again the unease and anxiety of the French at the rising numbers of Muslim immigrants. They were ruthlessly exploited by incumbent president Nicholas Sarkozy to provide high-octane fuel for his flagging re-election campaign. The first victims were soldiers, and the story line blamed neofascist paratroopers, supposedly expelled from the military for extremism. An unlikely story, given the pervasiveness of such views in the military, but one that might take votes away from Right-wing populist candidate Marine Le Pen in the April elections. As the hunt for the killers began, Sarkozy switched to the replacement line that the authorities 'knew' who they were looking for. The new suspect: a feeble-minded, 32-year-old small-time crook of Algerian origins called Mohammed Merah. In no time at all he was provided with a full identikit, as an Al Qaeda activist picked up by US forces in Afghanistan and expelled back to France. The media dutifully churned out the claim that he was allied with a terrorist cell in Morocco that had been planning attacks to disrupt the election campaign. Never mind the report in *The Guardian* that a witness saw the gunman had clear green eyes, when Merah's eyes are brown — nor that the ex-director of French intelligence revealed that Merah had been an informant for the agency.

Merah was hunted down to his apartment in a quiet quarter of Toulouse. The place was surrounded by a huge force of police, special forces, reporters and television cameras. Merah allegedly shot and slightly wounded one officer, before his senses snapped and he jumped out of his apartment window to his death, guns blazing. The important fact is that Toulouse and Merah between them *became* the French election campaign. All the candidates were instantly obliged to recognise the deadly events as symptoms of tensions raised by the presence of some five to six million Muslims in France. Sarkozy promised that if re-elected, he would make it a crime to visit 'Internet sites that promoted terrorism.' Few were in any doubt that another five years of NS in the Elysée Palace would bode ill for the Muslim minority, and for the hopes of tolerance and reason proclaimed by Sarkozy's chief opponent, the socialist contender François Hollande.

Toulouse counted as the classic Gladio outing. A masked man on a motor scooter, aiming with precision and skill. Targets selected to raise maximum racial tensions. Attacks on Jews in a country with a difficult history of anti-Semitism, perfectly timed in the throes of the presidential elections. The branding of the usual Gladio patsy, a drifter hearing voices in his head, well-known to police and intelligence services, easily marketed as the lone rogue gunman, who jumps from a window to his death. Vintage tactics copied straight from the the Strategy of Tension playbook. Sarkozy, the friend of NATO who brought France back into the alliance, was well informed when he blurted that the authorities knew who they were searching for.

XVIII.
22/7: The Massacre at Pleasure Island

'Now everybody's a terrorist — except the ruling class.' -Alex Jones at Prison Planet.com, following the Norwegian massacre, July 2011.

The carnage in Norway struck on 22nd July 2011, first in the central district of Oslo, the capital city, then on a sleepy little island camping retreat not far away. It marked a significant development in the use of synthetic terror as a means of social control, while advancing the agenda of global world power. First, to cut an awkwardly independent but immensely wealthy country down to size; second, to usher on stage the next phase of indefinite war waged on ordinary citizens, the familiar story of Gladio told throughout these pages. Within hours of the attacks, the EU's policing offshoot Europol announced a new multi-national task force, charged with investigating and infiltrating potentially hostile political movements deemed as potentially dangerous. In other words, exactly those groups which supposedly inspired the 33-year-old market gardener Anders Behring Breivik to kill 77 people, 55 of them teenagers. Another 62 suffered bullet wounds. The massacre commanded world headlines and news channels. But when the news leaked out six weeks later that Norway's crack anti-terrorist squad had just finished a 'training exercise' on the day, which exactly mirrored the bombing in downtown Oslo and the following shooting frenzy on Utøya Island, the only official response was silence. The bomb that practically wrecked a large area of the downtown business and government district exploded less than half an hour after the so-called drill ended. A senior police spokesman brushed it off as a mere 'co-incidence.'

The chances against such a random co-incidence are multiples of millions to one. The odds rose even further when it emerged that the first police officer who stepped ashore amid the bloodshed on Utøya Island not only recognised Breivik immediately, but addressed him directly by name. According to other reports in the media, Breivik had also called the police several times during the attack at Utøya. What these reports tell us is that whistle-blowers within police ranks are fully aware of the true story behind 22/7, and intended that it should come out. We are in the same territory as the NORAD drill involving the use of jets as weapons on 9/11, and the simulated terrorist attack on the London underground system, which 'just happened' to overlap with the real-time deadly bombings.

The investigative British author Nick Kollerstrom (*Terror on the Tube*, examining the July 2005 London underground attacks) surmises that Breivik was probably on the island, but cannot be conclusively traced to the explosions in Oslo that same morning. The only proof is in the form of a clearly photo-shopped image of a 'man in black' who was purportedly seen by one witness, although it appears that he may have subsequently assumed that it was Breivik, after the enormous propaganda blitz. The explosion left few discernible traces at ground level, which is very peculiar as we see in a moment. The serious damage mainly occurred at higher levels of the surrounding buildings, which which appears strange if it was a car bomb. The remnants of the car supposedly driven to the scene by Breivik did not appear until five days after the bombing. Forensic reports seemed not to indicate the tell-tale presence of ammonium nitrate, the high-nitrogen fertilizer the police alleged Breivik employed as an explosive or a trigger. If the bomb exploded at ground level, we should expect to see some kind of signature crater, conspicuous by its absence. While I was on active journalist service in Ulster in the '80s, it was not at all unusual to encounter craters that were made by car bombs or ground-planted explosives. In Oslo photographs depict streets filled with debris — but no sign at all of any large holes.

Some witnesses described more than a single explosion, which may account for the wide footprint of damage to the surrounding area, and the multiple fires located in the upper floors of buildings. The pictures taken in the immediate aftermath show smoke plumes near the tops of buildings, whereas the lower floors display the indications of collateral blast. The damage was unquestionably huge, so extensive that clearly a powerful device was involved, and possibly smaller incendiary devices. The footprint suggests the use of military-type high explosive. The line that there had been two big explosions, and not one, was the early story that reached the headlines, but later faded away. Taken together, the evidence points to a 'pancake effect,' a flattened profile rather than one immense centralised blast. The tangled wreckage of a car was mentioned in some early reports. Since there were a number of parked cars, this could not be taken as conclusive evidence. There were bound to be questions if anything at all might be found of a car after such a massive blast. The story of the man in black is another mystery, if he was supposed to be Breivik. Why would he hang around at the scene of crime? And in any event, he was supposed to be dashing to another grisly appointment elsewhere. It is plain to see that other hands must have been involved.

Among the buildings heavily damaged due to proximity to the explosion (or more probably, explosions) was the one housing the office and services of the socialist prime minister, Jens Stoltenberg. Providence had fortunately directed him to feel unwell, and work from home that day. The building housing the popular tabloid *Verdens Gang*, close to Mr. Stoltenberg's official quarters, was largely wrecked. The combination of Norway's mass-appeal newspaper and the prime ministerial suite suggests some high political intent. In yet another of the remarkable coincidences that dot this event, the prime minister was scheduled to visit Utøya Island, where many young socialists were on holiday, the following day.

Over the years, Norway strayed out of line across a wide range of US/NATO policies. Among them, driving Palestinian recognition in the UN, a firm anti-Zionist policy and pulling the plug on the war games in Libya. The Norwegians obstinately refuse to open their precious oil and gas fields and fishing grounds to foreigners. They cold-shoulder the EU. Wall Street cannot get its grimy hands on Norway's prized assets, especially the rich mineral resources and the national Sovereign Wealth Fund these thrifty Norsemen have built up to $1.3 trillion. It pays not to mention the Euro or privatisation among such gritty, self-reliant folk. The stubborn attachment of Norwegians to a socialistic, paternalist state replete with a vigorous public sector is regarded as an aberration by the world globalist juggernaut. Norway has virtually branded Israel as a pariah state, scarcely permitted to enter Norwegian markets. Taken overall, it is a substantial list of grievances, if you happen to dislike plucky pocket states with a strong penchant to do their own thing. However, the establishment policy of pursuing friendly relations with Arab states, backed by a liberal immigration policy, is far from universally popular among Norwegians. The ultra-Right, unashamedly populist Progress Party grew to the second largest force in the Storting (the national parliament) preaching an aggressive anti-immigration litany. Its leadership argues that Norway's overly liberal immigration policy failed because it penalised native-born families who worked hard and followed the law, while work-shy immigrants made no attempt to integrate or adopt Norwegian standards of thrift and hard work. Curiously, this was insufficiently tough for Breivik, the man portrayed as the monster of Utøya Island: he tore up his membership card and left the party.

First suspicions of responsibility fell naturally enough on some sleeping nest of Al Qaeda sympathisers. But as the television commentator Martin Jay was later to say in the wake of Norway's very own 9/11: 'Norwegians quickly discovered that terrorists could also be blond, blue-eyed men.' The Christian fundamentalist Breivik turned his weapons on fellow Norwegians, most of whom who were as fair-haired and light-skinned as he. His rambling, 1,500-page manifesto posted on the Web (plus a rather professionally assembled video) made it clear that his real targets were the global Islamic threat and multiculturalism plaguing his homeland. He warned his fellow countrymen: 'The time for dialogue is over.' In what became a popular refrain, Breivik's roots were instantly traced to the rising strength of xenophobic political parties, spreading like a black ink stain across Europe. In no time at all, Europol announced it was immediately recruiting senior counter-terrorism experts from a number of European countries to work at mission control in The Hague. Robert Wainwright, the organisation's British director, declared: 'As soon as it [22/7] happened we opened our operational centre to connect the investigation with an international platform of counter-terrorism analysts.' Was it yet another co-incidence that Europol seemed to be anticipating exactly such an atrocity in order to clamp down on awkward non-establishment political platforms?[78]

The bloody events of 22/7 began with the bomb placed in the capital's government quarter. The explosion went off with devastating force, killing eight people in the street or relaxing in the canteen of the popular daily tabloid *Verdens Gang*. In the shootings that followed on Utøya Island, a small wooded atoll situated in the picturesque Tyrifjord lake, about 30 kilometers from Oslo, another 69 — campers, their families and friends — were shot to death, supposedly by Breivik, the lone, crazed gunman. Among the victims was Trond Berntsen, the step-brother of Crown Princess Mette-Marit. He died as he tried to save his ten-year-old son by pushing him into thick bushes out of the line of fire.

All the tell-tale signs of a stage-managed Gladio event were apparent from the outset. The dummy or patsy, 32-year old British-born Breivik, was instantly ushered on parade, complete with the windy, incongruous epistle setting out his motivations. All the better that Breivik was a freemason (pictures of him in Masonic garb raced around the globe) and furthermore, exposed as a former supporter of the Progress Party. The story which duly did the rounds insisting that Breivik was also the bomber was soon compromised. Suspicious local reporters discovered the cause of mysterious explosions heard in the capital's downtown area in the previous 48 hours. It was an anti-terrorist squad, playing with live explosives as part of a security drill, a classic *modus operandi* of the Gladio repertoire. Anti-terrorist police staged a fake raid with live ammunition and explosives in a disused building used as a training centre barely 200 meters from the National Opera House, but curiously 'forgot' to warn the public. As Dr. Webster Tarpley observed, these security drills which frequently parallel so many so-called terrorist attacks (9/11, the London bombings, Times Square, the downtown Stockholm bombs in December 2010) serve a very practical purpose.

Once the drill has occurred, the capabilities, hardware, etc., which it has created can remain in place to be mobilised at the desired moment. The secret is that the legally sanctioned drill has been used to conduit or bootleg the actual butchery through a government bureaucracy whose resources are required to run the terror, but in which there are many officials who cannot be allowed to know what is happening.

The explosion mirrored precisely the scheme laid out in the famous training drill.

At this point it is worth briefly recalling the curious history of the local Gladio stay-behind network, code-named Rocambole (ROC), and the possible relevance to the 22/7 massacre. In the 1950's ROC was accused of spying on senior Left-wing Norwegian politicians. Vilhelm Evang, the Left-leaning head of Norwegian intelligence who discovered the plot, was forced from office by senior US spycatcher James Jesus Angleton, who falsely accused him of being a double agent for the KGB. Dr. Webster Tarpley believes on sound grounds that the United States has infiltrated anti-terrorist networks in Norway, ostensibly to look for threats to US citizens. But since the recruits include prominent former senior officers of Norwegian intelligence, the potential for using off-radar units to create false-flag terror incidents is too strong to be ignored. For reasons which become clear, 22/7 bore all the indications of synthetic terrorism, planned and carried out by the secret state.[79]

The strange response of the Norwegian police at all levels on Black Friday was more akin to a black parody of the Keystone Kops. The local detachment in Sandvika, the nearest mainland community, sat on their hands for about an hour while the shooting continued on the island, just a few rowing minutes (about 2,000 feet or 600 meters) from the shore. We are asked to believe that hearing the screams and the gunfire from the horrors being performed a short distance across the water, they felt no sense of pressing urgency, not even as the few who managed to swim to the mainland struggled ashore. Their excuse was that their only boat had sprung a leak. Why then did they not instantly commandeer a replacement in this popular lakeside location, crammed with floating craft of all shapes and sizes? The explanation was presented that local constables in Norway, unaccustomed to violent crime in this usually peaceful climate, are unarmed. Yet, this is a country of dedicated hunters. Are policemen any less enthusiastic about the national pastime? So why did the officers not resort to weapons kept at home, given such a terrible emergency?

The only available helicopter, it was later claimed, lay far to the south. So they drummed their fingers until the special Delta intervention squad arrived from Oslo. Strangely, this élite rapid intervention force seemed to be in no

---

[79] An interesting sense of humour behind the name: Rocambole comes from the stories of the 19th century French writer Pierre du Terrail about the fantastical adventures experienced by one of his fictional characters: *rocambolesque* has come to mean any kind of incredible exploits.

particular hurry either. The obviously begging question is therefore who exactly was giving the orders during Norway's worst emergency since WW2? The answer of course lies in the convenient training exercise that had just concluded in the capital, the overlying template of the events that were now occurring in real time. Officially, the Delta squad peeled off from the devastation in the government district on receiving reports of the shooting in Utøya at around 5.30 pm. They set off, not for the island (only thirty or so minutes away by the fast E16 lakeside road) but instead to a hilltop where they were supposed to rendezvous with a helicopter. This failed to arrive, so they shot off to the seashore, where they commandeered a pair of speedboats and finally got to the island at 6.25 pm.

The improbability factor now switches to overdrive. In late August 2011, sources at the most senior level of the Oslo city police force confirmed to the newspaper *Aftenposten* that a full-scale security drill had been in progress the same day, practically overlapping with the attacks attributed to Breivik. The investigating reporter Andreas Bakke Foss was informed that the official drill finished at 15:00 that same Friday. He wrote:

All of the officers from the anti-terror unit that later took part at the bomb site at the government buildings and [then] went out to Utøya to apprehend Anders Behring Breivik had been training on the exact same scenario earlier the same day and in the days preceding.

The Oslo city centre bomb attributed to Breivik went off just 26 minutes after the police drill finished, which as Dr. Tarpley observed, points towards explosives smuggled to the scene under cover of the drill. As *Aftenposten* was informed, the drill mirrored more or less precisely the carnage that the Delta squad encountered in the Tyrifjord lake later that very day. The exercise envisaged an attack, in which one or more perpetrators attempted to shoot as many people as they could manage, and then shoot at the police when they arrived (the only element of the pre-arranged script that did not play out).

Verdens Gang reported claims of survivors that shooting came 'from two different places on the island at the same time.' Nineteen-year-old Emilie Bersaas described the shooting as 'coming from all different directions.' Another fortunate survivor, Alexander Stavdal, said the other person stalking the campers and visitors like a single-minded hunter did not resemble Breivik in any manner. His thick mane of wavy dark hair was quite unlike the typical Scandinavian features of the alleged lone gunman. The police were noticeably reticent in following up this highly significant line of inquiry, confining themselves to waffling vaguely about 'reports' of another gunman at the crime scene. The eye-witness reports were then ignored by the judges, court lawyers and Breivik's doctors. The corporate media, in Norway and everywhere else, made some initial mention of other shooters present on the island, and then abandoned the angle which compromised the official story of a solo gunman. Since the orgy of killing continued for more than an hour, the witnesses who described this mysterious figure so clearly were unlikely to be mistaken as to what they had seen. Then, once Breivik had been formally charged and arraigned in court, he began to claim that he committed the murderous acts as part of a group, who were planning similar atrocities in the future. He was immediately silenced by the judge and packed off incommunicado for a month, subsequently extended until he was finally adjudged clinically insane on 30th November 2011. We recall that this is a close parallel to the treatment meted out to Volkert van der Graaf following the murder of Pim Fortuyn in the Netherlands. As we remember, Mehmet Ali Ağca too was hustled off to a jail far distant from Rome, where he underwent extensive coaching sessions as to what exactly he should say in open court concerning his role in the attack on Pope John Paul.

Utøya Island is managed by a charitable foundation associated with the Socialist party, Norway's largest political party and the main long-term anchor in national politics. The victims were mostly members of the party's youth wing, who repair to their very own Pleasure Island every summer for their annual camp. There are no permanent inhabitants, and the appeal is the typical Scandinavian out-of-doors attraction of back to nature, in this peaceful idyll scarcely 27 or so acres (a dozen hectares) in size.

There were approximately 170 people enjoying themselves in the balmy weather, most of them campers, others visiting for the day. Breivik supposedly selected the island because of its association with the socialist party, the same reason for the supposed fertiliser bomb that he allegedly set off close to the premier's office in Oslo. But it was also the ideal location where a gunman could run amok killing at will, the close confinement of the wooded islet forming a watertight shooting gallery. Among the dead and the injured victims were those who desperately attempted to escape by jumping into the water.

With this small nation paralysed by shock, few paid much initial notice to the early claims that pointed to at least one other gunman at the scene. This was exactly the scenario envisaged in the notorious parallel training drill, namely a massive explosion in the heart of the capital, followed shortly afterwards by mass homicide on the island. Breivik's arrival on the island is also interesting. He was dressed as a policeman — in fact he strongly resembled *The Terminator*, in the 1984 movie of that name starring Arnold Schwarzenegger, if not exactly in looks then certainly in terms of his heavy-duty ordnance. Tellingly Breivik told the first people he encountered that he had been 'sent from Oslo as a security guard after the bombings.' This was clearly a line adapted directly from the script of the parallel drill.

His subsequent expertise as a marksman suggested accumulated shooting skills of a high order, but how many single individuals are there in Norway — save among the armed forces and the police — who might be capable of such a coldly performed cull? Breivik, the draft dodger with no known military experience, seems a difficult fit in this frame. His subsequent outburst about accomplices appeared to answer these awkward questions. Moreover, since every gun leaves its own personal signature on spent cartridges, it should have been straightforward to discover if more than one weapon was in use, allowing for Breivik's supposed use of a pistol as well a high-velocity rifle.

Breivik was presented to the world as the perfect misfit, thanks to his rambling personal manifesto, large chunks of which were hacked in a random paste job from the famous testament of the American mail bomber Theodore Kaczynski. Over almost two decades between 1978 and 1995, the famously elusive 'Unabomber' mailed deadly packets to scientists of whom he disapproved. He admitted that the resulting deaths and injuries were morally reprehensible, but considered they were justified to awaken a society he regarded as sleepwalking into mass-induced hypnosis. Many intellectuals — although they shied from the violence — nonetheless empathised with Kaczynski's central ethos, the immoral perversion of science and the consequent rape of human minds and freedoms. Similarly, Breivik admitted in court that his acts were also morally wrong, but necessary as an alarm call to warn of the coming Islamic invasion. Kaczynski was a youthful prodigy, if also a social misfit and natural hermit. He slipped into Harvard at the age of 16, collected a maths doctorate before he was 20, and became an assistant professor at the University of California by his mid-twenties. He devoted his mind to baffling numerical theories of such complexity that it was thought there might be only a dozen or so initiates in the world who fully grasped them. His manifesto is studied widely as a brilliantly-argued essay in societal analysis from the perspective of primitive anarchism (that same driving ethos of the Propaganda of the Deed that we encountered in Chapter IV).

In stark contrast, Breivik was no such prodigy. As a younger man he was generally out of his step with his family. He shunned parental discipline, choosing to hang about with street gangs. He eventually found a niche in computer systems, and then shifted to farming vegetables. His 1,500-page personal cry of rage reads as a disorganised and disconnected harangue which includes — naturally enough for a man of the soil — a treatise on growing sugar beet. We are left to ponder whether he really was the sole author of the elephantine diatribe, or if other eyes fell upon the precious document from time to time, fine-tuning the nonsense to the perfect pitch of imbecility. The impression of a self-manufactured personality was in any event seriously compromised, if not entirely undermined, by the subsequent discovery of mysterious hands meddling with his Facebook profile. This suggests that even at this late stage, after the attacks, the personality moulding was still continuing, as though his credentials as a lone crazed terrorist still invited refinement and adjustment.

As with so many stooges studied in these pages, Breivik was well known to the police and secret services prior to the bombing and the massacre. The police began to question him after he purchased a large quantity of agricultural fertiliser from a supplier in Poland, where he was a regular customer. Market gardeners in Norway and everywhere else purchase fertiliser in large quantities all the time. What was it that made this consignment, ordered as it was by a legitimate commercial vegetable grower, apparently so suspicious? A brief police surveillance exercise was then abruptly dropped, after the initial excitement. But when did the surveillance begin, and was it really called off? The police could only have known about the fertiliser acquisition if they were watching him over an extended period, with the intention of establishing a profile of the future mass killer. Unsurprisingly, the fertiliser plot was subsequently guaranteed glaring headlines, with the story that Breivik spared his sugar beet and carrots from his Polish purchases and instead blew up a significant part of Oslo's central district.

The world was soon looking at the calmly composed and classically Nordic features of a blue-eyed, blonde-mopped figure in his early thirties, not altogether without a certain wholesome appearance. He seemed the image of serenity, like the state of composure he maintained after his arrest and according to survivors, his glacial demeanour amid the bloodbath on the camping island. Indeed his brief public appearances in court conveyed the impression of an individual transfixed in some entrancing dream. One of his closest friends wondered if he was drugged or brainwashed, finding his appearance eerie and quite untypical. Of course such conjecture will never be resolved one way or the other. But considering the history of Lee Harvey Oswald, to take but one example, was Breivik really the Manchurian Candidate rather than the patsy at Pleasure Island?

Invoking guilt by association, Breivik's flirting with the far Right Progress Party was clearly intended to cast doubts on similar populist forces in countries such as Switzerland, Finland, the Netherlands and Austria. As Alex Jones declared in the opening to this chapter, we are all terrorists now, in the minds of our increasingly authoritarian rulers. With indecent haste, America's Führerina of Homeland Security, Janet Napolitano, leapt before Americans to solemnly warn them of a wave of forthcoming attacks by Breivik-inspired fanatical conservative fundamentalists — or 'sovereign citizens' as they are beginning to be called in the United States. In the United States of today, this tends to suggest some world-startling event may be in the offing. We begin to glimpse an explanation for the secretive and hurriedly-constructed FEMA camps, which appear to be scarcely veiled interment centres, sprouting everywhere across the United States. The right to own and bear weapons is certain to be even more rigorously restricted, as indeed occurred in Norway and the US within days. In London, Scotland Yard urged curtain-twitchers to spy on neighbours for signs of 'suspicious anarchist anti-government behaviour'. My own guess is that the right to roam freely as one wills anywhere in the European Union without a passport (one of the genuine fruits of real liberty bestowed by the Brussels commissars) will face extinction. It is ironic indeed that populist parties whose principal plank is the return to crude nationalism are now the selected instrument to bring this about *en passant*.

Breivik was diagnosed as suffering from paranoid schizophrenia, by the psychiatrists paid by the state to understand his actions and motives. If we take his famous elegy at face value, then he certainly assembled an eclectic collection of grudges against society. These included a magnetism towards right wing politics, his affections for white supremacy and a suspiciously ill-defined attraction to 'cultural conservatism.' The image of Breivik's personality was further coloured by his disrespect for anything stained with womens' liberation, plus of course a good strong dose of Islamophobia thrown into the broth for good measure. The obvious problem attached to this brand of personality profiling is that the same clothes can easily be tailored for many others to wear, particularly anyone who might be similarly diagnosed as 'culturally conservative.' I can only define this to mean anyone who steps aside from the centre-of-the road mainstream, in which case the victims that might be caught in the dragnet could certainly include Margaret Thatcher, to give but one instance. I cannot think of a better description that might fit Mrs. Thatcher's record than 'culturally conservative.' She was also famously cool on the rights of women to enjoy fair treatment alongside men, herself of course the commanding exception. And while we are on the subject, to whom could we point in the United States as suffering from the contagion of 'cultural conservatism,' if not the entire massed ranks of the Republican Party?

There is also a great deal of mystery as to how an apparently witless loner came to acquire considerable sums of money, which seemed to be far in excess of his earning capacity. In 2008, for example, Breivik was supposed to have amassed $370,000 (£240,000) in profits generated by his self-established computer programming business. It was said that by 2002 he was a 'kroner millionaire.' However, by 2010 he was scraping along on his last $70,000 (£45,000). One could draw the conclusion that the market garden business that succeeded his brush with computers had not flourished as expected, which might be a fair one. But the subliminal implication behind the release of these figures seemed designed to impress on the public agora the picture of a deranged and obsessive lunatic exploiting his fortune and spending it on the means to commit a savage atrocity. As we saw, the police were alerted at one stage by the Norwegian customs service that he had bought or tried to buy explosive primers, but investigations had strangely revealed no need for further actions. At another level this implies that Breivik was being monitored — or manipulated — for much longer than later accounts suggested. In the eyes of his neighbours clustered around his isolated farm in the county of Hedmark, about 149 kilometers (85 miles) north-east of Oslo, he was a secretive city type, who always kept his windows curtained, and refrained from mixing with the locals. Rural Norwegians are not exactly cosmopolitan, so perhaps such behaviour by a stranger did seem odd. But in fact we see a common script in the portrayal of terrorists as isolated and insulated figures, which has spread into the mainstream stereotype. Anyone who lives at the bottom of your street, closes their curtains, and minds their own business is now being defined as a proto-terrorist by Orwellian official briefings issued by the police services in the United Kingdom and the US. In short, privacy and anonymity are now the subject of suspicion, and potentially crimes. This is an essential component of the modern Gladio Strategy of Fear.

There is an important dispute within the clinical community in Norway as to the actual extent of Breivik's mental incapacitation, in particular whether he fulfills the category of the criminally insane. An alternative view that he suffers from a milder condition of personality disorders has been proposed by an independent group of doctors, who want the government to commission a second opinion. The distinction is important, because a milder diagnosis would require that he served a sentence in a normal prison, after due adjudication in court. Diagnosed as criminally insane and thus not responsible for his actions, he can be detained in a secure institution or a mental hospital indefinitely. Hearings can be held behind closed doors. The clinical report delivered by the state-appointed psychiatrists is not, so far at any rate, to be subjected to such an independent test. Of course, if Breivik were to speak in open court instead of shuttered hearings, then he might reveal awkward evidence concerning the 'friends' who accompanied him that awful day in July 2011, and the role they played.[80]

Early in January 2012, Janne Kristiansen, Norway's internal security chief, unexpectedly submitted her resignation. Ostensibly, this was because she had let slip to parliament that officers of Norwegian home security were on active duty alongside American personnel in far-away Pakistan.

---

[80] Early in March 2012 the Norwegian authorities relented on this score. A second assessment did indeed reach the conclusion that Breivik was not criminally insane and that he was of fit mind to stand trial on criminal charges of murder. A judgement of guilty but insane would have resulted in confinement in an asylum for life. His sentence will now be served in prison.

Inadvertently she also confirmed the long-suspected close links between the CIA and Norway's internal security services. Kristiansen had previously come under fire from the Norwegian media for insisting that nobody could have predicted the attacks purportedly carried out by Breivik. How can this statement be made to square with the plain fact that Breivik had indeed been under suspicion by the police and the customs services, that his large shipments of fertiliser from Poland were deemed suspicious, and that he was also investigated on grounds of purchasing explosive primers?

It is now a matter of fact that since early 2000, a top secret unit called SDU routinely spied on thousands of Norwegians suspected of harboring intentions to attack Americans living or working in Norway and the US embassy in Oslo. What is especially interesting concerning this startling revelation is the initial efforts by the Norwegian government to deny that any such activities existed, even though the SDU was run by the country's former anti-terrorist chief, Olaf Johansen. Knut Storberget, the minister of defence, at first denied that he knew anything about secret spying on Norwegian citizens, but later changed his tune in a statement that he made to parliament. He got off the hook by claiming that the US authorities had formally notified the government of SDU's activities. This was a sticking plaster. The impression of panic at high levels was confirmed when Bjørn Erik Thon, the head of Norway's own internal surveillance agency — who was also obviously in the dark in this murky affair — gave his straightforward opinion that any such spying conducted on Norwegian territory was against the law. The excuses were stripped away one by one. It emerged that SDU employed the *crème de la crème* of Norway's police and intelligence services. SDU went for the top men at the highest levels of the Oslo police district and the Kriminalpolitisentralen (Kripos for easy consumption), supposedly to frustrate attacks on US citizens or interests. The unit, numbering around 20-25 individuals, was headquartered anonymously in a government-owned building in central Oslo.

Of course the interesting question is how such a specialized and well-organized clandestine unit, moving around the country in complete secrecy, tapping thousands of calls unknown to the authorities, managed to let Anders Behring Breivik slip through the net. After all, here was a man going about ordering suspiciously large quantities of fertilizer, who seemed to be looking for materials to set off bombs, and to cap it all, was tracked on an expedition to the Czech Republic, where he purportedly tried to buy weapons that were illegal in Norway. SDU was clearly a branch of US intelligence — the CIA, operating under the guise of the State Department (as we see below) — so it is indeed very curious that Breivik's activities, conducted as they were over a long period leading up the bombing in central Oslo and the massacre at Utøya Island, were either overlooked or ignored by supposedly the finest men in the field.

Peeling away the SDU onion revealed many more fascinating layers. It was by no means an isolated outfit confined to Norway. Again in 2010, the Finnish security police (SUPO) at first denied the existence of an SDU operation on Finnish soil, only to backtrack shortly afterwards. Not long after the original exposure in Norway, an operational SDU unit was uncovered in Sweden. The justice minister Beatrice Ask declared that she knew nothing of such activities, which gave to rise to more concerns of illegality.

The origins of the SDU units appear to lie in the bombing of the US embassy in Nairobi (212 killed) and Dar es Salaam, Tanzania (eleven victims) on 7th August 1998. In the wake of these deadly attacks, the State Department created a worldwide surveillance detection program, at the cost of some $80 million, to deter future terrorism aimed at US embassies and their personnel, whether at work or in their homes. The programme was put together in some haste and was active from 2000. The key words describing the programme were 'expansion of the surveillance perimeter' (beyond the strict confines of embassies), which was the actual wording employed when yet another Scandinavian SDU operation was exposed in Iceland, once again in the very busy SDU month of November 2010. There is a plain and obvious connecting thread here. This is the initial insistence of sovereign governments in each country that they were unaware of the United States employing well-trained counter-terrorism experts — nationals of each state concerned — to indulge in covert spying and information-gathering on their own citizens. The final reporting centre was a central data base called SIMAS, short for Security Incident Management Analysis Systems, developed by the Bureau of Diplomatic Security, a State Department subsidiary. The documents which are in the public realm do not specifically state that there was any intention to reveal the existence of the SDU programme to the relevant government authorities or law enforcement agencies in the countries concerned. Yet here was a virtual duplicate of national efforts in the field of counter-terrorism. SDU's were charged to construct a 'narrative of suspicious' activity, namely persons, race and appearance, vehicles, times, dates, locations and so forth, but not to share — if we are to believe the string of political denials — any of this with the relevant national agencies operating with identical tasks. There is a rather clear loophole. In each country, SDU was employing local nationals who were drawn from the local police and state counter-terrorism services. Could it really be that they withheld high-grade information gained by their activities from their own former colleagues and employers? And the same contradiction arises if we looked at the perspective from the reverse direction.

Another mystery centres on exactly how much free time Breivik actually had to manage his computer company and thereafter grow vegetables, given that he appeared to be an extremely busy frequent flyer. A rather different picture of the isolated loner starts to appear when his wide travels around Europe, his visits to the United States and apparently as far as China are taken into consideration. Breivik's pedigree — and especially his bank account — seems to fit a man involved with a global organization connected to both arms and narcotics trafficking on a very large scale. The location of Breivik's smallholding in the picturesque valley of Østerdalen, near the small mountain town of Rena, is another source of rather more than curiosity. The area is a paradise of isolated lakes, forests and mountains, which makes the perfect training ground for the Norwegian army's special forces units. From time to time the division's base camp hosts visiting forces from other NATO countries, which just happened to be the ones that Breivik visited so frequently. Like the training exercises which preceded the Oslo bombings and the subsequent massacre at Pleasure Island, Breivik's selection of pastures close to a military base specializing in counter-terrorism is another coincidence too far.

Time and again we have seen throughout this chapter that Breivik was considered a suspicious person, yet he was allowed to pursue his purportedly nefarious plans without hindrance. Yet again we are back in the territory of 'just let it happen.' The security drill that paralleled Breivik's efforts, his talk of other partners in crime, the long-winded and rambling elegy, his strange access to rather fabulous sums of money coming from such an unpromising background, suggest a manufactured personality in the pattern of so many stooges and patsies that we have studied in these pages.

As for Pleasure Island, this perfect gem set in a silver sea will be remembered forever as the silent witness to a day of infamy.

XIX.
Appointment at Račak

'We should remember what happened in Račak. Innocent men, women and children were taken from their homes to a gully, forced to kneel in the dirt and sprayed with gunfire.' — Bill Clinton, 19th March 1999

'Victims had their eyes gouged out, heads smashed in, faces blown away at close range, all farmers, workers, villagers, aged 12-74, men, women, children.' — London *Times*, January 1999

What happened in the small hillside village of Račak, tucked away in southern Kosovo on 15th January 1999, was to prove no exception to the classic bromide that in war, truth is always the first casualty. Within two months, the 'alliance for peace' went to war for the first time in its history, pulverising Serbia with a massive, almost three-month-long aerial blitzkrieg. The member states of NATO might just as well have collectively met in solemn conclave, torn up the Atlantic Charter and tossed it out of the nearest window. War fever blew aside the cardinal principle requiring an external attack or plausible threat before pistols should be cocked. In a scarcely subtle attempt to evade this legal quibble, President Bill Clinton declared a state of emergency of an 'unusual scale' to the physical land mass of the United States itself, as though Serbian battle fleets might charge up the Potomac at any moment to bombard Capitol Hill. No one banged the war drums louder than Clinton's Secretary of State, the hard-line neo-conservative Madeleine Albright, who used Račak to justify her grotesque rationalisation of 'bombing on humanitarian grounds.' Germany's Green Party foreign minister Joschka Fischer joined the chorus line. The former activist in a streetfighting terror gang known for attacks on policeman (one of them by him) solemnly told *Berliner Zeitung* that the massacre of Račak 'became the turning point for me.' Lest anyone should doubt the scale of the horrors, Human Rights Watch dutifully reported bodies of the dead exhibited signs of torture, such as fingernails torn out.

Račak was certainly a grisly business. But in the history of war it was remarkable in at least one unique respect. It seemed to be the first massacre conducted before an invited audience.

Atrocity stories are part of the armoury of war, a tried and tested method of arousing hatred. They supply 'proof' of the depravity of the enemy and his degenerate conduct of war, against the righteous cause of those who resist, as we saw again in the mass rape stories served up in the Libyan crusade. In the First World War, tall tales galvanised hostility to the Germans, while serving a second strategic aim, that of the French and British governments scheming to lure the neutrally-inclined Americans into the fray. Nothing, it was thought, could be more certain to tip the balance than horror stories of ruthless German soldiers spearing Belgian babies, and indulging in the mass rape of nuns and other innocent virgins in public squares. The venerable British peer Lord James Bryce was commissioned to investigate, and duly came up with a thick tome listing a catalogue of German barbarities. The war long over, and the document having served its purpose, the entire exercise was revealed as largely a fabrication. The Germans, in common with combatants on all sides, committed inhumanities, but on nothing like the scale that Bryce claimed. Moreover, his only evidence came from a few second-hand hearsay reports of dubious reliability.

In Račak, the main source for a Serbian atrocity story was an American diplomat with his own skeletons rattling in similar cupboards. William Walker was in charge of the peace monitors patrolling Kosovo under the OSCE (Organization for Security and Co-operation in Europe). He was the first to accuse the Serbian police of a massacre against the local Albanian population. His accusations of a 'crime against humanity' instantly rang around the world. This same Walker had made headlines concerning another crime against humanity, committed during his tenure as ambassador to El Salvador, in the late eighties. He was at the eye of the storm when a US-trained Right-wing death squad mercilessly butchered six Jesuit priests, together with their housekeeper and her young daughter. The plan to blame godless Left-wing revolutionaries soon backfired when the local Jesuit hierarchy openly accused Walker of 'personally hiding the real perpetrators by concealing evidence, obstructing the investigation, pressuring judges to impede the trial process and terrorising witnesses.'[81]

Walker's chief task in the Balkans was again more to do with peace-breaking than making. His main activity was to pull the plug on the stalemated talks droning on between the Serbs and Albanian Kosovars in the faraway French chateau of Rambouillet. There, NATO lorded the proceedings as a political power in its own right, with Supreme Commander General Wesley Clarke the puffed-up monarch in residence. He promised the Kosovars the earth, including the prize plum of independence, whenever they chose to pluck it. For their part, the Serbs were instructed to sign on the dotted line or face severe consequences, so the idea of negotiations as such was an anomaly. The humiliation of Serbia was virtually complete, although the image the world at large received was very different. The regime of Slobodan Milošević in Belgrade, the last visible façade of the now utterly

---

[81] As a consequence, Walker was blackballed by the Panamanians, normally docile to the demands of Washington, when Clinton tried to park him there as the new US ambassador.

shattered Yugoslav 'Switzerland of the Balkans,' was portrayed as the stubborn obstacle to self-determination of a long-oppressed people. In fact Milošević was not a despot but an uncompromising nationalist, burdened with the baggage of the ancient Serb inheritance. Yet even as Walker's claims of innocents executed by Serb death squads stirred the conscience of the world, a different story was already filtering up from the ground.[82]

We now have a clearer idea, from a variety of angles, of what really happened at Račak. Before the war began, it was a community of about 2,000 mainly Albanian Muslims, and a key stronghold of the US-backed Kosovar Liberation Army (KLA). By January 1999, most of the peacetime population had sensibly melted away, rather than remain trapped in the crossfire of an increasingly violent front line. When four Serbian policemen were ambushed and killed in two separate incidents in the course of a week, Serb security forces responded by surrounding Račak, and then attacked. The Serbs thought to protect themselves by tipping off foreign journalists and even OSCE observers, who appeared for a front row seat. Fighting between the Serbian police and KLA fighters was brief but savage. International reporters counted about 20 bodies strewn around the town centre, but none in the surrounding fields. At nightfall, they and the Serbs packed up and left, leaving the KLA in undisputed control.

A two-man television camera crew from the Associated Press news agency, and two teams of OSCE observers watching the scrap in Račak from the safety of a nearby hilltop, entered the largely silent and deserted town as soon as the Serb units did, and left with them. Another eyewitness, French journalist Reynaud Girard from *Le Figaro*, was puzzled that all reports failed to mention it was a 'fortified village with a lot of trenches.' His colleague Christophe Chatelet of *Le Monde* counted just one dead and four wounded when he left at dusk. The next day, KLA officials showed him bodies from 'a massacre' that had not been there before. He told his readers: 'I can't solve that mystery.' One man who did was the KLA commander-in-chief Hashim Thaci who foolishly crowed off-message to the BBC: 'We had a key unit in the region and had a fierce fight. Regrettably, we had many casualties, but so did the Serbs.' In September 2007, *Voice of Russia* quoted Thaci as admitting KLA guerrillas killed the Serbian policemen deliberately to goad the Serbs into an 'adequate reaction.' This squared exactly with the account wired by Chatelet describing a 'violent police attack on Friday [on a] stronghold of Albanian independence fighters.' As he pointed out, virtually all the inhabitants fled Račak during the Serb offensive in the summer of 1998.

---

[82] Arrested by the new authorities in charge of Serbia in 2001, Milošević was sent to the UN War Crimes Tribunal at The Hague. He was charged with war crimes. On May 11 2002, he was found dead in his cell at the Tribunal's detention centre. The cause of death was stated to be a heart attack brought on by high blood pressure.

With few exceptions, they had not come back. 'Smoke came from only two chimneys,' noted one of the two AP TV reporters.

The next morning, NATO sheriff William Walker strutted into town, counted the now much-swollen tally of 40 corpses, some occupying a shallow gully, and pronounced a massacre. His report to headquarters spoke of 'arbitrary arrests, killings and mutilations of unarmed civilians' (on which he was such an expert). The KLA and Walker alleged that masked Serb policemen had entered the village the previous day, and killed men, women and children at close range, after torturing and mutilating them. 'Chillingly, the Serb police were said to have whistled merrily as they went about their work of slaughtering the villagers.'[83]

Journalists long schooled in the mystifying ways of the Balkans scratched their heads. Where were the shell casings one would expect to find lying around after a mass execution? Why did none of the victims appear to be hit at close range, but instead from a distance, consistent with casualties from the previous day's much-observed battle? The mutilations seemed to have been caused by the gnawing teeth of hungry wild animals attracted to this irresistible feast of flesh during the night (as all the autopsies subsequently confirmed).

What really happened was this: the KLA stripped the uniforms off of their own casualties and dumped them in a ditch to look like the victims of a mass shooting. The Finnish forensic expert summoned by OSCE to perform an 'independent vetting' delivered a performance so confusing and at times contradictory, it bordered on the farcical. Dr. Helena Ranta was a curious choice, primarily accustomed to identifying victims from dental evidence rather than investigating ballistics. Clearly under considerable pressure to preserve the official line, she ducked and weaved, delivered a highly equivocal press statement and consistently refused to confirm if there had been a massacre or a battle. Unsurprisingly, both NATO and the EU quietly sat on her final report, while milking the Račak affair to justify the aerial bombardment of Belgrade. The silence was broken by *Berliner Zeitung* two years later. According to a leaked copy of the Finnish team's report which the newspaper obtained, it proved impossible to establish for certain that the victims were civilians, whether they were people from Račak, or even where they died. Furthermore, the investigators found only one body that showed traces of an execution-style killing, and no evidence at all that the bodies had

---

[83] In a speech at a mass rally for the Albanian National Self-Determination Party in Pristina on the eve of Kosovo's general election in 2010, Walker performed a startling somersault, accusing the Thaci regime of practicing the same abuse of power experienced under former Serbian repression. He further accused the NATO liberators of looking the other way while Kosovo morphed into a full-blown gangster state. Paul Lewis, London *Guardian*, 12th December 2010.

been mutilated, despite the trumpeting of Human Rights Watch and Bill Clinton. Moreover, gunpowder could be traced to the hands and clothes of some of the victims, suggesting involvement in paramilitary activity.

Waves of condemnation of the Belgrade government swept the western media, replete with interviews of the sorrowful survivors and demands for protection and retaliation. The words and images were harsh and charged with emotion. The rump Yugoslav government's explanation was routinely dismissed, even though the gaping holes in William Walker's story were already being picked over by increasingly suspicious reporters who had been on the spot.

On 17th February 2008 — which came close to marking the exact anniversary of the alleged atrocity ten years before — Kosovo finally snapped the link to Belgrade. 'The day has come,' Prime Minister Hashim Thaci, the former separatist guerrilla leader gushed to his pocket parliament. 'From this day forward Kosovo is proud, independent and free.' The parable of Račak is instructive at many levels. It demonstrated how the public mind was tutored to swallow the story of a pitiless massacre as a continuation of the wretched calamities that tortured the Balkans for a decade. Milošević was demonised to the point of sprouting horns. Louise Arbour, the Canadian-born chief war crimes prosecutor in The Hague, allowed Kosovo to stand as one of the major indictments against him, despite contrary evidence. Milošević was certainly no angel. He was an accustomed practitioner in rough tactics, in the traditional style of Balkan leaders. But essentially he was now the nationalist trapped in an extremely tight corner, facing an oncoming juggernaut approaching at terrifying speed. William Walker counted on that when the casualties of a fierce skirmish presented themselves as the perfectly landscaped opportunity to justify the long-sought NATO intervention.

As the media inquest wound on, the story line began to weaken. The suspicion grew that the Serbs had walked into a not-so-subtly-baited trap, primed with the deaths of their policemen. Wilfried Gimmer, a prominent German Christian Democrat politician and vice president of the parliamentary assembly of the OSCE, had intercepted interesting clues to the real course of events. He revealed that in 2002 he had heard 'much testimony' concerning American observers inciting KLA insurgents to deliberately break the cease-fire. This was to be achieved by targeting Serb targets, in order to provoke a crackdown. Herr Gimmer added; 'Everybody in the OSCE knew that NATO and the USA did not wish the mission [the cease-fire] to be a success.'

Račak was a false flag. It was a direct continuation of the black propaganda patents of that old standby, the Strategy of Tension (as indeed was the protracted break-up of the former Yugoslav federal state to meet western designs). Although his own observers knew the boss was lying, and responsible journalists on the spot could prove that he was, Walker's version of events was confirmed. These 'observers,' as it was later claimed, were actually CIA wolves in sheep's clothing (as a Swiss member of the OSCE team in Kosovo told the French Swiss newspaper *La Liberté*). Michel Chossudovsky, who is generally well ahead in the bowling averages in these matters, alleges a unique twist to Balkan conspiracies, namely a pre-war secret pact between the CIA and German intelligence BND, with the object of promoting a '*Lebensraum*' protectorate in Southeast Europe. The Kosovo Liberation Army figured prominently in that deal, as the storm troopers to lever Kosovo towards independence and provide the operational base. A shadow EU member state as it already is, with many benefits of full membership — including the Euro circulating as the local currency, a vital spigot of the drugs trade lubricating scores of European and US banks, providing huge quantities of liquidity in the markets — it looks like a deal that came off.

In 2007, the Left-wing Belgian investigative writer Michel Collon, who assembled a network of independent civil observers to work in the Balkans, published a book suggesting that the United States had similar designs. The Pentagon constructed an operational military plan, which included selecting targets for air attacks on Yugoslavia, long before NATO invented the pretext of an impending 'humanitarian catastrophe' in Kosovo. He independently corroborated an important Russian witness called to the stand in The Hague, who stated that Moscow had been aware of exactly such a secret National Security Council (NSC) decision dating from 1997. The former Russian premier Nikolai Ryzkhov pointed out that by any objective measure, the main humanitarian catastrophe in Kosovo was wrought on thousands forced to flee Secretary Madeleine Albright's humanitarian bombs.[84] Despite the chief prosecutor James Nice's lowball efforts to disparage him as a 'biased Slav' (a gratuitous racial slur), Ryzkhov also confirmed what is now a standard token: that 80% of the narcotics coming out of Afghanistan were trafficked across Turkey by mafia gangs connected with KLA freedom fighters. Moreover, KLA ranks were bolstered by '800 to 1,000' mercenaries recruited by the CIA, mainly ex-Mujahideen fighters — the Faustian 'pact with the devil' subsequently confirmed by Bill Clinton's chief emissary in the Balkans, Richard Holbrooke. Within two months of the attacks commencing, any informed reader of the *Washington Times* knew that many of the heroic resistance fighters known as the KLA had been to clandestine

---

[84] A strange way to repay hospitality, but typifying the well-fertilized Albright myth. Born in Prague to Jewish parents, her father a Czech diplomat, the family subsequently became reluctant Catholic converts, to escape the camps. As Marie Jana Korbelová, she was of course with them when they sought refuge in Belgrade from Nazi persecution 1936-8.

training camps in Afghanistan run by Osama bin Laden, who was suspected in the deadly bombing of U.S. embassies in Kenya and Tanzania in 1998.

So two more components of the old Gladio-Strategy of Tension blueprint fell into place: the alliance of NATO with organised crime specialising in narcotics trafficking, and the use of imported secret armies to manufacture terror for political ends. Račak was furthermore the classic psy-ops, false-flag incident designed to legitimise an otherwise illegal attack on a sovereign state. With an additional twist of melancholy brilliance that the principal actors at the crime scene, the sacrificial victims, were already dead.

As the political scientist Paul Treanor has argued, any modern power that seeks to engage in wars of conquest or ensure its continuing dominance needs an 'ideology of justification.' When the Berlin Wall collapsed, the US and its proxy acolyte NATO found themselves drifting in uncharted waters, until a lifeboat named 'human rights intervention' came to the rescue. The export of the American Dream to previously unexploited realms soon became the dominant consensus among the ruling Washington foreign policy cliques, many of whom — including Human Rights Watch — enjoyed strong ties to neocon camps such as the Council for Foreign Relations.

From the outset, the new policy was the velvet glove, the seemingly ideal guise for pursuing US military adventures under the banner of democracy and freedom. The first expedition went horribly astray. In 1992, Clinton tried to plant a US military colony in the ethnically-ravaged Horn of Africa, an old sparring ground with the Soviets. This was disguised as a humanitarian mission intended to rescue the broken-backed state of Somalia from famine and civil war. The enterprise ended abruptly two years later, with the gruesome television spectacle of unfortunate GI's dragged by their heels through the very same ocean surf where they had earlier splashed ashore.

When Clinton attempted a return bout in the Balkans, he fared better, because the cultural complexities could be exploited to advantage by prodding subliminal memories of the Holocaust. An oppressed religious minority, the Albanian Kosovars, were shown as getting the full Hitlerian treatment from the Serbs. To borrow from the old Leninist lexicon, this was now a war of 'popular liberation.' To make sure, Pentagonia's Fort Bragg psy-ops warfare department got to work fabricating stories of death camps, and freezer trucks stuffed with corpses supposedly driven into the Danube. The mainstream media breathlessly regurgitated each and every outlandish claim. American Exceptionalism always appeared to wire in the assumption of owning the moral high ground (in spite of skating past endemic slavery and the near extinction of the ethnic Indians). But as Paul Treanor noted, the vague assumption of organising crusades around the hugely undefined territory labelled as human rights is not the sole option for a general ideology of intervention. It belongs with the massive colonial expansion of the nineteenth century under the heading of a 'civilising mission.' Can we ignore the fact that Hitler, Mussolini and the fascist Japanese junta used precisely the same language, in pursuit of wider imperial aims unrelated to its real content?

Cui bono? The proceedings in The Hague, modelled as they were on the trials of Nazi war criminals staged at Nuremburg after WW2, were intended to demonstrate that NATO (viz. the United States) is incapable of doing wrong. Those of a more objective disposition will echo the thinking of the American novelist and military commentator Caleb Carr, who wrote, 'all too often the armies of modern democracies have tolerated and even initiated outrages against civilians, in manners uneasily close to those of their totalitarian and terrorist enemies.'

By the time NATO warplanes began swooping from the skies in the name of a humanitarian crusade, everyone in the US and European intelligence community already knew that the KLA — certain to be the chief beneficiary in the final outcome — was the key player in the rapidly expanding international drugs-for-arms cartel. Kosovo was the key transit camp on the chain, shipping some $2 billion worth of high-end narcotics annually into Western Europe alone. In 1998, none other than the US State Department — at the time under Madame Albright's supervision — formally branded the KLA as an international terrorist organisation, that bankrolled its operations with proceeds from global heroin rackets and subsidies from wanted terrorists such as bin Laden. It was actually worse, since the 'freedom fighters' were thoroughly loathed by many Kosovars for their criminal practices, such as forced tithes imposed on businessmen and 'taxes' of 3% levied on all remittances sent home by Kosovars who had flown abroad. In March 1999, the month the bombings commenced, the widely respected British-based *Jane's Intelligence Review* published a report stating that the KLA earned 'high tens of millions of dollars' every month from narcotics trafficking. Four years earlier the same magazine warned that 'Albanian narco-terrorism could lead to a Colombian syndrome in the southern Balkans, or the emergence of a situation in which the Albanian mafia becomes powerful enough to control one or more states in the region.' On 25th March 1999, just one day after NATO's bombardment began, drug enforcement experts from the Hague-based European Office of Police (Europol), met in an emergency closed session devoted solely to the threat posed by 'Kosovo narcotics trafficking networks.' The result was an extensive report for European interior ministers, confirming the KLA's dominant role as chief spigot of the Afghan heroin smuggling ring. According to Leonard Cohen, writing on racketeering and organised crime in the Balkans for the Italian daily *La Repubblica*, powerful KLA heroin gangs had successfully elbowed aside Albanian and Turkish rivals, and seized control of the fabled Balkan Route. Michel Koutouzis, the EU's future drugs czar (who was then working at Paris-based Geopolitical Drug Watch) explained how their Yugoslav passports allowed them to travel earlier and much more widely than rivals from Albania, another important but more isolated junction on the golden trail.

Yet in the face of this overwhelming evidence, the U.S. Congress solemnly debated a bill to arm ten battalions of the KLA to fight the Serbs. Lawmakers were prepared to vote taxpayer dollars to arm a branded terrorist movement in cahoots with the global Mafia, in order to skirt Clinton's reluctance to risk American boots on Serbian soil. As an official of the US Drug Enforcement Agency sourly observed, 'one man's terrorist today is another man's freedom fighter tomorrow.' In Milan, again according to Michel Chossudovsky, the Albanians became so powerful and feared that they deposed the long-established Calabrian mafia from control of the narcotics and vice rackets in Italy's financial capital. The connection with Kosovo was identified early in 2011, when a number of top secret reports dealing with NATO actions came to the hands of Paul Lewis, an investigative reporter at *The Guardian* newspaper in London. These documents indicated that NATO chiefs had known since at least 2004 that Hashim Thaçi was at the wheel of organized crime in Kosovo, this micro-state of 1.7 million people which is now recognized by 86 members of the UN. Shortly afterwards, the parliamentary chamber of the Strasbourg-based Council of Europe (the main human rights organization spanning the European Continent) voted to endorse a report claiming that senior officials of the KLA controlled a grisly trade in human organs and sex slaves. Thaci reacted furiously when he was directly accused by Dick Marty, the prominent Swiss politician who compiled the report, of permitting the peddling of transplantable body organs removed from the bodies of Serb war prisoners, in some instances while the victims were still alive. Marty's report seemed to echo the prophecy by *Jane's Intelligence Review* some five years earlier that burgeoning Albanian criminal activity could well lead to the establishment of a mafia-controlled narco pocket state.

As we noticed earlier, Madame Albright, the mission controller of the Balkans affair, was subsequently hired to chart the future course of NATO. No doubt James Burnham, surveying developments from his astral armchair, seized with delight on her conclusion that henceforth the alliance must concentrate on the necessity to 'secure vital resources.' It is after all the same judgement that he reached in his own famous exercise in clairvoyance, the seminal work he published in 1947 called *The Struggle for the World.* So be it, since Kosovo is also home to the last great unexploited mineral resource in Europe. This is the sprawling Trepča mining complex. Its Stygian depths are believed to hoard fabulous reserves of around sixty million tonnes of fine-grade ores containing lead, zinc, bauxite, nickel and gold. This great flagship of Serbian industry was chronically mismanaged by managers lacking independence and powers to push ahead. It was further hampered by the absence of systematic exploration. Prized from the grip of Slobodan Milošević, packaged and parcelled for 'privatisation' by global mining corporates, it was to no small extent worth the war in itself.

Račak, and the consequences, are the story of the Gladio Strategy of Tension pursued to its logical conclusion. All the salient features were present. The 'deep state' represented by the CIA's long-time conspiracies with organised crime and narcotics racketeers, shiploads of psychological and black warfare, the alliances with branded terrorists, and not least the overall guiding hand of NATO. The same terrorists the State Department accused of dealings with Al Qaeda, America's Public Enemy Number One, are now running the statelet of Kosovo. An uninvited NATO army vainly tries to stamp out the opium fields in Afghanistan (or so we are told; the Taliban had already done that, so is NATO fighting a new Opium War to protect the crop?) Meanwhile the main wholesalers of the heroin trade are comfortably ensconced in the quaintly-named Kosovan capital of Pristina, working the cash registers on overtime.

The US embassy in Belgrade was torched in the immediate aftermath of Kosovo independence. On 2nd August 2010, 30,000 people attended a public commemoration of the Gladio bombing of the Bologna railway station, thirty years before. Kosovo, Bologna: different tragedies, but the same unchanging story.

Short Story: The Strange Tale of Two Earls

In the notorious parlance of the British upper crust, popularised by Bertie Wooster and his likes, was he a cad, a bounder or simply a plain rotter? Or alternatively the pastiche British Führer in waiting? Which appellation might best suit the hereditary 7th Earl of Lucan (named for an undistinguished small town close to Dublin), one Richard John Bingham, the legendary vanishing playboy aristocrat. He disappeared on the night of 7th November 1974, leaving his battered wife and the mangled body of the family nanny in the blood-spattered basement of the family home in London's fashionable Belgravia quarter. Lord Lucan, never again seen in mortal form since that fatal night, is the veritable Bigfoot of British crime annals. He is regularly spotted everywhere from the Zambezi to the Orinoco, or the depths of the Australian outback. Occasionally, like the affair of Georgi Markov, he is exhumed by Scotland Yard to keep the myth alive. But, as we saw with Markov, it is preferable first to understand the man.

The six-foot-two (188 cm), Eton-educated, ex-Coldstream Guardsman was an establishment top-feeding drone with a purported penchant for gambling indifferently, while making rich and powerful friends. He was a proclaimed fascist, who often relaxed by listening to scratchy recordings of Hitler's wartime speeches at the Nazi party's Nuremburg rallies. His like-minded close associates included East African entrepreneur Roland 'Tiny' Rowland, the fanatically Right-wing casino entrepreneur and eclectic zoo proprietor John Aspinall, and the fabulously wealthy Sir James Goldsmith — another famous Right-wing reactionary. Lucan was among the co-founders of the exclusive Clermont gambling den, then owned by Aspinall, situated in London's Mayfair. Another was Col. Archibald David Stirling, the founder of the SAS regiment. He was one of the early protagonists of the stay-behind armies that subsequently evolved into Gladio. The clan warmed their hands at the hearth of MI5, and the same quintet was involved in the unfolding plot to stage a Gladio-managed British neofascist putsch, amid the pre-Weimar mood sweeping the UK in the mid-1970s. The conspiracy enjoyed the encouragement of a core group within the home secret service.

With his ram-rod guardsman posture, the statesmanlike photogenic glare at the camera, the immaculately cultivated moustache, Lucan consciously reflected Sir Oswald Mosley, the British Blackshirt leader at the height of his fame in the 1930s. Like Mosley, Lucan spoke in a hypnotically mesmerising manner, which undoubtedly appealed to the plotters, although he was nothing like as intelligent. He could however be reliably tutored to demonstrate the human face of the intended regime. Unlocking the strange myth of the vanishing earl will lead us to another extraordinary mystery, the brutal assassination of the Duke of Edinburgh's uncle, Earl Louis Mountbatten, who was killed by a bomb planted in his fishing boat at an Irish loch on 27th August 1979.

If the stories swirling around the plotters are correct, might Britons have awoken one morning to solemn music playing on the BBC, followed by the strikingly handsome, confident-sounding Earl of Lucan, proclaiming a state of national emergency 'in view of the grave peril facing the nation?' Far stranger things have happened in neighbouring countries. It is only that such remarkable dramas seem foreign to the English climate. Yet the Lucan story has much about it which suggests that he was being groomed by his well-heeled backers as the compliant front man, the pull-by-wire PR face of the junta. As we saw in Chapter XI, dealing with the 'soft' political assassination of Prime Minister Harold Wilson, it was clear that a small coterie of Right-wing officers in British intelligence were indeed sympathetic to the plotting within the Clermont set to overthrow the legitimate government. One man who certainly knew of these intrigues was the last Viceroy of British Imperial India, Lord Mountbatten, whom they approached to act as their regent in the Pétainist model.

Lord Lucan's troubles began as he passed the family home, No. 46 in Lower Belgrave Street, on that evening early in November 1974. The official account, based on the often equivocal evidence of Countess Lucan, states that around nine o'clock he quietly entered the terraced house, while his estranged wife and their three children were occupied watching television.[85] The family nanny, Sandra Rivett, aged 29, had gone to the kitchen located in the downstairs basement to make tea. Wondering why she was taking so long, Lady Lucan said that she went down to the kitchen, which she found to be in darkness. A man then emerged from the shadows and struck her hard with some kind of blunt object. When he spoke she recognised the voice as her husband's. He told his wife that the nanny was lying dead downstairs. Lady Lucan then insisted that he tried to choke her. Both engaged in a struggle. Lord Lucan then went upstairs to send their eldest daughter, Frances (then aged ten), who was still watching television and quite unaware of the *contretemps*, off to bed. Lady Lucan seized her chance and took flight to the local public house called the Plumber's Arms in the same street. Customers

---

[85] The West London coroner Gavin Thurston, who has already featured on questionable grounds in these chronicles, puts in a repeat appearance yet again, because he conducted the inquest on Sandra Rivett. His chief task was to convict Lord Lucan *in absentia*. Questioning Lady Lucan on the events of the night in question, he asked; 'You have no doubt it was he?' She replied: 'No doubt at all.' In legal terms this is the classic example of the leading question. Thurston's naming of Lord Lucan as the murderer was unprecedented for a coroner. The law was later changed to prevent a repetition, because of fury in the legal profession.

were astonished to see the distraught woman screaming and shouting that her husband had just tried to murder her. When the police arrived shortly afterwards, they found the nanny Sandra Rivett's battered corpse inside a canvas bag in the basement of the house. They also came upon the alleged murder weapon, a length of bloodstained pipe enclosed in medical plaster.

These are the forensic details of the affair. What never emerged from the accounts of his wife or the police investigations was the vaguest hint of a motive. The couple's difficult marriage had ended in legal separation. Lord Lucan had fought a legal battle for custody of their three children, a basically hopeless cause, on the grounds that his wife was mentally unstable.[86] But there seemed no grounds as to why he should enter the house, beat the nanny to death with a length of lead pipe, and then calmly stuff her body in something like a mail bag. The latter would seem to suggest an intention to remove the body from the house, a curious business given the fifteen minutes or so in which Mrs. Rivett was supposed to be occupied in brewing tea.

Shortly after the mayhem in No. 46, Lucan called a friend who lived nearby, to say that he had entered the house and discovered the slaughter in the kitchen. He asked her to rush to the house and take care of the children. Lucan's own car, a Mercedes, was garaged for repairs. He had borrowed a rather more modest black Ford Corsair from a friend, and used that to drive to the home of gambling friends, the Maxwell-Scotts, who lived about sixty miles away in the East Sussex town of Uckfield. There he delivered an expanded account of the night's bizarre events to Mrs. Susan Maxwell-Scott. He was passing the house in Lower Belgrave Street in an unhurried fashion when he heard some sort of fight or scramble. He entered, and found his distraught wife Veronica covered in blood. She declared there had been an assailant on the premises who attacked and killed Mrs. Rivett. His wife at first implied that the murderer was sent by Lucan, and got the wrong victim in the form of the nanny. He gave a similar account by telephone to his mother.

Lucan then began to lead a kind of charmed existence. One would expect a nationwide manhunt, and urgent calls to alert Interpol, involving a close watch on all air and sea ports. As we see in a moment, none of this happened, as Scotland Yard either dithered or were told to lay off. Four days later, on 11th November, the unprepossessing Ford was found abandoned at Newhaven, a modest cross-Channel ferry port, about twenty miles from the home of his friends at Uckfield. Conveniently another length of lead pipe

---

[86] Lady Lucan was subsequently to lose contact with her three children, and attempted to commit suicide in 1982. In 1983 she was committed temporarily to a mental hospital, after being found wandering in a confused state near her home. Her history of mental illness appears to bear out her husband's concerns in the bitter family struggle for custody of the children.

exactly like that found in Lower Belgrave Street, and similarly enclosed in medical plaster, was found in the car. What is more than curious is that the police did not issue a warrant for the Earl's arrest until five days after the murder, ostensibly because they thought he would give himself up. So there was no nationwide appeal to search for a suspected brutal murderer, which in itself is fairly remarkable in the annals of crime detection. Clearly, he was allowed the luxury of time to get away.

Lucan's whereabouts are thus enclosed by the interval between the murder on 7th November and the discovery of the abandoned car four days later. The Ford Corsair found at Newhaven was the only evidence from the authorities that he made his way aboard the Newhaven ferry to Le Havre in France. If this was the case, then the most dramatic vanishing act in British criminal history was remarkably accomplished by a celebrity killer using his own passport. The most important and invariably ignored background to the night's events is the subsequent leakage by certain Scotland Yard officers that they knew of urgent SOS calls made to friends of Lucan — undoubtedly members of the Clermont Set — made by officers of MI5. This accounts for the Yard seemingly moving in slow motion in the search for the missing peer. The alternative notion that Lucan drove to Newhaven where he stole a small motorboat (the starting key conveniently left in the engine), then tied a cord attached to a heavy stone around his neck and jumped into the sea, is the most improbable account. All of these improbabilities began with the allegation that Lord Lucan was seized with a sudden fit to butcher his estranged wife and by accident killed the nanny in mistake. The frenzied slaughter in Belgravia seems purposeless unless it is understood in the light of another individual altogether as the killer, upon whom the Earl chanced while passing by en route to his nightly rendezvous with the gaming tables.

To disappear so thoroughly, quickly and efficiently, Lucan urgently required the essential forged documents, including a replacement passport replete with a new identity, that he would require for the rest of his life. His own bank accounts shuttered, his other great necessity was money, in substantial quantities. The most obvious source to satisfy pressing needs was the London gambling set operating in the orbit of 'Tiny' Rowland, James Goldsmith and John Aspinall. Some accounts claimed that he owed these men large sums at the time that he disappeared. But given that 'Lucky' Lucan was party to the many swindles perpetrated at the tables, he was at little risk himself of losing real money.

Somewhere in the murky background Lucan was in the receipt of remarkable assistance in order to turn himself into the invisible man. That was almost certainly supplied by the six-footer-plus nicknamed 'Tiny' Rowland, a man who spent his entire adult life as the eternal outsider in elusive pusuit of an identity. The consequence was a burning inferiority complex which he fought to overcome with his stupendous wealth and endless struggles to be accepted, notably the famous battle for control of Harrods, the iconic London supermarket for the rich. He came out the loser after an epic encounter with Mohamed Al-Fayed, whose son, Dodi, was later to die with Princess Diana in Paris. *The Guardian*'s investigative reporter Nick Davies traced Rowland's connections to Sir George Joseph Ball, a rabid pro-fascist and one-time head of MI5's 'B' counter-espionage branch. As WW2 approached, the young Rowland clamoured to join British intelligence, but his somewhat compromising pedigree, as a Hitler Youth volunteer while living in Hamburg with his parents, blotted his copy book.[87] Ball however spotted a brilliant cover to despatch Rowland as his eyes and ears at an internment camp for Sir Oswald's Mosley supporters established in the Isle of Man during the war. Thereafter his intelligence career blossomed, in a business career which invariably lockstepped with British interests, particularly in Africa. He eventually hired the MI6 globetrotter Nicholas Elliot, his partner in many overseas escapades, as a board member of his flagship company Lonrho.

There is no evidence that Lucan remained in the country in the interval between the murder of Sandra Rivett and the discovery of the abandoned Ford Corsair at Newhaven docks. But it would in all likelihood require at least that amount of time to manufacture an entirely new personality from the wreckage of the old one. Moreover he would require a safe house. I believe that he found that, thanks to his closest friend in the Clermont set, the fabled casino impresario John Aspinall. He owned a luxurious country mansion called Howletts, situated close to the historic city of Canterbury, and about 60 miles across country from Uckfield. Lucan made his way there, and Rowland then took charge of the operation. Neither the British establishment nor the intelligence services wanted the trial of the century, starring a peer in the dock at the Old Bailey on a charge of murdering a family servant. Much better that he should simply disappear from the face of the earth. It is likely that Rowland employed his intelligence contacts to organise the paperwork, and then provided the final signal service. Over the years he owned a series of splendidly-appointed private aircraft which he used for jetting around Africa, and often to visit his close friend and ally, the late Libyan dictator

---

[87] Nothing was ever entirely straightforward with Tiny Rowland, which applied especially to his past. He was born Roland Walter Fuhrhop in a British detention camp in Calcutta during the First World War, to a German father and Anglo-Dutch mother. The future tycoon established a claim to a British passport on the somewhat tenuous grounds that he was an empire citizen. The family left India and moved to Hamburg. His parents were interned again when they fled the Nazis for sanctuary in England during WW2. His mother was poorly treated in an internment camp. These unsettling events served to inflame Rowland's subsequent passion to gain acceptance in a country that had never been his homeland.

Mu'ammar Gaddafi. It was a simple matter for Rowland to prevail on him to conceal Lord Lucan in his secretive desert kingdom. Thus the fugitive peer was smuggled on board the Lonhro company jet and flown at first to North Africa. The black Ford Corsair dumped at Newhaven was simply a decoy, and Lucan may have still been in the country when it was discovered. Aspinall himself later circulated the famous story of Lucan's rather comic suicide. But he spoilt it by a subsequent accidental confession to the somewhat unconventional journalist Lynn Barber that he had 'remained friendly' with Lord Lucan *after* the bogus suicide.

Aspinall always said that he would have 'done anything' that Lucan asked. Detective Chief Superintendent Roy Ranson, who led the original murder investigation, claimed in his book on the case that he believed Lucan did not kill himself but fled to Africa 'with the help of influential friends.' There is a strong indication here that he was muffled by his superiors from naming these figures.[88] Rowland was also in the position to provide the repackaged Earl with employment opportunities in his scattered business empire, had he need of them. In 1992, Richard John Bingham, Earl of Lucan, was presumed deceased in a legal judgment, and seven years later formally adjudicated to be dead. If he is still alive, as I believe that he is, barring ill health, then this year would be his 78th. Sir James Goldsmith died in 1997, after a brief if meteoric career as the leader of an independent anti-EU splinter party. The Earl of Lucan's great benefactor Tiny Rowland followed him in 1998. The vanishing peer's closest friend, John Aspinall, who also took to politics as a candidate for Goldsmith's private political party, died in 2002.

The great mystery of Lord Lucan is better understood by looking to the role of these men in the disturbed political climate hanging over the United Kingdom in 1974. The murder of Nanny Rivett at No. 46 Lower Belgrave Street overlaps with the plotting against the incumbent socialist prime minister Harold Wilson, and the infectious talk of an imminent coup which drenched the mainstream media. And of course, Lord Lucan's knowledge of these matters, which became a highly toxic business once he became a hunted killer. As to who really killed the unfortunate Sandra Rivett, we see all the hallmarks of what the French call a *crime passionnel*, intimately connected to the private affairs of the murdered woman herself. Like Lady Veronica Lucan, she was herself estranged from her husband.

---

[88] *Looking for Lucan, the Final Verdict*, 1984. The same officer took the lead in investigating the theft of Harold Wilson's personal tax documents. This was widely believed — and never effectively disputed — to be the work of the intelligence services.

We shift time gears, accelerating forward five years to the warm sunny morning of 29th August 1979. The weather on the Atlantic coast of Ireland had been typically capricious for some days. With calm waters and clear skies breaking through at last, Earl Louis Mountbatten was preparing a family fishing party, close to his much-loved summer retreat near the entrancing little harbour of Mullaghmore, County Sligo. The border with the British province of Ulster is scarcely a dozen miles off. In between lay the so-called bandit country, the badlands freely used by the Irish Republican Army to replenish guns and other supplies for the struggle in the North. Yet here, year after year, this ultimate patrician of the Royal Family repaired for an annual vacation, evidently without a care in the world for his personal safety.

That Mountbatten, towering scion of British imperialism, was allowed to relax in this way, at the height of an extremely violent anti-colonial rebellion, the war zone practically on his own doorstep, was itself remarkable. Even more extraordinary, the IRA having the means to tuck a radio-controlled bomb aboard the Earl's fishing wherry, without Irish State intelligence or MI6 having the slightest clue. Little moves in Mullaghmore without someone seeing it, given a tiny community numbering no more than 150 souls. The great rollers crashing from the Atlantic have long made the village a prime destination for surfers, but mostly people come for the quiet beauty of the place. More recently, newcomers made rich by the now-exhausted Gaelic Tiger boom paid astronomical sums for plots of land and humble properties. Tourists have been lured by Mullaghmore's charms since the early 1800's. The English patrician statesman Lord Palmerson was by far the most famous. He was responsible for commissioning the towering hulk of castellated granite called Classiebawn Castle, standing on a plain hillside with magnificent prospects of the wild seascape and the loch. Palmerston also built the stone-walled harbour, quite the most secure and sturdy in the county. The inheritance rights fell to Lord Mountbatten's future wife, Lady Edwina Ashley, when her grandfather, the 9th Earl of Shaftesbury, died in 1921. Mountbatten was thoroughly smitten by this idyllic Irish wedding present when he married Edwina a year later. 'I have a place in Eire, Classiebawn Castle in County Sligo,' he told a gathering of the Empire Club of Canada in 1967, 'and I and my family could not be treated with greater friendship by the Irish.' Twelve years later he was to die in Mullaghmore at the hands of the Irish Republican Army.

The story runs that Thomas McMahon, then 31 and one of the IRA's most experienced bomb-makers, had been able to step unchallenged down to the shore and ship the device on board the unguarded boat in the dead of night. The Garda (Irish state police) claimed that they had circulated advance warnings of a possible attack. Yet not a single British newspaper commented on this extraordinary negligence by the Irish security services. A 24-year-old gravedigger called Francis McGirl was also charged, but released because he could not be connected to the scene, whereas McMahon had paint splinters from the boat and traces of nitroglycerine on his clothes. The *Shadow V* had put to sea just before eleven o'clock when the explosion happened, about 200 yards (182 meters) from the shore. The device was set off by radio control from a hillside overlooking the harbour. Lord Mountbatten, 79, was so badly injured that he drowned. The victims included Nicholas Knatchbull, 14, one of the Earl's twin grandsons, and a fifteen-year-old local boat boy, Paul Maxwell. Another passenger on the boat, the Dowager Lady Brabourne, 82, was pulled alive from the shattered boat, but died in hospital the following day.

Freshly elected to the Strasbourg Euro Parliament, I was staying with my family not far away at the renowned Cashel House Hotel at Cashel Bay in Galway. The tearful manager came to me at lunchtime bearing the gloomy news that 'the Lord Mountbatten' and his family had just been blown up. She added tearfully: 'they should find them [the culprits] and string them up in their own villages.' Yet truthfully Her Majesty's Government could hardly be disappointed at the tidings from Ireland. The blowback in the wake of the tragedy, particularly against the IRA's political wing, Sinn Fein, reaped enormous rewards in the form of huge damage to the Republican cause. For their part, the media blinded themselves to the absence of a security detail for such a prominent potential target, the nonchalant way the terrorist planted his bomb or indeed why Mountbatten — who returned in such clockwork fashion for his annual retreat — was killed at precisely this moment. This was a common theme repeated in the Irish newspapers that I saw at the time. The Garda were on difficult ground, given their circulation of warnings that Earl Mountbatten might be attacked. Yet no special team was assigned to watch the harbour, even though the Earl's intentions to put to sea the following day were well known in the village. The grisly affair smacks of the intercepted plot, the old Strategy of Tension look the other way game of 'just let it happen,' common to so many black episodes of the Irish rebellion and the Gladio story. It is a highly plausible explanation, tantamount though it is to a degree of official complicity in the atrocity. Many Republicans indeed agreed that the killing of Lord Mountbatten and the innocents on board *Shadow V* was a profound tactical error and, for numerous reasons, did much lasting harm to their cause. Mullaghmore was home to many strong sympathizers with the IRA. Yet to a man they were in the lead at the rescue efforts.

Among the bulk of secrets Mountbatten took to the grave was the projected British putsch of 1974. He was undoubtedly privy to all the mechanics, including the necessary false-flag incidents that would be required to convey the necessary mood of disorder sweeping the realm. He would have known the probable role of Lord Lucan. Some of the key plotters, such as Col. Archibald David Stirling, Goldsmith, Rowland and Stirling, were all members of his own intimate private circle. Mountbatten, it appears, reluctantly balked at the honour that they proposed to heap on him, for fear of marginalising his nephew Prince Philip's consort, Queen Elizabeth. Certainly the secrets to which the earl had some exclusive access had a potentially long radiation life.

The vanishing earl and the murdered one may have shared another connection, namely the services of exclusive brothels, such as the reputed but never specifically named Golden Key Club, in the genteel West London suburb of Kensington. This was a rest and recuperation facility allegedly run by MI5/MI6 for the pleasure of highly-sheltered dignitaries, important foreign visitors and close allies of the secret services. There was common gossip around the newsrooms of London newspapers that important royals were patrons, either as guests or more discreetly, having the specialised services delivered elsewhere. It was open knowledge Earl Mountbatten was among these privileged persons. The existence of such an officially-condoned sex circuit exploded with the sensational Profumo Affair in 1963. The red top tabloids had a field day exposing a three-way link between the war (defense) minister John Profumo, the Russian naval attaché Yevgeny Ivanov and an attractive hooker called Christine Keeler. These were the star acts reported as sporting themselves in orgies conducted at the palatial late-Italian style Cliveden mansion in Berkshire, then owned by the second Lord Astor.

These high jinks held darker secrets: the leading pimp, a society osteopath called Stephen Ward, was either murdered or committed suicide while in prison (more likely the former), which effectively sealed the prospects of daylight exposing other shadowy figures party to the furious romping around the gilded pile's lavish swimming pool and numerous appealing chambers. The career of Profumo was wrecked and the prime minister, Harold Macmillan, resigned on grounds of ill health shortly afterwards. In 1964 the Conservatives were defeated by the Labour party after thirteen years in office, a slight widely thought to be connected in part to the backlash from the Cliveden scandal. It was known that Sir Roger Hollis (the director-general of MI5) and Sir Anthony Blunt, the Surveyor of the Queen's Pictures and a Soviet double agent, were among the frequent visitors to Cliveden on party days. Blunt, who was gay, was stripped of his knighthood when his treachery as a member of the legendary Cambridge Five nest of spies was exposed. He was another close intimate of Mountbatten. Hollis remains the most likely candidate for the Fifth Man in the Cambridge circle. The entertainments at Cliveden were also supplied to a long invitation list of important foreign leaders such as Willy Brandt of Germany.

In 1992 Ivanov published a memoir revealingly entitled *The Naked Spy,* in which he claimed that he supplied his KGB masters with enticing snapshots of extramarital activities indulged in at Cliveden by leading members of British high society. He further boasted that he collected 'compromising material on each of them,' which was taken to mean the royals. This seemed to confirm the samizdat gossip circulating in the media for many years concerning members of the royal family and their private lives, and swirling around Earl Mountbatten in particular. Both he and the Countess were 'swingers' in the formerly popular but now rather dog-eared parlance, noted for the 'informality' of their private lives and frequent amoral adventures. One of Mountbatten's innermost circle, the second Lord Astor (of the Waldorf Astor dynasty) lived at Cliveden, although he had assigned the title to the National Trust. One night in 1961 Astor ('Bill' to his intimates) gave a discreet dinner party attended by the cabinet minister John Profumo and a select group of high society figures, including Mountbatten. The conversation over the cutlets and the smoked salmon may well be imagined, given that two of the leading ladies of the forthcoming scandal were also sipping champagne from the fine crystal. They were Christine Keeler, then aged scarcely 19, and her companion *femme fatale*, Mandy Rice-Davies.

Another guest on that famous evening was the osteopath Stephen Ward, who was on close relations with Bill Astor and lived rent-free in a cottage set in the great estate's 350 acres of gardens and woods. From there he organised the match-making parties that would end with the fall of the Conservative government in the wake of the greatest political scandal since WW2 — and his own tragic death.

Very little in the way of hard new facts emerged from Ivanov's book, but the same could as well be said of the official Cliveden inquiry conducted by a prominent law lord, the Master of the Rolls Lord Denning. He devoted 49 days and 70,000 words to a splendid exercise in damage limitation. This is that same Lord Denning whom we previously encountered (Chapter X) who cheerfully sentenced men to years in prison for crimes they did not commit, solely to protect the reputation of the police. Denning's task was to brand the unfortunate dupe John Profumo as the scapegoat of the entire affair, due to his manifold 'errors of judgment,' and the lies that he told to members of the House of Commons concerning his liaisons with prostitutes at Cliveden.

At all costs the government and the security services must conceal Cliveden as nothing less than an enormous MI5 honey trap, in which the central figure was much less Profumo than the genuine pivotal actor, who was Stephen Ward. His social skills and immaculate manners ensured he was a gifted and natural mixer, always at consummate ease with the rich and famous. He was actually a symbol of the great glacier of the stratified and sexually repressive English social fabric, that began to melt into the famous Permissive Society of the 1960s. The story of generous royal patronage of courtesans was of course nothing new. But there now existed a strange stiffness in the organs of the media, to suppress the truth thanks to the re-deification of the monarchy for political ends. It required the emergence in 1961 of the establishment-baiting fortnightly magazine *Private Eye* to undertake the task from which which staid Fleet Street newspaper magnates shrank, due of course to their own incestuous entanglements with the royals. *Private Eye*'s instant success was due in no small part to its uncensored coverage and insights of the salacious Cliveden business, on behalf of virtually an entire nation hungering for the facts.

Ward took his ease with government ministers, royals, diplomats and high officials of the secret services. His relations with the latter are the key to the story. Ward is often painted as a petty retailer of prostitutes, catering to the varied and exotic tastes that his clients often demanded. However, the mystery of how he was elevated to Master of Ceremonies at Cliveden was not explained by Lord Denning. Only in the wake of his death has it finally emerged that Ward, who seemed to be largely penniless most of the time, despite all his wealthy friends and acquaintances, was an MI5/MI6 implant.

In June 1963 Ward was duly arraigned on charges of procuring prostitutes and living off the immoral earnings of Christine Keeler, Mandy Rice-Davies and two other women. The 51-year-old Ward, a slight and almost albino-like figure, appeared stunned by the charges, quite unable to understand why his official protection had now so suddenly collapsed. Where were the rich and famous now that he needed them? The trial was a sham. Ward was subjected to outrageous defamation by the prosecution team. British justice was enjoying another of its famous days in court. The evidence was paper-thin, the prosecution relied on innuendo and could not in any event call witnesses of substance against Ward. Having experienced a blistering attack by the lead prosecutor, the priggish QC and establishment clone John Griffith-Jones,[89] on the final day of the trial, Ward was said to have taken an overdose of

---

[89] Another Griffith-Jones star turn was his prosecution of Penguin Books in the autumn of 1960, on grounds of publishing salacious literature in the form of D.H. Lawrence's classic, *Lady Chatterley's Lover*. There was no better example of the other-wordliness of a post-Victorian prude when he advised the jury that such a novel was bound to induce 'lustful thoughts' in the minds of readers. He then inquired; 'When you have read it through, would you approve of your young sons, young daughters — because girls can read as well as boys — reading this book? Is it a book that you would have lying around in your own house? Is it a book that you would even wish your wife or your servants to read? (Wikipedia). He lost the case. Censorship of literature collapsed. In the circumstances, the 'lustful frolics' at Cliveden presented an ideal opportunity to redeem himself.

sleeping tablets that he was allowed to keep in his cell. This story is preposterous. Ward was an obvious candidate for suicide watch, yet had access to enough pills to kill himself. Alternatively, and this is the probable account, they were not self-administered. He lapsed into a coma in which he remained when sentence of living on immoral earnings was pronounced on 31st July 1963. Ward survived a few more days until 3rd August, but he never awoke to learn that he had been cleared of the charge of greater substance, namely procuring. Ward would have served a light sentence, about eighteen months, even less with remission, for acting as a pimp. With his passing, many secrets of Cliveden were buried with him. Had he lived, Ward would have shrugged off the discomforts of his short confinement to pick and choose between the many lucrative offers that he was certain to receive for his explosive memoirs. Instead he was given the ultimate pay-off.

You can always guarantee that crocodile tears are cheap and in plentiful supply after events like Ward's convenient 'suicide.' Sure enough, some rather peculiar off-the-record briefings subsequently emanated from MI5, which indicated at the least certain pangs of conscience hovering there. The usual anonymous officer ventured the somewhat remarkable opinion that the trial should have been informed of Ward's true role as a sleeper working for the secret services. Of course this was politically impossible, and the statement was either naive or simply intended to get the truth about Ward into open play. The same goes for the connected comment that Lord Denning ought to have said, at the conclusion of his famous exercise in whitewash, something along the lines of, 'Oh by the way, did I forget to mention that Stephen Ward, on whom I have had so much to say, was working for MI5 all along.' Reading between the lines, it becomes clear that all Ward's games with hookers and the high and mighty were intended as the usual tawdry stock in trade of the spy business; peccadillos that allowed the services to turn potential agents and expose or blackmail others. As is well known, sex is one of the most important tools of the intelligence trade. The honeytrap so often turns to blackmail, another important tactical weapon in the ensnare-ment game, as we saw in the chapter exposing the vice rings in Belgium.

The Mountbatten and Lucan affairs share the same frame with the Cliveden affair. Despite all the subsequent attempts to paint Lord Lucan as a dissolute and feckless groupie attached like a limpet to high society, the facts are that the great and the good looked kindly upon him as one of their own. He counted among his associates a glittering cast list; John Aspinall, who freely pilfered the rich at his gambling casinos, yet preserved their respect; the fanatically Right-wing SAS founder David Stirling; the bucolic Jewish Anglo-French billionaire tycoon and frantic womaniser 'Jimmy' Goldsmith; Edmund de Rothschild, scion of the banking dynasty; Cecil Harmsworth King, owner of the *Daily Mirror* group of titles and a longtime MI5 asset; George Kennedy Young, the ex-deputy director of MI6 and later a Right-wing activist; the famous Colditz escapee, Conservative MP and inner circle Thatcherite Airey Neave, a former member of MI9, British military intelligence (assassinated by Irish republicans at the House of Commons in 1979, the same year in which Mountbatten was murdered); the crown prince of the Lonrho conglomerate Roland 'Tiny' Rowland; General Sir Walter Walker, former NATO Gladio commander who set up the civilian activist prop to support the proposed coup against Harold Wilson; Roderick Blunt-Mackenzie, the fourth Earl of Cromartie, ex-Seaforth Highlander and a close friend of the leading Wilson coup plotter Col. Stirling; and finally, Earl Mountbatten himself.

If nothing else, this partial cast list of Lucan's associates serves to confirm that Lucan had at his disposal all the necessary high-grade connections to effect a total and complete disappearance. Without a doubt Cecil King (MI5), George Kennedy Young (MI6) and Airey Neave (ex-military intelligence) were splendidly placed to manufacture an entirely new replacement personality for the vanishing earl.

Officialdom subsequently overstretched itself not to find Lord Lucan, but rather to erase all traces of his existence. That remains the case to this day. Spluttering efforts by Scotland Yard to follow the trail (the same pattern with the Bulgarian émigré Georgi Markov four years later, and MI6 agent Ann Chapman earlier in 1971) ran into the sands. In all three cases, British intelligence played a leading role. Rarely indeed may so-called penniless 'bounders' such as Lucan count on a fully-equipped lifeboat in their hour of need. The projected coup against Harold Wilson is sometimes known as the Clermont Plot, since the key conspirators were either founders of the legendary casino, or regular visitors to Aspinall's succession of gaming houses. This accounts in no small part for the charmed exit of Richard John Bingham, Earl of Lucan. Unlike the lowly Stephen Ward, he was not to be thrown to the wolves. That is how it always works in the upper echelons of what they still call British high society.

Endnotes^(N)

Endnote reference numbers are given in the text with parentheses and a capital letter N, thus ^(N1), to distinguish them from footnotes.

Introduction – Lambs to the Slaughter

1) 1905-1987. A hugely complicated brilliant iconoclast, educated at Princeton and Balliol College, Oxford (where he studied Old English and knew Tolkien). *The Managerial Revolution* (John Day, 1941) is his masterpiece, a ground-breaking work of extraordinary and lasting perception, in which he noticed the striking similarities between National Socialism, Soviet Communism and the New Deal. Burnham believed with some justice he had discovered the New World Order composed of an emerging managerial class, who were just as likely to be found in a Soviet state monopoly as any American corporation. Who can dispute the managerial state Burnham envisioned is what we see around us today?

Chapter I – The Outcomes Business

1) Reports, various, European media, 21-25 January, 2008, following joint press conference in Brussels.

2) *CIA Clandestine Service History*, *"Overthrow of Premier Mossadegh of Iran, November 1952-August 1953,"* March 1954, by Dr. Donald Wilber. The writer was a key CIA planner and espionage figure in Operation Ajax.

3) Pulitzer prize reporter, pioneer in exposing the American deep state, author of *The Man Who Kept the Secrets: Richard Helms and the CIA* and the seminal *Intelligence Wars: American Secret History from Hitler to Al Qaeda.*

4) Fort Bragg is the command HQ of the US Army's 4th Psychological Operations Group. The 'Fourth' was an important strand of the Gladio psy-ops structure, and plays a similar role in the present activities of NATO, particularly in the Afghan theatre. MISO's new remit, *Persuade, Change, Influence* was the big idea of former Defense Secretary Robert Gates, to cast off the black-magic stigma attached to psy-warfare, dating back to Vietnam-era operations bordering on voodoo.

5) Dr. Ganser specialises in international history from 1945. He lists his research interests as geostrategic studies, secret warfare, resource wars, globalisation and human rights. He teaches at several Swiss universities. His current research is focusing on the 'war on terror' and peak oil forecasting. He is working on the impact of globalisation on war and peace, to demonstrate how Swiss and international companies support and profit from war. Benchmark work: *NATO's Secret Armies: Operation Gladio and Terrorism in Western Europe*, Frank Cass, January 2005, and subsequent translations.

6) Extracts from broadcast by London Weekend Television, 11th June 2000. Interviewer: David Dimbleby. Transcription by Dick Withecombe. Highlights as follows:

Dimbleby: "The NATO justification the next day was that the bombers had struck at, your phrase, NATO's phrase, the regime's ability I quote to transmit their version of the news. I ask you whether it constitutes formally a war crime or not — whether killing civilians for transmitting government propaganda is a justifiable act of war?

Robertson: [We said] all along that military infrastructure was going to be hit, military facilities were going to be hit, whether it was barracks, whether it was communications, radio relay points — that was and it is now widely acknowledged to have been part of the military superstructure, it was used, that building was used to communicate military instructions to the field. and remember the kind of killing that was going on.

[Author: No evidence of military installations in the building was ever produced. In any event, the NATO claim to have acted to silence either propaganda or instructions relayed to the field, was superfluous because the station was back on the air from another location inside 24 hours. Robertson's contempt for international law could not have been more obvious from a subsequent exchange on the legality of the war, with considerable bearing on Iraq.]

Dimbleby: Secretary-General, you also went to war without formally seeking the endorsement of the United Nations Security Council. Would you do that again?

Robertson: Well, I think it's an exception rather than the rule, because we were faced with the prospect that there would have been a veto on a specific UN Security Council Resolution. but it's worth remembering.

[Author: Memories conveniently lapsed when it came to Libya's turn].

7) *The Guardian*, London.

8) Numerous reports in the Turkish media from the moment the story broke early in January 2008. Non-Turkish speakers who want to know what is going on in Turkey will find the on-line English daily version published by *Zaman* both informative and provocative: www.todayszaman.com.

Chapter II – The Curse of the Two-edged Sword

1) William Scobie, *The Observer*, London, 18th November 1990.

2) *The Guardian*

3) President Cossiga's speech on Gladio (Bruce Johnston, *The Sunday Times*, 12th October 1990). This leading Christian Democrat was, ironically, cousin to the Communist leader, Enrico Berlinguer. Highly compromised in the murder of Moro, but later took a line close to his 'historic compromise,' insisting that Italian politics must adapt to the fall of the Berlin Wall and the end of the Cold War. On 30th November 2007, he puzzled many Italians with remarks in *Corriere della Sera* that 9/11 was planned and carried out by the CIA, in conjunction with Israel's Mossad, in order to justify the invasions of Afghanistan and Iraq, inferring that Italian intelligence knew this.

4) *The Guardian*, 12th January 1992.

5) On 28th April 1992, *Dagens Nyheter* headlined: 'A top-secret intelligence network within NATO is behind the death of Olof Palme.' Journalist Göran Beckérus stated: 'This has been leaked by several sources in Sweden and Germany.' Beckérus then described in precise detail how he uncovered a 'secret

Swedish resistance network under the command of one Alvar Lindencrona.' Subsequently Lindencrona (died 1981) was confirmed as former leader of the stay-behind unit. The newspaper uncovered the top-secret and hitherto unknown operating structure of ACC (Allied Clandestine Committee) and its tasks to 'plan and hide' certain actions. Beckérus went on to describe how delegates of ACC and a special operations support unit met every month in different European capitals, before he let off a real firecracker. '*Dagens Nyheter* is in the possession of information, that also Sweden at times regularly participated in ACC. During several meetings of the ACC/SOPS (Special Operations) committee an assassination plot was made code-named 'Operation Tree' [concerning Palme]. *Dagens Nyheter* is in possession of an alleged SOPS document which states 'project management is local, technician imported.' Alvar Lindencrona was reported as a regular attendee of ACC/SOPS gatherings.

6) Townley is currently on parole under the protection of a Federal Witness Program, thought to be at least partially in connection with information in his possession concerning a number of assassinations.

7) Belgian parliamentarians were treated with open contempt by their own security services. General Bernard Legrand, chief of the military secret service, steadfastly refused to co-operate. He defied the government by refusing to name names of the secret soldiers under his command. 'Whatever the ministers say, there remain very good reasons not to reveal the names of the clandestines.' Later, a mocking note appeared in *Le Soir* attributed to Legrand: 'Give us the names.' 'Never, reply the Gladiators.' This clear allusion to a Gladio operation in Belgium was signed off with the words, 'Adolf is well.' Daniele Ganser, NATO's Secret Armies, *Whitehead Journal of Diplomacy and International Relations,* 2005.

8) The two days of rioting that erupted in November 2000 led the Flemish federal premier of Belgium, Guy Verhofstadt, to cash political chips by forcing down the shutters at the Antwerp-based Arab European League. Professor Herman de Ley, director of the Centre for Islam in Europe at Ghent University, said that with sensitive elections forthcoming, 'paranoia and electoral opportunism were the main motives.' Reported by Khaled Diab, editor of the European public affairs commentary *Diabolical Dialogue,* Ghent.

9) Quotes from an interview Vinciguerra gave to *The Guardian* in 1984.

10) Law-and-order demagogue Sarkozy gained fame as mayor of Paris in 1993 when a man took kindergarteners hostage there. As interior minister in 2002, his handling of an attack on an elderly man three days before the election pushed the Left out of the race. In *The Guardian,* 24th March 2012, under the headline: 'The 23-year-old petty thief who killed three Jewish children and their teacher had accumulated a lethal arsenal and lived a life at odds with his unemployed status. How could this have happened under the nose of the intelligence services?'

Chapter III – May the Force be with You

1) *Justification for US Military Intervention in Cuba (TS),* a collection of draft proposals by the Department of Defense and the office of the Joint Chiefs of

Staff. 'TS' stands for top secret. The document was presented by the Joint Chiefs of Staff to Defense Secretary Robert McNamara on 13th March 1962. 'Appendix to Enclosure A' and 'Annex to Appendix to Enclosure A' of the Northwoods document were initially published online by the National Security Archive on 6th November 1998.

2) Northwoods included the archly cynical Operation Dirty Trick, a plot to blame Castro if the 1962 Mercury space shot carrying John Glenn crashed: 'The objective is to provide irrevocable proof that, should the Mercury manned orbit flight fail, the fault lies with the Communists et al Cuba. This to be accomplished by manufacturing various pieces of evidence which would prove electronic interference on the part of the Cubans.' Composed by Brigadier General Bill Craig and sent on 2nd February 1962, to his boss General Edward Lansdale, who oversaw the long (and completely fruitless) Cuban destabilisation programme called Operation Mongoose.

3) *Time*'s editorial generals forged a mood of hysteria. 'But what of the top Nazis who cannot hide? With a compact army of young SS and Hitler Youth fanatics, they will retreat, behind a loyal rearguard cover of *Volksgrenadiere* and *Volksstürmer*, to the Alpine massif which reaches from southern Bavaria across western Austria to northern Italy. If the retreat is a success, such an army might hold out for years.' *Time*, 12th February 1945.

4) The Strategy of Tension *par élégance*. Told by the CIA that Russia had at most twenty ICBM's, Eisenhower nonetheless signed off the 'cookbook for ending the world.' The first strike 'single integrated operations plan (SIOP-62)' was projected to throw up an explosive yield of 8,000 megatons. (Think the combined 40 or so *kilo*tons for the *bimbi* dropped on Hiroshima and Nagasaki). Some 175 million Russians and Chinese would be vaporized in the first strike, and another 285 million — no one explained how the figures were computed to such polished degrees of exactitude — in follow-up blows. It would take eons for the world to ever detoxify. Pax Americana therefore would be total, if purchased at the price of ridding the planet of all life forms. Foreshadowed by Nevil Chute's apocalyptic 1956 novel *On The Beach,* which features a dwindling band of survivors in Australia and an epic submarine quest to see if life had survived in America.

5) James Bamford, *Body of Secrets.*

Chapter V – God's Terrorist: Yves Guérin-Sérac and the Press Gang

1) Daniele Ganser, 2005, quoting from the Scottish anarchist Stuart Christie and the Italian terrorist Stefano Delle Chiaie.

2) In 2005, the same Judge Guido Salvini was responsible for issuing arrest warrants against 2022 CIA personnel involved in kidnapping Egyptian cleric Abu Omar in Milan in 2003 (the *Imam Rapito* ('kidnap') Affair). For these and other similar annoying actions, he was regularly singled out by the Berlusconi administration as a closet communist. On 4th November 2009, the CIA station chief in Milan, Robert Seldon Lady, was convicted in absentia of illegally kidnapping Abu Omar, together with 21 other agency operatives. They face

arrest if they step on Italian soil. Lady, who planned to retire to the villa that he purchased in Piedmont, later admitted the snatch was illegal. The judgment was a landmark decision against the 'rendition' of suspects who were then subjected to torture in the jails of sympathetic US allies.

3) Quoted by Ganser et al, extracts from an Aginter operations manual discovered in 1974 entitled *Our Political Activity*. Effectively, the document elaborates the main principles of the Strategy of Tension, and so reasonably qualifies as the Gladio psy-warfare order of battle. Clearly the inspiration can be traced back to the expertise of French counter-insurgency techniques practised in Vietnam, which in turn were adopted by prominent American practitioners including Col. Edward Lansdale.

4) Aginter Press: *Our Political Activity*. Cited by Ganser.

5) Stefano Delle Chiaie, quoted by Ganser.

6) An operation masterminded by Belgian neo-fascist Florimand Damman, 'the man of the shadows,' an intimate confidante of Guérin-Sérac. His network of connections extended to many of the highest figures in the Belgian state and the Catholic hierarchy. A third figure, Emile Lecerf, completed an intimate triangle. Lecerf was the force behind the CIA-Gladio-inspired attempted coup in 1973. Guérin-Sérac's arrival in Belgium in 1969 effectively kicked off the Belgian 'years of lead.'

7) *The Great Heroin Coup: Drugs, Intelligence and International Fascism*, 1976. English version occasionally available via Amazon or Bookfinder.com.

8) *The Yankee and The Cowboy*, Sheed Andrews and McMeel, 1975.

Chapter VI – One Last French Kiss

1) De Gaulle's early pronouncements on the Algerian crisis were necessarily ambiguous in the early days of the Fifth Republic. *Vive l'Algérie française* (6th June 1958) fell distinctly short of assuring two million French settlers their futures were secure. He may already have resolved to hold plebiscites in which the Metropolitan French had the overwhelming say on independence.

2) Challe, vaunted proponent of counter-insurgency, was responsible for the brutal pacification program — 'the reign of terror' — launched in 1959. Thousands of Algerians were thrown into concentration camps where they suffered hunger, torture and death. Relying on tactics honed in Indo-China, Challe created fast-moving raiding forces recruited from turncoat Algerians, disguised by FLN (liberation army) uniforms. The tactics stunted but failed to defeat the resistance movement. Challe was summoned back to Paris, fuming at such a snub to his Alpine self-importance.

3) *The Economist* noted when he died in 1997: 'In a theatrical gesture rather out of keeping with a life of discretion and secrecy, Jacques Foccart died at the moment French policy in Africa seems to be collapsing.' Typical of its rather sparse successes in the prediction game, the magazine suggested French influence in Africa would die with him. In fact, all successive presidents to date have firmly pursued Foccart's post-colonialism.

Chapter VII – The Devil in the Deep Blue Sea

1) Quoted by Cottrell, *Blood on Their Hands*. Extract from the report written by Alexander Matsos, the ambassador in question.

2) State Department telegram.

3-7) Cottrell, *Blood on Their Hands*.

Chapter VIII – Behind the Mask of the Red Death

1) Stated in the article published by Grivas in the Sunday weekly *To Proto Thema,* December 2005.

2) Cottrell, *Blood on Their Hands.*

3) Early in her career Ann Chapman spent an interlude in Paris attached to the well-known Berlitz language school. Constantine Karamanlis was there as well, enjoying his CIA-sponsored sabbatical. It seems that part of her duties may have included spying on members of his camp, as a useful preparatory exercise for her forthcoming mission to Greece.

4) State Department response.

5) *Blood on Their Hands.*

6) *The Reluctant Spy: My Secret Life in the CIA's War on Terror* (Random House)

Chapter IX – Goodbye Piccadilly

1) Extracts from a letter dated 18th February 1977 (eighteen months before his death) to Dimiter Bobchev, working for Radio Free Europe in Germany. Translated by Gordon Logan.

2) Extract from Politburo records: Cold War International History Project (CWIHP), Woodrow Wilson International Center for Scholars.

3) *West Europe Report, Case Study of Ağca Activities*, published internally by the Information Service of the US Department of Commerce, April 23rd 1983: Abstract of investigations by Uğur Mumcu appearing in the Turkish daily *Cumhuriyet.* Other information in this chapter has been extracted from Uğur Mumcu's investigations of Turkish-Bulgarian *derin devlet* connections published in the same document.

4) Cold War International History Project.

Chapter X – The Eye of the Serpent

1) The collapse of the fascist state in September 1943 left Borghese, literally, high and dry. He re-directed a strong force to his mentor Mussolini's rump *Repubblica Sociale Italiana.* There, Borghese's followers earned a reputation for cruel and violent repression. The RSI was better known as the Salo Republic, from the sleepy small town on the shores of renowned Lake Garda. It was there that *Il Duce* established the capital of his pocket state. Hitler refused to allow Mussolini to set up camp in the old Savoy capital of Milan, because it would make him seem too important. The area vaguely controlled by the Salo Republic was thick with partisans, who sooner or later were bound to get their man.

Chapter XI – Frolics in the Forest: A Very British Coup

1) Agee's 1975 book, *Inside The Company: CIA Diary*, was the most revealing work in its genre as then published, and earned a furious response from Washington for the scores of revelations concerning internal corruption, assassinations and conspiracy practiced by the Agency. Agee may have been provoked by internal rivalries and jealousies, but it hardly mattered. He certainly behaved like a man possessed. The book was a PR disaster for the United States. After relentless pressure from Washington, Agee was finally expelled from the UK in June 1977, after his protector Harold Wilson left office.

2) Angleton kept a file on Wilson code-named Oatsheaf. His suspicions relied on the vague theory propagated by Soviet defector Golitsyn that Labour leader Hugh Gaitskell, a Right-winger cool to the European project, was murdered to pave the way for the more pliable Wilson. (Tom Mangold: *Cold Warrior: James Jesus Angleton*, Simon & Schuster, 1991). Gaitskell's death in 1963 was attributed to natural causes, the auto-immune disease Lupus erythematosus.

3) General Walker was Commander-in-Chief of NATO forces in Northern Europe between 1969 and 1972. In this capacity he held oversight of NATO's secret armies and psy-operations of the Alliance in that sphere, including of course, the UK.

Chapter XII – St. Petersgate

1) In 2008, Roth's book, *The New Bulgarian Demons*, argued they were simply the leftovers from the Živkov regime 'dressed in new clothes.' A fresh work, *Gangster Economy* (2010), explained how the Bulgarian Mafia continued long-established rackets like smuggling amphetamines through Turkey, with the help of highly placed figures in political circles. He named the former socialist interior minister, Rumen Petkov, who took Roth to court. Roth won the case in absentia, saying he refused to travel to Bulgaria for fear of his life.

2) *Killing Hope*, William Blum, 2003 Common Courage Press.

3) Breakfast with Ledeen at the American Enterprise Institute, 27th March 2003. Topic: Iraq. 'I think the level of casualties is secondary. I mean, it may sound like an odd thing to say, but all the great scholars who have studied American character have come to the conclusion that we are a warlike people and that we love war. What we hate is not casualties but losing. And if the war goes well and if the American public has the conviction that we're being well-led and that our people are fighting well and that we're winning, I don't think casualties are going to be the issue.'

4) During the 1991 Congressional hearings on the confirmation of Robert Gates as CIA director, it emerged that for ten years the Agency had been trying to make the Russian slipper fit the Papal shooting and failed. (Professor Edward Herman (Pennsylvania University) and Frank Brodhead: *The Rise and Fall of the Bulgarian Connection,* Sheridan Square Publications, New York, 1986.)

5) *Riyadh Daily*, 21st March 21, from a *Moscow Times* piece on the background to the coup.

6) Cottrell. Unpublished research conducted in Poland, provisionally titled: *Hidden Hands: How The CIA Hijacked The Polish Revolution.*

Chapter XIII – Something Rotten in the State of Belgium

1) 1923-1995. German-born son of Jewish parents, Mandel (who used a string of pseudonyms) was among the most illuminating figures of the Left in post-war Europe. Survived the German forced-labor camp at Nordhausen, and went on to lead the militant Trotyskist faction of the Belgian socialist party. His influence ebbed after the traumatic national strike of 1960-61, a galvanising factor in the slow-motion break-up of Belgium. Passionate orator and writer, his personal orthodoxy of worker power blinded him to the terminal decay of the Left's traditional industrial power base in Wallonia. But he sure scared the entrenched élites.

2) Little of substance has been published in the mainstream media on the connections which drew together figures such as Violet (a long-time SDECE French intelligence sleeper); the Pinay Circle (as *Le Cercle* was also known); the Pan-European Movement created by the Belgian Count Richard Coudenhove-Kalergi and Otto von Habsburg; and not least the founding fathers of the EU, Jean Monnet and Robert Schumann. The Polish politician Jozef Retinger, a member of the wartime Free Polish government in London, went to Prince Bernhard of the Netherlands to interest him in the project for post-war European unity. Through Retinger, contact was made with Walter Bedell Smith, at the time head of the CIA. The fruits of these liaisons included the Bilderberg Club and the future European Union, which can now be glimpsed through the mists of history as products of the trans-Atlantic intelligence community. In terms of understanding Gladio, these structures are significant. Perhaps we have another reason why NATO fled to Brussels as first preference after the de Gaulle affair, and an explanation of the continuing preponderance of Belgian politicians at the summit of EU affairs. These connections are a legitimate subject of historical curiosity, but largely ignored because of the thickets of esoteric literature which surround them.

3) Published by Uitgeverij Houtekiet, Brussels, 1999, in Flemish and French editions; French title: *Les dossiers X: ce que la Belgique ne devait pas savoir sur l'affaire Dutroux.*

4) Barry James, *New York Times*, 16th December 1999. James predicted the Belgian statute of limitations, assisted by self-imposed media gags, would ensure that no high-profile cases would ever reach the courts. He was right. Just one patsy, Dutroux, was eventually sentenced.

Chapter XIV – If You Go Down to the Woods Today, Be Sure of a Big Surprise

1) The job lot swept up by BND recruiters included two notorious mass killers. SS Captain Johannes Clemens was one of the officers whose men shot 335 civilians in a mass reprisal at the disused marble quarries in Rome's Ardeatine quarter in 1944. The pitiless SS commander Georg Wilimzig of the death squad

code-named IV/2 was responsible for the murder of thousands of men, women and children as German troops marched into Poland. Another prize catch was Alfred Benzing, former NCO in the Secret Field Police (*Geheime Feldpolizei*) who was kitted out with a false business front selling roller blinds in the city of Karlsruhe. His scruffy backyard office was actually a job placement centre for ex-Nazis called Directorate 114, charged with identifying suitable candidates for counter-espionage, counter-sabotage, detection of treasonable activity and counter-propaganda. In short, all the qualities of a Third Reich secret soldier, transferred intact to the services of the BND and thereafter NATO.

Der Spiegel's report by Klaus Wiegrefe, on 16th January 2011, claimed the facts had been known for years, but successive chancellors, including Angela Merkel, had turned their backs on *glasnost* that would dim the glory of Germany's post-war rehabilitation.

2) Stefan Aust, *The Baader-Meinhof Complex.*

3) The memorable phrase to describe the RAF campaign coined by the German author and Nobel prize winner Heinrich Theodor Böll (1917-1985).

4) The order of fatalities was as follows. Ulrike Meinhof died first, dangling from a rope made of jail towels on 7th May 1976. On October 18 the following year the 'night of the long knives' claimed Baader from a gunshot to the back of his head. His girlfriend Gudrun Ensslin was found hanged in her cell (with electrical cord, and no explanation where she got it from). Jan-Carl Raspe died from a copycat head shot. Irmgard Muller alone survived, insisting her three partners were murdered. A month later, Ingrid Schubert died from hanging.

To the least sympathetic minds, much of the forensic and autopsy evidence looked crude and sloppy. It was later divulged the brains of some of those who died were removed, a bizarre eugenical quest for signs of mental illness, reminiscent of quack Nazi medical science. Old habits die hard.

5) Dr. Hoffman was foremost at issue with the insistence of the prosecutor's final report that the position of the pistol lying at the left side of Baader's head matched up with the entry hole of a bullet at the nape of the victim's neck. (My own inquiries demonstrate that shooting oneself in the back of the head is rarely a favoured option chosen by suicides, and unsurprisingly raises suspicions of another party.) The smoking gun, so to speak, lay in the examination of a fragment of skin taken from Baader's neck.

According to BKA specialists, the entry point was clearly indicated by 'a pressure mark whose outline corresponds with the mouth of the pistol....' Moreover, traces of powder smoke were found inside the cavity, consistent with the pistol pressed firmly to the flesh. All this was presented as proof that Baader contorted himself into that difficult position to end his life, for reasons of his own. Hoffman was not convinced.

He examined the skin again to ascertain the projectile's impact signature, which in turn tells an expert important information concerning the distance from which the shot was fired. He deduced an impulse rate of 14,300 per second. Taking a snippet of pigskin, very similar to human flesh, and using an identical pistol, he got a result of 74,000 ps. The lower figure could only be explained if the pistol were not pressed to the neck, but fired from some distance away, strongly implying someone else fired the fatal shot. The dogged Hoffman persisted with his tests and concluded that whoever fired the shot held the pistol thirty to forty centimeters from the point of impact.

So what about the powder traces in the wound? There must have been 'some dispersion,' said the BKA people, leaving the invitation open to conclude, as Aust himself proposed, that perhaps someone had 'been fingering the area around Baader's gunshot wound.' Aust poses the existential question that by now screams to be answered. How can it be possible for someone to fire a gun that was simultaneously pressed against the flesh and also thirty and possibly more centimeters away? Aust introduces and then leaves open another important gap in the official story. A pistol equipped with a silencer might leave less evidence of smoke compounds, but this could not be squared with the fact that the 7.65 pistol caliber found at Baader's side did not have a silencer. 'In that case,' muses Aust, 'it must have been murder.' And yet as he says, none of the other prisoners apparently heard a gunshot that night, so there must have been a silencer, which in turn rules out the gun in the cell. (Précis of Aust, pp 423-425 *The Baader-Meinhof Complex,* with my own additional remarks.)

The last word definitely belongs to Stefan Aust. 'The investigating public prosecutor received Dr. Hoffman's expert opinion on the distance from which the shot had been fired at Baader almost two months before the close of his inquiries — and never said a word about it.'

6) 'BND/Plutonium-Affäre' questions to the Government by Manfred Such, MP, 19.4.95; *Frankfurter Rundschau,* 18.4.94, 13.4.95, 12.4.95, 11.4.95; *Der Spiegel* 34/94, 22.8.94; 15/95, 9.4.95; 16/95, 15.4.95; *Frankfurter Allgemeine Zeitung,* 15-16.4.95, 11.4.95, 12.4.95. None produced convincing answers.

Chapter XV – Ghost Trains: Madrid, London and the Template of Tension

1, 2) The daily *El Mundo.*

3) Luis del Pino.

4) *El País.*

5) Luis del Pino.

6) It haunts him today in the form of the *Ludicrous Diversion* DVD, which became a massive YouTube hit.

7) Hayman left the force in December 2007, amid press publicity alleging lavish expense claims and an association with a female staff member of the Complaints Commission. Hayman's freelance contributions to Murdoch newspapers brought him into prominence again, because he was accused of soft-pedaling when he was running the Scotland Yard inquiry into the NewsCorp phone hacking scandal (2011). Tory MP Lorraine Fullbrook called the top ex-cop a 'dodgy geezer' at the formal Westminster inquisition. Other commentators were less generous.

8) The full account in *The Fourth Bomb: Inside London's Terror Storm*, written under his pseudonym Daniel Obachike. Floran, 2007.

9) Marie Fatayi-Williams' moving testament to her son *For the Love of Anthony* was published by Hodder and Stoughton in 2006.

10) The Reverend Nicholson resigned as the vicar of her Bristol parish shortly after her daughter's death. She wrote *A Song for Jenny: A Mother's Story of Love and Loss*, published by Harper Collins in 2010.

Chapter XVI – The Return of Gladio: Death in the Underworld

1) The SRR was actively deployed in Iraq, and reputed to be involved in the classic false-flag incident at Basra in September 2005, attacking a police post dressed in Arab clothing. The regiment's cap badge suggests a subliminal connection to the modern Gladio: the sword Excalibur borne by King Arthur, whose sleeping soldier-knights reputedly await the recall to arms.

Chapter XVII – The Return of Gladio: In the Shadow of the Minaret

1) *New York Times*, 10th September 2001.

2) 'What I didn't find in Niger,' *New York Times*, 6th July 2003.

3) Extract from the Congressional Records, 12th July 2007 (Senate) [Page S9155-S9184]: 'Since Mr. Barlow's separation from government service in 1992, five Senate and five House committees have intervened in support of his case on a bipartisan basis. Investigations by the Central Intelligence Agency, State Department Inspectors General, and the Government Accountability Office have corroborated Mr. Barlow's findings, or found that personnel actions were taken against him in reprisal.'

4) More details in 'The French Connection: Are we watching Gladio-style electioneering by terror?' by the author, at EndTheLie.com.

Sarkozy has been linked by family ties to the CIA, in an article by French writer Thierry Meyssan, "Operation Sarkozy: how the CIA placed one of its agents at the presidency of the French Republic." As a matter of public record, Sarkozy's stepmother Catherine de Ganay remarried Frank Wisner II, son of the iconic CIA figure. A member of the CFR, Wisner Jr. has held high posts in the CIA and State Department, was vice chairman of AIG Insurance, and is now U.S. special envoy to Kosovo. He is stepfather to Olivier Sarkozy, the half-brother of the French president and Managing Director of the Carlyle Group.

Bibliography

Ahmed, Nafeez Mossadeq. *The London Bombings: An Independent Inquiry*. The Bodley Head, 2009.

Aldrich, Richard J. *The Hidden Hand: Britain, America, and Cold War Secret Intelligence*. Overlook, 2002.

Alexander, Yonah; Brenner, Edgar H.; and Tetuncuoglu, Serhat. *Turkey: Terrorism, Civil Rights, and the European Union*. Routledge, 2008.

Ali, Tariq. *Masters of the Universe: NATO's Balkan Crusade*. Verso, 2000.

Aust, Stefan. *The Baader-Meinhof Complex*. The Bodley Head, 2008.

Aybet, Gülnur; Moore, Rebecca; and Freeman, Lawrence. *NATO in Search of a Vision*. Georgetown University Press, 2010.

Bamford, James. *Body of Secrets: the Anatomy of the Ultra Secret National Security Agency*. Anchor Books, 2007.

Baruma, Ian. *Murder in Amsterdam: Liberal Europe, Islam, and the Limits of Tolerance*. Penguin, 2007.

Beckett, Andy. *When the lights went out*. Faber and Faber, 2010.

Bereanu, Vladimir and Todorov, Kalin. *Who killed Georgi Markov?* Bulgaria, 1984. In English as *The Umbrella Murder*, 1991, unpublished.

Bernays, Edward. *Propaganda*. IG Publishing, re-issued, 2004.

Bondeson, Jan. *Blood on the Snow: The Killing of Olof Palme*. Cornell University Press, 2005.

Bulté, Annemie; de Coninck, Douglas; and van Heeswyck, Marie-Jeanne *Les dossiers X: Ce que la Belgique ne devait pas savoir sur l'affaire Dutroux*. (*The X-Dossiers: What Belgium was not supposed to know about the Dutroux affair*.) Compiled for the Institute for the Study of Globalization and Covert Politics. EPO, Bruxelles, 1999.

Burnham, James. *Suicide of the West*. Regnery Publishing, 1985.

Carr, Gordon. *The Angry Brigade: A History of Britain's First Urban Guerilla Group*. PM Press, 2010.

Chossudovsky, Michel. *America's 'War on Terrorism.'* Global Research (2nd edition), 2005.

Christie, Stuart. *Stefano Della Chiaie: Portrait of a Black Terrorist*. Anarchy Magazine/Refract, 2002.

Clark, Ramsay. *NATO in the Balkans: Voices of Opposition*. International Action Centre (New York) 1998 .

Coates, Tim. *The Scandal of Christine Keeler and John Profumo: Lord Denning's Report, 1963 (Moments of History)*. Self-published, 2003.

Colby, William. *Honorable Men: My Life in the CIA*. Hutchinson, 1978.

Curtis, Adam, *The Mayfair Set*. Series for BBC Television (DVD). 1999.

De Lutiis, Giuseppe. *I servizi segreti in Italia. Dal fascismo all'intelligence del XXI secolo (The Secret Services in Italy; Fascism and intelligence in the 21st Century)*. Sperling and Kupfer, 2008.

De Lutiis, Giuseppe. *Il Golpe di Via Fani (The Coup on the Via Fani)*. Sperling and Kupfer, 2007.

del Pino González, Luis Manuel. *11-M: Golpe de Régimen. (9/11: Coup d'État.)* In Spanish. Madrid, La Esfera de los Libros, 2007.

del Pino González, Luis Manuel. *Enigmas del 11-M: Conspiración o Negligencia? Con prólogo de César Vidal (The Enigmas of 9/11: Conspiracy or Negligence, with foreword by César Vidal).* In Spanish. Barcelona, Libros Libres, 2006.

del Pino González, Luis Manuel. *Las Mentiras del 11-M (The Lies of 9/11).* In Spanish. Barcelona, Libros Libres, 2006.

Demaret, Pierre. *Target de Gaulle: The true story of the 31 attempts on the life of the French president.* Dial Press, 1975.

Doulis, Thomas. *The Iron Storm: The Impact on Greek Culture of the Military Junta, 1967-1974.* Xlibris, 2011.

Duthel, Heinz. *Secret Organization Gladio: Western Union Clandestine Killer Organization.* IAC Society. Amazon Kindle edition, 2010.

Ebaugh, Helen Rose. *The Gülen Movement: A Sociological Analysis of a Civic Movement Rooted in Moderate Islam.* Springer, 2009.

Engdahl, F. William. *Full Spectrum Dominance: Totalitarian Democracy in the New World Order.* Edition-Engdahl, 2009.

Executive Intelligence Review. *Tiny Rowland: The Ugly Face of Neocolonialism in Africa.* EIR, 1993.

Eyerman, Ron. *The Assassination of Theo van Gogh: From Social Drama to Cultural Trauma.* Duke University Press, 2008.

Fallon, Ivan. *Billionaire: Life and Times of Sir James Goldsmith.* Hutchinson, 1991.

Fenby, Jonathan. *The General: Charles de Gaulle and the France He Saved.* Simon & Schuster, 2010.

Flamigni, Sergio. *La sfinge delle Brigate Rosse: delitti. segreti e bugie del capo terrorista Mario Moretti (The Sphinx of the Red Brigades: Crimes. Secrets and Lies of Terrorist Chief Mario Moretti).* Kaos, 2004.

Flamigni, Sergio. *Le idi di marzo: Il delitto Moro secondo Mino Pecorelli (The Ides of March: the Moro Crime according to Mino Pecorelli).* Kaos, 2006.

Flamigni, Sergio. *Trame Atlantiche: Storia della loggia massonica P2 (Atlantic Plots: The History of the P2 secret Masonic lodge).* Kaos, 2005 .

Flamini, Gianni. *La Banda della Magliana (the Magliana Band).* Kaos, 2002.

Gaffney, John. *Political Leadership in France: From Charles de Gaulle to Nicolas Sarkozy.* Palgrave Macmillan, 2010. French Politics. Society and Culture.

Ganser, Dr. Daniele. *NATO's Secret Armies: Operation Gladio and Terrorism in Western Europe.* Taylor and Francis, 2007.

Garcia-Abadillo, Casimiro. *11-M: La Venganza (9/11: The Vengeance).* In Spanish. La Esfera de los Libros, 2009.

Ginsborg, Paul. *Silvio Berlusconi: Television, Power and Patrimony.* Verso Books, 2005.

Grivas, Kleanthis. *Papandreism, a Dark Green Authoritarianism.* Athens, 1993.

Harrison, Alexander. *Challenging De Gaulle: The O.A.S. and the Counter-Revolution in Algeria, 1954-1962.* Praeger Publishers, 1989.

Herman, Edward S. and Broadhead, Frank. *The Rise and Fall of the Bulgarian Connection.* Sheridan Square Publications. New York, 1986. [The shooting of Pope John Paul II].

Jackson, Paul. *The Far Right in Europe: An Encyclopedia.* Greenwood, 2008.

Jenkins, Roy. *Churchill.* Macmillan, 2000.

Johnson, Chalmers. *The Costs and Consequences of American Empire* (Blowback Trilogy). Holt, 2001.

Johnson, Haynes. *Sleepwalking through History: America in the Reagan Years.* Anchor, 1992.

Kashneri, Sarwar A. *NATO 2.0: Reboot or Delete?* Potomac Books, 2011.

Kassimeris, George. *Europe's Last Red Terrorists: The Revolutionary Organization 17 November.* NYU Press, 2001.

Kelly, Daniel. *James Burnham and the Struggle for the World.* Intercollegiate Studies Institute, 2003.

Knatchbull, Timothy. *From A Clear Blue Sky: Surviving the Mountbatten Bomb.* Hutchinson, 2009.

Knightley, Phillip and Kennedy, Caroline. *An Affair of State: The Profumo Case and the Framing of Stephen Ward.* Jonathan Cape, 1987.

Kollerstrom, Nick. *Terror on the Tube: Behind the Veil of 7/7, an Investigation.* Progressive Press, 3rd edition, 2011.

Krüger, Henrik. *The Great Heroin Coup: Drugs, Intelligence, & International Fascism.* English, translated from Danish. South Beach Press, 1981.

Lane, David. *Berlusconi's Shadow: Crime, Justice and the Pursuit of Power.* Allen Lane, 2004.

Leigh, David *The Wilson Plot: How the Spycatchers and Their American Allies Tried to Overthrow the British Government.* Pantheon Press, 2008.

Lobster Magazine (UK) Journal of Politics, Intelligence, Parapolitics, and State Research.

McKee, Grant and Franey, Ross. *Timebomb: Irish Bombers, English Justice and the Guildford Four.* Bloomsbury, 1988.

McLaughlin, Duncan and Hall, William. *The Lucan Conspiracy.* Blake Publishing, 2004.

Mecklenburg, Jans. *Gladio.* Elefanten Press (Germany), 1997.

Meinhof, Ulrike; Bauer, Karin; von Flotow, Luise; and Jelinek, Elfriede. *Everybody Talks About the Weather . . . We Don't: The Writings of Ulrike Meinhof.* Seven Stories Press, 2008.

Mosca, Carla; Moretti, Mario; and Rossanda, Rossana. Brigate Rosse*: Una storia italiana (The Red Brigades: An Italian Story).* Mondadori, 1997.

Nicolas, Jean and Lavachery, Frederic. *Dossier Pedophilie (the scandal of the Dutroux affair).* In French. Flammarion, 2001.

Otello, Lupaccini. *Banda della Magliana: alleanza tra mafioso, terroristi, spioni, politici, prefati (Alliance between the Mafia, terrorists, spies, politicians and priests).* Koinè Nuove Edizioni, 2004.

Pearson, John. *The Gamblers.* Arrow, 2007.

Pimlott, Ben. *Harold Wilson.* Harper Collins, 1993.

Pincher, Chapman. *Treachery: Betrayals, Blunders and Cover-Ups: Six Decades of Espionage: The True history of MI5.* Mainstream Publishing, 2011 .

Prouty, L. Fletcher. *The Secret Team: the CIA and its Allies in Control of the United States and the World.* Skyhorse Publishing, 2008.

Red Army Faction. *The Urban Guerilla Concept.* Kersplebedeb, 2010.

Redlinger, Lawrence and Cooper, H.H.A. *The Murder of Olof Palme: A tale of Assassination, Deception and Intrigue.* Edwin Mellen, 2004.

Robin, Marie-Monique. *Escadrons de la mort: l'école française (Death squads: the French school).* Editions La Découverte, 2008.

Rosi, Francesco. *Salvatore Giuliano.* Film. 1962.

Ruggiero. L. *Dossier Brigate Rosse (the Red Brigades dossiers) 1976-1978*. Kaos, 2007.

Schiller, Margit. *Remembering the Armed Struggle*. Zidane Press, 2008.

Seagrave, Sterling. *The Yellow Rain, a Journey through Chemical Warfare*. M. Evans and Co, 1981.

Serrovalle, Garardo. *Gladio*. Edizioni Associate, 1991.

Sorrentino, Paolo. *Il Divo*. Film biography of Guilio Andreotti. 2008.

Talat, Turhan. *Özel Savas Terör ve Kontragerilla (Extraordinary war: Terror and Counter Terrorism)*. Turkish. Istanbul, 2009.

Temelkuran, Ece. *My son, my daughter, my state — The mothers of political detainees, from their homes to the streets (Oğlum Kızım Devletim-Evlerden Sokaklara Tutuklu Anneleri)*. In English. Metis, 1997.

Thompson, Douglas. *The Hustlers: Gambling, Greed and the Perfect Con*. Pan, 2008.

van Gogh, Theo. *06/05*. Film on the events leading up to the murder of Pim Fortuyn. 2004.

Walker, Clive. *Miscarriages of Justice: A Review of Justice in Error*. Blackstone Press 1999.

Wiebes, Cees. *Intelligence and the War in Bosnia: 1992-1995 (Studies in Intelligence History)*. Lit Verlag, 2003.

Willan, Philip. *Puppetmasters: The Political Use of Terrorism in Italy*. Universe, 2003.

Willan, Philip. *The Last Supper: The Mafia, the Masons and the Killing of Roberto Calvi*. Robinson Publishing, 2007.

Williams, Paul L. *The Vatican Exposed: Money, Murder and the Mafia*. Prometheus Books, 2003.

Wright, Peter. *Spycatcher*. Bantam Doubleday Dell, 1988.

Yallop, David. *The Power and the Glory: Inside the Dark Heart of John Paul II's Vatican*. Constable, 2007.

Index

IN MEMORIA DEL GIOVANE
COMUNISTA
LUIGI DI ROSA
ASSASSINATO QUI DA SQUADRE
FASCISTE IL 28 MAGGIO 1976
SEZZE 28 GIUGNO 1976 · L'AMMINISTRAZIONE COMUNALE

Parting shot in the Gladio War, Era One: a tragedy remembered in Sezze, mountain-top city in Italy's Lazio province.

Utøya Island. Paradise Lost, July 22, 2011.

Towards a World War III Scenario: The Dangers of Nuclear War. The Pentagon is preparing a first-strike nuclear attack on Iran. 103 pp, $15.95.

America's "War on Terrorism" Concise, wide-reaching, hard-hitting study on 9/11 in geopolitical context. 387 pp, $22.95.

History

Two by George Seldes, the great muckraking whistleblower journalist. ***1,000 Americans Who Rule the USA*** (1947, 324 pp, $18.95). Concentration of the corporatist media: Nothing has changed. ***Facts and Fascism*** (1943, 292 pp, $15.95). The Morgan plot, and sourcebook on the plutocrats who financed fascism.

Afghanistan: A Window on the Tragedy. Ninety-eight black and white photos, steeped in the pathos and predicament of the Afghan people, with commentary and poetry from thirteen distinguished contributors. 160 pp, $19.95.

Enemies by Design: Inventing the War on Terrorism. A century of imperialism in the Middle East. Biography of Osama bin Ladeen; Zionization of America; the Project for a New American Century; Afghanistan, Palestine, Iraq; 416 pp, $17.95.

Global Predator: US Wars for Empire. A damning account of the atrocities committed by US armed forces over two centuries. Also by Stewart H. Ross: ***Propaganda for War: How the US was Conditioned to Fight the Great War.*** Psychological warfare by Britain and her agents like Teddy Roosevelt sucked the USA into the war to smash the old world order. 350 pp and $18.95 each.

Inside the Gestapo: Hitler's Shadow over the World. Intimate, fascinating tale of ruthlessness, intrigue, and geopolitics, by a Nazi defector. 287 pp, $17.95.

The Nazi Hydra in America: Suppressed History of a Century by Glen Yeadon. US plutocrats launched Hitler, then recouped Nazi assets to erect today's police state. Fascists won WWII because they ran both sides. "The story is shocking and sobering and deserves to be widely read." – Howard Zinn. 700 pp, $19.95.

Sunk: the Story of the Japanese Submarine Fleet, 1941-1945. A tale of the bravery of doomed men in a lost cause, against impossible odds. 300 pp, $15.95.

Terrorism and the Illuminati, A 3000-Year History. "Islamic" terrorists are tentacles of western imperialism – the Illuminati. 332 pp, $16.95.

Witness in Palestine: A Jewish-American Woman in the Occupied Territories. The nuts and bolts of oppression. Packed with color photos. 400 pp, $28.95.

La France Conquise: Edouard VII et Clemenceau. (*Français, English.*) La main derrière les tragédies de l'histoire; l'empire britannique cherche les grandes guerres. Toujours actuel. With a 38-page essay in English by Tarpley. 255 pp, $12.95.

Psychology: Brainwashing

The Rape of the Mind: The Psychology of Thought Control, Menticide and Brainwashing. Conditioning in open and closed societies. With tools for self-defense against torture or social pressure. 320 pp, $16.95.

The Telescreen: An Empirical Study of the Destruction of Consciousness, by Prof. Jeffrey Grupp. How mass media brainwash us with consumerism and war propaganda. Fake history, news, issues, and reality steal our souls. 199 pp, $14.95.

Telementation: Cosmic Feeling and the Law of Attraction. Deep feeling rather than thought or faith is our secret nature and key to self-realization. Prof. Grupp, a long-time Buddhist, shows the way in this simple guidebook. 124 pp, $12.95.

Conspiracy, NWO

Two by Henry Makow: *Illuminati: Cult that Hijacked the World* tackles taboos like Zionism, British Empire, Holocaust denial. How international bankers stole a monopoly on government credit, and took over the world. They run it all: wars, schools, media. 249 pp, $19.95. *Illuminati 2: Deception & Seduction.* A satanic cult is out to enslave us. Totalitarianism by stealth, needless wars, porn, trivia, violence, dehumanization, and materialism are some of their tools. 285 pp, $19.95.

Corporatism: the Secret Government of the New World Order, by Prof. Jeffrey Grupp. Corporations control all world resources. Their New World Order is the "prison planet" that Hitler aimed for. 408 pp, $16.95.

Dope Inc.: Britain's Opium War against the United States. "The Book that Drove Kissinger Crazy." All-new edition of the underground classic. 320 pp, $12.95.

Final Warning: A History of the New World Order. In-depth research into the Great Conspiracy: the Fed, the CFR, Trilaterals, Illuminati. 360 pp, $14.95.

How the World Really Works, by A.B. Jones. Crash course in conspiracy: digests of 11 classics like *Tragedy and Hope, Creature from Jekyll Island.* 336 pp, $15.

The Triumph of Consciousness, by Chris Clark. The real Global Warming and Greening agenda: more hegemony by the NWO. 347 pp, $14.95.

Conspiracy: 9/11 False Flag

9/11 on Trial: The W T C Collapse. 20 closely-argued proofs that the World Trade Center was destroyed by controlled demolition. 192 pp, $12.95.

Conspiracies, Conspiracy Theories and the Secrets of 9/11. Fascinating best-seller from Germany explores the conspiracy principle in history and biology, before tackling 9/11. English translation, 274 pp, $14.95.

The War on Freedom. The seminal exposé of 9/11. "Far and away the best and most balanced analysis of September 11th." – Gore Vidal. 400 pp, $16.95.

Terror on the Tube: Behind the Veil of 7/7, an Investigation, by Nick Kollerstrom. This unique research work proves that the four young Muslim scapegoats were completely innocent. 3rd ed, 322 pp, $17.77.

Truth Jihad: My Epic Struggle against the 9/11 Big Lie. In this first humorous book on 9/11, Kevin Barrett sends Sean Hannity, the Secret Service and neocon politicians packing. 224 pages, $9.95.

9/11 Truth Novels

Instruments of the State, by Dave Aossey. Gripping thriller. 550 pp, $14.95.
Skulk, by Marc Estrin. Light romantic fiction with a twist. 182 pp, $14.95.

Coming Soon

The Real Pearl Harbor Conspiracy by Webster Tarpley.
Dixie Reckoning: the Lincoln Assassination and Lost Confederate Treasury.
Homeland and *Troublesome Country,* by James Hufferd.
In Search of the Truth, by Azar Mirza-Beg.

ProgressivePress.com
PO Box 12834,
Palm Desert, Calif. 92255-2834
info@progressivepress.com

THE "WAR ON TERROR" IS A HOAX
SUPPORT THE
TRUTH about 9/11 & 'NWO.'
Books & DVD's from
ProgressivePress.com
SEE HOW THE TOWERS FALL? THAT TELLS IT ALL!